# The Law of Hockey

**John Barnes**

Research Centre for Sport in Canadian Society
School of Human Kinetics
University of Ottawa

LexisNexis·

**The Law of Hockey**
© LexisNexis Canada Inc. 2010
March 2010

**Members of the LexisNexis Group worldwide**

| | |
|---|---|
| **Canada** | LexisNexis Canada Inc., 123 Commerce Valley Dr. E. Suite 700, MARKHAM, Ontario |
| **Australia** | Butterworths, a Division of Reed International Books Australia Pty Ltd, CHATSWOOD, New South Wales |
| **Austria** | ARD Betriebsdienst and Verlag Orac, VIENNA |
| **Czech Republic** | Orac sro, PRAGUE |
| **France** | Éditions du Juris-Classeur SA, PARIS |
| **Hong Kong** | Butterworths Asia (Hong Kong), HONG KONG |
| **Hungary** | Hvg Orac, BUDAPEST |
| **India** | Butterworths India, NEW DELHI |
| **Ireland** | Butterworths (Ireland) Ltd, DUBLIN |
| **Italy** | Giuffré, MILAN |
| **Malaysia** | Malayan Law Journal Sdn Bhd, KUALA LUMPUR |
| **New Zealand** | Butterworths of New Zealand, WELLINGTON |
| **Poland** | Wydawnictwa Prawnicze PWN, WARSAW |
| **Singapore** | Butterworths Asia, SINGAPORE |
| **South Africa** | Butterworth Publishers (Pty) Ltd, DURBAN |
| **Switzerland** | Stämpfli Verlag AG, BERNE |
| **United Kingdom** | Butterworths Tolley, a Division of Reed Elsevier (UK), LONDON, WC2A |
| **USA** | LexisNexis, DAYTON, Ohio |

**Library and Archives Canada Cataloguing in Publication**

Barnes, John
      The law of hockey / John Barnes.

Includes bibliographical references and index.
ISBN 978-0-433-45188-4

      1. Hockey — Law and legislation — Canada. 2. Hockey — Law and legislation — United States. I. Title.

KE3792.B37 2010       344.71'099       C2010-900530-9
KF3989.B37 2010

Printed and bound in Canada.

**THE LONEY TRIAL AT CORNWALL.**—In cross-examining witnesses for the defence, Mr. James Dingwall, Crown Attorney, associated with Mr. French, K.C., for the prosecution, demonstrated the various ways in which the fatal blow might have been struck. His tall figure, long flowing beard and patriarchal appearance generally were truly impressive, but the contrast implied in the barrister's gown he wore and the hockey stick he brandished murderously above his head, excited much amusement.

*The Montreal Daily Star*, March 30, 1905, p. 5.

The game commonly known as ice hockey is hereby recognized and declared to be the national winter sport of Canada....

*National Sports of Canada Act*, S.C., 1994, c. 16, s. 2.

# ABOUT THE AUTHOR

John Barnes is a member of the Research Centre for Sport in Canadian Society at the School of Human Kinetics, University of Ottawa, where he teaches graduate courses in sports law and sports policy. He took his B.A. and B.C.L. degrees in law from Oxford University and is a qualified barrister. Professor Barnes has taught at Carleton University and the University of Western Ontario and from 1981 to 1992 served as a research consultant with the Law Reform Commission of Canada. His work in law reform related to the comprehensive codification of criminal law and included particular studies dealing with assault, sexual offences and crimes involving cruelty to animals.

John Barnes is the author of *Sports and the Law in Canada*, 3rd ed. (Toronto: Butterworths, 1996) and numerous other texts and articles dealing with current and historical issues in sport. His research has considered the evolution of sport in Britain, Australia and North America and has dealt with a wide range of legal issues, including human rights, safety in sport, dispute resolution, and business structures and employment relations in professional leagues. He has over 30 years of experience in teaching sports law and assisting sports organizations in legal and administrative matters. With *The Law of Hockey*, the author now explores the varied elements of the essential Canadian game.

# PREFACE

In view of its official status, we need to get to grips with the legalities and illegalities of the national winter game. This work offers an introduction to the Canadian law of hockey and discusses legal and policy aspects in the context of social, economic and other issues. All levels of the game are considered, from community or minor play to the high finance of the National Hockey League.

The book opens with the challenge to the ownership of the Stanley Cup as delivered during the 2004-05 NHL lockout. This dispute serves to introduce the evolution of the game and the history of the associations and leagues that have controlled elite competition. Chapter 2 deals with the growth of sports law and the role of government in regulating sport. The chapter then addresses the various processes for protecting fundamental rights and considers equality of opportunity in hockey for different groups and minorities. Chapter 3 looks at the international and domestic organizations that are responsible for managing the game and deals with the various types of dispute that arise. Chapters 4 to 6 address the central issue of safety in hockey and consider the variety of risks on and off the ice, including the danger from flying pucks, "rink rage" and violent acts by players. These chapters deal with standards of safety at the rink and elsewhere and outline the remedies and procedures that come into play in the event of injury or misconduct. Money rears its head in a big way in Chapter 7 with a discussion of the business of hockey and the sources of revenue for the game. Chapter 8 outlines the general framework of competition law and labour law. Chapter 9 then focusses on the NHL with particular reference to labour relations and contractual rights as the players strive to take their share of the proceeds. Chapter 10 briefly meditates on the future by looking back to the start.

In decades past, *The Law of Hockey* might have been a candidate for "world's shortest book" since not invoking the law was part of the "code". In the words of Punch Imlach, "The law is the law and the hockey business is the hockey business".[1] Although the game's involvement in formal legal processes is now more familiar, and the cases sometimes serve a flagship role in legal developments, the unsuspecting puck chaser might still be surprised by the scale and variety of the material. While the dominating presence of the striped suit brigade throughout the sports system is regretted by many, it is perhaps the inevitable result of the serious interests at stake, and it will emerge that there have been legal problems from the early days. Study of the law of hockey

---

[1]    Imlach was responding to the policy of the Attorney General of Ontario, Roy McMurtry, to prosecute violent play and the decision to charge Dan Maloney, of the Detroit Red Wings; see, "Hockey reaction harsh on charge" *The Citizen* (Ottawa: November 7, 1975) at 17.

requires charging into just about every corner of the law syllabus and adapting the material to the peculiarities of the game. Along the way, I hope that non-lawyers will get a better sense of the Canadian legal system and that legal types will have a new resource for dealing with hockey issues. The "law" dealt with is widely conceived beyond cases and statutes. Besides the many unstated codes, it includes policies, regulations of associations, standard practices and cultural attitudes. The book seeks to serve all members of the hockey community and may also be read as a general introduction to Canadian law. If hockey can't stir interest in matters juridical, then there is no hope for the subject.

I am indebted to many friends and colleagues for information and assistance. Jeremy deBeer kindly shared his research into the Stanley Cup trust, a topic he has used to put a bit of spark into the law of property. Todd Jackson, Lisa Noseworthy, Glen McCurdie and Sean Kelly kept me on top of Hockey Canada regulations and risk management programs, and Richard Harkin was always able to track down exotic legal materials. I have benefited from comments and suggestions from fellow members of the Research Centre for Sport in Canadian Society, including Don Dawson, Jean Harvey, Marc Lavoie and Michael Robidoux. Help and advice on particular matters came from Ron Watson, Ed Ratushny and Gordon Kirke. I also acknowledge editorial support received from Gian-Luca DiRocco and Rina Ciriani of LexisNexis Canada.

This work is a successor to the various editions of *Sports and the Law in Canada* which dealt with legal issues in the administration of different sports and physical activities. Some of the material from the 3rd edition (1996) finds its way here, including modified and updated discussions of fundamental rights, commercial structures and liability for injuries. I have also revived the accounts of the hockey homicides of 1905 and 1907 included in the 1st (1983) and 2nd (1988) editions and have drawn on my detailed study in, *Two Cases of Hockey Homicide: The Crisis of a Moral Ideal* (1990). The shift to a work focussing on one sport reflects the massive growth of the global subject of sports law. It is not entirely possible to separate hockey law from sports law or from general law, but the time is due for specialist studies, and in Canada there is only one place to start. I know that I am daring to invade sacred cultural space, but skate out with head up fully aware of the risks.

John Barnes
Ottawa
January 2010

# TABLE OF CONTENTS

# TABLE OF CASES

**B**

# E

# F

## G

## H

# I

# J

# L

## N

# O

## Q

# R

## S

Seaton v. Gagnon, [1997] O.J. No. 3982, 74 A.C.W.S. (3d) 399 (Ont. Gen. Div.)........ 239
Seattle Totems Hockey Club, Inc. v. National Hockey League, 783 F.2d 1347 (9th
 Cir., 1986) ............................................................................................................ 351
See You In - Canadian Athletes Fund Corp. v. Canadian Olympic Committee,
 [2007] F.C.J. No. 541, 57 C.P.R. (4th) 287 (F.C.), affd [2008] F.C.J. No. 580, 65
 C.P.R. (4th) 421 (F.C.A.) ..................................................................... 40, 128, 273
Setana Sport Ltd. v. 2049630 Ontario Inc. (c.o.b. Verde Minho Tapas & Lounge),
 [2007] F.C.J. No. 1167, 2007 FC 899 (F.C.) .................................................... 309
Sexton v. Sutherland, [1991] O.J. No. 624, 26 A.C.W.S. (3d) 472 (Ont. Gen. Div.) ..... 239
Sharp v. B.C. School Sports, [2000] B.C.H.R.T.D. No. 49, 2000 BCHRT 49
 (B.C.H.R.T.) ........................................................................................................ 68
Sharpe v. Mikoula, [2006] B.C.H.R.T.D. No. 31, 2006 BCHRT 31 (B.C.H.R.T.) .......... 57
Sharpe v. National Football League Players' Assn., 941 F.Supp. 8 (D.D.C., 1996) ...... 362
Shaw v. Dallas Cowboys Football Club, Ltd., 172 F.3d 299 (3rd Cir., 1999) .............. 310
Shaw v. Gorter, [1977] O.J. No. 2243, 16 O.R. (2d) 19, 2 C.C.L.T. 111 (Ont. C.A.).... 235
Shayne v. National Hockey League, 504 F.Supp. 1023 (E.D.N.Y., 1980).................... 351
Sheddon v. Ontario Major Junior Hockey League, [1978] O.J. No. 3273, 19 O.R.
 (2d) 1 (Ont. H.C.J.) ................................................................... 96, 117, 325
Sheehan v. The San Francisco 49ers, Ltd., 62 Cal. Rptr. 3d 803 (C.A., 2007) .............. 144
Sheehy v. Edmonton World Hockey Enterprises Ltd., [1979] A.J. No. 867, 105
 D.L.R. (3d) 644 (Alta. Q.B.) ................................................................... 418, 425
Shoniker v. Ontario (Ministry of Education), [1986] O.J. No. 804, 17 O.A.C. 265
 (Ont. Div. Ct.) .................................................................................................. 122
Silva v. Winnipeg (City), [1992] M.J. No. 522, [1993] 1 W.W.R. 691 (Man. Q.B.) ..... 145
Silverman v. Major League Baseball Player Relations Comm., Inc., 516 F.Supp. 588
 (S.D.N.Y., 1981) .............................................................................................. 361
Silverman v. Major League Baseball Player Relations Comm., Inc., 880 F.Supp. 246
 (S.D.N.Y., 1995), affd 67 F.3d 1054 (2nd Cir., 1995)............................ 359, 361, 363
Simutenkov v. Ministerio de Educación y Cultura and Real Federación Española
 Fútbol, [2005] E.C.R. I-2579.............................................................................. 368
Skalbania v. Simmons, 443 N.E.2d 352 (C.A. Ind., 1982) .................................. 288, 378
Smith v. Horizon Aero Sports Ltd., [1981] B.C.J. No. 1861, 19 C.C.L.T. 89, 130
 D.L.R. (3d) 91 (B.C.S.C.)................................................................... 245, 251
Smith v. IMG Worldwide, Inc., 360 F.Supp. 2d 681 (E.D. Penn., 2005)...................... 449
Smith v. Pro Football Inc. 593 F.2d 1173 (D.C.Cir., 1978), varg 420 F.Supp. 738
 (D.D.C., 1976)..............................................................336, 338, 341, 346, 361
Smolden v. Whitworth, unreported, April 19, 1996 (Q.B.D.)............................... 249
Solin v. British Columbia Amateur Hockey Assn. (1988), 9 C.H.R.R. D/5266
 (B.C.H.R.C.)........................................................................... 42, 63, 116
Spain v. Houston Oilers, Inc., 593 S.W.2d 746 (Tex. Civ. App., 1979) .................. 419
Spath v. National Collegiate Athletic Assn., 728 F.2d 25 (1st Cir., 1984).................... 94
Speakers of Sport, Inc. v. Proserv, Inc., 178 F.3d 862 (7th Cir., 1999) .................. 449
Spencer v. Milton, 287 N.Y.S. 944 (S.C., 1936)....................................... 420, 431
Sport Maska inc. c. Canstar Sports Group inc., [1994] J.Q. no 2044, 57 C.P.R. (3d)
 323 (Que. S.C.)................................................................................... 272
Sportrust Associates International, Inc. v. Sports Corp., 304 F.Supp. 2d 789 (E.D.
 Va., 2004)........................................................................................ 449
Sports Corp. v. Svoboda, [2004] A.J. No. 728, 32 Alta. L.R. (4th) 272
 (Alta. Q.B.)................................................................................... 421, 449
Sprewell v. Golden State Warriors, 266 F.3d 979 (9th Cir., 2001)............................ 411
Spriggs and Riddell v. Commissioner of Taxation, [2009] HCA 22 (H.C. of Aust.) ..... 450

**T**

# W

# Y

# Z

# Chapter 1

# LORD STANLEY AND THE WEDNESDAY NIGHTERS

Who is the keeper of the game?[1]

The economists doubted the figures,[2] but a difference of USD $6.5 million for each team was enough to do it. The National Hockey League ("NHL")[3] wanted a salary cap of USD $42.5 million, the NHL Players' Association[4] insisted on USD $49 million. On February 16, 2005, league commissioner Gary Bettman duly announced that the "sad, regrettable day"[5] had arrived and the season would be cancelled.[6] The shock of grim finality inspired some further discussions involving Wayne Gretzky and Mario Lemieux,[7] but "Zeus and Poseidon coming down off Mount Olympus [could not] solve a problem among mortals".[8] The 2004-05 NHL season did not happen, and the owners' lockout brought the first year without the award of the Stanley Cup since the "Spanish" influenza epidemic halted the playoff series in 1919. As the labour lawyers took a breather before bargaining resumed,[9] it was time for the trusts lawyers to step up. The Stanley Cup predated the NHL by 25 years and was supposed to be a challenge trophy administered by trustees. How could the Cup be the property of one professional league and why should it be withheld because of stalled collective bargaining? In an application to the Ontario Superior Court of Justice,[10] these were some of the questions posed by the "Wednesday Nighters", a group of amateur hockey players attuned to the Cup's origins. In the absence of the NHL, the winter of 2005 may also have been the time that the game returned to its origins.

---

[1]  K. Dryden, *The Game* (Don Mills, ON: Totem Books, 1984) at 230.

[2]  See, "Economists question Bettman's calculations" *The Globe and Mail* (Toronto: February 17, 2005) at R7.

[3]  See generally, online: <www.nhl.com>.

[4]  See generally, online: <www.nhlpa.com>.

[5]  "League Cancels Hockey Season in Labor Battle", "This Is A Sad Regrettable Day" *The New York Times* (February 17, 2005) at A1, D1-D3.

[6]  See, "Canada's game lives on", "The End" *The Globe and Mail* (Toronto: February 17, 2005) at A1, A2, R1, R10.

[7]  See, "How the bottom line beat Gretzky and Mario" *The Globe and Mail* (Toronto: February 21, 2005) at A1, A8.

[8]  "Take a kick, Charlie" *The Globe and Mail* (Toronto: February 21, 2005) at A12.

[9]  On the settlement, see Chapter 9, "National Hockey League", section C.

[10]  *Burt v. O'Neill*, Notice of Application, Ont.S.C.J., 05-CV-287601PD3, April 13, 2005. See also, T. Gilbert, "Does the Stanley Cup belong to the NHL or the Canadian people?" *The Lawyers Weekly* (May 27, 2005) at 12.

## A.   THE GIFT

When the sixth Governor General of Canada, Baron Stanley of Preston,[11] brought his sporting family to Rideau Hall in 1888 they discovered a flourishing winter game and moved quickly to be involved in its organization. Lord Stanley's interest was certainly encouraged by his hockey-playing sons[12] and by a hockey-playing daughter.[13] The third son, Arthur Stanley, led the way by forming the Rideau Rebels team and in 1890 helped found the Ontario Hockey Association.[14]

In spite of his famous patronage, the Governor General never saw a Stanley Cup game and was not in Canada when the gift of the Dominion Hockey Challenge Cup was announced. On March 18, 1892, at a banquet of the Ottawa Amateur Athletic Club, Lord Stanley's representative, Lord Kilcoursie, read the following letter from His Excellency in response to a toast:

> I have for some time past been thinking that it would be a good thing if there were a challenge cup which should be held from year to year by the champion hockey team in the Dominion. There does not appear to be any such outward and visible sign of championship at present, and considering the general interest which the matches now elicit, and the importance of having the game played fairly and under rules generally recognized, I am willing to give a cup which shall be held from year to year by the winning team...[15]

Captain Charles Colville was commissioned to order a suitable cup, which he purchased in London for 10 guineas, and Sheriff J. Sweetland and P.D. Ross of Ottawa were appointed as the first trustees of the silver bowl. Lord Stanley returned to Britain in July 1893 having directed that the Cup should first be presented to the hockey team of the Montreal Amateur Athletic Association ("MAAA"),[16] which

---

[11]   Frederick Arthur Stanley (1841-1908), the 16th Earl of Derby, was a Conservative member of the British Parliament from 1865 to 1886 and held positions as secretary for war (1878), colonial secretary (1885) and president of the board of trade (1886). Lord Stanley served as Governor General of Canada from 1888 to 1893 and so was in office at the time of the death of Sir John A. Macdonald in 1891. Stanley Park in Vancouver is dedicated in his honour. On the life of Lord Stanley, see, K. Shea & J.J. Wilson, *Lord Stanley: The Man Behind the Cup* (Bolton, ON: Fenn Publishing, 2006).

[12]   See, P. Drackett, "Lord Stanley and Sons" in D. Diamond, ed., *The Official National Hockey League Stanley Cup Centennial Book* (Toronto: McClelland & Stewart, 1992) at 10.

[13]   See, R. Gruneau & D. Whitson, *Hockey Night in Canada: Sport, Identities and Cultural Politics* (Toronto: Garamond Press, 1993) at 48, referring to Isobel Stanley.

[14]   On the sporting Stanleys and the gift of the Cup, see: H. Roxborough, *The Stanley Cup Story* (Toronto: McGraw-Hill Ryerson, 1971) at 9-17; K. Shea & J.J. Wilson, *Lord Stanley: The Man Behind the Cup* (Bolton, ON: Fenn Publishing, 2006) at 348-86.

[15]   "The Champions Dined" *The Daily Citizen* (Ottawa: March 19, 1892) at 1. See also, "Oh, did we mention the Cup?" *Ottawa Citizen* (April 23, 2006) at A11.

[16]   The Montreal Hockey Club, connected to the MAAA, at first refused the Cup in 1893; see, D. Morrow, "The Little Men of Iron: The 1902 Montreal Hockey Club" (1981) 12 Can. J. of the History of Sport 51 at 55-56. The club officially accepted the Cup in February 1894 and won the

was the champion of the Amateur Hockey Association of Canada ("AHAC"). His Excellency laid down the following "preliminary conditions" for the award of the trophy:

1. The winners to give bond for the return of the cup in good order when required by the trustees for the purpose of being handed over to any other team who may in turn win.
2. Each winning team to have at their own charge engraved on a silver ring fitted on the cup for the purpose the name of the team and the year won...
3. The cup shall remain a challenge cup, and will not become the property of any team, even if won more than once.
4. In case of any doubt as to the title of any club to claim the position of champions, the cup shall be held or awarded by the trustees as they may think right, their decision being absolute.
5. Should either trustee resign or otherwise drop out, the remaining trustee shall nominate a substitute.[17]

Lord Stanley also noted that there were several hockey associations in Canada and "asked the trustees to suggest a means of making the cup open to all, and thus representative of the hockey championship as completely as possible, rather than of any one association".[18] According to the "Deed of Gift", consisting of "His Excellency's Conditions" and the "Trustees' Regulations", "Challenges from outside the A.H.A. of C. are recognized by the trustees only from champion clubs of senior provincial associations and in order received".[19]

Lord Stanley's gift envisaged an open challenge trophy for the amateur championship of the Dominion. As the game and its organization evolved in the following decades, each of these elements fell by the wayside and the trophy became emblematic of supremacy in one North American professional league.

---

first Stanley Cup game against the Ottawa Capitals in March 1894; see: H. Roxborough, *The Stanley Cup Story* (Toronto: McGraw-Hill Ryerson, 1971) at 14-15; D. Diamond, ed., *The Official National Hockey League Stanley Cup Centennial Book* (Toronto: McClelland & Stewart, 1992) at 14-15; K. Shea & J.J. Wilson, *Lord Stanley: The Man Behind the Cup* (Bolton, ON: Fenn Publishing, 2006) at 380-84.

17 "For Championship Hockey" *The Gazette* (Montreal: May 1, 1893) at 8; "The Stanley Hockey Cup" *The Gazette* (February 23, 1894) at 8. See also, "Stanley Cup Regulations" as reproduced in, J.C. Wong, *Lords of the Rinks: The Emergence of the National Hockey League, 1875-1936* (Toronto: University of Toronto Press, 2005) at 158.

18 "For Championship Hockey" *The Gazette* (May 1, 1893) at 8; "The Stanley Hockey Cup" *The Gazette* (February 23, 1894) at 8. See also, "Stanley Cup Regulations" as reproduced in, J.C. Wong, *Lords of the Rinks: The Emergence of the National Hockey League, 1875-1936* (Toronto: University of Toronto Press, 2005) at 159.

19 "Stanley Cup Rules" *The Ottawa Evening Journal* (January 6, 1903) at 10. See also, "Stanley Cup Regulations" as reproduced in J.C. Wong, *Lords of the Rinks: The Emergence of the National Hockey League* (Toronto: University of Toronto Press, 2005) at 159; K. Shea & J.J. Wilson, *Lord Stanley: The Man Behind the Cup* (Bolton, ON: Fenn Publishing, 2006) at 376-80.

## B. AMATEUR ASSOCIATIONS AND PROFESSIONAL LEAGUES

The game that so appealed to the vice-regal family is usually dated from the record of an exhibition presented by members of the Victoria Skating Rink in Montreal on March 3, 1875. Other locations have been suggested as the "birthplace" of organized hockey,[20] and there is a far older tradition of contests among native peoples,[21] informal stick games[22] and mass sessions of outdoor bandy and shinny.[23] The Montreal game was, however, recognizably modern in that there was a system of rules and a recorded score.[24] On that occasion, two identified teams of nine-a-side competed in a scheduled event on a confined rink of 200 feet by 85 feet. In the absence of boards or screens, the organisers also had a very modern concern for risk management.[25] Rather than use the usual flying ball, the game was played with a "flat circular piece of wood" likely to slide along the ice and so reduce "imminent danger" and "discomfort" among the spectators. The "block of wood" seemed to present no hazard, and the event was reported to be a "well-contested affair". The spectators "adjourned well satisfied with the evening's entertainment", having witnessed some "brilliant play" and a victory by the team of one of the chief organisers, James G.A. Creighton.[26]

The Victoria Rink had been built in 1862 as a fashionable venue for the wealthier members of the English community. The original preferred activity was skating, but this began to yield to stick-wielding during the 1880s. A set of rules from 1877 established that hockey had been formalized as an on-side game that allowed no forward passing. Those rules also specified that, "No player shall raise his stick above his shoulder" and disallowed the ungentlemanly acts of, "Charging from behind, tripping, collaring, kicking or shinning".[27] The standard team size was soon reduced to seven players and the wooden block gave way to a vulcanized rubber puck. In 1887, clubs in Ottawa and Montreal established the

---

[20] There are records of officers playing hockey in the garrison towns of Halifax and Kingston in the 1850s. Claims are also made for Dartmouth and Windsor, Nova Scotia.

[21] See, C.D. Howell, *Blood, Sweat, and Cheers: Sport and the Making of Modern Canada* (Toronto: University of Toronto Press, 2001) at 26-27, 44.

[22] The European tradition of stick games on ice is famously shown in the "Skating Scene" and the winter landscapes by the early seventeenth century Dutch master Hendrik Avercamp.

[23] See, W. Simpson, "Hockey" in D. Morrow *et al.*, eds., *A Concise History of Sport in Canada* (Toronto: Oxford University Press, 1989) at 169-71.

[24] On the distinction between traditional play and modern structures, see, A. Guttmann, *From Ritual to Record: The Nature of Modern Sports* (New York: Columbia University Press, 1978). The transformation from traditional to modern has its theoretical difficulties: see, D. Booth, *The Field: Truth and Fiction in Sport History* (London: Routledge, 2005) at 159-77.

[25] On flying pucks and other safety issues, see Chapter 4, "Build Safe: Rink Management and Risk Management".

[26] The game is described in, "Victoria Rink" *The Gazette* (Montreal: March 3, 1875) at 3 and "Hockey" *The Gazette* (Montreal: March 4, 1875) at 3, with an alternative version in, "Canadian" *The British Whig* (Kingston: March 5, 1875) at 2. On James Creighton's role, see, M. McKinley, *Putting a Roof On Winter* (Vancouver: Greystone Books, 2000) at 3-19.

[27] "Hockey On Ice" *The Gazette* (Montreal: February 27, 1877) at 4.

Amateur Hockey Association of Canada to organize local schedules of regular games. The Stanley Cup "Trustees Regulations"[28] recognized the early predominance of the AHAC champion as teams from Montreal took seven out of the first eight challenge series. The game had, however, spread well beyond its local roots and was being played in town leagues on the Prairies, in Ontario and in the Maritimes.[29] The Winnipeg Victorias broke Montreal's Stanley Cup monopoly when the trophy went west for the first time in February 1896.

Through the 1880s and 1890s, hockey organizations subscribed to codes of amateurism reflecting the sporting values of the middle class elite.[30] In 1881, the Montreal Amateur Athletic Association was incorporated to promote "physical and mental culture" and provide members with "rational amusements and recreation".[31] Sport was conceived as an improving and respectable activity that should be pursued for its physical and moral benefits. Members were expected to maintain standards of propriety and good conduct, avoiding any suspicion of drunkenness, violence, bribery or gambling. In particular, the reputable participant had to avoid the corrupting effects of money, so that a recognized amateur was,

> one who has never competed for a money prize, or staked bet, or with or against any professional for any prize, or who has never taught, pursued, or assisted in the practice of athletic exercise as a means of obtaining a livelihood.[32]

The MAAA was committed to sound financial management and received substantial gate receipts for its events, but drew the line at pay-for-play because sports participation should not be reduced to a mercenary vocation.[33] In 1884, members of the MAAA assisted in the formation of the Amateur Athletic Association of Canada ("AAAC"), which in 1898 reconstituted itself as the Canadian Amateur Athletic Union ("CAAU"). These bodies attracted the affiliation of clubs and associations in different sports by providing uniform definitions of amateurism and processes for adjudicating amateur status and reinstatement. The regulations incorporated strict rules of eligibility and a firm

---

[28] "Stanley Cup Rules" *The Ottawa Evening Journal* (January 6, 1903) at 10. See also, "Stanley Cup Regulations" as reproduced in J.C. Wong, *Lords of the Rinks: The Emergence of the National Hockey League, 1875-1936* (Toronto: University of Toronto Press, 2005) at 159.

[29] See: A. Metcalfe, *Canada Learns to Play: The Emergence of Organized Sport, 1807-1914* (Toronto: McClelland and Stewart, 1987) at 63-64; W. Simpson, "Hockey" in D. Morrow *et al.*, eds., *A Concise History of Sport in Canada* (Toronto: Oxford University Press, 1989) at 175-77.

[30] See, A. Metcalfe, *Canada Learns to Play: The Emergence of Organized Sport, 1807-1914* (Toronto: McClelland and Stewart, 1987) at 99-132.

[31] J.C. Wong, *Lords of the Rinks: The Emergence of the National Hockey League, 1875-1936* (Toronto: University of Toronto Press, 2005) at 20.

[32] J.C. Wong, *Lords of the Rinks: The Emergence of the National Hockey League, 1875-1936* (Toronto: University of Toronto Press, 2005) at 20-21.

[33] The contemporary judicial attitude was that play involved no proprietary interest and that the court would not assist teams who engaged professionals "to satisfy their pride in winning their matches". See, *Radford v. Campbell* (1890), 6 T.L.R. 488 (C.A.) (Nottingham Forest refused injunction against player jumping to Blackburn Rovers); *Rowe v. Hewitt*, [1906] O.J. No. 7, 12 O.L.R. 13 (Ont. Div. Ct.) (player expelled from OHA refused injunction).

position against any form of payment, but the moral ideal was threatened by the increasing commercialism of games and the tendency to resort to robust win-at-all costs tactics. The crisis had first been faced by lacrosse, which in the 1880s saw its senior leagues begin to disassociate from the authority of amateur governing bodies.[34] The same decade brought complaints about rough play in hockey, and the 1890s saw further examples of the evils associated with professionalism — incidents of brutality and poor sportsmanship, the use of "ringers" and misconduct by fans.[35] In 1895, the AHAC had to deal with a particularly ungentlemanly encounter between Ottawa and Quebec:

> Not only did several players exchange punches during the game, but the Quebec fans also dragged the officials back to the rink after the game was over and wanted them to declare the contest a draw. The Ottawa contingent further complained about the verbal abuse directed by the home fans towards them despite the presence of lady supporters.[36]

As newspapers devoted more attention to hockey, public interest in games increased and senior teams in the AHAC recognized the lucrative possibilities of successful performance. This led to the active recruiting of playing talent and the emergence of an elite level of competition. In 1898, five teams separated from the AHAC to establish a closed association known as the Canadian Amateur Hockey League ("CAHL"). This league operated for seven years with a variety of teams from eastern Ontario and Montreal and was usually successful in Stanley Cup challenges. Although the CAHL continued to subscribe to the amateur ethic, almost from the start there were rumours of payments to players. The first decade of the twentieth century then brought an alphabet soup of rival operations in central Canada, each looking to draw fans or accommodate disaffected teams.[37] The inevitable consequence was an incipient labour market for players. The rapid turnover of short-lived circuits can be summarised as follows:

CAHL : 1898-1905
IHL  : 1904-1907
FAHL : 1904-1907
ECAHA : 1906-1908
OPHL : 1908-1911
CHA  : 1909-1910
NHA  : 1909-1917

---

[34] See, A. Metcalfe, *Canada Learns to Play: The Emergence of Organized Sport, 1807-1914* (Toronto: McClelland & Stewart, 1987) at 181-218.

[35] See, A. Metcalfe, *Canada Learns to Play: The Emergence of Organized Sport, 1807-1914* (Toronto: McClelland & Stewart, 1987) at 69-71.

[36] J.C. Wong, *Lords of the Rinks: The Emergence of the National Hockey League, 1875-1936* (Toronto: University of Toronto Press, 2005) at 23.

Of these, the International Hockey League ("IHL") and the Ontario Professional Hockey League ("OPHL") were openly professional. The IHL operated in Sault Ste. Marie, Ontario and in Pittsburgh and Michigan but relied mainly on Canadian players. The OPHL was a "trolley league" consisting of teams in Toronto, Berlin (Kitchener), Brantford and Guelph. In March 1908, the first winner of the OPHL, the Toronto Maple Leafs, played a Stanley Cup challenge game against the Montreal Wanderers of the Eastern Canada Amateur Hockey Association ("ECAHA") and provided serious opposition in a losing cause.[38]

Stanley Cup series were usually contested by the recognised champions of the other circuits and by challengers from the west. From 1903 to 1905, the Cup was held by the Ottawa Silver Seven, who were originally located in the CAHL. In 1904, the Federal Amateur Hockey League ("FAHL") was established with the Ottawa Capitals, the Montreal Wanderers, the Montreal Nationals and Cornwall, the latter team having been refused admission to the CAHL. The Silver Seven resigned from their league in mid-season after refusing to accept a resolution to replay a game and subsequently joined the FAHL for the following season.[39] The CAHL contended that the Stanley Cup should be awarded to its champion, but the doubt was resolved by a challenge series won by Ottawa.[40] For 1906, the FAHL lost the services of the Silver Seven and the Wanderers when they joined four ex-CAHL teams in the newly formed ECAHA. By 1909, the ECAHA had dropped the amateur connection and reformed itself as the Canadian Hockey Association ("CHA"), and the rival National Hockey Association ("NHA") was similarly an acknowledged professional circuit. Now that the Stanley Cup was a contest between paid performers, the Allan Cup was donated in 1909 for the national senior championship.

This transformation in senior commercial hockey occurred against the background of the political infighting of the "Athletic War".[41] Recognizing the emerging professionalism in lacrosse and hockey and the common practice of under-the-table payments, the MAAA began to consider proposals in 1905 to allow amateurs to compete against professionals. The CAAU at first allowed this liberalization for lacrosse, but annulled the resolution in October 1906 when

---

[37] See, J.C. Wong, *Lords of the Rinks: The Emergence of the National Hockey League, 1875-1936* (Toronto: University of Toronto Press, 2005) at 28-45.

[38] See, C.L. Coleman, *The Trail of the Stanley Cup, Volume I, 1893-1926* (National Hockey League, 1966) at 158-63.

[39] The Ottawa Silver Seven were members of the FAHL when they played the challenge series against Dawson City. The FAHL is also remembered as the site of a "hockey homicide" in 1907; see Chapter 6, "Play Safe: On the Ice", sections B,1, 2 and Appendix I.

[40] See, J.C. Wong, *Lords of the Rinks: The Emergence of the National Hockey League, 1875-1936* (Toronto: University of Toronto Press, 2005) at 35-36. See also, D. Diamond, ed., *The Official National Hockey League Stanley Cup Centennial Book* (Toronto: McClelland & Stewart, 1992) at 52, arguing that the Montreal Canadiens could claim the Cup in 1919 even though the east-west playoff series was not completed.

[41] See: B. Kidd, *The Struggle for Canadian Sport* (Toronto: University of Toronto Press, 1996) at 30-37; D. Morrow, "A Case Study in Amateur Conflict: The Athletic War in Canada, 1906-1908" (1986) 3 British J. of Sport History 173; A. Metcalfe, *Canada Learns to Play: The Emergence of Organized Sport, 1807-1914* (Toronto: McClelland & Stewart, 1987) at 112-19.

Toronto-based purists carried the day. Opposition to the radical innovation was particularly strong in the Ontario Hockey Association ("OHA") which found itself threatened by the professional leagues. The MAAA then joined several clubs in resigning from the CAAU to form a new potential governing body known as the Amateur Athletic Federation of Canada ("AAFC"). During 1907 and 1908, the two warring factions manoeuvred for support and debated the merits of their positions. The traditionalists of the CAAU maintained that strict amateurism was needed to preserve sport as a community-based activity promoting fair play and character development. The AAFC responded that the mixing of amateurs and professionals had become a practical necessity and the prohibition would only perpetuate "shamateurism" and hypocrisy. After the AAFC committed a tactical error in supporting an American protest against the eligibility of marathon runner Tom Longboat for the 1908 London Olympics, increasing numbers of clubs from all regions of Canada chose to affiliate with the CAAU. The Union duly won the "Athletic War", although the AAFC was allowed to save face when a new organization, the Amateur Athletic Union of Canada ("AAUC"), was "amalgamated" at the end of 1909. The AAUC emerged as a national organization enforcing strict principles of amateurism, and the power base in association politics shifted to Toronto. In 1914, the AAUC was instrumental in establishing the Canadian Amateur Hockey Association ("CAHA") which subscribed to the newly confirmed tenets that games should not be prostituted and must always be an instrument for the moral good.

The victory by the amateur purists meant that the leading commercial leagues would continue on their separate path towards independent business operation and pay-for-play. The game lost the opportunity for coexistence under exclusively Canadian governing bodies, and elite hockey would eventually be drawn into American markets. For the 1907 season, the ECAHA voted to allow amateurs and professionals to play together, provided each team listed the status of their players.[42] The Stanley Cup trustees were now involved in disputes over the importing of players, but in March 1907 they effectively allowed the Montreal Wanderers of the ECAHA and the Kenora Thistles to settle their own differences over eligibility. The Stanley Cup was duly contested and resulted in a victory for the Wanderers, although a number of their players barely survived the violence of the series.[43] As mentioned, by 1908 there were Cup challenges involving declared professionals, including the series against the OPHL champion, and in 1909 the ECAHA rebranded itself as the Canadian Hockey Association ("CHA"). The CHA immediately faced competition from the National Hockey Association ("NHA") which included a promising group known as the Canadiens. The francophone community in Montreal now had the

---

[42] See, C.L. Coleman, *The Trail of the Stanley Cup, Volume I, 1893-1926* (National Hockey League, 1966) at 131-52. William A. Foran was now acting Stanley Cup trustee in the absence of P.D. Ross.

[43] See, "Kenoras Played Brutally Last Night But They Lost The Cup" *The Montreal Daily Star* (March 26, 1907) at 12; "Stanley Cup Winners Were In Town Today" *The Toronto Daily Star* (March 30, 1907) at 9 (rumours of death of Ernie Johnston).

Canadiens of the NHA and the Nationals of the CHA to match the Wanderers of the English.

The NHA was the creation of industrialists Michael J. O'Brien and his son J. Ambrose O'Brien, who mined Cobalt, Haileybury and Renfrew as the site for three of the original teams.[44] The other owners were also entrepreneurs or powerful business types with "few ties to the upper-class fraternal roots of the early hockey organizations".[45] These profit-oriented operators soon realised that the market in eastern Canada could not sustain both the CHA and the NHA, whose rivalry had driven the salaries of some players to the unsustainable range of CDN \$2500-\$3000 a year.[46] In January1910, the two circuits merged as the NHA, and for the 1911 season the owners adopted a league constitution that implemented a team salary cap of CDN \$5000. To compound the cash limit, there were job losses the following year when the game was reduced to six-a-side. A competing labour market was, however, emerging in the west since Lester and Frank Patrick established the Pacific Coast Hockey Association ("PCHA") in Vancouver and Victoria in 1911. The PCHA retained seven-man hockey and sought to offer a high standard of play in a new environment by raiding the rosters of the NHA: the greatest coup came in late 1912 when Fred "Cyclone" Taylor signed to play for the Vancouver Millionaires.[47] The Patricks were players and lumber barons who operated the league as a "syndicate", owning both the teams and the newly constructed rinks equipped with artificial ice. These arenas now offered the possibility of playing a Stanley Cup series after the end of the eastern season in mid-March, and cooperation between the PCHA and the NHA was enhanced in 1913 when both agreed to respect player contracts and suspension decisions.

The establishment of the PCHA confirmed the drift of the Stanley Cup away from an open challenge trophy for the amateur championship of the Dominion. The Cup became a "trustee-approved"[48] contest between the PCHA and the NHA, and the prospect of an American winner arose when the PCHA granted franchises to Portland (1914) and Seattle (1915). Portland duly played a Stanley Cup series in 1916, and the Cup was lifted by the Seattle Metropolitans in 1917 when they defeated the Canadiens. A further western circuit emerged in 1922 when the Western Canada Hockey League ("WCHL") was established with franchises in Edmonton, Calgary, Regina and Saskatoon. From 1914 to 1926, Cup series opposed the eastern and western champions of the dominant professional leagues, but this format terminated with the disbanding of both the

---

[44]  See, F. Cosentino, *The Renfrew Millionaires: The Valley Boys of Winter 1910* (Burnstown, ON: General Store Publishing House, 1990).

[45]  J.C. Wong, *Lords of the Rinks: The Emergence of the National Hockey League, 1875-1936* (Toronto: University of Toronto Press, 2005) at 55.

[46]  See, D. Guay, *L'Histoire du hockey au Québec: Origine et développement d'un phénomène culturel avant 1917* (Chicoutimi, QC: Les Éditions JCL, 1990) at 116-26.

[47]  See, E. Whitehead, *Cyclone Taylor: A Hockey Legend* (Toronto: Doubleday Canada, 1977) at 40-51.

[48]  D. Diamond, ed., *The Official National Hockey League Stanley Cup Centennial Book* (Toronto: McClelland & Stewart, 1992) at 46.

PCHA and the WCHL. The WCHL had become unprofitable, and according to one theory there was more money to be made from filling "their spacious rinks with grain rather than people".[49]

In the east, the franchises in the NHA from 1911 to 1917 included the Ottawa Senators, Montreal Canadiens, Montreal Wanderers, Quebec Bulldogs and an odd assortment of squads in Toronto. The gadfly of the Toronto scene was the highly litigious Edward J. Livingstone[50] who by 1915 had incurred the enmity of his colleagues through his ownership of the Shamrocks and other teams. League operations were further hampered by wartime conditions and especially by the loss of manpower to enlistment. In February 1917, the anti-Livingstone faction first resolved to exclude Toronto from the schedule and then suspended the entire league at the annual general meeting in November. Further meetings beginning on November 22, 1917 at the Windsor Hotel in Montreal then saw the four NHA teams from Ottawa, Montreal and Quebec reconstitute themselves as the National Hockey League ("NHL"). The Quebec franchise did not, however, appear in the NHL's inaugural season in 1917-18 because it was replaced by the Toronto Hockey Club owned by the Arena Gardens company. The NHL's "original four" were, therefore, the Ottawa Senators, Montreal Canadiens, Montreal Wanderers and the Toronto Hockey Club, of which only three completed the season. The NHL's troubled origins culminated in the loss of the Wanderers after the Montreal Arena burned down in January 1918:[51] arson by Livingstone was not suspected.

During the 1920s, the NHL continued with teams in Quebec and Ontario, including the Hamilton Tigers, and began expansion into the United States in 1924 with the admission of the Boston Bruins. When the western league folded in 1926, the NHL emerged as the dominant professional circuit, so that since 1927 the annual playoffs in the NHL have decided the Stanley Cup championship. The NHL may not have been claiming the Stanley Cup as its own, but the trophy had certainly moved into the league's possessive control because they viewed it as a badge of major league status and product superiority. In February 1932, the "rebellious" American Hockey League ("AHL")[52] issued a challenge in an attempt to boost its standing and fight off the financial effects of

---

[49]  H. Roxborough, *The Stanley Cup Story* (Toronto: McGraw-Hill Ryerson, 1971) at 68.

[50]  On litigation and reorganization in the early years of the NHL, see Chapter 9, "National Hockey League", section A, 1. See also, M. Holzman & J. Nieforth, *Deceptions and Doublecross: How the NHL Conquered Hockey* (Toronto: Dundurn Press, 2002).

[51]  See: "Wanderers Have Excuse To Quit" and "Montreal Arena Burns To Ground" *The Globe and Mail* (Toronto: January 3, 1918) at 12; "Red Bands Withdraw" *The Globe and Mail* (Toronto: January 4, 1918) at 9; "N.H.L. Again Topsy-Turvy" *The Globe and Mail* (Toronto: January 5, 1918) at 18 (action by Toronto club against the Wanderers for non-fulfilment of schedule date). See also, W. Brown, *The Montreal Maroons: The Forgotten Stanley Cup Champions* (Montreal: Véhicule Press, 1999) at 15-16, 27-28. The Montreal Maroons picked up the flag of the English community in 1924 and maintained a rivalry with the Canadiens until 1938.

[52]  See: M. Holzman & J. Nieforth, *Deceptions and Doublecross: How the NHL Conquered Hockey* (Toronto: Dundurn Press, 2002) at 311-28; J.C. Wong, *Lords of the Rinks: The Emergence of the National Hockey League, 1875-1936* (Toronto: University of Toronto Press, 2005) at 133-42.

the Depression. The trustees felt duty-bound to receive and consider the challenge, but NHL president Frank Calder refused to allow a series against what he viewed as a minor, "outlaw" circuit and said that the NHL would rather compete for a new trophy.[53] Calder pursued a strategy of allowing the AHL to die a natural death, and the trustees essentially cooperated by not pressing the presentation of the challenge.[54] The problem duly went away later in the year when the AHL affiliated with the NHL as a minor league.

## C.  A MATTER OF TRUST

In June 1947, trustees P.D. Ross and J. Cooper Smeaton[55] entered into a Memorandum of Agreement with the NHL that recited the evolution of the Stanley Cup series and recognized the NHL as "the world's leading professional hockey league".[56] The Agreement noted that "the original conditions of competition as set out by the donor have been amended from time to time to meet the changing conditions brought about by the expansion of the game of hockey". The main substantive provisions of the Agreement were as follows:

1. The Trustees hereby delegate the League full authority to determine and amend from time to time the conditions of competition for the Stanley Cup, including the qualifications of challengers, the appointment of officials, ...and

---

[53]  See: "Chihawks Action May Provoke War" *The Globe and Mail* (Toronto: February 5, 1932) at 8; "What Will They Do With the Stanley Cup?" *The Globe and Mail* (Toronto: February 8, 1932) at 12 ("no all-American loop ever had the cup in its possession"); "That Stanley Cup Argument Again" and "Another Trophy Offered To N.H.L." *The Globe and Mail* (Toronto: February 9, 1932) at 8 (AHL "is the weakest of all the minor loops"; trustee Foran said matter will be "thoroughly investigated" and "a fair decision" made).

[54]  Authors differ on the attitude of the Stanley Cup trustees towards the challenge: R. Gruneau & D. Whitson, *Hockey Night in Canada: Sport, Identities and Cultural Politics* (Toronto: Garamond Press, 1993) at 99 (trustees "accepted" the challenge); J.C. Wong, *Lords of the Rinks: The Emergence of the National Hockey League, 1875-1936* (Toronto: University of Toronto Press, 2005) at 141 (trustees "presented" the challenge) at 224, note 45 (trustees requested counterproposal); D. Cruise & A. Griffiths, *Net Worth: Exploding the Myths of Pro Hockey* (Toronto: Viking Press, 1991) at 33 (trustees "agreed to" the challenge); B. Kidd & J. MacFarlane, *The Death of Hockey* (Toronto: New Press, 1972) at 112 (trustees "refused" the challenge). According to B. Kidd, *The Struggle for Canadian Sport* (Toronto: University of Toronto Press, 1996) at 217, President Calder's refusal to permit a series with the AHL "was upheld by the cup's trustees"; Kidd observes at 305, note 71, that the "records of the Stanley Cup trustees have never been found".

[55]  The sequence of trustees has been: Phillip D. Ross (1893-1949); Sheriff John Sweetland (1893-1907); William A. Foran (1907-1945); J. Cooper Smeaton (1946-1978); N.A.M. "Red" Dutton (1950-1987); Clarence S. Campbell (1979-1984); Justice Willard Estey (1984-2002); Brian O'Neill (1988-present); and Ian "Scotty" Morrison (2002-present).

[56]  "Memorandum of Agreement, June 30, 1947 between Philip Dansken Ross and J. Cooper Smeaton of the First Part and National Hockey League of the Second Part". See, *Burt v. O'Neill*, Notice of Application, Ont.S.C.J., 05-CV-287601PD3, April 13, 2005, Exhibit O to Affidavit of David Burt.

distributions of all gate receipts, provided always that the winners of the trophy shall be the acknowledged World's Professional Hockey Champions.

2. The Trustees agree that during the currency of this agreement they will not acknowledge or accept any challenge for the Stanley Cup unless such challenge is in conformity with the conditions specified in paragraph (1) hereof...

.....

5. This agreement shall remain in force so long as the League continues to be the world's leading professional hockey league as determined by its playing calibre, and in the event of dissolution or other termination of the National Hockey League, the Stanley Cup shall revert to the custody of the Trustees.

6. In the event of default in the appointment of a new trustee by the surviving trustee the Trustees hereby delegate and appoint, the Governors of the International Hockey Hall of Fame, Kingston, Ontario, to name two Canadian trustees to carry on under the terms of the original trust and in conformity with this agreement.

Under the 1947 Agreement, the trustees undertook to transfer their powers and discretion to the NHL and now considered the Stanley Cup emblematic of a "world" professional championship. The Cup's evolution and the purported amendments began to be questioned during the 1960s as correspondence and legal opinions expressed doubts about the league's control and about the diminishing Canadian presence in the NHL.[57] The issues were further complicated in 1962 when the original trophy was retired to the Hockey Hall of Fame in Toronto. A replacement trophy was then manufactured, so that it is now necessary to distinguish control of the physical Stanley Cups from ownership of associated properties. These intellectual properties include the NHL's registered trade-marks[58] in the words "The Stanley Cup" and in the recognizable design showing the bowl, bands and base of the trophy.

The general validity of the 1947 Agreement may be doubted, but it supplied ammunition to the "Wednesday Nighters" when the NHL season was cancelled in February 2005: the league was obviously no longer "continuing" and the question arose as to whether this constituted a "termination" resulting in the reversion of the Cup to the trustees. In April 2005, David Burt and Gard Shelley on behalf of the group applied for declarations requiring the current trustees to perform their duties under the trust and declaring that the cancellation of the season did not prevent the awarding of the Stanley Cup. In particular, Burt and Shelley applied for,

A declaration that the agreements between the NHL and the Trustees do not prevent the Trustees from awarding the Cup in any year that the NHL does not have a season and a final playoff determining the champion hockey team.[59]

---

[57] See, *Burt v. O'Neill* Application, *ibid.*, Exhibits P, Q, S, T,Y.

[58] See, *National Hockey League (NHL) v. Pepsi-Cola Canada Ltd.*, [1992] B.C.J. No. 1221, 92 D.L.R. (4th) 349 (B.C.S.C.), affd [1995] B.C.J. No. 310, 122 D.L.R. (4th) 412 (B.C.C.A.). See Chapter 7, "The Business of Hockey", section A, 3.

[59] *Burt v. O'Neill*, Notice of Application, Ont.S.C.J., 05-CV-287601PD3, April 13, 2005, para. 1(e).

The grounds of the application were that the trust is a charitable purpose trust and that the "fundamental purpose of the Trust is to award the Stanley Cup every year so as to promote the sport of hockey."[60] Anticipating awkward questions during the 2004-05 lockout, trustee Brian O'Neill took the "parrot position" and maintained that the league was not dead, just resting.[61]

The application by the "Wednesday Nighters" raised the issue of the nature of the Stanley Cup trust and the fiduciary duties of the trustees.[62] In most cases, a gift creating a private purpose trust is invalid because the object is uncertain, there is no identifiable group of human beneficiaries[63] and a court is not in a position to enforce the trust.[64] The gift also fails because of the perpetual duration of the purpose. The property then reverts to the donor, which in this example would either be the office of the Governor General or the Stanley family. One possible basis for sustaining the donation would involve accepting that it created a "power" to award the Stanley Cup to a reasonably certain class of hockey associations and their winning teams.[65] If, however, the gift created a trust for charitable purposes,[66] it would be a valid public trust enforceable by the provincial Public Guardian and Trustee and by the Attorney General. By section 7 of the *Charities Accounting Act*,[67] "charitable purpose" means:

(a) the relief of poverty,

(b) education,

(c) the advancement of religion; and

(d) any purpose beneficial to the community not falling under clause (a), (b)  or (c).

---

[60]   *Burt v. O'Neill*, Notice of Application, Ont.S.C.J., 05-CV-287601PD3, April 13, 2005, para. 2(c).

[61]   See, "Stanley Cup likely won't be up for grabs" *The Globe and Mail* (Toronto: November 16, 2004) at R7. O'Neill is quoted as saying, "The National Hockey League is not extinct. It's on sabbatical ...it's still the premier league in the world and it's the one we have an agreement with".

[62]   See, R.C. Payne, "Opinion regarding Stanley Cup" (January 19, 2005), formerly online: <http://www.freestanley.com/legal_opinion2.pdf>.

[63]   But see, *Re Denley's Trust Deed*, [1968] 3 All E.R. 65, [1969] 1 Ch. 373 (Ch. D.).

[64]   See: D.W.M. Waters, ed., *Waters' Law of Trusts in Canada*, 3d ed. (Toronto: Thomson Carswell, 2005) at 625-40; A.J. Oakley, *Parker and Mellows: The Modern Law of Trusts*, 6th ed. (London: Sweet & Maxwell, 1994) at 111-29.

[65]   See now, *Perpetuities Act*, R.S.O. 1990, c. P.9, s. 16 (trusts for specific non-charitable purposes construed as powers of appointment for 21 years).

[66]   See: D.W.M. Waters, ed., *Waters' Law of Trusts in Canada*, 3d ed. (Toronto: Thomson Carswell, 2005) at 640-798; J. Warburton, *Tudor on Charities*, 9th ed. (London: Sweet & Maxwell, 2003). See also, *Vancouver Society of Immigrant and Visible Minority Women v. Canada (Minister of National Revenue - M.N.R.)*, [1999] S.C.J. No. 5, [1999] 1 S.C.R. 10 (S.C.C.) (general meaning of charitable purposes).

[67]   R.S.O. 1990, c. C-10. By s. 10 of the Act, two or more persons may apply to the Superior Court of Justice to seek an order for carrying out a trust for a charitable purpose.

Traditionally, trusts promoting sports[68] for their own sake have not been recognized as charitable. A gift to provide a prize for yacht racing has, for example, been held to be void.[69] But if the sporting objective is part of a wider charitable purpose, then the gift is valid. Gifts to encourage sport at a particular school or through programs operating in the education system have, therefore, been recognized as charitable.[70] More recently, in *Re Laidlaw Foundation*,[71] the Ontario Divisional Court recognized that some amateur athletic activities may be beneficial to the community in that they promote health and general education; certain national sports organizations serving a wide sector of the public were held to qualify as having charitable purposes and so could properly receive gifts from the foundation.[72]

The Stanley Cup provisions are arguably invalid as a perpetual purpose trust for the promotion of sport, but the original object of establishing a trophy for amateur hockey may have amounted to a public benefit sufficient to constitute a charity. Property in the Cup then vested in the trustees who were obliged to discharge their powers and obligations in accordance with the objects of the trust. As noted earlier, the original conditions and regulations granted the trustees absolute discretion to recognize eligible champion clubs, but required the competition to be a challenge cup "open to all".[73] Deviation from the founding goals began in 1908 when the trophy entered the preserve of commercially motivated professional leagues, and the 1947 Agreement is particularly suspect in that the trustees delegated their discretion to the NHL and agreed to limit challenges to NHL teams. If the Stanley Cup was properly donated for a charitable purpose, it might be appropriate for the Public Trustee to call for a 100-year accounting of profits and proceeds. The period of explanation for the NHL might be from its foundation in 1917, from its monopolization of the Cup in 1927 or from the 1947 Agreement. It is, however, open to the league to show that its teams are non-profit organizations dedicated to the relief of poverty or to advancing purposes beneficial to the community.

The application by the "Wednesday Nighters" was eventually settled in February 2006 when the NHL acknowledged that the trustees can award the Cup

---

[68] See: J. Barnes, *Sports and the Law in Canada*, 3d ed. (Toronto: Butterworths, 1996) at 31-33; D.W.M. Waters, ed., *Waters' Law of Trusts in Canada*, 3d ed. (Toronto: Thomson Carswell, 2005) at 724-43.

[69] See, *Re Nottage*, [1895] 2 Ch. 649 (C.A.).

[70] See: *Re Mariette*, [1915] 2 Ch. 284 (Ch. D.); *I.R.C. v. McMullen*, [1980] 1 All E.R. 884, [1981] A.C. 1 (H.L.).

[71] [1984] O.J. No. 3390, 48 O.R. (2d) 549, 13 D.L.R. (4th) 491 (Ont. Div. Ct.).

[72] See also: *Income Tax Act*, R.S.C. 1985, c. 1 (5th Supp.), ss. 110.1(1)(a)(ii), 248(1) (gifts to registered Canadian amateur athletic associations); *A.Y.S.A. Amateur Youth Soccer Assn. v. Canada (Revenue Agency)*, [2007] S.C.J. No. 42, [2007] 3 S.C.R. 217 (S.C.C.) (sports associations may qualify as charitable under the *Income Tax Act* if their activities are ancillary to a recognized charitable purpose).

[73] See Chapter 1, "Lord Stanley and the Wednesday Nighters", section A. The recognition of American-based challengers is arguably consistent with the trustees' authority and with the general goal of promoting the game in the Dominion.

to a non-NHL team in any year that the league does not operate.[74] It was, therefore, confirmed that the NHL has no exclusive claim to Lord Stanley's trophy, although trustee O'Neill insisted that potential recipients should be of a very high standard.[75] The settlement left many issues unresolved, and it remains open to other applicants to question the proprietary rights and legal arrangements that surround the award of the Cup. The "changing conditions" of the historical evolution of the trophy have tended to obscure the element of public obligation demanded by the original gift, and the new awareness of the founding purpose may be useful in reminding the NHL of its responsibilities. In his capacity as a keeper of the game, one of the "Wednesday Nighters" offered the following view:

> I believe the Cup is a symbol, not only of hockey, but also of Canadian culture. I am truly saddened by the fact that the awarding of the Cup is now treated as captive to purely commercial interests, and is totally dependent on the resolution of a private collective bargaining agreement process.[76]

The Stanley Cup is certainly symbolic, although it has represented only half of Canada's hockey world. During the lockout, Governor General Adrienne Clarkson suggested that women's teams compete for the Cup,[77] but subsequently resolved to donate a new trophy for the women's championship.[78] The Clarkson Cup was duly inaugurated in 2006 to be contested between the champions of the Women's Hockey Leagues of eastern and western Canada.[79] Since property rights are not the exclusive preserve of the men's game, the new trophy was quickly the subject of a licensing dispute as the designers and artists claimed a share of royalties from the marketing of the Cup or its image.[80]

---

[74] See, "Hockey buffs win faceoff with NHL over Stanley Cup" *The Globe and Mail* (Toronto: February 7, 2006) at A2. As part of the settlement, the NHL agreed that from 2006-2110 it would contribute CDN $100,000 a-year to hockey leagues for women and for underprivileged children.

[75] See, "Court: Non-NHL teams could vie for Cup" *Canadian Press* (February 7, 2006) reporting that a new clause will be included in the NHL's agreement with the trustees.

[76] *Burt v. O'Neill*, Notice of Application, Ont.S.C.J., 05-CV-287601PD3, April 13, 2005, Affidavit of David Burt.

[77] See: "Let women play for Stanley Cup, Clarkson says" *The Globe and Mail* (Toronto: February 22, 2005) at A1, A7; "Give the girls the glory of the game" *The Globe and Mail* (Toronto: February 26, 2005) at A15 (argument by Christie Blatchford that the NHL has merely "leased" the Stanley Cup and has proved to be a bad tenant).

[78] See, "Clarkson to reward women's champion" *The Globe and Mail* (Toronto: March 11, 2005) at R7. On trophies, see, Hockey Canada, Regulations (2008-2009), Regulation L, and "Trophies of the Association" (at 191-198).

[79] See, "Hockey's Newest Treasure" *The Globe and Mail* (Toronto: July 11, 2006) at A1. On women's hockey, see Chapter 2, "Legal Fundamentals and Equality Rights", section E, 1.

[80] See, "Lawyers, instead of hockey teams, to fight it out" *The Globe and Mail* (Toronto: November 13, 2007) at A14. The trophy shows the Inuit goddess Sedna rising through the ice.

# Chapter 2

# LEGAL FUNDAMENTALS AND EQUALITY RIGHTS

Our world of sports is constantly on trial.[1]

## A.  THE LAW OF SPORTS

Sports are subject to a double dose of rules and regulation and inevitably risk the attention of lawyers. As organized physical contests,[2] sports are constituted by an internal legal apparatus consisting of the playing rules and the administrative structures of the governing body.[3] The game rules define the contest, incorporate safety standards and grant supervisory and disciplinary power to officials. The administrative structure establishes a hierarchy of authority for running the sport and deals with matters such as the organization of competitions and the eligibility of participants. Games have always required contractual agreement,[4] and more uniform modern sports[5] have elaborated this into national or international charters,[6] constitutions and codes.[7] The stated rules are, however, only part of the text, which is also inscribed with a whole range of cultural and

---

[1]   P. Weiler, *Leveling the Playing Field: How the Law Can Make Sports Better for Fans* (Cambridge: Harvard University Press, 2000) at 341.

[2]   Sports usually require the competitive use of physical skills and are more structured and formalized when compared to general human movement, exercise or recreation. The distinction between "physical activity" and "sport" is recognized in ss. 3-4 of the *Physical Activity and Sport Act*, S.C. 2003, c. 2. For the purpose of Sport Canada's "Sport Funding and Accountability Framework", "Sport is a regulated form of physical activity organized as a contest between two or more participants for the purpose of determining a winner by fair and ethical means. Such contest may be in the form of a game, match, race or other event" (SFAF III, 2009-2013, A1, Annex A1). See further, Chapter 2, "Legal Fundamentals and Equality Rights", section B, 1, 4.

[3]   See, G.M. Kelly, *Sport and the Law: An Australian Perspective* (North Ryde: The Law Book Company, 1987) at 18-28.

[4]   See, A. Harvey, *The Beginnings of a Commercial Sporting Culture in Britain, 1793-1850* (Aldershot: Ashgate Publishing, 2004) at 115-20.

[5]   See, A. Guttmann, *From Ritual to Record: The Nature of Modern Sports* (New York: Columbia University Press, 1978).

[6]   For the *Olympic Charter* (July 2007), see online, <http://www.olympic.org>. For the *World Anti-Doping Code* (2009), see online: <http://www.wada-ama.org>.

[7]   The *Rule Book of Association Football* (1863) has been included in a selection of the world's most influential books: M. Bragg, *12 Books That Changed the World* (London: Hodder & Stoughton, 2006).

moral attitudes about the chivalrous playing of the game.[8] Sporting rivals try to "hurt the opposition", but there are unwritten codes and conventions as to how the beating may be inflicted. Although the sports field embodies a Darwinian survival of the fittest, there is behaviour that is "not cricket" and "not hockey".

To compound all this in-house legalism and sporting lore, the wider legal system also invades the field, because "[n]o rules or practice of any game whatever can make that lawful which is unlawful by the law of the land".[9] Sports law largely takes the form of a collision event in which players' conduct or decisions by leagues or associations run up against state institutions and public legal standards. The resulting law game can be played out in the relative privacy of committee rooms and arbitration hearings, but battle is also waged before judges, human rights tribunals, labour boards, commissions of inquiry and legislatures.[10] These and other agencies have a hand in regulating sport and resolving the disputes and conflicts that arise. Jurisdiction is sometimes limited because there is a tendency to defer to the voluntary processes and expertise of private associations, but no individual or organization can entirely escape state supervision and legal intervention. This public law of sports is a formal response to ethical problems as parties lay claim to equitable opportunities,[11] liberty of action,[12] safe playing conditions,[13] fair procedures,[14] property rights[15] or appropriate financial rewards.[16] The regulations and mechanisms of sports law strive for an approximation of sports justice and try to balance these competing demands for equality, freedom, fairness and security.

The interaction between sport and law is not new since there is a long tradition of societies exerting moral control over leisure in the interest of Sunday Observance,[17] public order and "rational recreation".[18] In the nineteenth century,

---

[8]    See, D. Fraser, *"The Man in White is Always Right": Cricket and the Law* (Sydney: Institute of Criminology, 1993/London: Routledge, 2005).

[9]    *R. v. Bradshaw* (1878), 14 Cox C.C. 83, 84 (Assize Ct.), *per* Bramwell L.J. (death in soccer game; accused acquitted of manslaughter). See Chapter 6, "Play Safe: On the Ice", section B.

[10]   For general legal research, including current federal and provincial legislation and recent case decisions, see, online: <http://www.lexisnexis.ca> or <http:www.canlii.org>. For information on the Sport Dispute Resolution Centre of Canada, see, online: <http://www.crdsc-sdrcc.ca/eng/home.jsp>, including "Resource and Documentation Centre" and "Jurisprudence Database"; see further, Chapter 2, "Legal Fundamentals and Equality Rights", section C.

[11]   See Chapter 2, "Legal Fundamentals and Equality Rights", sections B, 3; E.

[12]   See Chapter 3, "Organizations and Regulations"; Chapter 8, "Competition Law and Labour Law", sections A - C.

[13]   See, Chapters 4 - 6.

[14]   See Chapter 3, "Organizations and Regulations", section C; Chapter 8, "Competition Law and Labour Law"; Chapter 9, "National Hockey League", section D.

[15]   See Chapter 7, "The Business of Hockey", sections A; B.

[16]   See Chapter 8, "Competition Law and Labour Law"; Chapter 9, "National Hockey League".

[17]   The main federal legislation was the *Lord's Day Act*, S.C. 1906, c. 27. See in particular, *R. v. Icelandia Ltd.*, [1947] O.J. No. 536, [1947] O.R. 761 (H.C.) (hockey practices not an exempted "work of necessity").

[18]   Official action combined the suppression of vice with the provision or protection of approved leisure activities; see: R. Vorspan, "'Rational Recreation' and the Law: The Transformation of Popular Urban Leisure in Victorian England" (2000) 45 McGill L.J. 891; A. Harvey, *The*

state authorities looked to prohibit or tax disreputable activities,[19] and the criminal law was applied against animal sports[20] and prize fighting.[21] The early years of organized sport also saw a fair collection of incidents and cases. In 1884, an unruly lacrosse exhibition involving the Royal Caughnawagas was brought into line by a brawny New York policeman who raised his billy club as a regulatory incentive and threatened to stop the game.[22] The first hockey associations faced disputes relating to eligibility, players' contracts and business operations,[23] and there were instances of the criminal prosecution of players for assault and even manslaughter.[24] In 1909, in *Stewart v. Cobalt Curling and Skating Assn.*,[25] a spectator recovered damages from the owners of a rink after a gallery rail gave way under the press of eager "rooters" wanting to see a fight on the ice. The private lives of prominent professionals also brought their share of legal trouble, especially where behaviour was influenced by the drug of choice, alcohol. In 1918, Sprague Cleghorn was arrested on a charge of spousal assault after he was alleged to have struck his wife with the crutch he was using for his broken leg.[26]

In the 1970s, this legal heritage began to blossom into a more sustained and significant discipline as sport grew in both economic and political importance. The enhanced commercialisation of sport was a leading factor in the growth of sports law:

> The industrialization of sport and its expanded role as entertainment has been the main determinant in the explosive expansion of sports law. Sport marketing, sponsorship, advertising and media involvement now account for a substantial segment of economic activity. In those fields, the impact of the law is ubiquitous. The legal issues, moreover, reach across state frontiers because sport has an international focus.[27]

---

*Beginnings of a Commercial Sporting Culture in Britain, 1793-1850* (Aldershot: Ashgate Publishing, 2004) at 63-113.

[19] See, T. Joyce, "Canadian Sport and State Control: Toronto 1845-86" (1999) 16 Int. J. of the History of Sport 22.

[20] *An Act respecting Cruelty to Animals*, 32-33 Vict., c. 27 (1869); am. 33 Vict., c. 29 (1870). See now, *Criminal Code*, R.S.C. 1985, c. C-46, ss. 444-447.1.

[21] *An Act respecting Prize Fighting*, S.C. 1881, c. 30. See now, *Criminal Code*, R.S.C. 1985, c. C-46, s. 83. On illegal sports, see Chapter 6, "Play Safe: On the Ice", section B, 1.

[22] See, "The Indians Smile" *The New York Times* (July 25, 1884) at 3 (report of a game played at the Polo Grounds between the Royal Caughnawaga Indians of Canada and the Independents). The policeman's exact words were, "If yez don't stop this, begorra I'll stop the game". The incident is a rare recorded example of an Irishman actually saying "begorra".

[23] See Chapter 1, "Lord Stanley and the Wednesday Nighters", section B; Chapter 9, "National Hockey League", section A, 1.

[24] See Chapter 6, "Play Safe: On the Ice", section B; Appendix I.

[25] [1909] O.J. No. 170, 19 O.L.R. 667 (Ont. Div. Ct.) (plaintiff was thrown onto the ice from the gallery; CDN $850 in damages for serious injuries).

[26] See, "Sprague Cleghorn Arrested" *The Globe and Mail* (Toronto: January 5, 1918) at 18.

[27] M. Kelly, "The Sport Revolution and the Legitimation of Sport Law" (1991) 1(1) ANZSLA Newsletter 6.

As the sports business developed new revenue sources, more militant professional players claimed a due share of the proceeds and looked to protect their financial interests through legal and industrial relations processes. The formation of rival leagues created competing markets, and players achieved further mobility and prosperity through antitrust litigation and collective bargaining. Management had always relied on legal power to control the enterprise and retain the prime slice of the pie, but there was now a fairer fight over the spoils.[28] Other levels of sport also faced athlete emancipation movements seeking better protection of civil rights and playing opportunities,[29] and governments became increasingly involved in sports administration as they promoted activities, funded organizations and investigated problems.[30] The underpaid, the excluded and the injured acquired remedies and gained the organizational strength necessary to further claims. The sports lawyer was born,[31] and the law became a familiar feature of sporting culture as it tackled expected issues such as violence, discrimination, disciplinary action and contractual disputes.[32] The litigation record also extends to more unusual cases.[33] Quite apart from the contested ownership of the Stanley Cup, there have been altercations between hockey mothers,[34] a rioting Canucks fan has sued the police,[35] a player has sued a minor hockey association because he was not selected as MVP,[36] a

---

[28] On the formation of rival leagues, including the World Hockey Association, see, G. Davidson & B. Libby, *Breaking the Game Wide Open* (New York: Atheneum, 1974). On management domination of employment relations in professional hockey, see, D. Cruise & A. Griffiths, *Net Worth: Exploding the Myths of Pro Hockey* (Toronto: Viking, 1991). See further, Chapter 7, "The Business of Hockey", section C, 1; Chapter 8, "Competition Law and Labour Law"; Chapter 9, "National Hockey League", sections A-B.

[29] See, B. Kidd & M. Eberts, *Athletes' Rights in Canada* (Toronto: Ministry of Tourism and Recreation, 1982).

[30] See Chapter 2, "Legal Fundamentals and Equality Rights", section B (powers and policies); Chapter 3, "Organizations and Regulations", section A (reports on organization and administration); Chapter 6, "Play Safe: On the Ice", section B, 5 (reports on violence).

[31] On the rise and fall of Alan Eagleson, see Chapter 3, "Organizations and Regulations", section A, 4; Chapter 9, "National Hockey League", section B.

[32] See: J. Barnes, *Sports and the Law in Canada*, 3d ed. (Markham, ON: Butterworths, 1996); "Sports", *Canadian Encyclopedic Digest*, 4th ed., vol. 31, title 135.1 (Ontario), vol. 32, title 136.1 (Western) (Toronto: Thomson Carswell, 2008).

[33] There is a remarkable variety in "Rink Rage": see Chapter 5, "Be Safe: Off the Ice", section B. See, for example, *Reddemann v. McEachnie*, [2005] B.C.J. No. 1374, 2005 BCSC 915, 140 A.C.W.S. (3d) 766 (B.C.S.C.) (coach attacked mascot-fan who was banging drum).

[34] *de Groot v. Arsenault*, [1999] M.J. No. 489, 140 Man.R. (2d) 285 (Man. Q.B.), affd [2000] M.J. No. 487, 150 Man.R. (2d) 154 (Man. C.A.) (assault action dismissed on the basis of self-defence).

[35] *Berntt v. Vancouver (City)*, [2001] B.C.J. No. 2658, 209 D.L.R. (4th) 494 (B.C.S.C.) (action dismissed). See also: *Berntt v. Vancouver (City)*, [1999] B.C.J. No. 1257, 174 D.L.R. (4th) 403, additional reasons [1999] B.C.J. No. 2219, 179 D.L.R. (4th) 380 (B.C.C.A.); *R. v. Berntt*, [1997] B.C.J. No. 2301, 120 C.C.C. (3d) 344 (B.C.C.A.).

[36] *Croteau (tuteur d'instance de) c. Conseil du hockey mineur du Nouveau-Brunswick*, [2003] A.N.-B. no 292, 2003 NBBR 307 (N.B.Q.B.) (no bad faith in decision to make awards). See

novice player has attempted to bring an action for mental distress caused by his dismissal from the team,[37] and a disgruntled season-ticket holder has sued Alexei Yashin because of his holdout from the Ottawa Senators.[38] No one would suggest that lawyers have been stirring up sporting conflict: more probably it is a case of the combative tendencies of sports people being transferred to a new arena, especially when serious money or deeply felt principles were at stake. The legal profession does, however, have a good nose for a fee and a fight and has been happy to lend its services.

Commentators have debated whether the accumulation of jock-prudence constitutes a discrete subject area. Many issues are resolved according to ordinary legal principles so that the field seems to be a form of applied law best designated as "sports and the law". The growth of material and the enactment of dedicated legislation have, however, brought a preference for "sports law".[39] Proponents of this special *ius ludorum* (law of games) also maintain that sports present peculiar problems that call for distinct doctrines and expert consideration. The peculiar characteristics include the physical dimensions[40] of the contest and the inherent risks, the voluntary nature of the activity and the framework of rules. Professional leagues are a particularly unusual type of cartel in that they promote rivalry through co-operation.[41] The member teams may be sworn enemies but they are interdependent in offering a joint product: the Leafs would be nothing without the Canadiens. Leagues make arrangements to share wealth, maintain competitive balance and keep fans guessing as to which team will win. The game characteristics and monopoly structures sometimes call for economic and sporting sophistication, and courts are often divided and confused as to how to proceed in sports cases.[42] In response to the proliferation of conflict

---

also, *Croteau c. Hockey Canada*, [2005] A.C.F. no 883, 2005 CF 704 (F.C.) (Hockey Canada not federal agency subject to review by Federal Court).

[37] *Butrimas v. Applewood Hockey Assn.*, [2006] O.J. No. 3494, 147 A.C.W.S. (3d) 144 (Ont. S.C.J. Small Claims Ct.)(no reasonable cause of action for intentional infliction of emotional harm but case could proceed with respect to breach of fiduciary duty). See also, "Hockey dad launches $10,000 lawsuit" *The Globe and Mail* (Toronto, June 27, 2003).

[38] *Potechin v. Yashin*, [2000] O.J. No. 1660, 186 D.L.R. (4th) 757 (Ont. S.C.J.).

[39] See: S. Gardiner *et al.*, *Sports Law*, 3d ed. (London: Cavendish Publishing, 2006) at viii, 88-93; M.J. Beloff, T. Kerr & M. Demetriou, *Sports Law* (Oxford: Hart Publishing, 1999) at 1-6.

[40] See, for example: the special problems relating to discrimination on the basis of sex, disability and transgender status (sex change); Chapter 2, "Legal Fundamentals and Equality Rights", section E.

[41] See Chapter 7, "The Business of Hockey", section C; Chapter 8, "Competition Law and Labour Law".

[42] For major reversals in Australia, Canada and the United States, see, for example: *Rootes v. Shelton* (1967), 116 C.L.R. 383 (H.C. of Aust.), revg [1966] 2 N.S.W.R. 784, 86 W.N. Pt. 1 N.S.W. 94 (N.S.W.C.A.) (whether a participant owes a duty of care in negligence to another participant); *Crocker v. Sundance Northwest Resorts Ltd.*, [1988] S.C.J. No. 60, [1988] 1 S.C.R. 1186 (S.C.C.), revg [1985] O.J. No. 2607, 51 O.R. (2d) 608, 20 D.L.R. (4th) 552 (Ont. C.A.) (whether race organizers should be liable for injuries suffered by an inebriated inner-tube slider); *Clarett v. National Football League*, 369 F.3d 124 (2nd Cir., 2004), revg 306 F.Supp. 2d 379 (S.D.N.Y., 2004) (whether a player eligibility rule is protected from antitrust challenge by the non-statutory labour exemption). See also, *Association olympique canadienne c. Deschênes*, [1988] J.Q. no 1646, [1988] R.J.Q. 2389 (Que. C.A.) (whether courts should be involved in team selection disputes).

and grievances, many organizations have turned to alternative dispute resolution ("ADR") in the hope that specialized tribunals will render the correct and favourable decision.[43] This preference for private mechanisms does nothing to halt the "juridification" of sport, it merely limits athletes in their access to national courts and leaves them dependent on the justice of international federations.[44] The Court of Arbitration for Sport ("CAS") now carries a heavy case load in relation to high performance events and major Games and offers a process that can yield uniform, internationally-enforceable decisions. At the national level, athletes or officials affiliated with Canadian teams may be required to take disputes before the arbitrators or mediators of the Sport Dispute Resolution Centre of Canada ("SDRCC"). These tribunals endeavour to find solutions that are sensitive to the needs of sport, and there is an emerging jurisprudence that is sometimes labelled with the neologism, *lex sportiva*.[45] As to whether there is a discrete "sports law", suffice to say that special problems and processes do exist, but sports participants are also entitled to ordinary legal protections. The athlete does not cease to be a citizen, and the loaded theory that participation is a "privilege" does not justify any exclusion of basic rights.[46]

## B.   GOVERNMENT POWERS AND POLICIES

### 1.   *Physical Activity and Sport Act*

The sporting objectives of the Government of Canada are declared in the *Physical Activity and Sport Act*[47] ("PASA") of 2003, which is also the legislation that established the Sport Dispute Resolution Centre of Canada (see, PASA, ss. 9-35). The new Act repealed the *Fitness and Amateur Sport Act*[48] of 1961, although it incorporates many of the ministerial powers mentioned in the previous legislation. The federal government began to develop a significant presence in amateur sport in the 1970s when it assumed responsibility for national organizations and high-performance sport, while also expressing

---

[43]   See Chapter 2, "Legal Fundamentals and Equality Rights", section C; Chapter 9, "National Hockey League", sections C-G (forms of arbitration in the NHL).

[44]   See, K. Foster, "Alternative Models for the Regulation of Global Sport" in L. Allison, ed., *The Global Politics of Sport: The Role of Global Institutions in Sport* (London: Routledge, 2005) at 63 and 68-73.

[45]   This invented term is said to be inspired by the law merchant (*lex mercatoria*), but the adjective *sportivus, sportiva* is unknown to Latin. The Latin words *sportula* and *sportulo* do, however, have associations with the largesse handed out at the Roman Games; a *sportula* was a basket, and *sportulo* meant to take the dole. See further: J.A.F. Nafziger, "Lex Sportiva" [2004] (1-2) Int. Sports L.J. 3; K. Foster, "*Lex Sportiva* and *Lex Ludica*: The Court of Arbitration for Sport's Jurisprudence" and A. Erbsen, "The Substance and Illusion of *Lex Sportiva*" in I.S. Blackshaw, R.C.R. Siekmann and J. Soek, eds., *The Court of Arbitration for Sport 1984-2004* (The Hague: TMC Asser Press, 2006) at 420 and 441.

[46]   On rights in doping control, see Chapter 3, "Organizations and Regulations", section D.

[47]   S.C. 2003, c. 2.

[48]   R.S.C. 1985, c. F-25; repealed, S.C. 2003, c. 2, s. 39.

concerns over public health and fitness.[49] The purpose of PASA is to modernize the legislative framework that supports programs and to give formal expression to general policies adopted in 2002.[50]

In the preamble to PASA, the federal government recognizes, "that physical activity and sport are integral parts of Canadian culture and society and produce benefits in terms of health, social cohesion, linguistic duality, economic activity and quality of life". The government's policy objectives include promoting physical activity "as a fundamental element of health and well-being" and reducing barriers that prevent Canadians from being active (see, PASA, s. 3(a), (c)). In relation to sport, the objectives are to increase participation, support the pursuit of excellence and "build capacity" by developing the potential of the system (see, PASA, s. 4(2)). Section 4(1) incorporates a statement of policy principles declaring that,

> The Government of Canada's policy regarding sport is founded on the highest ethical standards and values, including doping-free sport, the treatment of all persons with fairness and respect, the full and fair participation of all persons in sport and the fair, equitable, transparent and timely resolution of disputes in sport.

To further the objectives of the Act, the responsible Minister has the mandate under section 5 to take appropriate measures and may "coordinate federal initiatives" relating to sports policies (see, PASA, s. 5(f)). In particular, the Minister may:

- undertake or assist in research or studies (see, PASA, s. 5(a));

- cooperate with interested groups (see, PASA, s. 5(e));

- provide for the training of coaches (see, PASA, s. 5(i));

- encourage the promotion of sport as a tool of individual and social development in Canada and abroad (see, PASA, s. 5(k));

- encourage financial contributions from the private sector (see, PASA, s. 5(l));

- facilitate the participation of under-represented groups (see, PASA, s. 5(m)); and

- encourage provincial and territorial governments to promote and develop sport (see, PASA, s. 5(n)).

---

[49] See: J. Barnes, *Sports and the Law in Canada*, 3d ed. (Toronto: Butterworths, 1996) at 11-17; D. Macintosh *et al.*, *Sport and Politics in Canada: Federal Government Involvement since 1961* (Montreal and Kingston: McGill-Queens University Press, 1987); D. Macintosh & D. Whitson, *The Game Planners: Transforming Canada's Sport System* (Montreal & Kingston: McGill-Queens University Press, 1990).

[50] See Chapter 2, "Legal Fundamentals and Equality Rights", section B, 3.

The Minister may provide financial assistance in accordance with the *Official Languages Act*[51] (see, PASA, s. 6) and may enter into international agreements with the government of any foreign state (see, PASA, s. 8). Since the regulation of sport and the delivery of sport programs are the responsibility of different levels of government, the Act also provides that the Minister may enter into agreements with any Province or Territory regarding the implementation of federal sport policy (see, PASA, s. 7(2)) and may pay contributions towards the costs of promoting physical activity or sport (see, PASA, s. 7(1)). Sport is, therefore, deeply affected by the recurring Canadian dilemma about constitutional roles.

## 2.    Division of Powers

Canada is constituted as a confederation that divides law-making power. The *Constitution Act, 1867*[52] assigns jurisdiction in different classes of subject matter between the provincial legislatures and the federal Parliament. The Act does not specifically refer to sports, although the failed Charlottetown Accord of 1992 did propose to list "recreation" as a matter of exclusive provincial authority subject to funding limitation agreements with the federal government.[53] Each level of government has enacted legislation incidental to its constitutional authority[54] to support, stimulate or regulate sports programs,[55] and each bureaucracy includes its Ministry of Vigorous Walks.

Primary responsibility for development and participatory aspects of sport, recreation and fitness lies with private and community agencies falling under the jurisdiction of the Provinces. Under section 92 of the *Constitution Act, 1867*, the Provinces have exclusive jurisdiction to make laws in relation to public land, hospitals, municipal institutions, property and civil rights, and general matters of a merely local or private nature in the Province. Section 93 gives the Provinces jurisdiction over education. Since sports and recreation are aspects of health, culture and education, the more general and direct responsibility falls to local, municipal and provincial bodies. Provincial legislation authorizes the support and operation of programs and provincial law sets regulatory standards of health,

---

[51]    R.S.C. 1985, c. 31 (4th Supp.).

[52]    (U.K.) 30 & 31 Vict., c. 3; R.S.C. 1985, App. II, No. 5. On the *Constitution Act, 1982* and the *Canadian Charter of Rights and Freedoms*, see Chapter 2, "Legal Fundamentals and Equality Rights", section D, 2.

[53]    See, "Consensus Report on the Constitution, Charlottetown", August 28, 1992, Final Text, at 11-12; "Draft Legal Text" October 9, 1992, s. 11 (proposed s. 93A in the *Constitution Act, 1867*).

[54]    See, D. Alhéritière, "La réglementation du loisir, des activités de plein air et des sports au Canada: aspects constitutionnels" (1973), 14 C. de D. 33. On legislation regulating safety standards, see Chapter 6, "Play Safe: On the Ice", section A, 3.

[55]    *Cf.* Canada, *Report of the Federal Cultural Policy Review Committee* (Ottawa: Supply and Services Canada, 1982) (Applebaum-Hébert report) at 72-90 (roles of government in cultural policy: patron, catalyst, regulator, proprietor and custodian).

safety and integrity; such control occurs under general private law or through statutory provisions or public commissions that license and supervise the activity. Sports litigation more commonly raises issues in provincial civil law, notably the general law of torts, contracts and administrative law.

The federal government or Parliament may supplement private or provincial support by making grants in exercise of the "spending power",[56] provided the intervention does not amount to a regulatory scheme relating to matters under provincial jurisdiction. This power has enabled the federal government to fund health and fitness programs and to offer research services.[57] Under section 91 of the *Constitution Act, 1867*, further federal intervention in sport may be based on the residual authority of Parliament to make "Laws for the Peace, Order, and good Government of Canada" and on Parliament's jurisdiction in trade and commerce, taxation, the military, shipping and inland fisheries, immigration and citizenship, and criminal law. More generally, whenever a matter is claimed to be of some national or international significance,[58] federal authorities may in practice assert an interest. The federal government therefore has important regulatory jurisdiction in areas such as commerce and communications and has an evolved responsibility in relation to national sport programs:

> The primary federal program areas include support for national team programs, team centralization, national coaching programs, national coaches, major Games and championships, research, and international competition.[59]

## 3.   Policies

In 2002, the different levels of government achieved a significant "first" when they approved a national policy[60] document presenting a shared vision and goals for the period 2002 to 2012. The "Canadian Sport Policy" "emphasizes increased communication and collaboration amongst all the stakeholders [and] commits all governments to setting targets".[61] While offering a national vision and a goal of world-class excellence, the document also points out that "[s]port is best developed at the local level where participation is provided through...community-based organizations".[62] The Policy recites the contributions of sport to health and culture and notes that sport and recreation account for

---

[56]   See, P.W. Hogg, *Constitutional Law of Canada*, 2004 Student Edition (Scarborough: Carswell, 2004) at 164-68.

[57]   See, M. Lalonde, Minister of National Health and Welfare, *A New Perspective on the Health of Canadians — A Working Document* (Ottawa: Information Canada, 1975) at 46.

[58]   See also, *Constitution Act, 1867*, (U.K.) 30 & 31 Vict., c. 3, R.S.C. 1985, App. II, No. 5, s. 132 (power of Parliament in relation to treaties with foreign countries).

[59]   "The Canadian Sport Policy" (May 24, 2002) at 22, online: <www.pch.gc.ca> "Sport Canada".

[60]   For comparative perspectives on sport policy, see: B. Houlihan, *Sport, Policy and Politics: A Comparative Analysis* (London: Routledge, 1997); B. Stewart *et al.*, *Australian Sport: Better by Design? The Evolution of Australian Sport Policy* (London: Routledge, 2004).

[61]   "The Canadian Sport Policy" (May 24, 2002) at 3, online: <www.pch.gc.ca>.

[62]   "The Canadian Sport Policy" (May 24, 2002) at 14, online: <www.pch.gc.ca>.

about 1.1 per cent of the gross domestic product and 2 per cent of jobs. Acknowledging the decline in physical activity, the various social barriers to access and the need to improve programs at all levels, the Policy sets four goals for 2012:

> Goal I: ENHANCED PARTICIPATION: A significantly higher proportion of Canadians from all segments of society are involved in quality sports activities at all levels and in all forms of participation.

> Goal II: ENHANCED EXCELLENCE: The pool of talented athletes has expanded and Canadian athletes and teams are systematically achieving world-class results at the highest levels of international competition through fair and ethical means.

> Goal III: ENHANCED CAPACITY: The essential components of an ethically based, athlete/participant-centred development system are in place and are continually modernized and strengthened as required.

> Goal IV: ENHANCED INTERACTION: The components of the sport system are more connected and coordinated as a result of the committed collaboration and communication amongst the stakeholders.[63]

The Policy therefore aims to promote participation and to establish an integrated sport development system that will ultimately yield results at the high-performance level.

The ethical component in the "Canadian Sport Policy" is complemented by the principles declared in the companion document, the "Canadian Strategy for Ethical Conduct in Sport",[64] which also offers a vision for 2012 and aims to promote ethical conduct in both "amateur" and professional sport. This Policy declares the goal of achieving a fair sport system that is free from discrimination and that accords respect to all participants. It is part of the vision that,

> Those who participate in sport receive from their fellow athletes, coaches and officials, and parents/guardians and spectators, fairness and ethical treatment in a safe and welcoming sport environment, free of harassment and abuse.[65]

In collaboration with sport communities, the "Strategy" envisages an action plan to raise awareness of ethical issues through education and prevention programs

---

[63]   "The Canadian Sport Policy" (May 24, 2002) at 16-19, online: <www.pch.gc.ca>. See also, "The Canadian Sport Policy: Federal-Provincial/Territorial Priorities for Collaborative Action 2007-2012" (2007).

[64]   "Canadian Strategy for Ethical Conduct in Sport: Policy Framework" (May 24, 2002), online: <www.pch.gc.ca> "Sport Canada". See also, "Canadian Policy Against Doping in Sport" (June 2004). On the True Sport Foundation, see online: <http://www.truesportpur.ca>.

[65]   "Canadian Strategy for Ethical Conduct in Sport: Policy Framework" (May 24, 2002) at 3, online: <www.pch.gc.ca> "Sport Canada".

and to "foster the next generation of value-based leaders in Canadian sport".[66] The "Strategy" offers a comprehensive statement of ethical goals and is particularly a response to recent crises relating to violence and sexual abuse.[67] The goals of promoting equity and eliminating discrimination are also stated in other federal policy documents dealing with women in sport, official languages, participation by aboriginal peoples and sport for persons with a disability.[68]

It is a longstanding policy of the federal government to encourage national sport organizations ("NSOs") to generate private funding[69] through sponsorships and other commercial contracts. Funded NSOs may not, however, associate with tobacco companies,[70] and various types of tobacco-related promotions and advertising are now prohibited under the *Tobacco Act*.[71] As health care systems deal with alcohol consumption, obesity and diabetes, further restrictions may be considered in relation to the staple sponsors of sport: breweries, manufacturers of soft drinks and purveyors of fast food.

## 4. Programs and Ministries

In the federal government, the former Fitness and Amateur Sport directorate, which consisted of Sport Canada and Fitness Canada (previously Recreation Canada), was traditionally located in the ministry responsible for national health. In 1993, the directorate was divided to reflect the separate functions, so that Sport Canada was relocated to the Department of Canadian Heritage and the smaller Fitness Canada program became part of the Health Canada ministry. Health Canada now includes the Public Health Agency of Canada, which incorporates the Physical Activity Unit.[72] This Unit is responsible for promoting active living and operates a contributions program that funds projects operated by not-for-profit, incorporated, national organizations. Historically the federal government has included ministers responsible for sport but has not operated a

---

[66] "Canadian Strategy for Ethical Conduct in Sport: Policy Framework" (May 24, 2002) at 4, online: <www.pch.gc.ca> "Sport Canada".

[67] See Chapter 5, "Be Safe: Off the Ice"; Chapter 6, "Play Safe: On the Ice", section B.

[68] "Actively Engaged: A Policy on Sport for Women and Girls" (2009); "Treasury Board Policy on Official Languages"; "Sport Canada's Policy on Aboriginal Peoples' Participation in Sport" (May 2005); "Policy on Sport for Persons with a Disability" (June 2006), online: <www.pch.gc.ca> "Sport Canada". See further, Chapter 2, "Legal Fundamentals and Equality Rights", section E.

[69] See Chapter 7, "The Business of Hockey", section A, 2, 3. See also, *Income Tax Act*, R.S.C. 1985, c. 1 (5th Supp.), ss. 110.1(1)(a)(ii), 248(1) (tax deductible gifts to registered Canadian amateur athletic associations).

[70] See, "Federal Government Policy on Tobacco Sponsorship of National Sport Organizations" (March 1985), online: <www.pch.gc.ca> "Sport Canada".

[71] S.C. 1997, c. 13, s. 24, re-enacted 1998, c. 38, s. 1. On the constitutionality of the prohibitions, see, *Canada (Attorney General) v. JTI-MacDonald Corp.*, [2007] S.C.J. No. 30, [2007] 2 S.C.R. 610 (S.C.C.).

[72] See online: <http://www.phac-aspc.gc.ca/>.

full, unified "sports ministry".[73] The structures have also not followed the model of providing grants through a quasi-independent, statutory council or commission.

At the federal level, the promotion of sport policies and the delivery of sport programs are the responsibility of Sport Canada, which is now a branch of the International and Intergovernmental Affairs Sector in the Department of Canadian Heritage.[74] Sport Canada contributes funding through three programs (Athlete Assistance, Hosting and Sport Support) and makes grants to the Provinces. In 2006-07, the total funding was CDN $138.3 million (compared to CDN $79.5 million in 2002-03), of which the major share went to different types of organization through Sport Support. The Athlete Assistance Program provided CDN $25.3 million in living and training allowances to "carded" athletes in different sports. Sport Support contributions include allocations to national sport organizations ("NSOs"), to multi-sport service organizations and to Canadian Sport Centres. NSOs are responsible for administering particular sports, and in 2006-07, 40 NSOs received contributions over CDN $400,000, while lesser lights received smaller amounts (*e.g.*, CDN $73,000 to the Canadian Broomball Federation). In 2004, there were particular increases in allocations towards athlete assistance and coaching. The federal budget in 2005 approved annual funding of CDN $140 million for Sport Canada programs and provided an additional CDN $87 million in support of the 2010 Vancouver Olympics.

Recent contributions to Hockey Canada (or the "Canadian Hockey Association") have been as follows:

2007-08: CDN $3.7 million

2006-07: CDN $3.2 million

2005-06: CDN $3.5 million

2004-05: CDN $2.3 million

2003-04: CDN $1.8 million

2002-03: CDN $1.5 million

2001-02: CDN $1.6 million

2000-01: CDN $1.3 million

---

[73]  In the original cabinet of Prime Minister Stephen Harper in 2006, Tony Clement was designated as Minister of Health, Bev Oda as Minister of Canadian Heritage, and Michael Chong as Minister of Intergovernmental Affairs and Sport. The various ministerial responsibilities of David Emerson included the 2010 Vancouver-Whistler Olympics. Health subsequently passed to Leona Aglukkaq (2008), Heritage to Josée Verner (2007) and James Moore (2008), and Sport to Helena Guergis (2007) and Gary Lunn (2008).

[74]  See, <www.pch.gc.ca>. See also, *Department of Canadian Heritage Act*, S.C. 1995, c. 11. On the recent evolution of program priorities, see, L. Thibault & K. Babiak, "Organizational Changes in Canada's Sport System: Toward an Athlete-Centred Approach" (2005) 5 Euro. Sport Management Q. 105.

Hockey Canada's revenue is mainly derived from commercial sources, so that in 2008-09 the contribution from the federal government represented 12 per cent of total funding.[75]

The funding of NSOs is subject to the "Sport Funding and Accountability Framework" (SFAF, 2009-2013) which defines basic eligibility and includes a process for evaluating whether NSOs are contributing towards the goals of the "Canadian Sport Policy". The NSO must be an incorporated entity that is the recognized national governing body for the sport. This recognition may be shown either by the size of its membership and provincial affiliations or by affiliation with an international federation. The NSO must have a democratically elected leadership structure and a bilingual constitution and must present independently audited financial statements. It must have a multi-year plan and be committed to technically and ethically sound and safe programs, including the use of certified coaches. The NSO must have formally adopted the "Canadian Policy Against Doping in Sport" (2004) and must have formal policies demonstrating commitment to the use of official languages and to equity and access. It must be "athlete-centered", including the requirement that high-performance athletes are involved in decision-making. Further requirements are that the NSO have policy and procedures in relation to harassment and abuse and have fair internal appeal procedures that allow disputes to be referred to the Sport Dispute Resolution Centre of Canada. In summary, funded NSOs are instruments of federal government policy and are eligible for support only where they show commitment to those policies. Since the federal government only associates with approved private bureaucracies representing established professional interests, the support system may be fairly styled as "corporatist".[76]

In provincial governments, there is a wide fragmentation of responsibility for sport and recreation because particular aspects fall within different ministerial mandates. These portfolios include, education, colleges and universities, health, municipal affairs, tourism, culture, parks, environment, natural resources, and directorates concerned with special population groups. Provincial governments do, however, include departments or divisions with a general responsibility to promote activity or to provide funding to provincial sport organizations and elite athletes.[77] In Ontario, the Ministry of Health Promotion, created in June 2005,

---

[75]  See, Hockey Canada, *2009 Annual Report*, at 25. See further, Chapter 3, "Organizations and Regulations", section B, 2; Chapter 7, "The Business of Hockey", section A, 2.

[76]  See, B. Houlihan, *Sport, Policy and Politics: A Comparative Analysis* (London: Routledge, 1997) at 29-31; J. Harvey, L. Thibault & G. Rail, "Neo-Corporatism: The Political Management System in Canadian Amateur Sport and Fitness" (1995) 19 J. of Sport and Social Issues 249.

[77]  The provincial Departments or Ministries are as follows: British Columbia, Healthy Living and Sport (online: <http://www.gov.bc.ca/hls/>); Alberta, Tourism, Parks and Recreation and the Alberta Sport, Recreation, Parks and Wildlife Foundation (online: <http://tpr.alberta.ca/>); Saskatchewan, Tourism, Parks, Culture and Sport (online: <http://www.tpcs.gov.sk.ca/>); Manitoba, Culture, Heritage and Tourism and Sport Manitoba (online: <http://www.gov.mb.ca/>); Ontario, Health Promotion (online: <http://www.mhp.gov.on.ca/>); Québec, Ministère de l'Éducation, du Loisir et du Sport (online: <http://www.gouv.qc.ca/>); New Brunswick, Wellness, Culture and Sport (online: <http://www.gnb.ca/>); Nova Scotia, Health Promotion and Protection (online: <http://www.gov.ns.ca>); Newfoundland, Tourism,

aims for healthier lifestyles by encouraging involvement in sport, recreation and physical activity.[78] The Ministry has adopted, "Active 2010: Ontario's Sport and Physical Activity Strategy", which is a comprehensive plan that looks to increase participation and enhance sport development leading up to the 2010 Winter Olympics. The strategy is to be implemented in partnership with other ministries and with community groups and sport organizations.

Provincial governments may fund programs and projects from the general tax base or through the substantial revenues from approved lotteries and similar gambling operations.[79] Under the public gambling business, sedentary players of long-odds games voluntarily pay taxes to assist more active participants. In Ontario, the *Ontario Lottery and Gaming Corporation Act, 1999*,[80] provides for dedicated allocations from lottery tickets, charity casinos and slot machine facilities. In 2007-08, the lotteries of the Ontario Lottery and Gaming Corporation ("OLG")[81] generated CDN $709 million in net proceeds to be applied by the Province for sporting, cultural and charitable purposes. In 2006, the OLG introduced "Quest for Gold" lottery tickets to provide financial aid to high-performance athletes and ensure that Ontario is well represented on national teams. Based on the location of the head office in Calgary, "Alberta Lotteries" provides CDN $400,000 in annual funding to Hockey Canada.

## C.   DISPUTE RESOLUTION

To avoid expensive and unproductive litigation, the "Canadian Sport Policy" calls for "alternative avenues that ensure the orderly, effective, fair, and efficient resolution of sport disputes".[82] In pursuit of this goal, the major part of the *Physical Activity and Sport Act* ("PASA")[83] is dedicated to establishing the Sport Dispute Resolution Centre of Canada ("SDRCC"), which offers alternative dispute resolution ("ADR") in relation to decisions by different types of national

---

Culture and Recreation (online: <http://www.tcr.gov.nl.ca/>); and Prince Edward Island, Community, Cultural Affairs and Labour (online: <http://www.gov.pe.ca/>). In the Territories, the responsible Departments are as follows: Yukon, Community Services (online: <http://www.community.gov.yk.ca/>); Northwest Territories, Municipal and Community Affairs (online: <http://www.maca.gov.nt.ca/>); and Nunavut, Culture, Language, Elders and Youth (online: <http://www.gov.nu.ca/>).

[78] See online: <http://www.mhp.gov.on.ca/>. See also, *Ministry of Tourism and Recreation Act*, R.S.O. 1990, c. M.35.

[79] Provincially licensed "lottery schemes" are permitted under s. 207 of the *Criminal Code*, R.S.C. 1985, c. C-46. The federal government withdrew from operating lotteries in 1985 in exchange for CDN $100 million and an annual indexed payment from the Provinces which in 2003 had reached CDN $60 million. See further, Chapter 7, "The Business of Hockey", section A, 5.

[80] S.O. 1999, c. 12, Schedule L, s. 14(2)(a). Under s. 14(2)(b), payments may also be made to the Ontario Trillium Foundation whose activities include making grants in support of sport and recreation.

[81] See, "OLG Gives Back", online: <http://www.olg.ca>. The OLG notes that from 1975 to 2008 gaming operations generated more than CDN $28 billion for Ontario.

[82] "The Canadian Sport Policy" (May 24, 2002), at 10, online: <www.pch.gc.ca> "Sport Canada". See also, "Canadian Strategy for Ethical Conduct in Sport" (May 24, 2002).

[83] S.C. 2003, c. 2, ss. 9-35.

organization, including service organizations such as the Canadian Centre for Ethics in Sport ("CCES").[84] In relation to international events or international federations, cases may fall within the jurisdiction of the Court of Arbitration for Sport ("CAS").[85] Issues such as eligibility disputes or doping appeals are now regularly referred to these agencies, and sports organizations have a decided preference for ADR. Many types of case do, however, remain subject to the civil court system, and a particular incident may give rise to a proliferation of parallel proceedings. A case of alleged sexual assault might, for example, prompt sports-related disciplinary processes, investigations by professional associations, complaints to human rights commissions or other boards, civil actions, and criminal prosecutions.

The obligation to refer certain types of dispute to mediation or arbitration is based on contractual agreement, either through special reference or through the application of the regulations of the organization. These processes normally come into play once the issues have been considered by domestic tribunals and once internal appeals have been exhausted. In mediation, a third-party intervener assists the parties in their negotiations by suggesting solutions and attempting to bring about an acceptable settlement. In arbitration, the parties argue the case before a chosen adjudicator and agree to abide by the decision, the arbitrator's "award" being enforceable by court order.[86] In mediation, the authority to settle remains with the parties; in arbitration, they put their fate in the hands of the umpire. Although conceptually different, the two processes may be combined as "Med/Arb" by which a neutral intervener initially functions as a mediator but ultimately may conclude the dispute through an arbitration decision. These processes offer advantages in terms of speed, flexibility, cost-saving, confidentiality and the specialist expertise of the intervener. Mediators and arbitrators attempt to fashion solutions that are suitable to the circumstances and try to preserve a degree of harmony in future relations between the parties. A particular advantage of arbitration is finality: the arbitral award is usually the end of the matter since it is judicial policy to encourage private resolution, and courts exercise very limited review of arbitrators' decisions.[87]

The *Physical Activity and Sport Act* establishes the SDRCC as a not-for-profit corporation and requires that it include a dispute resolution secretariat and a resource centre (see, PASA, s. 9(1)).[88] The mission of the Centre is to

---

[84] See Chapter 3, "Organizations and Regulations", section C, 5.

[85] By article 13.2.1 of the "World Anti-Doping Code" (2009), CAS has exclusive jurisdiction in relation to appeals by "international-level athletes", online: <http://www.wada-ama.org/>.

[86] See, *Arbitration Act, 1991*, S.O. 1991, c. 17, s. 50. In *Moscow Dynamo v. Ovechkin*, 412 F.Supp. 2d 24 (D.D.C., 2006), the court was not satisfied that there was a written agreement that Alexander Ovechkin would submit a contractual dispute to the Arbitration Committee of the Russian Ice Hockey Federation; see Chapter 3, "Organizations and Regulations", section C, 2, a.

[87] See, for example, *Raguz v. Sullivan* (2000), 50 N.S.W.L.R. 236 (N.S.W.C.A.) (arbitrator's decision in relation to team selection in judo; "exclusion agreement" precluded appeal to court).

[88] See online: <http://www.crdsc-sdrcc.ca/eng/home.jsp>. This website includes general information about the SDRCC program, a "Jurisprudence Database" and the text of the "Canadian Sport Dispute Resolution Code" (January 1, 2009).

provide a national ADR service for sport disputes and to provide expertise and assistance regarding ADR (see, PASA, s. 10(1)), including programs designed to prevent disputes arising in the first place. The services include the office of "Resolution Facilitator" who advises the parties about the process and chances of success and attempts to resolve the dispute on agreeable terms.[89] The arbitrators and mediators are required to be qualified, independent, and able as a group to provide services in both official languages (see, PASA, s. 29). The Canadian Sport Dispute Resolution Code ("Code") includes the rules of procedure for filing and hearing cases and by article 6.17 grants arbitration panels full scope to review and rectify the previous decision:

> The Panel shall have full power to review the facts and the law. In particular, the Panel may substitute its decision for:
>
> (i) the decision that gave rise to the dispute; or
>
> (ii) in case of Doping Disputes, the CCES' assertion that a doping violation has occurred and its recommended sanction flowing therefrom,
>
> and may substitute such measures and grant such remedies or relief that the Panel deems just and equitable in the circumstances.[90]

By section 10(2) of PASA, a "sport dispute" includes, "disputes among sport organizations and disputes between a sport organization and persons affiliated with it, including its members". By article 1.1(ll) of the Code, it is also provided that:

> "Sports related dispute"...may include...:
>
> (i) team selection;
>
> (ii) a decision made by a NSO board of directors, a committee thereof or an individual delegated with authority to make a decision on behalf of a NSO or its board of directors, which affects any Member of a NSO;
>
> (iii) any dispute for which an agreement to conduct a Mediation, Arbitration or Med/Arb or use the services of the Resolution Facilitator has been entered into by the Parties; and
>
> (iv) any dispute arising out of the application of the Anti-Doping Program.[91]

---

[89] The role of the Resolution Facilitator (RF) is dealt with in Article 4 of the Code; the services of the RF are free. Advice and assistance to athletes is provided by the "Sport Solution", affiliated with The University of Western Ontario, Faculty of Law, online: <http://www.law.uwo.ca/>.

[90] Canadian Sport Dispute Resolution Code, January 1, 2009, online: <http://www.crdsc-sdrcc.ca/eng/dispute-resolution-code.cfm>, at article 6.17.

[91] Canadian Sport Dispute Resolution Code, January 1, 2009, online: <http://www.crdsc-sdrcc.ca/eng/dispute-resolution-code.cfm>, at article 1.1(ll).

Besides the mentioned categories, the SDRCC recognizes disputes related to Athlete Assistance funding, harassment, discipline, eligibility, interpretation of contracts, and "field of play" decisions.

The Court of Arbitration for Sport[92] is based in Lausanne (with regional registries in New York and Sydney) and was originally established in 1983 on the initiative of the International Olympic Committee ("IOC"). A decision of a Swiss civil court in 1993 recognized CAS as a true arbitral tribunal but expressed reservations about its institutional independence should the IOC be a party to a case.[93] The IOC and various international federations then established the International Council of Arbitration for Sport ("ICAS") to administer CAS and draw up the list of arbitrators.[94] CAS has emerged as a leading source of sports law doctrine[95] and has the advantage of overcoming jurisdictional disputes that may arise in international competition. CAS decisions are enforceable under legislation and international conventions dealing with the recognition of foreign arbitral awards.[96] Under the Statutes 54-57 of the International Ice Hockey Federation, appeals of decisions of IIHF bodies and disputes "concerning the interpretation or application of the Statutes, Bylaws, Regulations and playing rules" must be submitted to CAS.[97]

The jurisdiction, powers and procedures of CAS are prescribed in its "Code of Sports-Related Arbitration" which recognizes various "Divisions" of the court. CAS services also include mediation and advisory procedures. The Ordinary Arbitration Division deals with first instance cases such as contractual or commercial disputes, the Appeals Arbitration Division hears appeals from decisions of sports federations, and Ad Hoc Divisions are set up at major

---

[92]  See online: <http://www.tas-cas.org/>. See: M. Holmes, "The CAS: A Case Study of an International Arbitration Institution" (2005), 27 Australian Bar Rev. 56; I.S. Blackshaw, R.C.R. Siekmann & J. Soek, eds., *The Court of Arbitration for Sport 1984-2004* (The Hague: TMC Asser Press, 2006).

[93]  *Gundel v. Fédération Equestre Internationale*, Swiss Federal Tribunal, March 15, 1993, appeal from CAS 92/63, October 15, 1992.

[94]  The new structure was largely approved in, *A., B. v. International Olympic Committee*, Swiss Federal Tribunal, May 27, 2003, appeal from CAS 2002/A/370-371, November 29, 2002 (Larissa Lazutina and Olga Danilova).

[95]  See, M. Reeb, ed., *Digest of CAS Awards*, vol. I (1986-1998), vol. II (1998-2000), vol. III (2001-2003) (The Hague: Kluwer Law International, 1998, 2002, 2004).

[96]  See: *Commercial Arbitration Act*, R.S.C. 1985, c. 17 (2nd Supp.); *International Commercial Arbitration Act*, R.S.O. 1990, c. I-9. On the jurisdictional difficulties of the Butch Reynolds saga (1991-1994), see, J. Barnes, *Sports and the Law in Canada*, 3d ed. (Toronto: Butterworths, 1996) at 104-05. On jurisdiction over the IOC, see, *Sagen v. Vancouver Organizing Committee for the 2010 Olympic and Paralympic Winter Games*, 2009 BCCA 522 (B.C.C.A.), affg [2009] B.C.J. No. 1393, 2009 BCSC 942 (B.C.S.C.); leave to appeal to S.C.C. refused December 22, 2009, [2009] S.C.C.A. No. 459.

[97]  See, for example, *Finnish Ice Hockey Assn. v. International Ice Hockey Federation*, CAS 2004/A/757, October 25, 2005 (payments under international transfer agreement). On IIHF Bylaws and Regulations, see Chapter 3, "Organizations and Regulations", sections B, 1; C, 2, a; 5, a; D, 2.

international Games.[98] By article R57 of the Code, a panel of the Appeals Division,

> shall have full power to review the facts and the law. It may issue a new decision which replaces the decision challenged or annul the decision and refer the case back to the previous instance.[99]

The Code makes provision for the laws or legal system to be applied by the various Divisions.[100] By article R45, a panel of the Ordinary Division must decide the dispute according to the law chosen by the parties or, failing such choice, according to Swiss law. By article R58, a panel of the Appeals Division,

> shall decide the dispute according to the applicable regulations and the rules of law chosen by the parties or, in the absence of such a choice, according to the law of the country in which the federation, association or sports-related body which has issued the challenged decision is domiciled or according to the rules of law, the application of which the Panel deems appropriate.[101]

Under Ad Hoc Rules for particular Games or championships, a panel of the Ad Hoc Division must apply regulations such as the *Olympic Charter*, "general principles of law" and appropriate rules of law. As specialist tribunals, CAS panels consider the sporting context and consider the rationale and purposes underlying rules of competition.[102]

## D.   FUNDAMENTAL RIGHTS

## 1.   Human Rights in Sport

A "right" is a just claim or recognized interest: it is a moral or legal entitlement that others are duty-bound to respect. A particular function of rights is that they

---

[98]   See, *Olympic Charter* (July, 2007), rule 15(4) (jurisdiction of CAS in "certain cases"), rule 59 (exclusive jurisdiction of CAS in relation to disputes in connection with the Olympic Games); see online: <http://www.olympic.org>. See also, R. McLaren, "Introducing the Court of Arbitration for Sport: The Ad Hoc Division at the Olympic Games" (2001) 12 Marquette Sports L. Rev. 515; R. McLaren, "The CAS Ad Hoc Division at the Athens Olympic Games" (2004) 15 Marquette Sports L. Rev. 175.

[99]   Code of Sports – Related Arbitration, article R57.

[100]   In *Rebagliati v. International Olympic Committee*, CAS 002, O.G. Nagano, February 12, 1998, dealing with the detection of traces of marihuana, the court emphasised (at para. 26) that, "CAS is not ...a criminal court and can neither promulgate nor apply penal laws. We must decide within the context of the law of sports, and cannot invent prohibitions or sanctions where none appear."

[101]   Code of Sports — Related Arbitration, article R58.

[102]   See, for example, *Czech Olympic Committee v. International Ice Hockey Federation*, CAS 004-005, O.G. Nagano, February 18, 1998 (team ranking system and sanction for using ineligible player); see further, Chapter 3, "Organizations and Regulations", section C, 2.

are able to trump the will of the majority because a just society requires both democratic rule and the protection of minorities.

Some legal rights are based on rules of law or specific transactions, while others have the status of fundamental safeguards necessary to ensure human dignity. These basic "human rights" are the claim of all humankind and are articulated in international documents and conventions[103] such as the United Nations' *Universal Declaration of Human Rights* (1948).[104] The Universal Declaration proclaims what should be a "common standard of achievement for all peoples" and expresses entitlement to liberal values such as freedom and equality and fair treatment in legal proceedings. It also recognizes that human dignity requires an adequate standard of living, so that human rights should include provision for economic and social security through work, leisure, medical care and education. At the national level, the high ideals of the Universal Declaration receive partial expression in constitutional guarantees and other state legislation.

Some sports-related rights are recognized in the international conventions, while more elaborate declarations are included in association documents, in policy statements and in legislation. The *Olympic Charter* declares that the "practice of sport is a human right" and that any form of discrimination is "incompatible with belonging to the Olympic Movement".[105] In the context of employment in the National Hockey League ("NHL"), article 7.2 of the Collective Bargaining Agreement (2005) between the league and the NHL Players' Association ("NHLPA") similarly prohibits discrimination on specified grounds:

> Neither the NHLPA, the NHL, nor any Club shall discriminate in the interpretation or application of this Agreement against or in favor of any Player because of religion, race, disability, color, national origin, sex, sexual orientation, age, marital status, or membership or non-membership in or support of or non-support of any labor organization.[106]

---

[103] See, for example, *Convention on the Rights of the Child* (United Nations General Assembly, resolution 44/25, November 20, 1989, ratified by Canada, December 13, 1991), art. 31 (child's right to leisure, play and recreational activities), see online: <www.unhchr.ch>. See also, P.J. Galasso, "Children in Organized Sport: Rights and Access to Justice" in P.J. Galasso, ed., *Philosophy of Sport and Physical Activity: Issues and Concepts* (Toronto: Canadian Scholars' Press, 1988) at 324. On discrimination through date of birth, see: M. Lavoie, *Désavantage numérique: les francophones dans la LNH* (Hull, QC: Éditions Vents d'Ouest, 1998) at 21-22, 141-43; W. Hurley, D. Lior & S. Tracze, "A Proposal to Reduce Age Discrimination in Canadian Minor Hockey" (2001) 27 Can. Public Policy 65; *Aitken v. Yellowknife School Dist. No. 1* (2001), 44 C.H.R.R. D/288 (N.W.T.F.P.O.).

[104] See online: <www.unchr.ch/udhr>.

[105] *Olympic Charter* (July 2007), "Fundamental Principles of Olympism", Principles #4 and #5 at 11; see online: <http://www.olympic.org/>. See also, IIHF Statutes and Bylaws (2008-2012) (July 2008), Statute 7.

[106] Collective Bargaining Agreement, 2005, online: <http://www.nhl.com/cba/2005.CBA.pdf>, at article 7.2.

The *Physical Activity and Sport Act*[107] and the "Canadian Sport Policy" reflect a commitment to human rights in sport by promoting participation and declaring the goals of equal access under conditions of fairness and respect.

The quest for human rights is particularly associated with enhancing sporting opportunities for disadvantaged social groups[108] and maintaining a safe playing environment,[109] although sports-related rights should also extend to the working conditions of the employees who manufacture the equipment[110] and to political rights and freedoms under regimes hosting major Games. The campaign for "athletes' rights"[111] combines the assertion of human rights with the claim to proper treatment as contractual members of sports organizations. Whether the "right to play" is realized is a matter of sport politics:

> Rights are inherently political and contingent...their articulation, acceptance and realization involves complex, ongoing processes of assertion, struggle and negotiation between competing interests in the context of changing social, economic, political and ideological circumstances.[112]

The goal of a just and accessible sports system is pursued through political engagement and the policy process, where representative organizations serve an important function in applying pressure on behalf of particular interests. In sport, these lobby groups include Sport Matters, Athletes Can, the Canadian Association for the Advancement of Women in Sport ("CAAWS") and the Ontario Women's Hockey Association ("OWHA"). Litigation and the more formal legal remedies also have their place. In 2002, there was a threat to a fundamental rite of childhood when a father and son in Hamilton were charged with illegally playing ball hockey and football on a city street. The charges were dismissed when the Justice of the Peace ruled that there were reasonable doubts as to whether the alleged incidents had taken place.[113]

In Canadian law, basic rights are protected by two types of legislation: general charters or bills guaranteeing fundamental rights, and human rights codes prohibiting discrimination in services and employment. The most important

---

[107] S.C. 2003, c. 2. On legislation, policies and programs, see Chapter 2, "Legal Fundamentals and Equality Rights", section B.

[108] See Chapter 2, "Legal Fundamentals and Equality Rights", section E. See also, M.J. Cozzillio & R.L. Hayman, eds., *Sports and Inequality* (Durham: Carolina Academic Press, 2005).

[109] See Chapters 4-6.

[110] See: B. Kidd & P. Donnelly, "Human Rights in Sport" (2000) 35 Int. Rev. for the Sociology of Sport 131 at 141-42; G.H. Sage, "Justice Do It! The Nike Transnational Advocacy Network: Organization, Collective Actions, and Outcomes" (1999) 16 Sociology of Sport J. 206.

[111] See: J. Barnes, *Sports and the Law in Canada*, 3d ed. (Toronto: Butterworths, 1996) at 47-106; B. Kidd & M. Eberts, *Athletes' Rights in* Canada (Toronto: Ministry of Tourism and Recreation, 1982). See further, Chapter 3, "Organizations and Regulations".

[112] B. Kidd & P. Donnelly, "Human Rights in Sport" (2000) 35 Int. Rev. for the Sociology of Sport 131, 133.

[113] See, "Street hockey charge tossed out of court" *The Globe and Mail* (Toronto: January 8, 2002) at A7.

general charter ("the *Charter*") is now the *Canadian Charter of Rights and Freedoms* in Part I of the *Constitution Act, 1982*.[114]

## 2. *Canadian Charter of Rights and Freedoms*

By section 52 of the *Constitution Act, 1982*, the *Charter* is part of the Constitution of Canada and has primacy as a supreme law, so that "any law that is inconsistent with the provisions of the Constitution is, to the extent of the inconsistency, of no force or effect". The power to strike down laws belongs to the courts, and anyone whose rights or freedoms under the *Charter* "have been infringed or denied may apply to a court of competent jurisdiction to obtain such remedy as the court considers appropriate and just in the circumstances" (see, s. 24(1)).

The fundamental freedoms guaranteed in the *Charter* include "freedom of conscience and religion" in section 2(a), "freedom of thought, belief, opinion and expression" in section 2(b) and "freedom of association" in section 2(d). Section 6(2) guarantees mobility rights to move to any Province and pursue a livelihood there. Legal rights include "the right to life, liberty and security of the person and the right not to be deprived thereof except in accordance with the principles of fundamental justice" (see, s. 7) and "the right to be secure against unreasonable search and seizure" (see, s. 8). Further specific legal rights detailed in section 11 of the *Charter*, such as the right to be tried in a reasonable time and the presumption of innocence, apply to the criminal process or to similar public proceedings that may lead to punitive sanctions. By section 15(1) of the *Charter* (which came into operation in 1985),

> Every individual is equal before and under the law and has the right to the equal protection and equal benefit of the law without discrimination and, in particular, without discrimination based on race, national or ethnic origin, colour, religion, sex, age or mental or physical disability.[115]

By section 15(2), this protection of equality rights[116] does not preclude affirmative action programs designed to ameliorate conditions of disadvantaged individuals or groups.

---

[114] *Constitution Act, 1982*, Schedule B of the *Canada Act, 1982* (U.K.), 1982, c. 11.

[115] *Constitution Act, 1982*, Schedule B of the *Canada Act, 1982* (U.K.), 1982, c. 11, s. 15(1).

[116] See: *Andrews v. Law Society of British Columbia*, [1989] S.C.J. No. 6, [1989] 1 S.C.R. 143 (S.C.C.) (requirement of citizenship for admission to practice of law; s. 15 prohibits discrimination that imposes disadvantages on individuals or groups); *Law v. Canada (Minister of Employment and Immigration)*, [1999] S.C.J. No. 12, [1999] 1 S.C.R. 497 (S.C.C.) (age distinctions in pension benefit; no violation of human dignity); *Sagen v. Vancouver Organizing Committee for the 2010 Olympic and Paralympic Winter Games*, [2009] B.C.J. No. 1393, 2009 BCSC 942 (B.C.S.C.) (men's ski jumping was a tradition but women's ski jumping had to meet criteria for new events; exclusion was discrimination but did not equate to breach of s. 15); *Sagen v. Vancouver Organizing Committee for the 2010 Olympic and Paralympic Winter Games*, 2009 BCCA 522 (B.C.C.A.) (absence of women's ski jumping was not denial of

The guarantees in the *Charter* are subject to wide interpretation and are not absolute. Exceptionally, Parliament or a provincial legislature may exclude fundamental freedoms and legal and equality rights by declaring under section 33 that an Act or provision shall operate "notwithstanding" the *Charter*. More importantly, section 1 of the *Charter* allows rights and freedoms to be restricted by "such reasonable limits prescribed by law as can be demonstrably justified in a free and democratic society". In *R. v. Oakes*,[117] decided in 1986, the Supreme Court of Canada held that limits under section 1 must satisfy a "stringent standard of justification" and must be designed to achieve a significant or fundamentally important social objective that would warrant overriding a constitutional right. The objective had to relate to concerns that were "pressing and substantial" and the means had to be reasonable, demonstrably justified and proportional. Proportionality required that the means be carefully designed in purpose and effects, be rationally connected to the objective and "impair as little as possible the right or freedom in question".[118] The Supreme Court continues to adhere to the tests in *Oakes* as a general framework, but has also applied a weaker, more flexible standard of justification[119] and has repeatedly deferred to legislation thought to be reasonable in the context.[120]

By section 32(1), the *Charter* applies to the Parliament and government of Canada and to the legislatures and governments of the Provinces in respect of all matters within the authority of each level of government. The *Charter* is a constitutional constraint on laws,[121] statutory powers and actions by agencies of public government. It applies to government entities discharging government functions or state responsibilities and does not apply to autonomous institutions such as universities that are not engaged in public regulation.[122] The *Charter* does not in general apply to actions by private individuals or to private

---

"benefit of law"); leave to appeal to S.C.C. refused December 22, 2009, [2009] S.C.C.A. No. 459.

[117] [1986] S.C.J. No. 7, [1986] 1 S.C.R. 103 (S.C.C.).

[118] *R. v. Oakes*, [1986] S.C.J. No. 7, [1986] 1 S.C.R. 103 at 139 (S.C.C.), *per* Dickson C.J.C.: "Although the nature of the proportionality test will vary depending on the circumstances, in each case courts will be required to balance the interests of society with those of individuals and groups".

[119] See, *Irwin Toy Ltd. v. Québec (Attorney General)*, [1989] S.C.J. No. 36, [1989] 1 S.C.R. 927 (S.C.C.) (commercial advertising directed at children; legislature mediating competing claims).

[120] In *R.J.R.-MacDonald Inc. v. Canada (Attorney General)*, [1995] S.C.J. No. 68, [1995] 3 S.C.R. 199 (S.C.C.), the court did not defer to the ban on tobacco advertising in the *Tobacco Products Control Act* of 1988, R.S.C. 1985 c. 14 (4th Supp.), c. T-11.7. It subsequently upheld the constitutionality of the *Tobacco Act*, S.C. 1997, c. 13; see, *Canada (Attorney General) v. JTI-MacDonald Corp.*, [2007] S.C.J. No. 30, [2007] 2 S.C.R. 610 (S.C.C.).

[121] *Blainey v. Ontario Hockey Assn.*, [1986] O.J. No. 236, 54 O.R. (2d) 513, 26 D.L.R. (4th) 728 (Ont. C.A.), revg [1985] O.J. No. 2645, 52 O.R. (2d) 225, 21 D.L.R. (4th) 599 (Ont. H.C.J.), leave to appeal refused [1986] 1 S.C.R. xii, 58 O.R. (2d) 274*n* (challenge to sports exception in human rights code; one party in litigation acted on the authority of the statute).

[122] *McKinney v. University of Guelph*, [1990] S.C.J. No. 122, [1990] 3 S.C.R. 229 (S.C.C.); *Harrison v. University of British Columbia*, [1990] S.C.J. No. 123, [1990] 3 S.C.R. 451 (S.C.C.); *Stoffman v. Vancouver General Hospital*, [1990] S.C.J. No. 125, [1990] 3 S.C.R. 483 (S.C.C.).

litigation.[123] Neither does it extend to contractual rights or to domestic proceedings involving private voluntary associations, including incorporated bodies. *Charter* scrutiny does, however, apply where a private entity serves as a government delegate and is used to implement a government policy or program.[124]

In relation to sport, the *Charter* applies to legislative provisions, actions by government departments or public agencies, and to policies or programs implemented under government direction or control. Relevant *Charter* rights may, for example, be invoked in doping control proceedings since section 4(1) of the *Physical Activity and Sport Act* declares an official government policy of doping-free sport and Sport Canada mandates that national sports organizations adopt the anti-doping policy.[125] In *Sagen v. Vancouver Organizing Committee for the 2010 Olympic and Paralympic Winter Games* ("VANOC"), it was found that the decision not to include women's ski jumping had been made by the International Olympic Committee ("IOC") which was not subject to the *Charter*:

> Regardless of whether VANOC's hosting of the Games can properly be considered to be a governmental activity because of the substantial commitments made by the several levels of government to secure and hold the Games in Vancouver, it is clear on the facts that neither government nor VANOC had any authority either to make or to alter the decision of the IOC not to include a women's ski jumping event in the 2010 Games. The decision of the IOC not to add women's ski jumping as an event in the 2010 Games is not a "policy" choice that could be or was made by any Canadian government and the staging by VANOC of only those events authorized by the IOC cannot reasonably be viewed as furthering any Canadian government policy or program.[126]

The *Charter* does not in general apply to eligibility or similar disputes involving private sports organizations even when these are supported by public grants.[127] National sports organizations have nevertheless been

---

[123] *R.W.D.S.U. v. Dolphin Delivery Ltd.*, [1986] S.C.J. No. 75, [1986] 2 S.C.R. 573 (S.C.C.). See also, *Hill v. Church of Scientology of Toronto*, [1995] S.C.J. No. 64, [1995] 2 S.C.R. 1130 (S.C.C.).

[124] *Eldridge v. British Columbia (Attorney General)*, [1997] S.C.J. No. 86, [1997] 3 S.C.R. 624 (S.C.C.) (failure by hospitals to provide sign language interpreters).

[125] See Chapter 2, "Legal Fundamentals and Equality Rights", section B, 1, 4; Chapter 3, "Organizations and Regulations", section D. For the view that the *Charter* does not apply to doping control, see: *Canadian Centre for Ethics in Sport v. Adams*, SDRCC DT-06-0039 (June 11, 2007, R.H. McLaren, arb.); *Adams v. CCES*, CAS 2007/A/1312, May 16, 2008.

[126] *Sagen v. Vancouver Organizing Committee for the 2010 Olympic and Paralympic Winter Games*, [2009] B.C.J. No. 2293, 2009 BCCA 522 at para. 49 (B.C.C.A.); leave to appeal to S.C.C. refused December 22, 2009, [2009] S.C.C.A. No. 459.

[127] *Morrison v. British Columbia Amateur Hockey Assn.*, [1986] B.C.J. No. 1881, 13 C.P.R. (3d) 556 (B.C.S.C.) (zoning dispute); *Blainey v. Ontario Hockey Assn.*, [1986] O.J. No. 236, 54 O.R. (2d) 513, 26 D.L.R. (4th) 728 (Ont. C.A.) (male-only eligibility rule); *Kanigan (Guardian*

encouraged to respect *Charter* rights,[128] and Olympic organizations claiming to be a "public authority" for the purpose of the *Trade-marks Act* must explain why they are so private for the purpose of the *Charter*.[129] The liberal application of the *Charter* is consistent with the principles declared in the *Physical Activity and Sport Act* and Sport Canada policies, and given the public commitment to athletes' rights, government lawyers should not be devoting all their energies to restrictive interpretations.

## 3. Human Rights Codes

Illegal discrimination in the private, commercial or public sectors is prohibited by human rights legislation, which also declares the right to be free from harassment in the workplace or other contexts.[130] Human rights codes have been enacted in each of the Provinces and the *Canadian Human Rights Act*[131] prohibits discrimination in areas subject to federal jurisdiction. Depending on the circumstances of the case and the terms of the legislation, the human rights process may be the exclusive or preferred mechanism for enforcing the right, although the case may also be suitable for a civil action[132] or may fall under the jurisdiction of a labour arbitrator.[133]

---

*ad Litem) v. Castlegar Minor Hockey Assn.*, [1996] B.C.J. No. 2431, 141 D.L.R. (4th) 563 (B.C.S.C.) (application for try-out in higher age division).

[128] See, *Sport: The Way Ahead*, The Report of the Minister's Task Force on Federal Sport Policy (Minister of State, Fitness and Amateur Sport, May 1992) at 140-41.

[129] See: *Canada (Registrar of Trade Marks) v. CDN Olympic Assn.*, [1982] F.C.J. No. 174, [1983] 1 F.C. 692, 139 D.L.R. (3d) 190 (F.C.A.) (forms of government control); *See You In - Canadian Athletes Fund Corp. v. Canadian Olympic Committee*, [2007] F.C.J. No. 541, 57 C.P.R. (4th) 287 (F.C.); *Sagen v. Vancouver Organizing Committee for the 2010 Olympic and Paralympic Winter Games*, [2009] B.C.J. No. 1393, 2009 BCSC 942 (B.C.S.C.), affd 2009 BCCA 522 (B.C.C.A.); leave to appeal to S.C.C. refused December 22, 2009, [2009] S.C.C.A. No. 459.

[130] See Chapter 5, "Be Safe: Off the Ice", section C. In *Madsen v. Torry (No. 4)*, [2005] B.C.H.R.T.D. No. 144, 52 C.H.R.R. D/131 (B.C.H.R.T.), it was held that alleged sexual harassment by a bowling tournament director did not occur in the context of a service customarily available to the public.

[131] R.S.C. 1985, c. H-6. See, for example: "Female ski jumpers set to take on IOC" *The Globe and Mail* (Toronto: December 20, 2006) at A1, A7 (absence of women's ski jumping from 2010 Vancouver Olympic Games; compliant against VANOC and federal government); "Olympic dreams of female ski jumpers take flight" *The Globe and Mail* (Toronto: January 7, 2008 (settlement)) at A1, A6; *Sagen v. Vancouver Organizing Committee for the 2010 Olympic and Paralympic Winter Games*, [2009] B.C.J. No. 1393 at paras. 119-120, 2009 BCSC 942 (B.C.S.C.).

[132] See, for example: *Lehman v. Davis*, [1993] O.J. No. 2891, 16 O.R. (3d) 338 (Ont. Gen. Div.) (wrongful dismissal action); *Farris v. Staubach Ontario Inc.*, [2004] O.J. No. 1227 (Ont. S.C.J.) (simultaneous civil action); *Sulz v. British Columbia (Minister of Public Safety and Solicitor General)*, [2006] B.C.J. No. 3262, 43 C.C.L.T. (3d) 187 (B.C.C.A.), affg [2006] B.C.J. No. 121, 263 D.L.R. (4th) 58 (B.C.S.C.) (actions in tort and contract based on harassment by RCMP supervisors).

[133] See: *Weber v. Ontario Hydro*, [1995] S.C.J. No. 59, [1995] 2 S.C.R. 929 (S.C.C.); *Parry Sound (District) Social Services Administration Board v. Ontario Public Service Employees*

Human rights legislation typically establishes a complaint procedure by which cases are referred to a human rights commission that conducts a preliminary investigation. If the issues are not resolved by conciliation and settlement, the case is brought before a tribunal that may order remedial action and compensation. Since 2007,[134] the Ontario Human Rights Commission has assumed a proactive educational function and works to prevent discrimination and promote human rights; it is also authorized to conduct inquiries into rights issues. Particular cases are filed directly with the Human Rights Tribunal of Ontario, and claimants receive advice and representation from the Human Rights Legal Support Centre. The claim may result in a hearing before an adjudicator of the Tribunal or an alternative form of resolution. By section 46.1 of the amended legislation, a court in civil proceedings may order monetary compensation or restitution where a right has been infringed.

In Ontario, the *Human Rights Code*[135] declares a right to equal treatment and prohibits discrimination with respect to "services, goods and facilities" (see, s. 1), accommodation (see, s. 2), employment (see, s. 5) and membership in a trade union or occupational association (see, s. 6). By section 16(2) of the Code, the right to be free from discrimination is not infringed where a requirement of Canadian citizenship or permanent residence in Canada is "adopted for the purpose of fostering and developing participation in cultural, educational, trade union or athletic activities". Similarly, special religious, fraternal or social organizations may limit services or facilities to persons identified with the group (see, s. 18). The use of services and facilities may be limited to one sex on the grounds of public decency (see, s. 20(1)), and recreational clubs may restrict or qualify access or give preferences "with respect to membership dues and other fees because of age, sex, marital status or family status" (see, s. 20(3)). The right to equal treatment in employment is not infringed where age, sex or record of offences is a reasonable and *bona fide* qualification because of the nature of the employment (see, s. 24(1)(b)). Such a qualification is recognized only where the employer would suffer "undue hardship" in accommodating the circumstances of the employee (see, s. 24(2)).

In the area of services and facilities, human rights legislation in most jurisdictions (and formerly in Ontario) limits protections to services that are

---

*Union, Local 324*, [2003] S.C.J. No. 42, [2003] 2 S.C.R. 157 (S.C.C.) (grievance arbitrator had jurisdiction to enforce human rights code); *Quebec (Commission des droits de la personne et des droits de la jeunesse) v. Quebec (Attorney General)*, [2004] S.C.J. No. 34, [2004] 2 S.C.R. 185 (S.C.C.) (age discrimination dispute fell under jurisdiction of human rights tribunal). See also, *British Columbia (Public Service Employee Relations Commission) v. B.C.G.E.U.*, [1999] S.C.J. No. 46, [1999] 3 S.C.R. 3 (S.C.C.) (*Meiorin* case; aerobic standard for firefighters discriminated against women and was not a *bona fide* occupational requirement).

[134] See, *Human Rights Code*, R.S.O. 1990, c. H.19, amended S.O. 2006, c. 30.

[135] See, R.S.O. 1990, c. H.19, amended S.O. 2006, c. 30. The prohibited grounds of discrimination generally include: race, ancestry, place of origin, colour, ethnic origin, citizenship, creed, sex, sexual orientation, age, marital status, family status, disability, receipt of public assistance and record of offences. On alleged discrimination based on family status, see, *Paisley v. Kerry Park Minor Hockey Assn.*, [2007] B.C.H.R.T.D. No. 218, 2007 BCHRT 218, application to dismiss [2007] B.C.H.R.T.D. No. 443, 2007 BCHRT 443 (B.C.H.R.T.).

customarily available to the public. Public recreation facilities and social clubs[136] are therefore prohibited from practising discrimination. A complaint may, however fail if the organization or activity is not public in character.[137] Complaints in Ontario involving minor hockey[138] and softball[139] were formerly denied because of the constitutions of the associations and the scope of the services provided. More recently, however, services customarily available to the public have been held to include amateur[140] and school[141] hockey and an armed forces parachuting course.[142] In *University of British Columbia v. Berg*,[143] the Supreme Court of Canada held that internal services at a university are protected by provincial human rights legislation.

In Ontario, section 1 of the *Human Rights Code* now refers to "services, goods and facilities" and makes no reference to public access. From 1982 to 1986, the application of section 1 was limited by section19(2) of the Code which declared that the right "to equal treatment with respect to services and facilities is not infringed when membership in an athletic organization or participation in an athletic activity is restricted to persons of the same sex". This statutory exception was successfully challenged as a denial of the equality rights guaranteed by the *Charter*.[144]

---

136  *Letendre v. Royal Canadian Legion, South Burnaby Branch No. 83* (1988), 10 C.H.R.R. D/5846 (B.C.H.R.C.) (wheelchair dancing). In *Stopps v. Just Ladies Fitness (Metrotown) Ltd.* (2006), 58 C.H.R.R. D/240 (B.C.H.R.T.), no discrimination was found when a male was denied membership in a women-only gymnasium; other co-ed facilities were available, and the gymnasium addressed special disadvantages experienced by women.

137  *Gould v. Yukon Order of Pioneers*, [1996] S.C.J. No. 29, [1996] 1 S.C.R. 571 (S.C.C.) (fraternal historical organization); *Buntain v. Marine Drive Golf Club*, [2007] B.C.J. No. 37, [2007] 2 W.W.R. 575, 278 D.L.R. (4th) 309 (B.C.C.A.), affg [2005] B.C.J. No. 2181, [2006] 5 W.W.R. 560, 50 B.C.L.R. (4th) 167 (B.C.S.C.), revg (2005), 52 C.H.R.R. D/111 (B.C.H.R.Trib.) (men's lounge in private golf club), leave to appeal refused [2007] S.C.C.A. No. 112, 374 N.R. 395 (*note*) (S.C.C.).

138  *Cummings v. Ontario Minor Hockey Assn.*, [1979] O.J. No. 4357, 26 O.R. (2d) 7, 104 D.L.R. (3d) 434 (Ont. C.A.), affg [1978] O.J. No. 3548, 21 O.R. (2d) 389, 90 D.L.R. (3d) 568 (Ont. Div. Ct.), revg (1977), 29 R.F.L. 259 (Board of Inquiry).

139  *Ontario Human Rights Commission v. Ontario Rural Softball Assn.*, [1979] O.J. No. 4375, 26 O.R. (2d) 134, 102 D.L.R. (3d) 303 (Ont. C.A.), affg [1978] O.J. No. 3549, 21 O.R. (2d) 395, 90 D.L.R. (3d) 574 (Ont. Div. Ct.), revg, unreported, May 19, 1977, Board of Inquiry (Lederman).

140  *Solin v. B.C. Amateur Hockey Assn.* (1988), 9 C.H.R.R. D/5266 (B.C.H.R.C.) (Finnish national seeking to play Midget AAA). See also, *Beacon Hill Little League Major Girls Softball Team - 2005 v. Little League Canada (No. 2)*, [2009] B.C.H.R.T.D. No. 12, 2009 BCHRT 12 (B.C.H.R.T.) (travel fund policy had adverse effect on girls' softball teams).

141  *Pasternak v. Manitoba High Schools Athletic Assn. Inc.*, [2006] M.H.R.B.A.D. No. 2 (M.H.R.B.A.D.) (Decision of M. Lynne Harrison, adjudicator, September 22, 2006); *Manitoba High Schools Athletic Assn. Inc. v. Pasternak*, [2008] M.J. No. 10, [2008] 10 W.W.R. 729, 222 Man.R. (2d) 288 (Man. Q.B.) (judicial review denied).

142  *Rosin v. Canadian Armed Forces*, [1990] F.C.J. No. 1104, [1991] 1 F.C. 391 (Fed. C.A.). See also, *J.S. v. Brooker*, [2005] F.C.J. No. 1865, 2005 FC 1510 (F.C.) (alleged sexual harassment in jiu-jitsu club operated by armed forces).

143  [1993] S.C.J. No. 55, [1993] 2 S.C.R. 353 (S.C.C.).

144  *Blainey v. Ontario Hockey Assn.*, [1986] O.J. No. 236, 54 O.R. (2d) 513, 26 D.L.R. (4th) 728 (Ont. C.A.), revg [1985] O.J. No. 2645, 52 O.R. (2d) 225, 21 D.L.R. (4th) 599 (Ont. H.C.J.),

Where a complaint of discrimination relates to an inter-provincially organized professional league, the Canadian Human Rights Commission has jurisdiction to hear the case.[145] Normally, however, complaints relating to employment,[146] services or facilities are dealt with under provincial legislation. In *Wood v. Canadian Soccer Assn.* ("CSA"),[147] a 16-year-old girl from Denmark was prevented from participating in the boys' division of an international invitational soccer tournament organized by the Scarborough Youth Soccer Association and sanctioned by the CSA. The organizers allowed a 10-year-old girl to play in another age sector, but denied the opportunity in the older age group because of more pronounced physical differences and greater risk of injury. When a complaint was brought under the *Canadian Human Rights Act*, a tribunal of the federal commission found that primary responsibility for organizing the competition lay with the local soccer association. The tribunal held that the CSA's involvement in the exclusion did not have the character of an inter-provincial undertaking or national concern and did not qualify as commercial or corporate activity so as to give the commission constitutional jurisdiction. Any remedy had to be pursued under the Ontario *Human Rights Code*.

## E.  EQUALITY RIGHTS

Western sport owes a good deal to male, able-bodied, WASP heterosexuals, but there is no reason why these types should have all the fun. Excluded and disadvantaged groups seek the chance to play and to enjoy the benefits of sport. While the various campaigns for access and recognition focus on sporting opportunities, athletic achievement can also be the way for outsiders to "prove themselves", "enter the mainstream" or "gain acceptance". The campaigns then symbolise wider political struggles as sporting protest offers a visible reminder of real-world problems. Even if there is "acceptance" in sport, this may not be matched in society at large, and in the case of women's sport there is the further risk that "entering the mainstream" means "entering the malestream".

The basis of the disadvantage may be physical, as in the case of gender and disability, or there may be discrimination based on race, colour, nationality or language. Further issues relate to the ethics of the body, as in the case of religion,

---

leave to appeal refused [1986] 1 S.C.R. xii, 58 O.R. (2d) 274*n* (S.C.C.); see further, Chapter 2, "Legal Fundamentals and Equality Rights" section E, 1. Section 19(2) was repealed by *Equality Rights Statute Law Amendment Act, 1986*, S.O. 1986, c. 64, s. 18(12).

[145] *Canadian Football League v. Canada (Human Rights Commission)*, [1980] F.C.J. No. 47, [1980] 2 F.C. 329, 109 D.L.R. (3d) 397 (F.C.T.D.) (challenge by James Bone to CFL's designated import rule; alleged discrimination on the basis of national origin).

[146] See, for example, *Bone v. Hamilton Tiger-Cats Football Club Ltd.* (Ont. Board of Inquiry, J.D. McCamus, August 16, 1979) (complaint by James Bone against Hamilton Tiger-Cats); *Rossi v. School District No. 57*, [1985] B.C.C.H.R.D. No. 21, 7 C.H.R.R. D/3237 (B.C.H.R.C.) (man denied position teaching girls physical education; supervision and decency did not require female appointment).

[147] (1984), 5 C.H.R.R. D/2024 (C.H.R.T.). On provincial jurisdiction, see also, *Sahyoun v. Atlantic Colleges Athletic Assn.*, [2004] N.B.H.R.B.I.D. No. 3 (N.B. Labour and Employment Board, Board of Inquiry, Decision of G.G. Couturier, July 20, 2004).

sexual orientation and sexual identity. It might be thought that elite sport would be free of discrimination on non-physical grounds since teams should value superior athletic contribution from persons of any race, language, religion or orientation. At the same time, the hiring of coaches should be based exclusively on effectiveness and performance. The source of the discrimination in elite sport lies in cultural attitudes and perceptions about the consumer market. Team operators have tended to have fixed ideas about who the spectators might want to see.

When considering differences and disadvantages in the sports system, a distinction can be drawn between "equality" and "equity".[148] "Equality" focusses on creating the same opportunities through freedom of access and the elimination of arbitrary barriers to entry. "Equity" is concerned more with actual participation and the quality of programs and takes account of different needs and circumstances. A program is equitable when it achieves an appropriate level of participation and a fair allocation of resources and facilities. Areas of potential inequity in women's sport may be illustrated by the case initiated in 2000 against the University of Saskatchewan. In a complaint filed with the Saskatchewan Human Rights Commission, a group alleged that there was violation of the human rights code in the funding and operation of the Huskies' hockey program:

> It is our belief that the women's hockey program is treated in an inferior manner as compared to the men's program. For example, funding is allocated inequitably; the men's team receives greater public recognition by the university, and the travel budget is less for the women's team. Men have greater access to more competitive events. The qualifications, experience and numbers of coaches are greater for men's hockey than women's, and the men's team has paid assistants whereas the women's team does not. Fund-raising is greater for men's hockey. The number and duration of practice times is greater for men. The allocation of scholarships is greater for men. We believe that these factors and more result in an inferior program for women wishing to play hockey...[149]

Rather than focus on an individual instance of exclusion, the *University of Saskatchewan* case alleged ongoing and systemic discrimination in the quality of the program.

## 1.   Gender Equity and Sex Discrimination

Gender-based equality and equity are now required by the *Convention on the Elimination of All Forms of Discrimination Against Women*,[150] which was

---

[148]   See, M.A. Hall, *The Girl and the Game: A History of Women's Sport in Canada* (Peterborough, ON: Broadview Press, 2002) at 202-11.

[149]   *University of Saskatchewan v. Women 2000*, [2006] S.J. No. 231, 268 D.L.R. (4th) 558 (Sask. C.A.), affg [2005] S.J. No. 504, 267 Sask.R. 33, 54 C.H.R.R. D/210 (Sask. Q.B.), affg (2005), 52 C.H.R.R. D/231 (S.H.R.T.).

[150]   See online: <www.unhchr.ch>. The Convention was adopted by United Nations General Assembly resolution 34/180, December 18, 1979. By 2004, 176 countries had ratified the Convention.

ratified by Canada in December 1981 after the federal and provincial governments agreed to adopt the measures needed for implementation.[151] Parties to the Convention agree to "take all appropriate measures to eliminate discrimination against women" and ensure equal rights in areas such as education, employment and economic and social life (see, articles 10, 11, 13). Parties specifically agree to ensure the "same opportunities to participate actively in sports and physical education" (see, article 10(g)) and the "right to participate in recreational activities, sports and all aspects of cultural life" (see, article 13(c)). These special protections reflect the fact that sport has been a leading institution of male privilege and a conspicuous example of discrimination. In the case of hockey, "Canada's national pastime has come to epitomize an almost gross caricature of maleness: on-ice violence and off-ice wheeling and dealing".[152]

Women's sport has suffered from the warped view that it is a physical anomaly or odd imitation — an inappropriate substitute for the real thing. The cultural ambivalence about female athleticism was embodied in the 1890s in the founding principles of the modern Olympic movement. The Games at first reflected Victorian ideas of "manliness" and "separate spheres" in seeking the outright exclusion of women. It was only in 1924 that a limited number of women's events received official recognition. Women's hockey had to wait until the Nagano Winter Olympics of 1998, after the International Ice Hockey Federation ("IIHF") had sanctioned the first women's world championship in 1990.

Various forms of game and recreation have always been available to girls and women, but many societies have recognized male contests as the dominant form and have contrived to marginalise women's sport through medical mythology, moral and aesthetic concerns and other systems of control.[153] The powerful and seriously competitive female has even been viewed as "gender suspect", an idea that formerly received official sanction in sex testing at major events. Although the athletic gap between the sexes is diminishing, after puberty men can outperform women in activities requiring size, strength and speed. Sport has,

---

[151] See, *Convention on the Elimination of All Forms of Discrimination against Women: Fifth Report of Canada* (2002), online: <http://www.pch.gc.ca/> "Human Rights Program".

[152] E. Etue & M.K. Williams, *On the Edge: Women Making Hockey History* (Toronto: Second Story Press, 1996) at 157. The victims of this male culture include the men who work in it; see, M.A. Robidoux, *Men at Play: A Working Understanding of Professional Hockey* (Montreal & Kingston: McGill-Queen's University Press, 2001). See also: R. Gruneau & D. Whitson, *Hockey Night in Canada: Sport, Identities and Cultural Politics* (Toronto: Garamond Press, 1993); V. Burstyn, *The Rites of Men: Manhood, Politics, and the Culture of Sport* (Toronto: University of Toronto Press, 1999). On politics, violence and wheeling and dealing, see, in particular, Chapters 3, 5, 6, 7 and 9.

[153] See: A. Guttmann, *Women's Sport: A History* (New York: Columbia University Press, 1991); J. Hargreaves, *Sporting Females: Critical Issues in the History and Sociology of Women's Sport* (London: Routledge, 1994); A. Harvey, *The Beginnings of a Commercial Sporting Culture in Britain, 1793-1850* (Aldershot: Ashgate Publishing, 2004) at 196-98 (women professionals, including Mrs. Thornton in 1804 and the "first great national sporting event").

therefore, been a prime site for the construction of gender differences and the assertion of male superiority. The disadvantaged status of women's sport cannot, however, be explained by mere physical differences since it is common to recognize multiple categories of valid competition. Furthermore, maximum athletic ability ought not to affect rates of recreational participation or competence in coaching or administration. The disparities are rooted in attitudes, social factors and economic control. Expectations regarding sex roles, appearance and behaviour have tended to restrict women's recreational opportunities and limit involvement to socially acceptable activities. Professional opportunities have also been restricted because the prevailing model of elite sport in North America has been the commercial spectacle of men's leagues.

The history of women's sport in Canada[154] reveals a rise and fall of programs as social structures affected opportunities and new campaigns were launched to claim a fair share of the field. From the late nineteenth century, private schools offered gymnastics and calisthenics to upper- and middle-class girls. More popular participation included games such as basketball, whether played in its original version or in the less robust adaptation of "girls' rules". The newly invented safety bicycle was an instrument of liberation and dress reform,[155] although social approval tended to be reserved for more refined pursuits such as tennis, skating and golf. The Ontario Department of Education gave permission for physical education for girls in 1913, and activities in the public schools evolved from regimented drill to more appealing games and athletic activities. The years from 1915 to 1940 are usually characterised as a productive era for women's sport when opportunities were offered through community-based teams and national associations. Extraordinary competitive success was achieved by Canadian track athletes and by teams such as the Edmonton Grads, and there was informed and supportive media coverage of women's events. This era came to an end with the disruptions of the Second World War and its "baby boom" aftermath. During the 1950s, the forces of suburban domesticity, the feminine mystique and televised sport largely relegated women to the sidelines, in spite of some famous incidents of girls swimming against the conservative tide. It was not until the late 1960s that second-wave feminism addressed the inequitable distribution of opportunities and drew renewed attention to the importance of physical activity for women's health.

The pattern of rise, fall and renewal applies particularly to women's hockey.[156] A game was first recorded in Ottawa in 1889, so that women's hockey

---

[154] See: H. Lenskyj, *Out of Bounds: Women, Sport and Sexuality* (Toronto: The Woman's Press, 1986); B. Kidd, *The Struggle for Canadian Sport* (Toronto: University of Toronto Press, 1996) at 94-145; K. Young & P. White, eds., *Sport and Gender in Canada*, 2d ed. (Don Mills, ON: Oxford University Press, 2007); M.A. Hall, *The Girl and the Game: A History of Women's Sport in Canada* (Peterborough, ON: Broadview Press, 2002). On sexual orientation and gender definition, see Chapter 2, "Legal Fundamentals and Equality Rights", section E, 8.

[155] See, *R. v. Sprague* (1899), 63 J.P. 233 (Surrey Quarter Sessions) (lady in "rational dress" refused permission to enter hotel coffee room but offered refreshment in the bar).

[156] See: D. Guay, *L'Histoire du hockey au Québec: Origine et développement d'un phénomène culturel avant 1917* (Chicoutimi, QC: Les Éditions JCL, 1990) at 150-59; E. Etue & M.K. Williams, *On the Edge: Women Making Hockey History* (Toronto: Second Story Press, 1996);

predates the Stanley Cup by four years. University teams were formed in the 1890s, and women's community and professional games achieved particular popularity during the First World War when the star skaters included Albertine Lapensée of Cornwall. By the 1930s, there was an established system of provincial, regional and Dominion championships in which the Preston Rivulettes were the dominant dynasty.[157] After the Second World War, these opportunities had largely disappeared, and minor hockey was apparently the exclusive preserve of boys. In 1956, the enterprising nine-year-old, Abby "Ab" Hoffman, responded by resorting to disguise and playing on defence for an entire season, although the game was up when birth certificates had to be submitted following her selection for the local all-star team.[158] National and international tournaments were revived in 1967 as the number of women's teams grew and new facilities became available. The female game mainly came to be integrated with the dominant provincial and national governing bodies, but in 1975 the Ontario Women's Hockey Association ("OWHA") was created as a special "separatist" organization.[159] While remaining a separate structure, the OWHA affiliated with the Ontario Hockey Association in 1980 and so formed a link with the Canadian Amateur Hockey Association, which established a Women's Hockey Council in 1981. The new Canadian national championship for the Abby Hoffman Cup followed in 1982, women's hockey was included in the Canada Winter Games from 1991, and the junior championship was established in 1993. In 2006, the elite National Women's Hockey League was re-organized as a unified competition between East and West divisions, and former Governor General Adrienne Clarkson donated the Clarkson Cup as the championship trophy. Subsequent changes then occurred in relation to the participating leagues and the format of the championship.

Although women's participation has greatly increased, the benefit of sports programs (which may be supported by public funds, lottery proceeds or student fees contributed by both sexes) still largely accrues to males. Statistics Canada's survey of participation in organized sport in 2005 indicated that more men (36 per cent) than women (21 per cent) were regularly involved.[160] Female

---

N. Theberge, *Higher Goals: Women's Ice Hockey and the Politics of Gender* (Albany: State University of New York Press, 2000); J. Stevens, "Women's Hockey in Canada: After the 'Gold Rush'" in D. Whitson & R. Gruneau, *Artificial Ice: Hockey, Culture, and Commerce* (Peterborough, ON: Broadview Press, 2006) at 85.

[157] See, C. Adams, "'Queens of the Ice Lanes': The Preston Rivulettes and Women's Hockey in Canada, 1931-1940" (2008), 39 Sport History Review 1.

[158] Abigail Hoffman subsequently became a track star and was director of Sport Canada during the 1980s. Her infiltration of minor hockey in 1956 was treated as an isolated and amusing novelty and there was no chance that "Ab" would be able to compete the following season: "Girl, 9, Hockey League Star Never Spotted Among 400 Boys" *The Toronto Daily Star* (March 8, 1956) at 1-2; "No Time for Girls - Abby" *The Toronto Daily Star* (March 9, 1956); "Dresses Are Stupid" *Time* (March 19, 1956) at 36.

[159] See online: <http://www.owha.on.ca>. For Hockey Canada, see online: <http://www.hockeycanada.ca>.

[160] See, Statistics Canada, *Sport Participation in Canada, 2005* (February, 2008). In 2005, there were 1.3 million hockey players aged 15 or over. With the aging of the population, the report indicated substantial declines in participation in organized sport since 1998, although figures

registration in organized hockey has risen from 7000 in 1989 to 85,000 in 2008, but this still represents only 17 per cent of the total registration of 585,000. Upon entering high school in Quebec, only 46 per cent of girls engage in physical activity, as compared to 68 per cent for boys, and there is a general progressive decline in taking physical education classes in Ontario after Grade 9.[161] At the university level, a survey by Canadian Interuniversity Sport ("CIS") in 2005[162] revealed that athletics departments were less likely to have equity statements than the institution as a whole, although operations funded directly by the department's budget or influenced by university standards were most often reported to be occurring equitably. The percentages of CIS members reporting equitable practices in relation to conditions or facilities were as follows: compensation of coaches (65 per cent), modes of team travel (84 per cent), meal allowances (76 per cent), equipment (79 per cent) and exhibition competition opportunities (72 per cent). Inequitable practices were more common in relation to external fundraising, alumni contributions, marketing and promotional efforts and athletic financial awards.

At the national and international levels, surveys of Canadian National Sports Organizations ("NSOs") since 2003 revealed that women constituted 32 per cent of registered competitors, 49 per cent of recipients of Athlete Assistance grants, 50 per cent of athletes on teams at Summer Olympics, 22 per cent of coaches, 28 per cent of technical officials and 37 per cent of senior administrative staff.[163] Following significant increases in the number of available events,[164] female athletes at the Athens Olympics in 2004 represented 41 per cent of the total of competitors. The leadership of international federations does, however, remain predominantly male, and progress is also required in the relation to officiating and prize money. In 2006, only two of the 35 international federations participating in the Summer and Winter Olympics had women presidents, and of the 114 members of the International Olympic Committee only 14 were women.

---

on involvement in physical activity were not included. Participation is particularly affected by income and educational attainment.

[161] See: *Convention on the Elimination of All Forms of Discrimination Against Women: Fifth Report of Canada* (2002), "Report of Quebec", para. 704; "Ontario teens taking fewer physical education classes" *The Globe and Mail* (Toronto: July 26, 2006) at A3.

[162] See, Canadian Interuniversity Sport, *2005 Equity Practices Questionnaire* (CIS, May 2005). On gender equity programs in universities, see also: *University of Saskatchewan v. Women 2000*, [2006] S.J. No. 231, 268 D.L.R. (4th) 558 (Sask. C.A.), affg [2005] S.J. No. 504, 267 Sask.R. 33, 54 C.H.R.R. D/210 (Sask. Q.B.), affg (2005), 52 C.H.R.R. D/231 (S.H.R.T.); E. Etue & M.K. Williams, *On the Edge: Women Making Hockey History* (Toronto: Second Story Press, 1996) at 76-78, 180-83.

[163] See, Sport Canada, "Actively Engaged: A Policy on Sport for Women and Girls" (2009), online: <www.pch.gc.ca>.

[164] On the exclusion of women's ski jumping from the 2010 Olympics, see, *Sagen v. Vancouver Organizing Committee for the 2010 Olympic and Paralympic Winter Games*, [2009] B.C.J. No. 2293, 2009 BCCA 522 (B.C.C.A.), affg [2009] B.C.J. No. 1393, 2009 BCSC 942 (B.C.S.C.), leave to appeal to S.C.C. refused December 22, 2009, [2009] S.C.C.A. No. 459. See Chapter 2, "Legal Fundamentals and Equality Rights", section D, 2. See also, *Martin v. International Olympic Committee*, 740 F.2d 680 (9th Cir., 1984) (civil rights legislation did not require IOC to include certain events for women).

The greatest inequities occur in professional playing opportunities and media exposure, so that female role models remain relatively scarce. There are few leagues offering employment in women's sport, and women's events receive minimal coverage in print and electronic media. In Canada, viewership of sports specialty channels is 70 per cent male, so that programming is oriented towards men's sport and a channel dedicated to women's sport is unlikely to be commercially viable.[165] Media coverage also tends to be afflicted by the sexist or sexualised representation of female athletes,[166] and special "eligibility criteria" apply to the employment of female reporters.

Since the 1970s there has been increased study of all aspects of women's sport, and various strategies have been applied to achieve equitable funding and representation. The leading advocacy agency is the publicly funded Canadian Association for the Advancement of Women and Sport and Physical Activity ("CAAWS").[167] Sport Canada established a women's program in 1980 to provide employment internships for women and to promote increased participation in NSOs and in 1986 formalized the goal of achieving equal opportunity in the, "Sport Canada Policy on Women in Sport". The policy was renewed in 2009 in, "Actively Engaged: A Policy on Sport for Women and Girls" which includes an "Action Plan" seeking to develop awareness and knowledge and achieve improvements in relation to programs, participation and leadership. In the United States, Title IX of the *Education Amendments Act* of 1972[168] requires equity in educational programs and threatens the sanction of loss of federal funding. In Canada, sports development is not concentrated in the schools and colleges, and the constitutional system does not allow direct federal funding control of educational institutions. Financial sanctions could nevertheless be applied

---

[165] See, "CTV's women's sports network was doomed from beginning" *The Globe and Mail* (Toronto: September 3, 2003) (closure of WTSN). In 2006, an Australian Senate committee found that women's competitions constituted about a third of national coverage on the public ABC television network, but that the percentage was far lower in relation to commercial systems. Print media stories might be as low as 4% and overall television coverage as low as 2%. The committee considered the possibility of regulatory changes to require more programming and recommended government funding to promote the broadcasting of women's events. See, *About Time! Women in Sport and Recreation in Australia*, Report of the Senate Environment, Communications, Information Technology and Arts Committee (Commonwealth of Australia, September 2006), paras. 6.6-6.55.

[166] It is discrimination on the basis of sex to require female employees to wear "more sexy" dress: *Québec (Comm. des droits de la personne et des droits de la jeunesse) c. 2632-1661 Québec Inc.* (1997), 31 C.H.R.R. D/481 (Que. Trib.) (improper dress code for waitresses; short skirts, tight tops and high heels). On media coverage and the attention paid to Manon Rhéaume, see, E. Etue & M.K. Williams, *On the Edge: Women Making Hockey History* (Toronto: Second Story Press, 1996) at 191-230, 248-49.

[167] See online: <http://www.caaws.ca>. In 2007-08, the Sport Canada contribution to CAAWS was CDN $519,000. On the evolution of CAAWS, see, M.A. Hall, *The Girl and the Game: A History of Women's Sport in Canada* (Peterborough, ON: Broadview Press, 2002) at 172-77.

[168] 20 U.S.C., s. 1681 (prohibition against discrimination), s. 1687 (Act applies throughout institution receiving federal financial assistance). On gender equality in American sport, see, M.J. Cozzillio & R.L. Hayman, eds., *Sports and Inequality* (Durham, NC: Carolina Academic Press, 2005) at 347-832.

against NSOs or through the regulation of government grants and contracts.[169] In 2002, CAAWS initially proposed amendments to Bill C-54, the *Physical Activity and Sports Act,* to include further gender equity provisions.[170] This position was subsequently withdrawn when the federal government provided assurances that equity standards in areas such as funding, coaching and staffing would be required through the NSOs' accountability framework.[171]

In addition to the government initiatives, equity has been pursued through litigation and complaints to human rights commissions,[172] including cases where participants were excluded from programs because they were pregnant.[173] After inconsistent results in early cases, this strategy has served to vindicate individual rights. The decision of the Ontario Court of Appeal in *Blainey v. Ontario Hockey Association* removed a major obstacle in that Province's legislation.

In *Forbes v. Yarmouth Minor Hockey Assn.,*[174] a board of inquiry in Nova Scotia held that house league hockey is a service or facility customarily provided to the public, so that the *Human Rights Act*[175] was breached when 11-year-old Tina Forbes was denied registration in an association that had previously catered only to boys. The Yarmouth association was community-based and publicly supported and did not qualify as a private group exclusively for boys. External regulations that limited eligibility to "male persons" did not apply because the association did not qualify as a member of the Nova Scotia Minor Hockey Council and because Canadian Amateur Hockey Association ("CAHA") rules had no application to local competition; those rules would be in issue only in the case of all-star or inter-zone play. In *Commission des droits de la personne v. Fédération québécoise de hockey sur glace inc.,*[176] 13-year-old Françoise Turbide was excluded from a "Bantam" team at the instance of the Quebec Ice Hockey Federation. The Superior Court ordered her reinstated, noting that the federation's constitution did not limit membership to males. Distinguishing cases decided under other legislation, the court held that the federation was subject to

---

[169] *Canadian Human Rights Act*, R.S.C. 1985, c. H-6, s. 23.

[170] See, "Minister opposes enshrining women" *The Globe and Mail* (Toronto: May 30, 2002) at S7.

[171] See further, Chapter 2, "Legal Fundamentals and Equality Rights", section B, 1, 4.

[172] See: M.A. Hall, *The Girl and the Game: A History of Women's Sport in Canada* (Peterborough, ON: Broadview Press, 2002) at 177-82, 192; E. Etue & M.K. Williams, *On the Edge: Women Making Hockey History* (Toronto: Second Story Press, 1996) at 73, 160-64; N. Theberge, *Higher Goals: Women's Ice Hockey and the Politics of Gender* (Albany: State University of New York Press, 2000) at 150-52.

[173] See: *Barclay v. Peverill,* [1986] N.S.J. No. 296, 75 N.S.R. (2d) 208 (N.S.S.C. (T.D.)) (unauthorized exclusion of pregnant player from softball league); *Duxbury v. Gibsons Landing Slo-Pitch League* (1997), 28 C.H.R.R. D/441 (B.C.H.R.C.). See also, *Gardner v. All Australia Netball Association Ltd.* (2003), 197 A.L.R. 28 (Fed. Mag. Ct.).

[174] Unreported, October 27, 1978, N.S. Board of Inquiry (Kimball).

[175] S.N.S. 1969, c. 11 (now, R.S.N.S. 1989, c. 214).

[176] [1978] C.S. 1076. Turbide was first excluded in 1976 and unsuccessfully applied for an interlocutory injunction in *Commission des droits de la personne c. Fédération québécoise de hockey sur glace,* unreported, December 20, 1977 (Que. S.C.), Bard C.J., C.S. 500-05-024964-775.

the broader protections of the Quebec *Charter of Human Rights and Freedoms*[177] so that a competent female player could not be excluded. The federation was unable to prove that there were "separate but equal" facilities available for the age group. The court ordered Turbide's admission for the 1978-79 season and declared that regulations that discriminated on the basis of sex were inoperative in Quebec.

Contrary results were reached in two infamous Ontario decisions. In *Cummings v. Ontario Minor Hockey Assn.*,[178] ten-year-old Gail Cummings was barred from further participation on an all-star team when her CAHA registration was rejected by the Ontario Minor Hockey Association ("OMHA"). A board of inquiry held that this action constituted discrimination in the provision of "services and facilities available in any place to which the public is customarily admitted" and so was contrary to Ontario's former *Human Rights Code*.[179] The board rejected arguments seeking to justify the exclusion for social or physical reasons or on the grounds of public decency. The Divisional Court reversed this decision, holding that the OMHA, as a private voluntary organization promoting boys' hockey in certain age categories, was not a service available to the public in the sense contemplated by the Code. The Court of Appeal affirmed the dismissal of the complaint on the technical ground that the unincorporated OMHA did not qualify as a "person" under the definition in the Code; the complaint should have been laid against named officers or directors of the association. In *Ontario Human Rights Commission v. Ontario Rural Softball Assn.*,[180] nine-year-old Debbie Bazso was refused a certificate to play on a boys' all-star softball team. The Divisional Court, reversing the decision of the board of inquiry, noted that the association operated separate teams and competitions for boys and girls and held that an integrated team was not eligible to use its facility. A majority of the Court of Appeal then affirmed the dismissal of the complaint. Houlden J.A. held that the association's structured program could not qualify as a service or facility subject to the *Human Rights Code* in the absence of clear and unequivocal statutory language; his brother, Weatherston J.A., held that groups could be excluded from an organization provided there was a valid reason such as the desire to achieve fairness in competition. Madam Justice Wilson, dissenting, noted that the competitions were held in public parks so that the facility could not be defined according to prohibited criteria; the case was exactly the same as that of a boy denied registration because he was black. Wilson J.A. held that there was nothing in the Code to warrant a restrictive interpretation of "services and facilities" so as to exclude the association's activities. Had it been intended to exclude amateur sport, a particular exception should have been enacted.[181]

---

[177] R.S.Q. 1977, c. C-12.

[178] [1979] O.J. No. 4357, 26 O.R. (2d) 7, 104 D.L.R. (3d) 434 (Ont. C.A.), affg [1978] O.J. No. 3548, 21 O.R. (2d) 389, 90 D.L.R. (3d) 568 (Ont. Div. Ct.); revg (1977), 29 R.F.L. 259 (Board of Inquiry).

[179] R.S.O. 1980, c. 340, s. 2(1)(b).

[180] [1979] O.J. No. 4375, 26 O.R. (2d) 134, 102 D.L.R. (3d) 303, affg [1978] O.J. No. 3549, 21 O.R. (2d) 395, 90 D.L.R. (3d) 574 (Ont. Div. Ct.), revg unreported, May 19, 1977, Board of Inquiry (Lederman).

[181] See, for example, *Sex Discrimination Act*, 1975 (U.K.) c. 65, s. 44.

When the Ontario *Human Rights Code* was revised in 1981, public access ceased to be a requirement for the protection of equality of treatment with respect to services, goods and facilities.[182] At the same time, section 19(2) of the new Code excluded protection where "membership in an athletic organization or participation in an athletic activity is restricted to persons of the same sex". This statutory limitation operated until 1986 when the Ontario Court of Appeal in *Blainey v. Ontario Hockey Assn.*[183] ("OHA") found it contrary to the equality rights guaranteed in section 15 of the *Canadian Charter of Rights and Freedoms.*[184] In this case, 12-year-old Justine Blainey was selected in 1985 to play on a team in the Metro Toronto Hockey League, but was rejected for registration by the OHA which restricted eligibility to males. Blainey wished to develop her skills and take advantage of the levels of competition in the larger OHA, rather than play in the OWHA. The Court of Appeal, reversing the High Court, held that section 19(2) was inconsistent with section 15 of the *Charter* in that it permitted direct sex-based discrimination in athletic activity. Section 19(2) was not demonstrably justifiable under section 1 of the *Charter* since its terms and effects were disproportionate to any reasonable objective such as promoting public decency or protecting participants from injury:

> It prescribes no limits and provides no guidelines....it permits the posting of a "no females allowed" sign by every athletic organization in this province....it is somewhat of an anomaly to find in a statute designed to prohibit discrimination a provision which specifically permits it.[185]

The *Charter* did not apply directly to a private entity such as the OHA, but could be used to strike down the statutory provision. Blainey's remedy was to resubmit a complaint to the Human Rights Commission. When that complaint was heard, the board of inquiry found that discrimination had occurred.[186] The team, the league and the OHA were then ordered to pay Blainey CDN $3,000 for the anxiety suffered, and she was entitled to the cost of attending hockey school as a means of maintaining her skills.[187] The OHA was ordered to allow equal playing opportunities to both sexes and ordered to make this policy apparent in its

---

[182]   *Human Rights Code*, R.S.O. 1990, c. H.19, s. 1.

[183]   [1986] O.J. No. 236, 54 O.R. (2d) 513, 26 D.L.R. (4th) 728 (Ont. C.A.), revg [1985] O.J. No. 2645, 52 O.R. (2d) 225, 21 D.L.R (4th) 599 (Ont. H.C.J.), leave to appeal refused [1986] 1 S.C.R. xii, 58 O.R. (2d) 274n (S.C.C.). See also, S. Vella, *"Re Blainey and Ontario Hockey Association*: Removing "No Females Allowed" Signs in Ontario" (1989-90), 3 C.J.W.L. 634.

[184]   Part I of the *Constitution Act, 1982*, Schedule B of the *Canada Act, 1982* (U.K.), c. 11. See Chapter 2, "Legal Fundamentals and Equality Rights", section D, 2.

[185]   *Blainey v. Ontario Hockey Assn.*, [1986] O.J. No. 236, 54 O.R. (2d) 513, at 529, 530, 26 D.L.R. (4th) 728 at 744, 746 (C.A.), *per* Dubin J.A. On injury protection, see: *Barclay v. Peverill*, [1986] N.S.J. No. 296, 75 N.S.R. (2d) 208 (N.S.S.C. (T.D.)) (unauthorized exclusion of pregnant player from softball league); *Savard c. Fédération québécoise du sport étudiant*, unreported, April 23, 1993 (Que. C.S.) C.S. Hull 550-05-000517-931 (12-year-old refused order to allow play in older age group).

[186]   *Blainey v. Ontario Hockey Assn.* (1987), 9 C.H.R.R. D/4549 (Ont. Board of Inquiry).

[187]   *Blainey v. Ontario Hockey Assn. No. 2* (1988), 9 C.H.R.R. D/4972 (Ont. Board of Inquiry).

published materials. The OHA's legal costs had to be partially borne by the OWHA which had joined in opposing the integration of teams because it feared large-scale defection from the female game.

In Ontario, since the *Blainey* litigation, "the right to equal treatment under the *Human Rights Code* means that in sports, girls and women have access to the team of their choice, provided they can make the grade athletically".[188] This will not, however, result in a total integration of teams.[189] In the post-puberty age group, few female athletes will qualify for traditionally male levels of competition, and no comparable cross-over right applies to males (except for cases of gender re-alignment through sex-change). Separate female teams may continue to operate as special programs or affirmative action programs[190] for a group that would otherwise be at a physical disadvantage.[191] The existence of the special program does not, however, mean that all females have to play in it or that other programs are free to discriminate.[192] A further favoured solution is to have integrated play up to the age of 12, followed by competitive structures based on skill level.[193]

In 2006, an adjudicator appointed under the *Human Rights Code*[194] of Manitoba addressed similar issues in *Pasternak v. Manitoba High School Athletic Assn. Inc.*[195] In this case, the 17-year-old twin sisters, Amy and Jesse Pasternak, had played minor hockey with boys until the age of 15 and wished to try out for the boys' team at their school because the girls' team was a developmental program offering a significantly lower level of play. The adjudicator determined that it was unlawful to exclude the Pasternaks

---

[188] *Casselman v. Ontario Soccer Assn.* (1993), 23 C.H.R.R. D/397 (Ont. Board of Inquiry), at para. 31, *per* Lorne Slotnick (rights infringed when girls from mixed team disqualified).

[189] On integration strategies, see also, J. Sopinka, *Can I Play? Report of the Task Force on Equal Opportunity in Athletics*, vol. 1 (September 1983) at 89-113; vol. 2 (December 1984) at 121-25 (Ontario Task Force report; views on human rights remedies, separation, integration and role of an Equality Co-ordinator).

[190] See: *Canadian Charter of Rights and Freedoms*, Part I of the *Constitution Act, 1982*, being Schedule B to the *Canada Act 1982* (U.K.), 1982, c. 11, s. 15(2); *Human Rights Code*, R.S.O. 1990, c. H.19, s. 14; *Canadian Human Rights Act*, R.S.C. 1985, c. H-6, s. 16.

[191] See: *Blainey v. Ontario Hockey Assn.* (1987), 9 C.H.R.R. D/4549 (Ont. Board of Inquiry); *Ontario Women's Hockey Assn. v. Ontario Human Rights Commission*, [1987] O.J. No. 444, 59 O.R. (2d) 492 (Ont. H.C.J.). In *Stopps v. Just Ladies Fitness (Metrotown) Ltd.* (2006), 58 C.H.R.R. D/240 (B.C.H.R.T.), a women-only gymnasium was recognized as serving a special social need.

[192] See, *Blainey v. Ontario Hockey* Assn. (1987), 9 C.H.R.R. D/4549 (Ont. Board of Inquiry), at para. 35402; *Pasternak v. Manitoba High Schools Athletic Assn. Inc.*, [2006] M.H.R.B.A.D. No. 2 at 37 (Man. H.R.Comm.) (Decision of M. Lynne Harrision, adjudicator, September 22, 2006).

[193] This approach was endorsed in the "Sport Canada Policy on Women in Sport" (1986) at para. 6.2.

[194] S.M. 1987-88, c. 45, C.C.S.M., c. H175.

[195] [2006] M.H.R.B.A.D. No. 2 (Man. H.R.Comm.) (Decision of M. Lynne Harrison, adjudicator, September 22, 2006); *Manitoba High Schools Athletic Assn. Inc. v. Pasternak*, [2008] M.J. No. 10, [2008] 10 W.W.R. 729, 222 Man.R. (2d) 288 (Man. Q.B.) (judicial review denied). See also, "After 2-year wait, twins break a hockey barrier" *The Globe and Mail* (Toronto: September 23, 2006) at A3.

and ruled that the Association was guilty of a discriminatory practice in maintaining that they should assist in improving the girls' team:

> It was suggested that there would have been other or different opportunities available to the twins in the women's program, such as the opportunity to be leaders and to help other girls to learn the game. That may be so, but it was not their choice, and does not justify denying them the opportunity to participate and compete at their level in the game they were familiar with, and to be treated on the basis of their personal merit.
>
> I do not believe it would be considered acceptable to force a boy to play on a lower calibre team on the basis that he could help less skilled players to play better. Similarly, it is not acceptable to force a girl to play on a lower calibre team on the basis that she can help others to play better.[196]

The Pasternaks were entitled to participate in try-outs for the boys' team, and the Association was ordered to pay CDN $3500 damages to each girl and ordered to pay the costs of individual coaching to make up for their lost playing opportunities in the past few years.

Complaints under human rights legislation can serve a useful purpose in opening access to the established system, combatting sexual harassment[197] and focusing attention on the status of women's sport. The human rights process has been applied to remedy inequitable municipal subsidies that provided disproportionate support for male-dominated sports,[198] and the process may even have positive social effects when it is directed at equalizing opportunities at upper social levels.[199] Legal remedies do, however, tend to follow liberal theory and merely aim to eliminate arbitrary distinctions and establish genderless practices. This "me too" feminism barely transforms male-defined activities and runs the risk of reinforcing male control by co-opting women into the commercial structures that push an aggressive style of play.

In hockey, the human rights process has given women the choice of teams and has been used to remedy inequities in the allocation of ice time.[200] This process is, however, hardly the fast track to the transformation of hockey programs: the complaint involving the University of Saskatchewan was filed in 2000, and by 2006 the Saskatchewan Court of Appeal had decided that there

---

[196] *Pasternak v. Manitoba High Schools Athletic Assn. Inc.*, [2006] M.H.R.B.A.D. No. 2 at 31-32 (Man. H.R. Comm.) (Decision of M. Lynne Harrison, adjudicator, September 22, 2006).

[197] See Chapter 5, "Be Safe: Off the Ice", section C.

[198] "Mediated Settlement Between David Morrison, the City of Coquitlam, and the Deputy Chief Commissioner", B.C. H.R. Comm., March 8, 1999 (complaint on behalf of female gymnasts in gymnastics club; settlement designed to eliminate systemic barriers to female participation); see, L. Robinson, *Black Tights: Women, Sport, and Sexuality* (Toronto: HarperCollins Publishers, 2002) at 36-43. On differences in amenities, see also, *Anderson and O'Neill v. The YMCA of Barrie* (Ont. Board of Inquiry, 00-020, December 6, 2000) (YMCA ordered to build comparable women's facility).

[199] *Quon c. Club de golf de la vallée du Richelieu inc.* (1994), 21 C.H.R.R. D/55 (Que. Trib.) (golf club membership; inequality caused by denial of discount to spousal member).

[200] See, E. Etue & M.K. Williams, *On the Edge: Women Making Hockey History* (Toronto: Second Story Press, 1996) at 169-76.

was no procedural impediment to the case being heard.[201] The development of the game remains a matter of sport politics, and women's hockey must address whether the traditional "boys club" associations are an effective route to significant change. The provincial bodies, Hockey Canada and the IIHF offer the advantages of professional management and established business structures, but the women's game is not the priority when it is incorporated as a "little sister".[202] The "separatist" OWHA, which accounts for half of all national registrations, presents one alternative model for creating a characteristic style of on-ice play and association governance. To remedy continuing inequities in funding, promotion and professional opportunities, it may be necessary to combine legal and political strategies with organizational change.

## 2.    Athletes with Disabilities[203]

Disabilities may be physical (locomotor), sensory or intellectual, and issues of access may relate either to participants or to spectators.[204] Athletes with disabilities include those in wheelchairs, amputees, blind or deaf athletes, and athletes with cerebral palsy or mental disability. Issues of discrimination and liability can also occur in relation to the exclusion of participants suffering from infectious diseases[205] or the mandatory testing of groups

---

[201]    *University of Saskatchewan v. Women 2000*, [2006] S.J. No. 231, 268 D.L.R. (4th) 558 (Sask. C.A.), affg [2005] S.J. No. 504, 267 Sask.R. 33, 54 C.H.R.R. D/210 (Sask. Q.B.), affg (2005), 52 C.H.R.R. D/ 231 (Sask. H.R. Trib.).

[202]    On the status of the women's game within national organizations, see: E. Etue & M.K. Williams, *On the Edge: Women Making Hockey History* (Toronto: Second Story Press, 1996) at 48-66 (Female Council, playing opportunities and promotion) at 240-45 (promotional efforts for the first world championship in 1990, including the pink uniforms); J. Stevens, "Women's Hockey in Canada: After the 'Gold Rush'" in D. Whitson & R. Gruneau, *Artificial Ice: Hockey, Culture, and Commerce* (Peterborough, ON: Broadview Press, 2006) at 85, 96-97. On strategies of organizational change, see, *Towards Gender Equity for Women in Sport: A Handbook for National Sport Organizations* (CAAWS, March 1993) at 9-27.

[203]    By s. 9 of the *Declaration on the Rights of Disabled Persons* (United Nations General Assembly, resolution 3447 (XXX), December 9, 1975), "Disabled persons have the right...to participate in all social, creative or recreational activities". See also: *Convention on the Rights of the Child* (United Nations General Assembly, resolution 44/25, November 20, 1989, ratified by Canada, December 13, 1991), art. 23(3) (right of disabled child to special assistance in access to recreation opportunities); *Palik v. Lloydminster Public School Div. No. 99*, Sask. H.R. Trib., September 18, 2006 (diabetic child's participation in hockey tournament was discretionary recreational activity; refusal of leave to parent was not discrimination on the basis of family status).

[204]    On spectator access in movie theatres, see: *Canadian Odeon Theatres Ltd. v. Saskatchewan (Human Rights Commission)*, [1985] S.J. No. 268, 18 D.L.R. (4th) 93, [1985] 3 W.W.R. 717 (Sask. C.A.); *Turnbull v. Famous Players Inc.* (2001), 40 C.H.R.R. D/333 (Ont. Board of Inquiry) and [2003] O.H.R.T.D. No. 10, 2003 HRTO 10 (Ont. H.R.Trib.) (remedy). On discrimination in employment, see also, *De Souza v. 1469328 Ontario Inc.*, [2008] O.H.R.T.D. No. 20, 2008 HRTO 23 (Ont. H.R.Trib.) (tennis coach with epilepsy).

[205]    See: "Gymnast files complaint against Cirque du Soleil" *The Globe and Mail* (Toronto: July 16, 2003); "Cirque offers to rehire HIV-positive gymnast" *The Ottawa Citizen* (January 31, 2004) at A5.

perceived to be at greater risk of carrying the disease.[206] The development of opportunities requires flexible strategies in recreational or fitness programs[207] and in the organization of competitive sport. Various models of inclusion are available to promote acceptance and to improve the experience for the athlete.[208] Particular progress is required in fully recognizing the achievements of all classes of athlete.[209]

Sport Canada's "Policy on Sport for Persons with a Disability" (2006), "envisions the full and active participation of persons with a disability in Canadian sport at all levels and in all forms, to the extent of their abilities and interests".[210] This document follows the objectives of the "Canadian Sport Policy"[211] by seeking to promote participation, excellence, capacity and interaction and sets the objective of increased participation at both the recreational and competitive levels. The Policy's action plan anticipates improvements in coaching and competitive structures and looks to increase development projects and bilateral agreements with provincial and territorial governments. In 2007-08, Sport Canada funded six national organizations for athletes with disabilities. The Canadian Paralympic Committee serves as a co-ordinating and fundraising body for member associations, and the sport organizations include multi-sport organizations for a single disability (*e.g.*, blind sports, deaf sports) and Games organizations (*e.g.*, Special Olympics Canada). Separate organizations are presently needed to serve an advocacy role, and some groups prefer to maintain a separate sporting culture. There is, however, a widely held goal of integrating all athletes into the administration of sports organizations, while preserving special competitive categories either in separate competitions or in mixed events. The Sport Funding and Accountability Framework requires NSOs to have a formal policy demonstrating commitment to equity and access for persons with a disability. Hockey Canada's programs include the promotion of sledge hockey, where Canada has a strong record of performance in world championships and in the Paralympic Winter Games.

Besides the policy initiatives and funding programs, equity has also been pursued through complaints under human rights legislation. In Ontario, sections 1

---

[206] See, R.S. Magnusson & H. Opie, "HIV and Hepatitis in Sport: A Legal Framework for Resolving Hard Cases" (1994), 20 Monash U. L. Rev. 214, esp. at 234-37, 258-60.

[207] See, *Active Living for Canadians with a Disability: A Blueprint for Action* (Government of Canada, Fitness and Amateur Sport, 2001). On special supervision and liability, see: *Dziwenka (Next Friend of) v. Alberta*, [1971] S.C.J. No. 121, [1972] S.C.R. 419 (S.C.C.); *Bain (Guardian ad litem of) v. Calgary Board of Education*, [1993] A.J. No. 952, [1994] 2 W.W.R. 468 (Alta. Q.B.).

[208] See, *Sport: The Way Ahead*, Report of the Minister's Task Force on Federal Sport Policy (Minister of State, Fitness and Amateur Sport, May 1992) at 157-61.

[209] See, for example, "Paralympic star rejects shared award" *The Globe and Mail* (Toronto, December 4, 2004) at S1 (Chantal Petitclerc, having won five gold medals at the Paralympic Games, rejects shared award from Athletics Canada).

[210] "Policy on Sport for Persons with a Disability" (June 2006), para. 4.0 "Vision", online: <http://www.pch.gc.ca> "Sport Canada".

[211] See Chapter 2, "Legal Fundamentals and Equality Rights", section B, 3.

and 5 of the *Human Rights Code*[212] prohibit discrimination on the basis of disability, which is defined in section 10 to include physical, mental, developmental and learning disabilities. Section 3(1) of the *Canadian Human Rights Act*[213] also proscribes discrimination based on disability, which means "any previous or existing mental or physical disability and includes disfigurement and previous or existing dependence on alcohol or a drug" (see s. 25).[214] Cases relating to physical activity programs have dealt with the exclusion of blind and visually impaired participants,[215] persons with intellectual and learning disabilities,[216] wheelchair users[217] and paraplegics.[218] In Ontario, rights are not infringed if the disability renders the person "incapable of performing or fulfilling the essential duties or requirements attending the exercise of the right".[219] There is, however, a duty to accommodate the needs of persons with disabilities up to the point of "undue hardship".[220] The similar duty under American law was famously considered in the case of the professional golfer, Casey Martin, whose circulatory disorder prevented him from walking the courses. Martin successfully argued that the game would not be fundamentally altered by his use of a golf cart.[221]

---

[212] R.S.O. 1990, c. H.19. See also, *Accessibility for Ontarians with Disabilities Act, 2005*, S.O. 2005, c. 11.

[213] R.S.C. 1985, c. H-6.

[214] Most provincial Commissions operate a policy of accepting complaints relating to discrimination based on alcohol and drug dependency. On doping control, see, Chapter 3, "Organizations and Regulations" section D.

[215] *Rogers v. Newfoundland (Department of Culture, Recreation and Youth)*, [1994] N.J. No. 355, 120 D.L.R. (4th) 326 (Nfld. C.A.), affg [1991] N.J. No. 271, 93 Nfld. & P.E.I.R. 121 (Nfld. S.C. (T.D.)) (denial of hunting licence to blind man; complaint dismissed); *Rosin v. Canadian Armed Forces*, [1990] F.C.J. No. 1104, [1991] 1 F.C. 391 (F.C.A.) (monocular cadet could remain on armed forces parachuting course).

[216] *Saskatchewan High Schools Athletic Assn., Re* (1994), 23 C.H.R.R. D/159 (Sask. H.R.Comm.) (effect of "under 19" rule on students with learning disabilities); *Corp. du Collège Notre-Dame du Sacré Coeur c. Québec (Commission des droits de la personne)*, [2001] J.Q. no 6014, [2002] R.J.Q. 5 (Que. C.A.), varg [1994] R.J.Q. 1324 (Que. S.C.) (discrimination found when student with mild cerebral palsy denied admission to private school emphasising physical education); see, W.F. Foster & W.J. Smith, "*Québec v. Collège Notre-Dame du Sacré-coeur*: Justice Delayed, but Injustice Denied" (2002), 12 E.L.J. 75. See also, *Sharpe v. Mikoula*, [2006] B.C.H.R.T.D. No. 31, 2006 BCHRT 31 (B.C.H.R.T.) (person with physical and mental disabilities; membership in fitness facility terminated).

[217] *Letendre v. Royal Canadian Legion, South Burnaby Branch No. 83* (1988), 10 C.H.R.R. D/5846 (B.C.H.R.C.) (dancing); *Munsch v. York Condominium Corp. No. 60* (1992), 18 C.H.R.R. D/339 (Ont. Bd. of Inquiry) (need for bench in shower area of swimming pool); *Québec (Commission des droits de la personne et des droits de la jeunesse) c. Repentigny (Ville)*, [2003] J.T.D.P.Q. no 1 (T.D.P.Q.) (no obligation to admit wheelchair onto ice rink).

[218] *McDeere v. British Columbia Kart Club Assn.* (2004), 49 C.H.R.R. D/237 (B.C.H.R.T.) (denial of licence to race go-kart with gear shift).

[219] *Human Rights Code*, R.S.O. 1990, c. H.19, s. 17(1).

[220] *Human Rights Code*, R.S.O. 1990, c. H.19, s. 17(2). See also, *Canadian Centre for Ethics in Sport v. Adams*, SDRCC DT-06-0039 (June 11, 2007, R.H. McLaren, arb.); *Adams v. CCES*, CAS, 2007/A/1312, May 16, 2008 (no obligation on doping control organization to provide sterile catheter to athlete in wheelchair).

[221] *PGA Tour, Inc. v. Martin*, 2001 U.S. LEXIS 4115, 532 U.S. 661 (S.C.) (obligations under the *Americans with Disabilities Act* of 1990; tournament was not fundamentally altered because

In *Youth Bowling Council v. McLeod*,[222] 11-year-old Tammy McLeod, who suffered from cerebral palsy, was excluded from a zone tournament in children's bowling because she used a wooden ramp to deliver the ball from her wheelchair. The Ontario Divisional Court recognized that "Tammy is not able, because of handicap, to perform the essential act of bowling — manual control and release of the ball".[223] This rule of the game was, however, found to have adverse impact on the disabled, so that an obligation arose to accommodate persons affected by it:

> .... the *Code* imposes upon those who offer services in the sports field the obligation of making accommodations to the needs of handicapped persons who wish to participate, up to the point of undue hardship. That point is reached, in my opinion, when the proposed accommodation would impact significantly upon the way in which other participants would be required to play or would give the accommodated person an actual advantage over others in such participation. The *Code* does not require that the essential elements of a sport be altered for the participants in order to accommodate those who for whatever reason cannot perform those essential elements.[224]

Since bowling is an individual sport, use of the ramp did not affect the way others played; neither did it give McLeod any unfair advantage over the other children, who in fact completely accepted her. The Court found no undue hardship to the Bowling Council or the competitors and upheld the finding that there had been a denial of equal treatment.

## 3. Aboriginal Peoples

Discrimination on the basis of race is prohibited in human rights codes[225] and in section 15 of the *Canadian Charter of Rights and Freedoms*, although the rights of Aboriginal Peoples are also subject to special legal provision. The *Charter* recognizes the unique historical status by affirming the "existing aboriginal and treaty rights of the aboriginal peoples of Canada" (see, s. 35), and the *Canadian Human Rights Act* now provides for the application of the Act in a manner that

---

walking rule is peripheral and essence of golf is shot-making). See also, M.J. Cozzillio & R.L. Hayman, eds., *Sports and Inequality* (Durham, NC: Carolina Academic Press, 2005) at 929-1038.

[222] (1988), 9 C.H.R.R. D/ 5371 (Ont. Bd. of Inquiry), affd [1990] O.J. No. 2047, 75 O.R. (2d) 451, 74 D.L.R. (4th) 625 (Ont. Div. Ct.), affd [1994] O.J. No. 4420, 20 O.R. (3d) 658, 121 D.L.R. (4th) 187 (Ont. C.A.).

[223] *Youth Bowling Council v. McLeod*, *ibid.*, at 75 O.R. (2d) 460, 74 D.L.R. (4th) 633, *per* Lane J.

[224] *Ibid.*, at 75 O.R. (2d) 458, 74 D.L.R. (4th) 631. See also, *Rogers v. Newfoundland (Department of Culture, Recreation and Youth)*, [1991] N.J. No. 271, 93 Nfld. & P.E.I.R. 121 (Nfld. S.C. (T.D.)) (licence system for active hunters; inappropriate to change public policy).

[225] See, *Baptiste v. Napanee and District Rod & Gun Club* (1993), 19 C.H.R.R. D/246 (Ont. Bd. of Inquiry) (native fisherman denied prize in fishing derby). In *Richard v. Brandon Youth Hockey Assn. Inc.*, Man. H.R. Comm., Decision of M. Lynne Harrison, October 16, 2006 (adjudicator found unlawful reprisal against a player of aboriginal ancestry who was denied registration because he had filed a human rights complaint).

respects the rights and traditions of the First Nations.[226] International documents similarly acknowledge the particular rights of indigenous peoples.[227] In 2006, 1.17 million people identified themselves as Aboriginal, representing 3.8 per cent of Canada's total population. Of this group, 60 per cent are North American Indian, 33 per cent are Métis and 4 per cent are Inuit.

Games and contests form an important part of the Aboriginal heritage,[228] and *baggataway* or lacrosse is the particular gift of this culture.[229] There is a long record of participation in both traditional and modern sports and a short list of famous performers in the NHL,[230] where the first recognized aboriginal player was Fred Sasakamoose of the Chicago Blackhawks. In spite of the potential positive effects of sports activities, native communities have not been saved from endemic social problems. The Aboriginal population is much younger than the general population, but suffers serious disadvantages in income, educational attainment and health:

> Aboriginal people have a poverty rate comparable to that found in developing countries, an unemployment rate among adults of almost 25%, a poorly educated population and a dramatic suicide rate, which among 10-19 year-olds is more than 5 times higher than their non-Aboriginal counterparts....Forty-four percent of Aboriginal people smoke daily, 61% report problems with alcohol abuse and 48% report problems with drug abuse.[231]

Recent reports dealing with sport policy have drawn attention to the particular needs of Aboriginal Peoples[232] and have suggested that suitable recreation

---

[226] *An Act to amend the Canadian Human Rights Act*, S.C. 2008, c. 30 (repealing s. 67 of the *Canadian Human Rights Act*). On Métis hunting rights, see, *R. v. Powley*, [2003] S.C.J. No. 43, [2003] 2 S.C.R. 207 (S.C.C.).

[227] The *Declaration on the Rights of Indigenous Peoples* was adopted by the United Nations General Assembly on September 13, 2007 (GA resolution 61/295), with Canada voting against the Declaration. See also, *International Convention on the Elimination of All Forms of Racial Discrimination*, adopted by UN General Assembly resolution 2106 (XX), December 21, 1965; ratified by Canada, October 14, 1970.

[228] See, C.D. Howell, *Blood, Sweat, and Cheers: Sport and the Making of Modern Canada* (Toronto: University of Toronto Press, 2001) at 26-27.

[229] See: A. Metcalfe, *Canada Learns to Play: The Emergence of Organized Sport, 1807-1914* (Toronto: McClelland and Stewart, 1987) at 181-218; D.M. Fisher, *Lacrosse: A History of the Game* (Baltimore: The Johns Hopkins University Press, 2002).

[230] See, D. Marks, *They Call Me Chief: Warriors on Ice* (Winnipeg: J. Gordon Shillingford Publishing, 2008), noting the careers of George Armstrong, Blair Atcheynum, Henry Boucha, John Chabot, Ron Delorme, Theoren Fleury, Stan Jonathan, Reggie Leach, Jim Neilson, Ted Nolan, Gino Odjick, Everett Sanipass, Gary Sargent, Fred Sasakamoose and Bryan Trottier.

[231] Subcommittee on the Study of Sport in Canada, *Sport in Canada: Everybody's Business* (Dennis Mills, M.P., chair) (House of Commons Canada, November 1998) at 87.

[232] See, for example, *Sport: The Way Ahead*, Report of the Minister's Task Force on Federal Sport Policy (Minister of State, Fitness and Amateur Sport, May 1992) at 153-57, 161-63. On ethnocentric bias in earlier programs, see, V. Paraschak, "The Native Sport and Recreation Program, 1972-1981: Patterns of Resistance, Patterns of Reproduction" (1995) 26 Can. J. of History of Sport 1.

programs can contribute to spiritual and cultural renewal and to alleviating the range of social and economic difficulties. The Aboriginal Sport Circle ("ASC")[233] was established in 1995 to promote participation, and competitive opportunities are offered at major Games such as the North American Indigenous Games and the Arctic Winter Games.[234]

The goal of an inclusive sport system is now declared in "Sport Canada's Policy on Aboriginal Peoples' Participation in Sport" (2005),[235] which aims to reduce barriers to participation and emphasizes the potential of sport as a means of driving social development and economic change. The current barriers include inadequate infrastructure and facilities, the remote location of communities and the lack of coaches who are sensitive to Aboriginal sporting traditions. The Policy aims to work with the ASC to enhance participation and excellence and realize social improvements in association with other programs and agencies. It also calls for a holistic approach that recognizes the special circumstances of the Aboriginal experience and respects the diversity of Canada's Aboriginal Peoples.

The Policy identifies racism as an alienating factor that prevents full participation in Canadian society. Racist attitudes may be manifested in the adoption of native names and insignia in association with amateur or professional teams.[236] This concern has led to widespread review of mascots and team names in North America,[237] although change may be contested by "traditionalists"[238] or by those who find nothing offensive in the images. The intended meaning of a sign suffers further complication when it is promoted and endorsed by Aboriginal Peoples themselves.[239] Various legal remedies are available to address questionable forms of communication,[240] including the

---

[233] See online: <http://www.aboriginalsportcircle.ca/>. In 2007-08, the Sport Canada contribution to the ASC was CDN $684,000.

[234] See also, "All-native national hockey team planned" *The Globe and Mail* (Toronto: December 9, 1999) at A1 (proposed Aboriginal team to compete in international events). On the experiences of aboriginal players in organized hockey, see, R. Pitter, "Racialization and Hockey in Canada: From Personal Troubles to a Canadian Challenge" in D. Whitson and R. Gruneau, eds., *Artificial Ice: Hockey, Culture, and Commerce* (Peterborough, ON: Broadview Press, 2006) at 123, 129-31 (referring to, *They Call Me Chief*).

[235] "Sport Canada's Policy on Aboriginal Peoples' Participation in Sport" (May 2005), online: <http://www.pch.gc.ca> "Sport Canada".

[236] See: C.R. King & C.F. Springwood, eds., *Team Spirits: The Native American Mascots Controversy* (Lincoln: University of Nebraska Press, 2001); Special Issue, (2004) 28(1) J. of Sport and Social Issues 3-87.

[237] See, C. Dennie, "Native American Mascots and Team Names: Throw Away the Key; the Lanham Act is Locked for Future Trademark Challenges" (2005) 15 Seton Hall J. of Sports and Entertainment L. 197, at 200 (changes to names of teams and mascots at over 600 high schools and colleges).

[238] See, for example, "Manitoba school rethinks Mohawk mascot" *The Globe and Mail* (Toronto: March 23, 2004) at A9 (students protest to keep the name "Morden Mohawks").

[239] See, M.A. Robidoux, "The Nonsense of Native American Sport Imagery: Reclaiming a Past that Never Was" (2006) 41 Int. Rev. for the Sociology of Sport 201.

[240] See, C.L. Claussen, "Ethnic Team Names and Logos - Is There a Legal Solution?" (1996) 6 Marquette Sports L.J. 409.

denial of public funding or official permits, cancellation of rights under trademark legislation,[241]and criminal prosecution for incitement to hatred.[242] Human rights legislation also prohibits the "display before the public of any notice, sign, symbol, emblem, or other similar representation" that indicates an intention to practice prohibited discrimination.[243] The legal texts are not always appropriate to deal with the controversy, which is best resolved through informed and culturally sensitive debate. The community discussion should address the significance of the name or image, who is in control of it, and how any stereotype would be received if it related to another minority group.

## 4.   Colour

The *Physical Activity and Sport Act*[244] and the accompanying policy statements declare the goals of reducing barriers to participation and promoting ethical standards.[245] The elimination of discrimination and vilification based on colour or race is a central objective that can be pursued through government programs, policies of organizations and legal remedies.[246]

Many studies have considered the historical emancipation of black athletes and the current status of African Americans in collegiate and professional sport in North America.[247] Entry barriers to major league baseball and football began to be eliminated in the 1940s and 1950s,[248] but there are continuing issues in relation to the "stacking" or segregation of playing positions, differentials in salaries and other earnings, and career

---

[241]   *Trade-marks Act*, R.S.C. 1985, c. T-13, s. 9(1)(j) (prohibited marks; "any scandalous, obscene or immoral word or device").

[242]   *Criminal Code*, R.S.C. 1985, c. C-46, s. 319 (crimes involving public incitement of hatred against any identifiable group). See also, Law Reform Commission of Canada, *Hate Propaganda*, Working Paper 50 (Ottawa: Law Reform Commission of Canada, 1986).

[243]   *Human Rights Code*, R.S.O. 1990, c. H.19, s. 13. See also, *Hagan v. Trustees of the Toowoomba Sports Ground Trust* (2001), 105 F.C.R. 56 (Fed. C. of Aust.) (community did not regard person's name on grandstand as offensive).

[244]   S.C. 2003, c. 2. See Chapter 2, "Legal Fundamentals and Equality Rights", section B, 1.

[245]   See Chapter 2, "Legal Fundamentals and Equality Rights", section B, 3, 4.

[246]   See, for example, *Jones v. Cluff* (1982), 3 C.H.R.R. D/959 (Ont. Bd. of Inquiry) (alleged discrimination in treatment of blacks at public golf course).

[247]   For recent studies, see: D.K. Wiggins & P.B. Miller, eds., *The Unlevel Playing Field: A Documentary History of the African American Experience in Sport* (Urbana, IL: University of Illinois Press, 2003); P.B. Miller & D.K. Wiggins, eds., *Sport and the Color Line: Black Athletes and Race Relations in Twentieth-Century America* (New York: Routledge, 2004); M.J. Cozzillio & R.L. Hayman, eds., *Sports and Inequality* (Durham, NC: Carolina Academic Press, 2005) at 69-346. On race and genetics, see: J. Hoberman, *Darwin's Athletes: How Sport Has Damaged America and Preserved the Myth of Race* (Boston: Houghton Mifflin, 1997); J. Entine, *Taboo: Why Black Athletes Dominate Sports and Why We're Afraid to Talk About It* (New York: Public Affairs, 2000).

[248]   Jackie Robinson played his first game for the Montreal Royals, a farm team of the Brooklyn Dodgers, in April 1946. He joined the Dodgers the following year.

opportunities as coaches and senior administrators. A particular field of concern is the low academic attainment of African American student athletes in revenue-producing sports and the tendency of schools to lower educational expectations.[249] Sport also continues to be marred by incidents of racist outbursts by fans and racist remarks by coaches, media commentators and others.[250]

The NHL was late in admitting black players[251] and remains predominantly white compared to other major leagues.[252] The pool of elite hockey players is largely Canadian and European,[253] and hockey is not the game of cultural choice for African Americans, partly because of the cost of participation. The first black player in the NHL was Willie O'Ree, from Fredericton, who played professional hockey for 25 years and played for the Boston Bruins in 1958 and 1960-61.[254] Many commentators believe that the colour barrier should have been broken 10 years earlier by Herbert Carnegie, from Toronto, who excelled in a career that was mainly played in the Quebec Senior League. Carnegie performed well in a tryout with the New York Rangers in 1948, but was offered only a minor league contract.[255] Conn Smythe is reputed to have said, "I'd give anyone $10,000 if he could turn Herb Carnegie white".[256]

---

[249] See, C.K. Harrison & A. Valdez, "The Uneven View of African American Ballers" in C.K. Ross, ed., *Race and Sport: The Struggle for Equality on and off the Field* (Jackson: University Press of Mississippi, 2004) at 183-87 (the "illusion of integration").

[250] See, for example: "Racial epithet costs coach his job" *The Globe and Mail* (Toronto, March 11, 2003) at S1, S3 (comments directed at Trevor Daley); *Rudder (Litigation guardian of) v. Ontario Amateur Softball Assn.*, [2005] O.J. No. 3358 (Ont. S.C.J.) (racist remark by coach; order to allow release of 11-year-old player). On "Rink Rage", see Chapter 5, "Be Safe: Off the Ice", section B, 1.

[251] On the experiences of blacks in organized hockey, see: C. Harris, *Breaking the Ice: The Black Experience in Professional Hockey* (Toronto: Insomniac Press, 2003); G. & D. Fosty, *Black Ice: The Lost History of the Colored Hockey League of the Maritimes, 1895-1925* (New York: Stryker-Indigo Publishing, 2004); R. Pitter, "Racialization and Hockey in Canada: From Personal Troubles to a Canadian Challenge" in D. Whitson & R. Gruneau, eds., *Artificial Ice: Hockey, Culture, and Commerce* (Peterborough, ON: Broadview Press, 2006) at 123, 131-34.

[252] On hiring practices in different leagues, see, R.E. Lapchick, *2005 Racial and Gender Report Card*, Institute for Diversity and Ethics in Sports, University of Central Florida, online: <http://www.tidesport.org/>.

[253] On other winter sports, see also, A.G. Coleman, "The Unbearable Whiteness of Skiing" in J. Bloom & M.N. Willard, eds., *Sports Matters: Race, Recreation, and Culture* (New York: New York University Press, 2002) at 141.

[254] See, "O'Ree knows black can be hell on ice" *The Globe and Mail* (Toronto: October 31, 1990) at A14; "NHL to honour its first black player" *The Globe and Mail* (Toronto: January 17, 1998) at A30. Willie O'Ree was named to the Order of Canada in 2009.

[255] See, "Colour bar shattered one Canadian's NHL dream" *The Globe and Mail* (Toronto: April 5, 1997) at A1. See also, H. Carnegie, *A Fly in a Pail of Milk* (Toronto: Mosaic Press, 1997).

[256] This remark (or "I'll pay anyone $10,000 to turn Herbie white") is attributed to Conn Smythe after he watched Herbert Carnegie play as a teenager: "Colour bar shattered one Canadian's NHL dream" *The Globe and Mail* (Toronto: April 5, 1997) at A1; "A muted message" *The Globe and Mail* (Toronto: September 3, 1997) at A22.

## 5. National Origin

Under the eligibility rules of the International Ice Hockey Federation ("IIHF"), citizenship is one of the primary qualifications for membership of national representative teams participating in international tournaments.[257] Restrictions on "imports" also operate at other levels of competition in hockey and other sports. The eligibility criteria of the Canadian Football League ("CFL") and of men's basketball in Canadian Interuniversity Sport ("CIS")[258] limit the number of roster places available to non-Canadian (usually American) athletes.[259] These rules potentially amount to discrimination based on national or ethnic origin, ancestry, place of origin or citizenship, and they may also constitute a quota on the number of African American players.[260] The preference for Canadian players has, however, been justified as a special program or arrangement designed to reduce disadvantages in training and experience in particular sports.[261] In Ontario, the *Human Rights Code* specifically permits preferences for Canadian citizens and permanent residents where the purpose is to foster participation in cultural, educational or athletic activities.[262]

In the NHL, there is no quota limiting the signing of players from outside North America, so that by 2006 team rosters were around 30 per cent European (compared to 52 per cent Canadian and 18 per cent American). The Major Junior teams of the Canadian Hockey League ("CHL") have been limited to two non-North American "imports", and it has been the practice of CHL teams to

---

[257] See, IIHF Statutes and Bylaws (2008-2012) (July 2008), Bylaw 205. See further, Chapter 3, "Organizations and Regulations", section C, 2.

[258] By CIS Eligibility Policy, 40.10.4.4 (September 2008), men's basketball teams are limited to three players who are not Canadian citizens or landed immigrants. In *Beattie v. Acadia University*, [1976] N.S.J. No. 32, 72 D.L.R. (3d) 718 (N.S.C.A.), it was held that a limit based on place of training was discriminatory, but that the right to play at a private university was not protected by human rights legislation. The latter aspect of the decision was disapproved in *Berg v. University of British Columbia*, [1993] S.C.J. No. 55, [1993] 2 S.C.R. 353 (S.C.C.).

[259] The quarterback position is, however, usually reserved for Americans. See: *Bone v. Hamilton Tiger-Cats Football Club Limited* (Ont. Board of Inquiry, J.D. McCamus, August 16, 1979); *Canadian Football League v. Canada (Human Rights Commission)*, [1980] F.C.J. No. 47, [1980] 2 F.C. 329 (F.C.T.D.); Canadian Human Rights Commission, *Release* (February 20, 1981) and *Summary of Decisions* (January & February, 1981).

[260] See, N. Longley, "The Professional Football Industry in Canada: Economic and Policy Issues" in R. Fort & J. Fizel, eds., *International Sports Economics Comparisons* (Westport: Praeger, 2004) at 209, 218-19.

[261] See, *Canadian Human Rights Act*, R.S.C. 1985, c. H-6, s. 16; Canadian Human Rights Commission, *Release* (February 20, 1981) and *Summary of Decisions* (January & February, 1981) (complaint of George O'Leary, import quotas).

[262] *Human Rights Code*, R.S.O. 1990, c. H.19, s. 16(2). See also, *Solin v. British Columbia Amateur Hockey Assn.* (1988), 9 C.H.R.R. D/5266 (B.C.H.R.C.) (residence rules not discriminatory); *Sahyoun v. Atlantic Colleges Athletic Assn.*, [2004] N.B.H.R.B.I.D. No. 3 (N.B. Labour and Employment Board, Board of Inquiry, Decision of G.G. Couturier, July 20, 2004) (services may be denied on the basis of citizenship).

maximize their permitted European content. Hockey Canada Regulations[263] now provide that as of 2012-13 Major Junior teams can have only one non-North American player and must establish the maximum number of American players who can register and play on teams based in Canada (see, F, 53(f), (g)). By Regulation K.26(b), the permitted use of non-North American "imports" at other level is as follows: below Major Junior (none), Senior and above (one within the current season), Senior female (two within the current season) and female hockey (two).

In 2006, a study by the IIHF suggested that European players should develop their skills at home and indicated that most Europeans drafted by the NHL achieved only marginal careers.[264] The study suggested that the CHL and the minor professional leagues were not productive routes and recommended that both the NHL and the European leagues would be strengthened through more selective drafting. The study therefore proposed reducing the European presence in the NHL to 20 per cent. It is commonly alleged that Europeans receive preferential treatment in North American hockey, although based on NHL performance they are in fact the victims of discrimination.

## 6.    Francophone Interests and *l'affaire* Cherry

French is the first language of 24 per cent of Canadians, and linguistic issues are a central theme in national politics. Sport has been regularly implicated in the debate over language through prominent controversies that offered opportunities for partisan advantage. Tensions were stirred in 1991 when Eric Lindros refused to report to the Quebec Nordiques after they had drafted him,[265] and a Parliamentary committee received mixed reviews in 2007 when it revived old allegations that Shane Doan had made insulting remarks to a referee.[266] Besides the famous *affaires*, there has been detailed study of participation by francophones and of their experience in sports organizations.

Issues relating to the equitable treatment of francophones involve national sport organizations ("NSOs"), which are required to be bilingual, and the NHL, where the working language is English. (The standard player contract in the NHL ends with the declaration that, "Les parties ont par les présentes exprimé

---

[263]  See, Hockey Canada, Regulations (amended to June 2009). On Major Junior hockey, see Chapter 3, "Organizations and Regulations", sections A, 1-2; B, 3; C, 2; Chapter 7, "The Business of Hockey", section A, 2.

[264]  See: "Study critical of NHL drafting Europeans" *The Globe and Mail* (Toronto: October 26, 2006) at R6, R10; "IIHF study criticizes flight of players to North America" *The Globe and Mail* (Toronto: October 27, 2006) at R7. On discrimination in the evaluation of European players, see, M. Lavoie, "The Entry Draft in the National Hockey League: Discrimination, Style of Play, and Team Location" (2003) 62 Am. J. of Econ. and Soc. 387, at 390, 395, 405. On international transfers, see Chapter 3, "Organizations and Regulations", section C, 2.

[265]  See, D. Cruise & A. Griffiths, *Net Worth: Exploding the Myths of Pro Hockey* (Toronto: Viking, 1991) at 339-56. See further, Chapter 8, "Competition Law and Labour Law", section A, 3.

[266]  See: "MPs bodycheck Team Canada's captain" *The Globe and Mail* (Toronto: May 2, 2007) at A1; "Doan offers to step down as captain" *The Globe and Mail* (Toronto: May 3, 2007) at A4.

leur volonté expresse que ce contrat soit rédigé en anglais.") English comprehension may be a job requirement in professional hockey, although general prejudice against francophones would qualify as discrimination on the basis of national or ethnic origin. A slightly sub-par NHL salary is not the worst form of suffering, but it may reflect a wider pattern of disadvantage in the labour market.[267] Francophones have historically been under-represented on national teams in high performance sports and have been disadvantaged when administrative and technical services were not available in French.[268] There was particular controversy in 1998 when a pre-Olympic reception in Nagano organized by the Canadian Olympic Association included barely a word of French.[269] By November 2004, 18.5 per cent of athletes "carded" under the Athlete Assistance Program were francophone,[270] but anglophones made up 90 per cent of "carded" players in team sports, where discretion in the selection process may bring linguistic favouritism.[271]

The goals of reducing linguistic barriers and facilitating participation are now addressed in legislation and in the policy requirements demanded of NSOs. The *Physical Activity and Sport Act*[272] emphasizes the importance of linguistic duality and recognizes the obligations under the *Official Languages Act*.[273] Sport Canada's "Sport Funding and Accountability Framework" (SFAF, 2009-2113) now requires NSOs to have a formal policy providing for communications in both Official Languages,[274] so that funded NSOs must make reasonable provision to deliver services to athletes and to the public in both English and French. A study in 2005 found that these requirements were more easily satisfied by the

---

[267] See, M. Lavoie, *Désavantage numérique: les francophones dans la LNH* (Hull, QC: Éditions Vents d'Ouest, 1998) at 139-40.

[268] See: R. Boileau, F. Landry & Y. Trempe, "Les Canadiens français et les grands jeux internationaux (1908-1974)" in R.S. Gruneau & J.G. Albinson, eds., *Canadian Sport: Sociological Perspectives* (Don Mills, ON: Addison-Wesley (Canada), 1976) at 141; D. Macintosh & D. Whitson, *The Game Planners: Transforming Canada's Sport System* (Montreal & Kingston: McGill-Queen's University Press, 1990) at 82-84; Sub-Committee on the Study of Sport in Canada, *Sport in Canada: Everybody's Business* (Dennis Mills, M.P., Chair) (House of Commons Canada, November 1998) at 171-72 (Bloc Québécois Dissenting Report); M. Lavoie, *Désavantage numérique: les francophones dans la LNH* (Hull, QC: Éditions Vents d'Ouest, 1998) at 24-26.

[269] See: "Language politics rears its head at Games" *The Globe and Mail* (Toronto: February 9, 1998) at A1, A9; "COA chastised for language faux pas" *The Globe and Mail* (Toronto: March 18, 1998) at A4.

[270] See, M. Svoboda & P. Donnelly, "Linguistic Barriers to Access to High Performance Sport Study – 2005" (2006), at II, C "Carded Athletes", online: <http://www.pch.gc.ca> "Sport Canada - Official Languages".

[271] See: *Assn. olympique canadienne c. Deschênes*, [1988] J.Q. no 1646, [1988] R.J.Q. 2389 (Que. C.A.); *St. Hilaire c. Assn. canadienne d'athlétisme*, [1990] J.Q. no 42 (Que. C.A.). On team selection disputes, see Chapter 3, "Organizations and Regulations", section C, 3.

[272] S.C. 2003, c. 2. See Chapter 2, "Legal Fundamentals and Equality Rights", section B, 1.

[273] R.S.C. 1985, c. 31 (4th Supp.). On reports by the Commissioner of Official Languages, online: <http://www.ocol-clo.gc.ca/>.

[274] See, <http://www.pch.gc.ca> "Sport Canada" and "Official Languages". See also, Chapter 2, "Legal Fundamentals and Equality Rights", section B, 4.

larger and wealthier NSOs that were less dependent on volunteers.[275] Compliance was also easier in the case of NSOs with a history of bilingualism based on their sport's popularity in Quebec, although Hockey Canada was not always efficient in translating and delivering documents. The study concluded that a knowledge of English was still essential in order to function and advance in the high performance system. NSOs had made considerable progress in head office administration, but the study identified a continuing need for improved bilingualism in direct athletic services such as coaching. At the same time, it warned that Sport Canada should not be "overly prescriptive" for fear of losing the most qualified specialist coaches.[276]

A particular area of research has been the status of francophone players in the NHL and the historical reluctance of teams in English Canada to hire francophone coaches and general managers. Data from 1977-78 suggested a pattern of entry barriers, performance differentiation, positional segregation and salary discrimination,[277] but more recent studies have found less evidence of discrimination in relation to admission and pay.[278] The leading commentator, Marc Lavoie, has identified some of the myths and reality about francophone players in the league.[279] It is, for example, a myth that francophones abandon NHL careers because of language difficulties: francophones begin playing in the NHL at a younger age than anglophones, so it is unlikely that they have been despatched to the minors to improve their language skills. It is also a myth that francophones in the NHL are smaller than anglophones. Lavoie notes that the drafting of players is a chancy and subjective business that allows scope for pre-conceived ideas:

Sauf pour les premiers choix au repêchage, les dépisteurs sont incapables de prédire correctement la performance future des jeunes joueurs. En raison du

---

[275] M. Svoboda & P. Donnelly, "Linguistic Barriers to Access to High Performance Sport Study – 2005" (2006), at IV, C, 1 "Language of Operations".

[276] M. Svoboda & P. Donnelly, "Linguistic Barriers to Access to High Performance Sport Study – 2005" (2006), at VI, "Recommendations".

[277] See, M. Boucher, "Les Canadiens français dans la Ligue nationale de hockey: une analyse statistique" (1984) 60 L'Actualité économique 308; M. Lavoie *et al.*, "Discrimination and Performance Differentials in the National Hockey League" (1987) 13 Can. Public Policy 407; M. Krashinsky, "Do Hockey Teams Discriminate Against French Canadians?: A Comment on 'Discrimination and Performance Differentials in the National Hockey League'" (1989) 15 Can. Public Policy 94; M. Lavoie *et al.*, "Discrimination versus English Proficiency in the National Hockey League: A Reply" (1989) 15 Can. Public Policy 98; M. Lavoie, "Stacking, Performance Differentials and Salary Discrimination in Professional Ice Hockey: A Survey of the Evidence" (1989) 6 Sociology of Sport J. 17.

[278] See, M. Lavoie & G. Grenier, "Discrimination and Salary Determination in the National Hockey League: 1977 and 1989 Compared" in G.W. Scully, ed., *Advances in the Economics of Sport* (Greenwich: Jai Press, 1992) at 151. On continuing patterns of entry discrimination, see, M. Lavoie, "The Entry Draft in the National Hockey League: Discrimination, Style of Play, and Team Location" (2003) 62 Am. J. of Econ. and Soc. 387.

[279] M. Lavoie, *Désavantage numérique: les francophones dans la LNH* (Hull, QC: Éditions Vents d'Ouest, 1998) at 129-35.

principe de l'incertitude, c'est une activité qui peut facilement donner libre cours aux préjugés ou au favoritisme.[280]

Lavoie's research reveals that there is a low proportion of francophone defensemen and an elevated proportion of goalkeepers. This hiring pattern is sometimes related to perceptions about the style of play in the Quebec Major Junior Hockey League ("QMJHL"), where it is supposed that games are all offense, giving goalkeepers a lot of practice in shot-blocking. The statistics in fact reveal a lower rate of goal-scoring in the QMJHL. The prominent "Block *québécois*" of goalkeepers are not star players since their performance is similar to that of the anglophones, indicating that there is less discrimination in hiring for a position that allows for objective evaluations (*e.g.*, goals against average and saves percentage). True status is reflected in the employment market, where francophone goalkeepers are sometimes less well paid than anglophones, while the salaries of francophone defensemen and forwards tend to exceed those of anglophones. However, in relation to performance, francophone defensemen have been underpaid, and francophone forwards have been underpaid by Canadian teams outside Quebec. According to Lavoie, the NHL's scouting system underestimates the performance of francophone players, so that they tend not to be taken at an appropriate point in the Entry Draft. In 2008, NHL teams selected 27 QMJHL players (19 from Quebec), but no QMJHL player was taken in the first round; in 2009, 23 QMJHL players were selected, with four in the first round.

Although there have been advances in NHL employment practices, media commentary remains an area of concern since CBC broadcasts allow a platform for the personal wisdom of the opinionated Mr. Don Cherry.[281] In 2004, the popular and perceptive dandy made observations about "Europeans and French guys" protecting themselves with visors and seemed to disregard the importance of safety.[282] The CBC responded with a temporary seven-second delay on the "Coach's Corner" segment to screen for objectionable remarks.

---

[280] M. Lavoie, *Désavantage numérique: les francophones dans la LNH* (Hull, QC: Éditions Vents d'Ouest, 1998) at 134. For recent statistical analysis, see, B. Sirois, *Le Québec mis en échec: La discrimination envers les Québécois dans la LNH* (Montréal: Les Éditions de l'Homme, 2009).

[281] In *National Hockey League v. Pepsi-Cola Canada Ltd.*, [1992] B.C.J. No. 1221, 92 D.L.R. (4th) 349 (B.C.S.C.), Hardinge J. commented (at 354) on the "very distinctive public character" of Mr. Cherry, a former coach of the Boston Bruins: "He dresses in a manner calculated to catch attention and excite comment. His manner of speech is turgid. He projects a 'tough guy' image and appears to favour a violent brand of hockey that includes on-ice fights between players."

[282] See, "Language watchdog to review Cherry diatribe" *The Globe and Mail* (Toronto: February 5, 2004) at A1, A9; "'Reprehensible' Cherry put on a short leash" *The Globe and Mail* (Toronto: February 7, 2004) at A1; "7-second solution draws criticism" *The Globe and Mail* (Toronto: February 10, 2004) at A1, A2; "Minister chastises Cherry, CBC over comment" *The Globe and Mail* (Toronto: February 12, 2004) at A9. On the statistics of visor use, see, "Visor rant backed by numbers" *The Globe and Mail* (Toronto: February 12, 2004) at S3. On the size and aggressiveness of players, see, M. Lavoie, *Désavantage numérique: les francophones dans la LNH* (Hull, QC: Éditions Vents d'Ouest, 1998) at 39-55.

## 7.    Religion[283]

Sport may be a religion but it is sometimes at odds with creeds or spiritual belief systems. Sports organizations should be sensitive to religious diversity and should try to avoid compromising the beliefs and observances of players and other participants. Sports can conflict with religious obligations when events are scheduled on days of worship or during holy festivals. Potential discrimination can also occur in relation to dress regulations,[284] the mixing of the sexes,[285] and other requirements or rituals,[286] including drug testing procedures. The responsibility to accommodate religious principles was considered in the case of the boxer, Pardeep Singh Nagra, whose Sikh religion required him to wear a beard. Nagra boxed through the provincial trials using a net to gather his beard and then obtained court orders against the Canadian Amateur Boxing Association to allow him to participate in the national championships.[287] The Association was prevented from enforcing the international rule requiring fighters to be clean shaven,[288] and Boxing Canada's national rules now provide an exemption for cases where a beard is a *bona fide* religious requirement.[289]

---

[283] See, for example, *Sharp v. B.C. School Sports*, [2000] B.C.H.R.T.D. No. 49, 2000 BCHRT 49 (B.C.H.R.T.) (student lost athletic eligibility when he transferred school for religious reasons; student was not required to act contrary to his religious beliefs and appeal processes found no "extraordinary circumstances"). On freedom of religion in general, see: *Commission scolaire régionale de Chambly v. Bergevin*, [1994] S.C.J. No. 57, [1994] 2 S.C.R. 525 (S.C.C.) (leave for Yom Kippur); *Syndicat Northcrest v. Amselem*, [2004] S.C.J. No. 46, [2004] 2 S.C.R. 551 (S.C.C.) (right of orthodox Jews to set up "succahs" on balconies); *Multani v. Commission scolaire Marguerite-Bourgeoys*, [2006] S.C.J. No. 6, [2006] 1 S.C.R. 256 (S.C.C.) (Sikh kirpans at school); *R. v. Badesha*, [2008] O.J. No. 854 (Ont. C.J.) (motorcycle helmet law reasonably necessary for safety); Ontario Human Rights Commission, "Policy on Creed and the Accommodation of Religious Observances", online: <http://www.ohrc.on.ca/>.

[284] On wearing the hijab for soccer and tae kwon do, see: "Red card renews hijab debate" *The Globe and Mail* (Toronto: February 27, 2007) at A1; "Quebec leaders seize hijab issue" *The Globe and Mail* (Toronto: February 28, 2007) at A9; "Quebec tae kwon do team knocked out for wearing hijab" *The Globe and Mail* (Toronto: April 16, 2007) at A1, A6.

[285] *Kingston (Guardian ad litem of) v. Central Okanagan School District No. 23*, [1984] B.C.J. No. 3040 (B.C.S.C.) (religious objection to co-ed physical education). See also, "Gym, Jews don't see eye to eye" *The Globe and Mail* (Toronto: November 8, 2006) at A1 (synagogue in Montreal adjacent to YMCA exercise room used by women).

[286] *Akiyama v. Judo B.C. (No. 2)* (2002), 43 C.H.R.R. D/425 (B.C.H.R.T.) (requirement to bow in judo has moral rather than religious dimension; no discrimination found). See also, K.B. Koenig, "Mahmoud Abdul-Rauf's Suspension for Refusing to Stand for the National Anthem: A 'Free Throw' for the NBA and Denver Nuggets, or a 'Slam Dunk' Violation of Abdul-Rauf's Title VII Rights? (1998) 76 Washington U. L. Rev. 377.

[287] See, "Beard knocks out boxer's ring plans" *The Globe and Mail* (Toronto: December 2, 1999) at S1 (order by Somers J.); "Bearded Sikh boxer can compete" *The Globe and Mail* (Toronto: January 13, 2000) at S4 (order by Low J. based on agreement).

[288] See also, *Barnard v. Australian Soccer Federation* (1988), 81 A.L.R. 41 (Fed.C. of Aust.) (court prohibited the enforcement of a labour market restriction required by FIFA).

[289] Boxing Canada, *Articles and Rules Governing Amateur Boxing in Canada*, rule 4.1m.

Controversies within the Church of England in the mid-nineteenth century produced a faith in athleticism[290] as a means of promoting "manliness" and improving moral character. The "Broad Church" movement of Thomas Arnold of Rugby[291] gave way to broad shoulders as "Muscular Christians"[292] focused on putting the body to clean and useful purposes. By exercising the body and submitting to the discipline of sport, the athlete was supposed to purify mind and soul.[293] This optimistic Victorian ethic is contradicted by all the bad behaviour in sport,[294] and it has difficulty accommodating the athletic traditions of ancient Greece and the homoeroticism of the exposed and developed body.[295] The unintended consequence of evangelical Muscular Christianity is that the gym, the locker room and the YMCA are the logical place for homosexuals to meet.[296]

## 8. LGBT: Sexual Orientation and Transgender Status

The Gay Games (founded in 1982) and the Outgames (first held in Montreal in 2006) offer a forum for the Lesbian, Gay, Bisexual and Transsexual ("LGBT") sports movement. LGBT organizations[297] promote sports opportunities for

---

[290] See, J.A. Mangan, *Athleticism in the Victorian and Edwardian Public School: The Emergence and Consolidation of an Educational Ideology* (Cambridge: Cambridge University Press, 1981). See also, B. Haley, *The Healthy Body and Victorian Culture* (Cambridge: Harvard University Press, 1978).

[291] In the 1830s, the liberal "Broad Church" faction was at odds with strict Evangelicals and with the High Church ritualists of the Oxford or Tractarian movement. Sport was not Arnold's priority, but he did oversee some sport-related reforms at Rugby; see, E. Dunning and K. Sheard, *Barbarians, Gentlemen and Players: A Sociological Study of the Development of Rugby Football* (New York: New York University Press, 1979) at 72-78.

[292] See, C. Putney, *Muscular Christianity: Manhood and Sports in Protestant America, 1880-1920* (Cambridge: Harvard University Press, 2001). See also, Thomas Hughes, *Tom Brown's Schooldays* (Oxford: Oxford University Press World's Classics, 1989), originally published in 1857.

[293] "[I]n the mid-nineteenth century, sport became accepted as the clean, manly, 'character-building', Christian way to have physical fun and avoid bad forms of sex": V. Burstyn, *The Rites of Men: Manhood, Politics, and the Culture of Sport* (Toronto: University of Toronto Press, 1999) at 110. On "bad forms of sex", see: *R. v. Brown*, [1993] 2 All E.R. 75, [1994] 1 A.C. 212 (H.L.) (sado-masochistic sex distinguished from "manly diversion"); *Sahaydakivski v. YMCA of Greater Toronto*, [2006] O.J. No. 1368 (Ont. S.C.J.) (member expelled because of indecent conduct).

[294] See, for example, Chapters 5-6 (abuse and violence); Chapters 7-9 (greed).

[295] See: B. Pronger, *The Arena of Masculinity: Sport, Homosexuality, and the Meaning of Sex* (Toronto: Summerhill Press, 1990); T.F. Scanlon, *Eros & Greek Athletics* (New York: Oxford University Press, 2002).

[296] See, J.D. Gustav-Wrathall, *Take the Young Stranger by the Hand: Same-Sex Relationships at the YMCA* (Chicago: University of Chicago Press, 1999). See also, M. Houlbrook, *Queer London: Perils and Pleasures in the Sexual Metropolis, 1918-1957* (Chicago: University of Chicago Press, 2005).

[297] See, for example, the Gay and Lesbian International Sport Association (GLISA), online: <http://www.glisa.org>. On sports and sexual orientation, see, M.J. Cozzillio & R.L. Hayman, eds., *Sports and Inequality* (Durham, NC: Carolina Academic Press, 2005) at 833-927.

homosexual athletes and address issues of discrimination, homophobia[298] and harassment.[299] A particular target of abuse is the referee since it is common to attribute all adverse decisions to his or her orientation. The lesbian has traditionally been victimized as the threatening "bogey woman" of female sport,[300] although alleged discrimination can go the other way when a heterosexual claims that a team or sport is a lesbian clique.[301]

Discrimination on the basis of sexual orientation is prohibited under the general terms of section 15[302] of the *Canadian Charter of Rights and Freedoms* and is specifically prohibited in human rights codes. It is, therefore, unlawful to discriminate in public programs or deny employment or opportunities to a person on the grounds that he or she is homosexual. For the 2010 Winter Olympics, a Canadian court might have been asked to order the organizing committee and international federation to add same-sex events. Very cosy rides such as two-person luge and bobsled are currently same-sex, but ice dancing and pairs figure skating are limited to opposite-sex couples. The omission is arguably contrary to both the *Olympic Charter* and to Canadian law, but national courts are "wary of applying a state statute to alter the content" of international Games.[303]

---

[298] See: G. Demers, "Homophobia in Sport — Fact of Life, Taboo Subject", (2006) 6(2) Can. J. of Women in Coaching; "Gay group outraged by CBC's use of 'pansification'" *The Globe and Mail* (Toronto: January 29, 2009) at R7 (objections by Égale Canada in context of debate over fighting); *Newman v. Ontario Hockey Assn.*, [2009] O.H.R.T.D. No. 1655 (Ont. H.R.Trib.) (alleged slurs at minor game).

[299] The victim of the harassment need not in fact be homosexual: *North Vancouver School District No. 44 v. Jubran*, [2005] B.C.J. No. 733, [2005] 9 W.W.R. 242, 253 D.L.R. (4th) 294 (B.C.C.A.), affg [2002] B.C.H.R.T.D. No. 10, 2002 BCHRT 10 (B.C.H.R.T.). See also, Chapter 5, "Be Safe: Off the Ice", sections B; C.

[300] See: P. Griffin, *Strong Women, Deep Closets: Lesbians and Homophobia in Sport* (Champaign: Human Kinetics, 1998); N. Theberge, *Higher Goals: Women's Ice Hockey and the Politics of Gender* (Albany: State University of New York Press, 2000) at 91-99, 108-111; L. Robinson, *Black Tights: Women, Sport and Sexuality* (Toronto: HarperCollins Publishers, 2002) at 59-76; B. Osborne, "'No Drinking, No Drugs, No Lesbians': Sexual Orientation Discrimination in Intercollegiate Athletics" (2007) 17 Marquette Sports L. Rev. 481. On false allegations of sexual behaviour with a student, see: *In the matter of Lindsay Jane Willow against Halifax Regional School Board* (N.S. Human Rights Commission, May 10, 2006); "Rights board vindicates gay N.S. teacher" *The Globe and Mail* (Toronto: May 12, 2006) at A10.

[301] In January 1994, the Australian media took a rare interest in women's cricket when Denise Annetts claimed that she was not selected because she is heterosexual; see: P. Griffin, *Strong Women, Deep Closets: Lesbians and Homophobia in Sport* (Champaign: Human Kinetics, 1998) at 60-61; R. Cashman, *Paradise of Sport: The Rise of Organised Sport in Australia* (Melbourne: Oxford University Press, 1995) at 81-82.

[302] *Egan v. Canada*, [1995] S.C.J. No. 43, [1995] 2 S.C.R. 513 (S.C.C.) (sexual orientation is analogous to the listed forms of discrimination). See also: *Vriend v. Alberta*, [1998] S.C.J. No. 29, [1998] 1 S.C.R. 493 (S.C.C.) (sexual orientation "read into" human rights legislation); *Trinity Western University v. British Columbia College of Teachers*, [2001] S.C.J. No. 32, [2001] 1 S.C.R. 772 (S.C.C.) (freedom to adhere to religious beliefs); *Reference re Same-Sex Marriage*, [2004] S.C.J. No. 75, [2004] 3 S.C.R. 698 (S.C.C.).

[303] *Martin v. International Olympic Committee*, 740 F.2d 670, at 677 (9th Cir., 1984) (civil rights legislation did not require the IOC to include certain events for women); see also, *Reynolds v.*

There are prominent gay and lesbian athletes[304] in tennis, figure skating and other sports,[305] but gays and lesbians are rarely "out" at the Olympics or in the leading professional leagues. In particular, no male professional hockey player has been openly homosexual, so that the sport lacks a leading gay role model. In 1976, representatives of the league's security department were emphatic that there were "no homosexuals in the NHL", while also expressing confidence that drugs, alcohol and gambling were not a problem.[306] The gay athlete does not conform to the hyper-masculine image of the major leagues,[307] where men perform homosocial rituals[308] to prove that they are straight. Coming out may make the player a marked man and is also likely to diminish prospects for commercial and endorsement income. In all probability, there are more gays in the majors than meet the eye:

> [A]n estimate that 2 per cent of the total population is gay would translate to seven gay players in the NBA, 12 in the NHL, 15 in major league baseball, 28 in the NFL and eight in the CFL.[309]

Until 1999, the International Olympic Committee subjected women athletes to gender verification in an attempt to ensure the "femininity" of events.[310] Gender categories are, however, unclear since there are different sex types and different criteria of determination.[311] Whatever one's original category, some measure of realignment is now possible through a combination of hormone treatment and surgery. Discrimination against transsexuals or against persons

---

*International Amateur Athletic Federation*, 23 F.3d 1110 (6th Cir., 1994) (Ohio court lacked jurisdiction). See also, *Sagen v. Vancouver Organizing Committee for the 2010 Olympic and Paralympic Winter Games*, [2009] B.C.J. No. 2293, 2009 BCCA 522 (B.C.C.A.), affg [2009] B.C.J. No. 1393, 2009 BCSC 942 (B.C.S.C.), leave to appeal to S.C.C. refused December 22, 2009, [2009] S.C.C.A. No. 459 (IOC, not VANOC, took decision to exclude women's ski jumping from 2010 Olympics; IOC not subject to *Canadian Charter of Rights and Freedoms*). See Chapter 2, "Legal Fundamentals and Equality Rights", sections, D, 2; E, 1.

[304] For a list, see online: <http://www.outsports.com/>. An early example was the tennis player Bill Tilden.

[305] See, for example, M. Tewksbury, *Inside Out: Straight Talk from a Gay Jock* (Mississauga, ON: John Wiley & Sons Canada, 2006). See also, "Out and In" *Ottawa Citizen* (July 23, 2006) at B1, B4, B5.

[306] See, "No drugs, gambling or alcoholics; NHL players portrayed as Mr. Kleen" *The Globe and Mail* (Toronto: April 29, 1976) at 48.

[307] These sports tend to be "space invading" and "space protecting": the object is to penetrate the opponent's zone and protect your own; see, B. Pronger, "Outta My Endzone: Sport and the Territorial Anus" (1999) 23 J. of Sport & Social Issues 373. On hyper-masculinity, see further, Chapter 5, "Be Safe: Off the Ice".

[308] See, M.A. Robidoux, *Men at Play: A Working Understanding of Professional Hockey* (Montreal & Kingston: McGill-Queen's University Press, 2001) at 100-150. On hazing, see Chapter 5, "Be Safe: Off the Ice", section E.

[309] "Rainbow warriors: gay and lesbian athletes" *The Toronto Star* (August 26, 2005).

[310] See, P.B. Fastiff, "Gender Verification Testing: Balancing the Rights of Female Athletes with a Scandal-Free Olympic Games" (1992) 19 Hastings Constitutional L.Q. 937.

[311] See, D.L. Hawley, "The Legal Problems of Sex Determination" (1977) 15 Alta. L. Rev. 122.

undergoing gender change is a form of discrimination on the basis of sex.[312] In sport, it may be claimed that the person going from male to female retains a physical advantage and so should be excluded from women's competition.[313] However, since 2004 transsexual athletes are eligible for the Olympics, and a number of former males now compete in women's events in different sports.[314] Male hockey players therefore have the option of making the surgical cut prior to trying out for a women's team.

---

[312] See, for example, *Forrester v. Peel (Regional Municipality) Police Services Board*, [2006] O.H.R.T.D. No. 13, 2006 HRTO 13 (Ont. H.R.Trib.) (person being strip-searched by police can choose sex of officers).

[313] Jurisdictions in Australia prohibit discrimination on the basis of transgender status. The legislation in New South Wales, Victoria, Queensland and Western Australia includes various types of exception for sporting activity.

[314] An early pioneer was Renee Richards (originally Richard Raskind); see, *Richards v. United States Tennis Assn.*, 1977 N.Y. Misc. LEXIS 2670, 400 N.Y.S. 2d 267 (S.C.).

## Chapter 3

# ORGANIZATIONS AND REGULATIONS

The International Ice Hockey Federation is dedicated to the worldwide growth and development of ice hockey and in-line hockey, providing exemplary leadership and governance by diligently observing the principles of democracy, fairness, solidarity and transparency for its member national associations.[1]

Hockey Canada is a voluntary Association of members and individuals, structured to promote and foster amateur hockey throughout Canada.[2]

This chapter considers the organizations and associations that govern hockey at the international and national levels and deals with different types of dispute that may arise in the administration of the game. Organizations operate by virtue of domestic constitutions and regulations that define the rights of members and provide authority for action in particular cases.[3] Some disputes relate to player participation and eligibility, while others involve allegations of misconduct. There are general disciplinary processes to sanction wrongdoers, and special regimes mandated by government apply in the case of doping violations. While many disputes involve individual claims to playing opportunities, the differences and conflicts sometimes assume the status of public policy problems. It is a measure of hockey's importance that the game is often contested in the wider political arena.[4]

## A. POWER PLAYS: A BRIEF HISTORY OF ASSOCIATION POLITICS

### 1. The CAHA and the Problem of Dependence

As noted in Chapter 1, "Lord Stanley and the Wednesday Nighters", various associations in eastern Canada took responsibility for the organization of men's

---

[1]  IIHF Statutes and Bylaws, 2008-2012 (July 2008), preamble.

[2]  Hockey Canada, Articles (amended to June 2008), preamble.

[3]  See, Chapter 3, "Organizations and Regulations", sections B; C.

[4]  According to one commentator, "Both the federal government and the Ontario government have spent more time on hockey as a problem than all other sports put together": D. Fisher, *The Policy and Programs of the Ontario Government for Recreation, Sport and Fitness, 1980* (Toronto: Ontario Ministry of Culture and Recreation, 1980) at 81. For further politics, see, for example: Chapter 2, "Legal Fundamentals and Equality Rights", section E (equality); Chapter 6, "Play Safe: On the Ice", section B (player violence); Chapter 7, "The Business of Hockey", sections A; B (business issues).

amateur hockey in the 1880s and 1890s, and the Allan Cup was donated in 1909 for the senior national championship after the Stanley Cup had passed into the possession of professional leagues. By 1909, the code of amateurism was enforced by the Amateur Athletic Union of Canada ("AAUC"), whose meeting in Ottawa in December 1914 played a role in the creation of the Canadian Amateur Hockey Association ("CAHA") since many delegates were present in the capital for both the annual gathering of the AAUC and the planned establishment of a national organization for hockey.[5] Dr. W.F. Taylor of Winnipeg was elected as the first president of the CAHA, and the founding associations were those from western Canada, together with the Ontario Hockey Association ("OHA"); the association from Quebec joined in 1919. A national junior trophy was inaugurated in 1919 when the OHA Memorial Cup was presented in honour of players who had died in the First World War.

The CAHA participated in the AAUC's "Canadian Parliament of Sport" from 1919 and subscribed to the Union's strict code prohibiting any form of monetary reward for play.[6] The affiliation continued until 1936 when the CAHA adopted a liberalized four-point eligibility rule that allowed payments to players and permitted association with professionals:

i.    Hockey players may capitalize on their ability as hockey players for the purpose of obtaining legitimate employment.

ii.   Hockey players may accept from their clubs or employers payment for time lost from work while competing for amateur clubs (*i.e.*, "broken-time").

iii.  Amateur hockey teams may play exhibition games against professional teams under such conditions as may be laid down by the individual branches of the CAHA.

iv.   Professionals in other branches of sport may be permitted to play on amateur hockey teams.[7]

Economic conditions during the Depression had rendered a pure amateurism unrealistic, and the new eligibility rules helped to maintain the senior leagues that offered a popular alternative to the National Hockey League ("NHL"). While assisting community hockey, the CAHA also forged links with the NHL by entering into an agreement to promote uniformity in playing rules and control the signing of CAHA players by professional teams.[8]

The senior leagues were weakened after the Second World War, and the emphasis in player development shifted to junior players holding the potential to

---

[5]   See, J. Wong, "Sport Networks on Ice: The Canadian Experience at the 1936 Olympic Hockey Tournament" (2003) 34 Sport History Review 190.

[6]   See, B. Kidd, *The Struggle for Canadian Sport* (Toronto: University of Toronto Press, 1996) at 44-93.

[7]   B. Kidd, *The Struggle for Canadian Sport* (Toronto: University of Toronto Press, 1996) at 86-87.

[8]   See, B. Kidd, *The Struggle for Canadian Sport* (Toronto: University of Toronto Press, 1996) at 84-85, 226. See also, J.C. Wong, *Lords of the Rinks: The Emergence of the National Hockey League, 1875-1936* (Toronto: University of Toronto Press, 2005) at 143-51.

serve in the professional leagues. The amateur game therefore tended to become "a vast feeder system [for]...a continental labour market".[9] The co-ordination between the CAHA and the NHL included the sponsorship system which had originated in the 1920s through financial support provided to individual amateur players. By the late 1940s, this evolved into sponsorship of entire junior teams, and NHL teams achieved controlling influence and exclusive signing rights for another 20 years:

> ...at the height of the sponsorship system, 27 professional teams in North America, all but five of which were located in the United States, owned 50 Canadian junior teams. The system was sanctioned by the NHL-CAHA agreements of 1947 and 1958, and it gave the pros control over virtually every amateur player in the country.[10]

NHL teams gained rights to minor players affiliated with the junior club, conducted a trade in teenage prospects and generally shuttled sponsored players around the country. They also gained lifetime control of professional careers when players signed the standard "C form" try-out contract as part of the CAHA's registration system. "As a result, every boy in Fredericton grew up knowing he was 'Black Hawk Property', every boy in Winnipeg 'belonged' to the Boston Bruins".[11]

When the NHL expanded from its core of six teams in 1967,[12] the sponsorship system was abolished since the league now required a new means to allocate junior talent. By agreement between the NHL and CAHA,[13] a universal junior draft was established and the age limit for junior hockey was reduced from 21 to 20 years to accommodate the league's need for a wider pool of players. The Pro-Am Agreement of 1967 established a joint development committee for "the purpose of maintaining a closer liaison between the NHL and the CAHA in the conduct of an efficient player development program" (see, s. 17). It also provided that the NHL pay annual assessments, player development grants, and draft claim payments to the CAHA (see, s. 18). The Agreement established a formula by which NHL teams paid for players drafted in various rounds. The payments were placed in the CAHA's player development fund to be distributed to the junior or affiliated team that had brought the player along.

The Pro-Am Agreement was immediately condemned in various government reports as not in the best interests of the game, the players or the community. A report by an Alberta government committee[14] castigated the restrictive and self-serving control exercised by the NHL and criticised the CAHA's financial

---

9    B. Kidd, *The Struggle for Canadian Sport* (Toronto: University of Toronto Press, 1996) at 264.

10   B. Kidd & J. Macfarlane, *The Death of Hockey* (Toronto: New Press, 1972) at 55.

11   B. Kidd & J. Macfarlane, *The Death of Hockey* (Toronto: New Press, 1972) at 56.

12   See Chapter 9, "National Hockey League", section A.

13   "Agreement made between the NHL, the CAHA and the AHA of US, May 15, 1967". An amateur draft for unsponsored players was originally held in 1963.

14   See, *Final Report of the Alberta Department of Youth Hockey Study Committee* (November 15, 1967).

dependence on professional leagues. Similarly, a committee of the National Advisory Council on Fitness and Amateur Sport recommended abolishing the joint committee to give the CAHA independence in its program development. The Advisory Council committee favoured 21 years as the draft age, while recognizing that "a limited number of exceptional 18-21-year-old juniors should be permitted to negotiate contracts with professional hockey".[15] This group felt that legislation was needed to protect individual rights and community interests and recommended federal laws to guarantee "amateur hockey freedom from any kind of interference from the National Hockey League or its agents".[16] The Alberta committee recognized that amendments to the federal *Combines Investigation Act*[17] would be helpful, but considered that action could most effectively be taken at the provincial level.[18] Both committees made the following recommendation for changes in provincial law:

> That Provincial Governments consider the enactment of legislation for the protection of young athletes of eighteen years of age and under from contracts with professional hockey which will in any way interfere with their pursuit of amateur hockey interests, their education, or their moral and physical well-being.[19]

Changes in organization and administration started to emerge following the decision by the federal government to play a larger and more direct role in sport policy. The federal government's extensive presence in funding and regulating national sport organizations[20] has its origins in the *Report of the Task Force on Sports for Canadians* in 1969 and the establishment of the Administrative Centre for Sport and Recreation in 1970. Sport Canada and Recreation Canada followed in 1971 as units of the government's Fitness and Amateur Sport ("FAS") Directorate.[21] The Task Force paid particular attention to hockey and noted that amateur players fell into two classes: a large group of recreational participants

---

[15]   See, Hockey Study Committee of the National Advisory Council on Fitness and Amateur Sport, *Report on Amateur Hockey in Canada* (January 1967) at 55 (Recommendation 6(e)).

[16]   See, Hockey Study Committee of the National Advisory Council on Fitness and Amateur Sport, *Report on Amateur Hockey in Canada* (January 1967) at 55 (Recommendation 11).

[17]   R.S.C. 1970, c. C-23. See now, *Competition Act*, R.S.C. 1985, c. C-34. See further, Chapter 8, "Competition Law and Labour Law", section A.

[18]   See, *Final Report of the Alberta Department of Youth Hockey Study Committee* (November 15, 1967) at 21.

[19]   *Final Report of the Alberta Department of Youth Hockey Study Committee* (November 15, 1967) at 20. See also, Hockey Study Committee of the National Advisory Council on Fitness and Amateur Sport, *Report on Amateur Hockey in Canada* (January 1967) at 55 (Recommendation 12).

[20]   See Chapter 2, "Legal Fundamentals and Equality Rights", section B.

[21]   See: J. Munro, *A Proposed Sport Policy for Canadians* (Government of Canada, Department of Health and Welfare, 1970); J. Munro, *Sports Canada: Recreation Canada* (Government of Canada, Department of National Health and Welfare, 1971); D. Macintosh, T. Bedecki & C.E.S. Franks, *Sport and Politics in Canada: Federal Government Involvement since 1961* (Kingston and Montreal: McGill-Queen's University Press, 1987) at 68-82.

under the age of 15, and a small, elite group, aged 16 or over, with professional ambitions. The Task Force was concerned about the drop in participation and did not regard the fact that the game quickly became "the exclusive property of a relative handful of players and promoters"[22] as a reason for government not to take an interest. The *Report* commented on "the irony that the ruling body in a national sport, the CAHA, should have to have an agreement with an international industry, most of which operates in the United States, as to when its players reach the end of a certain stage in their hockey careers".[23]

The *Report of the Task Force* agreed with many of the findings of the Advisory Council committee and recommended that the federal government assist with the administrative costs of the CAHA in order to end the association's reliance on specific payments from the NHL.[24] The CAHA had began to centralize its operations in 1967 by establishing a national office in Winnipeg and in 1970 moved to the Administrative Centre in Ottawa. The CAHA duly received grants of CDN $6,733 in 1970-71 and CDN $17,119 in 1971-72 from the FAS Directorate.[25] The Task Force had also recommended the establishment of "Hockey Canada" to develop and operate national teams.[26] The FAS Directorate qualified this new organization as a "Special Project" and it benefited to the extent of CDN $476,227 in 1970-71 and CDN $175,000 in 1971-72.[27]

## 2. "What's Wrong with Canadian Hockey?"

The 1970s and 1980s were characterised by further angst over perceived deficiencies in domestic hockey programs, especially in light of continuing frustration in men's Olympic and international competition. Investigations and discussions analysed the values and structures of the home game at the minor and junior levels. Some inquiries focussed on violence,[28] and a series of reports addressed issues related to participants' rights and player development. A force for change in the pro-am relationship was the presence of the World Hockey Association ("WHA") which operated from 1972 to 1979.[29]

---

[22] See, *Report of the Task Force on Sports for Canadians* (Ottawa: Department of National Health and Welfare, 1969) at 27.

[23] *Report of the Task Force on Sports for Canadians* (Ottawa: Department of National Health and Welfare, 1969) at 32.

[24] *Report of the Task Force on Sports for Canadians* (Ottawa: Department of National Health and Welfare, 1969) at 32.

[25] See, Fitness and Amateur Sport Directorate, *Annual Report 1971-72* (Health and Welfare Canada, 1972) at 19. The Administrative Centre for Sports and Recreation received total grants of CDN $430,976 in 1970–1971 and CDN $671,146 in 1971–1972. The Administrative Centre, housing various national associations, was incorporated as the National Sport and Recreation Centre in 1974.

[26] See Chapter 3, "Organizations and Regulations", section A, 3.

[27] See, Fitness and Amateur Sport Directorate, *Annual Report 1971-72* (Health and Welfare Canada, 1972) at 22.

[28] See Chapter 6, "Play Safe: On the Ice", section B, 5.

[29] See Chapter 9, "National Hockey League", section A, 2. See also, *Philadelphia World Hockey Club, Inc. v. Philadelphia Hockey Club, Inc.*, 351 F.Supp. 462 (E.D. Pa., 1972).

Many issues related to individuals' rights were addressed in a comprehensive report prepared by L.W. Downey for the Alberta government in 1973.[30] Downey noted that hockey had developed as a private voluntary system largely free of government regulation and had possibly turned to professional leagues for assistance because government lent only modest support. In the absence of public control, the evolved rules, structures and "team property rights" infringed participants' freedom to choose where and when they would play. At the "pre-professional" level,[31] Downey addressed junior teams' "protected lists", their restrictive and discretionary powers, the limits on the freedom to transfer and the contractual claims to recover development costs. Strong criticism was also reserved for the powers and procedures of the CAHA.[32] Downey deplored the monopolistic control claimed by the association and was particularly critical of appeal procedures that attempted to deny any recourse to the courts.[33] The report favoured legislation to protect players' rights and the opportunity to participate, it also recommended setting up an amateur sport or hockey ombudsman or commission. No immediate action was taken on these recommendations.[34]

The process of graduating from junior hockey to the professional level was modified when the WHA disturbed the NHL's major league monopoly. The Pro-Am Agreement of 1967 originally required the NHL to pay development fees to the CAHA in respect of drafted junior players, these payments were then distributed to the junior teams. "From 1969 to 1973 under the NHL-CAHA agreement a total of $7.3 million was paid to the CAHA, approximately $1.2 million per year".[35] The NHL terminated payments in 1974 when doubts developed whether the system was in breach of American antitrust law[36] and proceeded to deal directly with the Canadian Major Junior Hockey League ("CMJHL"),[37] first by providing a scale of payments and in 1981 by making a general grant to the league in recognition of development services. The WHA originally agreed to match NHL arrangements in support of Canadian amateur hockey and by 1978 was still making payments to the CAHA. WHA teams also undertook to pay development costs directly to junior teams, although the payments were not always forthcoming. The general policy of the WHA was to respect the draft age of 20, but some of their teams

---

30  See, L.W. Downey, *Report of an Inquiry into the Rights of Individuals in Amateur Sports (Hockey)* (Alberta Department of Culture, Youth and Recreation, 1973).

31  See, L.W. Downey, *Report of an Inquiry into the Rights of Individuals in Amateur Sports (Hockey)* (Alberta Department of Culture, Youth and Recreation, 1973) at 31-35.

32  See, L.W. Downey, *Report of an Inquiry into the Rights of Individuals in Amateur Sports (Hockey)* (Alberta Department of Culture, Youth and Recreation, 1973) at 27-31.

33  Under the current Hockey Canada By-Law 1007 (amended to June 2008), members are required to accept the "final and binding authority of all rules and decisions" and are prohibited from taking action in court until all internal remedies and appeals have been exhausted.

34  See, Canadian Hockey Review, *Interim Report on Minor Amateur Hockey in Canada* (1979) at 95.

35  See, Canadian Hockey Review, *Interim Report on Minor Amateur Hockey in Canada* (1979) at 69.

36  See further, Chapter 8, "Competition Law and Labour Law", section C.

37  See further, Chapter 3, "Organizations and Regulations", section B, 3 (Canadian Hockey League).

were prepared to enlist "underage" talent and successfully argued that a restrictive age rule was an illegal restraint of players' freedom under antitrust law.[38] Recognizing the right of capable juniors to enjoy the benefits of professional play, the NHL instituted an underage draft in 1980 and agreed to pay $70,000 over four years for each such player selected in the first round who signed a contract and played 200 games.

The "raiding" for "underage" players elicited little sympathy in the various reports and inquiries since the junior leagues were regularly condemned as "hard knocks" operations whose gruelling schedules were likely to disrupt the education of the young players.[39] The charge that the game was violent, overly-competitive, "over-organized" and a bad moral influence even extended to minor hockey.[40] In 1976, a press account reported that nine-year-olds were being offered "signing bonuses" such as bicycles to induce them to play for specific teams in Toronto.[41] In a prolonged public debate over the perceived failings in the children's game, many observers criticised the parental and structural pressures that emphasised championships and winning at the expense of fundamental skills. Critics deplored the absence of adequate instruction in basic techniques and the failure to develop proper systems of physical conditioning, and reports consistently recommended less competitiveness, improved coaching, greater involvement by schools and a renewed emphasis on safety and equal opportunity.[42]

In 1977, a committee report focussing on international participation[43] included numerous comments on the organization of domestic hockey. The

---

[38]    See, *Linseman v. World Hockey Assn.*, 439 F. Supp. 1315 (D. Conn., 1977). The WHA sought to maintain the age rule and unsuccessfully argued that it was compelled by the Canadian government as an act of state: see, H.T. Ricks, Note, "International Law — Antitrust Law — Immunities to Extraterritorial Application of United States Antitrust Law: Linseman v. World Hockey Association" (1977-78), 12 J. Int'l L. & Econ. 487.

[39]    See: *Report of the Task Force on Sport for Canadians* (Ottawa: Department of National Health and Welfare, 1969) at 33; L.W. Downey, *Report of an Inquiry into the Rights of Individuals in Amateur Sports (Hockey)* (Alberta Department of Culture, Youth and Recreation, 1973) at 22-23; Canadian Hockey Review, *Interim Report on Minor Amateur Hockey in Canada* (1979) at 144-52.

[40]    See: *Report of the Task Force on Sport for Canadians* (Ottawa: Department of National Health and Welfare, 1969) at 27 (noting criticisms in the *United Church Observer*); L.W. Downey, *Report of an Inquiry into the Rights of Individuals in Amateur Sports (Hockey)* (Alberta Department of Culture, Youth and Recreation, 1973) at 7-13; Canadian Hockey Review, *Interim Report on Minor Amateur Hockey in Canada* (1979) at 24-55.

[41]    See, "'Signing bonuses' for 9-year-olds to play hockey" *The Globe and Mail* (Toronto: March 22, 1976) at 1, 2.

[42]    See, Canadian Hockey Review, *Interim Report on Minor Amateur Hockey in Canada* (1979) at 88-89 (summaries of various government studies). See also: B.D. McPherson & L. Davidson, *Minor Hockey in Ontario: Toward a Positive Learning Environment for Children in the 1980s* (Toronto: Ontario Ministry of Culture and Recreation/Ontario Hockey Council, 1980); D. Fisher, *The Policy and Programs of the Ontario Government for Recreation, Sport and Fitness, 1980* (Toronto: Ontario Ministry of Culture and Recreation, 1980) at 81-82 ("hockey's inadequacies").

[43]    See, *Report by the Committee on International Hockey* (Government of Canada, 1977) (report to the Minister of State, Fitness and Amateur Sport).

committee was surprised that the CAHA sanctioned the CMJHL since it regarded the league as a professional organization closely connected to the major leagues:

> It should be recognized that major junior hockey is a professional operation. Hence the individual player should be able to bargain for the team of his choice, remuneration, or perquisites in education...Frankly, we are chilled by the thought of 16 to 19 year olds travelling scores of thousands of miles to play as many as 100 games a season...Do the entrepreneurial gains and developmental worth of junior hockey justify such an exploitive arrangement?[44]

The committee criticised the interference with players' freedom of choice and educational opportunities and called for a major federal study of junior hockey. The report also recommended that the federal government make a stronger financial commitment towards development programs of the CAHA and that hockey scholarships subject to academic standards be recognized in Canadian universities.[45]

Subsequently, the Minister of State for Fitness and Amateur Sport established the Canadian Hockey Review, under the chairmanship of Mr. Justice John J. Urie, to consider the "malaise permeating the entire Canadian hockey system commencing from the time that a child enters that system".[46] In its *Interim Report*,[47] the Review surveyed the level of participation, the organization of associations, financing, government involvement, legal issues and civil liberties (including equality rights), physiological aspects, coaching and officiating, violence, and the problem of combining hockey participation with schooling. The report also compared Canadian amateur hockey with the game's organization in leading European countries. The Review's investigations confirmed the prevalence of many of the defects noted by earlier reports, and the Review proposed further studies including a "major project" inquiring into junior hockey.

The Canadian Hockey Review was unable to complete its work since it was terminated by the Progressive-Conservative government in 1979 at a time when its studies had dealt only with rules and officiating, coaching and organizations. The inquiry into junior hockey was not begun. The recommendations in the Review's *Final Report*[48] included support for the creation of a national university hockey league.

The critique of domestic hockey continued during the 1980s as registration in minor hockey decreased to 400,000. Commentators deplored the influence of the professional game and called for technical improvements and academic

---

[44]  *Report by the Committee on International Hockey* (Government of Canada, 1977) at 6.

[45]  See, *Report by the Committee on International Hockey* (Government of Canada, 1977) at 4, 5.

[46]  Canadian Hockey Review, *Interim Report on Minor Hockey* (1979), at iv.

[47]  Canadian Hockey Review, *Interim Report on Minor Hockey* (1979). See also, Mr. Justice J.J. Urie & L.E. Regan, *A Status Report on the Canadian Hockey Review* (Government of Canada, May 1979).

[48]  See, Mr. Justice J.J. Urie & L.E. Regan, *Final Report on the Canadian Hockey Review* (Government of Canada, 1980).

assistance programs. The CAHA responded with development programs for both elite teams and minor hockey and introduced organizational changes through reforms to the appeal system and the creation of the Female Hockey Council in 1981. There were particular initiatives emphasising basic skills and fun for players aged 5-10, although the decision in 1985 to reinstate bodychecking in the peewee division (11-year-olds) raised concerns about safety and the increased rate of injury.[49] In Quebec, the influential report by Robert Thérien in 1988 recommended a less structured and competitive model for young players in which the objectives would include the acquisition of skills, good sportsmanship and having fun.[50] The Province subsequently implemented the Hockey 2000 program focussing on participation and recreational play in the under-12 age group. A new *orientation philosophique* was beginning to work its way into the home game, but co-ordinated organization and competitive success continued to remain elusive so far as international events were concerned.

## 3.  International Participation and "Hockey Canada" (1969)

A world men's championship was held in association with the Antwerp Summer Olympics in 1920 when the tournament was won by Canada represented by the Winnipeg Falcons.[51] The first official Olympic competition for men was played at the 1924 Winter Olympics in Chamonix when the Toronto Granites outscored European opponents 104-2 and took the gold medal by defeating the Americans 6-1. Except for a dubious loss in 1936,[52] gold remained Canada's Olympic colour until 1952. The annual men's championships of the International Ice Hockey Federation ("IIHF") were established in 1930, although the Olympic competition doubled as the world championship in Olympic years. Out of 19 non-Olympic championships played between 1930 and 1961, the gold medal went to a Canadian senior amateur team on 13 occasions. However, by the mid-1950s domination of the world tournaments shifted to European teams and to the Soviet Union as these benefited from the IIHF's political regime and were able to use "professional amateurs" or "state athletes".[53] (North American professional

---

[49]  On the more recent debate about body checking, see Chapter 6, "Play Safe: On the Ice", section, A, 2.

[50]  See: Groupe de travail sur le hockey mineur, *Rapport préliminaire* (Gouvernement du Québec, 1988); *Vers un développement harmonieux du hockey au Québec*, Rapport Thérien, Rapport final du groupe de travail sur le hockey au Québec (Gouvernement du Québec, juin 1989). See also, *Le développement du hockey mineur au Québec*, Plan d'action gouvernemental (Gouvernement du Québec, avril 1990).

[51]  See: R. Eyford, "From Prairie Goolies to Canadian Cyclones: The Transformation of the 1920 Winnipeg Falcons" (2006) 37 Sport History Review 5; D. Square, *When Falcons Fly: The Story of the World's First Olympic Gold Hockey Team* (Vancouver: Poppy Productions, 2007).

[52]  See, J. Wong, "Sport Networks on Ice: The Canadian Experience at the 1936 Olympic Hockey Tournament" (2003) 34 Sport History Review 190.

[53]  See, H. Cantelon, "Have Skates, Will Travel: Canada, International Hockey, and the Changing Labour Market" in D. Whitson & R. Gruneau, eds., *Artificial Ice: Hockey, Culture, and Com-*

players were not eligible for the men's world championships until 1977, and Canada's victory drought at that tournament lasted until 1994. The 50–year Olympic drought ended in 2002.)

By the 1960s, as the senior representative clubs came to be outperformed on the world stage, it was recognized that preparation for international men's events required an established program. From 1962 to 1969, the CAHA, in conjunction with Father David Bauer, operated a national team assembled from eligible players graduating from junior and university teams. This program was effectively killed by the NHL as it resisted the loss of amateur talent and draft selections and particularly resented the bargaining leverage provided by the national team alternative.[54] The Task Force on Sports for Canadians then recommended the creation of a new non-profit agency to manage and finance national teams and recommended that the CAHA initiate with the IIHF the possibility of an "open" world championship.[55] "Hockey Canada" was duly incorporated in 1969 with a board of directors that included representatives of the federal government, the CAHA, Canadian universities, the NHL and the NHL Players' Association ("NHLPA"). When the NHL persisted in obstructing the release of players to a standing team, "Hockey Canada" petitioned the IIHF to allow the use of NHL players, and the IIHF tentatively agreed that some professionals would be eligible for a proposed world championship to be held in Canada in 1970. This decision was soon revoked after backroom influence persuaded European countries that Olympic eligibility would be threatened by competing against professionals. The result was that Canada cancelled the 1970 tournament and withdrew from all levels of international competition.[56]

The opportunity to use top professionals came in 1972 after Joe Krycza and Gordon Juckes of the CAHA conducted negotiations that led to the first "open" tournament with the Soviets.[57] "Hockey Canada" established a management committee for this famous 8-game series, but operations soon came to be dominated by R. Alan Eagleson, executive director of the NHLPA, whose market skills yielded a profitable television contract. Domination was also exerted by the NHL since WHA players were excluded from Team

---

*merce* (Peterborough, ON: Broadview Press, 2006) at 215-21 (noting the influence of IIHF president John "Bunny" Ahearne).

[54]   See: H. Cantelon, "Have Skates, Will Travel: Canada, International Hockey, and the Changing Labour Market" in D. Whitson & R. Gruneau, eds., *Artificial Ice: Hockey, Culture, and Commerce* (Peterborough, ON: Broadview Press, 2006) at 221-22; B. Kidd & J. Macfarlane, *The Death of Hockey* (Toronto: New Press, 1972) at 79-85; R. Gruneau & D. Whitson, *Hockey Night in Canada: Sport, Identities, and Cultural Politics* (Toronto: Garamond Press, 1993) at 260-62.

[55]   See, *Report of the Task Force on Sports for Canadians* (Ottawa: Department of National Health and Welfare, 1969) at 31. See also, Hockey Study Committee of the National Advisory Council on Fitness and Amateur Sport, *Report on Amateur Hockey in Canada* (January 1967) at 55-56 (Recommendations 13-20).

[56]   See, B. Kidd & J. Macfarlane, *The Death of Hockey* (Toronto: New Press, 1972) at 88-89.

[57]   See: D. Cruise & A. Griffiths, *Net Worth: Exploding the Myths of Pro Hockey* (Toronto: Viking Penguin, 1991) at 216-19; W. Houston & D. Shoalts, *Eagleson: The Fall of a Hockey Czar* (Toronto: McGraw-Hill Ryerson, 1993) at 75-77; M. Jokisipilä, "Maple Leaf, Hammer, and Sickle: International Ice Hockey During the Cold War" (2006) 37 Sport History Review 36.

Canada. Following his appointment as chief international negotiator for "Hockey Canada", Alan Eagleson went on to organize the first of the Canada Cup series in 1976. This six-nation, "open" tournament was sanctioned by the IIHF and paved the way for Canada's re-entry into the world championships. Since 1977, Canada has competed at the annual IIHF competition mainly using players from teams that have been eliminated from the NHL play-offs.

The CAHA, Canada's official member of the IIHF, was soon in conflict with the rival organization as it questioned the jurisdiction and administration of "Hockey Canada". Some disputes related to the new agency's role in domestic hockey development and the CAHA's right to share in proceeds from international series. More generally, the established association was concerned at its loss of control as private and professional interests came to be increasingly represented in the membership of "Hockey Canada", the hostility being compounded by the professional leagues' signing of "underage" players and the difficulties in recovering development fees. In 1977, following a truculent and undistinguished performance by Team Canada at the world championships in Vienna, the Minister of State for Fitness and Amateur Sport formed a committee to study the arrangements for international participation. The *Report by the Committee on International Hockey* recommended a "National Team structure", including a permanent coach and manager, and called on "Hockey Canada" to take various steps to improve the preparation and management of national teams; release clauses in professional players' contracts would also be useful in giving players the freedom to play for Canada. Anticipating the return to Olympic competition in 1980, the committee noted the need for a co-ordinated program of assistance and recruitment to prepare the Olympic team. On the issue of representation at the IIHF, the committee insisted on the need for able negotiators and called for a realignment of Canada's delegation "to ensure that all factions of Canadian Hockey are heard"; the committee recommended that the Canadian nominee to the IIHF Council "be selected by Hockey Canada and nominated and endorsed by the two Canadian delegates" to the IIHF Congress.[58]

This report did nothing to unite the factions, and in October 1979 the CAHA withdrew its representatives from "Hockey Canada" arguing that the agency had ceased to be needed since the NHL and the NHLPA had made arrangements for attractive international series. "Hockey Canada" promptly stopped making interest payments to the CAHA on CDN $1 million of the receipts from the 1976 Canada Cup, and the CAHA responded with a civil action to recover what it claimed was owing. The two organizations then found themselves in a jurisdictional conflict over responsibility for preparing the 1984 Olympic team. Peace was finally restored in March 1982 through a formal agreement that settled the financial difference and allocated responsibility for national teams for the next six years, so that "Hockey Canada" would manage Olympic teams and national teams above the junior level (*e.g.*, world championships and Canada Cup). The CAHA retained its place on the IIHF but agreed to vote according to the wishes of "Hockey Canada". "Hockey Canada" undertook to co-operate with

---

[58]   *Report by the Committee on International Hockey* (Government of Canada, 1977) at 5.

the CAHA's development programs, while also offering its own system of scholarships for potential Olympic players attending Canadian universities.

By the mid-1980s, Canada was represented by the best NHL players during pre-season Canada Cup events and by available NHL players at the annual world championships. At the same time, the national team coached by Dave King participated in invitational tournaments and competed at the 1988 Olympics in Calgary where it finished fourth. Enhanced by the presence of professionals and 19-year-old Eric Lindros,[59] this team moved up to the silver medal position at Albertville in 1992. A second agreement in 1988 had extended "Hockey Canada's" management of senior national teams, but by the 1990s the CAHA was reconsidering arrangements[60] and was particularly resolved to recover control of the Olympic team. That competition then took a new form as different countries looked forward to icing "dream teams". During 1994, negotiations involving the NHL, the IIHF and the IOC led to the availability of NHL players for the Nagano Olympics in 1998. The NHLPA also entered the picture in 1995 by negotiating the terms of the break in the 1997-98 NHL schedule and by agreeing to forego a clause allowing the early termination of the collective bargaining agreement. The need for "Hockey Canada" now came into question, and questions were also being asked about one member of its board of directors.

## 4.   R. Alan Eagleson

Alan Eagleson was an accomplished deal-maker whose multi-faceted career included activities as a lawyer, conservative politician, player agent and executive director of the NHLPA.[61] Lacrosse and swimming were the main sports of his student days, when it was also apparent that he had a preference for team management and money-making schemes.[62] Having originally focussed on the player representation business, from 1975 to 1992 the "Eagle" also served as chief international negotiator for "Hockey Canada" and was instrumental in organizing the Canada Cups of 1976, 1981, 1984, 1987 and 1991. Profits from these tournaments were shared between "Hockey Canada", the NHL and the NHL players' pension fund.[63] From an early date, there was criticism of

---

[59]   In February 1992, Lindros was in contractual limbo after he had declared his unwillingness to sign with the Quebec Nordiques who had selected him in the first round of the 1991 NHL entry draft. See further, Chapter 8, "Competition Law and Labour Law", section A, 3.

[60]   See, "Overhaul seen by CAHA head for national team" *The Globe and Mail* (Toronto: December 15, 1990) at A14.

[61]   See further, Chapter 9, "National Hockey League", section B.

[62]   See: D. Clayton, *Eagle: The Life and Times of R. Alan Eagleson* (Toronto: Lester & Orpen Dennys, 1982) at 25-39 ("it was generally felt among the faculty that we'd hear more about Al" (at 34)); R.A. Eagleson with S. Young, *Power Play: The Memoirs of Hockey Czar Alan Eagleson* (Toronto: McClelland & Stewart, 1991) at 35-44 ("If there was any chance of making a dollar or two I'd deal with anybody" (at 36-37)); W. Houston & D. Shoalts, *Eagleson: The Fall of a Hockey Czar* (Toronto: McGraw-Hill Ryerson, 1993) at 28-32 ("Eagleson's sense of invincibility not only meant defending himself, but also playing the role of the aggressor" (at 29-30)).

[63]   On international participation, see now, CBA of NHL (2005), article 24.

Eagleson's personal control of Canada Cup business,[64] but his pugnacious style reaped unexpected television revenue and advertising contracts.[65] With his "many hats" or multiple roles,[66] Eagleson earned the title "czar of hockey" and moved in the Canadian political establishment. Cracks began to appear in the empire during the 1980s, and there was a serious unravelling in the mid-1990s when the Eagle finally fell. Alan Eagleson resigned from the "Hockey Canada" board in July 1993 as allegations of irregularity in financial dealings accumulated, and investigations and litigation ultimately shed light on improprieties in a variety of Eagle enterprises.

The NHLPA had shown a less than vigorous approach to free agency rights after the demise of the WHA in 1979, so that some members were dissatisfied with the union's performance in collective bargaining.[67] Complaints about the services and management of the NHLPA culminated at the annual general meeting in June 1989 when a group of players and agents commissioned a special investigation and tabled a 60-page document alleging "financial misconduct, conflict of interest, charging excessive rent and expenses, and that [Eagleson] had not consulted the executive on some financial decisions".[68] Eagleson received votes of support from player representatives, but agreed to audits of accounts and to the formation of a committee to find his successor as executive director of the NHLPA. After yielding this position to Robert Goodenow in 1991, Eagleson's affairs, including his role in international events, became the subject of intense scrutiny by investigative reporters,[69] police authorities and the Law Society of Upper Canada.[70] In February 1993, "Hockey Canada" agreed to release its general financial records and commissioned a review of accounts that revealed a CDN $100,000 mortgage loan, payments of

---

[64]    See, D. Clayton, *Eagle: The Life and Times of R. Alan Eagleson* (Toronto: Lester & Orpen Dennys, 1982) at 173-75, 191-93. See also, *The Globe and Mail* (Toronto: September 2, 3, 7, 8, 1977) (articles by Christie Blatchford), at 27, 39, 29, 41.

[65]    See, W. Houston & D. Shoalts, *Eagleson: The Fall of a Hockey Czar* (Toronto: McGraw-Hill Ryerson, 1993) at 80-83 (Canada Cup revenue and expenses), 154-58 (pension fund). See also, D. Clayton, *Eagle: The Life and Times of R. Alan Eagleson* (Toronto: Lester & Orpen Dennys, 1982) at 80-92, 110-27 (1972 Series), 170-74, 181-84 (1976 Canada Cup).

[66]    See, J. Papanek & B. Brubaker, "The Man Who Rules Hockey" *Sports Illustrated* (July 2, 1984) at 60. On Eagleson's role as an agent, see Chapter 9, "National Hockey League", section G, 2.

[67]    See, *Forbes v. Eagleson*, 19 F.Supp. 2d 352 (E.D. Pa., 1998), affd 228 F.3d 471 (3rd Cir., 2000). See further, Chapter 9, "National Hockey League", section B.

[68]    R.A. Eagleson with S. Young, *Power Play: The Memoirs of Hockey Czar Alan Eagleson* (Toronto: McClelland & Stewart, 1991) at 209. See also, D. Cruise & A. Griffiths, *Net Worth: Exploding the Myths of Pro Hockey* (Toronto: Viking Penguin, 1991) at 300-19.

[69]    See: "Eagleson tried to deal for NHL franchise" *The Globe and Mail* (Toronto: February 20, 1993) at A1, A4; "Collecting for disability cost some players extra" "Gifts, apartment billed to NHLPA" *The Globe and Mail* (Toronto: February 23, 1993) at A1, A4, A13. See also, R. Conway, *Game Misconduct: Alan Eagleson and the Corruption of Hockey* (Toronto: Macfarlane, Walter & Ross, 1995, revised 1997).

[70]    See, "Ontario law society charges Eagleson" *The Globe and Mail* (Toronto: November 12, 1994) at A1, A2.

CDN \$2 million in administration costs and management services in 1991, and the hiring out to "Hockey Canada" of employees of Eagleson's management company.[71] Following police investigations in Canada and the United States, in March 1994 a federal grand jury in Boston brought a 32-count indictment against Eagleson alleging the misuse of funds and private profiteering from the management of the NHLPA.[72] In December 1996, Eagleson was charged in Toronto with eight counts of theft and fraud in relation to three of the Canada Cup tournaments.[73] The criminal proceedings eventually terminated in January 1998 when Eagleson consented to an unusual cross-border plea bargain[74] and admitted to three charges involving mail fraud and the making of false claims. Eagleson waived his extradition rights and presented himself in a federal court in Boston where he pleaded guilty to misuse of airline passes and the diversion of advertising profits from international tournaments; he also pleaded guilty to charges relating to the use of NHLPA funds for personal expenses and the retention of an insurance payment that should have gone to a player.[75] Under the plea arrangement, Eagleson was fined USD \$700,000, which was placed in a trust fund for the benefit of NHLPA members, and was required to plead guilty in Canada to related charges and receive a sentence of at least 18 months imprisonment. Eagleson duly returned to Toronto to accept his sentence from the Ontario Court,[76] although the early release program enabled him to leave the provincial jail after only six months. The Eagle's fall was completed when he was disbarred by the Law Society,[77] expelled from the Order of Canada and the Sports Hall of Fame and when he chose to resign from the Hockey Hall of Fame.

---

[71] See: "Hockey Canada keeps Eagleson, but plans probe" *The Globe and Mail* (Toronto: February 12, 1993) at A12; "Hockey Canada calling in help to probe books" *The Globe and Mail* (Toronto: February 25, 1995) at A4; "Eagleson benefited from Hockey Canada contracts" *The Globe and Mail* (Toronto: March 5, 1993) at A1, A2. See also: W. Houston & D. Shoalts, *Eagleson: The Fall of a Hockey Czar* (Toronto: McGraw-Hill Ryerson 1993) at 85-102; R. Conway, *Game Misconduct: Alan Eagleson and the Corruption of Hockey* (Toronto: Macfarlane, Walter & Ross, 1995, revised 1997) at 213-42, 267.

[72] See, "Eagleson accused of racketeering" "Eagleson's biggest face-off" *The Globe and Mail* (Toronto: March 4, 1994) at A1, A2, C14.

[73] See: "Eagleson faces eight charges" *The Globe and Mail* (Toronto: December 4, 1996) at A1, A5 (fraud and theft charges); *Eagleson (Re)*, [1998] L.S.D.D. No. 35, 1998 ONLSDC 10038 (L.S.U.C. Discipline Committee).

[74] See, P. Boisseau, "Global Resolution: The International Plea Bargain That Put Away Alan Eagleson" (May 1998) 22:5 Canadian Lawyer 24.

[75] See: "Eagleson may do only 90 days" *The Globe and Mail* (Toronto: January 6, 1998) at A1, A7; "Eagleson admits his guilt" *The Globe and Mail* (Toronto: January 7, 1998) at A1, A6. Eagleson was directed to reimburse the former player Glen Sharpley for the amount owing on the insurance policy.

[76] See, "Eagleson brought to earth hard" *The Globe and Mail* (Toronto: January 8, 1998) at A1, A7.

[77] See, *Eagleson (Re)*, [1998] L.S.D.D. No. 35, 1998 ONLSDC 10038 (L.S.U.C. Discipline Committee). Eagleson had been called to the Ontario Bar in 1959. He joined with the Law Society's counsel in submitting that he should be disbarred.

The rise and fall of Alan Eagleson is the story of an energetic operator who turned player representation and international tournaments to his own interests[78] during a period of intense and unconstrained commercialization in hockey. As a global practitioner of sports law, his status was heroic, and when disbarred by the Law Society he had no prior record of disciplinary infractions. Eagleson thrived for 25 years as he benefited from the passivity of professional players,[79] useful connections in the corridors of power and media coverage that remained sympathetic until late in the day. Under the corporate structure of "Hockey Canada", the board offered only general guidance, so that "staff experienced significant autonomy to carry out operational responsibilities."[80] The low level of control in this small agency especially suited one powerful director.

By 1994, there was impetus to reorganize hockey's national organizations by integrating the positive business elements of the original "Hockey Canada". It was the time for a united structure and a new brand.

## 5. Unification

In July 1994, the CAHA and "Hockey Canada" agreed in principle to merge as the "Canadian Hockey Association" ("CHA") and so consolidate the governing body for the newly declared "national winter sport".[81] To symbolize the way forward, a new logo was adopted showing the outline of a player skating out of a maple leaf. The merger announcement anticipated a strengthening of operations as each organization brought its own qualities:

> Hockey Canada has in its portfolio entrepreneurial abilities, its full-time national team program, world class Centre of Excellence facilities, and extensive involvement in international hockey...The CAHA is the sport governing body for hockey, brings federal government revenues, membership on the International Ice Hockey Federation and Canadian Olympic Association, a national delivery system to over four million Canadians involved in hockey, and successful development and national team...programs.[82]

Since 2003, the new association has functioned as both the CHA and as Hockey Canada. Article One of the constituting documents now declares:

> This organization shall be registered as the Canadian Hockey Association. The Association is registered with the business name "Hockey Canada". For legal

---

[78] On assets and asset dealing, see, "Where's the money?" *Maclean's* (February 9, 1998) at 16.

[79] See, in particular, D. Cruise & A. Griffiths, *Net Worth: Exploding the Myths of Pro Hockey* (Toronto: Viking Penguin, 1991).

[80] J. Stevens, "The Canadian Hockey Association Merger and the Emergence of the Amateur Sport Enterprise" (2006) 20 J. of Sport Management 74 at 83.

[81] See, *National Sports of Canada Act*, S.C. 1994, c. 16, s. 2.

[82] Canadian Hockey Association, News Release, "CAHA and Hockey Canada Announce Plans To Create New Organization" (July 14, 1994).

purposes, the name shall be the Canadian Hockey Association, but for all other purposes, this organization shall be known as Hockey Canada.[83]

As noted, the former CAHA was regularly torn between commitment to community play and the need to co-operate with commercial and professional elements. The CAHA's organizational model nevertheless remained that of a volunteer association providing structures and services to different levels of the game. By contrast, the "Hockey Canada" of 1969 followed a corporate design and served to arrange elite contests for commercial consumption and broadcasting. One was a community-oriented "sport provider", the other a victory-seeking, profit-oriented "sport marketer".[84] Since the merger or takeover of 1994, the challenge for the CHA has been to balance the traditional development model with the newly incorporated business elements. While members and volunteers are well served by an efficient enterprise, their interests should not be entirely lost in the drive to serve sponsors and put on profitable events.[85]

The debate about player development continued in the late 1990s as many commentators affirmed that safety,[86] education and fun should be the primary goals in the early years. There was a familiar ring to the critique of the on-ice environment.[87] The standard recitation of problems in minor hockey included the failure to teach skills, the incidence of injuries from body checking, competitive pressures and intimidation, and the dropout rate. Junior hockey had also not shaken its image as a gruelling business that shopped teenagers around at an unconscionably young age. The issues were thoroughly aired in August 1999 at the "Open Ice" summit, which was particularly inspired by the declining Canadian presence in the early rounds of the NHL entry draft and the domination by European players of the leagues's "skill positions".[88] Ken Dryden and other leaders called for change[89] and presented a plan to offer "master coaches" to minor associations.[90] With skill development as the basis of reform, the recommended ratio of practices to game was three to one. "Open Ice" produced 11 recommendations and was also conscious that effective development required

---

[83]   Hockey Canada, Articles (amended to June 2009), Article One, 1.

[84]   See, J. Stevens, "The Canadian Hockey Association Merger and the Emergence of the Amateur Sport Enterprise" (2006) 20 J. of Sport Management 74. On issues of mandate and mission, see also, M. Robidoux & P. Trudel, "Hockey Canada and the Bodychecking Debate in Minor Hockey" in D. Whitson & R. Gruneau, eds., *Artificial Ice: Hockey, Culture, and Commerce* (Peterborough, ON: Broadview Press, 2006) at 101; on body checking, see Chapter 6, "Play Safe: On the Ice", section A, 2.

[85]   On the business of hockey, see Chapter 7, "The Business of Hockey".

[86]   On the particular concern about physical and sexual abuse, see Chapter 5, "Be Safe: Off the Ice".

[87]   See, for example, W. Houston, "A Game in Crisis" (Parts 4, 6, 7 and 8) *The Globe and Mail* (Toronto: April 8, 10, 11, 13, 1998). See also, "Putting the Canadian back in hockey" *The Globe and Mail* (Toronto: April 25, 1998) at D6.

[88]   See, "Leading hockey figures gather to deal with development system" *The Globe and Mail* (Toronto: August 24, 1999) at S2.

[89]   See, "Hockey must change: Dryden" *The Globe and Mail* (Toronto: August 26, 1999) at S1.

[90]   See, "Open Ice plan emphasizes practices, skills" *The Globe and Mail* (Toronto: August 28, 1999) at A28.

adequate funding.[91] The dependence on commercialized championship events and payments from the NHL had not gone away.

## B.  ORGANIZATIONS

### 1.  International Ice Hockey Federation ("IIHF")[92]

The IIHF is the governing body for international ice hockey and in-line hockey and by 2007 included 65 member countries. The International Olympic Committee ("IOC") recognizes the IIHF as the governing body for ice hockey (see, IIHF Statute 4), so that the federation conducts the competitions at the Olympics Games (see, IIHF Bylaw 204). The IIHF also organizes world championships at different levels and runs various European club competitions.

The IIHF celebrated its centenary in 2008,[93] having been founded in 1908 as the *Ligue Internationale de Hockey sur Glace* ("LIHG"). The organization was the initiative of Louis Magnus of France who wished to popularize Canadian ice hockey in Europe.[94] The founding countries were Belgium, France, Great Britain and Switzerland, which were soon joined by Bohemia (1908), Germany (1909), Russia (1911), Austria (1912), Sweden (1912) and Luxembourg (1912). Canada and the United States were admitted to official membership in 1920. The first European men's championships were played in 1910 and included a team of "Oxford Canadians" participating as unofficial competitors, and a less prominent LIHG championship operated from 1912 to 1914. As noted earlier, a world men's championship was held in association with the Summer Olympics in 1920, and the official Winter Olympic tournament for men followed in 1924; the annual men's world championships date from 1930. The women's world championships (1990) and Winter Olympics competition (1998) are more recent arrivals.[95] To mark the centenary of the federation, the Victoria Cup competition between European and NHL clubs was inaugurated in 2008.

The IIHF is based in Zürich, Switzerland and is designated as an "association" under Swiss law.[96] The IIHF is constituted by its Statutes,

---

[91]  See, "Youth hockey needs more cheques, summit concludes" *The Globe and Mail* (Toronto: August 27, 1999) at S1. On the implementation of recommendations, see, *Five Years in the Making: A Report on the Open Ice Initiatives* (Hockey Canada, August 2005).

[92]  Online: <http://www.iihf.com>. The IIHF is located at Brandschenkestrasse 50, Postfach, 8027 Zürich, Switzerland.

[93]  See, A. Podnieks & S. Szemberg, eds., *World of Hockey: Celebrating a Century of the IIHF* (Bolton, ON: HB Fenn and Company, 2007).

[94]  See, A. Podnieks *et al.*, *Kings of the Ice: A History of World Hockey* (Richmond Hill, ON: NDE Publishing, 2002) at 155-60.

[95]  See Chapter 2, "Legal Fundamentals and Equality Rights", section E, 1.

[96]  See, *Code civil suisse*, art. 60.

Bylaws and Regulations[97] and is a "non-profit organization functioning as trustee in financial matters for its member national associations" (see, IIHF Statute 6). The primary language of the federation is English (see, IIHF Statute 8). Membership may be either "full", "associate" or "affiliate", depending on participation standards and whether the association is an independent body and responsible solely for ice hockey (see, IIHF Statute 20).

The objectives of the IIHF (see, IIHF Statute 2) include to organize international competition and,

- to govern, develop and promote ice and in-line hockey throughout the world;
- to develop and control international ice and in-line hockey;
- to promote friendly relations among the member national associations; and
- to operate in an organized manner for the good order of the sport.

The IIHF is administered through legislative bodies such as the Annual Congress, executive bodies such as the Council and various operational committees chaired by Council members (see, IIHF Statutes 29-53). The "Directorates" are temporary executive bodies responsible for conducting championships. In 2009, the president of the IIHF was René Fasel and the general secretary was Horst Lichtner. The responsibilities of the president include acting as the chief representative of the IIHF and serving as chairman of meetings of Congress and Council (see, IIHF Statute 46). The Council serves to enforce the regulations and policies of the Federation and makes proposals to Congress; it is also responsible for appointments to committees and approving agreements (see, IIHF Statute 44). The operational committees are established at the discretion of Council as recommending bodies. In addition there is an independent Disciplinary Committee that may not include Council members (see, IIHF Statute 52).[98]

The IIHF president is authorized to negotiate broadcasting, advertising, sponsorship and merchandising contracts on behalf of the federation (see, IIHF Statute 46). The IIHF is the sole owner of commercial rights related to IIHF competitions and activities (see, IIHF Statute 13; Bylaw 410), although television and advertising rights from national and international games also attach to participating national associations (see, IIHF Bylaw 309). The IIHF shares in revenue from the Olympic Games and has other sources of income such as fees related to memberships, transfers and participation in competitions (see, IIHF Bylaw 404).

---

[97]    See, IIHF Statutes and Bylaws, 2008-2012 (July 2008). The Regulations are supplementary to the Statutes and include: International Transfer Regulations (May 2009); Championship Regulations (May 2007); and Medical Regulations (July 2007).

[98]    On different types of dispute and hearing processes, see Chapter 3, "Organizations and Regulations", section C.

## 2. Hockey Canada (Canadian Hockey Association)[99]

Hockey Canada is the national governing body for hockey, holding responsibilities in relation to domestic play, research and development, and the management of various national teams performing in international competitions. Hockey Canada is constituted by its Articles, By-Laws and Regulations[100] which deal particularly with the organization of competitions and issues related to eligibility and discipline.[101] The association works in conjunction with its member organizations and with the Major Junior leagues participating in the Canadian Hockey League ("CHL").[102] The CHL is responsible for the Memorial Cup competition and is involved in selecting the team for the world junior tournament. Eligibility for junior and Major Junior competitions is subject to Hockey Canada Regulations and to the "Canadian Development Model"[103] which recognizes the educational needs of players.

The "objects" of Hockey Canada (see, Article Three) include to:

a.   Foster and encourage the sport of amateur hockey throughout Canada;

...

c.   Recognize and sanction the establishment of governing bodies...;

...

e.   Establish and maintain uniform playing rules for amateur hockey;

...

h.   Conduct Inter-Branch and international contests of amateur hockey;

i.   Provide representation for international open hockey competition.[104]

The member Branches are the provincial and regional hockey associations which are obliged to control amateur hockey in accordance with the constitution, policies, playing rules and decisions of Hockey Canada (see, Article Four: 8, 10(a); By-Law One: 101,103). Branches have sole discretion in classifying teams consistent with Hockey Canada's age limits (see, By-Law One: 104). The "Associate Members" of Hockey Canada are the Canadian Armed Forces, Canadian Inter-University Sport,

---

[99]   Online: <http://www.hockeycanada.ca>. Hockey Canada's main offices are located at 801 King Edward Avenue, Suite N204, Ottawa, ON, K1N 6N5 and 2424 University Drive NW, Calgary, AB, T2N 3Y9.

[100]   See, Hockey Canada, Articles, By-Laws, Regulations (amended to June 2008). Articles may be amended only by a two-thirds majority of a quorum of the Annual General Meeting following prescribed notice (see, Article Five). Subject to requirements with respect to notice and timing, By-Laws or Regulations may normally be amended at other meetings by majority vote (see, By-Law Eleven).

[101]   See Chapter 3, "Organizations and Regulations", section C.

[102]   See Chapter 3, "Organizations and Regulations", section B, 3. The CHL is a "named insured" under Hockey Canada's Commercial General Liability Policy; see Chapter 4, "Build Safe: Rink Management and Risk Management", section D.

[103]   See, Hockey Canada Information Manual for the Canadian Development Model (June 2008).

[104]   Online: <http://www.hockeycanada.ca/index.php/ci_id/66601/la_id/1.htm>, Article 3.

the NHL and NHLPA, the Canadian Ball Hockey Association, the Aboriginal Sport Circle, the Canadian Deaf Ice Hockey Federation, the Canadian Amputee Hockey Committee and the National In-line Hockey Association (see, Article Four: 11).

Hockey Canada is governed through its officers (see, By-Law Four) and through meetings of the Board of Directors and various specialist councils and committees (see, By-Laws Five-Seven). In 2008, the officers and directors of Hockey Canada included Allan Morris (chair of the Board), Bob Nicholson (president) and Murray Costello (director, international operations). The president is appointed by the Board of Directors and is responsible for the day-to-day operations of the Association and for the initial interpretation of regulations (see, By-Law Four: 403). The Board of Directors is authorized to enforce the constitution and adjudicate disputes between Branches and in By-Law 502(l) claims the remarkable power to,

> solely, finally, absolutely and exclusively...establish and define the rules and laws of amateur hockey in Canada.[105]

The Board may also enter into agreements with the NHL and members of the IIHF to regulate matters of common interest such as the transfer of players (see, By-Law Five: 502(p)(q)). The councils of Hockey Canada are those dealing with development, female hockey, and junior, minor and senior hockey (see, By-Law Five: 504). The committees are organized into groups dealing with governance, risk and safety,[106] management, and high performance (see, By-Law Five: 505-523).

In accordance with By-Law 902, Hockey Canada may derive its income from,

> ...grants, annual membership fees, annual team assessments for national competitions, gate receipts, performance bonds, sanction fees, appeals and protest fees, proceeds from sale of goods, products and educational resources, marketing proceeds, and the sale of broadcasting and television rights.[107]

Hockey Canada reserves the broadcasting rights to national championships and international games and reserves other media rights such as Internet and digital rights (see, By-Law Nine: 905). As noted elsewhere,[108] the major funding sources of the association are commercial revenues from sponsorship, events and the sale of goods and services.[109]

---

[105] *Ibid.*, By-Law 502(l).
[106] On safety, conduct and liability on and off the ice, see Chapters 4-6.
[107] Online: <http://www.hockeycanada.ca/index.php/ci_id/66601/la_id/1.htm>, By-Law 902.
[108] On government regulation and funding, see Chapter 2, "Legal Fundamentals and Equality Rights", section B. On business aspects, see Chapter 7, "The Business of Hockey", section A, 1.
[109] See, Hockey Canada, *2009 Annual Report*, at 19-27. Long term investment and endowment are maintained through donations to the Canadian Hockey Foundation ("CHF") which provides

## 3. Canadian Hockey League

The Canadian Hockey League ("CHL")[110] coordinates the national Major Junior competition, which is a classification established in 1970 through the division of Junior A play. The member regional leagues are the Western Hockey League ("WHL"),[111] the Ontario Hockey League ("OHL"),[112] and the Quebec Major Junior Hockey League ("QMJHL")[113] which include a total of 60 teams located in ten Provinces and five American states. The CHL is a significant business operation[114] and player development system that "mirrors the style of play, rules, practice and game schedule of the NHL".[115] In 2008, about 54 per cent of NHLers were products of Major Junior hockey, although the professional alumni are the chosen few since the conventional estimate is that less than five per cent (<5 per cent) of Major Junior players advance to significant playing careers.[116] CHL players do, however, feature prominently in the NHL's Entry Draft, accounting for 110 of the 210 selections in 2008 and 99 in 2009. The member leagues of the CHL operate in professional form with mechanisms such as entry drafts and standard player contracts. There is, however, only a minimal market for players' services since "salaries are fixed"[117] and compensation is limited to modest stipends and allowances for accommodation and schooling.

Major Junior competition consists primarily of players aged 16 to 20, with teams limited to registering a maximum of four 16-year-olds (Regulation F.53(d)). It is the general policy of the Hockey Canada development model that first year Midget players (aged 15) should register and compete in minor hockey, although "players who believe they are 'exceptional'"[118] may apply to play at the

---

particular assistance for development and participation projects that would not otherwise be funded.

[110] The CHL is located at 201-305 Milner Ave., Scarborough, ON, M1B 3V4. Besides the OHA Memorial Cup, the Major Junior trophies include the George T. Richardson Memorial Trophy (eastern Canada championship) and the Athol Murray Trophy (western Canada championship).

[111] Online: <http://www.whl.ca>.

[112] Online: <http://www.ontariohockeyleague.com>.

[113] Online: <http://www.lhjmq.qc.ca> (Ligue de hockey junior majeur du Québec).

[114] See further, Chapter 7, "The Business of Hockey", section A, 1, b.

[115] *National Hockey League Players' Assn. v. Plymouth Whalers Hockey Club*, 325 F.3d 712 at 716 (6th Cir., 2003), *per* Gibbons Cir. J.

[116] See, "System's culture of silence hides flaws" *The Globe and Mail* (Toronto: May 13, 1997) at A18, at A19. On the career prospects of Joshua Morrow drafted in the seventh round in 2002, see, *Morrow v. Outerbridge*, [2009] B.C.J. No. 640, 2009 BCSC 433 (B.C.S.C.).

[117] *National Hockey League Players' Assn. v. Plymouth Whalers Hockey Club*, 419 F.3d 462 at 476 (6th Cir., 2005), *per* Clay Cir. J. In the OHL, "Overage players receive a stipend of $150 per week; players under twenty receive fifty dollars per week" at 419 F.3d 470, note 2. For a higher scale of pay in the WHL, see, *McCrimmon Holdings Ltd. v. M.N.R.*, [2000] T.C.J. No. 823 (T.C.C.).

[118] On the eligibility of John Tavares, see, "Governors reject OHL proposal to drop draft age" *The Globe and Mail* (Toronto: March 24, 2005) at R11; "Hockey Canada sets junior age restrictions" *The Globe and Mail* (Toronto: May 24, 2005) at R10. For a critical account of the Canadian Development Model and its effect on Junior A operators, see, K. Campbell, "Junior-A Leaders Feeling the Freeze" *The Hockey News* (February 26, 2008) at 14.

Major Junior level in accordance with Hockey Canada Regulations and special appeal procedures (see, Regulation F.53(b)).[119] Junior teams may affiliate no more than five 15-year-olds for a maximum of five games during the season, may use only one such player per game and are subject to other restrictions in relation to the "call-up" (see, Regulation F.53(c)). At the upper age level, the eligibility rules of the OHL[120] allow teams only three 20-year-old or "overage" players, and the so-called "Van Ryn Rule"[121] excludes any 20-year-old coming from competition in the National Collegiate Athletic Association ("NCAA"). No "overage" player can be signed unless he was previously registered under Hockey Canada or USA Hockey, and the NCAA rules do not permit participation by players holding either type of registration.[122]

The decision around the age of 15 to "go junior" has important consequences as the player chooses a tough apprenticeship in the hope of professional success, and there is long-standing concern over the effects of this decision on general education. In the OHL, teams play 68 games in the regular season, although 90 per cent are scheduled around the weekend in an attempt to reduce the interference with school. CHL players are excluded from the NCAA and the associated scholarships since NCAA regulations classify Major Junior teams as professional and impose restrictions on the restoration of eligibility.[123] CHL teams do, however, cover educational costs while players are playing and provide scholarships for post-secondary study.[124] Former Major Junior players

---

[119] See also, "Hockey Canada Direction and Notes for Transfers and Appeals" (June 2008).

[120] According to the *Plymouth Whalers* decisions, *infra*, the use of "overage" players is dealt with in "OHL Rule" 7.4.

[121] See: *National Hockey League Players' Assn. v. Plymouth Whalers Hockey Club*, 325 F.3d 712 (6th Cir., 2003); *National Hockey League Players' Assn. v. Plymouth Whalers Hockey Club*, 419 F.3d 462 (6th Cir., 2005). Mike Van Ryn, who had been drafted by the New Jersey Devils in 1998, achieved free agent status in the NHL by staying at the University of Michigan and then joining the Sarnia Sting of the OHL for 1999–2000. The Devils failed to sign Van Ryn by June 1, 2000, with the result that he was able to negotiate attractive terms with the St. Louis Blues. See, *In the Matter of...NHLPA and NHL, Grievances Concerning Ben Clymer and Mike Van Ryn* (June 22, 2000, L.T. Holden, arb.) (players were not "defected players" since CHL is an affiliated league).

[122] Particular eligibility rules of the NCAA prohibit participation in outside or noncollegiate competition during the academic year; see, *2007-08 NCAA Division 1 Manual*, Operating By-laws, 14.7.1, 17.14.8.1.1 (ice hockey), online: <http://www.ncaa.org>.

[123] See: *2007-08 NCAA Division 1 Manual*, Operating By-laws, 12.1.2 (Amateur Status), 12.2.3.2.4/4.1 (Major Junior A Ice Hockey); "USAH/HC/CHL/ Transfer & Release Agreement" (2008) Article II. C.2. See also: *Buckton v. National Collegiate Athletic Assn.*, 366 F.Supp. 1152 (D. Mass., 1973); *Jones v. National Collegiate Athletic Assn.*, 392 F.Supp. 295 (D. Mass., 1975); *Colorado Seminary (University of Denver) v. National Collegiate Athletic Assn.*, 417 F.Supp. 885 (D. Col., 1976); *Spath v. National Collegiate Athletic Assn.*, 728 F.2d 25 (1st Cir., 1984).

[124] See also, *McCrimmon Holdings Ltd. v. M.N.R.*, [2000] T.C.J. No. 823 (T.C.C.) (players of Brandon Wheat Kings are employees and not in "a form of private education").

are eligible for competition in Canadian Interuniversity Sport ("CIS")[125] where they represent a leading source of hockey talent.

Entry into the Major Junior leagues is subject to regional drafts or systems of "Priority Selection" as member teams choose new players for their rosters. The legal status of one draft was considered in *Greenlaw v. Ontario Major Junior Hockey League*,[126] where a 16-year-old from St. Catherines, who wished to play in Toronto, was refused an interlocutory injunction to preclude his selection by North Bay. The draft was defended as necessary to enable small, remote cities to compete with larger centres. Playing opportunities were not being completely denied to Greenlaw, and the injunction was refused on the balance of convenience. Montgomery J. was persuaded that defiance of the draft was destructive of the league and might reduce the scale of career development provided.

The CHL maintains agreements with the NHL relating to its professional training function and dealing with the return of players to Major Junior teams. As noted earlier,[127] the payment of development fees began in 1967 when the NHL replaced the sponsorship of junior teams with an entry draft allowing the selection of players at the age of 20. Until 1975, compensation provisions were included in the joint development agreement between the NHL and the Canadian Amateur Hockey Association, and the CAHA distributed fees to the junior team from which a player had been selected.[128] The agreement was then superseded by periodic arrangements made directly between the NHL and the Major Junior leagues. The World Hockey Association (1972 - 1979) originally undertook to observe the draft age and pay development fees, but after 1974 some WHA teams began to sign "underage" juniors and failed to make payments. Junior teams then rewrote their players' contracts to place an obligation on individual players who signed with professional teams. In *Toronto Marlboro Major Junior "A" Hockey Club v. Tonelli*,[129] the defendant signed a multi-year contract with the Marlboros at the age of 17. Being an "infant" in law, the contract was binding only if it was for his benefit. On reaching the age of majority, Tonelli repudiated the contract and signed a lucrative agreement to play for the Houston Aeros of the WHA. The junior contract obliged Tonelli to pay USD $64,000 in development fees which represented a portion of his first three years of gross professional earnings. The junior contract was found to have various unbeneficial terms and so was unenforceable against the "infant" defendant. When dismissing the Marlboros' preliminary application for an interim injunction, Morden J. commented:

---

[125] On CIS rules related to professional leagues and participation in hockey outside the CIS during the same season, see, Canadian Interuniversity Sport, Eligibility Policy (September 2009), 40.10.6.2.3.6/7; 40.10.6.3.2, online: <http://www.universitysport.ca/e/pol_proc/index.cfm>.

[126] [1984] O.J. No. 3373, 48 O.R. (2d) 371 (Ont. H.C.J.).

[127] See Chapter 3, "Organizations and Regulations", section A, 1, 2.

[128] See, *Regina Pats Hockey Club v. Wilson*, [1974] S.J. No. 82, 15 C.P.R. (2d) 16 (Sask. Q.B.) (claim by vendor of junior team against purchaser for draft payments).

[129] [1979] O.J. No. 4054, 23 O.R. (2d) 193, 96 D.L.R. (3d) 135 (Ont. C.A.), affg [1977] O.J. No. 2464, 18 O.R. (2d) 21, 81 D.L.R. (3d) 403 (Ont. H.C.J.). See further, Chapter 9, "National Hockey League", section E.

...the amount of the contribution appears to be out of all proportion to what the amateur club should be entitled to in this respect, if it is fairly entitled to anything, from the player. It puts a gigantic premium on the value of the training imparted to the player and the exposure given to him and pays little, if any, heed to the contribution to the player's success resulting from his own natural ability, hard work and desire to succeed.[130]

Morden J. did, however, recognize the legitimacy of junior hockey's claims to some contribution and favourably contrasted the sum of CDN \$25,000 in a revised version of the junior contract.[131]

The NHL's draft age of 20 allowed for the maturing of players and protected the commercial interests of owners of Major Junior teams who were able to offer a higher standard of competition. The age rule did, however, delay opportunities for exceptional young players and was suspect under competition law as an unreasonable limitation on participation.[132] In *Linseman v. World Hockey Assn.*,[133] an American federal court granted an injunction ordering the WHA not to prevent a member team using an "underage" player. The age rule was found to be an illegal boycott contrary to antitrust law that could not be justified by the need to support Canadian junior leagues or the possibility of international sanctions against the WHA.

From 1979-80, the NHL began drafting 18- and 19-year-olds and agreed to pay special compensation for first-round selections who played specific numbers of games. After the collective bargaining in 1986, the NHL modified the age rules in its by-laws to require normally three years of Major Junior service before a player qualified for the entry draft; 18-or 19-year olds could be selected only in the first three rounds.[134] Since the collective bargaining in 1992, "underage" players may be drafted in any round, the CHL having become concerned about the increased tendency to draft players from American schools and colleges. By relating age limitations to the collective bargaining agreement ("CBA"), the NHL relies on the "labour exemption"[135] from antitrust liability which has been applied to restraints on potential players as well as on present members of the bargaining unit.[136] The CBA negotiated in

---

[130] *Toronto Marlboro Major Junior "A" Hockey Club v. Tonelli*, [1975] O.J. No. 2618, 11 O.R. (2d) 664 at 682 (Ont. H.C.J.).

[131] *Toronto Marlboro Major Junior "A" Hockey Club v. Tonelli*, [1975] O.J. No. 2618, 11 O.R. (2d) 664 at 682 (Ont. H.C.J.). *Cf.* "\$25,000 is no small value to place on the privilege of playing in the league...": *Sheddon v. Ontario Major Junior Hockey League*, [1978] O.J. No. 3273, 19 O.R. (2d) 1 at 4 (Ont. H.C.J.), *per* Reid J. In more recent versions of the OHL Standard Player Contract, the player has acknowledged the club's material contributions to his development.

[132] See Chapter 8, "Competition Law and Labour Law".

[133] 439 F.Supp. 1315 (D. Conn., 1977). Linseman's contract with the Birmingham Bulls would pay USD \$500,000 over six years.

[134] See, NHL By-Laws (November 1991), sec. 16B.2(a)(v) (deleted in 1992).

[135] See, Chapter 8, "Competition Law and Labour Law", section C, 3.

[136] See: *Wood v. National Basketball Assn.*, 602 F.Supp. 525 (S.D.N.Y., 1984), affd 809 F.2d 954 (2nd Cir., 1987); *Zimmerman v. National Football League*, 632 F.Supp. 398 (D.D.C., 1986); *Clarett v. National Football League*, 369 F.3d 124 (2nd Cir., 2004).

2005 specifies that 18 is the age of eligibility for the entry draft (see, article 8.4) and that "age 18" means reaching that birthday between January 1 and September 15 of the draft year (see, article 8.10). During the first two seasons following the signing of an 18-year-old to a standard player contract, a NHL team must first offer him back to the junior team before loaning him to a minor-professional affiliate, except where the junior team is no longer in competition (see, article 8.7). The exclusive negotiation rights of the drafting NHL team normally extend until June 1 of the next calendar year, or until the second June 1 where the team has made a "Bona Fide Offer" (see, article 8.6). In the case of a drafted 18-year-old who ceases to play in the juniors, the rights extend to the fourth June 1 following the initial selection (see, article 8.6(b)). The same period also applies to a drafted 18-or 19-year-old "bona fide college student" who ceases to be a student (see, article 8.6(c)(ii)); in the case of the student who remains in college, the drafting team retains rights until the August 15 following the graduation of his class (see, article 8.6(c)(i)).

## C. ISSUES AND DISPUTES

## 1. Private Associations

### a. *Decisions and Remedies*

Hockey organizations have the status of private, voluntary associations, as opposed to public authorities exercising statutory powers.[137] A statutory basis for decisions only arises in relation to disputes that are taken to arbitration.[138] An association is a self-governing body whose members are in an on-going contractual relationship defined by the rules, agreements and customs of the fellowship.[139] Formal regulations in constitutions and by-laws assign specific authority to officers, committees or tribunals,[140] and associations develop standard practices based on the culture and objectives of the voluntary union. Courts are reluctant to supervise the decision-making of domestic bodies and will refrain from acting as courts of appeal on the merits of

---

[137] On the choice between judicial review and action, see, S. Blake, *Administrative Law in Canada*, 4th ed. (Markham, ON: LexisNexis Butterworths, 2006) at 180-83. See also: *Croteau v. Hockey Canada*, [2005] F.C.J. No. 883, 2005 FC 704 (F.C.) (Hockey Canada is not a federal board or agency subject to review by the Federal Court); *Duguay v. Hockey Canada*, [2005] F.C.J. No. 884, 2005 FC 705 (F.C.).

[138] On the Sport Dispute Resolution Centre of Canada and the Court of Arbitration for Sport, see Chapter 2, "Legal Fundamentals and Equality Rights", section C. On the rights of members of incorporated associations, see: *Trudelle (Litigation guardian of) v. Saskatchewan Hockey Assn.*, [2003] S.J. No. 207, 233 Sask.R. 51 (Sask. Q.B.); *Garcia v. Kelowna Minor Hockey Assn. (Inc. No. S-17423)*, [2009] B.C.J. No. 316, 2009 BCSC 200 (B.C.S.C.).

[139] See, *Lakeside Colony of Hutterian Brethren v. Hofer*, [1992] S.C.J. No. 87, [1992] 3 S.C.R. 165 (S.C.C.). On the value of voluntary community associations, see, *West Hill Minor Hockey Assn. v. Scarborough Hockey Assn.*, [2009] O.J. No. 2171 (Ont. S.C.J.).

[140] See, J.R.S. Forbes, *Justice in Tribunals*, 2d ed. (Sydney: Federation Press, 2006).

cases.[141] The refusal to second-guess "consensual tribunals" applies especially where officers have made an honest attempt to resolve technical matters falling within their expertise or discretion.[142] Although there is a preference for resolving matters in-house, courts hold the ultimate authority to determine whether a tribunal exceeded its jurisdiction or acted illegally, and a general provision that an association's rulings are "final" is insufficient to oust the authority of the courts. This judicial supervision is especially required in relation to established organizations that hold near-monopoly powers. Where a sport governing body controls advancement to higher levels of competition, the interested player has little choice about membership. The voluntary nature of associations is a matter of degree.

Remedies are available when important property or contractual rights are at stake,[143] including the right to earn a living.[144] A court will consider whether an association exceeded its powers, deviated from its rules, acted oppressively or in bad faith,[145] committed fraud on a minority[146] or based its decision on irrelevant or extraneous considerations. It is a particular requirement that tribunals follow a fair procedure or observe the "rules of natural justice". In matters of law and fairness, a tribunal must get it right: it must be "correct".[147]

---

[141]   See, for example: *Posluns v. Toronto Stock Exchange*, [1964] O.J. No. 792, [1964] 2 O.R. 547 at 610, 46 D.L.R. (2d) 210 at 273 (Ont. H.C.J.); *Vancouver Hockey Club Ltd. v. 8 Hockey Ventures Inc.*, [1987] B.C.J. No. 2074, 47 D.L.R. (4th) 51 at 56 (B.C.S.C.); *Trudelle (Litigation guardian of) v. Saskatchewan Hockey Assn.*, [2003] S.J. No. 207, 233 Sask.R. 51 (Sask. Q.B.) (suspension for head-butting; appeal committee was in the best position to judge); *Bowman v. B.C. Amateur Hockey Assn.* (October 21, 2005), Kamloops, Powers J. (B.C.S.C.) (applications to transfer to junior teams; interim injunctions denied); *Garcia v. Kelowna Minor Hockey Assn. (Inc. No. S-17423)*, [2009] B.C.J. No. 316, 2009 BCSC 200 (B.C.S.C.) (parent who made unsubstantiated allegations related to fundraising could be suspended in best interests of association).

[142]   See, for example: *Toronto Hockey Club Ltd. v. Ottawa Hockey Assn. Ltd.*, [1918] O.J. No. 293, 15 O.W.N. 145 (Ont. C.A.) (decision to exclude team from new schedule); *Weir v. Saskatchewan Amateur Baseball Assn.*, [1978] S.J. No. 333, 90 D.L.R. (3d) 707 (Sask. Q.B.) (continuation or replay of interrupted game).

[143]   See, *Lakeside Colony of Hutterian Brethren v. Hofer*, [1992] S.C.J. No. 87, [1992] 3 S.C.R. 165 (S.C.C.).

[144]   See: *Lee v. Showmen's Guild of Great Britain*, [1952] 2 Q.B. 329 (C.A.); *Nicholson v. Haldimand Norfolk (Regional) Police Commissioners*, [1978] S.C.J. No. 88, [1979] 1 S.C.R. 311 (S.C.C.) (dismissal of probationary employee; duty to be fair even though regulation provided that employee was not entitled to a hearing).

[145]   See: *Baird v. Wells* (1890), 44 Ch. D. 661; *Warkentin v. Sault Ste. Marie Board of Education*, [1985] O.J. No. 1616, 49 C.P.C. 31 (Ont. Dist. Ct.) (10-semester limit on participation; rule reasonable and no evidence of bad faith); *Walton (Litigation guardian of) v. Saskatchewan Hockey Assn.*, [1998] S.J. No. 125, [1999] 1 W.W.R. 135 (Sask. Q.B.) (no illegality, bad faith or oppression).

[146]   See, *Weir v. Saskatchewan Amateur Baseball Assn.*, [1978] S.J. No. 333, 90 D.L.R. (3d) 707 (Sask. Q.B.) (no allegation of fraud).

[147]   "The standard of review in determining whether the Appeal Panel acted within its jurisdiction is one of correctness": *McGarrigle v. Canadian Interuniversity Sport*, [2003] O.J. No. 1842 at para. 24, 123 A.C.W.S. (3d) 6 (Ont. S.C.J.), *per* Aitkin J.

The proceedings and decisions of private associations are normally subject to challenge by ordinary action,[148] although the special process of "judicial review" is applicable in some Provinces and Territories.[149] The usual remedy is a declaration of legal rights, but an injunction may be issued to protect proprietary interests[150] or other important opportunities to participate.[151] Issues are often addressed in the context of an application for an interim or interlocutory injunction seeking a preliminary order that the respondent do or refrain from doing something. The injunction is a discretionary remedy and courts take great care in granting it because of the serious consequences of the order.[152] In the context of sport, a directive to permit participation or lift a suspension largely resolves the main matter. The Supreme Court of Canada has outlined three general tests for determining whether it is just and equitable to grant the remedy.[153] First, there must be a preliminary assessment of the merits of the case. Traditionally, this required applicants to make out a *prima facie* case,[154] but in some circumstances they need only show that the case is not frivolous and that there are serious issues to be tried. Second, applicants must show that if the injunction is not granted they will suffer irreparable injury that cannot be compensated by damages. And, third, the court must consider the balance of convenience to determine which of the parties will suffer the greater harm from the grant or refusal of the injunction.

Associations and arbitrators deal with a variety of disputes, including issues relating to funding, contracts or harassment. For present purposes, it is useful to note four types of case:

---

[148] See: *Warren v. Hampton Country Club Inc.*, [1995] N.B.J. No. 608, 173 N.B.R. (2d) 241 (N.B.C.A.); *Vessie (Litigation guardian of) v. Swimming New Brunswick Inc.*, [1997] N.B.J. No. 313, 191 N.B.R. (2d) 323 (N.B.Q.B.); *Parks (Guardian ad litem of) v. B.C. School Sports*, [1997] B.C.J. No. 440, 145 D.L.R. (4th) 174 (B.C.S.C.); *Walton (Litigation guardian of) v. Saskatchewan Hockey Assn.*, [1998] S.J. No. 125, [1999] 1 W.W.R. 135 (Sask. Q.B.). See also, *Trudelle (Litigation guardian of) v. Saskatchewan Hockey Assn.*, [2003] S.J. No. 207, 233 Sask.R. 51 (Sask. Q.B.) (application under *The Non-profit Corporations Act, 1995*, S.S. 1995, c. N-4.2).

[149] On the *Alberta Rules of Court*, see, *Rankin v. Alberta Curling Federation Appeals Committee*, [2005] A.J. No. 1759, 262 D.L.R. (4th) 484 (Alta. Q.B.).

[150] See, *Rowe v. Hewitt*, [1906] O.J. No. 7, 12 O.L.R. 13 (Ont. Div. Ct.) (loss of playing opportunity held to be trivial and non-proprietary).

[151] See, *MacDougall v. Ontario Federation of School Athletic Assns.*, [1987] O.J. No. 1728, 27 C.P.C. (2d) 326 (Ont. Dist. Ct.) ("bureaucratic bungling" in interpretation of transfer rule).

[152] See, *Yule Inc. v. Atlantic Pizza Delight Franchise (1968) Ltd.*, [1977] O.J. No. 2429, 17 O.R. (2d) 505 (Ont. Div. Ct.).

[153] *Manitoba (Attorney General) v. Metropolitan Stores Ltd.*, [1987] S.C.J. No. 6, [1987] 1 S.C.R. 110 (S.C.C.); *RJR-MacDonald Inc. v. Canada (Attorney General)*, [1994] S.C.J. No. 17, [1994] 1 S.C.R. 311 (S.C.C.); see also, *American Cyanamid Co. v. Ethicon Ltd.*, [1975] A.C. 396 (H.L.). See, for example, *West Hill Minor Hockey Assn. v. Scarborough Hockey Assn.*, [2009] O.J. No. 2171 (Ont. S.C.J.) (order requiring continued membership and operation of house league program).

[154] Proof of a strong case is still required where the injunction will enforce a restrictive covenant in an employment contract; see, *Drake International Inc. v. Wortmann*, [1980] O.J. No. 3533, 27 O.R. (2d) 707, 108 D.L.R. (3d) 133 (Ont. Div. Ct.).

1.   eligibility;

2.   selection;

3.   event outcome; and

4.   discipline.

1. *Eligibility*: An eligibility dispute deals with fundamental qualifications for admission to a particular level of competition. Typical eligibility requirements include nationality, residence or period of residence, gender, possession of a disability, age, academic standing and amateur status. In this type of case, there is an allegation that a participant does not meet the necessary qualification, and eligibility is often questioned following a transfer of allegiance.

2. *Selection*: In a selection dispute, a player or officer claims the right to be nominated for a team place, position or award. Claimants allege that because of superior athletic performance or working experience, they are the ones who deserve to be chosen. The claim is usually based on the text of prescribed selection criteria or on other representations made by an organization.

3. *Event outcome*: A "field of play" case involves a challenge to the result of a game or competition and is a form of "game protest". The losing side alleges that there was an error by officials or a misapplication of playing rules.

4. *Discipline*: In a disciplinary case, an accused party is alleged to have engaged in wrongdoing contrary to a code of behaviour. A charge of undisciplined conduct carries an element of moral stigma and exposes the accused to sanctions imposed by the sports association. Doping infractions involve a form of disciplinary proceedings, although they are subject to a special regime of investigation and control required by government policy. Certain doping activities are also subject to statutory regulation and punishment through the criminal justice system.

In eligibility and selection disputes, claimants are typically "applicants" on the outside trying to get in. In disciplinary and doping cases, claimants have been on the inside and may now find themselves expelled.[155] Although conceptually different, the various categories can be mingled in particular circumstances. Eligibility is subject to "take-away" proceedings since previous status or registration might be rescinded,[156] and the use of an ineligible player can lead to disciplinary action against a coach or team.[157] A disciplinary suspension might

---

[155] The distinction between a decision-maker's duties on applications, expectation cases and forfeitures is considered in *McInnes v. Onslow-Fane*, [1978] 3 All E.R. 211 (Ch. Div.) (denial of boxing manager's licence).

[156] See, for example: *Levasseur c. Assoc. du hockey mineur Chaudière-Ouest*, [2007] J.Q. no 13414, 2007 QCCS 5510 (Que. C.S.) (re-registration refused); *Eikelenboom (c.o.b. Eiklyn Farms) v. Holstein Assn. of Canada*, [2004] N.S.J. No. 330, 226 N.S.R. (2d) 235 (N.S.C.A.) (prize cow stripped of purebred status). On the use of the human rights process to restore membership, see, *Paisley v. Kerry Park Minor Hockey Assn.*, [2007] B.C.H.R.T.D. No. 218, 2007 BCHRT 218 (B.C.H.R.T.) and [2007] B.C.H.R.T.D. No. 443, 2007 BCHRT 443 (B.C.H.R.T.).

[157] See, *McGarrigle v. Canadian Interuniversity Sport*, [2003] O.J. No. 1842, 123 A.C.W.S. (3d) 6 (Ont. S.C.J.).

render a player "ineligible", with the result that he or she is not selected,[158] and the presence of ineligible or doped players can have consequences for the outcome of a game. Where that game is a selection trial, the selections may also be thrown into doubt.

### b. Playing by the Rules

Whatever the dispute, the primary right of members is to see association business conducted according to properly adopted[159] regulations and procedures. Courts are prepared to oversee the observance of contractual rights and the correct interpretation of rules[160] and will also consider whether rules are "reasonable".[161] In a disciplinary case, for example, an association's action must be based on a valid rule prohibiting the act in question,[162] and any mental or conduct elements in the prohibition must be satisfied.[163] The power to impose particular penalties must similarly derive from established rules,[164] and the accused is entitled to a reasoned explanation when a harsh penalty or maximum suspension is imposed.[165] Besides having substantive authority, an association is bound to follow prescribed procedures in matters such as notice periods or the proper composition of tribunals, and the powers of review panels or appeal committees are confined to those set out in the authorising rules.

---

[158] See, for example: *In the Matter of Eric Lamaze* (September 19, 2000), Canadian Centre for Ethics in Sport (E. Ratushny, adj.) (non-selection for Sydney Olympics even though arbitrator overruled suspension for use of cocaine); *Hooper v. Canadian Soccer Assn.* (SDRCC-07-0051, June 15, 2007, J. Welbourne, arb.) (players suspended for not taking part in series of games).

[159] For a failure to enact eligibility rules properly, see, *University of Windsor v. Canadian Intercollegiate Athletic Union*, [1975] O.J. No. 2551, 11 O.R. (2d) 119 (Ont. H.C.J.). On unauthorized amendment of rules, see, *Kane v. Canadian Ladies' Golf Assn.*, [1992] P.E.I.J. No. 110, 102 Nfld. & P.E.I.R. 218 (P.E.I.T.D. (In Chambers)) (team selection criteria).

[160] See: *Lee v. Showmen's Guild of Great Britain*, [1952] 2 Q.B. 329 (C.A.) (showman charged with "unfair competition"); *Baker v. Jones*, [1954] 2 All E.R. 553 (Q.B.D.) (rules of British Amateur Weightlifters' Association); *Australian Football League v. Carlton Football Club*, [1998] 2 V.R. 546 (C.A.) (charge of "unduly" interfering with umpire).

[161] See, *Hanson v. Ontario Universities Athletic Assn.*, [1975] O.J. No. 2557, 11 O.R. (2d) 193 (Ont. H.C.J.) (rule restricting participation to five years).

[162] See, for example, *Rebagliati v. International Olympic Committee*, CAS 002, O.G. Nagano, February 12, 1998 (in the absence of agreement with the Fédération Internationale de Ski, marijuana was not a banned substance).

[163] See, *McGarrigle v. Canadian Interuniversity Sport*, [2003] O.J. No. 1842, 123 A.C.W.S. (3d) 6 (Ont. S.C.J.) (whether coach "knowingly" allowed use of ineligible athlete). On the elements of doping infractions, see Chapter 3, "Organizations and Regulations", section D, 1.

[164] See, *Vancouver Hockey Club Ltd. v. 8 Hockey Ventures Inc.*, [1987] B.C.J. No. 2074, 47 D.L.R. (4th) 51 (B.C.S.C.) (NHL attempted to impose a fine of USD $310,000; league by-laws allowed a maximum of USD $10,000).

[165] See, *Rankin v. Alberta Curling Federation Appeals Committee*, [2005] A.J. No. 1759, 262 D.L.R. (4th) 484 (Alta. Q.B.) (code of conduct; varying levels of misconduct when curlers caused disruption at tournament).

The obligation to observe rules and follow procedures also applies to members. Courts often refuse relief when a decision-making process of the association is still available to the complainant.[166] Someone who has expressly agreed to exhaust internal remedies must justify going to court,[167] and the *Arbitration Act, 1991*[168] limits jurisdiction where a dispute is subject to an arbitration agreement. Recourse to the courts will not be rejected if a domestic process can be shown to be futile or unfair.[169] Long delay in a hearing may, for example, involve undue hardship,[170] and a court order may be the only appropriate remedy where there is an urgent need for a determination or where participation rights are at risk. There is also no obligation to exhaust a process that does not comply with the rules of the association or the jurisdiction of a committee.[171]

By-Law Ten of Hockey Canada emphasizes that membership is voluntary and that the organization is self-governing. The first recourse of members "in the event of any dispute, difference or question" is the rights of appeal and procedures outlined in the constitutional documents and other rules (see, By-Law 1003), including the general procedures of the National Appeals Committee (see, By-Law Twelve). By-Law 1007 further provides that it is a violation of the Hockey Canada constitution to have recourse to the courts prior to exhausting domestic remedies and rights of appeal. Breach of this By-Law potentially exposes a member to suspension and the payment of legal costs (see, By-Law 1007(a)-(d)). Similarly, Statute 21 of the IIHF provides that,

---

[166] See, for example: *Gretzky v. Ontario Minor Hockey Assn.*, [1975] O.J. No. 2540, 64 D.L.R. (3d) 467 (Ont. H.C.J.); *Trumbley v. Saskatchewan Amateur Hockey Assn.*, [1986] S.J. No. 151, 49 Sask.R. 296 (Sask. C.A.); *Fox c. Club communautaire hockey mineur Edmundston*, [2007] A.N.-B. no 490, 2007 NBBR 278 (N.B.Q.B.) (court ordered hearing before appeal committee).

[167] See: *Lawlor v. Union of Post Office Workers*, [1965] Ch. 712; *Leigh v. National Union of Railwaymen*, [1970] Ch. 326. A complaint of discrimination may, however, be taken to a human rights commission; see, *Richard v. Brandon Youth Hockey Assn.* (October 16, 2006, File No. 04 EN 467, Manitoba Human Rights Commission, M. Lynne Harrison, adj.) (unlawful reprisal).

[168] S.O. 1991, c. 17, ss. 6-8. On alternative dispute resolution, see Chapter 2, "Legal Fundamentals and Equality Rights", section C.

[169] See: *White v. Kuzych*, [1951] A.C. 585 at 601, [1951] 3 D.L.R. 641 at 651 (P.C.) (no reason to believe appeal would have been useless; federation capable of giving honest attention to complaint); *Harelkin v. University of Regina*, [1979] S.C.J. No. 59, [1979] 2 S.C.R. 561 at 587-94 (S.C.C.) (adequacy of alternative remedy; breach of natural justice curable on appeal); *Lawson v. Atlantic Federation of Musicians, Local 571*, [1986] N.S.J. No. 214, 74 N.S.R. (2d) 131 (N.S.T.D.) (improper notice and apprehension of bias).

[170] See: *Orchard v. Tunney*, [1957] S.C.J. No. 26, [1957] S.C.R. 436 (S.C.C.) (appeal to union's international executive in Miami); *Barrieau v. United States Trotting Assn.*, [1987] N.B.J. No. 110, 78 N.B.R. (2d) 128 (N.B.T.D.) (time and location of appeal from suspension of licence).

[171] See, *Vancouver Hockey Club Ltd. v. 8 Hockey Ventures Inc.*, [1987] B.C.J. No. 2074, 47 D.L.R. (4th) 51 at 67 (B.C.S.C.), *per* Dohm J.: "...there is no jurisdiction for the President to provide for 'appeals' from his own Order. ... there is no obligation to exhaust internal remedies if the remedy 'is unreasonable, impractical and ineffective'".

IIHF member national associations are obliged to abide by the Statutes, Bylaws, Regulations and decisions of the IIHF and to undertake not to involve any third party whatsoever outside of the IIHF in the resolution of any dispute arising and to submit any such dispute to the jurisdiction of the IIHF as specified in the IIHF Statutes, Bylaws and Regulations.[172]

The Disciplinary Committee of the IIHF is constituted by Statute 52 and is bound to act in accordance with the Disciplinary Regulations. Appeals from the committee and from other bodies of the IIHF are lodged with the Council (see, IIHF Statute 44). Once appeal and review processes within the IIHF have been fully exercised, disputes concerning the interpretation or application of IIHF regulations and disputes between member national associations must be settled by arbitration before the Court of Arbitration for Sport (see, IIHF Statutes 54-57).[173]

## c.  *Fairness and Natural Justice*

Besides conforming to established rules, a decision must be fair. Fairness is a flexible standard that depends on the nature of the dispute, the structure of the organization and the interests at stake.[174] A fair determination is one made by an impartial tribunal honestly applying the relevant material and giving due consideration to different points of view.[175] In eligibility and selection cases, fairness calls for timely disclosure of the applicable regulations, criteria or objections to make candidates aware of where they stand. Disgruntled applicants should also be given the opportunity to present their case. A full hearing is particularly required in disciplinary proceedings, since membership rights are liable to be forfeited and there is an accusation of blameworthiness. Where a member risks sanction, suspension or expulsion, a voluntary association is bound to observe the "rules of natural justice":[176]

> The content of the principles of natural justice is flexible and depends on the circumstances...the most basic requirements are...notice, opportunity to make representations, and an unbiased tribunal. A member must be given notice of the cause for which he is to be expelled. It is insufficient merely to give notice that the conduct of a member is to be considered at a meeting...The member who is to be expelled must also be given an opportunity to respond to the allegations...an

---

[172]  IIHF Statutes and Bylaws, Statute 21, online: <http://www.iihf.com>.

[173]  See Chapter 2, "Legal Fundamentals and Equality Rights", section C.

[174]  See, *Kane v. University of British Columbia*, [1980] S.C.J. No. 32, [1980] 1 S.C.R. 1105 at 1112-13 (S.C.C.) (trappings of a court are not required but there must be a high standard of justice when professional interests are at stake).

[175]  *Cf.* "...the board were under a duty to reach an honest conclusion without bias and not in pursuance of any capricious policy": *McInnes v. Onslow-Fane*, [1978] 3 All E.R. 211 at 221 (Ch. Div.), *per* Megarry V-C.

[176]  See, R. Dussault & L. Borgeat, *Administrative Law: A Treatise*, 2d ed., vol. 4 (Toronto: Carswell, 1990) at 243-336.

unbiased tribunal is one of the central requirements of natural justice. However, given the close relationship amongst members of voluntary associations, it seems rather likely that members of the relevant tribunal will have had some previous contact with the issue in question, and... will have at least an indirect interest.[177]

The accused party is entitled to an accessible[178] hearing with an adequate period of notice. There should be proper notice of the facts and offence alleged, and only those allegations may form the basis of the decision.[179] The essence of a fair hearing is that it gives a reasonable opportunity to rebut or challenge the case being made, for example by allowing cross-examination of those who are making accusations.[180] The hearing does not have to conform to the procedures of a formal trial[181] with strict application of the rules of evidence, and it need not be "live" since a conference session or documentary process may be fair in the circumstances. Legal representation is also not necessary.[182] Associations are free to adopt rules disallowing the use of counsel, although it is advisable to allow parties to bring lawyers when the case turns on legal issues or when serious interests are at stake. Greater procedural protection is required in relation to final decisions, as opposed to interim hearings. Where an initial determination has been made unfairly, it is possible for an association to cure defects through further notice[183] or through a review hearing. A court will evaluate the overall process and may recognize that original irregularities were ironed out in the association's system of appeals.[184] A decision will, however, be quashed if an appeal panel only serves to compound errors or acts without authority.[185]

---

[177] *Lakeside Colony of Hutterian Brethren v. Hofer*, [1992] S.C.J. No. 87, [1992] 3 S.C.R. 165 at 195-97 (S.C.C.), *per* Gonthier J.

[178] "To set up a hearing at a time and place and in such a manner that one party can not afford to be heard is clearly a denial of justice": *Barrieau v. United States Trotting Assn.*, [1987] N.B.J. No. 110, 78 N.B.R. (2d) 128 at 134 (N.B.T.D.), *per* Meldrum J.

[179] See, *McGarrigle v. Canadian Interuniversity Sport*, [2003] O.J. No. 1842, 123 A.C.W.S. (3d) 6 (Ont. S.C.J.) (use of ineligible basketball player; penalty imposed on coach for behaviour not raised in original charge). See also, *D'Arcy v. Adamson* (1913), 29 T.L.R. 367 (Ch. Div.) (injunction granted when club member expelled without hearing and for reasons of which he had no notice).

[180] See, *Paterson v. Skate Canada*, [2004] A.J. No. 1542, [2006] 3 W.W.R. 158 (Alta. Q.B.) (allegations of dishonesty and harassment against professional skating coaches).

[181] See: *Stachiw v. Saskatoon Softball Umpires Assn.*, [1985] S.J. No. 531, [1985] 5 W.W.R. 651 (Sask. Q.B.) (suspension for beer drinking during game; reasonable opportunity given to refute allegation); *Street v. B.C. School Sports*, [2005] B.C.J. No. 1523, 2005 BCSC 958 (B.C.S.C.) (coach suspended for recruiting violations; errors in procedure did not amount to denial of natural justice).

[182] See, *Enderby Town Football Club. v. Football Association Ltd.*, [1971] 1 Ch. 591 (C.A.).

[183] See, *Dunford (Litigation guardian of) v. Springers Gymnastics Club Inc.*, [2001] M.J. No. 399, [2002] 1 W.W.R. 480 (Man. Q.B.) (decision not to renew memberships).

[184] See: *Calvin v. Carr*, [1979] 1 N.S.W.L.R. 1 (P.C.); *Harelkin v. University of Regina*, [1979] S.C.J. No. 59, [1979] 2 S.C.R. 561 (S.C.C.).

[185] See, *McGarrigle v. Canadian Interuniversity Sport*, [2003] O.J. No. 1842, 123 A.C.W.S. (3d) 6 (Ont. S.C.J.).

As noted, in the closed world of sports organizations, it is difficult to empanel tribunal members who are entirely removed from the dispute. Members may bring their general knowledge and expertise to the case, but must be free from bias or an appearance of bias.[186] Fairness requires panels that are independent in their constitutional structures and composed of members who are able to make their own decision: the institutional arrangement is particularly suspect where one group is called upon to review its own decision. Bias may be manifested by a hostile attitude, by pre-judging the case and not bringing an open mind to the issues, or by private or unilateral dealings with one side.[187] Bias is also apparent when an officer has a conflict of interest or stake in the outcome,[188] and there is particular risk of partiality when there is a personal or professional relationship with a party or with a rival competitor.[189]

## 2. Eligibility and Transfer

### a. *International*

Eligibility for international and Olympic competition is subject to Bylaws 204-212 of the International Ice Hockey Federation ("IIHF")[190] and the IIHF International Transfer Regulations ("IT Reg.").[191] Participation in championships is subject to minimum standards, and the eligibility of players for the Olympics is "as permitted by the IIHF and accepted by the IOC" (see, IIHF Bylaw 204). Given the constant movement of players between Canada and the United States, the "USAH/HC/CHL Transfer & Release Agreement"[192] makes special provision

---

[186]  See, S. Blake, *Administrative Law in Canada*, 4th ed. (Markham, ON: LexisNexis Butterworths, 2006) at 101-16. In Australia, only actual bias will invalidate the decision of a private tribunal, although a test of reasonable suspicion of bias may apply to the conduct of tribunal members during the hearing; see: *Maloney v. New South Wales National Coursing Assn. Ltd.*, [1978] 1 N.S.W.L.R. 161 (C.A.); *Dale v. New South Wales Trotting Club Ltd.*, [1978] 1 N.S.W.L.R. 551 (C.A.).

[187]  See, *Kane v. University of British Columbia*, [1980] S.C.J. No. 32, [1980] 1 S.C.R. 1105 (S.C.C.).

[188]  See, *Hooper v. Canadian Soccer Assn.* (SDRCC 07-0051, June 15, 2007, J. Welbourn, arb.) (no bias, conflict of interest or improper motive in decision to suspend players).

[189]  The issue of bias must be raised at the tribunal hearing; see, *Eikelenboom (c.o.b. Eiklyn Farms) v. Holstein Assn. of Canada*, [2004] N.S.J. No. 330, 226 N.S.R. (2d) 235 (N.S.C.A.).

[190]  See, IIHF Statutes and Bylaws, 2008-2012 (July 2008); see further, Chapter 3, "Organizations and Regulations", section B, 1. Under By-law 205.3, players who are eligible for in-line are not necessarily eligible to play for their country in ice hockey competitions. An earlier version of By-law 205.1.3 was considered in *Nabokov v. International Ice Hockey Federation*, CAS/2001/A/357, January 31, 2002 (player had previously represented Kazakstan and was ineligible to play for the Russian Olympic team).

[191]  See, IIHF International Transfer Regulations (May 2009). See also, Hockey Canada, Regulations (amended to June 2008), K, Appendix K1; "Hockey Canada Direction and Notes for Transfers and Appeals" (July 2007).

[192]  See, Hockey Canada, Regulations (amended to June 2008), K, Appendix K2.

for eligibility and transfer mainly in relation to players of junior age or younger. This Agreement is made between USA Hockey Inc., Hockey Canada and the Canadian Hockey League ("CHL") and runs from year to year unless amended (see, Article VIII). Special appeal, mediation and arbitration processes are established to deal with disputes, subject to teams paying an initial cost bond of USD $1000 when filing appeals (see, Article VI). (A further aspect of international movement is the organization of incoming and outgoing tours which are subject to sanction and approval by Hockey Canada.[193])

To compete in IIHF or Olympic competition, a player "must be under the jurisdiction of a member national ice hockey association of the IIHF and be a citizen of the country he represents" (see, IIHF Bylaw 205.1.1). Players who have represented a country and who later acquire another citizenship are not disqualified provided they are still citizens of the original country (see, IIHF Bylaw 205.1.4). Players who have changed citizenship or who hold multiple citizenships may represent an association for the first time after playing in national competition for two consecutive years (see, IIHF Bylaw 205.1.6-7). Once a player has played for a country, a change in representation is permitted, provided the player has the required citizenship, receives an IIHF transfer card, and participates for four consecutive years exclusively in the national competition of the new country while not representing the previous country (see, IIHF Bylaw 205.1.3). This change may be made only once and is "final and irrevocable". There is no waiting period when a change of citizenship results from the partitioning or uniting of countries (see, IIHF Bylaw 2005.1.5).

The registration of an ineligible player carries "disciplinary consequences" for the national association and player. Under IIHF Bylaw 205.2.1,

> If the ineligibility of one or more players is proved during a championship then the games played by the team with an ineligible player shall be forfeited and the ineligible player dismissed from the tournament.[194]

An earlier version of this rule was considered in *Czech Olympic Committee v. IIHF*,[195] where Ulf Samuelsson had played for Sweden at the 1998 Winter Olympics in Nagano despite losing his citizenship under Swedish law after he acquired American citizenship. The results and ranking in preliminary division play were challenged by the Czechs with a view to changing the draw of opponents in the quarter finals, but the IIHF Directorate responsible for the Olympics decided to maintain "the ranking as from the games results". Although Samuelsson was found to be "clearly ineligible", the Court of Arbitration for Sport held that the Czechs did not have standing to challenge game results since

---

[193] Hockey Canada, Regulations (amended to June 2008), K, Appendix K2, Regulation A (definition), D. An "international tour" relates to games involving teams from outside Hockey Canada or USA Hockey.

[194] IIHF Statutes and Bylaws, Bylaw 205.2.1, online: <http://www.iihf.com>.

[195] CAS 004-005, O.G. Nagano, February 18, 1998.

they had not played Sweden. It would be unfair to allow them to improve their position, and it would distort the purpose of the rule to punish teams other than the one at fault by causing them to be drawn against stronger opponents. Bylaw 205.2.1 now provides that,

> In exceptional circumstances, the Directorate may vary the application of this clause in the best interests of the competition applying the principle that the team at fault should not take benefit of any ranking and with the objective not to disadvantage, even indirectly, other teams taking part in the competition. Any decision taken by the Directorate in this respect shall not be regarded as a precedent.[196]

Under the "USAH/HC/CHL Transfer & Release Agreement", players claiming dual citizenship must, at their first registration or affiliation in junior hockey, choose their citizenship for playing purposes. Once declared, no change is permitted (see, Article II, B.5). This Agreement governs the movement of eligible players between member leagues and teams and places the main responsibility for enforcement on the two federations (see, Article I). A team's nationality depends on its geographical location, and all transfers must be processed through its home federation (see, Article X, G). The transnational operation of the CHL is subject to particular provision, including rules relating to involuntary movement and trades by CHL teams (see, Article II, C). Special rules also deal with temporary affiliation with junior teams (see, Article V) and end-of-season release from junior teams (see, Article IV, B.5). The general principle of the Agreement is that movement by eligible players requires a properly completed release from the player's outgoing team, a transfer from the outgoing federation and the payment of sums due (see, Article II, A). The categories of players ineligible for transfer include those under suspension, provided rights of hearing and appeal have been afforded (see, Article II, B.1.2). The general period for transfers is between June 1 and February 10 in each playing season since rosters are frozen at the latter date; players may be contacted after their team has been eliminated from competition, and there is a designated tryout period for initiating the transfer process (see, Article III). Release fees are paid by the incoming team to the outgoing team, although payments at the Major Junior level are made through the CHL office (see, Article III, D.1). Each federation establishes its transfer fees (see, Article IV, A.2), while off-season releases are subject to a schedule of maximum fees varying according to the level of play (see, Article IV, B.1). This schedule also applies to junior age players securing release from NCAA programs during their first season of participation on the NCAA team (see, Article IV, B.7).

The IIHF seeks to maintain "good order" in the international transfer of players, while also regulating eligibility and enforcing suspensions (see, IIHF Bylaw 206). The IT Regulations also deal with the obligation to release players who have been selected for national teams and with the obligation of players to

---

[196] IIHF Statutes and Bylaws, Bylaw 205.2.1, online: <http://www.iihf.com>.

respond (see, IT Reg. I, 10). Players cannot transfer during the period when they are under a recognized suspension (see, IT Reg. I, 2.8), although arrangements may be made for serving the suspension with the new team and federation (see, Hockey Canada, Regulation H.,5). A move to a new country requires an International Transfer Card ("ITC") signed by the player and the national associations involved and confirmed by the IIHF.[197] Playing without a valid card is subject to disciplinary procedures (see, IIHF Bylaw 210), and the player who moves without approval must establish 18 months of residence before being permitted to play in the new member association (see, IIHF Bylaw 211). Breach of the bylaws or transfer regulations is subject to special disciplinary provisions allowing the IIHF Disciplinary Committee to impose sanctions such as caution, censure, fine or suspension (see, IT Reg. III).

The transfer process begins with negotiations between the teams and preparation of the ITC by the new team. Where a national association refuses to sign an ITC, the player may appeal to the IIHF which must resolve the case in accordance with the IT Regulations (see, IIHF Bylaw 209). The player and new team are entitled to be informed of the refusal and basis of objection (see, IT Reg. I, 2.3). An association may refuse to sign where a player has not fulfilled contractual or financial obligations to the former team, but the failure of the two teams to agree on compensation is not a ground of refusal (see, IT Reg. I, 2.2). A transfer may be unlimited, or it may be limited to a specified team and specific duration (see, IIHF Bylaw 208; IT Reg. I, 3). A limited transfer may be changed to unlimited by following regular transfer procedures (see, IT Reg. I, 3.10). The transfer deadline for associations in the Northern Hemisphere is January 31 of the applicable season (see, IT Reg. I, 3.11).[198]

Players under 18 may complete international transfers in accordance with regular procedures, but are also permitted to move through a letter of approval from their former association (see, IT Reg. I, 4.1). Children under 10 who moved to a new country with their families may play in the new country without approval of the transfer (see, IT Reg. I, 4.6). The national eligibility of a player who moved before the age of 18 may be proved by adequate documentation and is subject to the requirement of two years participation within the new association (see, IT Reg. I, 4.7). Hockey Canada Regulations restrict the international transfer of players of minor hockey age, except that players residing with their parents may move with their parents (see, Regulations H.8(b), K.5, K.18). Special provision is made for residential schools, and transfer is permitted for players of Midget age where they will be playing Major Junior hockey (see, Regulation K.6). By Hockey Canada Regulation K.6(b),

> No player of second year Midget eligibility or under may be transferred from Hockey Canada to USA Hockey unless a player resides with his parent and the

---

[197] The service fees charged should reflect the costs of executing the transfer, and the former association shall not charge more than CHF 500 to complete the procedure: IT Reg. I, 8.2. On incoming and outgoing transfer fees, see, Hockey Canada, Regulations (amended to June 2008), K.24-25.

[198] On further release dates and conditions, see, Hockey Canada Regulations, F.45, F.46, F.47.

parent changes his place of residence to the USA and the player continues to reside with his parent.[199]

Section II of the International Transfer Regulations includes additional "Provisions on Stability of Professional Player Contracts" and focuses on moves made in breach of contracts.[200] These rules were specially modified in 2009 and supplement the general approval processes. Section II applies to players who have concluded written contracts of specific duration that provide for payments beyond expenses (see, IT Reg. II, 1). Professionals are considered to be in breach of contract unless there is just cause for termination or the contract has been brought to an end through the expiry of its term or mutual agreement (see, IT Reg. II, 2). A player in breach of contract is liable to suspension, and disciplinary measures may be applied against persons, teams or organizations that attempt to induce a breach of contract (see, IT Reg. II, 3, 4). A transfer during the term of the contract may occur where the former team, the new team and the player reach an agreement (see, IT Reg. II, 4.4). Where a transfer is refused because an association claims that a player is still under contract, the regulations provide for the dispute to be referred to the General Secretary and to the Executive Committee of the IIHF (see, IT Reg. II, 5).

The international transfer process was considered in *Labbé c. Assoc. Canadienne de Hockey*,[201] where François Labbé obtained an interlocutory injunction against Hockey Canada, Hockey Québec and the Quebec Senior League to prevent any interference with his playing for Le Garaga of Saint-Georges-de-Beauce. Labbé had previously signed with Lada Togliatti of the Super League, but lawfully terminated this contract when the Russian team failed to pay salary and was USD $101,000 in arrears. The Russian Ice Hockey Federation made no mention of these circumstances when it advised the IIHF that Labbé still had contractual obligations and should not be allowed to play elsewhere. The court found that the IT Regulations had not been followed, that Labbé was not obliged to work for an employer who did not pay and that Hockey Canada had not properly informed Labbé of his status and rights of appeal. The injunction was granted because of the breach of Labbé's rights and the potential irreparable harm to him and to Le Garaga. Orders have similarly been granted to allow transfers to Canadian teams where players under the age of 18 signed contracts without independent legal advice and where the contracts made inadequate provision for remuneration.[202]

---

[199] Online: <http://www.hockeycanada.ca/index.php/ci_id/66601/la_id/1.htm>, Regulation K.6(b).

[200] See further: Chapter 8, "Competition Law and Labour Law", section E (issues in competition law, including out-of-contact restraints); Chapter 9, "National Hockey League", section E (professional players' contracts and remedies for enforcement).

[201] [2004] J.Q. no 727 (Que. C.S.).

[202] See: *Kitchener Dutchmen Inc. v. Russian Ice Hockey Federation*, [1998] O.J. No. 970 (Ont. Gen. Div.) (contracts with Torpedo Yaroslavl; on application for interlocutory injunction, Ontario court has jurisdiction to consider enforcement of contracts); *Kootenay Ice Hockey Club Ltd. v. Slovak Ice Hockey Assn.*, [2001] B.C.J. No. 99, 2001 BCSC 51 (B.C.S.C.) (Kosice refused further release unless paid USD $10,000; contract with Kosice was probably void).

The entry of Russian and European players into the NHL was accelerated in the early 1990s following the collapse of the Soviet Union, when CSKA Moscow ("Central/Red Army") was a particular focus of recruiting.[203] In 1993, Moscow Dynamo agreed to release Alexei Yashin to the Ottawa Senators in exchange for four annual payments of CDN $100,000. When a payment was overdue in October 1995, Yashin briefly joined CSKA in furtherance of one of his recurring salary and contractual disputes with the Senators, and the IIHF duly threatened sanctions against both the player and the Russian Ice Hockey Federation since Yashin's contract with the Senators rendered him ineligible to play elsewhere.[204] From 1994, entry into the NHL by players under contract with teams within the IIHF was subject to the "Memorandum of Agreement" between the NHL and the IIHF,[205] although Russia declined to participate in later versions. The Agreement covering 1994-97 provided that players under contract could be released to NHL teams in consideration of payment to the IIHF of a general fee of USD $10.4 million to support the development of hockey outside North America. Under this system, where a player signed with a NHL team, payments were distributed to the originating national association and its member team. Subsequent negotiation to renew the Agreement focussed on the level of payments, the number of players leaving Europe and the practice of assigning the vast majority of players to the North American minor leagues.[206] A two-year Agreement in 2005 provided for a basic payment of USD $200,000 for each of the first 45 players signed; this deal was ratified by the IIHF member associations of the Czech Republic, Slovakia, Sweden, Finland, Germany and Switzerland.

By 2007, average salaries in the former Russian Super League had reached USD $400,000, so that the teams and the Russian Ice Hockey Federation preferred to negotiate vastly increased compensation. Teams attempted to have their employment contracts recognized and enforced, but were frustrated by

---

[203] See, *Professional Hockey Club Central Sports Club of the Army v. Detroit Red Wings, Inc.,* 787 F.Supp. 706 (E.D. Mich., 1992) (rights, remedies and jurisdiction in relation to Viacheslav Kozlov; contracts with CSKA allegedly signed under duress). On the signing of an agency agreement at this time, see, *Gandler v. Nazarov,* 1995 WL 363814 (S.D.N.Y., 1995).

[204] See: "Russians take offensive in war of words with NHL" *The Globe and Mail* (Toronto: October 11, 1995) at C8; "Red Army ends battle with NHL temporarily" *The Globe and Mail* (Toronto: October 16, 1995) at D6. On free agency rights under Yashin's 1995 contract, see, *Yashin v. National Hockey League,* [2000] O.J. No. 3306, 192 D.L.R. (4th) 747 (Ont. S.C.J.); see further, Chapter 9, "National Hockey League", section B, 3.

[205] See, A.N. Wise & B.S. Meyer, *International Sports Law and Business,* vol. 1 (The Hague: Kluwer Law International, 1997) at 655-59. See also: *Central Sports Army Club v. Arena Associates, Inc.,* 952 F.Supp. 181 (S.D.N.Y., 1997) (team and International Hockey League were not members of IIHF); *Finnish Ice Hockey Assn. v. International Ice Hockey Federation,* CAS 2004/A/757, October 25, 2005 (Sean Bergenheim drafted and signed by N.Y. Islanders from Jokerit Helsinki; half-payment when player returns to previous team).

[206] On quotas and the European presence in North American hockey, see Chapter 2, "Legal Fundamentals and Equality Rights", section E, 5.

article 80 of the *Labour Code of the Russian Federation*[207] that permitted employees to terminate contracts by giving two-weeks' written notice. Teams also had little success in obtaining injunctions from American courts to prevent players joining the NHL.[208] Two prominent cases involved the top picks in the 2004 NHL entry draft. Alexander Ovechkin had been selected first overall by the Washington Capitals but signed with Moscow Dynamo during the lost lockout season of 2004-05.[209] Dynamo sent Ovechkin a qualifying offer for 2005-06, when he preferred to join Avangard Omsk subject to a power of termination should he sign with a NHL team before July 20, 2005. When Ovechkin exercised this power and signed with the Capitals, Dynamo argued that under league regulations their matching offer gave them exclusive rights to the player's services. This claim was upheld by the arbitration committee of the Russian Ice Hockey Federation after a hearing at which Ovechkin was not represented. In *Moscow Dynamo v. Ovechkin*,[210] the team was unsuccessful in enforcing the award because the court was not satisfied that the expired contract and "patchwork of documents" constituted evidence of a written agreement to submit the case to arbitration. In August 2006, Evgeni Malkin was spirited into the hands of the Pittsburgh Penguins even though he had signed a contract with Metallurg Magnitogorsk, which suffered the further loss of the standard USD $200,000 when they signed a replacement from Sparta Prague.[211] Malkin gave the statutory two-weeks' notice and was able to remain with the Penguins when Magnitogorsk were denied a preliminary injunction. In exercising its discretion, the court considered a verbal promise that Malkin would be allowed to play in the NHL and evidence of duress when he was required to sign a second contract.[212]

---

[207] Federal Law No. 197-FZ of 2001 (December 31, 2001). In the Evgeni Malkin case, Metallurg Magnitogorsk objected to the fax giving the notice of termination; see, "Russian team claims Malkin's resignation is unreadable, illegal" *The Globe and Mail* (Toronto: August 19, 2006) at S5.

[208] Lokomotiv Yaroslavl filed suit in 2006 in relation to Andrei Taratukhin, of the Calgary Flames, and Alexei Mikhnov, of the Edmonton Oilers. CSKA Moscow was unsuccessful in 2005 in an action involving Nikolai Zherdev of the Columbus Blue Jackets. See also, *Central Sports Army Club v. Arena Associates, Inc.*, 952 F.Supp. 181 (S.D.N.Y., 1997) (elements of interference with contract not shown).

[209] See also, *Lincoln Hockey, LLC v. Semin*, No. 05-02094, 2005 U.S. Dist. LEXIS 34047 (D.D.C., 2005) (player signed with Capitals returned to Russia during lockout rather than play in minors; injunction denied).

[210] 412 F.Supp. 2d 24 (D.D.C., 2006) (the documents showed "that Ovechkin wished to end his relationship with Dynamo once and for all" at 29, *per* Sullivan U.S. Dist. J.).

[211] See: "Malkin's great escape ends in L.A." *The Globe and Mail* (Toronto: August 18, 2006) at R5, R10 (passport manoeuvring at the Helsinki airport); "Malkin's departure has ripple effect" *The Globe and Mail* (Toronto: September 6, 2006) at R8 (comments by Dave King, coach of Magnitogorsk).

[212] See: "Penguins get to keep Malkin" *The Globe and Mail* (Toronto: November 15, 2006) (online); "Judge's Ruling on Malkin a Victory for NHL" *The Globe and Mail* (Toronto: November 16, 2006) at R11. The federal court dismissed the action on February 1, 2007. See generally: C. Miller, "Hockey's Cold War — Russia's Defiance of the IIHF and the Evgeny Malkin Affair" (2007) 17.1 Seton Hall J. of Sport and Ent. L. 163; J.P. Gleason, "From Russia with

In July 2007, the countries that had signed the 2005 agreement ratified a conditional transfer Agreement for 2007-11[213] prescribing deadlines for signing players who were under contract or subject to the NHL draft and anticipating an annual development fee of USD $9 million. A rate between USD $50,000 and USD $100,000, depending on draft round, would apply to players who are not on the NHL roster for at least 30 games in their first season. The associations subsequently exercised a right of renegotiation, so that a new Agreement was required after the 2007-08 season.[214] A meeting in January 2008 proposed that, except for first-round picks in the NHL draft, players under 22 (rather than 20) should first be offered back to their European teams before being sent to the minors. The age rules were then opposed by NHL teams that feared losing negotiation rights, since players drafted from outside North America must now be signed within the same two-year period allowed for signing Major Junior players (see, CBA (2005), article 8.6(a)). A new agreement failed to materialize following initial opposition by the Swedish association and a decision taken by teams in the Czech league. Negotiation with individual teams would, therefore, be required when a NHL team proposed to sign a player who was under contract.[215]

In 2008, the Russian Super League was reconstituted in expanded form as the 24-team Continental Hockey League ("KHL") under the presidency of oil and gas magnate, Alexander Medvedev. At a meeting of the IIHF in July 2008, the KHL and the NHL apparently agreed to respect each other's contracts, and in September 2008 the KHL withdrew objections to five transfers to NHL teams. Any accord was, however, undermined when Alexander Radulov, who was under contract with the Nashville Predators, signed with Salavat Yulaev Ufa for USD $13 million tax-free over three years. The NHL refused to consider compensation, insisting that Radulov honour his remaining obligation to the Predators, and the IIHF was unable to resolve Radulov's status. He duly played for Salavat Yulaev Ufa during the 2008-09 season, having been suspended by the Predators.

In the absence of a transfer agreement and with the KHL available as a rival employer, only seven Russian players were selected in the NHL's 2009 Entry Draft. In 2009, Article I, 5.3 of the IIHF International Transfer Regulations also assumed importance:

> Any player of a non-member organisation, without an IIHF transfer agreement, who wishes to join an IIHF member national Association (regardless of whether he is seeking to return to his former member national association) must apply for an

---

Love: The Legal Repercussions of the Recruitment and Contracting of Foreign Players in the National Hockey League" (2008) 56 Buff. L. Rev. 599.

[213] See, "European hockey federations, leagues ratify new agreement" *Associated Press* (July 13, 2007).

[214] See, "European countries reopen transfer agreement with NHL" *Canadian Press* (December 13, 2007).

[215] See, "Europe Opts Out" *The Hockey News* (May 27, 2008) at 9.

ITC from the member national association of the country of his non-member organisation.[216]

Since the NHL was a "non-member organization" without a transfer agreement, players moving from the NHL to European teams would need an International Transfer Card signed by Hockey Canada or USA Hockey. Those associations would be in a position to determine whether contractual obligations had been met, and IIHF regulations and sanctions would be applicable.

## b. National

Eligibility for Hockey Canada competitions is a matter of time, space and registration. Hockey Canada Regulations establish divisions based on age (see, B.1), and teams are normally under the jurisdiction of the Branch in the geographic area in which they play their home games (see, B.7). It is the responsibility of Branches to implement residency registration regulations for the formation of teams within their Branch (see, F.1), although residential qualifications are not required for players registered with senior and junior teams (see, F.5). Senior competition is open to players of any age, so that the main eligibility rules are the general qualifications in Regulation F.6 that players must be amateurs, not subject to a recognized suspension and not members of a team under the jurisdiction of any other member of the IIHF. "Amateur" is defined as "one who is not participating in organized professional hockey" (see, A.3). "Participation" in this context is usually shown by the signing of a valid professional contract, so that in 2005 locked-out NHL players were not eligible for Allan Cup competition.[217]

Players below the junior division must play in the Branch that is the usual residence of their parents or of the parent or guardian holding legal custody as appointed by a court (see, F.2-3). On application, Hockey Canada may deem a player resident "in a Branch other than that where his parent is resident" and a Branch may deem a player resident "in a place within the Branch other than that where his parent is resident" (see, F.4). Until 2007, player qualification regulations required that the parent of a registered player live in the same "geographic sub-division" as the team.[218] This was then amended to give Branches flexibility in their registration systems, although zoning and territorial division[219] continue as the main means of allocation.[220] The local residence rule

---

[216] Online: <http://www.p2hl.org.pl/trasfery-miedzynarodowe.pdf>, Article I 5.3.

[217] In January 2005, Hockey Alberta held that Theo Fleury was not a locked-out player and so could play for the Horse Lake Thunder; see: "'They're going to pay', Fleury says after senior hockey appeal denied" *The Ottawa Citizen* (January 15, 2005) at C3; "Fleury gets OK to play senior" *The Ottawa Citizen* (January 22, 2005) at C2.

[218] For the previous qualifications, see, Hockey Canada, Regulations (amended to June 2006), F.3, F.6.

[219] On the reclassification of teams, see: *Dickie (Re)*, [1984] B.C.J. No. 439, 28 A.C.W.S. (2d) 177 (B.C.S.C.) (boundaries in lacrosse); *Missal (Litigation guardian of) v. Saskatchewan Amateur Hockey Assn.*, [1993] S.J. No. 38, 110 Sask.R. 247 (Sask. Q.B.); *Cranberry Portage Midget*

has been seen to promote community loyalty, balanced competition and fair opportunities, while avoiding "bidding wars", "raiding" and other abuses associated with win-at-all-costs strategies.[221] The general purpose of residence requirements and restrictions on transfers is to combat the disruptions in home and school life that occur when a player relocates in order to play for a team in the area.

A "team" normally consists of a group of qualified[222] team officials in charge of not less than 15 registered players in one age division (see, E.1). To maximize the availability of players, there is provision for team-to-team affiliation, special affiliation of players and the operation of multi-team "clubs" (see, E.9-39). By Hockey Canada Regulation F.11,

> Every player competing in the games provided by this Association and its Branches shall be a member of a team which is a member of this Association and shall, prior to competing in any league or championship game, be registered by the Branch and duly validated by the Branch Executive Director or his designate for the current playing season.[223]

Once registered, players remain members of their team until released or until they otherwise move in accordance with Regulations (see, F.13). When players are over-age within a club structure, they are considered to advance to the team of the next higher age division (see, F.13). The system of established registration is supported by prohibitions against "tampering", so that written permission from the current team is required before another team in a Hockey Canada Branch may invite a registered player to participate in training camp activities or games (see, J).

By Regulation H.1, a player desiring to transfer from one team to another within the Branch must first secure a release in writing from the club or team of which he is a member. "Release" means the unconditional discharge of a player from team or club membership (see, A.26). Even though a release has been obtained, the Branch Executive may disallow a transfer within the Branch (see, H.2). No release is required in certain circumstances, including where players were not registered during the previous season, where they change residence with their parents and where a higher age division is not available in the community (see, H.8). The Regulations also prescribe circumstances where returning players are deemed to be members of their previous team (see, H.9). The release deadline is January 10, so that players are ineligible to play with other teams in the current season after this date (see, F.45, 46; H.7).

---

*Winterhawks Hockey Team v. Manitoba Amateur Hockey Assn.*, [1990] M.J. No. 148, 20 A.C.W.S. (3d) 258 (Man. Q.B.); *Miramichi Minor Hockey Club Inc. v. New Brunswick Amateur Hockey Assn.*, [1999] N.B.J. No. 631, 95 A.C.W.S. (3d) 799, [1999] N.B.R. (2d) (Supp.) No. 26 (N.B.Q.B.) (boundary change was a constitutional matter requiring proper meeting).

[220] See for example, Hockey PEI Constitution (amended to August 2008), Regulation 20, Association Boundaries.

[221] See, *You and Your Child in Hockey* (Toronto: Ministry of Culture and Recreation/ Ontario Hockey Council, 1975) at 18-19.

[222] The qualifications include certification in relation to "Speak Out" and safety programs; see further, Chapter 5, "Be Safe: Off the Ice" and Chapter 6, "Play Safe: On the Ice".

[223] Online: <http://www.hockeycanada.ca/index.php/ci_id/66601/la_id/1.htm>, Regulation F.11.

Transfers between Branches[224] are conducted through the Hockey Canada Intranet system. The player is ineligible to compete in the new Branch until the transfer is approved or the appeal is allowed (see, K.17; By -Law 1212). The player first obtains the release from the current team and then delivers the application form to the Executive Director of the new Branch who makes application to the home Branch (see, K.8-10). The home Branch has five business days to reply and must state reasons when the application is rejected (see, K.11); no reply within the five days is taken as acceptance (see, K.12).[225] The appeal of Branch decisions is subject to the procedures of the National Appeals Committee prescribed in By-Law Twelve. Appeals must be brought within seven days of the impugned decision and must be in writing and accompanied by a fee of CDN $300 (see, By-Law 1203). Particular documentation is required for registration appeals relating to Inter-Branch transfers or the refusal of releases (see, By-Laws 1207-1208). The nature of the hearing is at the discretion of the National Appeals Committee and may include written presentations, conference calls or face-to-face hearings (see, By-Law 1218), although registration appeals are conducted primarily through written submissions. The appellant seeks to offer "compelling reasons" for the move, including reference to the position of the parents and academic considerations; the respondent refers to opportunities available in the home Branch.[226]

In spite of the availability of domestic appeals and the prohibition on premature recourse to the courts (see, By-Law 1007),[227] release and transfer cases have a history of litigation as frustrated players look to complete moves.[228] One case in 1975 involved a 14-year-old named Wayne. In *Gretzky v. Ontario Minor Hockey Assn.*,[229] the plaintiff-applicant, described as "exceptionally gifted", had left Brantford and was now living and attending school in Toronto. One purpose of the new residence was to play for the Toronto Nationals of the Metropolitan Toronto Hockey League, but Gretzky was yet to have his transfer approved. When the Metro League refused to accept Gretzky's playing card, Southey J. declined to grant an injunction to allow him to play because the case had not been taken to the appeal tribunal[230] and because Gretzky's age meant that

---

[224] See further, "Hockey Canada Direction and Notes for Transfers and Appeals" (July 2007).

[225] In contract law, silence does not normally amount to acceptance; see, *Felthouse v. Bindley* (1862), 11 C.B. (N.S.) 869, 142 E.R. 1037 (C.C.P.), affd (1863), 1 New Rep. 401 ("If I hear no more about him, I shall consider the horse mine").

[226] See, "Hockey Canada Direction and Notes for Transfers and Appeals" (July 2007), Appendix 1, "Appeal Submissions Information". See, *Steffes (Litigation guardian of) v. Hockey Canada*, [2003] O.J. No. 5885 (Ont. S.C.J.) (application to move from Michigan to Stratford; interim injunction refused).

[227] See Chapter 3, "Organizations and Regulations", section C, 1, b.

[228] On jurisdictions in Ontario and the MTHL, see, "Rival leagues fight for turf" *The Globe and Mail* (Toronto: June 8, 1996) at A24.

[229] [1975] O.J. No. 2540, 10 O.R. (2d) 759 (Ont. H.C.J.). Wayne Gretzky's fellow plaintiff was Brian Rorabeck, a 10th round pick in the 1980 NHL Entry Draft.

[230] See also: *Cummings v. McCallum*, [1981] O.J. No. 940, 11 A.C.W.S. (2d) 107 (Ont. H.C.J.) (hearing to decide whether prejudice caused by publication and termination of buffer zone);

any contractual rights were not mutually enforceable. Southey J. was also sympathetic to the arguments that it was undesirable to have teenage boys "induced to go from one city to another away from their homes for the purpose of playing hockey" and that a requirement of *bona fide* residence "could mean a residence that is not primarily for the purpose of playing hockey in a different municipality".[231]

Courts have recognized that associations need reasonable qualification rules for the orderly conduct of competition and have denied injunctions allowing free movement by players on the basis that regulations must be observed[232] and that courts should not assist breaches of agreement.[233] The balance of convenience[234] is often seen to favour retaining the residence and release system, which has been held not to involve any illegal combination[235] or prohibited discrimination.[236] Courts are nevertheless prepared to interpret rules to see that proper decisions have been made.[237]

---

*Godin c. Hockey Outaouais* (February 26, 2001, C.S. Hull, 550-05-010662-016, Trudel J.) (appeal and arbitration available; "Le tribunal ne doit pas s'ingérer dans les politiques du sport").

[231] *Gretzky v. Ontario Minor Hockey Assn.*, [1975] O.J. No. 2540, 10 O.R. (2d) 759 at 761 (Ont. H.C.J.).

[232] See: *Strummer Holdings Ltd. v. Costello*, [1982] S.J. No. 905, 19 Sask.R. 297 (Sask. Q.B.) (Midget AA Inter-Branch transfers not allowed); *McDowell v. Belleville Bobcats Junior B Hockey Club* (1986), 35 A.C.W.S. (2d) 149 (Ont. Dist. Ct.) (no release for playoffs); *Morrison v. British Columbia Amateur Hockey Assn.*, [1986] B.C.J. No. 1881, 13 C.P.R. (3d) 556 (B.C.S.C.) (changed zoning rules enforceable; majority's interpretation accepted); *Walton (Litigation guardian of) v. Saskatchewan Hockey Assn.*, [1998] S.J. No. 125, [1999] 1 W.W.R. 135 (Sask. Q.B.) (no illegality in committee's finding that player violated population subdivision guidelines); *Martino c. Hockey région Laval*, [2006] J.Q. no 14158, 2006 QCCS 5737 (Que. C.S.) (attempt to move from Midget A to Bantam CC).

[233] See: *Thornhill Islanders Hockey Club Inc. v. Metropolitan Toronto Hockey League*, [1985] O.J. No. 563, 33 A.C.W.S. (2d) 289 (Ont. H.C.J.) (participation in league contrary to association agreement and residency rule); *McLean v. Metropolitan Toronto Hockey League*, [1988] O.J. No. 1408, 11 A.C.W.S. (3d) 393 (Ont. H.C.J.) (plaintiff had lied about residency on document; no irreparable harm if he did not play in league). In *Bowman v. B.C. Amateur Hockey Assn.* (October 21, 2005), Kamloops, (B.C.S.C.), Powers J., the applicants alleged that the association was interfering with their agreements with junior teams; interim injunctions were denied.

[234] See: *Boduch v. Harper*, [1974] O.J. No. 2273, 10 O.R. (2d) 755 (Ont. H.C.J.) (player was not being put out of hockey); *Cummings v. McCallum*, [1981] O.J. No. 940, 11 A.C.W.S. (2d) 107 (Ont. H.C.J.) (players merely required to play in zone); *McDowell v. Belleville Bobcats Junior B Hockey Club* (1986), 35 A.C.W.S. (2d) 149 (Ont. Dist. Ct.).

[235] See, *Boduch v. Harper*, [1974] O.J. No. 2273, 10 O.R. (2d) 755 (Ont. H.C.J.) (mandatory injunction striking down system refused).

[236] See: *Strummer Holdings v. Costello*, [1982] S.J. No. 905, 19 Sask.R. 297 (Sask. Q.B.); *Solin v. B.C. Amateur Hockey Assn.* (1988), 9 C.H.R.R. D/5266 (B.C.H.R. Council) (parents lived in Finland; no discrimination in holding Midget AAA player ineligible); *Kanigan (Guardian ad litem of) v. Castlegar Minor Hockey Assn.*, [1996] B.C.J. No. 2431, 141 D.L.R. (4th) 563 (B.C.S.C.); *Beauchamp (Litigation guardian of) v. North Central Predators AAA Hockey Assn.*, [2004] O.J. No. 5275, 247 D.L.R. (4th) 745 (Ont. S.C.J.) (no breach of *Discriminatory Business Practices Act*), affd [2006] O.J. No. 2432 (Ont. C.A.) (appeal moot since appellant changed residence). It is, however, an unlawful reprisal to refuse a registration or transfer because a player has filed a human rights complaint; see, *Richard v. Brandon Youth Hockey Assn.*

In some cases, courts have allowed transfers to teams of choice or have acted to protect playing opportunities by preventing the removal of players from teams. An injunction may be issued when rules have been improperly altered,[238] when there is a *bona fide* reason for switching team[239] or when serious contractual issues are raised and the year's play is at risk.[240] The remedy will be allowed where a transfer involves no harm to the league and enables the player to pursue school work more conveniently.[241] An injunction may also issue to prevent irreparable injury in the form of lost professional opportunities.[242] If the player is the innocent victim of an internal dispute among association members or officers, an order will be granted to allow participation.[243]

Besides the Hockey Canada registration system, further eligibility issues may arise in relation to particular competitions or Games. An appeal adjudicator has, for example, refused to disallow a rule of the Canada Games limiting participation in one sport, so that an athlete was not permitted to compete in both hockey and ringette.[244] In the case of school[245] and university[246] competitions,

---

(October 16, 2006, File No. 04 EN 467, Manitoba Human Rights Commission, M. Lynne Harrison, adj.).

[237] See, for example, *Strummer Holdings v. Costello*, [1982] S.J. No. 905, 19 Sask.R. 297 (Sask. Q.B.). However, "minute legalistic analysis" is not favoured: *Gretzky v. Ontario Minor Hockey Assn.*, [1975] O.J. No. 2540, 10 O.R. (2d) 759 (Ont. H.C.J.); *Chantler v. Metropolitan Toronto Hockey League*, [1983] O.J. No. 3240, 44 O.R. (2d) 85 (Ont. H.C.J.).

[238] See, *North Shore Winter Club v. Pacific Coast Amateur Hockey Assn.*, [1985] B.C.J. No. 773, 35 A.C.W.S. (2d) 281 (B.C.S.C.) (conflict in residence rules; financial hardship).

[239] See, *McDonald v. Edmonton Metropolitan Hockey Assn.* (June 1, 1970), unreported (Alta. S.C.), Liberman J. (player began attending Catholic school out of community; release ordered to allow play for parochial team).

[240] See, *Holmes v. Metropolitan Toronto Hockey League*, [1984] O.J. No. 263, 24 A.C.W.S. (2d) 185 (Ont. H.C.J.).

[241] See, *Hebert v. Shawinigan Cataractes Hockey Club*, [1978] O.J. No. 3659, 22 O.R. (2d) 654 (Ont. H.C.J.) (transfer from QMJHL to Hawkesbury Hawks in Ottawa association; player could attend high school and play fewer games in smaller geographical area). See also, *Solin v. B.C. Amateur Hockey Assn.* (1988), 9 C.H.R.R. D/5266 (B.C.H.R. Council) at 5270 (residence based on avoiding parental abuse or obtaining better educational opportunities).

[242] See: *Sheddon v. Ontario Major Junior Hockey League*, [1978] O.J. No. 3273, 19 O.R. (2d) 1 (Ont. H.C.J.); *Kootenay Ice Hockey Club Ltd. v. Slovak Ice Hockey Assn.*, [2001] B.C.J. No. 99, 2001 BCSC 51 (B.C.S.C.) (international release; reduced chance of being drafted into NHL if season is lost).

[243] See: *Sheddon v. Ontario Major Junior Hockey League*, [1978] O.J. No. 3273, 19 O.R. (2d) 1 (Ont. H.C.J.) (dispute between commissioner and board of governors over trade); *Chantler v. Metropolitan Toronto Hockey League*, [1983] O.J. No. 3240, 44 O.R. (2d) 85 (Ont. H.C.J.).

[244] See, *Hekle and Team Manitoba v. Canada Games Council* (November 6, 2002, Internal Appeal Committee, D.W. Lech, adj.) (appeal adjudicator had no authority to change rule; rule benefited other athletes by creating opportunities).

[245] See, *St. Andrews College v. York Region Athletic Assn.*, [2000] O.J. No. 637, 95 A.C.W.S. (3d) 415 (Ont. S.C.J.) (clerical error in player eligibility list; executive exceeded its jurisdiction by thwarting discretion of league convenors).

[246] See, Canadian Interuniversity Sport, Eligibility Policy (September 2008). See also, *Hanson v. Ontario Universities Athletic Assn.*, [1975] O.J. No. 2557, 11 O.R. (2d) 193 (Ont. H.C.J.).

eligibility and transfer are subject to the rules and procedures of the relevant athletic associations.[247]

## 3.    Selection and Nomination

Selection disputes regularly occur in one-on-one sports and other events involving races or measured performances. Selections for major Games have been a significant source of litigation[248] and arbitral decisions[249] as athletes claim that the association deviated from established performance criteria, failed to select according to designated results or otherwise operated in an unfair manner. Coaches, officers and association representatives have also been aggrieved at not being nominated for positions. A tribunal, court or arbitrator is well placed to determine the issues when there is a clear contractual right to participate based on objective, published criteria.

In the case of team sports, choices are largely at the discretion[250] of the head coach or selection committee, leaving less scope for contesting the decision.[251] Choosing the right squad can be an art rather than a science, and the coach is entitled to pursue hunches about "chemistry". Some recourse is, however, available. Selections must not be based on discriminatory grounds,[252] and in the context of contract termination grievances[253] it has been suggested that releasing a player must not be "arbitrary or capricious".[254] The

---

[247] On eligibility in various sports, see, for example: *MacDougall v. Ontario Federation of School Athletic Assns.*, [1987] O.J. No. 1728, 27 C.P.C. (2d) 326 (Ont. Dist. Ct.); *Parks (Guardian ad litem of) v. B.C. School Sports*, [1997] B.C.J. No. 440, 145 D.L.R. (4th) 174 (B.C.S.C.); *Peerless (Guardian ad litem of) v. B.C. School Sports*, [1998] B.C.J. No. 673, [1998] 10 W.W.R. 104 (B.C.C.A.); *Milne v. Nipissing District Secondary School Athletic Assn.*, [1998] O.J. No. 4678, 15 Admin. L.R. (3d) 126 (Ont. Div. Ct.); *Johnson (Litigation guardian of) v. Ontario Federation of School Athletic Assn.*, [2000] O.J. No. 4994, 29 Admin. L.R. (3d) 204 (Ont. S.C.J.).

[248] See, J. Barnes, *Sports and the Law in Canada*, 3d ed. (Toronto: Butterworths, 1996) at 76-78.

[249] For appeal decisions and arbitrations associated with the Sport Dispute Resolution Centre of Canada, see online: <http://www.sdrcc.ca>. In the Canadian Sport Dispute Resolution Code (January 1, 2009), see, in particular: article 6.7 (onus of proof in team selection disputes), articles 6.12, 6.14 (participation by "affected party"). Although selection is usually contested at the national level, the Court of Arbitration for Sport has dealt with cases dealing with quota allocations at major Games and other opportunities to participate.

[250] On selectors' discretion in professional cricket, see, *Greig v. Insole*, [1978] 1 W.L.R. 302 at 354 (Ch. Div.).

[251] For cases involving team sports, see: *Maesson v. Canadian Volleyball Assn.* (1984), 26 A.C.W.S. (2d) 279 (Ont. H.C.J.) (injunction to require try-out for Olympic team denied); *Forbes v. Australian Yachting Federation Inc.* (1996), 131 F.L.R. 241 (N.S.W.S.C.) (discretion in relation to composition of crews). See also, *Hooper v. Canadian Soccer Assn.* (SDRCC 07-0051, June 15, 2007, J. Welbourne, arb.).

[252] See Chapter 2, "Legal Fundamentals and Equality Rights", sections D; E.

[253] See Chapter 9, "National Hockey League", section E, 4.

[254] See, *Hawes v. Sherwood-Parkdale Metro Junior Hockey Club*, [1991] P.E.I.J. No. 145, 88 D.L.R. (4th) 439 (P.E.I.C.A.), affg [1990] P.E.I.J. No. 109, 86 Nfld. & P.E.I.R. 342 (P.E.I.T.D.) (player's claim for season's salary failed because contract was ambiguous). See also, *Di Ruocco*

composition of the playing line-up should also be genuinely related to considerations of performance and skill.[255] Although courts exercise limited review of the decisions of private associations, a full rehearing and the substitution of players may be permitted under rules of arbitration.[256]

Minor hockey has faced unusual litigation when players have received limited playing time or have been dropped from teams. The coach's failure to put kids on the ice is sometimes the cause of violent incidents,[257] and dissatisfied parents may also attempt to recover registration fees.[258] In *Butrimas (Litigation Guardian of) v. Applewood Hockey Assn.*,[259] an eight-year-old had been dismissed from a novice team because his father had been "confrontational" with the association.[260] In the ensuing action, the court struck out various claims in tort, but recognized that negligence and breach of fiduciary duty were possible causes of action. A claim based on abuse of authority could not succeed because the association was not exercising statutory powers, and a claim for intentional infliction of emotional harm was disallowed because there was no evidence that the exclusion from the team caused mental distress requiring medical help. In *Croteau (tuteur d'instance de) c. Conseil de hockey mineur du Nouveau-Brunswick*,[261] the lack of recognition took the form of a Bantam AAA player receiving the "Top Scorer" trophy but not being nominated as "Top Playmaker" and MVP. He then sued for damages for stress or "psychological trauma" and looked to receive the awards and be included on New Brunswick's team at the Canada Games. Croteau had led the league with 45 goals and 42 assists, while the MVP award went to a player with 21 goals and 39 assists.[262] The claims were denied when the court found no evidence that awards were motivated by bad faith or an intention to harm, the MVP award being based on a democratic process involving voting by coaches representing teams in the league.

---

c. *Association de hockey mineur Les Étoiles de l'Est inc.*, [2007] J.Q. no 5725, 2007 QCCQ 5921 (C.Q.).

[255] See, *Lamp v. Toronto Blue Jays* (December 30, 1986; February 20, 1987, G. Nicolau, arb.) (failure to play Dennis Lamp prevented his earning a contract extension).

[256] See, Canadian Sport Dispute Resolution Code (January 1, 2009), article 6.17 (scope of panel's review).

[257] On the various forms of "rink rage", see Chapter 5, "Be Safe: Off the Ice" section B, 1.

[258] See, *Dagenais c. Association de hockey mineur de St-Hyacinthe inc.*, 2007 QCCQ 7188 (C.Q.).

[259] [2006] O.J. No. 3494, 147 A.C.W.S. (3d) 144 (Ont. S.C.J. (Small Claims Ct.)).

[260] See, "Demoted 10-year-old sues hockey league" *The Globe and Mail* (Toronto: June 20, 2005) at A13.

[261] [2003] A.N.-B. no 292, 2003 NBBR 307 (N.B.Q.B.). Justice McIntyre recommended that a suspension of Croteau be lifted. See also, *Croteau v. Hockey Canada*, [2005] F.C.J. No. 883, 2005 FC 704 (F.C.).

[262] See: "Father files suit after son fails to win MVP award" *The Globe and Mail* (Toronto: November 7, 2002) at S1; "Anglophone factor raised by father" *The Globe and Mail* (Toronto: November 9, 2002) at S1; "Hockey dad pulls no punches in legal fight" *The Globe and Mail* (Toronto: June 1, 2005) at A3.

## 4.   Event Outcome

Hockey Canada Regulations provide that Branches may adopt procedures for handling protests of games (see, C.9).[263] With regard to Inter-Branch games above the minor level (see, C.1-6), protests must be presented to the Hockey Canada officer in charge of the series who then delivers the protest to the opposing team; both sides pay a deposit of CDN $100 which is forfeited by the loser of the protest. By Regulation C.7, the Hockey Canada officer and the chair or vice-chair of the board "shall have full power to rule on the protest" and their decision "shall be final".

Courts and arbitrators are reluctant to be involved in "field of play" decisions by game officials since they do not regard themselves as qualified or well-placed to review calls of a purely technical nature relating to the playing rules of the sport.[264] A finding of fraud would normally be required to reverse an official's decision.[265] Event results may, however, be reviewed where there has been legal error in relation to the authority of officials.[266] The court or arbitrator may also take jurisdiction when scores or competitive results are intermixed with questions of eligibility, selection or discipline.

## 5.   Discipline

### a.   International

The IIHF has the authority to sanction associations and other members (see, IIHF Bylaw 1001), and Council and Congress may order suspensions or expulsions for actions such as failing to meet constitutional responsibilities or bringing the sport into disrepute (see, IIHF Statutes 24, 25). Gambling activities by players and officials are specifically prohibited (see, IIHF Bylaw 1004). Disciplinary authority with respect to IIHF championships is held by the responsible Directorate (see, IIHF Statute 49; IIHF Bylaw 615). Under Statute 52, the IIHF Disciplinary Committee is appointed by Council and consists of a chairman, deputy chairman and four other members. Committee members are to be "independent, not bound by instruction and... not accountable to anyone for their decisions". Decisions may be appealed

---

[263]  See, for example, *Walton (Litigation guardian of) v. Saskatchewan Hockey Assn.*, [1998] S.J. No. 125, [1999] 1 W.W.R. 135 (Sask. Q.B.) (protest based on use of player ineligible because of residence).

[264]  See: *Mendy v. Association internationale de boxe amateur*, CAS, O.G. Atlanta, August 1, 1996 (referee's decision to disqualify boxer involved a technical standard and not a "violation of the law, social rules or general principles of law"); *Yang v. International Gymnastics Federation*, CAS 2004/A/704, October 21, 2004 (marking error by judges).

[265]  See, *Weir v. Saskatchewan Amateur Baseball Assn.*, [1978] S.J. No. 333, 90 D.L.R. (3d) 707 (Sask. Q.B.) (continuation or replay of interrupted game; interpretation of tournament rules).

[266]  See, for example, *Comité national olympique et sportif français v. Fédération equestre* internationale, CAS 04/007, O.G. Athens, August 21, 2004 (Appeal Committee had no authority to reverse decision of Ground Jury regarding time penalty).

to Council, and such appeal is mandatory prior to any application for arbitration (see, IIHF Statute 54; IIHF Bylaw 1005). National associations must honour IIHF suspensions, and there is an obligation to report penalties that may affect a player participating for his national team (see, IIHF Bylaw 302). Player suspensions apply to participation in both ice hockey and in-line hockey.

The responsibilities and procedures of the Disciplinary Committee are specified in the Disciplinary Regulations,[267] which require the Committee "to act as the sole decider of the matter brought before it, as if they were judges in a civil proceeding" (see, Article 2.1). The Committee is authorized to sanction violations of "good order" in ice hockey and in-line and is responsible for doping cases (see, Articles 1.5, 3.8-10, 5) and "Supplementary Discipline" arising from breaches of playing rules (see, Article 1.2). Hearings are conducted before a panel of three members (see, Article 2.2), and the Regulations list the types of disciplinary measure that may be imposed (see, Articles 4.1, 5). The general limitation period is two years from the date of the alleged infringement or eight years in the case of doping violations (see, Articles 3.7, 3.11).

## b.   *National*

The Board of Directors of Hockey Canada has the power to impose and enforce appropriate penalties for violations of the constitution or rules of the association and may remove or remit penalties (see, By-Law 502(c)(d)). Any player, coach or official who is under suspension by a member Branch, league or association is excluded from all games sanctioned by Hockey Canada (see, Regulation O.6). Hockey Canada also recognizes and enforces suspensions imposed by associate members, international federations and professional leagues (see, Regulation O.7).

Where the Board of Directors is of the opinion that a member or individual "has been guilty of conduct detrimental to the welfare of amateur hockey", it may suspend the right to participate in games or activities sponsored by Hockey Canada or a Branch (see, By-Law 1005(c)). The decision requires a meeting of the Board and proper notice, and the accused is entitled to address the Board and be represented by counsel (see, By-Law 1005(c)). Under By-Law Two, there is also special provision for the immediate indefinite suspension of members, individuals, clubs or teams. By-Law 401(d) further provides that,

> The Chair of the Board or designate shall have the power to suspend summarily any player, coach, manager, club, team, member or individual for any breach or violation:
>
> > i) of the provisions of the Articles, By-Laws, Regulations, Playing Rules;
> >
> > ii) of any decision or ruling of the Board of Directors;

---

[267]   See, 2009 IIHF, Disciplinary Regulations (September 2008).

iii) involving unsportsmanlike conduct on or off the ice;

iv) involving abusive language to any of the officials; or

v) involving an alleged infraction of the amateur definition.[268]

Rulings by Branches may be appealed to the National Appeals Committee in accordance with procedures set-out in By-Law Twelve. A Branch member may allege that the decision was in conflict with rules of Hockey Canada, that there was procedural error or unfairness or that the Branch did not have authority to make the decision (see, By-Law 1201).

Hockey Canada Regulations provide for disciplinary sanctions against teams or individuals that are responsible for using suspended or ineligible players or that participate in unsanctioned events (see, Regulation O). By Regulation F.12,

A Branch or the Officers of Hockey Canada, as applicable, may take disciplinary action against:

 a)   Any team found to be in violation of any Hockey Canada registration regulation, and/or;

 b)   Any individual found guilty of having falsified or forged any document that would make that individual eligible to play hockey in any IIHF member federation.[269]

Similarly, a player who falsifies registration information or competes under a false name is liable to an automatic suspension for up to three years (see, Regulation F.22). Further prohibitions, procedures and sanctions relate to harassment, bullying and hazing.[270]

Disciplinary decisions have prompted extensive litigation as members question the fairness of proceedings or challenge the authority of Branches or associations to impose sanctions. The actions usually fail as courts defer to the discretion of the organizations to manage affairs in the best interests of the game. Players accused of acts of violence,[271] other game infractions[272] or general misconduct[273] have been unsuccessful in having their suspensions

[268]   Online: <http://www.hockeycanada.ca/index.php/ci_id/66601/la_id/1.htm>, By-Law 401(d).

[269]   *Ibid.*, Regulation F.12.

[270]   See Chapter 5, "Be Safe: Off the Ice", sections C, E.

[271]   See: *Lecuyer v. Alberta Junior "A" Hockey League*, [1977] A.J. No. 580, 3 A.R. 213 (Alta. T.D.) (injunction to prevent enforcement of league suspension for spearing denied); *Trudelle (Litigation guardian of) v. Saskatchewan Hockey Assn. Inc.*, [2003] S.J. No. 207, 233 Sask.R. 51 (Sask. Q.B.) (head butt against linesman; no error by appeal committee).

[272]   See, *Shoniker v. Ontario (Ministry of Education)*, [1986] O.J. No. 804, 17 O.A.C. 265 (Ont. Div. Ct.) (secondary schools association had authority to suspend student).

[273]   See: *Lemieux c. Organisation de hockey mineur de la Pointe-Lévy inc.*, [2007] J.Q. no 1815, 2007 QCCS 996 (Que. C.S.) (personality conflicts and other complaints involving 11-year-old player and father; association's decision was reasonable); *Levasseur c. Assn. du hockey mineur*

lifted. Attempts to recover compensation or receive reimbursement of registration fees have also failed.[274] Suspensions of teams and coaches have been confirmed in cases where ineligible players were used[275] or where teams participated in unsanctioned tournaments.[276]

## D.   DOPING CONTROL

## 1.   Organizations and Codes

Anti-Doping Codes[277] are special disciplinary systems required by government and enforced in conjunction with organizations dedicated to a vision of "ethics in sport". In an attempt to bring uniformity to doping control, the World Anti-Doping Agency ("WADA")[278] was founded in 1999 and established its headquarters in Montreal in 2001. The first version of the World Anti-Doping Code ("WADC") was adopted in 2003 and revised in 2007 and 2009. In Canada, the domestic equivalent of the WADC is the Canadian Anti-Doping Program of 2009 ("CADP") which is monitored and enforced through investigations conducted by the Canadian Centre for Ethics in Sport ("CCES").[279] In 2007-08, the CCES was maintained through a contribution of CDN \$5.3 million from Sport Canada. The WADC is endorsed by international sports organizations such as the International Ice Hockey Federation ("IIHF"), and governments agree to bring their controls into harmony with it. By Article 22.6 of the WADC, sanctions may be applied against governments that fail to ratify or accept the *International Convention against Doping in Sport*[280] which requires States Parties to adopt appropriate measures consistent with the Code.

Under the WADC, there is no systematic definition of "doping", which is referred to in Article 1 as "the occurrence of one or more of the anti-doping violations" specified in the Code. A doping infraction is the breach of a technical

---

*Chaudière-Ouest*, [2007] J.Q. no 13414, 2007 QCCS 5510 (Que. C.S.) (re-registration refused; interim injunction denied).

[274]  See: *Lagüe c. Hockey West Island inc.*, [2002] J.Q. no 10427 (C.Q.) (request for reimbursement was late; no proof that player was expelled by team-mates); *Trachtenberg c. Assn. de hockey Dollard inc.*, [2002] J.Q. no 10426 (C.Q.) (player was not expelled from organization; playing suspension was matter for referees and discipline committee).

[275]  See: *Walton (Litigation guardian of) v. Saskatchewan Hockey Assn.*, [1998] S.J. No. 125, [1999] 1 W.W.R. 135 (Sask. Q.B.) (application dismissed); *Fox c. Club communautaire hockey mineur Edmundston*, [2007] A.N.-B. no 490, 2007 NBBR 278 (N.B.Q.B.) (court ordered hearing before appeal committee).

[276]  See, *Trumbley v. Saskatchewan Amateur Hockey Assn.*, [1986] S.J. No. 151, 49 Sask.R. 296 (Sask. C.A.) (coach should have proceeded with hearing offered by appeals committee).

[277]  See: J. O'Leary, ed., *Drugs and Doping in Sport: Socio-Legal Perspectives* (London: Cavendish Publishing, 2001); W. Wilson & E. Derse, eds., *Doping in Elite Sport: The Politics of Drugs in the Olympic Movement* (Champaign: Human Kinetics Publishers, 2001).

[278]  Online: <http://www.wada-ama.org>.

[279]  Online: <http://www.cces.ca>.

[280]  UNESCO, *International Convention against Doping in Sport* (October 19, 2005), accepted by Canada, November 29, 2005, entered into force, February 1, 2007.

prohibition and is based on a constantly changing list of banned substances and practices. If a product or method is deleted, it regains ethical status and becomes "sport science" again. The general drift of the list has been towards expansion as training techniques and the intake of substances undergo moral evolution. Supplementation, ergogenic assistance or medication become "cheating" once they are scheduled, although it is possible to obtain a Therapeutic Use Exemption (see, Article 4.4). The list can be applied only in the case of known, disapproved techniques and is only meaningful when there is an effective test or other means of detection. Athletes are subject to testing of urine and blood samples in and out of competition and must provide information as to their whereabouts (see, Article 14.3). The urine collection process requires that a Doping Control Officer or chaperone witness the sample leaving the athlete's body (see, CADP, Rule 6, Annex 6D).

Under Article 4.3, a substance or method may be placed on the Prohibited List where it has a masking effect or where it meets two out of the following three criteria:

> evidence suggests that alone or in combination it has the potential to enhance sport performance;
> evidence suggests that it represents an actual or potential health risk to athletes; or
> WADA determines that its use violates the spirit of sport.

Given that the goal is "Faster, Higher, Stronger" and given the risks and technological methods of elite sport, these criteria are obviously inadequate and constitute a very weak basis for condemning a technique as unethical.[281] The introductory text of the Code recites the "spirit of sport" as the "Fundamental Rationale" for doping control and states that the purpose of the Code is to "promote health, fairness and equality for Athletes worldwide". Many philosophers doubt whether any principled rationale can be found,[282] and it is far from clear that prohibition, surveillance and punishment are the best way to health and justice. Doping control is fundamentally a conservative[283] project using crime control techniques to preserve a nostalgic vision of athletic competition and gender types. The priority and cost of sport's "War on Drugs"

---

[281] See, S.J. Mulhall, "A Critique of the World Anti-Doping Code" (2006) 64 Advocate 29.

[282] See, for example: J. Barnes, *Sports and the Law in Canada*, 3d ed. (Toronto: Butterworths, 1996) at 95-99; B. Houlihan, *Dying to Win: Doping in Sport and the Development of Anti-Doping Policy* (Strasbourg: Council of Europe Publishing, 1999) at 107-28; C.M. Tamburrini, "What's Wrong with Doping?" in T. Tännsjö & C. Tamburrini, *Values in Sport: Elitism, Nationalism, Gender Equality and the Scientific Manufacture of Winners* (London: E & F N Spon, 2000) at 200.

[283] The Dubin Report famously extolled "the necessity of order" and the need for loyalty to the "established hierarchy" and our "current leaders": Canada, *Commission of Inquiry into the Use of Drugs and Banned Practices Intended to Increase Athletic Performance* (Ottawa: Minister of Supply and Services, 1990) (The Honourable Charles L. Dubin Commissioner) at 499-500. The Report was making bizarre use of a passage from J.-M. Brohm, *Sport – A Prison of Measured Time* (London: Ink Books, 1978) at 75-76.

must be questioned since the presence of traces of obscure bio-chemical combinations is probably not the leading safety problem in sport. It is a bizarre feature of the Olympics that neck-risking stunts are encouraged but medications are condemned.[284] Rather than enforcing safety standards, organizations such as the CCES are better understood as agencies of sports marketing and medal retention: their goal is to ensure that the country's athletes do not get caught using disapproved science or the wrong stuff.

The 2010 Prohibited List distinguishes substances and methods prohibited at all times from substances and methods prohibited in-competition. Other substances are prohibited in particular sports (*e.g.*, alcohol in motor sports and karate), and there is a further category of "Specified Substances" such as stimulants that are susceptible to unintentional use because of their presence in medicines so that the athlete may credibly claim to have had no intention to enhance performance (see, Article 10.4). The substances and methods prohibited at all times are:

PROHIBITED SUBSTANCES
S1. Anabolic Agents
   1. Anabolic Androgenic Steroids (AAS)
      a. Exogenous AAS not normally capable of natural production by the body are prohibited. These include, 1-androstendiol, stanozolol, 1-testosterone "and other substances with a similar chemical structure or similar biological effect(s)".
      b. Endogenous or naturally occurring AAS (*e.g.*, testosterone) are prohibited when administered exogenously.
   2. Other Anabolic Agents (*e.g.*, clenbuterol).
S2. Peptide Hormones, Growth Factors and Related Substances (*e.g.*, erythropoietin ("EPO"), insulin, growth hormone).
S3. Beta-2 Agonists, except for some inhalers.
S4. Hormone Antagonists and Modulators (*e.g.*, anti-estrogenic substances).
S5. Diuretics and other Masking Agents.
PROHIBITED METHODS
M.1. Enhancement of Oxygen Transfer
   1. Blood doping.
   2. Artificially enhancing the uptake, transport or delivery of oxygen.
M.2. Chemical and Physical Manipulation.
   1. Tampering or attempting to tamper with samples.[285]
   2. Intravenous infusions, except as used in surgery, medical emergencies or clinical investigations.

---

[284] See, for example, *Andreea Raducan v. International Olympic Committee*, CAS 00/011, O.G. Sydney, September 28, 2000 (positive test for Pseudoephedrine; doctor prescribed Neurofen flu tablet for gymnast). On safety issues in hockey, see Chapters 4-6.

[285] See, for example, *Michelle Smith-de Bruin v. Fédération Internationale de Natation*, FINA Panel, August 6, 1998; CAS 98/211, June 7, 1999 (sample spiked with alcohol).

M.3. Gene Doping (*e.g.,* transfer of cells or genetic elements).[286]

The additional substances prohibited during competitions are:

S6.  Stimulants (*e.g.,* amphetamine, cocaine;[287] strychnine (specified)).

S7.  Narcotics (*e.g.,* heroin, methadone, morphine).

S8.  Cannabinoids.[288]

S9.  Glucocorticosteroids when administered by oral, intravenous, intramuscular or rectal routes.

Article 2 of the WADC establishes the following violations (which have their domestic equivalent in Rules 7.23-7.37 of the CADP):

2.1. The presence of a Prohibited Substance or its Metabolites or Markers in an Athlete's Sample.

2.2. Use or Attempted Use by an Athlete of a Prohibited Substance or a Prohibited Method.

2.3. Refusing or failing without compelling justification to submit to Sample collection after notification as authorized in applicable anti-doping rules, or otherwise evading Sample collection.[289]

2.4. Violation of applicable requirements regarding Athlete availability for Out-of Competition Testing.

2.5. Tampering or Attempted Tampering with any part of Doping Control.

2.6. Possession of Prohibited Substances and Methods.

2.7. Trafficking or Attempted Trafficking in any Prohibited Substance or Prohibited Method.

2.8. Administration or Attempted administration to any Athlete.

The violation in Article 2.1 is a strict liability infraction so that the athlete is responsible for the presence of the substance regardless of knowledge, intent or

---

[286]  See: C. Munthe, "Selected Champions: Making Winners in the Age of Genetic Technology" in T. Tännsjö & C. Tamburrini, *Values in Sport: Elitism, Nationalism, Gender Equality and the Scientific Manufacture or Winners* (London: E & F N Spon, 2000) at 217; B. Sellenger, "Genetic Testing: The Future of Athlete Selection?" (2003) 2 Virginia Sports and Ent. L. J. 207; A. Miah, *Genetically Modified Athletes* (London: Routledge, 2004).

[287]  See, *In the Matter of an Application by Eric Lamaze for a Category II Reinstatement* (September 19, 2000, CCES, (E. Ratushny, arb.).

[288]  See, *Rebagliati v. International Olympic Committee*, CAS 002, O.G. Nagano, February 12, 1998 (snowboard gold medal restored; marijuana was not banned at the time).

[289]  See, for example: *World Anti-Doping Agency v. International Ice Hockey Federation & Busch*, CAS 2008/A/1564, June 23, 2009; *World Anti-Doping Agency v. Deutscher Eishockey-Bund e.v. & Busch*, CAS/A/1738, June 23, 2009 (player received suspension for two years after he declined to be tested for a few hours; test was negative).

negligence.[290] Sanctions may, however, be eliminated under Article 10.5 where athletes establish how the substance entered their system and establish that they bear no fault or negligence.[291] Sanctions may be reduced where athletes establish that they bear no "significant" fault or negligence.

The person accused of a doping violation is entitled to a fair hearing (see, Article 8), and the Code prescribes rights of appeal for different parties and organizations, including WADA (see, Article 13). The ultimate destination for appeals, especially in cases arising from international competition, is the Court of Arbitration for Sport ("CAS"). The issues subject to appeal include the grant or refusal of a Therapeutic Use Exemption (see, Articles, 4.4, 13.4).

Violations by individual athletes result in disqualification, forfeiture of results and loss of prize money (see, Articles 9, 10.1, 10.8). The consequences in team sports are prescribed in Article 11.2:

> If more than two members of a team in a Team Sport are found to have committed an anti-doping rule violation during an Event Period, the ruling body of the Event shall impose an appropriate sanction on the team (*e.g.*, loss of points, Disqualification from a Competition or Event, or other sanction) in addition to any Consequences imposed upon the individual Athlete(s) committing the anti-doping rule violation.

For most violations, the sanction for a first offender is suspension or ineligibility for two years (see, Articles 10.2, 10.3). Lesser sanctions, such as warning or reprimand, are permitted for first violations involving "Specified Substances" (see, Article 10.4). In cases of trafficking or "administration", the minimum is ineligibility for four years (see, Article, 10.3.2). Higher penalties, including lifetime ineligibility, apply to multiple violations or where there are aggravating circumstances (see, Articles 10.6, 10.7). A first violation of the requirement to provide information as to whereabouts formerly resulted in ineligibility for a minimum of three months;[292] a combination of three filing failures and missed tests over an 18 month period is now subject to a minimum penalty of one year and a maximum of two years (see, CADP, Rule 7.41).

In an attempt to insulate doping cases from review, the Introduction to the WADC presents anti-doping rules as "competition rules... [or] sport rules governing the conditions under which sport is played". The rules are adopted by private organizations, and doping cases are normally brought before domestic

---

[290] See, J. Soek, *The Strict Liability Principle and the Human Rights of Athletes in Doping Cases* (The Hague: TMC Asser Press, 2006), esp. at 131-228. See, in particular, *Aanes v. Fédération Internationale de Luttes* Associées, CAS 2001/A/317, July 9, 2001.

[291] See: *Pobyedonostev v. International Ice Hockey Federation*, CAS 2005/A/990, August 24, 2006 (player was unaware that hospital had used steroid during emergency treatment); *Adams v. CCES*, CAS 2007/A/1312, May 16, 2008 (catheter contaminated following cocaine assault).

[292] See, "Sledge Hockey Athlete Commits Anti-Doping Violation", CCES Media Release (December 5, 2007).

tribunals and national[293] or international[294] arbitration systems rather than the court system.[295] The public law and public policy basis of the controls is, however, a peculiarity of the system, and investigations are increasingly coordinated with state authorities.[296] In Europe, the police raid is a regular side-attraction in bicycle racing,[297] and the athletes of the United States have been increasingly caught up in that country's "War on Drugs".[298] In Canada, the government presence takes various forms, including obligations under international agreements and Conventions.[299] The policy of "doping-free sport" receives statutory expression in section 4(1) of the *Physical Activity and Sport Act*.[300] Sport Canada introduced its first policy in 1983 in the wake of disqualifications at the Pan American Games and revised the controls in 1991 after the Dubin Inquiry[301] had investigated drug use by Canadian athletes and Ben Johnson's disqualification at the 1988 Seoul Olympics.[302] The current government policy dates from 2004,[303] and national sports

---

[293]  See, Canadian Sport Dispute Resolution Code (January 1, 2009), article 7, online: <http://www.sdrcc.ca>. See further, Chapter 2, "Legal Fundamentals and Equality Rights", section C.

[294]  On cases before the Court of Arbitration for Sport, see, M. Reeb, ed., *Digest of CAS Awards*, vol. I (1986–1998), vol. II (1998–2000), vol. III (2001–2003) (The Hague: Kluwer Law International, 1998, 2002, 2004). See also, online: <http://www.tas-cas.org/>.

[295]  The Canadian litigation includes: *Gray v. Canadian Track & Field Assn.*, [1986] O.J. No. 893, 39 A.C.W.S. (2d) 483 (Ont. H.C.J.); *Johnson v. Athletics Canada*, [1997] O.J. No. 3201, 41 O.T.C. 95 (Ont. Gen. Div.), affd [1998] O.J. No. 3757, 114 O.A.C. 388 (Ont. C.A.); *Chevrier c. Canadian Weightlifting/Fédération haltérophilie canadienne* (November 5, 1998), C.S. Montréal 500-05-044493-987, J.E. 99-26, Lanctôt J.; *Loranger v. Mount Allison University*, [1998] N.B.J. No. 473, 206 N.B.R. (2d) 96 (N.B.Q.B.); *Canadian Centre for Ethics in Sport v. Russell*, [2007] O.J. No. 2234 (Ont. S.C.J.).

[296]  The Canadian Olympic Committee is recognized as a "public authority": *Registrar of Trade Marks v. Canadian Olympic Assn.*, [1982] F.C.J. No. 174, [1983] 1 F.C. 692 (F.C.A.); *See You In - Canadian Athletes Fund Corp. v. Canadian Olympic Committee*, [2007] F.C.J. No. 541, 57 C.P.R. (4th) 287 (F.C.A.). See also, *Sagen v. Vancouver Organizing Committee for the 2010 Olympic and Paralympic Winter Games*, [2009] B.C.J. No. 1393, 2009 BCSC 942 (B.C.S.C.), affd 2009 BCCA 522 (B.C.C.A.), leave to appeal to S.C.C. refused December 22, 2009, [2009] S.C.C.A. No. 459.

[297]  On performance and suffering in the leading race, see, C.S. Thompson, *The Tour de France: A Cultural History* (Berkeley: University of California Press, 2006).

[298]  See, for example, "Jones sentenced to six months in jail" *The Globe and Mail* (Toronto: January 12, 2008) at S7 (Marion Jones convicted of lying to federal agents).

[299]  The extensive range of government programs related to doping control is set out in, *Canadian Centre for Ethics in Sport v. Adams*, SDRCC DT-06-0039 (June 11, 2007, R.H. McLaren, arb.), Attachment A, Affidavit of Lane MacAdam.

[300]  S.C. 2003, c. 2.

[301]  Canada, *Report of the Commission of Inquiry into the Use of Drugs and Banned Practices Intended to Increase Athletic Performance* (Ottawa: Minister of Supply and Services, 1990) (The Honourable Charles L. Dubin, Commissioner). See also, J. Barnes, "Recent Developments in Canadian Sports Law" (1991) 23 Ottawa L. Rev. 623.

[302]  See, C. Francis with J. Coplon, *Speed Trap: Inside the Biggest Scandal in Olympic History* (Toronto: Lester & Orpen Dennys, 1990).

[303]  See, "The Canadian Policy Against Doping in Sport" (June 2004), online: Canadian Heritage <http://www.pch.gc.ca>.

organizations are required to adopt and comply with the policy as a condition of funding.[304] The sanctions in the Program include the loss of direct financial support provided by the Government of Canada (see, CADP, Rule 7.57). The products subject to doping control range from alcohol, to over-the-counter medications, to prescription drugs, to substances that are regulated or prohibited by legislation.[305] Where the violation relates to an illegal drug, the accused risks both sport sanctions and penalties imposed by the criminal justice system. In Canada, the CCES works in association with the RCMP,[306] and the WADC requires reporting to public authorities where violations also involve breach of laws or regulations (see, Article 10.3.2); public agencies are also encouraged to share information with anti-doping agencies (see, Article 22.2).

Where a person is accused of a statutory offence, the full protection of the *Canadian Charter of Rights and Freedoms*[307] is applicable. Given the governmental and statutory basis of doping control, it is also strongly arguable that the *Charter* applies to anti-doping violations and the associated procedures of sports organizations. The legal rights in sections 7 and 8 are particularly relevant,[308] as is the guarantee of equality in section 15. One arbitrator has characterised doping violations as merely disputes arising "from the contractual arrangements between private non-governmental entities",[309] and the accused faces the hurdle that *Charter* rights may be waived by consenting to a system of controls.[310] The Privacy Commissioner of Canada has, however, questioned the genuineness of any "consent":

> ...athletes should not be forced to abandon their Charter rights at the locker room door – no matter how many may be willing to do precisely that in order to compete...The federal government dictates athlete drug testing policy. If those policies fail to measure up to Charter requirements, they will be subject to challenge even if a non-governmental agency actually conducts the tests.[311]

---

[304] See, "Sport Funding and Accountability Framework (SFAF III, 2009-2113)", A11. See further, Chapter 2, "Legal Fundamentals and Equality Rights", section B, 4.

[305] See, *Controlled Drugs and Substances Act*, S.C. 1996, c. 19. Anabolic steroids are, for example, included in Schedule IV, s. 23.

[306] See, *Drugs and Sport: The Score* (Ottawa: RCMP, 1993).

[307] Part I of the *Constitution Act, 1982*, being Schedule B to the *Canada Act, 1982* (U.K.), 1982, c. 11. Rights in s. 10 of the Charter apply on "arrest or detention", and rights in s. 11 apply to persons "charged with an offence" of a criminal nature. On the Charter, see further, Chapter 2, "Legal Fundamentals and Equality Rights", section D, 2.

[308] The mandatory, random testing of prisoners has been struck down: *Dion c. Canada (Procureur général)*, [1986] J.Q. no 2768, 30 C.C.C. (3d) 108 (Que. S.C.); *Jackson v. Joyceville Penitentiary*, [1990] F.C.J. No. 134, [1990] 3 F.C. 55 (F.C.T.D.).

[309] See, *Canadian Centre for Ethics in Sport v. Adams*, SDRCC DT-06-0039, R.H. McLaren, arb., June 11, 2007, at para. 157. See also, *Adams v. CCES*, CAS 2007/A/1312, May 16, 2008.

[310] See, *Ozubko v. Manitoba Horse Racing Commission*, [1986] M.J. No. 500, [1987] 1 W.W.R. 149 (Man. C.A.).

[311] *Drug Testing and Privacy* (Ottawa: Privacy Commissioner of Canada, 1990) at 43.

The Supreme Court of Canada has, furthermore, held that the *Charter* applies where government policies or programs are implemented through private agencies.[312] By section 24 of the *Charter*, rights may be enforced by applying to a "court of competent jurisdiction". The arbitration system of the Sport Dispute Resolution Centre of Canada has been held not to be "competent" for this purpose.[313] Where a person accused of a doping violation wishes to raise constitutional issues or obtain the protection of the *Charter*, the avenue of redress is the ordinary courts which can function as the forum in which to balance the dictates of doping control with other values.

The classification and regulation of drugs present difficult policy problems that are not necessarily solved by the strategy of prohibition used in the wider "War on Drugs". In sport, doping may be contractual "cheating" but it is entirely consistent with the commercial and competitive environment that demands size, speed, strength, aggression and the enhancement of performance. The government-financed laboratory is now the foundation of victory, and any nation looking to "Own the Podium" must be prepared to do everything to get the technological edge.[314] "Doping" therefore seems to be no more than the continuation of science-based training by other means. The demands of many sports often make drug use a matter of physical survival, and in the age of Viagra it is difficult to say that it is wrong to get a boost for the good of the country.

## 2.  Doping Control in Hockey

Except for the debate about testing programs in professional leagues,[315] hockey has not been the sport of focus with respect to the use of performance enhancing drugs. The testing of players in national associations such as Canadian Interuniversity Sport has resulted in some violations,[316] and a sledge hockey athlete has received a brief suspension for failing to provide whereabouts information.[317] Prominent cases have occurred when players have been subject to national or international standards applied in association with Major

---

[312] See, *Eldridge v. British Columbia (Attorney General)*, [1997] S.C.J. No. 86, [1997] 3 S.C.R. 624 (S.C.C.).

[313] See, *Canadian Centre for Ethics in Sport v. Adams*, SDRCC DT-06-0039, R.H. McLaren, arb., June 11, 2007, at para. 164.

[314] See, for example, "Testing the truth about altitude training for athletes" *The Globe and Mail* (Toronto: November 11, 2006) at A3 (increase in oxygen and red blood cells through use of hypoxic tents simulating high altitude).

[315] On the famous guess by Richard Pound, former chairman of WADA, and other aspects of doping control in the NHL, see Chapter 9, "National Hockey League", section D, 3.

[316] See: "Sport ban on cocaine keys on advantage" *The Globe and Mail* (Toronto: April 13, 1995) at A15; CCES Media Release, "University of Alberta Athlete Commits Anti-Doping Violation" (February 25, 2005) (positive test for "Specified Substances" cannabis and ephedrine; ineligibility for four months); CCES Media Release "CIS Hockey Athlete Commits Anti-Doping Violation" (February 9, 2007) (cocaine; ineligibility for two years).

[317] See, CCES Media Release, "Sledge Hockey Athlete Commits Anti-Doping Violation" (December 5, 2007) (ineligibility for three months).

Games. In 1999, Canada forfeited the roller hockey gold medal at the Pan American Games in Winnipeg after Steve Vézina recorded a spectacularly high level of the anabolic steroid Nandrolone.[318] In 2006 in pre-Olympic testing, José Théodore was nabbed for improper hirsuteness after he followed a prescription to stimulate hair growth.[319]

Under IIHF Bylaw 607, national associations entering teams in IIHF championships[320] must fulfil all conditions relating to anti-doping. Doping control is maintained in accordance with a Drug Testing Service Agreement signed with WADA, and the IIHF Council asserts the right to test players participating in IIHF competitions and to order that doping control be carried out on players affiliated with national associations (see, IIHF Bylaw 1401). The IIHF Disciplinary Regulations[321] incorporate sanctions for violations corresponding with the World Anti-Doping Code ("WADC") and allow for the fining of national associations and changing the announced results of competitions (see, Articles 6.13-14). Doping Control Regulations are included in the IIHF Medical Regulations[322] and provide for sample collection, analysis and results management. The testing is to be conducted in conformity with the International Standards for Testing and Laboratories. The Medical Regulations refer to the violations set out in the WADC and note that the Prohibited List is established by WADA.

The controls maintained by the CCES relate to athletes at the national and international levels, so that testing programs have not usually been applied in amateur hockey. In 2003, there were reports that the exhausting bus travel associated with the schedule of the Quebec Major Junior Hockey League ("QMJHL") gave rise to a culture of widespread use of stimulants and relaxants.[323] The QMJHL and other development leagues in Quebec introduced a new testing program in 2004 in association with the CCES providing for ineligibility at the national level and league suspensions for up to 10 games for a first violation.[324] In 2007, a policy was adopted by the entire Canadian Hockey League incorporating education programs, testing and a system of

---

[318] See: "Canadian goalie posts record high for steroids" *The Globe and Mail* (Toronto: August 2, 1999) at A1; "Many pro athletes just doing what comes naturally" *The Globe and Mail* (Toronto: August 4, 1999) at S2.

[319] See, "Theodore caught in doping test" *The Globe and Mail* (Toronto: February 10, 2006) at R6 (CCES testing of players on preliminary list for Olympic team; positive test for the hair loss drug Propecia which is banned as a masking agent).

[320] On the "pre-testing" of Soviet players and urine substitution at the 1986 World Championships, see, C. Francis with J. Coplon, *Speed Trap: Inside the Biggest Scandal in Olympic History* (Toronto: Lester & Orpen Dennys, 1990) at 284-85.

[321] See, 2009 IIHF Disciplinary Regulations (September 2008), Article 5; IIHF Bylaws 1402, 1407.

[322] See, 2010 IIHF Medical Regulations, II, at 30-43.

[323] See: "Drug use rife in QMJHL: report" *The Globe and Mail* (Toronto: December 9, 2003) (online) (reports in *La Presse* suggesting use of ephedrine, marijuana and other substances); "QMJHL planning drug-test program" *The Globe and Mail* (Toronto: December 10, 2003) at S2.

[324] See, CCES Advisory Note, "Quebec Hockey Doping-Free Sport Program" (November 25, 2004).

sanctions. By article 3.07.7.1 of the "CHL Anti-doping Policy", the main suspension periods for "the presence or use of a prohibited substance or prohibited method" are as follows: 1st infraction, 8 games; 2nd infraction, 25 games; 3rd infraction, 2 years.[325]

---

[325] CHL Anti-doping Policy (June 2008), Article 3.07.7.1, online: <http://www.lhjmq.qc.ca /lang_en/?page=1245574>.

## Chapter 4

# BUILD SAFE: RINK MANAGEMENT AND RISK MANAGEMENT

It is to be expected that when any quarrel or ruction arises during the game the people will look over the rail and press forward to the rail to see what is going on below, and this rail was not constructed with a view to withstanding any outward thrust whatever.[1]

## A.   ARENAS OF DANGER AND CIVIL LIABILITY

### 1.   Introduction: Varieties of Risk

This is the first of three chapters exploring the risks and dangers of hockey and the potential for legal liability and financial loss. The physical risks are not limited to the action between players on the ice surface, but include the threat of violence or abuse in the wider setting of the game.[2] A rink may also present design faults and environmental dangers putting spectators or arena personnel at risk. The flying puck is one well-known hazard, but this is not the only pitfall lurking at the facility,[3] and there is a growing problem of municipal ice arenas reaching their "life expectancy".[4] The risks faced by participants and fans require preventive measures, and various remedies and sanctions are available to victims and public authorities.[5] Where it is alleged that injury was caused by negligence

---

[1]    *Stewart v. Cobalt Curling and Skating Assn.*, [1909] O.J. No. 170, 19 O.L.R. 667 at 671 (Ont. Div. Ct.), *per* Boyd C. (gallery railing broke under the press of "rooters"; spectator "rather seriously injured" when thrown onto the ice). For a similar fall out of the press box at Maple Leaf Gardens in 1949, see, L. Scanlan, *Grace Under Fire: The State of Our Sweet and Savage Game* (Toronto: Penguin Canada, 2002) at 2 (hockey hack or "sports reporter" fell onto pregnant woman with happy results).

[2]    See, Chapter 5, "Be Safe: Off the Ice" (off-ice risks); Chapter 6, "Play Safe: On the Ice" (risks in play).

[3]    See, Chapter 4, "Build Safe: Rink Management and Risk Management", section B. The committed fan watching the big game at home also has an increased risk of heart attack; see: D. Carroll *et al.*, "Admissions for Myocardial Infarction and World Cup Football: Database Survey" (2002) 325 British Medical J. 1439 ("challenging events can perturb neuroendocrine, haemodynamic and endothelial systems, resulting in rupture of vulnerable atherosclerotic plaques"); U. Wilbert-Lampen *et al.*, "Cardiovascular Events during World Cup Soccer" (2008) 358:5 New England J. Med. 475.

[4]    The "life expectancy" is 32 years, and 73 per cent of arenas in Canada were built before 1980. See, "National Arena Census" (Canadian Recreation Facilities Council/Hockey Canada, 2005).

[5]    See, for example, Chapter 5, "Be Safe: Off the Ice", section C (screening systems, complaint processes, civil actions and criminal offences relating to sexual misconduct). See also, Chapter 6, "Play Safe: On the Ice", section A (regulatory standards applying to player safety).

or other default, the victim may initiate a civil claim for damages and bears the burden of proving the case on the balance of probabilities. Deliberate or serious misconduct may also warrant criminal prosecution, where the Crown must prove the accused's guilt beyond reasonable doubt.

The present chapter offers a general introduction to safety and security issues and considers means of limiting the costs of liability through risk management programs.[6] Hockey Canada's guide book, *Safety Requires Teamwork & Safety For All*, explains that when risks materialize, hockey must minimize:

> Risk management is the process by which an organization identifies, assesses, controls and minimizes the risk of bodily injury or financial loss arising from its activities. In organized hockey, risk management is the process by which a Branch, Association, League or Team reviews its activities, programs and operating procedures...to identify, understand and insure against the everyday risks confronted in operating an organized hockey program.[7]

Risk management is linked to the objectives of the organization and calls for policies, standards and procedures in relation to all spheres of operation.[8] Control systems and supervision can go some way towards preventing incidents, but it is in the nature of hockey that "stuff happens". When the inevitable risks translate into injuries and other adverse consequences, the object is to limit the losses. The costs of litigation and liability can be reduced through waivers[9] and insurance,[10] and liability can often be avoided by showing the operation and enforcement of a suitable program adapted to an identified risk.[11] Where injury has been caused by physical plant or structures, it is useful to show an efficient system of inspection and maintenance. Reasonable care for player safety is shown by proper equipment, appropriate rules, good coaching and a commitment to fair play. In the event of injury or illness, there should also be an emergency action plan and satisfactory medical treatment.[12] Similarly, off-ice dangers and the risk of abuse may be addressed through education programs, disciplinary action and systems for screening personnel.

---

[6]   Risk management and loss prevention are also relevant to other types of dispute and litigation. See, for example: Chapter 2, "Legal Fundamentals and Equality Rights", section E (equality rights and discrimination); Chapter 3, "Organizations and Regulations" (powers and procedures of organizations, including disciplinary cases).

[7]   Hockey Canada, *Safety Requires Teamwork & Safety For All* (2009–2010) at 23.

[8]   See: S. Bird & J. Zauhar, *Recreation and the Law*, 2d ed. (Scarborough, ON: Carswell, 1997) at 121-41, 155-61; R. Corbett & H.A. Findlay, *Your Risk Management Program: A Handbook for Sport Organizations* (Ottawa: Centre for Sport and Law, 1998); R. Corbett, H.A. Findlay & D.W. Lech, *Legal Issues in Sport: Tools and Techniques for the Sport Manager* (Toronto: Emond Montgomery Publications, 2008) at 229-47.

[9]   See Chapter 4, "Build Safe: Rink Management and Risk Management", section C.

[10]  See Chapter 4, "Build Safe: Rink Management and Risk Management", section D.

[11]  See, in particular: Chapter 5, "Be Safe: Off the Ice", section C (risk of sexual abuse); Chapter 6, "Play Safe: On the Ice", section A (on-ice player safety).

[12]  On the liability of organizations and medical negligence, see Chapter 6, "Play Safe: On the Ice", sections A; C, 5, 6.

Risk and danger therefore derive from a range of sources, whether the built environment, playing activities and team travel or the general culture of the game. The responsibility to prevent injury and limit liability falls to all members of the hockey community serving in different roles and performing different functions.[13] Legal duties attach to organizations and administrators, arena managers and employees, coaches, medical personnel, officials, volunteers, parents, spectators and players.

## 2. Torts on Ice

In the common law Provinces of Canada,[14] civil actions dealing with liability for injury are brought under the law of torts, which includes liability for "sports torts".[15] In a tort action, a person who has suffered damage or loss (the plaintiff) claims that the defendant is responsible for causing the injury and so should pay compensation through an award of damages assessed by the court.[16] The form of the proceedings is one of corrective justice[17] — the person who has wrongfully caused injury is required to pay for it. Tort actions attempt to shift the burden of the loss from the victim to the defendant by claiming that the defendant was at fault. In theory, tort law operates to deter harmful conduct, so that the possibility of civil liability may be seen as one device to promote safety in sport: the individual cases are supposed to warn and educate both the parties and the public. Torts involving personal injury[18] fall into two categories: intentional torts and negligence.

Intentional torts, such as battery and assault, involve an allegation of deliberate interference with the person either through direct contact or physical

---

[13] See, Hockey Canada, *Safety Requires Teamwork & Safety For All* (2009–2010) at 23-33.

[14] On liability for sports injuries under the civil law of Quebec, see: R. Joyal-Poupart, *La responsabilité civile en matière de sports au Québec et en France* (Montréal: Les Presses de l'Université de Montréal, 1975); *Guide en responsabilité civile* (Service juridique, Régie de la sécurité dans les sports du Québec, 1990). See also, *Civil Code of Québec*, R.S.Q. c. C-1991, c. 64.

[15] See: A.M. Linden & B. Feldthusen, *Canadian Tort Law*, 8th ed. (Markham, ON: LexisNexis Butterworths, 2006); L. Klar, *Tort Law*, 3d ed. (Toronto: Thomson Carswell, 2003); J. Barnes, *Sports and the Law in Canada*, 3d ed. (Toronto: Butterworths, 1996) at 269-315.

[16] See: K.D. Cooper-Stephenson, *Personal Injury Damages in Canada*, 2d ed. (Scarborough, ON: Carswell, 1996); C.J. Bruce, *Assessment of Personal Injury Damages*, 4th ed. (Markham, ON: LexisNexis Butterworths, 2004). On the assessment of damages for injured players, see Chapter 6, "Play Safe: On the Ice", section C, 1.

[17] E.J. Weinrib, "Toward a Moral Theory of Negligence Law" (1983) 2 Law & Phil. 37.

[18] The tort of libel relates to damage to reputation. See, for example: *McCann v. The Ottawa Sun*, [1993] O.J. No. 3103, 16 O.R. (3d) 672 (Ont. Gen. Div.) (claim based on libel of a group struck out); *Eagleson v. Dowbiggan*, [1996] O.J. No. 89, 47 C.P.C. (3d) 236 (Ont. Gen. Div.), affd [1998] O.J. No. 3919, 31 C.P.C. (4th) 181 (Ont. C.A.) (action by T. Allen Eagleson, son of R. Alan Eagleson); "Hull launches lawsuit against two newspapers" *The Globe and Mail* (Toronto: November 21, 1998) at A29 (action by Bobby Hull based on stories attributing racist remarks); *Burke v. NYP Holdings, Inc. (c.o.b. New York Post)*, [2005] B.C.J. No. 1993, 48 B.C.L.R. (4th) 363 (B.C.S.C.) (jurisdiction for action by Brian Burke against *New York Post* for suggestion that he "personally challenged" the Vancouver Canucks to "get" Steve Moore).

threats. Assault is both a crime and a civil wrong, so that acts of violence or interference may be remedied by both criminal prosecution and by civil action. In either case, it is usually necessary to prove that the defendant's conduct exceeded the express or implied consent of the victim.

In a negligence action, the plaintiff alleges that there was a breach of a duty to exercise due care — a failure to take reasonable precautions to prevent foreseeable harm. The plaintiff must show a duty owed, breach of duty and resultant injury. The defendant is liable if the plaintiff proves that the defendant's actions, objectively considered, fail to meet the standard of care that could reasonably be required in the circumstances. The appropriate precautions and responsibilities vary according to the defendant's role, the relationship with the victim and the nature and context of the activity:

> To avoid liability, a person must exercise the standard of care that would be expected of an ordinary, reasonable and prudent person in the same circumstances. The measure of what is reasonable depends on the facts of each case, including the likelihood of a known or foreseeable harm, the gravity of that harm, and the burden or cost which would be incurred to prevent the injury. In addition, one may look to external indicators of reasonable conduct, such as custom, industry practice, and statutory or regulatory standards.[19]

Victims are also required to show due care for their own safety, so that an action will be dismissed in its entirety if injuries were caused by the plaintiff's own carelessness. In *Resurfice Corp. v. Hanke*,[20] the Supreme Court of Canada dismissed the claim by a Zamboni driver who was severely burned by an explosion: the ice-resurfacing machine would not have gone up in flames "but for" the driver's carelessness in attaching the hot water hose to the gasoline tank. Even when some liability does attach to the defendant, "contributory negligence" by the plaintiff will result in damages being reduced in proportion to the plaintiff's fault.[21]

When a player or spectator sues for negligence, the defendant usually answers that there was voluntary assumption of risk. This doctrine has two distinct meanings that are often mingled and confused in sports cases:

1. voluntary assumption of risk as a defence; and

2. inherent risks in sport.

1. *Voluntary assumption of risk as a defence*: In its strict sense, voluntary assumption of risk is a defence of consent applicable to a negligence action. As a

---

[19]   *Ryan v. Victoria (City)*, [1999] S.C.J. No. 7, [1999] 1 S.C.R. 201 at 222 (S.C.C.), *per* Major J.

[20]   [2007] S.C.J. No. 7, [2007] 1 S.C.R. 333 (S.C.C.) ("but for" and "material contribution" tests). On causation issues, see also, *Hussack v. Chilliwack School District No. 33*, [2009] B.C.J. No. 1271, 2009 BCSC 852 (B.C.S.C.) (blow from field hockey stick and subsequent medical conditions).

[21]   See, for example, *Negligence Act*, R.S.O. 1990, c. N.1, s. 3.

defence, it operates to defeat the claim after breach of duty is shown.[22] To rely on it, the defendant must show that the plaintiff willingly ran a risk that was fully understood and agreed to give up any cause of action. Such willing acceptance may be an express contracting out of the right to sue through waivers, exclusions or tickets.[23] Or, the assumption of legal risk and forfeiture of rights may be implied from willing participation in a dangerous joint venture such as a drinking and driving expedition.

2. *Inherent risks in sport*: Playing sports or attending events involve certain necessary and inevitable risks from flying objects or flying bodies. Where injury arises from a normal and reasonable practice inherent in the game, there will be no liability. Such incidents are regarded as mere accidents whose costs must be borne by the victim. The value of sports derives from their inherent conflict, speed, exertion and physical contact. The occasional accident is the price paid by player or spectator for the benefits of sport.[24]

The primary issue in sports cases is whether there has been negligence by an administrator, player or other party: liability is fixed by determining whether the defendant met the standard of care appropriate to the relationship with the plaintiff. Where negligence is found, it is unusual for a court to hold that the plaintiff waived any legal claim through a bargain to give up rights of action. Where no negligence is found or where injury arises from an inherent risk, the plaintiff's case fails for that reason, and there is no need to consider voluntary assumption of risk as a special defence.

## 3.   Occupiers' Liability[25]

Occupiers' liability refers to the duty of care owed to visitors by persons or organizations controlling land or premises.[26] This topic has been subject to

---

[22]   In *Hagerman v. Niagara Falls (City)*, [1980] O.J. No. 3699, 29 O.R. (2d) 609 (Ont. H.C.J.), dealing with a spectator hit in the eye by puck, Labrosse J. observed (at 611),

> Only if negligence is proved is it necessary to consider whether the defendant has successfully asserted either of the possible defences of voluntary assumption of risk and contributory negligence. A finding of voluntary assumption of risk would completely negative the plaintiff's claim, whereas a finding of contributory negligence would result in an apportionment of damages.

[23]   See Chapter 4, "Build Safe: Rink Management and Risk Management", section C.

[24]   See, for example, *Crocker v. Sundance Northwest Resorts Ltd.*, [1988] S.C.J. No. 60, [1988] 1 S.C.R. 1186 at 1192 (the "run of the mill sports accident" usually entails no liability and the victim must rely on private insurance and public health care).

[25]   See: A.M. Linden & B. Feldthusen, *Canadian Tort Law*, 8th ed. (Markham, ON: LexisNexis Butterworths, 2006) at 711-58; L. Klar, *Tort Law*, 3d ed. (Toronto: Carswell, 2003) at 525-52. See further: Chapter 4, "Build Safe: Rink Management and Risk Management", section B (injuries to spectators); Chapter 6, "Play Safe: On the Ice", section C, 3 (injuries to players).

[26]   On status as an "occupier", see: *MacDonald v. Goderich (Town)*, [1949] O.J. No. 474, [1949] O.R. 619 (Ont. C.A.), affg [1948] O.J. No. 495, [1948] O.R. 751 (Ont. H.C.J.) (injury to spectator; liability of persons leasing rink); *Olinski v. Johnson*, [1997] O.J. No. 926, 32 O.R. (3d) 653 (Ont. C.A.), affg (1992), 36 A.C.W.S. (3d) 1054 (Ont. Gen. Div.) (attack on lacrosse referees; team's obligation to provide policing and supervision extended beyond playing surface to corridor outside locker room).

special common law rules, but reforming statutes in most Provinces[27] now bring occupier' liability closer to the general standards of negligence. Although differing in some important details, each piece of legislation imposes on occupiers a duty to take reasonable care for the safety of most visitors.[28]

Section 1 of the Ontario *Occupiers' Liability Act* provides that occupiers include: persons in physical possession of premises; persons responsible for and controlling the condition of the premises or the activities carried on; and persons controlling entry. "Premises" means land and structures and includes water, vessels and portable structures; it also includes vehicles when not in operation. The Act does not apply to the Crown or to any municipal corporation where either of these is the occupier of a public highway or public road (see, s. 10(2)). Where it is claimed that a street hockey injury was caused by a defective surface or other feature of the road, the case would be subject to the limitations on liability governing public authorities' responsibility for highway maintenance.[29]

By section 3(1) of the Ontario *Occupiers' Liability Act*, the occupier

> ...owes a duty to take such care as in all the circumstances of the case is reasonable to see that persons entering on the premises, and the property brought on the premises by those persons are reasonably safe while on the premises.[30]

This general duty applies to dangers caused by the condition of the premises or by the activity carried on (see, s. 3(2)). The occupier may restrict, modify or exclude the duty (see, s. 3(3)), for example by notices or warnings, but must take "reasonable steps" to bring the limitation to the visitor's attention (see, s. 5(3)). A landlord under a duty to repair premises owes the same duty towards a visitor as would be owed by the occupier (see, s. 8(1)). Nothing in the Act relieves an occupier from showing any higher standard of care required by a rule of law (see, s. 9(1)),[31] and the Act does not affect rights, duties and liabilities resulting from the relationship of employer and employee (see, s. 9(2)).

---

27   *Occupiers Liability Act*, R.S.B.C. 1996, c. 337; *Occupiers' Liability Act*, R.S.A. 2000, c. O-4; *The Occupiers' Liability Act*, C.C.S.M. c. O8; *Occupiers' Liability Act*, R.S.O. 1990, c. O.2; *Occupiers' Liability Act*, S.N.S. 1996, c. 27; *Occupiers' Liability Act*, R.S.P.E.I. 1988, c. O-2. In New Brunswick and Newfoundland and Labrador, the common law rules of occupiers' liability are now superseded by the general obligation in the law of negligence to exercise reasonable care for the safety of visitors: see: *Law Reform Act*, S.N.B. 1993, c. L-1.2, s. 2; *Murphy v. St. John's (City)*, [2001] N.J. No. 119, 200 Nfld. & P.E.I.R. 181 (Nfld. C.A.).

28   The legislation in Alberta prescribes a low standard of care in relation to trespassers and makes special provision for child trespassers; see, *Occupiers' Liability Act*, R.S.A. 2000, c. O-4, ss. 12, 13.

29   See, for example: *Municipal Act, 2001*, S.O. 2001, c. 25, ss. 44-46; *Winter v. London (City)*, [2002] O.J. No. 3724, 32 M.P.L.R. (3d) 219 (Ont. S.C.J.) (debris on sidewalk and pothole on roadway; action by in-line skater dismissed). See also, *Jetz v. Calgary Olympic Development Assn.*, [2002] A.J. No. 1470, 328 A.R. 265 (Alta. Q.B.) (cyclist injured hitting speed bump in Canada Olympic Park; common law occupiers' liability applicable).

30   *Occupiers' Liability Act*, R.S.O. 1990, c. O.2, s. 3(1).

31   In Manitoba, it has been held that the legislation does not preserve the higher standard owed to contractual visitors; see, *Wolf v. Airliner Motor Hotel (1972) Ltd.*, [1988] M.J. No. 351, 54 Man.R. (2d) 169 (Man. Q.B.) (hotel guest slipped and fell on steps leading to swimming pool; poor condition of abrasive strips).

By section 4(1) of the Act, the general duty of care does not apply in respect of risks "willingly assumed". This provision embodies the common law defence of voluntary assumption of risk and requires the defendant to show that the plaintiff waived legal rights and absolved the defendant of responsibility.[32] However, in the case of such a fully consenting visitor, the occupier may not create a danger with deliberate intent and may not act with reckless disregard of people's presence (see, s. 4(1)). This limited duty applies to persons who enter premises to commit criminal acts (see, s. 4(2)). It also applies in relation to certain rural or undeveloped premises entered by trespassers or by persons who enter to engage in recreational activity without paying a fee (see, s. 4(3)(4)). The person who without permission skates on a frozen pond in a farmer's field willingly assumes all risks and can claim only the duty of care in section 4(1).

Prior to the reforming legislation, occupiers' liability was governed by the common law rules that distinguish duties to different categories of visitor. This approach continues to be the law in the hockey heartland of Saskatchewan.[33] At common law, entrants may be either contractual visitors, invitees, licensees or trespassers. The highest standard is owed to *contractual visitors* such as members, patrons or ticket holders who are present as a matter of paid entitlement. These visitors have the benefit of any express obligations in the contract and also enjoy an implied warranty that the premises are reasonably fit for the intended purpose and are as safe as reasonable care and skill can make them.[34] Entrants are *invitees* if the occupier has an economic interest in their presence; the occupier's duty is then to "use reasonable care to prevent damage from unusual danger which he knows or ought to know".[35] A *licensee* is someone whom the occupier permits to enter the premises for the visitor's own purposes. Originally, occupiers had a duty towards the licensee to see that there were no traps or concealed dangers of which they had actual or imputed knowledge but which were not apparent to the visitor. Judicial decisions then largely assimilated the duty owed to a licensee with that owed to an invitee.[36] The person who enters without the occupier's express or implied permission is a *trespasser*. Those who enter in the face of warnings or exclusions are trespassers, but if the occupier acquiesces in their presence they become licensees. A licence will often be implied where an occupier maintains an allurement, such as a piece of

---

[32] *Waldick v. Malcolm*, [1991] S.C.J. No. 55, [1991] 2 S.C.R. 456 (S.C.C.). On the limited duty in s. 4(1), see, *Schneider v. St. Clair Region Conservation Authority*, [2009] O.J. No. 3667, 2009 ONCA 640 (Ont. C.A.), revg [2007] O.J. No. 5325, 89 O.R. (3d) 150 (Ont. S.C.J.) (cross-country skier struck hidden wall at frozen lake).

[33] Although it is the heartland, since 2001 the official sport of the Province has been curling; see, *The Provincial Emblems and Honours Act*, S.S. 1988-89, c. P-30.2, s. 9.1 (am. S.S. 2001, c. 4, s. 6).

[34] *Francis v. Cockrell* (1870), L.R. 5 Q.B. 501 (Ex. Ch.); *Maclenan v. Segar*, [1917] 2 K.B. 325; *Finigan v. Calgary*, [1967] A.J. No. 75, 65 D.L.R. (2d) 626 (Alta. C.A.).

[35] *Indermaur v. Dames* (1866), L.R. 1 C.P. 274 at 288, *per* Willes J., affd L.R. 2 C.P. 311 (Ex.Ch.).

[36] *Bartlett v. Weiche Apartments Ltd.*, [1974] O.J. No. 2246, 7 O.R. (2d) 263 (Ont. C.A.); *Mitchell (Guardian ad litem of) v. Canadian National Railway Co.*, [1974] O.J. No. 67, [1975] 1 S.C.R. 592 (S.C.C.); *Alaica v. Toronto (City)*, [1976] O.J. No. 2366, 14 O.R. (2d) 697 (Ont. C.A.); *McErlean v. Sarel*, [1987] O.J. No. 873, 61 O.R. (2d) 396 (Ont. C.A.).

equipment, that is likely to attract children. Generally, an occupier does not owe an onerous duty towards trespassers and need not anticipate their presence. A duty to treat the trespasser with "ordinary or common humanity" may, however arise "if the owner of the land knew of, or from all the surrounding circumstances ought reasonably to have foreseen, the presence of the trespasser".[37] Otherwise, the duty is not to cause injury intentionally or to act with reckless disregard of safety.

## 4.   Security[38]

The occupier of an arena must operate a reasonable system of supervision to maintain order on the premises and to respond to incidents.[39] This requires establishing adequate procedures and surveillance mechanisms and using an appropriate number of trained security personnel, whether stewards, private security agents or police officers.[40] The supervisors should not themselves be the source of violence,[41] and an employer may be vicariously liable when staff use excessive force. The necessary measures will vary according to the size of the crowd and the likelihood of trouble. Special precautions would, for example, be required for intense rivalries with a potential to be marred by fisticuffs or other disturbances. The risk to visitors may come from incidents of "rink rage"[42] or other deliberate assaults directed against players, spectators,[43] officials,[44] police

---

[37]   *Veinot v. Kerr-Addison Mines Ltd.*, [1974] S.C.J. No. 99, [1975] 2 S.C.R. 311 at 322 (S.C.C.), *per* Dickson J.

[38]   On types of security measure, see, M.J. Pantera *et al.*, "Best Practices for Game Day Security at Athletic & Sport Venues" (2003) 6:4 The Sport Journal (online). Under National Hockey League Official Rules (2009-2010), Rule 41.8, "All clubs shall provide adequate police or other protection for all players, goalkeepers and officials at all times", online: <http://www.nhl.com/league/ext/rules/2009-2010_Rule_Book.pdf>. There has been particular concern for the protection of players in different sports since tennis player Monica Seles was stabbed by a spectator in 1993.

[39]   On security in a movie theatre, see, *Mitchell v. Famous Players Inc.*, [2005] O.J. No. 4453 (Ont. S.C.J.) (one patron assaulted by another; theatre's duty under the *Occupiers' Liability Act* and obligations of employees to assist).

[40]   See, for example, *Francis v. Miramichi (City)*, [2000] N.B.J. No. 130 (N.B.Q.B.) (disturbance at hockey game; spectator's action for false arrest dismissed; police officers acted on reasonable grounds).

[41]   See, for example, *Lundy v. Shields*, [1996] O.J. No. 57, 60 A.C.W.S. (3d) 433 (Ont. Gen. Div.) (plaintiff alleged assaults by off-duty constable acting as "beer watchers" at baseball game).

[42]   See Chapter 5, "Be Safe: Off the Ice", section B.

[43]   See, for example, "Scotiabank Place offers regrets, return trip to attacked Sabres fan" *Ottawa Citizen* (May 18, 2007) (online) (visitor from Buffalo knocked down after suggesting that fans of the Ottawa Senators should put away their "sweep" brooms).

[44]   *Olinski v. Johnson*, [1997] O.J. No. 926, 32 O.R. (3d) 653 (Ont. C.A.), affg (1992), 36 A.C.W.S. (3d) 1054 (Ont. Gen. Div.) (liability of arena and other defendants for attacks on referees in Junior B lacrosse; no security provided; arena unsuccessful in claiming contribution from team).

officers[45] or others. An arena may be liable when boisterous or drunken behaviour has been tolerated or condoned,[46] and home-town partisanship should not extend to generating feelings of hatred towards supporters of the opposing team. Where the occupier operates a reasonable security system, it would not be liable for an out-of-the-blue act of violence, but could be held responsible for misconduct that could reasonably be foreseen. The loss of inhibition associated with alcohol is a particular source of danger,[47] and a licensed arena has statutory obligations under liquor control legislation to maintain safety and supervise consumption.[48]

Security is also maintained by prohibiting entry, which is achieved by notice to that effect or by enclosing premises "in a manner that indicates the occupier's intention to keep persons off the premises".[49] The right to prohibit entry includes banning re-entry once a visitor has stepped outside,[50] and an occupier may also limit access to parts of the premises and prohibit particular activities. By section 2 of the Ontario *Trespass to Property Act,*

> Every person who is not acting under a right or authority conferred by law and who,
>
> (a) without the express permission of the occupier, the proof of which rests on the defendant,
>
>     (i) enters on premises when entry is prohibited under this Act, or
>
>     (ii) engages in an activity on premises when the activity is prohibited under this Act, or

---

[45]   *Cunningham v. Reading Football Club,* [1992] P.I.Q.R. P141 (Q.B.D.) (police officer injured when fans threw pieces of loose concrete from terrace).

[46]   See, for example, *Jacobson v. Kinsmen Club of Nanaimo,* [1976] B.C.J. No. 343, 71 D.L.R. (3d) 227 (B.C.S.C.) (roof-beam swinger fell on plaintiff).

[47]   On the liability of a bar, see, for example: *Mellanby v. Chapple,* [1995] O.J. No. 1299 (Ont. Gen. Div.) (Scott Mellanby slashed on arm with broken beer bottle; share of liability and assessment of damages); *Renaissance Leisure Group Inc. (c.o.b. Muskoka Sands Inn) v. Frazer,* [2004] O.J. No. 3486, 242 D.L.R. (4th) 229 (Ont. C.A.). See also, *Donaldson v. John Doe,* [2007] B.C.J. No. 829, [2008] 1 W.W.R. 426 (B.C.S.C.), affd [2009] B.C.J. No. 154, 2009 BCCA 38 (B.C.C.A.) (no evidence that Oktoberfest patron posed risk).

[48]   See, for example, *Liquor Licence Act,* R.S.O. 1990, c. L.19, s. 29 (sale to intoxicated person), s. 30 (sale to person under 19), s. 34 (removing persons from premises). See also: *Liquor Control Act,* R.S.O. 1990, c. L.18; *Alcohol and Gaming Regulation and Public Protection Act, 1996,* S.O. 1996, c. 26.

[49]   *Trespass to Property Act,* R.S.O. 1990, c. T.21, s. 3(1)(b). On necessary notice under the *Petty Trespass Act,* R.S.A. 2000, c. P-11, see, *R. v. MacKenzie,* [1990] A.J. No. 1156, 115 A.R. 296 (Alta. Prov. Ct.) (skier who entered closed area acquitted). The playing area is a "'tabooed' spot" in the possession of the home club, but a forcible ejection must be justified; see, *Holmes v. Bagge* (1853), 1 E. & B. 782 (Q.B.D.) (substitute cricketer ejected for non-removal of coat).

[50]   See, *Aspden v. Maniaci and Niagara (Regional Municipality) Police Services Board,* [2005] O.J. No. 969 (Ont. S.C.J.) (false arrest after plaintiff re-entered grape harvest festival; plaintiff not given reasonable opportunity to leave).

(b)  does not leave the premises immediately after he or she is directed to do so by the occupier of the premises or a person authorized by the occupier,

is guilty of an offence and on conviction is liable to a fine of not more than $2,000.[51]

By section 9 of the Act,

A police officer, or the occupier of premises, or a person authorized by the occupier may arrest without warrant any person he or she believes on reasonable and probable grounds to be on the premises in contravention of section 2.[52]

The offences and arrest powers[53] in the Act and in equivalent statutes in other Provinces are "the workhorse of private security services in their patrol of the shopping malls, airports, sports stadiums and other private spaces where the public tends to congregate".[54]

A spectator usually gains lawful access to an arena or stadium by the purchase of a ticket, which serves as a temporary, revocable licence[55] to view the game from a particular seat and to enter designated parts of the premises. This "licence for value" creates an enforceable right to attend the event to the end, provided the ticket holder complies with all conditions and observes the management's rules of good behaviour.[56] At commercialized events, the conditions may include not displaying anything likely to offend the official sponsors. Once the patron has shown the ticket on admission and on being seated, there is generally no further requirement to make it available for inspection on demand. A SkyClub season ticket holder with the Toronto Blue Jays duly recovered damages against the club and the police following his unlawful arrest and "violent ejection" after he refused to show his ticket on leaving a SkyClub bar at the SkyDome. The circumstances created no grounds for revoking the plaintiff's licence and the Blue Jays' personnel unnecessarily escalated the dispute.[57]

---

[51]  R.S.O. 1990, c. T.21, s. 2. On legislation in Manitoba, see, *Gameday Publication(s) Ltd. v. Keystone Agricultural and Recreational Centre Inc.*, [1999] M.J. No. 57, 170 D.L.R. (4th) 617 (Man. C.A.) (arena entitled to prohibit distribution of rival magazine).

[52]  *Trespass to Property Act*, R.S.O. 1990, c. T.21, s. 9.

[53]  See also, *Criminal Code*, R.S.C. 1985, c. C-46, s. 494 (arrest without warrant by citizens and property owners). An arrest by a private citizen has been held to be a governmental function; see, *R. v. Lerke*, [1986] A.J. No. 27, 25 D.L.R. (4th) 403 (Alta. C.A.) (arrest and search by tavern employee).

[54]  *R. v. Asante-Mensah*, [2003] S.C.J. No. 38, [2003] 2 S.C.R. 3 at 8 (S.C.C.), *per* Binnie J. (arrest at airport). See also, G.S. Rigakos & D.R. Greener, "Bubbles of Governance: Private Policing and the Law in Canada" (2000) 15 C.J.L.S. 145.

[55]  See, for example, *Potechin v. Yashin*, [2000] O.J. No. 1660, 186 D.L.R. (4th) 757 at 762-63 (Ont. S.C.J.) (ticket terms and season ticket policies of the Ottawa Senators).

[56]  *Hurst v. Picture Theatres Ltd.*, [1915] 1 K.B. 1 (C.A.); *Heller v. Niagara Racing Assn.*, [1924] O.J. No. 136, [1925] 2 D.L.R. 286 (Ont. C.A.); *Winter Garden Theatre (London) Ltd. v. Millenium Productions Ltd.*, [1948] A.C. 173 (H.L.).

[57]  *Davidson v. Toronto Blue Jays Baseball Ltd.*, [1999] O.J. No. 692, 170 D.L.R. (4th) 559 (Ont. Gen. Div.).

To enhance safety and security and to control the consumption of alcohol, an arena may wish to search the persons and bags of patrons prior to allowing admission onto the premises. The management is supposedly looking for weapons, explosives and other items that pose a threat to the crowd, although the focus on food and drink raises the suspicion that the investigations have more to do with protecting the monopolies of the concession stands, where the prices are the most obvious form of crime at the arena. A rink may also want to avoid disruptions to the game by discouraging the celebratory practice of throwing octopus, toy rodents or other creepy or creamy projectiles.[58] (The illicit carrying of urns to spread loved-ones' ashes is mainly associated with football fields, although there is no discounting Canadians' devotion to hockey.[59]) Where there is a genuine goal of enforcing regulations and excluding dangerous or unsavoury items, unintrusive searches would seem to be an appropriate contractual condition of entry and a valid exercise of control over private property. The occupier has a civil "duty to ensure the safety of those attending...the search [is] a condition precedent to entry, [and the visitor has] the obvious choice of submitting to the search or declining to enter".[60] Interference with the person is, however, subject to special constitutional protection, and section 8 of the *Canadian Charter of Rights and Freedoms*[61] specifically declares that, "Everyone has the right to be secure against unreasonable search or seizure." Searches conducted by police or other public authorities are subject to *Charter* challenge, and searches by private security personnel[62] may also trigger *Charter* rights because an arena's power to limit entry, prohibit activities and prevent offences derives from statutory powers such as the *Trespass to Property Act*. Section 8 of the *Charter* serves to protect reasonable expectations of privacy appropriate to the context.[63] An expectation of privacy applies to the body and to personal belongings, although there is no breach of rights when a search is

---

[58]  On peanut butter projectiles supplied to fans, see, *R. v. Vandergraaf*, [1994] M.J. No. 503, 93 C.C.C. (3d) 286 (Man. C.A.).

[59]  See, "Man at Eagles Game Says He Was Spreading Mom's Ashes" *The Washington Post* (November 29, 2005) at E02.

[60]  *R. v. Roy*, [1985] O.J. No. 633, 25 C.C.C. (3d) 473 at 477 (Ont. H.C.J.), *per* O'Brien J. (search before concert at Maple Leaf Gardens revealed marijuana).

[61]  Part I of the *Constitution Act, 1982*, being Schedule B of the *Canada Act 1982* (U.K.), 1982, c. 11. On the application of the Charter, see Chapter 2, "Legal Fundamentals and Equality Rights", section D, 2.

[62]  Searches by private companies or by security guards do not usually constitute government action: *Khan v. El Al Israel Airlines*, [1991] O.J. No. 1267, 4 O.R. (3d) 502 (Ont. Gen. Div.) (security search by airline; action for battery and false imprisonment dismissed); *R. v. Buhay*, [2003] S.C.J. No. 30, [2003] 1 S.C.R. 631 (S.C.C.) (search of locker at bus station). On citizen's arrest and associated search powers, see *R. v. Lerke*, [1986] A.J. No. 27, 25 D.L.R. (4th) 403 (Alta. C.A.).

[63]  See, S.A. Cohen, *Privacy, Crime and Terror: Legal Rights and Security in a Time of Peril* (Markham, ON: LexisNexis Butterworths, 2005) at 9-48. On searches in schools, see: *R. v. R.M. (M.)*, [1998] S.C.J. No. 83, [1998] 3 S.C.R. 393 (S.C.C.); *R. v. A.M.*, [2008] S.C.J. No. 19, [2008] 1 S.C.R. 569 (S.C.C.) (court disallowed random search of students' backpacks using police sniffer dog).

conducted with the informed consent of the subject.[64] A search as a condition of admission is probably constitutional when it is announced in advance and involves only the visual inspection of patrons and their carry-in items.[65] Mandatory strip searches at the rink entrance would go too far,[66] and opinions are likely to differ on the intrusiveness and constitutionality of "mass suspicionless pat-downs" in response to a general fear of terrorist attack.[67] An arena is always free to offer cavity searches to volunteers as part of special medical campaigns such as "prostate awareness".[68] In such a case, the patrons are definitely entitled to know where the probe is leading.

## B.   INJURIES TO SPECTATORS: FLYING PUCKS AND OTHER HAZARDS[69]

An arena presents potential hazards to fans from the mass movement of the crowd,[70] the condition of the building and its surroundings, and the action on the ice.[71] Program operators and the occupiers of premises must anticipate the associated dangers and exercise reasonable care in the organization of games and in the design and maintenance of the facility. There is, however, no absolute guarantee of safety in all circumstances, and "there is no obligation to protect against a danger incident to the entertainment which any reasonable spectator foresees and of which he takes the risk".[72] The required standard of care and

---

[64]   See, for example, *R. v. Borden*, [1994] S.C.J. No. 82, [1994] 3 S.C.R. 145 (S.C.C.) (information to be supplied to suspect).

[65]   See, *Jensen v. City of Pontiac*, 317 N.W.2d 619 (C.A. Mich. 1982). In *Berthiaume c. Cinéma Guzzo inc. (Cinéma Méga-plex Marché central 18)*, [2009] J.Q. no 4933, 2009 QCCQ 4419 (C.Q.), damages were awarded to the patrons of a movie theatre who, without their consent, were subject to an intrusive search of their bags. The theatre was concerned about the use of camcorders and piracy equipment but had failed to give timely notice that searches would be conducted.

[66]   See, for example, *R. v. Golden*, [2001] S.C.J. No. 81, [2001] 3 S.C.R. 679 (S.C.C.) (strip search in sandwich shop incidental to arrest).

[67]   See: *State of North Dakota v. Seglen*, 700 N.W.2d 702 (N.D., 2005) (college hockey game); *Johnston v. Tampa Sports Authority*, 530 F.3d 1320 (11th Cir., 2008), revg 442 F.Supp. 2d 1257 (M.D. Fla., 2006) (season ticket holder consented to pat-down searches at professional football games); *Sheehan v. The San Francisco 49ers, Ltd.*, 62 Cal. Rptr. 3d 803 (C.A., 2007) (no breach of rights of privacy). See also, C.L. Claussen, "Mass Searches of Sports Spectators in the United States" (2007) 3:4 Int. Sports L.J. 76.

[68]   Major League Baseball began its "Take a Swing Against Prostate Cancer" program in 2003.

[69]   See, G.E. Siskind, "Liability for Injuries to Spectators" (1968) 6 Osgoode Hall L.J. 305. On case law and legislation in the United States, see, C.P. Goplerud & N.P. Terry, "Allocation of Risk between Hockey Fans and Facilities: Tort Liability after the Puck Drops" (2003) 38 Tulsa L.J. 445; see also, *Carver v. Niedermayer*, 920 So. 2d 123 (Dist. C.A. Fla., 2006) (examination of jurors).

[70]   See, *Hosie v. Arbroath Football Club*, [1978] S.L.T. 122 (Outer House) (Scottish fans seeking free entry; spectator trampled when crowd forced defective gate).

[71]   The action in a stage play can also be unduly realistic; see, *Cox v. Coulson*, [1916] 2 K.B. 177 (C.A.) (audience member hit by live pistol cartridge fired by actor).

[72]   *Hall v. Brooklands Auto Racing Club*, [1933] 1 K.B. 205 at 207 (C.A.), *per* Scrutton L.J.

precaution usually depends on the status of the patron for the purpose of occupiers' liability.[73] The paying customer is normally a contractual visitor or invitee at common law or a general visitor for the purpose of statutory occupiers' liability, although a reduced standard may apply when a spectator enters a restricted area in spite of clear warnings and prohibitions.[74] The defendant is often a public authority since 86 per cent of ice arenas in Canada are municipally owned and operated. In the event of injury caused by an object or body leaving the ice surface, the spectator is not limited to an action against the facility but may also sue individual players for assault or negligence.

Where a visitor alleges that injuries were caused by the state of premises or structures, there is often no issue as to the inherent risks of the game. Liability turns on the physical condition of the facility and the standards of construction, maintenance or inspection. The quality of the floor surface may, for example, be the determining factor, together with issues relating to the adequacy of lighting, warning signs, rails, barriers or doorways. Cases commonly deal with patrons who have suffered falls on parking lots,[75] walkways,[76] steps[77] or other parts of the premises.[78] Similarly, it may be alleged that injuries were caused by unsafe stands

---

[73]   On occupiers' liability, including duties owed to trespassers, see Chapter 4, "Build Safe: Rink Management and Risk Management", section A, 3. Where an activity is conducted illegally on the highway, there is no element of invitation to premises, so that liability for injury to a spectator is determined on the basis of negligence and nuisance; see, *Chubaty v. McCulloch*, [1955] B.C.J. No. 135, [1955] 5 D.L.R. 520 (B.C.C.A.) (soap-box derby in the street).

[74]   See, *Deyo v. Kingston Speedway Ltd.*, [1953] O.J. No. 723, [1954] 2 D.L.R. 419 (Ont. C.A.), affd [1955] 1 D.L.R. 718 (S.C.C.) (spectators at stock-car track moved outside roped-off area towards guard rail).

[75]   On maintenance standards, see: *Gould v. Amherst (Town)*, [1991] N.S.J. No. 455, 109 N.S.R. (2d) 439 (N.S.T.D.); *Breau v. Amherst (Town)*, [1996] N.S.J. No. 452, 155 N.S.R. (2d) 161 (N.S.S.C.); *Hawman v. Regina Exhibition Assn. Ltd.*, [1999] S.J. No. 700, [2000] 2 W.W.R. 669 (Sask. Q.B.); *Dhalla v. York (City)*, [2001] O.J. No. 3989, 24 M.P.L.R. (3d) 44 (Ont. S.C.J.); *McKay v. Prince Albert (City)*, [2003] S.J. No. 422, 235 Sask.R. 295 (Sask. Q.B.).

[76]   *Silva v. Winnipeg (City)*, [1992] M.J. No. 522, [1993] 1 W.W.R. 691 (Man. Q.B.) (icy sidewalk; arena corporation was occupier); *Larson v. Thunder Bay (City)*, [2000] O.J. No. 2125, 14 M.P.L.R. (3d) 79 (Ont. C.A.), affg [1999] O.J. No. 96, 50 M.P.L.R. (2d) 228 (Ont. Gen. Div.) (icy walkway was not a public sidewalk; duty of care in *Occupiers' Liability Act* applied.); *Josephson v. Merritt (City)*, [2003] B.C.J. No. 2282, 44 M.P.L.R. (3d) 257 (B.C.S.C.) (instructor at hockey school stepped on parking sign on sidewalk; city not liable).

[77]   *St. Amant (Litigation guardian of) v. Penetanguishene (Town)*, [1996] O.J. No. 1038, 32 M.P.L.R. (2d) 190 (Ont. Gen. Div.) (steps crowded during intermission). See also, *Wallach v. Garside*, [1993] B.C.J. No. 1422 (B.C.C.A.) (fall into open service bay).

[78]   *Rees v. B.C. Place Ltd.*, [1986] B.C.J. No. 2594 (B.C.S.C.) (puddle of beer on surface of stadium concourse); *Bolschetschenko v. London (City)* (1989), 18 A.C.W.S. (3d) 1029 (Ont. Dist. Ct.) (ice outside boards in aisle); *Landrey v. North Vancouver (City)*, [1993] B.C.J. No. 69, 37 A.C.W.S. (3d) 962 (B.C.S.C.) (loose plywood covering rotting platform at curling rink); *Economopoulos v. Doug Tarry Ltd. (c.o.b. London Ice House)*, [2001] O.J. No. 3598, 107 A.C.W.S. (3d) 1128 (Ont. S.C.J.) (condensation on freshly waxed floor; no warning signs or pylons); *Mott v. Brantford (City)*, [2008] O.J. No. 241, 42 M.P.L.R. (4th) 261 (Ont. S.C.J.) (city not liable when horseplay led to contact with plate glass window outside entrance door to arena).

or bleachers[79] or defective seats.[80] The playing of the game can, however, be relevant to the general safety of the facility because in some locations spectators' attention will be distracted by the action on the ice or by other interesting spectacles on offer.[81]

The direct risk from the game comes from escaping pucks or sticks and from players crashing into the glass or over the boards. Where the spectator's injury flows from an aspect of play, it is necessary to consider whether the incident was an ordinary and accepted risk or the result of negligence. The occupier's responsibility is to locate spectators safely[82] and to provide reasonable protection by using warnings and appropriate screens or barriers. Liability does not turn on the injured fan's personal understanding of the risks, but on the general standard of safety at the arena.[83] Where normal and satisfactory screening is used or where spectators choose to locate themselves in unprotected or more risky areas,[84] there normally will be no liability for flying pucks[85] or stray sticks.[86] The risk of some

---

[79]   *Francis v. Cockrell* (1870), L.R. 5 Q.B. 501 (Ex. Ch.) (collapse of grandstand at race course); *Stewart v. Cobalt Curling and Skating Assn.*, [1909] O.J. No. 170, 19 O.L.R. 667 (Ont. H.C.J.) (gallery railing broke); *Starkebaum v. Regina (City)*, [1995] S.J. No. 326, 130 Sask.R. 290 (Sask. Q.B.) (no unusual danger in bleacher); *Leweke v. Saanich School District No. 63)*, [2005] B.C.J. No. 1213, 2005 BCCA 304 (B.C.C.A.) (bleachers in school gym met reasonable standard); *Hollett v. St. John's (City) (No. 2)*, [2008] N.J. No. 114, 276 Nfld. & P.E.I.R. 54 (N.L.T.D.) (plaintiff fell climbing bleachers in hockey arena; no evidence of defect or inadequate maintenance); *Goodman v. Porcupine Plain (Town)*, [2008] S.J. No. 824, 2008 SKQB 416 (Sask. Q.B.) (no unusual danger in floor at arena).

[80]   *Cisecki v. Nipawin (Town)*, [2000] S.J. No. 238, [2000] 7 W.W.R. 376 (Sask. Q.B.) (goal judge's seat collapsed; town and team liable); *McLean v. London (City)*, [2001] O.J. No. 4366, 24 M.P.L.R. (3d) 141 (Ont. S.C.J.) (plaintiff stepping over benches; no negligence in design or construction of seating).

[81]   See, *Edwards v. Tracy Starr's Shows (Edmonton) Ltd.*, [1984] A.J. No. 2538, 13 D.L.R. (4th) 129 (Alta. Q.B.), vard [1987] A.J. No. 1424, 61 Alta. L.R. (2d) 233 (Alta. C.A.) (nightclub patron fell on poorly lit steps when distracted by naked dancer).

[82]   *Welsh v. Canterbury* (1894), 10 T.L.R. 478 (Q.B.D.) (chair dropped from Blondin's tightrope onto seats below).

[83]   *Murray v. Harringay Arena Ltd.*, [1951] 2 K.B. 529 (C.A.) (puck struck six-year-old boy).

[84]   *Elliott v. Amphitheatre Ltd.*, [1934] M.J. No. 19, [1934] 3 W.W.R. 225 (Man. Q.B.); *Klyne v. Indian Head*, [1979] S.J. No. 437, [1980] 2 W.W.R. 474 (Sask. C.A.).

[85]   *Gervais v. Can. Arena Co.* (1936), 74 C.S. 389; *Hagerman v. Niagara Falls (City)*, [1980] O.J. No. 3699, 29 O.R. (2d) 609 (Ont. H.C.J.); *Waselenkoff v. Hughes*, [1988] B.C.J. No. 2191 (B.C.S.C.). See also, *Yablonski v. Cranbrook (City)*, [2002] B.C.J. No. 3214, 2002 BCSC 1875 (B.C.S.C.). On escaping balls, see: *Noonan (Litigation guardian of) v. Exhibition Place*, [1991] O.J. No. 421 (Ont. Gen. Div.) (10-year-old hit by baseball at American League game; screening met industry standard); M. Conrod, "Blue Jays provided 'acceptable standard' of protection" *The Lawyers Weekly* (May 3, 1991) at 8; *Dyke v. British Columbia Amateur Softball Assn.*, [2005] B.C.J. No. 2187, 2005 BCSC 1422 (B.C.S.C.), affd [2008] B.C.J. No. 13, [2008] 9 W.W.R. 646 (B.C.C.A.) (ball hit scorekeeper; protective fencing made premises reasonably safe); *Harting v. Dayton Dragons Professional Baseball Club, LLC*, 870 N.E.2d 766 (Ohio App., 2007) ("fowl" ball; spectator alleged she was distracted by the San Diego Chicken).

[86]   *Payne v. Maple Leaf Gardens Ltd.*, [1948] O.J. No. 515, [1949] O.R. 26 (Ont. C.A.). But see, *Carson v. Thunder Bay (City)*, [1985] O.J. No. 2638, 52 O.R. (2d) 173 (Ont. Dist. Ct.) (hockey

escapes cannot reasonably be prevented, and a facility is not bound to take every conceivable precaution against a generally known hazard. Neither is the occupier liable where an incident is so unusual and unexpected that it could not be reasonably anticipated.[87] The spectator "takes upon himself the risk of unlikely or improbable accidents, provided there has not been on the part of the occupier a failure to take usual precautions."[88]

An individual player can be liable for intentionally shooting the puck at a spectator[89] or for negligently shooting over the glass during a pause or intermission when the puck is not expected.[90] Where a fan is injured during the heat of the action of a game, it is necessary to show that the player's conduct was in serious disregard of spectator safety. While play is in progress, players' attention must be directed primarily towards the game, and the stress of competition must be taken into account when assessing errors of judgment or lapses in skill.[91] Players are nevertheless bound to show some regard for the known proximity of fans and may be held liable for conduct that is irregular, incompetent or unreasonable in the circumstances.[92] In *Payne v. Maple Leaf Gardens Ltd.*,[93] the plaintiff sued two professional hockey players when she sustained injuries while sitting in a rink-side seat; the front-row was about 60cm (2 feet) back from the boards, which were about 1.2m (4 feet) in height. The plaintiff was struck by a hockey stick when the defendant player, Stewart, attacked his opponent, Marucci, in an attempt to take the latter's stick. This struggle occurred outside the proper course of play, and the plaintiff's attention was directed to the opposite side of the rink. While the court found no fault on the part of Marucci, it held Stewart liable for showing reckless disregard for the safety of front-row spectators. The plaintiff season ticket holder assumed the ordinary risks of the game, but did not accept the risk of injuries resulting from negligence or improper conduct by a player.

The required standard of screening and protection was the subject of review in 2002 after 13-year-old Brittanie Cecil was struck and killed by a puck while attending a game at the arena of the Columbus (Ohio) Blue Jackets.[94] This was apparently the first such fatality during a game in the National Hockey League

---

stick came through open mesh screen not of reasonable standard; no warnings; plaintiff 50 per cent responsible).

[87] *Payne v. Maple Leaf Gardens Ltd.*, [1948] O.J. No. 515, [1949] O.R. 26 (Ont. C.A.) (fight between hockey players for possession of stick).

[88] *Hall v. Brooklands Auto Racing Club*, [1933] 1 K.B. 205 at 224 (C.A.), *per* Greer L.J.

[89] On criminal liability, see, *R. v. Kemp*, [1993] S.J. No. 62, 107 Sask.R. 304 (Sask. Q.B.) (accused acquitted; insufficient evidence that player intended to fire puck at spectators).

[90] *Lewis v. Soucie*, [1990] B.C.J. No. 2283 (B.C.S.C.) (practice shot during intermission went over low portion of plexiglass shield).

[91] *Wooldridge v. Sumner*, [1963] 2 Q.B. 43 (C.A.) (photographer injured by show horse); A.L. Goodhart, "The Sportsman's Charter" (1962) 78 L.Q. Rev. 490; *Wilks v. Cheltenham Home Guard Motor Cycle and Light Car Club*, [1971] 2 All E.R. 369 (C.A.).

[92] Such conduct might include reckless or undisciplined behaviour in breach of game rules; see, *Wooldridge v. Sumner*, [1963] 2 Q.B. 43 at 57 (C.A.).

[93] [1948] O.J. No. 515, [1949] O.R. 26 (C.A.).

[94] See: "Hockey fan's death decried" *The Globe and Mail* (Toronto: March 20, 2002) at A1, A15; "Teen's death stuns Ohio village" *The Globe and Mail* (Toronto: March 21, 2002) at A7.

("NHL"), although deaths have occurred in community arenas and at minor league games, where there are also regular reports of serious injuries to bystanders.[95] At the time of the tragedy in Columbus, NHL arenas commonly had 2.4m (8 feet) of protective glass (usually Plexiglas) behind the goals, while the tempered glass along the side boards varied between 1.2m and 1.8m (4-6 feet). It was also the practice to print warnings on tickets and to use the scoreboard and public-address system to remind patrons to be on the alert for the flight of the puck. In June 2002, the NHL ordered its clubs to maintain a minimum of 1.5m (5 feet) of glass along the sides and required the installation of protective "spectator netting" above the end boards.[96] Similar mesh systems have been a common practice in Europe, and government publications in Quebec have recommended the use of fireproof netting sufficient to stop a puck at 160km/h.[97] In 2004, the Canadian Standards Association ("CSA") proposed voluntary standards of protection to be used in new indoor arenas. These guidelines aim to minimize interaction with spectators, while also reducing the risk of injury to participants if they accidentally leave the playing area. The CSA recommended that board and glass systems should be subject to impact testing at a velocity of 130 km/h and proposed that the appropriate heights measured from the ice should be 2.4m (8 feet) at the sides and 3m (10 feet) at the ends.[98] The CSA recommended that these systems permanently surround each playing area and favoured the use of spoken or written warnings:

> Prior to a game or event, and before the beginning of each period of any sporting event, the following announcement (or something equivalent) should be broadcast over the public address system: "Attention Fans! Be aware that pucks/balls/sticks/equipment may leave the surface at any time, which can cause serious injury. Please pay attention to the activities on the playing surface at all times!"

---

[95]   See, for example: "Hockey's worst injuries are in the stands" *The Globe and Mail* (Toronto: March 18, 2000) at A1, A4; "Injuries to spectators are hockey's 'dark' secret'" *The Globe and Mail* (Toronto: March 28, 2002) at A4.

[96]   "NHL's move to netting applauded" *The Ottawa Citizen* (June 22, 2002) at F2. See now, *National Hockey League Official Rules* (2009-2010), 1.3 (Boards and Glass) (boards of not less than 40 inches; 8 feet of approved safety glass at the ends, 5 feet along both sides), 1.4 (Spectator Netting), online: <http://www.nhl.com/league/ext/rules/2009-2010_Rule_Book.pdf>. The IIHF "Rules for Ice Rinks" require end zone nets and protective glass 160-200 cm in height at the ends and 80-120 cm along the sides.

[97]   *Sécuri-Sport Express - Hockey Sur Glace* (Secrétariat au loisir et au sport du gouvernement du Québec, mars 2000) at 6. This study also recommends 178 cm of glass along the sides of the rink and 224 cm at the ends. See also, *Guide de sécurité et de prévention dans les arénas* (Association des arénas du Québec/Ministère de l'Éducation, du loisir et du Sport); *Picotte c. Fédération québécoise de hockey sur glace Inc.*, [2000] J.Q. no 3144 (C.Q.) (spectator struck by puck during Pee Wee practice session).

[98]   *Guidelines for Spectator Safety in Indoor Arenas* (CAN/CSA-Z262.7-04) (Mississauga, ON: Canadian Standards Association, March 2004), clause 5.2.2 (amended June 2004), clause 6.

Where no public address system is feasible or available, signage should be used to convey the same message.[99]

With the renewed awareness of the dangers and the various safety initiatives, it is probable that the acceptable standard of care is now modified for the purpose of civil liability.[100] Improved protection may also be mandated by the increased speed of shots unleashed by a stronger breed of player using modern equipment. Venerable or modest community facilities are not required to match the cutting-edge precautions built into new NHL arenas, but the warning systems and the size and quality of screening will now be closely evaluated to see that they conform to evolving ideas of what is reasonably safe "in all the circumstances". The elite facilities will also have to reconsider the array of commercial clutter and other distractions that take fans' eyeballs away from the danger zone.

A rink presents further environmental hazards from deafening noise[101] and from the chemical stew required to lay down and maintain artificial ice. Ice-making equipment uses systems of filtration and refrigeration,[102] and harmful levels of carbon monoxide and nitrogen dioxide can be generated by machinery powered by gasoline or propane. The ice-grooming or resurfacing vehicle is commonly identified as the source of emissions and pollutants,[103] so that a move to electric models is desirable. The dangers of gas inhalation apply to rink staff and spectators, although the risks are particularly acute in the case of players because of their intense physical activity and high rates of breathing. The risk of gas poisoning can be reduced by proper maintenance of machinery, adequate

---

[99] *Guidelines for Spectator Safety in Indoor Arenas* (CAN/CSA-Z262.7-04) (Mississauga, ON: Canadian Standards Association, March 2004), clause 7.2.

[100] See: M. Hirshfeld, "Do spectator safety standards miss the net" *The Lawyers Weekly* (June 2, 2002) at 9; M. Hirshfeld, "Do Current Safety Standards Miss The Net? A Review of Canadian Law with Regard to Spectator Injuries at Sporting Events" (October-December), 13:4 *For The Record* 2 (The Official Newsletter of the National Sports Law Institute).

[101] W.E. Hodgetts & R. Liu, "Can hockey playoffs harm your hearing?" (2006) 175 Can. Medical Assn. J. 1541 (study using Edmonton Oilers' "loud" arena). See also, "Playoffs' din can damage your hearing" *The Globe and Mail* (Toronto: December 5, 2006) at A17 (noise level equal to chainsaw at 1½ m).

[102] According to the "National Arena Census" (Canadian Recreation Facilities Council/Hockey Canada, 2005) at 3, 65 per cent of arenas use ammonia as the primary refrigerant and 25 per cent use freon. See also: "Technical guidelines of an ice rink" in "Arena Development Manual", online: <http://www.iihf.com>; "How Ice Rinks Work", online: <http://www.howstuffworks.com/ice-rink>.

[103] See: M. Brauer *et al.*, "Air Pollutant Exposures Inside Ice Hockey Rinks: Exposure Assessment and Reduction Strategies" in C.R. Castaldi, P.J. Bishop & E.F. Hoener, eds., *Safety in Ice Hockey: Second Volume* (Philadelphia: ASTM, 1993) 142; "Watch Out for That Ice Cleaning Machine!" (March-May 1991) 1:3 Safety Net 1 (C.A.H.A.). See also, *Zurich Insurance Co. v. 686234 Ontario Ltd.*, [2002] O.J. No. 4496, 62 O.R. (3d) 447 (Ont. C.A.) (carbon dioxide poisoning in apartment complex; pollution liability exclusion in insurance contract did not apply). On other dangers related to the Zamboni, see, *Resurfice Corp. v. Hanke*, [2007] S.C.J. No. 7, [2007] 1 S.C.R. 333 (S.C.C.) (driver of ice-resurfacing machine badly burned by gas tank explosion).

ventilation and regular testing of air quality,[104] and it is particularly important that the air standard take account of the regular presence of young participants. The signs of carbon monoxide poisoning include headaches, fatigue, nausea and dizziness. Nitrogen dioxide poisoning is characterized by flu-like, respiratory conditions such as coughing and bronchitis, and the effects may be delayed for several days. Arena staff must be trained to identify symptoms, and the emergency action plan must include appropriate first aid.

## C.  WAIVERS, EXCLUSIONS AND INDEMNITIES[105]

Arenas and program operators often try to avoid liability through notices, tickets or entry forms that disclaim responsibility and indicate that all risks are assumed by the visitor or participating player. Registration documents may, for example, include an acknowledgment of the inherent dangers of the game together with a standard form waiver or release of liability. A defendant relying on such an agreement claims that the plaintiff, as a condition of entry, has given up the right to sue with respect to damage, death or injury. The waiver is, therefore, something more than a warning sign or consent form: it is an exclusion establishing a contractual defence to liability in tort. A further mechanism is a contract of indemnity or "hold harmless agreement" by which one person promises to reimburse another for losses incurred through specified actions or activities. Participants or other parties may, for example, be required to sign undertakings that they will indemnify rink owners or program operators for any liability award or other costs resulting from participation. Where the potential award is in favour of the participant who has agreed to the indemnity, the promise-to-reimburse constitutes a defence to the action. Hockey Canada advises that rink rental agreements should not include a "hold harmless" clause because of the potential to

---

[104]  See: *Sécuri-Sport Express - Hockey Sur Glace* (Secrétariat au loisir et au sport du gouvernement du Québec, mars 2000) at 7-8; M. Brauer *et al.*, "Air Pollutant Exposures Inside Ice Hockey Rinks: Exposure Assessment and Reduction Strategies" in C.R. Castaldi, P.J. Bishop & E.F. Hoener, eds., *Safety in Ice Hockey: Second Volume* (Philadelphia: ASTM, 1993) 142 at 155. On workplace safety, see, *Occupational Health and Safety Act*, R.S.O. 1990, c. O.1, s. 70, para. 21 (power to issue regulations relating to atmospheric conditions).

[105]  See: J.J. Neumann, "Disclaimer Clauses and Personal Injury" (1991) 55 Sask. L. Rev. 312; Law Reform Commission of British Columbia, *Consultation Paper No. 70, Recreational Injuries: Liability and Waivers in Commercial Leisure Activities* (Vancouver, August 1993); D. Healey, "Disclaimers, Exclusion Clauses, Waivers and Liability Release Forms in Sport: Can They Succeed in Limiting Liability?" in M. Fewell, ed., *Sports Law: A Practical Guide* (Sydney: LBC Information Services, 1995) 194; J. Barnes, *Sports and the Law in Canada*, 3d ed. (Toronto: Butterworths, 1996) at 276-79; J. Weir & S.A. Thiele, "Making Sense of Exemption Clauses" (1998) 21 Advocates' Q. 71; F.D. Cass, *The Law of Releases in Canada* (Aurora, ON: Canada Law Book, 2006) at 151-76, 191-93, 321-25; Manitoba Law Reform Commission, *Waivers of Liability for Sporting and Recreational Injuries* (Report #120, January 2009).

transfer liability even when the fault lay with the facility or with individuals who are not members of Hockey Canada or any of its Branches.[106]

In the case of visitors or participants who are over the age of majority, premises and programs are able to exclude liability because it is permissible to require adults to assume all risks when they voluntarily engage in recreational activities that entail known hazards.[107] Even when documentation is presented on a take-it-or-leave-it basis, waivers can be effective provided they accurately refer to the circumstances of the injury and provided their legal effect has been properly communicated.[108] A suitably drafted and administered waiver can preclude action by an adult,[109] but fair dealing is required and various tests must be satisfied:

1. interpretation and application;

2. forms of liability;

3. signing and notice;

4. reasonable steps; and

5. timing.

1. *Interpretation and application*: Exclusionary contract clauses are construed in their plain terms and according to the context in which they are used, but the meaning is not extended in favour of the party drafting them and relying on them. The provisions are construed *contra proferentem*. If the language is ambiguous or non-inclusive, the exclusion does not apply. For example, a release referring to claims by players would not preclude claims by spectators or officials, and a release referring to injuries on the ice would not apply to injuries in the stands. Similarly, a release mentioning named defendants would not preclude action against other parties. A registration form naming

---

[106] See, Hockey Canada, *Safety Requires Teamwork & Safety For All* (2009–2010) at 52. In *Griffiths v. New Westminster (City)*, [2001] B.C.J. No. 2274, 25 M.P.L.R. (3d) 31 (B.C.S.C.), it was held that an individual renting a rink was not required to indemnify the city for its own acts or omissions. The confusing licence agreement contemplated rental by an organization, and an individual would not expect to become the insurer of the city.

[107] Under Quebec civil law, material injury caused by "gross fault" (*faute lourde*) may not be excluded, and there can be no exclusion of liability for bodily injury; see, *Civil Code of Québec*, R.S.Q. c. C-1991, art. 1474.

[108] An indemnity must also be written in clear terms, and the party imposing the obligation must take reasonable steps to draw the attention of the person signing to the onerous provision; see, *Griffiths v. New Westminster (City)*, [2001] B.C.J. No. 2274, 25 M.P.L.R. (3d) 31 (B.C.S.C.).

[109] On effective exclusions in entry forms, see, for example: *Delaney v. Cascade River Holidays Ltd.*, [1983] B.C.J. No. 476, 44 B.C.L.R. 24 (B.C.C.A.) (rafting); *Dyck v. Manitoba Snowmobile Assn. Inc.*, [1985] S.C.J. No. 34, [1985] 1 S.C.R. 589 (S.C.C.) (snowmobile race); *Karroll v. Silver Star Mountain Resorts Ltd.*, [1988] B.C.J. No. 2266, 33 B.C.L.R. (2d) 160 (B.C.S.C.) (downhill ski race); *Ocsko v. Cypress Bowl Recreations Ltd.*, [1992] B.C.J. No. 1962, 95 D.L.R. (4th) 701 (B.C.C.A.) (skiing); *Schuster v. Blackcomb Skiing Enterprises Limited Partnership*, [1994] B.C.J. No. 2602, [1995] 3 W.W.R. 443 (B.C.S.C.) (skiing).

"USA Hockey, its Affiliates, their sponsors, event organizers and officials" provided no protection for the city that owned and operated the rink.[110]

2. *Forms of liability*: If the release can apply only to actions for negligence, the clause will be held to cover negligence, but if some other cause of injury is possible (*e.g.*, inherent risks in the game) or if some other ground of liability is available, negligence liability will be excluded only if clear terms are used. A common form of words is to release liability "due to any cause whatsoever, including negligence, breach of contract, breach of statutory or other duty of care or breach of the *Occupiers' Liability Act*".

3. *Signing and notice*: In the absence of fraud or misrepresentation, adults who sign contractual documents are bound by their terms even though they have not read them. Signers must, however, be given reasonable opportunity to see that the contract contains an exclusion and attention must be directed to that clause.[111] A common practice is to begin the document with conspicuous lettering boldly indicating that it involves a release or waiver affecting legal rights.

4. *Reasonable steps*: Where a contract is made without signing, an exclusion clause will be incorporated if the party relying on it took reasonable steps to bring it to the other party's attention. Similarly, under occupiers' liability legislation, "reasonable steps" must be taken to bring signed or unsigned exclusions to the attention of visitors to premises.[112]

5. *Timing*: The exclusion must be clearly written on a contractual document, not on a mere voucher or receipt. The steps notifying the other party of the terms must be taken at or before the time of contracting.

A valid waiver must, therefore, be comprehensive in its terms, and the person affected must be carefully alerted as to the contents of the document. Where an injured participant sues a program operator in spite of the presence of a waiver, the defendant often moves for summary dismissal on the basis that there is no possibility that the action will succeed or that there is no genuine issue for trial.[113] In *Pascoe v. Ball Hockey Ontario Inc.*,[114] the plaintiff alleged that his broken leg was caused by the negligence of Ball Hockey Ontario in failing to clear ice from the rink surface. Prior to participation, the plaintiff had read and willingly signed a waiver in the following terms:

> I/we assume all risk and hazards incidental to such participation, including transportation to and from the activities and I/we hereby waive, release,

---

[110]  *Wyrembelski v. City of St. Clair Shores*, 553 N.W.2d 651 (Mich. C.A., 1996) (plaintiff broke leg when skate caught in rut near boards; city was not "Affiliate" of USA Hockey).

[111]  See, *Crocker v. Sundance Northwest Resorts Ltd.*, [1988] S.C.J. No. 60, [1988] 1 S.C.R. 1186 (S.C.C.) (release not drawn to attention of participant in race on inner tubes down mogulled ski hill).

[112]  See, for example, *Occupiers' Liability Act*, R.S.O. 1990, c. O-2, s. 5(3). On notice given to a first-time visitor from England, see, *Greeven v. Blackcomb Skiing Enterprises Ltd.*, [1994] B.C.J. No. 2056, 22 C.C.L.T. (2d) 265 (B.C.S.C.).

[113]  See, for example, *Rules of Civil Procedure*, R.R.O. 1990, Reg. 194, r. 20.04(2).

[114]  [2005] O.J. No. 520, 137 A.C.W.S. (3d) 74 (Ont. S.C.J.).

absolve...and agree to hold harmless the supervisors, participants, officials, sponsors, organizers and corporation owners of the premises.[115]

The plaintiff alleged that he fell and was injured because of an unexpected hazard in the form of the condition of the rink and claimed that it was not contemplated that the waiver would provide protection when the "risk and hazards" were created and perpetuated by Ball Hockey Ontario. The court agreed that a trial was needed, so that the defendant's application for summary judgment was refused. There were issues to be determined relating to negligence and the applicability of the waiver.

A waiver was held not to apply in *Leonard v. Dunn*[116] when a player lost two teeth as a result of a punch from an opponent during recreational non-contact hockey. The game sheet used at a village sports facility incorporated an ungrammatical printed form in which signers acknowledged understanding the waiver, freely agreed to assume the risk of serious injury and agreed to withdraw themselves from participation on observing any "unusual significant hazard". The form then continued with the following release:

> I, for myself and on behalf of my heirs, assigns, personal representative and next of kin, HEREBY RELEASE AND HOLD HARMLESS THE VAUGHAN SPORTS VILLAGE, their officers, officials, agents and/or employees, other participants, sponsoring agencies, sponsors, advertisers and if applicable, owners and lessors of premises used to conduct the event ("Releasees"), WITH RESPECT TO ANY AND ALL INJURY, DISABILITY, DEATH, or loss or damage to person or property, WHETHER CAUSED BY THE NEGLIGENCE OF THE RELEASES (*sic*) OR OTHERWISE.[117]

The court recognised that injuries might occur from rule violations and objectionable play even in non-contact hockey, but held that the terms of the release did not clearly extend to injuries caused by battery. Deliberate unilateral attack was not within the implied consent and as a matter of public policy the waiver should not be construed as extending to unprovoked assaults. Low J. commented as follows:

> However fraught with potential for injury, hockey is nevertheless a sport, a contest of skill and strategy to be carried out in competitive but sportsmanlike manner. It is not a bar room brawl. When a player signs the game sheet agreeing to the terms of the waiver, he is assuming the risks inherent in playing the game; he is not volunteering to be the recipient of a battery.[118]

---

[115] *Pascoe v. Ball Hockey Ontario Inc.*, [2005] O.J. No. 520 at para. 18, 137 A.C.W.S. (3d) 74 (Ont. S.C.J.).

[116] [2006] O.J. No. 3941, 151 A.C.W.S. (3d) 1172 (Ont. S.C.J.), affd [2008] O.J. No. 2051, 167 A.C.W.S. (3d) 227 (Ont. Div. Ct.).

[117] *Leonard v. Dunn*, [2006] O.J. No. 3941 at para. 13, 151 A.C.W.S. (3d) 1172 (Ont. S.C.J.).

[118] *Leonard v. Dunn*, [2006] O.J. No. 3941 at para. 20, 151 A.C.W.S. (3d) 1172 (Ont. S.C.J.).

Although waivers can be effective in the case of adults, they cannot exclude liability towards persons who are under the age of majority, which is now attained at 18 or 19 years depending on the Province.[119] To be valid, most contracts made by minors (or "infants") must be for their benefit, and since a release or exclusion of rights is to the minor's disadvantage, such contracts are not enforceable.[120] Similarly, signing by a parent or guardian does not waive the minor's right to bring an action.[121] Where the program seeks to protect itself through an indemnity signed by the parent or guardian, that agreement may also be held to be unenforceable as a matter of public policy because the adult representatives are unlikely to initiate action to secure compensation for the minor when faced with the threat of indemnification.[122]

Proper documentation excluding liability to adult participants can serve as an effective risk management technique by putting some control on the costs of operating programs. The use of exclusions on spectators' tickets is less likely to affect liability because the texts are rarely conspicuous and it is not the practice to draw fans' attention to them. Similarly, fans are not usually required to sign comprehensive waivers as a condition of admission. Although waivers have no legal effect where minors suffer injuries as a result of negligence, they serve to discourage litigation and are commonly used as evidence that the parent and child had full appreciation of the inherent risks of the game. Waivers, exclusions and indemnities have their role in program administration, but should not displace efficient systems of injury prevention. Permitting the use of waivers carries the risk that too much effort will go into garish lettering and cunning drafting and not enough into safety.

---

[119] See, for example, *Age of Majority and Accountability Act*, R.S.O. 1990, c. A-7, s. 1 (age 18).

[120] *Butterfield v. Sibbitt and Nipissing Electricity Supply Co.*, [1950] O.J. No. 459, [1950] O.R. 504 (Ont. H.C.J.); *Swanson v. Hanneson*, [1972] M.J. No. 67 (Man. Q.B.); *Sterna v. Henkel Enterprises Ltd.*, [1972] M.J. No. 67, [1972] 3 W.W.R. 241 (Man. Q.B.), affd [1973] M.J. No. 27, [1973] 6 W.W.R. 179 (Man. C.A.); *Miller (Next friend of) v. Sinclair (c.o.b. Sinclair's Riding Stables)*, [1980] O.J. No. 209, 15 C.C.L.T. 57 (Ont. H.C.J.).

[121] See, *Wong (Litigation guardian of) v. Lok's Martial Arts Centre Inc.*, [2009] B.C.J. No. 1992, 2009 BCSC 1385 (B.C.S.C.). On minors' contracts and indemnities in British Columbia, see, *Infants Act*, R.S.B.C. 1996, c. 223, ss. 18-27. A release signed by a parent may be binding under the law of Ohio; see, *Mohney v. USA Hockey, Inc.*, 77 F.Supp. 2d 859 (N.D. Ohio, 1999), vard 5 Fed. Appx 450 (6th Cir., 2001) (collision with boards as players raced for puck under "touch icing" rules).

[122] *Stevens v. Howitt*, [1969] O.J. No. 1282, 4 D.L.R. (3d) 50 (Ont. H.C.J.) (injuries suffered in automobile accident; indemnity for insurer would effectively destroy the minor's potential cause of action); see also, Law Reform Commission of British Columbia, *Consultation Paper No. 70, Recreational Injuries: Liability and Waivers in Commercial Leisure Activities* (Vancouver, August 1993) at 40-41. The enforcement of waivers and indemnities presents particular difficulties when minors participate in research into the effects of body checking; see Chapter 6, "Play Safe: On the Ice", section A, 2.

## D.   INSURANCE[123]

A contract of insurance spreads the risk and burden of loss throughout the many subscribers to the insurance company. In exchange for the insured's payment of a premium, the company undertakes to pay for specified losses,[124] subject to maximum limits and prescribed exclusions.[125] Two types of loss may be covered:

> Liability insurance, which refers to costs and obligations derived from the insured's legal liability to others, including the cost of defending the lawsuit; and
>
> Accident, disability or medical insurance, which refers to expenses and payments related to personal injury or illness suffered by the insured.

Accident and medical insurance operate as private arrangements providing benefits and treatment additional to those available under provincial health care plans. The provincial plans cover medical expenses incurred in other Provinces, but additional health insurance is required for travel outside Canada.

The Hockey Canada Insurance Program[126] includes both liability coverage and benefits payable in the event of serious accidents. To keep premium costs down, the Program operates as secondary coverage[127] supplementing participants' individual protection provided by homeowners' or motor vehicle policies, private medical plans or similar coverage.[128] The Program also

---

[123]  See, S. Bird & J. Zauhar, *Recreation and the Law*, 2d ed. (Scarborough, ON: Carswell, 1997) at 163-76. On benefits available to NHL players, see Chapter 6, "Play Safe: On the Ice", section A, 4; Chapter 9, "National Hockey League", sections C; E.

[124]  On claims and payouts, see: *Jones v. Saskatoon Minor Hockey Assn.*, [2002] S.J. No. 376, 2002 SKQB 230 (Sask. Q.B.); *Pouliot c. Ligue de hockey mineur de St-Jean Inc.*, [2002] J.Q. No. 10429 (C.Q.); *Gosselin c. Association du hockey mineur Ste-Foy-Sillery inc.*, 2006 QCCQ 17244 (C.Q.).

[125]  See, for example, *Dawson Creek (City) v. Zurich Insurance Co.*, [2000] B.C.J. No. 463, [2000] 5 W.W.R. 311 (B.C.C.A.) (arena roof collapsed under weight of snow; faulty construction was not an excluded "inherent vice or latent defect").

[126]  See, Hockey Canada, *Safety Requires Teamwork & Safety for All* (2009–2010) at 36-57. The precise terms of the master policies are available for inspection at Branch offices. See also: "Insurance Program — Insurance FAQ's", available online: <http://www.hockeycanada.ca>; Ontario Hockey Federation, *Insurance Guide* (2006), available online: <http://www.ohf.on.ca> (under the "Risk Management" and "Insurance" tabs).

[127]  On overlapping coverage and contribution between insurers, see, *Canadian Universities Reciprocal Insurance Exchange v. CGU Insurance Co. of Canada*, [2007] O.J. No. 3612, 87 O.R. (3d) 672 (Ont. C.A.) (injury in judo class at university; club continued to be a member of Judo Ontario so that coverage was provided to volunteers; insurer was required to make equitable contribution).

[128]  Where insurance is absent or insufficient, a participant may claim that a program operator was under an obligation to advise of the need for coverage; see, *Oldfield v. MacMillan*, [1998] N.B.J. No. 103, 78 A.C.W.S. (3d) 1246 (N.B.Q.B. (T.D.)). But see, *Van Oppen v. Bedford Charity Trustees*, [1989] 3 All E.R. 389 (C.A.), affg [1989] 1 All E.R. 273 (Q.B.D.) (rugby injury; school under no duty to advise parents of need to take out accident insurance).

supplements insurance maintained by municipalities and other owners of arenas, so that it is common for owners to require teams or associations to show proof of their own insurance when renting facilities. Each member of Hockey Canada pays into the Program or has a fee paid on his or her behalf, and the payments contribute to the administrative costs of the risk management program. The basic fee can vary according to the number of claims in different parts of the country and may be supplemented by Branch administration fees and provincial taxes. In 2009, the basic fee was CDN $16.15, the major part of which contributed towards the liability insurance element. For the period, 2007 to 2012, the Commercial General Liability Policy called for the "Canadian Amateur Hockey Association" to pay an annual premium of CDN $4.8 million (a reduction from the previous rate of CDN $5.5 million).

The Commercial General Liability Policy provides up to CDN $20 million in coverage with respect to a single incident and applies to claims alleging liability for bodily injury, personal injury (*e.g.*, libel) or property damage; the Policy would, for example, apply where a lawsuit alleges that injuries were the result of negligence by a player, coach or official. Under the Policy, coverage does not extend to bodily injury or property damage "expected or intended from the standpoint of the insured", although this exclusion does not extend to injury or damage:

> resulting from the use of reasonable force to protect persons or property, or...
> resulting from the rendering of or failure to obtain "first aid treatment" ...[129]

It is also provided that "on ice" altercations are not considered to be excluded intentional acts, and the "ice" for this purpose includes the arena premises and adjacent parking lot. Special exclusions in the Policy relate to "any injury sustained by any person arising out of or resulting from the physical and/or sexual abuse of any person".[130] The general liability insurance coverage is subject to a deductible of CDN $100,000 in relation to each "occurrence".[131] Except for participants in "athletics" in "restricted areas", this Policy also offers up to CDN $25,000 in medical expenses.[132]

---

[129] Commercial General Liability Policy No. 0511578 (Canadian Amateur Hockey Association, September 1, 2007 – September 1, 2012), Section I, Coverage A, clause 2(a), as amended by Endorsement No. 14. See also, *Thorne v. Royal & SunAlliance Insurance Co. of Canada*, [2003] N.B.J. No. 322, 230 D.L.R. (4th) 587 (N.B.C.A.) (company had duty to defend player sued by an opposing player; insured claimed that his punch to the opponent's face was in self-defence).

[130] Commercial General Liability Policy No. 0511578 (Canadian Amateur Hockey Association, September 1, 2007 – September 1, 2012), Endorsement No. 12.

[131] Commercial General Liability Policy No. 0511578 (Canadian Amateur Hockey Association, September 1, 2007 – September 1, 2012), Endorsement No. 4.

[132] Commercial General Liability Policy No. 0511578 (Canadian Amateur Hockey Association, September 1, 2007 – September 1, 2012), Section I, Coverage C; Endorsement No. 13.

Under the Policy, the "named insured"[133] are the "Canadian Amateur Hockey Association", Hockey Canada, Branch associations and federations and the Canadian Hockey League. The in-line program is excluded, although the exclusions no longer refer to "CHA Adult Recreational Hockey". Besides the "named insured", coverage extends to the following individuals provided they are "acting at the direction of, or within the scope of their duties for the CAHA":

> owners, officers, directors, shareholder, members of committees, registered members, sponsors, employees, players, managers, staff members, team workers, officials, cheerleaders, referees, coaches, trainers, instructors, volunteers, and spouses of any of the foregoing ...[134]

Volunteers and off-ice officials assigned specific duties are included, provided premiums have been paid on their behalf and provided their names have been placed on lists approved by local associations and forwarded to Branch offices.

Additional liability coverage relates to directors' and officers' liability (D. & O.) and to sexual misconduct liability. The D. & O. insurance covers liability costs arising from official decisions taken by directors and officers of associations, teams or Branches; this program provides coverage to board members in defending actions and in paying any liability award. The sexual misconduct insurance covers the costs of defending civil actions brought by members, but not the cost of defending criminal charges.[135]

The accident insurance program offers supplementary coverage relating to accidental death or dismemberment ("A.D. & D.") and to major medical or dental costs. The A.D. & D. insurance applies to serious, permanent injuries suffered within a year of the accident, where the scale of benefits includes CDN $1 million for paralysis, CDN $50,000 for the loss of both eyes and CDN $25,000 for loss of life. The medical and dental plans offer coverage of reasonable expenses incurred within a year of the accident, subject to various maximum amounts. The expenses that may be reimbursed include the costs of nursing and hospital services, dental treatment, professional therapy, rental of equipment and transportation. The plan also covers some lost income during a 30-day period.

---

[133] Commercial General Liability Policy No. 0511578 (Canadian Amateur Hockey Association, September 1, 2007 – September 1, 2012), Endorsement No. 1.

[134] Commercial General Liability Policy No. 0511578 (Canadian Amateur Hockey Association, September 1, 2007 – September 1, 2012), Section II, 1. See also: *Gosselin c. Association du hockey mineur Ste-Foy-Sillery inc.*, 2006 QCCQ 17244 (C.Q.) (coverage for volunteer coach); *Canadian Universities Reciprocal Insurance Exchange v. CGU Insurance Co. of Canada*, [2007] O.J. No. 3612, 87 O.R. (3d) 672 (Ont. C.A.) (coverage for volunteer instructors at member club in judo).

[135] On processes and remedies in relation to sexual harassment and abuse, see Chapter 4, "Build Safe: Rink Management and Risk Management", section C.

Coverage under the Program applies during sanctioned events between member teams,[136] including the time spent staying in hotels or other accommodation. Insured players and personnel are covered with respect to travel to or from the arena or venue, although in the case of injuries suffered while travelling in a rented vehicle the primary insurance is the coverage placed by the owner of the vehicle.[137] The Program is designed to provide protection for activities directly related to the playing of hockey,[138] so that special provisions and exclusions apply in relation to social events and fundraisers. Coverage is usually excluded in relation to high risk events involving the consumption of alcohol.

Claims under the Program are made by filing a Hockey Canada Injury Report detailing the nature of the injury and how and when it occurred. The formal report requires the signature of a team official, health insurance information and statements from a physician or dentist. The completed claim must be submitted to the Branch office within 90 days of the accident. From 2001 to 2006, there was an average of 45 claims each year of which the majority related to on-ice incidents. In 2005, out of a total of 41 claims, the distribution was: 26 (on-ice), 4 (off-ice), 3 (spectator injuries) and 8 (rights claims).[139]

After 2000, the Hockey Canada Insurance Program became financially sound and had recovered from the serious strain caused by well-publicised liability cases.[140] The early 1990s had seen massive claims based on catastrophic injuries to players,[141] and there were subsequent crises based on the incidence of sexual abuse. Liability and health care costs have been addressed through a range of prevention and risk management programs applying to both the off-ice environment and the game itself.

---

[136] In relation to international competitions and events, IIHF Bylaws 408-409 (July 2008) provide that national associations and their teams are responsible for insurance coverage and the "IIHF is neither responsible for insurance nor for any liability". See also, IIHF International Transfer Regulations (May 2009), I 10.3, 10.5 (responsibility of team releasing player for international matches).

[137] On the scope of insurance coverage related to the use or operation of a motor vehicle, see: *Citadel General Assurance Co. v. Vytlingam*, [2007] S.C.J. No. 46, [2007] 3 S.C.R. 373 (S.C.C.); *Lumbermans Mutual Casualty Co. v. Herbison*, [2007] S.C.J. No. 47, [2007] 3 S.C.R. 393 (S.C.C.). See also, *Morrow (Litigation guardian of) v. Symons*, [2007] O.J. No. 662, 85 O.R. (3d) 365 (Ont. S.C.J.) (plaintiff injured while being towed on inline skates).

[138] See also, *Marcoccia (Litigation guardian of) v. Ontario Soccer Assn. Inc.*, [1995] O.J. No. 1894, [1995] I.L.R. ¶1-3228 (Ont. Gen. Div.) (coverage for soccer did not include baseball game).

[139] J. Sharoun, Hockey Canada Risk Management & Insurance Committee Meetings (October 12-13, 2007).

[140] On the general insurance crisis in Canadian sport, see, G. Hanna, *Outdoor Pursuits Programming: Legal Liability and Risk Management* (Edmonton: University of Alberta Press, 1991) at 138-58.

[141] See, for example: *Unruh (Guardian ad litem of) v. Webber*, [1994] B.C.J. No. 467, [1994] 5 W.W.R. 270 (B.C.C.A.), affg [1992] B.C.J. No. 2336, 98 D.L.R. (4th) 294 (B.C.S.C.) (player rendered quadriplegic in Midget AA game; award of CDN $3.7 million plus costs); see further, Chapter 6, "Play Safe: On the Ice", section C. In 1993, the CAHA had to increase its insurance rate for players from CDN $3 to CDN $20.

# Chapter 5

# BE SAFE: OFF THE ICE

Once outside the hockey enclosure, the physically dominant model of masculinity loses its validity, and these young men are often left with only physical dominance to compensate for their sudden powerlessness.[1]

## A.  OFF-ICE RISKS, SPORTING EXCESS AND MASCULINITY

This chapter deals with conduct and safety in the wider setting of hockey and considers how physical contact can spill out of bounds. Besides the hazards of the arena and the risks of play,[2] there is danger in the off-ice environment from deliberate assaults and other criminal acts,[3] including the full scale riot. The tribalism and hyper-masculinity of the game can stray beyond the boards into "rink rage", sexual assault and other forms of violence and abuse.[4] Partisan hostility is directed against those in stripes or opposing colours, but there is also danger within the victim's own organization from both authority figures and teammates. Relationships of power may be exploited for sexual purposes, and it is fellow players who like to welcome rookies with humiliating hazing rituals. With friend and foe alike, the zone of risk and misconduct extends beyond the ice surface, and even the annual awards ceremony can be marred by serious brawling.[5]

The various examples of deliberate violence and abuse may be linked to "negative imperatives"[6] in modern sport and its inherent tendency to carry things too far. Sport has the potential to offer a constructive experience, but can also be

---

[1]    M.A. Robidoux, *Men at Play: A Working Understanding of Professional Hockey* (Montreal & Kingston: McGill-Queens University Press, 2001) at 30. See further, D. Storey, *This Sporting Life* (London: Longmans, 1960) and film version (1963).

[2]    See: Chapter 4, "Build Safe: Rink Management and Risk Management"; Chapter 6, "Play Safe: On the Ice".

[3]    On the definitional elements of assault and other crimes, see Chapter 6, "Play Safe: On the Ice", section B, 2, 3, discussing violence involving players.

[4]    See Chapter 5, "Be Safe: Off the Ice", sections B-E.

[5]    *R. v. Lynch*, [1989] P.E.I.J. No. 177, 75 Nfld. & P.E.I.R. 351 (P.E.I.S.C.T.D.) (fighting at awards dinner and dance; accused convicted of aggravated assault).

[6]    S. Kirby, L. Greaves & O. Hankivsky, *The Dome of Silence: Sexual Harassment and Abuse in Sport* (Halifax: Fernwood Publishing, 2000) at 104-116 (seven negatives in modern sport). See also, W.R. McMurtry, *Investigation and Inquiry into Violence in Amateur Hockey* (Toronto: Ministry of Community and Social Services, 1974) at 20-35 (seven causes of violence in amateur hockey).

the breeding ground for anti-social behaviour and undue risk-taking.[7] The negative features include chauvinism and overly intense group loyalty, destructive competitiveness and abusive forms of sexuality. Violent behaviour can be seen as following from the social norms, commercial imperatives or power structures of sports organizations and may also be the expression of an exaggerated form of heroic masculinity[8] that is often fuelled by alcohol and other drugs. Far from being the deviant misdeeds of a few "bad apples", the claim is that misconduct is endemic to male sport and an extension of its values and culture. To make the point about men, it is useful to take the famous and rare example that involved a woman. When Tonya Harding acquiesced in the off-ice clubbing of her rival Nancy Kerrigan,[9] she was merely behaving like a man and using all aggressive means to whack the opposition. The incident became a made-for-media triumph, illustrating that nothing succeeds like excess, and figure skating was reborn as a popular full-contact sport.[10]

Since fanaticism, hard play and team culture can easily be transported into crime, it is the responsibility of teams and associations to consider the purpose of play and the values learned. The "Canadian Strategy for Ethical Conduct in Sport"[11] addresses the role and behaviour of various participants, including players, spectators, coaches, officials, volunteers and parents. The responsible parties also include the owners and operators of rinks and other facilities. The "Strategy", in combination with Hockey Canada programs, relies on education and prevention to realise the vision of a safer and less exploitive sports environment. The goal of renewed respect for all participants can also be addressed through legal regulation, criminal prosecution and civil remedies. In Canada, the applicable legal standards

---

[7]    On men taking risks, see: K. Young, "Violence, Risk, and Liability in Male Sports Culture" (1993) 10 Soc. of Sport J. 373; P. White & K. Young, "Masculinity, Sport and the Injury Process: A Review of Canadian and International Experience" (1997) 3(2) Avante 1.

[8]    On sport and masculinity, see: B. Pronger, *The Arena of Masculinity: Sport, Homosexuality, and the Meaning of Sex* (Toronto: Summerhill Press, 1990); M.A. Messner, *Power at Play: Sports and the Problem of Masculinity* (Boston: Beacon Press, 1992); M.A. Messner & D.F. Sabo, *Sex, Violence & Power in Sports: Rethinking Masculinity* (Freedom: The Crossing Press, 1994); M.B. Nelson, *The Stronger Women Get, The More Men Love Football: Sexism and the American Culture of Sport* (New York: Harcourt, Brace & Co., 1994); V. Burstyn, *The Rites of Men: Manhood, Politics, and the Culture of Sport* (Toronto: University of Toronto Press, 1999); M.A. Robidoux, *Men at Play: A Working Understanding of Professional Hockey* (Montreal & Kingston: McGill-Queens University Press, 2001).

[9]    See: "Kerrigan Attacked After Practice; Assailant Flees" *The New York Times* (January 7, 1994) at B7, B9; "Harding pleads guilty to role in coverup" *The Globe and Mail* (Toronto: March 17, 1994) at E6; *Harding v. U.S. Figure Skating Assn.*, 851 F.Supp. 1476 (D. Ore, 1994). In 2000, Harding pleaded guilty to an alcohol-related attack on her boyfriend.

[10]   In a further example of attempting to disable the opposition, a father in France has been convicted of drugging his children's tennis opponents with the result that one player died in a car crash: "The pushy tennis dad and the drugs in the drinks" *The Guardian* (London: March 1, 2006) "Man jailed for drugging his children's tennis rivals" *The Globe and Mail* (Toronto: March 10, 2006) at A3.

[11]   "Canadian Strategy for Ethical Conduct in Sport: Policy Framework" (May 24, 2002), online: <http://www.pch.gc.ca>; see Chapter 2, "Legal Fundamentals and Equality Rights", section B, 3. On the True Sport Foundation, see online: <http://www.truesportpur.ca>.

are usually those of the general law rather than special legislation adopted to deal with dangers peculiar to the sports setting.[12]

## B.   RINK RAGE AND RIOTS: "RELAX, IT'S JUST A GAME"

One of the functions of the glass barrier around a rink is to protect small-fry players from the mayhem in the stands.[13] Spectators, coaches and mascots are always liable to mix it up verbally and physically, and officials and security personnel may also be on the receiving end.[14] The seating area and other parts of the arena then becomes the site for various crimes of violence, disorder, indecency and intimidation.[15] It is, for example, not a good idea to equip spectators with jars of peanut butter since disappointed fans will only use them to pelt the rink surface when the home team loses.[16] In Canada, the off-ice anger and brawling are more contained than the mass "football hooliganism" of Europe and elsewhere. There have, however, been examples of major sports riots, and "rink rage", "parental rage" or "ugly parent syndrome"[17] can also have tragic consequences.

## 1.   Rink Rage

In July 2000 in Reading, Massachusetts, hockey dad Thomas Junta expressed his opposition to violence by beating another father to death. Junta was watching a

---

[12]   In the case of hazing, many American states have special legislation; see, R.B. Crow & D.R. Phillips, "Hazing – What the Law Says" in J. Johnson & M. Holman (eds.), *Making the Team: Inside the World of Sport Initiations and Hazing* (Toronto: Canadian Scholars' Press, 2004) at 19. On hazing, see Chapter 5, "Be Safe: Off the Ice", section E.

[13]   See, "Gable" cartoon, "Thankfully There's A Protective Glass Barrier", *The Globe and Mail* (Toronto: November 11, 2002) at A12.

[14]   On general safety and security at rinks, see Chapter 4, "Build Safe: Rink Management and Risk Management", section A. For early examples of ungentlemanly conduct, see Chapter 1, "Lord Stanley and the Wednesday Nighters", section B. On brawls involving Jimmy Skinner in the 1950s, see, "Red Wings coach won Stanley Cup without ever playing in the NHL" (obituary) *The Globe and Mail* (Toronto: July 20, 2007) at R5.

[15]   See, *Criminal Code*, R.S.C. 1985, c. C-46, ss. 63-69 (unlawful assemblies and riots), s. 173(1) (indecent acts), s. 174 (nudity), s. 175 (causing disturbance), s. 264.1 (uttering threats). On assault and homicide, see Chapter 6, "Play Safe: On the Ice", section B, 2, 3. On causing a disturbance, see, *R. v. Gallant*, [1992] P.E.I.J. No. 136, 101 Nfld. & P.E.I.R. 232 (P.E.I.S.C.T.D.), leave to appeal refused, [1993] P.E.I.J. No. 91, 110 Nfld. & P.E.I.R. 88 (P.E.I.C.A.) (derogatory comments at university game, conviction set aside). Criminal prosecution is not a suitable mechanism for dealing with minor verbal altercations; see, *R. v. Wright*, [2002] B.C.J. No. 1877, 2002 BCSC 1198 (B.C.S.C.).

[16]   See, *R. v. Vandergraaf*, [1994] M.J. No. 503, 34 C.R. (4th) 266, 93 C.C.C. (3d) 286 (Man. C.A.) (accused acquitted of assault because he intended his jar to hit the ice and not a front row spectator).

[17]   See: J. Deacon *et al.*, "Rink Rage" *Maclean's* (March 26, 2001); D.K. Fiore, "Parental Rage and Violence in Youth Sports: How Can We Prevent 'Soccer Moms' and 'Hockey Dads' from Interfering in Youth Sports and Causing Games to End in Fistfights Rather Than Handshakes?" (2003) 10 Vill. Sports & Ent. L.J. 103.

game involving his 10-year-old son and shouted to protest at the slashing and hitting. Junta ran onto the ice to remonstrate with the supervising coach, Michael Costin, and later engaged him in a fight where he delivered repeated blows to Costin's head. After Costin died of his injuries, Junta was convicted of involuntary manslaughter and sentenced to imprisonment for from six to 10 years.[18]

The Junta case represented rink rage in its most extreme form and seemed the culmination of a worsening problem of aggressive sideline confrontations in local games. The problem is shared by other sports,[19] and even curling has had to face "broom rage" in the form of "[b]anging the ice with a broom, swearing, and prolonged and repeated chattering at officials".[20] Hockey does, however, offer a particular wealth of incidents to complement the in-play confrontations involving players. The Canadian law reports reveal spectators assaulting players[21] and blows struck to coaches,[22] referees[23] and spectators.[24] There is a case of a fight between

---

[18]  See: "Hockey dad from hell goes on trial", *The Globe and Mail* (Toronto: January 4, 2002) at A3; "Hockey dad guilty in beating death" and "Parents link fame, money to rink rage" *The Globe and Mail* (Toronto: January 12, 2002) at A1, A12; "Harsh term in rink killing" *The Globe and Mail* (Toronto: January 26, 2002) at A15.

[19]  See: *Larin v. Goshen*, [1974] N.S.J. No. 248, 56 D.L.R. (3d) 719 (N.S.C.A.) (collision by wrestling referee following attacks by spectators); *R. v. Richardson*, [1995] N.B.J. No. 536, 170 N.B.R. (2d) 388 (N.B.Q.B.) (threats by parent in soccer); *Olinski v. Johnson*, [1997] O.J. No. 926, 32 O.R. (3d) 653 (Ont. C.A.) (occupiers' liability for attacks on lacrosse referee); *Sage v. Renner*, [2007] B.C.J. No. 1992, 2007 BCSC 1357 (B.C.S.C.) (head-butt by parent after lacrosse game).

[20]  *Rankin v. Alberta Curling Federation Appeals Committee*, [2005] A.J. No. 1759, 262 D.L.R. (4th) 484 at 508 (Alta. Q.B.), *per* Germain J. See also, "Bonspiel donnybrook raises eyebrows" *The Globe and Mail* (Toronto: December 10, 1997) at A20 (fight involving players and icemaker).

[21]  *Karpow v. Shave*, [1974] A.J. No. 215, [1975] 2 W.W.R. 159 (Alta. S.C.) ("hockey culture" does not excuse any violence exhibited by spectators to players); *Francis v. Miramichi (City)*, [2000] N.B.J. No. 130, 96 A.C.W.S. (3d) 332 (N.B.Q.B.) (altercation between players and fans; spectator's action for false arrest dismissed).

[22]  *Villeneuve v. Nolet*, [1981] C.P. 198 (father punched volunteer coach after game); *R. v. Buonassisi*, [2003] B.C.J. No. 2846, 2003 BCPC 408 (B.C. Prov. Ct.) (punch by one coach to another was in self-defence); *Hodgins v. Barnes*, [2007] O.J. No. 2072, 157 A.C.W.S. (3d) 964 (Ont. S.C.J.) (player struck coach with stick during brawl in junior game). See also: *R. v. Aussem*, [1997] O.J. No. 5582, 36 W.C.B. (2d) 335 (Ont. Prov. Div.) (player punched opposing coach before game); "Coaches under fire after teams of 8-year-olds brawl on ice" *The Globe and Mail* (Toronto: November 27, 2007) at A1 (police later decided not to lay charges in relation to the "Battle of Guelph").

[23]  *Cutler v. Smith*, [1977] N.S.J. No. 617, 25 N.S.R. (2d) 5 (N.S.T.D.) (assaults by spectator and referee); *R. v. Musselman*, [1999] O.J. No. 4666, 44 W.C.B. (2d) 339 (Ont. S.C.J.) (referee "tossed around" after he ejected accused's son); *R. v. Wright*, [2002] B.C.J. No. 1877, 2002 BCSC 1198 (B.C.S.C.) (minor altercation in officials' dressing room; new trial ordered); *R. c. Quessy*, [2002] J.Q. no 3810 (Que. S.C.) (professional player watching game punched referee); *Deshaies c. Asnong*, [2003] J.Q. no 150, [2003] R.R.A. 697 (Que. S.C.) (compensatory and exemplary damages awarded when 49-year-old father punched 17-year-old referee). See also, "Ex-hockey player jailed for attacking linesman" *The Globe and Mail* (Toronto: July 31, 2008) (ejected player came out of stands; 30 days in jail).

hockey mothers,[25] and a coach has hit a mascot because of his disruptive drum-banging.[26] In addition, a hockey dad-police officer has threatened death to the referee,[27] and an Ontario Superior Court judge has considered a case in which it was alleged that a minor hockey coach placed a bounty on the head of a nine-year-old after his own son was hit during the friendly post-game handshake.[28] A particular hazard for coaches is the failure to give sufficient playing time to a child who is an obvious prodigy.[29]

Unlike mass sports riots that may be rooted in wider economic or political conditions, rink rage is usually related to incidents in the arena or to past sporting antagonism. The context is usually minor play, rather than well-policed professional circuits,[30] and the offenders tend to have a personal link to the game. The outbreak may have been incited by fans as they exhort players to nail the enemy, and there may also be elements of racist or sexist abuse.[31] In the typical case, an incensed and offended family member confronts rival spectators or shows vociferous displeasure at the actions of players, coaches or officials.[32] The verbal hostility and physical violence come from a combination of fanatical enthusiasm, family pride, vicarious involvement and material ambition. Where minor leagues are structured according to a competitive and physically

---

[24]   *R. v. Hinz*, [2000] S.J. No. 42, 190 Sask.R. 297 (Sask. Prov. Ct.) (fan was cheering "kill #57"; father of player #57 assaulted fan); *R. c. Canale*, [2001] J.Q. no 3895 (C.Q.) (coaches wielded sticks at spectator in brawl at end of QMJHL game); *R. v. Goudey*, [2007] N.S.J. No. 287, 258 N.S.R. (2d) 201 (N.S.S.C.) (throwing water bottle was self-defence).

[25]   *de Groot v. Arsenault*, [1999] M.J. No. 489, 140 Man.R. (2d) 285 (Man. Q.B.), affd [2000] M.J. No. 487, 150 Man.R. (2d) 154 (Man. C.A.) (altercation outside arena; children were on same team).

[26]   *Reddemann v. McEachnie*, [2005] B.C.J. No. 1374, 2005 BCSC 915 (B.C.S.C.) (compensatory and punitive damages awarded against coach; team not liable). On coaches allegedly assaulting their own players, see: *Paisley v. Kerry Park Minor Hockey Assn.*, [2007] B.C.H.R.T.D. No. 218, 2007 BCHRT 218; [2007] B.C.H.R.T.D. No. 443, 2007 BCHRT 443 (B.C.H.R.T.); "Toronto coach charged for allegedly hitting teen players with hockey stick" *The Globe and Mail* (CP online) (Toronto: January 26, 2008).

[27]   See: "Hockey dad on trial for death threat" *The Globe and Mail* (Toronto: January 8, 2003) at A9; "Policeman found guilty of threats to referee" *The Globe and Mail* (Toronto: May 1, 2003) at A9 (Montreal detective sergeant given absolute discharge and CDN $50 fine).

[28]   See, "Hockey madness ruled offside" *The Globe and Mail* (Toronto: November 8, 2002) at A1, A11 (small claims court action dismissed).

[29]   *Villeneuve v. Nolet*, [1981] C.P. 198. See also: "Hockey dad chokes son's coach" *The Globe and Mail* (Toronto: January 17, 2005) (father choked volunteer coach into unconsciousness after son was told to sit out a few shifts; father was subsequently fined CDN $2000); *Sage v. Renner*, [2007] B.C.J. No. 1992, 2007 BCSC 1357 (B.C.S.C.) (playing time in lacrosse).

[30]   The peanut butter protest in *R. v. Vandergraaf*, [1994] M.J. No. 503, 34 C.R. (4th) 266, 93 C.C.C. (3d) 286 (Man. C.A.) followed a game between the Winnipeg Jets and the Ottawa Senators.

[31]   See, E. Etue & M.K. Williams, *On the Edge: Women Making Hockey History* (Toronto: Second Story Press, 1996) at 186-88. On equality rights and discrimination, see Chapter 2, "Legal Fundamentals and Equality Rights", section E.

[32]   See: M.A. Robidoux & J.G. Bocksnick, "Playing Behind the Glass: How Parents Support Violence in Minor Hockey" in L.K. Fuller (ed.), *Sexual Sports Rhetoric: Historical and Media Context of Violence* (New York: Peter Lane Publishing, 2009); *R. v. Hinz*, [2000] S.J. No. 42, 190 Sask.R. 297 (Sask. Prov. Ct.).

aggressive model, parents often have delusions of riches as they reinvent the local rink as a training ground for an athletic scholarship or a career in the NHL. It is to be expected that fans will show loyalty, arousal and support, but the line has to be drawn at intimidation, disorderly conduct or assault.

Although rage and disorder occur at very few games, the reported incidents have damaged the reputation of hockey and have made it difficult to recruit and retain volunteer coaches and officials.[33] Recognition of the risks also exposes associations and facility operators to liability for injuries suffered in out-of-play brawling.[34] Faced with possibly deteriorating standards of behaviour, Hockey Canada responded with the programs, "Safe and Fun Hockey" and "It's a New Game"[35] to give proper perspective to the purpose of play. City councils have also adopted "behaviour management" policies to enforce appropriate conduct and a safe environment at their recreational facilities. The initiatives by Hockey Canada include information packages and fair play codes to address the roles and responsibilities of parents, coaches and officials. These materials include the important reminder that only one per cent of children who start hockey go on to make a living at it.[36] In the "Relax, it's Just a Game" advertising campaign, aggressive parents make idiots of themselves with their competitiveness, and the campaign has also used scenes of role reversal to show children heaping pressure on parents. Besides education programs and moral persuasion, clubs and associations also have the power to implement disciplinary controls,[37] and the ultimate sanction under codes of conduct is to visit the sins of the parent on the child by banning the child. Such a measure would, however, require a fair and properly authorized process.[38]

---

[33] See, "Losing officials to abuse" *The Globe and Mail* (Toronto: March 12, 2001) at S3 (annual loss of 10,000 officials by CHA; turnover of nearly 30 per cent).

[34] See Chapter 4, "Build Safe: Rink Management and Risk Management", section A. See, in particular, K.P. Polansky, "Parental Violence at Youth Sporting Events: Should Landowners Be Liable?" (2006) 39 Suffolk U.L. Rev. 561.

[35] See online: <http://www.hockeycanada.ca> "Parent Program" and "It's a New Game"; see also the Hockey Canada CD, *A Minor Hockey Toolbox for Parents*. On the need for codes of ethics and a "philosophie de hockey mineur", see, Commission de l'aménagement du territoire, *La problématique de la violence dans le hockey mineur* (Québec: Assemblée nationale, octobre 2001).

[36] See, *Safe & Fun Hockey: A Parent's Approach* (Toronto: Hockey Canada and General Motors of Canada Limited, 2004) at 5.

[37] On fairness in disciplinary proceedings, see Chapter 3, "Organizations and Regulations", section C. See also, *Rankin v. Alberta Curling Federation Appeals Committee*, [2005] A.J. No. 1759, 262 D.L.R. (4th) 484 (Alta. Q.B.) (code of conduct in curling).

[38] In cases of personality conflicts, associations usually have broad authority not to renew memberships, but the exclusion of customers thought to be "difficult" is likely to be contested in different types of proceeding: *Tkachuk (Litigation guardian of) v. Bridge City Cosmo Aqualene Synchronized Swimming Club Inc.*, [1998] S.J. No. 196, 166 Sask.R. 55 (Sask. Q.B.) (complaints and "unpleasant encounters" involving swimmer's mother; no oppression or unfairness); *Dunford (Litigation Guardian of) v. Springers Gymnastics Club Inc.*, [2001] M.J. No. 399, [2002] 1 W.W.R. 480 (Man. Q.B.) (problems between parents and coaches; incorporated club's action was authorized); *Paisley v. Kerry Park Minor Hockey Assn.*, [2007] B.C.H.R.T.D. No. 218, 2007 BCHRT 218; [2007] B.C.H.R.T.D. No. 443, 2007 BCHRT 443 (B.C.H.R.T.) (parent had complained that coach had assaulted his daughter; alleged discrimination). On the dismissal of a

Legal remedies and codes of ethics address the worst forms of misconduct, but the imposed norms are unlikely to be effective where the game is structured as a celebration of dominance and aggression.[39] If the game requires the players to hit, the spectators will encourage them to do so and will be tempted to get in on the action. The quest for a solution is also not aided by the practice of suspending coaches if they pull their team from the ice in protest over dangerous play.[40]

## 2.   Riots

Besides the small scale brawling of rink rage, there are examples of much larger "hockey riots" where an excited crowd descends into mass disorder. The *Criminal Code* defines a riot as "an unlawful assembly that has begun to disturb the peace tumultuously", and it is an offence to participate in a riot or to fail to disperse following a "Riot Act" proclamation by a justice.[41] Sports riots and hooliganism are usually associated with professional events,[42] although the sports context may be merely a staging ground for gang wars or for playing out racial, economic or other divisions.[43] The riots fall into different categories[44] and should be distinguished from disasters caused by dangerous and unsuitable stadium facilities. Some riots begin as protests or demonstrations, some involve

---

player from a novice team, see: *Butrimas (Litigation Guardian of) v. Applewood Hockey Assn.*, [2006] O.J. No. 3494, 147 A.C.W.S. (3d) 144 (Ont. S.C.J.); "Demoted 10-year-old sues hockey league" *The Globe and Mail* (Toronto: June 20, 2005) at A13 (association claimed that father was "confrontational").

[39] See, M.A. Robidoux & J.G. Bocksnick, "Playing Behind the Glass: How Parents Support Violence in Minor Hockey" in L.K. Fuller (ed.), *Sexual Sports Rhetoric: Historical and Media Context of Violence* (New York: Peter Lang Publishing, 2009). On the influence of professional hockey and "undue pressure from parents and coaches", see, W.R. McMurtry, *Investigation and Inquiry into Violence in Amateur Hockey* (Toronto: Ministry of Community and Social Services, 1974) at 20-35.

[40] On suspensions by the Edmonton Minor Hockey Association, see: "Minor hockey coaches suspended for protests against rough play" *The Globe and Mail* (Toronto: January 15, 2003) at A12; "Minor-hockey coach suspended" *The Globe and Mail* (Toronto: February 7, 2003) at S5. On the OHA's suspension of the Bramalea Junior B club following their withdrawal from a violent series in 1974, see, W.R. McMurtry, *Investigation and Inquiry into Violence in Amateur Hockey* (Toronto: Ministry of Community and Social Services, 1974) at 17-19.

[41] See, *Criminal Code*, R.S.C. 1985, c. C-46, ss. 64, 65, 67-68.

[42] But see, W.R. McMurtry, *Investigation and Inquiry into Violence in Amateur Hockey* (Toronto: Ministry of Community and Social Services, 1974) (inquiry into player and fan violence at the Bramalea-Hamilton Junior B game of April 16, 1974). For an early example of fans of local teams engaging in a "continuous melee" and smashing a train, see, "Fought on a Train. Disgraceful Scenes on a Hockey Special Near Brockville" *The Globe* (Toronto: February 6, 1909) at 1.

[43] On theories of soccer hooliganism, see, "Football Violence and Hooliganism in Europe" online: <http://www.sirc.org> (Social Issues Research Centre, Oxford).

[44] See, W. Vamplew, "Sports Crowd Disorder in Britain, 1870-1914: Causes and Control" (1980) 7 J. of Sport History 5 at 9-11 (FORCE classification: frustration, outlawry, remonstrance, confrontation and expressive emotion). See also, M.D. Smith, *Violence and Sport* (Toronto: Butterworths, 1983) at 144-52.

confrontations between rival ethnic groups and some are victory celebrations. In each case, the conduct of the sports crowd and its fellow travellers can evolve into looting, vandalism, disorderly conduct and other forms of violent criminal behaviour. The recurring type of disturbance in North America has been celebration riots following successful championship series.[45] Vancouver was also struck by a "disappointment riot" in 1994 after the Canucks lost in the Stanley Cup.[46] The most famous Canadian hockey riot was of a more political character and dates from 1955. On that occasion, NHL president Clarence Campbell had suspended Maurice Richard for the remainder of the season and for the playoffs after the frustrated hero of the Canadiens had struck a linesman. The heavy sanction hampered the team's campaign for the Stanley Cup and deprived Richard of the chance to win the scoring title. The "Richard Riot"[47] of St. Patrick's night 1955 began when Campbell boldly presented himself at the Montreal Forum. After a smoke bomb put an end to the evening's game against the Detroit Red Wings, there was a night of rampaging and mob violence on Ste. Catherine Street as francophone fans condemned the injustice of the suspension and raged against the English power structure that had imposed it. Since boss Campbell had victimized two focal points of loyalty and identification in Quebec, the anger clearly held significance well beyond the confines of the game.[48]

---

[45]   For obvious reasons, Edmonton and Montreal have been the susceptible cities. On Stanley Cup disturbances in Montreal in 1986 and 1993, see: "Montreal police off guard as Cup celebrants run wild" *The Globe and Mail* (Toronto: May 26, 1986) at A1, A2; "Security to reign on Habs' parade" *The Globe and Mail* (Toronto: June 11, 1993) at A1, A3; "Inquiry scolds police for rampage inaction" *The Globe and Mail* (Toronto: October 12, 1993) at A16; *Aetna compagnie d'assurance du Canada c. Communauté urbaine de Montréal*, [1993] J.Q. no 851, [1993] R.J.Q. 1813 (Que. S.C.) (claims by store owners and insurance companies against police department with respect to losses in 1986). See also, "How a Habs playoff win became Montreal's loss" *The Globe and Mail* (Toronto: April 23, 2008) at A5 (vandalism and looting following series victory in first round).

[46]   On the Robson Street riot, see: "Probe ordered into hockey riot" *The Globe and Mail* (Toronto: June 16, 1994) at A1, A4; "Vancouver tries to learn from riot" *The Globe and Mail* (Toronto: November 3, 1994) at E7; "Riot spurred by drunkenness, report says" *The Globe and Mail* (Toronto: November 19, 1994) at A4. On charges against one rioter and his civil litigation against the police after being shot with plastic batons fired from an Arwen gun, see: *R. v. Berntt*, [1997] B.C.J. No. 2301, 120 C.C.C. (3d) 344, 11 C.R. (5th) 131 (B.C.C.A.); *Berntt v. Vancouver (City)*, [1999] B.C.J. No. 1257, 174 D.L.R. (4th) 403 (B.C.C.A.); *Berntt v. Vancouver (City)*, [2001] B.C.J. No. 2658, 209 D.L.R. (4th) 494 (B.C.S.C.).

[47]   See: "Richard Riot Ends Game" *The Globe and Mail* (Toronto: March 18, 1955) at 1, 23; M. McKinley, *Putting a Roof on Winter* (Vancouver: Greystone Books, 2000) at 184-90.

[48]   See: S. Katz, "The strange forces behind the Rocket Richard Riot" *Maclean's Magazine*, September 17, 1955; J-M Pellerin, *L'idole d'un peuple: Maurice Richard* (Montréal: Les éditions de l'homme ltée, 1976) at 253-342; J.R. Duppereault, "Affaire Richard: A Situational Analysis of the Montreal Hockey Riot of 1955" (1981) 12(1) Can. J. of History of Sport 66; S. Laberge & A. Dumas, "L'affaire Richard/Campbell: un catalyseur de l'affirmation des Canadiens français" (2003) 11 Bulletin d'histoire politique 30; "Not quite the birth of a nation" and "Quebec unrest boiled over in Richard riot" *The Globe and Mail* (Toronto: March 17, 2005) at A19, R8.

## C. SEXUAL HARASSMENT AND ABUSE: "SPEAK OUT"

## 1. Introduction: The Crisis Year

The masculine sports culture for many years tolerated the sexual exploitation of female victims as senior figures took advantage of positions of power and opportunities for physical contact.[49] Following various investigations by CBC television in 1993, the Canadian Association for the Advancement of Women and Sport ("CAAWS") addressed the issue in partnership with other associations,[50] and in 1996 Sport Canada required national sport organizations to adopt policies condemning harassment and establishing complaint procedures for dealing with cases.[51] One survey had revealed that 22 per cent of national team athletes had had sexual relations with persons in positions of authority in the sport.[52] It was, however, only in 1997 that there was serious public interest in the problem and sustained attempts to implement reforms.[53] The precipitating factor was the revelation of criminal cases related to hockey. A crisis was declared when the abuse affected the national sport and male victims. Some junior players had endured years of abuse as team culture made them reluctant to show disloyalty or to admit to conduct that might threaten professional careers.[54]

---

[49] See: S. Kirby, L. Greaves & O. Hankvivsky, *The Dome of Silence: Sexual Harassment and Abuse in Sport* (Halifax: Fernwood Publishing, 2000); C.H. Brackenridge, *Spoilsports: Understanding and Preventing Sexual Exploitation in Sport* (London: Routledge, 2001); C. Brackenridge & K. Fasting (eds.), *Sexual Harassment and Abuse in Sport: International Research and Policy Perspectives* (London: Whiting & Birch, 2002).

[50] See, *Harassment in Sport: A Guide to Policies, Procedures and Resources* (Gloucester: CAAWS, September 1994); see online: <http://www.caaws.ca>. On the recognition of the problem in the mid-1990s, see, A.P. Aggarwal & M.M. Gupta, *Sexual Harassment in the Workplace*, 3d ed. (Toronto: Butterworths, 2000) at 80-86.

[51] See, Sport Funding and Accountability Framework (SFAF IV, 2009-2013), A16; see further, Chapter 2, "Legal Fundamentals and Equality Rights", section B, 4. See also, Hockey Canada, "Recognition and Prevention of Abuse Policy" (revised, May 2008), "Bullying and Harassment Policy" (revised, May 2008) and "Harassment/Bullying Complaint Procedure", online: <http://www.hockeycanada.ca>.

[52] S. Kirby & L. Greaves, "Le jeu interdit: Le harcèlement sexuel dans le sport" (1997) 10 Recherches feministes 5. On the prevalence and incidence of exploitation, see: C.H. Brackenridge, *Spoilsports: Understanding and Preventing Sexual Exploitation in Sport* (London: Routledge, 2001) at 54-63; P. Donnelly, "Who's Fair Game? Sport, Sexual Harassment, and Abuse" in K. Young & P. White (eds.), *Sport and Gender in Canada*, 2d ed. (Don Mills, ON: Oxford University Press, 2007) at 279.

[53] The other influential case in 1997 involved allegations of sexual harassment against Liam Donnelly, the swim coach at Simon Fraser University. After initially being dismissed from the university, Donnelly was rehired following a review of evidence and procedures. See: "SFU report details sex allegations" *The Globe and Mail* (Toronto: July 17, 1997) at A4; "SFU rehires dismissed swim coach" *The Globe and Mail* (Toronto: July 26, 1997) at A8.

[54] On sport and sexual orientation, see Chapter 2, "Legal Fundamentals and Equality Rights", section E, 8. On the general organization of minor and junior hockey, see, Chapter 3, "Organizations and Regulations", sections A; B.

A series of prosecutions begun in February 1997 related to abuse that occurred at Maple Leaf Gardens ("MLG") during the 1970s and 1980s. Two staff members had lured boys into sex acts through gifts of equipment or the promise of access to the building.[55] Allegations of abuse were known to MLG in 1993 when they paid a confidential settlement to one victim. In *R. v. Stuckless*,[56] the Ontario Court of Appeal imposed a sentence of five years imprisonment after the accused pleaded guilty to 24 charges of indecent and sexual assault committed over a 20-year period. The court noted that the accused had exploited a position of trust and used the "irresistible lure" or "magnetic aura of Maple Leaf Gardens rather than a more overtly forceful form of manipulation to prey on these children".[57] The MLG cases followed the equally prominent conviction of Graham James, a successful coach in the Western Hockey League. James was sentenced to three-and-a-half years imprisonment after pleading guilty to charges of sexual assault relating to two junior hockey players; Sheldon Kennedy of the Boston Bruins then identified himself as one of the victims.[58] The Canadian Hockey League responded by commissioning its lawyer to propose procedures and measures to prevent further incidents,[59] and Kennedy subsequently led campaigns and programs to educate participants about the risk of abuse.[60] In 2009, Theoren Fleury alleged that he too had been the victim of abuse by James.[61]

## 2. Conduct, Processes and Remedies

Sexual misconduct involves a continuum of behaviour ranging from verbal harassment, to showing pornographic materials, to abusive physical contact. Some behaviour may be subject to sanctions under policies of organizations or collective

---

[55] See: "Scandal slams Gardens into the boards" *The Globe and Mail* (Toronto: February 22, 1997) at A1, A6 (charges against John Paul Roby and George Stuckless); "Abuse victim commits suicide" *The Globe and Mail* (Toronto: October 31, 1997) at A1, A8; C. Vine & P. Challen, *Gardens of Shame: The Tragedy of Martin Kruze and the Sexual Abuse at Maple Leaf Gardens* (Vancouver: Greystoke Books, 2002).

[56] [1998] O.J. No. 3177, 41 O.R. (3d) 103, 127 C.C.C. (3d) 225 (Ont. C.A.).

[57] *R. v. Stuckless*, [1998] O.J. No. 3177, 41 O.R. (3d) 103, at 116, 127 C.C.C. (3d) 225, at 241 (Ont. C.A.), *per* Abella J.A.

[58] See: "Hockey coach pleads guilty to sexual assault charges" *The Globe and Mail* (Toronto: January 3, 1997) at A1; "Kennedy hailed for going public" *The Globe and Mail* (Toronto: January 7, 1996) at A18; S. Kennedy with J. Grainger, *Why I Didn't Say Anything: The Sheldon Kennedy Story* (Toronto: Insomniac Press, 2006); M.B. Preston, "Sheldon Kennedy and a Canadian Tragedy Revisited: A Comparative Look at U.S. and Canadian Jurisprudence on Youth Sports Organizations' Civil Liability for Child Sexual Exploitation" (2006), 39 Vanderbilt J. of Transnational L. 1333.

[59] G.I. Kirke, *Players First: A Report Prepared for the Canadian Hockey League* (August 7, 1997). See further, L. Robinson, *Crossing the Line: Violence and Sexual Assault in Canada's National Sport* (Toronto: McClelland & Stewart, 1998) at 153-218.

[60] See now, online: <http://www.respectinsport.com>.

[61] See: "Fleury opens up about sexual abuse" *The Globe and Mail* (Toronto: October 10, 2009) at S2; T. Fleury & K.M. Day, *Playing with Fire: The Highest Highs and the Lowest Lows of Theo Fleury* (Toronto: HarperCollins Publishers, 2009).

bargaining agreements, and a particular incident may trigger a variety of processes before courts, professional bodies,[62] disciplinary panels or arbitrators of the Sport Dispute Resolution Centre of Canada.[63] A complaint of sexual harassment is primarily a breach of public rights calling for investigation by the relevant human rights commission,[64] although it may also fall under the jurisdiction of a labour arbitrator.[65] Criminal sanctions apply to the more serious forms of abuse such as sexual assault, sexual exploitation of young victims or making child pornography. In cases of "historical" abuse,[66] the relevant charge may be crimes such as rape or indecent assault that are no longer included in the *Criminal Code*.[67] Civil liability actions alleging harassment[68] or abuse can be brought against individual perpetrators or against employers or organizations that tolerated or facilitated the conduct. The person accused may also reply with an employment grievance challenging disciplinary sanctions or with an action for defamation, wrongful dismissal[69] or false arrest.[70]

---

[62] See, for example, *Re Cwinn and the Law Society of Upper Canada*, [1980] O.J. No. 3548, 28 O.R. (2d) 61, 108 D.L.R. (3d) 381 (Ont. Div. Ct.) (lawyer disbarred following convictions under the *Mann Act*; lawyer had sexual relations with teenage girls riding and assisting at horse shows).

[63] See, for example, *Canadian Amateur Diving Association v. Miranda* (SDRCC No. 05-0030, E. Ratushny, arbitrator, October 4, 2005) (consensual sex between athletes, age 32 and 15; suspension reversed because there was no coaching relationship). On the SDRCC, see Chapter 2, "Legal Fundamentals and Equality Rights", section C. On hearings and disputes, see Chapter 3, "Organizations and Regulations", section C.

[64] See: *Mohammed v. Canada (Treasury Board); Canada (Treasury Board) v. Boutilier; O'Hagan v. Canada (Treasury Board)*, [1999] F.C.J. No. 1867, 181 D.L.R. (4th) 590 (F.C.A.); leave to appeal to S.C.C. refused without reasons, [2000] S.C.C.A. No. 12 (S.C.C.); *Cadillac Fairview Corp. v. Saskatchewan (Human Rights Commission)*, [1999] S.J. No. 217, [1999] 7 W.W.R. 517 (Sask. C.A.). But see, *Labour Relations Act*, S.O. 1995, c. 1, Sch. A, s. 48(12)(j) (arbitrator may apply human rights statutes). See further, Chapter 2, "Legal Fundamentals and Equality Rights", sections D; E.

[65] See, for example, *A.(K.) v. Ottawa (City)*, [2006] O.J. No. 1827, 269 D.L.R. (4th) 116 (Ont. C.A.).

[66] See: *R. c. Fillion*, [1989] J.Q. no 809, 22 Q.A.C. 19 (Que. C.A.) (hockey coach convicted of gross indecency involving teenage boys); *R. v. Ledinski*, [1991] S.J. No. 196, 95 Sask.R. 1 (Sask. Q.B.) (accused teacher and coach committed indecent assaults on male children 25 years previously); *R. c. Le Coz*, [2001] J.Q. no 7000, [2001] R.J.Q. 2023 (C.Q.) (indecent assaults between 1977 and 1981 by coach of Canadian fencing team; suspended sentence).

[67] See, R.S.C. 1985 c. C-46, s. 161(1.1) (current and historical crimes for the purpose of a sex offender prohibition order).

[68] See: *Lajoie v. Kelly*, [1997] M.J. No. 52, [1997] 3 W.W.R. 181, 32 C.C.L.T. (2d) 115 (Man. Q.B.) (sexual harassment as a tort); *Sulz v. British Columbia (Minister of Public Safety and Solicitor General)*, [2006] B.C.J. No. 3262, [2007] 2 W.W.R. 419, 43 C.C.L.T. (3d) 187 (B.C.C.A.), affg [2006] B.C.J. No. 121, 263 D.L.R. (4th) 58, 37 C.C.L.T. (3d) 271 (B.C.S.C.) (damages awarded for harassment by RCMP supervisor).

[69] In 1994, the Canadian Cycling Association dismissed head coach Desmond Dickie after sexual assault charges were brought by two female cyclists. Dickie sued the association in 1995 and was acquitted at his criminal trial in 1996; see, "Acquittal no victory, Dickie says" *The Globe and Mail* (Toronto: October 11, 1996) at A15. See also, L. Robinson, *Black Tights: Women, Sport, and Sexuality* (Toronto: HarperCollins Publishers, 2002) at 106-07.

Sexual harassment[71] is usually dealt with under codes of conduct or human rights legislation,[72] but may amount to criminal "stalking" where a person is put in fear through repeated following or communicating or through watching or threatening.[73] Under the Ontario *Human Rights Code*,[74] "harassment" is defined as, "engaging in a course of vexatious comment or conduct that is known or ought reasonably to be known to be unwelcome" (see, s. 10). The *Code* treats sexual harassment as a form of discrimination and declares the right to be free from such harassment in accommodation and the workplace (see, s. 7(1)(2)). It is the particular responsibility of employers to prevent harassment,[75] but the protections also apply in other contexts. Section 7(3) of the *Code* declares a more general right to be free from,

> (a) a sexual solicitation or advance made by a person in a position to confer, grant or deny a benefit or advancement to the person where the person making the solicitation or advance knows or ought reasonably to know that it is unwelcome; or

> (b) a reprisal or a threat of reprisal for the rejection of a sexual solicitation or advance...[76]

Under human rights legislation, sexual harassment primarily takes the form of an unwelcome, humiliating or uncomfortable[77] environment created by co-workers or authority figures. Harassment includes unwelcome physical contact[78] or

---

[70]   See, *Trudgian v. Bosche*, [2005] S.J. No. 80, [2005] 5 W.W.R. 199, 249 D.L.R. (4th) 674 (Sask. C.A.), revg in part [2003] S.J. No. 311, [2004] 1 W.W.R. 324 (Sask. Q.B.) (RCMP cadets playing broom ball hockey; accusation of sexual assault).

[71]   See: A.P. Aggarwal & M.M. Gupta, *Sexual Harassment in the Workplace*, 3d ed. (Toronto: Butterworths, 2000); A.P. Aggarwal & M.M. Gupta, *Sexual Harassment: A Guide for Understanding and Prevention*, 2d ed. (Markham, ON: LexisNexis Butterworths, 2006). See also, *Janzen v. Platy Enterprises Ltd.*, [1989] S.C.J. No. 41, [1989] 1 S.C.R. 1252 (S.C.C.) (obligation of employer to protect employees from sexual harassment).

[72]   On the jurisdiction of the Canadian Human Rights Commission, see, *S.(J.) v. Brooker*, [2005] F.C.J. No. 1865, 2005 FC 1510 (F.C.) (Jiu-jitsu club operated by Canadian Armed Forces).

[73]   See, *Criminal Code*, R.S.C. 1985, c. C-46, s. 264.

[74]   R.S.O. 1990, c. H-19. See also, *Canadian Human Rights Act*, R.S.C. 1985, c. H-6, s. 14; *Canada Labour Code*, R.S.C. 1985, c. L-2, ss. 247.1-247.4 (definition of sexual harassment and duty of employer under federal jurisdiction to make reasonable efforts to combat harassment and establish a policy).

[75]   See, A.P. Aggarwal & M.M. Gupta, *Sexual Harassment in the Workplace*, 3d ed. (Toronto: Butterworths, 2000) at 249-327. See also: "Rangers cheerleader files sexual harassment lawsuit" *The Globe and Mail* (Toronto: October 19, 2004) at R9 (federal court action against Madison Square Garden ("MSG") following determination by U.S. Equal Employment Opportunity Commission); "Jury awards $11.6 million (U.S.) to former Knicks exec" *The Globe and Mail* (Toronto: October 2, 2007) (action against MSG involving Isiah Thomas). Both of the cases involving MSG were settled in December 2007.

[76]   Ontario *Human Rights Code*, R.S.O. 1990, c. H-19, s. 7(3).

[77]   See, for example, *Mahmoodi v. Dutton*, [2001] B.C.J. No. 1794, 95 B.C.L.R. (3d) 186 (B.C.S.C.), affg (1999), 36 C.H.R.R. D/8 (B.C.H.R.T.) (sexualized atmosphere of dinner at professor's home).

[78]   See, *Ha v. Harnois*, [2004] S.J. No. 211, 247 Sask.R. 18 (Sask. Q.B.), affd [2004] S.J. No. 813, 257 Sask.R. 69 (Sask. C.A.) (grabbing by martial arts expert during dancing; letter of complaint

repeated invitations, sexual language or insulting behaviour. It also includes *quid pro quo* propositions in which a position, team place or promotion is promised in exchange for sexual favours. Specially adopted policies may extend prohibitions to other types of activity such as having consensual relationships with subordinates, and special provision may also be needed to deal with conduct between "social equals" outside the workplace such as fellow students or teammates in recreational or amateur sport. Where an institution purports to apply a private disciplinary process, the special policy must be in force[79] and the activity must fall within the jurisdiction of the relevant committee. Sanctions are authorized only where the conduct amounts to a breach of the terms of the policy or is otherwise prohibited.[80]

The Hockey Canada "Bullying and Harassment Policy"[81] applies to officers and volunteers of the national organization. Each Branch and affiliate association has the responsibility to adopt a similar policy that conforms to provincial or local requirements. The national Policy declares a commitment to an environment that is free from discrimination and bullying, and defines "harassment" as:

> conduct, gestures or comments which are insulting, intimidating, humiliating, hurtful, malicious, degrading or otherwise offensive to an individual or group of individuals, and which create a hostile or intimidating environment for work or sports activities, or which negatively affect performance or work conditions.[82]

Hockey Canada's "Recognition and Prevention of Abuse Policy", condemns abuse and neglect and requires every parent, volunteer and staff member to take

---

to Tae Kwon Do Canada was protected by qualified privilege). See also, *Madsen v. Torry (No. 4)* (2005), 52 C.H.R.R. D/131 (B.C.H.R.T.) (attempted kiss; bowling tournament director had no power or authority in relation to participant).

[79] See, *Gleason v. Lethbridge Community College*, [1995] A.J. No. 1199, [1996] 3 W.W.R. 377 (Alta. Q.B.) (policy was unadopted and process was unfair because of lack of notice to accused student). On fairness in disciplinary proceedings, see Chapter 2, "Legal Fundamentals and Equality Rights", section B. See also, *Butler v. USA Volleyball*, 673 N.E.2d 1063 (Ill.App., 1996).

[80] See, for example: *Okanagan University College and Okanagan University College Faculty Assn. (Craig Grievance)*, [1997] B.C.C.A.A.A. No. 313, 64 L.A.C. (4th) 416 (B.C.C.A.A.) (professor dismissed for having sexual relationship with two students; conduct did not fall within definition but discipline was warranted because of breach of trust); *Mpega v. Université de Moncton*, [2001] N.B.J. No. 246, 240 N.B.R. (2d) 349 (N.B.C.A.) (committee exceeded its jurisdiction in investigating alleged criminal assault; policy applied to off-campus incidents but referred only to repeated acts); *Lethbridge College v. Lethbridge College Faculty Assn.*, [2008] A.J. No. 740, 96 Alta. L.R. (4th) 168 (Alta. Q.B.) (lack of express policy, but suspension warranted).

[81] Hockey Canada, "Bullying and Harassment Policy" (revised, May 2008). See also, Hockey Canada, "Recognition and Prevention of Abuse Policy" (revised, May 2008). Both Policies are available online: <http://www.hockeycanada.ca>.

[82] Hockey Canada, "Bullying and Harassment Policy", online: <http://www.hockeycanada.ca>.

all reasonable steps to safeguard the welfare of participants. The Policy[83] defines "child abuse" as "any form of physical, emotional and/or sexual mistreatment or lack of care which causes physical injury or emotional damage to a child". Emotional abuse refers to,

> a chronic attack on a child's self-esteem; it is psychologically destructive behaviour by a person in a position of power, authority or trust. It can take the form of name-calling, threatening, ridiculing, berating, intimidating, isolating, hazing or ignoring the child's needs.[84]

The Policy supplements provincial and territorial legislation providing for child protection services up to the ages of between 16 and 19 and including powers to extend the care.[85]

Further age distinctions apply in relation to federal criminal law. The *Criminal Code*[86] establishes various categories of sexual assault (see, ss. 265(1),(2), 271-273) and sets out special rules relating to consent and evidence (see, ss. 265(3),(4), 273.1-278.91). The *Criminal Code* also includes crimes of exposure (see, s. 173(2)) and sexual interference and exploitation (see, ss. 151-153.1) in relation to children, young persons and persons with a disability. Since 2008, the defence of consent[87] does not apply where the complainant is under the age of 16 (see, s. 150.1(1)), having formerly been set at age 14.[88] Certain exceptions apply in relation to accused who are less than two years or five years older than the complainant provided they are not in a position of trust or authority towards the complainant (see, s. 150.1(2)(2.1) (2.2.)).

---

[83] See also, *Participant's Workbook: Speak Out! It's more than just a game*, 3d ed. (Canadian Red Cross RespectED/Hockey Canada, 2005) at 33-34.

[84] Hockey Canada, "Recognition and Prevention of Abuse Policy", online: <http://www.hockeycanada.ca>.

[85] See, *Participant's Workbook: Speak Out! It's more than just a game*, 3d ed. (Canadian Red Cross RespectED/Hockey Canada, 2005) at 16. See, for example, *Child and Family Services Act*, R.S.O. 1990, c. C.11, s. 3. See also, *Convention on the Rights of the Child* (United Nations General Assembly, resolution 44/25, November 20, 1989, ratified by Canada, December 13, 1991).

[86] R.S.C. 1985, c. C-46. The age of criminal responsibility is 12 (see, s. 13). Additional relevant offences include: anal intercourse (see, s. 159), bestiality in the presence of a person under 16 (see, s. 160(3)), voyeurism or surreptitious visual recording (see, s. 162), crimes in relation to "child pornography" which relates to sexual activity involving persons under 18 (see, s. 163.1), luring a child by means of a computer system (see, s. 172.1) and obtaining sexual services for consideration from a person under 18 (see, s. 212(4)). By s. 161 of the *Criminal Code*, a person convicted of specified offences in respect of a person under 16 may be prohibited from attending recreational facilities or working or serving as a volunteer in a position of trust.

[87] See, *Tackling Violent Crime Act*, S.C. 2008, c. 6, ss. 13, 14, 54.

[88] See: *R. v. Oliver (G.)*, [1997] O.J. No. 1911, 99 O.A.C. 234 (Ont. C.A.) (relationship with boy under 12; recreation programmer sentenced to 15 months imprisonment); *R. v. W.R.A.*, [1997] B.C.J. No. 973, 89 B.C.A.C. 250 (B.C.C.A.) (13-year-old girl; gymnastics coach sentenced to eight months imprisonment); *R. v. Hall*, [2000] B.C.J. No. 441, 2000 BCCA 148 (B.C.C.A.) (13-year-old boys; hockey volunteer sentenced to probation and conditional sentence of two years imprisonment).

Sexual assault, which may be committed against a victim of any age, consists of intentional sexual touching of another person without that person's consent.[89] Consent requires "the voluntary agreement of the complainant to engage in the sexual activity in question" (see, s. 273.1(1)), and no consent is obtained where "the accused induces the complainant to engage in the activity by abusing a position of trust, power or authority" (see, s. 273.1(2)(c)).[90] An assault is "sexual" when in all the circumstances it can objectively be considered of a sexual nature.[91] In a sports context, it will be necessary to distinguish valid coaching technique or the ordinary incidental contact of the activity from inappropriate sexual touching.[92]

Sections 151 and 152 of the *Criminal Code* establish crimes of interference, invitation or incitement "for a sexual purpose" where the touching relates to a person under the age of 16.[93] The crime of sexual exploitation in section 153 deals with touching, invitation or incitement "for a sexual purpose" in relation to a "young person" who is 16 or more but under 18. Sexual exploitation may be committed by a person,

> ... who is in a position of trust or authority towards a young person, who is a person with whom the young person is in a relationship of dependency or who is in a relationship with a young person that is exploitive of the young person ...[94]

---

[89] See, *R. v. Ewanchuk*, [1999] S.C.J. No. 10, [1999] 1 S.C.R. 330 (S.C.C.). On the general elements of criminal assault, see Chapter 6, "Play Safe: On the Ice", section B, 3. For an example of sex at the rink, see, *R. v. R.J.S.*, [1994] P.E.I.J. No. 109, 123 Nfld. & P.E.I.R. 317 (P.E.I.S.C.T.D.) (Crown failed to prove lack of consent in homosexual encounter between night watchmen).

[90] Under s. 265(3) of the *Criminal Code*, consent is vitiated by the use of force, fraud or "the exercise of authority". Consent in sexual assault is also vitiated by special factors listed in ss. 273.1 and 273.2.

[91] See, *R. v. Chase*, [1987] S.C.J. No. 57, [1987] 2 S.C.R. 293 (S.C.C.).

[92] See: *R. v. M.(S.I.)*, [1994] A.J. No. 660, 158 A.R. 81 (Alta. Prov. Ct.) (sexual assault; dancing teacher cupped victim's breasts); *R. v. Gauthier*, [1995] O.J. No. 4239, 5 O.T.C. 44 (Ont. Gen. Div.) (charge of sexual interference; no sexual purpose in slap on buttocks as team left field); *R. v. R. (J.C.)*, [1995] A.J. No. 1117, 176 A.R. 108 (Alta. Prov. Ct.) (no sexual connotation in touching by teacher); *Trudgian v. Bosche*, [2005] S.J. No. 80, [2005] 5 W.W.R. 199, 249 D.L.R. (4th) 674 (Sask. C.A.), revg in part [2003] S.J. No. 311, [2004] 1 W.W.R. 324 (Sask. Q.B.) (action for false arrest; accusation of sexual assault during broom ball hockey game).

[93] See, *R. v. Rhynes* (2004), 236 Nfld. & P.E.I.R. 265, 186 C.C.C. (3d) 29 (P.E.I.S.C.T.D.); affd [2004] P.E.I.J. No. 55, 239 Nfld. & P.E.I.R. 89 (P.E.I.C.A.) (girls performed oral sex on baseball prospect Cass Rhynes; Rhynes acquitted of charge under s. 152 because he did not "incite" touching).

[94] *Criminal Code*, R.S.C. 1985, c. C-46, s. 153(1).

Persons in positions of trust and authority include parents, teachers,[95] coaches,[96] recreational supervisors and senior managers or officials. A teacher who has been informed that his contract will be renewed remains in a position of trust during the summer holidays.[97] A judge may infer that a relationship is exploitive based on factors such as age difference and the degree of control or influence that is being exerted (see, s. 153(1.2)). A former coach is no longer in a position of trust and authority, and it is a question of fact whether there is a continuing relationship that is "exploitive":

> I consider an exploitive relationship to exist where there is a power imbalance between the accused and the younger person...The evidence must demonstrate or, it must be possible for the court to draw the inference from all the circumstances of the relationship and in particular those factors listed in s. 153(1.2) that the young person is, as the result of this power imbalance, vulnerable to the actions and conduct of the accused who is taking advantage of the young person for his or her own benefit.[98]

The victim of sexual abuse can bring a civil liability action[99] against the individual offender[100] and against the club, school or other institution where the

---

[95] *R. c. Sénécal*, [1996] J.Q. no 4517, 3 C.R. (5th) 261 (C.Q.) (martial arts teacher began relationship with female student when she was 12; conditional sentence of 15 months imprisonment and probation); *R. c. Colas*, [1997] J.Q. no 2890, 37 W.C.B. (2d) 471 (Que. C.A.) (20 months imprisonment for school teacher who had repeated intercourse with 15-year-old student).

[96] *R. c. Guilmette*, [2005] J.Q. no 4799 (C.Q.) (speed skating coach and masseur pleaded guilty to two charges of sexual exploitation; sentenced to eight months imprisonment and three years probation). See further, Chapter 5, "Be Safe: Off the Ice", section F (charges against David Frost).

[97] *R. v. Audet*, [1996] S.C.J. No. 61, [1996] 2 S.C.R. 171 (S.C.C.) (physical education teacher and 14-year-old female student).

[98] *R. v. Anderson*, [2009] P.E.I.J. No. 7 at para. 74, 2009 PECA 4 (P.E.I.C.A.), *per* McQuaid J. (former soccer coach; female accused acquitted ).

[99] See: E.K.P. Grace & S.M. Vella, *Civil Liability for Sexual Abuse and Violence in Canada* (Toronto: Butterworths, 2000); M.B. Preston, "Sheldon Kennedy and a Canadian Tragedy Revisited: A Comparative Look at U.S. and Canadian Jurisprudence on Youth Sports Organizations' Civil Liability for Child Sexual Exploitation" (2006), 39 Vanderbilt J. of Transnational L. 1333. Actions for sexual assault are subject to the ordinary civil standard of proof on the balance of probabilities: *F.H. v. McDougall*, [2008] S.C.J. No. 54, 297 D.L.R. (4th) 193 (S.C.C.).

[100] See: *M.(L.N.) v. Green Estate*, [1996] B.C.J. No. 8 (B.C.S.C.) (action against estate of baseball coach); *W.M.Y. v. Duncan Scott, B.C. Soccer Assn.*, [2000] B.C.J. No. 1939, 2000 BCSC 1294 (B.C.S.C.); *H.(T.E.G.) v. K.(P.)*, [2001] A.J. No. 59, [2001] 6 W.W.R. 546 (Alta. Q.B.) (sports centre manager liable; action against city dismissed); *D.B. v. Parkland School Division No. 63*, [2004] S.J. No. 537, 244 D.L.R. (4th) 629 (Sask. C.A.) (action against coach and school board; third party notice to parents struck out); *H.(S.G.) v. Gorsline*, [2004] A.J. No. 593, [2005] 2 W.W.R. 716, 23 C.C.L.T. (3d) 65 (Alta. C.A.) (physical education teacher liable; action against school board dismissed). On the Hockey Canada Liability Insurance Program, see Chapter 4, "Build Safe: Rink Management and Risk Management", section D.

incidents occurred.[101] The individual is usually sued for civil assault or for breach of fiduciary duties where there is a position of trust.[102] The organization's liability can be based on negligence, breach of fiduciary duty or vicarious liability for the misconduct of employees. Numerous actions were filed based on the assaults committed by Graham James[103] and those committed at Maple Leaf Gardens.[104] An organization may be liable in negligence when officials knew[105] or ought to have known of the abusive conduct or of the likelihood that a particular individual may offend. Similarly, a victim has successfully sued a provincial government because a probation officer negligently failed to warn a hockey association that one of its volunteer assistant coaches was a convicted paedophile.[106] An organization is subject to strict vicarious liability where the employer has significantly increased the risk of abuse by putting the employee in a position that enhances opportunities for abuse; such liability requires a strong connection between the employee's tasks or authority and the wrongful act. In *Bazley v. Curry*,[107] the Supreme Court of Canada held that a non-profit children's home could be vicariously liable for sexual abuse committed by a paedophile working as a supervisor in one of its residential care facilities. The employee's duties included quasi-parental responsibilities such as supervising bathing and bedrooms. The court held that the employer can be vicariously liable when the empowerment of the employee in the enterprise materially increases the risk of sexual assault. In *Jacobi v. Griffiths*,[108] a bare majority of the court held that a

---

[101] See, *L.(H.) v. Canada (Attorney General)*, [2001] S.J. No. 298, [2001] 7 W.W.R. 722, 5 C.C.L.T. (3d) 186 (Sask. Q.B.), additional reasons [2001] 11 W.W.R. 727 and 737 (Sask. Q.B.), revd in part [2002] S.J. No. 702, [2003] 5 W.W.R. 421 (Sask. C.A.), revd in part [2005] S.J. No. 24, [2005] 1 S.C.R. 401 (S.C.C.) (boxing club for native boys operated by Government of Canada; action against government allowed).

[102] See: *Frame v. Smith*, [1987] S.C.J. No. 49, [1987] 2 S.C.R. 99 (S.C.C.) (fiduciary duties apply where there is a discretionary power to affect the interests of a vulnerable beneficiary); *M.(K.) v. M.(H.)*, [1992] S.C.J. No. 85, [1992] 3 S.C.R. 6 (S.C.C.). In the tort of sexual assault or battery, consent operates as a defence and must be proved by the defendant; see, *Non-Marine Underwriters, Lloyd's of London v. Scalera*, [2000] S.C.J. No. 26, [2000] 1 S.C.R. 551 (S.C.C.).

[103] See, for example, "Deal reached in James lawsuit" *The Globe and Mail* (Toronto: April 10, 2003) at S3 (settlement of actions against the Swift Current Broncos, WHL and other defendants).

[104] See: *K.(A.) v. Roby*, [1999] O.J. No. 4822, 46 C.P.C. (4th) 110 (Ont. S.C.J.); "Abuse ended dream" *The Globe and Mail* (Toronto: October 19, 2002) at S3 (allegations by four claimants against Maple Leaf Sports and Entertainment Ltd. and two employees).

[105] *S.(C.) (Next Friend of) v. Miller*, [2002] A.J. No. 173, [2002] 6 W.W.R. 148, 11 C.C.L.T. (3d) 136 (Alta. Q.B.), additional reasons [2004] A.J. No. 177, [2004] 5 W.W.R. 282, 22 C.C.L.T. (3d) 21 (Alta. Q.B.) (camp supervisor did not report molestations).

[106] *D.N. and D.S.G. v. Oak Bay (District)*, [2005] B.C.J. No. 2268, 261 D.L.R. (4th) 692 (B.C.S.C.). See also, *D.H. (Guardian ad litem of) v. British Columbia*, [2008] B.C.J. No. 921, [2008] 9 W.W.R. 82 (B.C.C.A.).

[107] [1999] S.C.J. No. 35, [1999] 2 S.C.R. 534 (S.C.C.).

[108] [1999] S.C.J. No. 36, [1999] 2 S.C.R. 570 (S.C.C.). See also, *G.(E.D.) v. Hammer*, [2003] S.C.J. No. 52, [2003] 2 S.C.R. 459 (S.C.C.); *Blackwater v. Plint*, [2005] S.C.J. No. 59, [2005] 3 S.C.R. 3 (S.C.C.); *E.B. v. Order of the Oblates of Mary Immaculate in the Province of British Columbia*, [2005] S.C.J. No. 61, [2005] 3 S.C.R. 45 (S.C.C.).

club providing recreational activities and "mentoring" was not liable for two instances of sexual assault by its program director, but sent the case back to trial to determine if there was fault-based liability. A sports organization may, therefore, be liable in negligence if it was aware of misconduct by its employee or, for example, failed to respond to complaints. It is also subject to strict liability when a coach or other role model is able to take advantage of supervisory power in intimate settings.

## 3.    Risk and Response

The incidence of sexual abuse is related to extreme risk factors created by the sports environment and by the traditional power structures in organizations. The abuse has operated within private clubs and associations that have a distinct preference for loyalty and good publicity, and compared to the workplace there has been less enforcement of regulatory standards. Young athletes are consigned[109] to the care of trusted male technicians who have hands-on authority and whose word is law. The heroic figure of the coach is often a volunteer whose background and qualifications have not been subject to close scrutiny, and a relationship is established within the intense and erotic setting of sport. The predatory supervisor is presented with classic opportunities through general access, travel arrangements and the physical contact and state of undress associated with training and medical treatment. Children and younger athletes are vulnerable because of immaturity, and athletes of any age may experience emotional dependency. Performers in competitive sport may be reluctant to complain when a place on the team depends on the coach's favour or on continuing a relationship with another officer associated with the squad.[110]

Faced with these inherent structural problems, the main administrative response has been to establish preventive measures through policies, codes of conduct, and reporting[111] and disciplinary procedures.[112] Various professionals

---

[109]   On the disruption of home life caused by entry drafts, see, G.I. Kirke, *Players First: A Report Commissioned by the Canadian Hockey League* (August 7, 1997) at 8-9. The report took the view that all players, whether close to home or at a distance, are best served by a framework of preventive measures.

[110]   See, L. Robinson, *Black Tights: Women, Sport, and Sexuality* (Toronto: HarperCollins Publishers, 2002) at 137.

[111]   In Ontario, the *Student Protection Act, 2002*, S.O. 2002, c. 7, introduced special duties and reporting requirements applying to school boards and employers of teachers or support personnel. By s. 170(1), para. 12.1 of the *Education Act*, R.S.O. 1990, c. E.1, a school board must suspend from duties any teacher who has been charged with a sex crime or other offence that may indicate that pupils are at risk. By ss. 43.2-43.3 of the *Ontario College of Teachers Act, 1996*, S.O. 1996, c. 12, employers must report to the College of Teachers the termination, resignation or restriction of duties of members for reasons of professional misconduct and must report relevant charges, convictions or conduct; see also, s. 1 (definition of "sexual abuse").

[112]   See: *Harassment in Sport: A Guide to Policies, Procedures and Resources* (CAAWS, September 1994); G.I. Kirke, *Players First: A Report Commissioned by the Canadian Hockey League* (August 7, 1997) at 23-38; L. Robinson, *Crossing the Line: Violence and Sexual*

and recreation workers are subject to established duties under provincial legislation to report suspected cases of child abuse,[113] and association policies may extend the responsibility to recognize and report improper behaviour. Both government departments[114] and sports organizations have promoted programs to set standards and educate participants. Hockey Canada's "Speak Out: Abuse and Harassment Can Be Stopped!"[115] program includes resource materials and workshops to raise awareness of different types of humiliation and abuse and offers a confidential counselling service. The information includes detailed guidelines outlining the supervisory responsibilities of coaches and staff and setting behavioural boundaries.[116] Hockey Canada's "Harassment/Bullying Complaint Procedures" encourages prompt and informal resolutions, while also providing for incidents to be reported to an "Official" such as a harassment advisor. Where either the complainant or the Official files a formal written complaint, the president of Hockey Canada appoints an independent "Investigator" who may determine that the case merits a hearing before a three-person Panel; the parties may also agree to waive the investigation stage and go directly to the hearing. After conducting a private hearing, the Panel issues a written decision that may include disciplinary "action" against the respondent (*i.e.*, the person accused) or disciplinary "sanctions" against the complainant. The Panel's decision is subject to appeal to a three-person Board that includes external representatives. The record of the procedures is usually private, but Hockey Canada recognizes that absolute confidentiality cannot be guaranteed where criminal conduct is involved or where it is necessary to protect others.

An important mechanism of prevention has been the introduction of employee screening, including criminal record checks and the use of the Canadian Police Information Centre ("CPIC"). Such "police clearance" is usually conducted through the services of a company providing search and investigation services. A

---

*Assault in Canada's National Sport* (Toronto: McClelland & Stewart, 1998) at 205-18; T. Kinsman, "Complaints Reviews: Ensuring Fairness" (1999) 6(2) Coaches Report 4. See, for example, *Paterson v. Skate Canada*, [2004] A.J. No. 1542, [2006] 3 W.W.R. 158, 26 Admin. L.R. (4th) 147 (Alta. Q.B.) (right of coaches to respond to allegations and cross-examine complainants).

[113] See, for example, *Child and Family Services Act*, R.S.O. 1990 c. C.11, s. 37(1)(2) (child under 16 in need of protection), s. 72 (duty to report). In Ontario, the duty to report applies to "every person who performs professional or official duties with respect to children" and includes health care professionals, teachers, social workers, day nursery operators, members of the clergy, peace officers and solicitors; a "youth and recreation worker" is included, but not a volunteer. On unfounded reports, see: *Carter v. NSW Netball Assn.*, [2004] NSWSC 737 (N.S.W.S.C.) (breach of natural justice; reporting of coach as child abuser was "riddled with injustice and illegality"); *Young v. Bella*, [2006] S.C.J. No. 2, [2006] 1 S.C.R. 108 (S.C.C.) (university liable for negligence).

[114] See, for example, *Making It Safer: Preventing Sexual Abuse of Children* (Ministry of Health Promotion, Ontario); see online: <http://www.mhp.gov.on.ca>.

[115] See online: <http://www.hockeycanada.ca>. See also, *Duguay v. Hockey Canada*, [2005] F.C.J. No. 884, 2005 FC 705 (F.C.) (court has no jurisdiction to order compliance).

[116] See, *Participant's Workbook: Speak Out! It's more than just a game*, 3d ed. (Canadian Red Cross RespectED/Hockey Canada, 2005) at 55-79.

search requires the agreement of the applicant or staff member,[117] and Hockey Canada has developed a "Consent For Criminal Record Search" form. Hockey Canada requires a criminal record check for its staff and representatives and recommends that Branches adopt similar policies. It is lawful for an employer to ask about criminal charges or a criminal record, although some human rights codes prohibit the exclusion of candidates when a past conviction is unrelated to the duties of the job.[118] In the case of occupations such as school employees, there is an obligation on the school board to collect personal information relating to "criminal history".[119] The sources of data include federal[120] or provincial[121] sex offender registries and child abuse registries.[122] Searches of criminal records and formal registries may yield important information about previous charges and convictions, but do not necessarily paint a full picture because the record may be incomplete or a person may be using an alias. More comprehensive screening includes interviewing candidates, checking references and conducting on-going evaluations of conduct and performance. Procedures of this sort increase the likelihood that the workplace will be safe and provide some protection to the organization in the event of a civil action.

The leading commentator on sexual abuse in sport has noted that the range of remedial responses "indicates that there is no consensus on either the origins of the problem or the best course of intervention".[123] Exclusionary measures and screening treat abusers as deviant or pathological cases, while other policies emphasise process failures and the need for declarations and bureaucratic procedures.[124] Sometimes sports administrators recognize that their own cultural

---

[117]   See, for example, *Privacy Act*, R.S.C. 1985, c. P-21, s. 8 (consent of individual for disclosure of personal information), s. 12 (individual's right of access). See also, "The Police Records Check" *Safety Net* (Hockey Canada), 3d ed., at 6.

[118]   See: *Human Rights Act*, R.S.B.C. 1996, c. 210, s. 13(1); *Woodward Stores (British Columbia) Ltd. v. McCartney* (1982), 3 C.H.R.R. D/1113 (B.C. Bd. of Inquiry), affd [1983] B.C.J. No. 40, 145 D.L.R. (3d) 193 (B.C.S.C.); *Griffiths v. Coquitlam (District)* (1988), 10 C.H.R.R. D/5852 (B.C.H.R.C.) (fire service justified in refusing position to person admitting indecent exposure); *Dunphy v. British Columbia (Minister of Public Safety and Solicitor General) (No. 2)* (2005), 51 C.H.R.R. D/320 (B.C.H.R.T.) (convictions for steroid trafficking were related to horse racing licence). See also: *Human Rights Code*, R.S.O. 1990, c. H.19, s. 5 (discrimination in employment based on "record of offences"); *Montréal (City) v. Québec (Commission des de la personne et des droits de la jeunesse*, [2008] S.C.J. No. 49, 295 D.L.R. (4th) 577 (S.C.C.) (employment of police officer).

[119]   See, *Collection of Personal Information*, O. Reg. 521/01 (regulation under the *Education Act*; school boards must collect a personal criminal history for board employees and service providers).

[120]   See, *Criminal Code*, R.S.C. 1985, c. C-46, ss. 490.001-032; *Sex Offender Information Registration Act*, S.C. 2004, c. 10.

[121]   See, *Christopher's Law (Sex Offender Registry), 2000*, S.O. 2000, c. 1.

[122]   See, *Child and Family Services Act*, R.S.O. 1990, c. 11, s. 75.

[123]   C.H. Brackenridge, *Spoilsports: Understanding and Preventing Sexual Exploitation in Sport* (London: Routledge, 2001) at 169.

[124]   Investigative and disciplinary processes should be more than public relations exercises and should take account of the needs and experiences of the athletes: S. Kirby, L. Greaves & O.

practices give rise to abuse and they "focus on 'how' their sport is coached, managed and administered".[125] Significant reform ultimately requires new forms of leadership, democratic structures and "changing the power relations between athletes and authority figures, and between men, women and children in sport".[126] A power shift in favour of responsible parents would be particularly useful since parents need to be "assured that the sport organization has the best interests of the whole child in mind (rather than just the issue of successful athletic performance)."[127]

## D. CRIMES BY ATHLETES

> I would there were no age between ten and three-and-twenty, or that youth would sleep out the rest; for there is nothing in the between but getting wenches with child, wronging the ancientry, stealing, fighting.[128]

Besides being the victims of crime, athletes can also be the perpetrators. Athlete criminality is not limited to violent attacks on playing opponents, but includes the many instances of misconduct in private and social life,[129] where a record of transgression during the playing career sometimes continues into a troubled retirement. With rare exceptions,[130] the athletes charged or convicted are male, so that problematic masculinity once again rears its head. Some behaviour can be put down to the folly of wild youth, but the source of the problem may also lie in the values of the sports world and culture of men's teams, not to mention the example set by some parents and coaches.

The irony of athlete criminality is that the athlete is supposed to be a role model who has learned all the right lessons. The incidence of irresponsibility and sexual misconduct would cause great distress to the Victorian headmasters who promoted sport to develop character and provide a healthy outlet for bodily

---

Hankivsky, *The Dome of Silence: Sexual Harassment and Abuse in Sport* (Halifax: Fernwood Publishing, 2000) at 151-52, 166.

[125] C.H. Brackenridge, *Spoilsports: Understanding and Preventing Sexual Exploitation in Sport* (London: Routledge, 2001) at 170.

[126] C.H. Brackenridge, *Spoilsports: Understanding and Preventing Sexual Exploitation in Sport* (London: Routledge, 2001) at 231. On systemic abuse of power in residential schools and other institutions, see, S. McIntyre, "Guardians of Privilege: The Resistance of the Supreme Court of Canada to Institutional Liability for Child Sexual Abuse" in S. Rogers, R. Ruparelia & L. Bélanger-Hardy (eds.), *Critical Torts* (Markham, ON: LexisNexis Canada, 2009) at 1.

[127] P. Donnelly, "Who's Fair Game? Sport, Sexual Harassment, and Abuse" in K. Young & P. White (eds.), *Sport and Gender in Canada*, 2d ed. (Don Mills, ON: Oxford University Press, 2007) at 279 and 295.

[128] W. Shakespeare, *The Winter's Tale* (1611), Act III, scene iii.

[129] On violence during play, see Chapter 6, "Play Safe: On the Ice", section B. On disciplinary proceedings, see Chapter 3, "Organizations and Regulations", section C; Chapter 9, "National Hockey League", section D.

[130] See, for example: "Panthers cheerleaders face charges after bar arrest" (Associated Press) *The Globe and Mail* (Toronto: November 7, 2005); "Bédard guilty of abducting daughter" *The Globe and Mail* (Toronto: September 21, 2007) at A5 (retired biathlete Myriam Bédard; abduction in breach of custody order).

energy,[131] and there is no easy explanation for why things go wrong. Where there is a crime of violence, it might seem to be a spill-over from the field of play,[132] but any account must also be grounded in the athlete's social origins, sense of identity and working environment. In the case of professional athletes,[133] economic prosperity and celebrity status do not seem to be the cure for crime and may even contribute to a feeling of being above the law. When the elite athlete is separated from the rest of the community, a different system of values and social relations is likely to prevail.[134]

"Crime" is a fluid concept so that the *Criminal Code*[135] and related legislation[136] criminalize an odd accumulation of acts not all of which carry great stigma; it is a manufactured product generated by the politics of prohibition, police priorities and working methods, and patterns of reporting crime. There is, however, a general idea of crime as seriously anti-social behaviour that deserves to be denounced or punished. Criminal conduct by players is an international and long-standing phenomenon,[137] and there is a particularly long parade of collegiate and professional athletes implicated in offences in the United States.[138]

---

[131] See, Chapter 2, "Legal Fundamentals and Equality Rights", section E, 7. See, for example, J. Gathorne-Hardy, *The Old School Tie: The Phenomenon of the English Public School* (New York: The Viking Press, 1978) at 68-93, 144-80.

[132] On spill-over from the rink, see, G.A. Bloom & M.D. Smith, "Hockey Violence: A Test of the Cultural Spillover Theory" (1996) 13 Soc. of Sport J. 65. See also: *Chiasson c. Roy*, [2007] A.N.-B. no 91, 312 N.B.R. (2d) 377 (N.B.Q.B. (T.D.)) (plaintiff attacked by group of hockey players renting cottage); *R. v. Ray*, [2008] O.J. No. 4185, 79 W.C.B. (2d) 556 (Ont. S.C.J.) (attack following party).

[133] The professional athlete who is protecting a business reputation may have a tax deduction for legal expenses incurred in defending criminal charges: J.R. Dorocak, "Sports and Entertainment Figures (and Others) May be Able to Deduct Legal Expenses for Criminal Prosecutions (and Wrongful Death Suits)" (1997), 13 Akron Tax J. 1. But see, *Harden v. Commissioner of Internal Revenue*, 62 T.C.M. (CCH) 756, T.C.M. (RIA) 91454 (payment of USD $25,000 to drop complaint of sexual assault not deductible).

[134] See, J. Coakley, *Sport in Society: Issues and Controversies*, 8th ed. (Boston: McGraw Hill, 2004) at 218.

[135] R.S.C. 1985, c. C-46. On the variety of crime, see: *R. c. Lafleur*, [2009] J.Q. no 4212, 2009 QCCQ 3785 (C.Q.); *R. c. Lafleur*, [2009] J.Q. no 6769, 2009 QCCQ 6274 (C.Q.) (sentencing); "Lafleur convicted of misleading Quebec court" *The Globe and Mail* (Toronto: May 2, 2009) at A7 (Guy Lafleur convicted of giving contradictory evidence contrary to s. 136).

[136] See, for example, *Controlled Drugs and Substances Act*, S.C. 1996, c. 19.

[137] See, for example: "Sprague Cleghorn Arrested" *The Globe and Mail* (Toronto: January 5, 1918) at 18 (professional hockey player alleged to have struck his wife with the crutch he was using for a broken leg); M. Houlbrook, *Queer London: Perils and Pleasures in the Sexual Metropolis, 1918-1957* (Chicago: The University of Chicago Press, 2005) at 28-29, 208-09 (charge of soliciting against cricketer Frank Champain in 1927).

[138] On racial factors and the politics of representation, see: V. Burstyn, *The Rites of Men: Manhood, Politics, and the Culture of Sport* (Toronto: University of Toronto Press, 1999) at 169-73, 201-13; B. Berry and E. Smith, "Race, Sport, and Crime: The Misrepresentation of African Americans in Team Sports and Crime" (2000) 17 Soc. of Sport J. 171. On the crime of "driving while black", see also, "Alouettes blame racism for traffic stop" *The Globe and Mail* (Toronto: November 10, 2006) at A10.

American football players[139] tend to lead the way, with O.J. Simpson the most notorious example, although there is also a record of serious crimes by players in the National Basketball Association.[140] Among Canadian athletes, the prominent cases include the conviction for sexual assault of boxer Dave Hilton,[141] the homicide conviction of football player Tommy Kane[142] and the conviction for aggravated sexual assault of football player Trevis Smith.[143] Between 1993 and 1997, numerous charges of assault and sexual assault were brought against the junior hockey player Jarret Reid.[144] A domestic disturbance in 2000 led to charges against Patrick Roy, but the Colorado Avalanche player was acquitted because no one was injured and the property damaged belonged to Roy himself.[145] In 2004, Mike Danton was convicted of conspiring to arrange the murder of someone he thought was a threat to him; the target has usually been identified as his agent David Frost, but may have been Danton's father.[146] In 2005 Dany Heatley pleaded guilty to second degree vehicular homicide with respect to the car crash that killed his Atlanta Thrashers' teammate Dan Snyder in 2003.[147]

Minor misdemeanours by celebrities can attract undue publicity, and allegations often turn out to be unfounded, but the problem of athlete criminality

---

[139] See: J. Benedict & D. Yaeger, *Pros and Cons: The Criminals Who Play in the NFL* (New York: Warner Books, 1998); G. Falk, *Football and American Identity* (Binghamton: The Haworth Press, 2005) at 199-220.

[140] See, J. Benedict, *Out of Bounds: Inside the NBA's Culture of Rape, Violence, and Crime* (New York: HarperCollins, 2004).

[141] See, "Unrepentant Hilton begins 7-year term" *The Globe and Mail* (Toronto: May 10, 2001) at A3; "Former boxer's daughter breaks silence on incest" *The Globe and Mail* (Toronto: October 14, 2004) at A9.

[142] *R. v. Kane*, [2005] Q.J. No. 12354, 202 C.C.C. (3d) 113, 34 C.R. (6th) 378 (Que. C.A.); "Wife-killer sentenced to 18 years" *The Globe and Mail* (Toronto: November 6, 2004) at A8. See also, "Wrestler strangled himself with pulley" *The Globe and Mail* (Toronto: June 27, 2007) at A3 (double murder and suicide involving Chris Benoit).

[143] *R. v. Smith*, [2008] S.J. No. 283, 310 Sask.R. 230 (Sask. C.A.); "Smith guilty, faces prison" *The Globe and Mail* (Toronto: February 9, 2007) at A7 (unprotected sex with two women while infected with HIV/AIDS).

[144] See, L. Robinson, *Crossing the Line: Violence and Sexual Assault in Canada's National Game* (Toronto: McClelland & Stewart, 1998) at 15-55.

[145] See: "Solemn Roy appears in court" *The Globe and Mail* (Toronto: October 24, 2000) at S1, S3; "Avs Roy cleared of charge" *The Globe and Mail* (Toronto: February 1, 2001) at S3. See also, "Brashear receives discharge" *The Globe and Mail* (Toronto: December 5, 2001) at S2 (Donald Brashear admitted grabbing a man by the throat in an altercation in the exercise room at his residential complex).

[146] See, "Danton jailed for 7½ years in murder plot" *The Globe and Mail* (Toronto: November 9, 2004) at R6, R11. At a parole hearing in Canada in September 2009, Danton testified that the murder-for-hire was directed against his father. See further, Chapter 5, "Be Safe: Off the Ice", section F.

[147] See, "Heatley avoids jail time with guilty plea" *The Globe and Mail* (Toronto: February 5, 2005) at S3. See also: "As families continue to suffer, there is plenty enough tragedy for everyone" *The Globe and Mail* (Toronto: October 11, 2007) at R8; "Ramage's exemplary career blackened by 4-year sentence" *The Globe and Mail* (Toronto: January 18, 2008) at A1, A6 (former NHL player Rob Ramage convicted of driving offences relating to death of Keith Magnuson).

cannot be dismissed as media exaggeration. Many of the quoted examples involve convictions for serious crimes, and one study produced the remarkable statistic that nearly a third of National Football League players had criminal arrest records.[148] Delinquency rates for athletes and non-athletes are best explained by family background, educational achievement and social conditions, so that it is probably not the game itself that sets someone on the path of either virtue or crime, and a variety of precipitating factors may explain particular incidents. There is, however, evidence that athletes tend to aggression and rule violation in sports that emphasize competitive results and the domination of opponents.[149] Moral development[150] is particularly weak among male athletes practising power sports at higher levels of performance, where the mind set is to win at all costs and never take "no" for an answer. In brief, the nearer you get to the pros or the Olympics, the more your ethical standards are compromised.

There are many reports of athletes committing sexual assaults and other crimes of violence against women,[151] although there are empirical difficulties in showing causal connection with sports participation. A leading study revealed a high number of student athletes implicated in sexual assaults, but when compared to non-athletes there were no significant differences in reported incidents.[152] Arrest rates in cases of alleged rape may be higher for athletes, although the conviction rate is particularly low.[153] The incidence of sex crimes by athletes is best understood as revealing the general factors and types of behaviour that may contribute to violence against women.[154] Aggressive hyper-

---

[148] See: J. Benedict & D. Yaeger, *Pros and Cons: The Criminals Who Play in the NFL* (New York: Warner Books, 1998) (509 out of 1590 players and draftees; 109 players had been arrested or indicted for a "serious" crime and had a total of 264 arrests); B. Berry & E. Smith, "Race, Sport, and Crime: The Misrepresentation of African Americans in Team Sports and Crime" (2000) 17 Soc. of Sport J. 171 at 188-92. See also, National Coalition Against Violent Athletes, online: <http://www.ncava.org>.

[149] See, J.J. Coakley, *Sport in Society: Issues and Controversies*, 6th ed. (Boston: Irwin McGraw-Hill, 1998) at 160-61, 164-65.

[150] See: D.L.L. Shields & B.J.L. Bredemeier, *Character Development and Physical Activity* (Champaign: Human Kinetics, 1995), especially at 122-23, 184-95; J. Bouton, *Ball Four* (New York: Dell Publishing, 1970) at 36-38 ("the crazy things ballplayers do", including Peeping Tom activities). Germaine Greer has commented, "They are 'lads' or 'boys' to be bought and sold, transferred or dropped or left on the bench; as they are denied autonomy, we can't be surprised if they lack responsibility": "Nothing new about ugly sex" *The Guardian* (London: December 16, 2003).

[151] See: J. Benedict, *Public Heroes, Private Felons: Athletes and Crimes against Women* (Boston: Northeastern University Press, 1997); M. Walsh, "Violence against Women by Professional Football Players: A Gender Analysis of Hypermasculinity, Positional Status, Narcissism, and Entitlement" (1997) 21 J. of Sport & Social Issues 392 (100 NFL players, through June 1996).

[152] T. Crosset *et al.*, "Male Student-Athletes Reported for Sexual Assault: Survey of Campus Police Departments and Judicial Affairs" (1995) 19 J. of Sport & Social Issues 126.

[153] See, J. Benedict & A. Klein, "Arrest and Conviction Rates for Athletes Accused of Sexual Assault" (1997) 14 Soc. of Sport J. 14.

[154] See, T. Crosset, "Male Athletes' Violence Against Women: A Critical Assessment of the Athletic Affiliation, Violence Against Women Debate" (1999) 51 Quest 244.

masculinity is reinforced in the closed culture of sports such as junior hockey[155] that honour chauvinism and the use of personal violence. This type of environment fosters toughness and alcoholic consumption and tends to reinforce misogyny as women are viewed as mere "groupies", "puck bunnies" or "goal diggers" willingly participating in the party atmosphere of the team. The successful athlete may be an egoist who is used to getting his own physical way and who enjoys the approval of his peers. He may also have been protected and tolerated by institutions that are reluctant to invite bad publicity or impose sanctions on their own player.[156] Sports such as hockey or football do not necessarily brutalize the player, but the macho and sexist values of the team fraternity illustrate the type of social structure that can breed sexual violence.

In spite of the links with team culture, teams do not normally bear civil responsibility for private-life crimes committed by their players,[157] although a school or university could be liable where student athletes are guilty of a pattern of violence against members of the institution.[158] A team could be implicated where it is in a proximate relationship with the victim and failed to respond to known examples of abusive behaviour, and a team might also be liable when incidents occur on its premises.

Given the repeated instances of crime and the excesses of hyper-masculinity, it is the responsibility of professional leagues and other organizations to implement preventive measures and adequate disciplinary systems.[159] Care should also be taken to see that there is a sound basis to

---

[155] See, L. Robinson, *Crossing the Line: Violence and Sexual Assault in Canada's National Sport* (Toronto: McClelland & Stewart, 1998) at 98-152.

[156] On institutional tolerance and the persecution of complainants, see, P. Safai, "Boys Behaving Badly: Popular Literature on the Mis/behaviour of Male Team Sport Athletes in North America" (2002) 37 Int. Rev. for the Soc. of Sport 97, at 100-01. On appropriate criminal sanctions, see, M.M. O'Hear, "Blue-Collar Crimes/White Collar Criminals: Sentencing Elite Athletes Who Commit Violent Crimes" (2001) 12 Marquette Sports L. Rev. 427.

[157] On allegations of a "culture of lawlessness" in the NBA, see, *Cimpean v. Payton*, [2008] O.J. No. 2665, 168 A.C.W.S. (3d) 445 (Ont. S.C.J.), leave to appeal granted [2008] O.J. No. 4713 (Ont. S.C.J.) (alleged assaults by Milwaukee Bucks' players at an adult entertainment lounge). On vicarious liability for the conduct of employees in supervisory positions, see Chapter 5, "Be Safe: Off the Ice", section C, 2. On liability for violence during play, see Chapter 6, "Play Safe: On the Ice", section C, 2.

[158] See: G.B. Fried, "Illegal Moves Off-the-Field: University Liability for Illegal Acts of Student-Athletes" (1997) 7 Seton Hall J. of Sport L. 69; T. Davis & T. Parker, "Student Athlete Sexual Violence Against Women: Defining the Limits of Institutional Responsibility" (1998) 55 Wash. & Lee L. Rev. 55; T.N. Sweeney, "Closing the Campus Gates — Keeping Criminals Away From The University — The Story of Student-Athlete Violence And Avoiding Institutional Liability For The Good of All" (1999) 9 Seton Hall J. of Sport L. 226; J.E. Spies, "Winning at All Costs: An Analysis of a University's Potential Liability for Sexual Assaults Committed by its Student Athletes" (2006) 16 Marquette Sports L. Rev. 429.

[159] See: "Out of Bounds: Professional Sports Leagues and Domestic Violence" (1996) 109 Harv. L. Rev. 1048; A.L. Jefferson, "The NFL and Domestic Violence: The Commissioner's Power to Punish Domestic Abusers" (1997) 7 Seton Hall J. of Sport L. 353; E.E. Dabbs, "Intentional Fouls: Athletes and Violence Against Women" (1998) 31 Columbia J. of L. & Social Problems 167.

accusations.[160] In 2007, both the NFL and NHL renewed their policies in relation to personal misconduct and suspended players convicted of criminal offences.[161] There is, however, little prospect of a sustained public campaign to demand significant reforms. Paying customers have proved themselves indifferent to the morals of their heroes, and athlete criminality has done nothing to harm the commercial viability of professional leagues, where a "rebel" image can be a good marketing device. If a player has the skills, neither coaches nor fans ask too many questions, and sponsors of teams rarely withdraw support because of "player transgressions".[162]

## E.  HAZING

Sometimes the victim of athlete misconduct is one of their own. Hazing usually refers to a humiliating initiation[163] rite marking entrance into groups such as teams, fraternities or military units. The ritual is designed to create a new identity and bond the novice with the team: the rookie proves loyalty and commitment by being prepared to suffer the worst indignity for the new community.[164] Through the initiation, the rookie yields to established values and authority:

> Rookies who have been hazed are less likely to pose any threat to the power struc-
> ture because they have conformed to the group by following orders and placing
> themselves in compromising positions for the perceived good of the group. In the
> eyes of the veterans, the rookies have participated in male solidarity, and have thus
> earned "their place" on the team.[165]

---

[160]  See, "Duke lacrosse players sue school, city" *Associated Press*, February 21, 2008 (university cancelled team's season following accusation's of rape; charges were dismissed and District Attorney disbarred).

[161]  See, "Union rushes to Bell's defence" *The Globe and Mail* (Toronto: September 13, 2007) at R10 (15-game suspension for Mark Bell who had pleaded no contest in California to drunk driving and hit-and-run charges). On disciplinary processes, see Chapter 9, "National Hockey League", section D.

[162]  See, K. Westberg, C. Stavros & B. Wilson, "An Examination of the Impact of Player Transgressions on Sponsorship B2B Relationships" (2008) 9 Int. J. of Sports Marketing & Sponsorship 125.

[163]  Hazing activities can also be ongoing; see, S. Kirby & G. Wintrup, "Running the Gauntlet: An Examination of Initiation/Hazing and Sexual Abuse in Sport" in C. Brackenridge & K. Fasting (eds.), *Sexual Harassment and Abuse in Sport: International Research and Policy Perspectives* (London: Whiting & Birch, 2002) at 65.

[164]  See, M.A. Robidoux, *Men at Play: A Working Understanding of Professional Hockey* (Montreal & Kingston: McGill-Queen's University Press, 2001) at 100-26, 189.

[165]  E.I. Allan & G. DeAngelis, "Hazing, Masculinity, and Collision Sports: (Un)Becoming Heroes" in J. Johnson & M. Holman (eds.), *Making the Team: Inside the World of Sport Initiations and Hazing* (Toronto: Canadian Scholars' Press, 2004) at 61, 73.

The rituals of men's[166] teams usually involve a perverse form of masculinity that mixes alcohol with nudity, pain, disgusting degradation or sexual activity.[167] The "sweatbox" of the washroom on the team bus has been a common practice,[168] and some form of simulated bodily penetration may also be involved.[169] The ceremony is sometimes recorded on video, and there may be a further loss of privacy when a newspaper conducts interviews with the participants and reports on the initiation.[170]

It is the official policy of leagues, associations and universities to forbid hazing, although team communities continue to find ways to initiate their newcomers. The Hockey Canada regulation, as amended in 2006, aims to sanction perpetrators rather than victims and is now in the following terms:

> Any player, team official, executive member, team, club or association or any other Hockey Canada member found, by an investigative process, to have con-doned, initiated or, to the detriment of another, participated in hazing actions or behaviours shall be subject to discipline up to and including expulsion from Hockey Canada registered programs. Discipline must relate to the degree of sever-ity of the incident(s).[171]

Hazing is defined as "an initiation practice that may humiliate, demean, degrade, or disgrace a person regardless of location or consent of the participant(s)".[172]

---

[166] On bonding in women's teams, see, N. Theberge, *Higher Goals: Women's Ice Hockey and the Politics of Gender* (Albany: State University of New York Press, 2000) at 101-11. See also, J. Bryshun & K. Young, "Hazing as a Form of Sport and Gender Socialization" in K. Young & P. White (eds.), *Sport and Gender in Canada*, 2d ed. (Don Mills, ON: Oxford University Press, 2007) at 302.

[167] On hazing in junior hockey, see: L. Robinson, *Crossing the Line: Violence and Sexual Assault in Canada's National Sport* (Toronto: McClelland & Stewart, 1998) at 65-97; L. Robinson, "Hazing — A Story" in J. Johnson & M. Holman (eds.), *Making the Team: Inside the World of Sport Initiations and Hazing* (Toronto: Canadian Scholars' Press, 2004) at 1.

[168] See, "Sidelined for standing up to his teammates" *The Globe and Mail* (Toronto: October 19, 2005) at A1, A8 (OHL sanctions against the Windsor Spitfires).

[169] See, for example: "Student quits McGill over hazing" *The Globe and Mail* (Toronto: September 23, 2005) at A1, A6; "McGill cuts its season short" *The Globe and Mail* (Toronto: October 19, 2005) at A1, A8; "McGill gets tough with hazing" *The Globe and Mail* (Toronto: January 11, 2006) at A1, A7 (hazing by football team and new policy).

[170] See, *Marquis c. Journal de Québec*, [2002] J.Q. no 3813, 219 D.L.R. (4th) 305 (Que. C.A.) (no breach of privacy when 17-year-old hockey players consented to be interviewed about video of initiation).

[171] See, Hockey Canada, Regulations (amended to June 2008), O.4 (Discipline of Clubs, Teams, Players and Officials).

[172] See, Hockey Canada, Regulations (amended to June 2008), O.4 (Discipline of Clubs, Teams, Players and Officials), Regulation A.15.

Besides being exposed to domestic sanctions, participants risk criminal[173] and civil[174] liability, and there may be further legal issues relating to the use of alcohol. Where the hazing involves physical contact or sexual activity, the case may allege that there was an assault or sexual offence,[175] although defendants will commonly argue that the victim voluntarily participated in the ritual and so consented. Where the hazing involves public nudity or disorderly conduct, those being hazed may face charges related to public indecency or causing a disturbance.[176] Workplace initiations have been held to constitute sexual harassment,[177] and an organization subject to a duty of care may be liable in negligence when the victim suffers physical or emotional injury. In the leading decision in *Powlett v. University of Alberta*,[178] a freshman was reduced to insanity by a series of indignities involving pain and nudity. The university was held liable for its "tacit approval" or "studied ignorance" of initiation practices that were so risky that members of the football team were excused. One judge in the Alberta Court of Appeal commented:

> In all Universities rough games are to be expected...but a system whereby the bullying of one or more boys by a superior number of other boys is permitted is, in my opinion, in quite a different category and is something, to put it very mildly, which does not appeal to my sense of fair play.[179]

## F.   THE TRIALS OF DAVID FROST

In November 2008, former junior hockey coach, David Frost, was found not guilty of four counts of sexual exploitation contrary to section 153 of the

---

[173]   See, for example, "Fourteen high-school students charged in Alberta hazing" *The Globe and Mail* (Toronto: September 2, 2008) (paddling with hockey sticks and cricket bats). On various offences, see, *Criminal Code*, R.S.C. 1985, c. C-46, s. 162 (voyeurism or surreptitious recording), ss. 219-221 (causing death or bodily harm by criminal negligence), s. 271 (sexual assault); see further, Chapter 6, "Play Safe: On the Ice", section B.

[174]   See, *Kinver v. Phoenix Lodge, I.O.O.F.*, [1885] O.J. No. 335, 7 O.R. 377 (Ont. H.C.J.) (action for trespass to the person; Oddfellows lodge liable for injuries suffered during initiation; "sport to the one party, may be very hurtful to the other").

[175]   See, "Quebec teen secretly taped having sex with player" *The Globe and Mail* (Toronto: December 22, 2006) at R7 (charges against four junior AAA players).

[176]   See, *Criminal Code*, R.S.C. 1985, c. C-46, ss. 173-175. But see, *R. v. Springer*, [1975] S.J. No. 55, 24 C.C.C. (2d) 56 (Sask. Q.B.) ("streaking" at football stadium held to be a "sport and a ritual").

[177]   See: *MacMillan Bloedel Ltd. v. IWA-Canada, Local 363 (Bowerman)*, [1997] B.C.C.A.A.A. No. 807, 69 L.A.C. (4th) 111 (B.C.) (discipline grievance); R.B. Crow & D.R. Phillips, "Hazing — What the Law Says" in J. Johnson & M. Holman, *Making the Team: Inside the World of Sport Initiations and Hazing* (Toronto: Canadian Scholars' Press, 2004) at 19, 26. On sexual harassment, see Chapter 5, "Be Safe: Off the Ice", section C.

[178]   [1934] A.J. No. 14, [1934] 2 W.W.R. 209 (Alta. C.A.), affg in part [1934] A.J. No. 6, [1933] 3 W.W.R. 322 (Alta. S.C.).

[179]   *Powlett v. University of Alberta*, [1934] A.J. No. 14, [1934] 2 W.W.R. 209, at 240 (Alta. C.A.), *per* McGillivray J.A. See also, *Kinver v. Phoenix Lodge, I.O.O.F.*, [1885] O.J. No. 335, 7 O.R. 377 (Ont. H.C.J.).

*Criminal Code.* Although the final verdict was an acquittal, the trial heard disturbing evidence of sexual conduct involving teenage participants, and Ontario Court Justice Griffin commented that the case had "exposed a dark and very unhealthy side of hockey."[180] Frost came to prominence in 2004 when he was serving as a "certified agent" under the auspices of the National Hockey League Players' Association.[181] He was then the apparent target of a weak murder plot by his client, Mike Danton of the St. Louis Blues,[182] who was sentenced to seven-and-a-half years in prison.[183] Danton was born in 1980 to Susan and Steve Jefferson of Brampton, but became increasingly estranged from his family and changed his name in 2002.[184] (At a parole hearing in Canada in September 2009, Danton testified that the actual target of the murder-for-hire was his father.) Danton was coached by Frost from the age of 11 and spent a great deal of time in his company. Frost's career in minor hockey was marred by suspensions by the Ontario Hockey Association and various leagues in Toronto,[185] and further investigations involved an alleged hazing incident in which a 13-year-old boy was tied to a bed.[186] Frost's technical ability and uncompromising style did, however, bring success in 1996 when he won the all-Ontario bantam championship using a core of players from Brampton. Frost maintains a website consisting of hockey commentary and describes himself as a "bad boy controversial figure" but "highly successful" in winning championships and developing players for elite levels of competition.[187]

In 1996, Frost moved to Deseronto, Ontario to coach the Quinte Hawks Junior A team, which soon improved their standings through an aggressive style of play that was sometimes modelled on coaching technique: in 1997, Frost received a conditional discharge for assault after he had punched one of his own players.[188] Frost was provided with accommodation at a motel that he shared with three of his teenage players. Room 22 then acquired the reputation as the site of regular sexual encounters with local high school girls. Frost's trial in 2008 related to the alleged sexual exploitation of his own players, either by touching the players himself or inviting others to touch; witnesses for the prosecution

---

[180] See, "Frost not guilty of sexual exploitation" *The Globe and Mail* (Toronto: Canadian Press online, November 28, 2008).

[181] See Chapter 9, "National Hockey League", section G.

[182] See, "How a hockey prospect fell under a coach's unshakable spell" *The Globe and Mail* (Toronto: April 24, 2004) at A2-A3.

[183] See: "Danton pleads guilty to plotting agent's murder" *The Globe and Mail* (Toronto: July 17, 2004) at A1, A2; "Danton jailed for 7½ years in murder plot" *The Globe and Mail* (Toronto: November 9, 2004) at R6, R11.

[184] See, "Why David Frost 'became my father'" *Ottawa Citizen* (April 29, 2006) at A1-A2, B1-B4.

[185] See, "The perfect place for a coach in exile" *Ottawa Citizen* (April 19, 2006) at A8.

[186] See, "The Frost boys" *Ottawa Citizen* (May 1, 2004) at A1, A2. The alleged incident gave rise to no criminal charges.

[187] See online: <http://www.hockeygodonline.com>.

[188] See: "How a hockey prospect fell under a coach's unshakable spell" *The Globe and Mail* (Toronto: April 24, 2004) at A2-A3; "The perfect place for a coach in exile" *Ottawa Citizen* (February 7, 2007) at A8, A9.

maintained that sexual activity occurred at Frost's direction.[189] The allegations of homosexual contact were denied by the players, who nevertheless admitted that there were "bonding" incidents of group sex involving two teammates and one female.[190] Since the alleged victims testified in Frost's favour, he was acquitted of the charges.[191]

In view of the sequence of peculiar circumstances, it is difficult to draw any general conclusion from this strange saga. A brief moral might be that further vigilance is required to deal with the potential for different forms of violence or misconduct by either coaches or players. The policy objectives remain those expressed in the "Canadian Strategy for Ethical Conduct in Sport"[192] as it envisions the ethical treatment of participants in a safe environment and declares the goal of promoting "excellence in sport by fair and ethical means".

---

[189] See, "Coach 'in control of every action the boys made'" *The Globe and Mail* (Toronto: October 29, 2008) at A9.

[190] See, "Hockey coach's alleged victims refuse to speak evil against him in sex case" *The Globe and Mail* (Toronto: October 31, 2008) at A1, A6.

[191] See, "Players' fierce denials deliver victory for ex-coach" *The Globe and Mail* (Toronto: November 29, 2008) at A7.

[192] See, "Canadian Strategy for Ethical Conduct in Sport: Policy Framework" (May 24, 2002), online: <http://www.pch.gc.ca>.

# Chapter 6

# PLAY SAFE: ON THE ICE

Any sport that is played at high speed in a confined area and that permits body contact is susceptible to a high injury rate among its participants.[1]

...there are some actions...that are so violent it would be perverse to find that anyone taking part in a sporting activity had impliedly consented to subject himself to them.[2]

## A. ON-ICE RISK AND INJURY

## 1. General

This chapter considers the risks of active participation and legal liability in relation to injuries suffered by players. Injuries occur accidentally in the ordinary course of play, but may also be the result of intentional or negligent conduct on the part of various defendants, and there is potential for both criminal and civil liability.[3] The impacts include high-mass collisions such as hitting the boards or checking and low-mass/high-speed blows from a puck, stick, skate, elbow, fist or helmet. Risk management in relation to player safety begins with surveillance of the incidence of injuries, including their mechanism, characteristics, circumstances and timing. There is a lack of systematic data on hockey injuries, but the following information outlines some of the available studies.

In 2002-03, hockey players in Ontario accounted for at least 8,000 presentations at hospital emergency departments, which would equate to 25,000 cases nationally. More than half (57 per cent) of the injuries in Ontario were suffered by persons under 20, and almost three-quarters (73 per cent) resulted from collisions with another person.[4] In 2002-03, the game brought nearly 500 hospitalizations in Ontario, over half of which involved victims under 19.[5] The

---

[1]   W.N. Widmeyer & E.J. McGuire, "Reducing Injury in Ice Hockey by Reducing Player Aggression" in C.R. Castaldi, P.J. Bishop & E.F. Hoerner (eds.), *Safety in Ice Hockey: Second Volume* (Philadelphia: American Society for Testing and Materials (ASTM), 1993) at 109.

[2]   *R. v. Cey*, [1989] S.J. No. 264, 48 C.C.C. (3d) 480 at 488 (Sask. C.A.), *per* Gerwing J.A.

[3]   See: Chapter 6, "Play Safe: On the Ice", section B (criminal liability); Chapter 4, "Build Safe: Rink Management and Risk Management", section A; Chapter 6, "Play Safe: On the Ice", section C (civil liability).

[4]   Canadian Institute for Health Information ("CIHI"), "Hockey injuries in Ontario" (July 28, 2003) (estimate based on hospitals accounting for about 60 per cent of ER visits). For the figures in soccer, see, "Soccer Injuries" (June 2007) 4(6) Ontario Injury Focus (SmartRisk).

[5]   "Hockey Injuries" (January 2006) 3(1) Ontario Injury Compass (SmartRisk).

impacts causing these acute care hospitalizations were as follows: contact with another object (45 per cent), with another person (35 per cent), with the puck (10 per cent) or with a stick (10 per cent). Collisions with the boards, including checks from behind, account for most major spinal injuries.[6] At the junior level and higher, collisions and body checking are the greatest cause of injury (31.7 per cent), followed by contact with the stick (18.2 per cent), puck (14 per cent) or boards (10.5 per cent) and by "no-contact" injuries (8.8 per cent).[7] There has been an evolution in the main types of injury and the part of the body affected:

> ...between 1952 and 2000...the percentages of head and face injuries, lacerations and injuries caused by the stick have decreased substantially. Conversely, shoulder and knee injuries, contusions, as well as injuries caused by player-player contacts...have substantially increased.[8]

The percentage of eye injuries has, for example, been significantly reduced by the introduction of helmets equipped with wire cages or visors.[9] Injuries in hockey are more associated with games than with practice sessions,[10] and studies have considered the site of incidents on the ice surface and their possible relation to rink configuration and rink size.[11] A study of youth hockey

---

[6]   See: C.H. Tator *et al.*, "Spinal Injuries in Canadian Ice Hockey: Documentation of Injuries Sustained from 1943-1999" (2004) 31 Can. J. of Neurological Sciences 460; C.H. Tator, J.D. Carson & R. Cushman, "Hockey Injuries of the Spine in Canada, 1966-1996" (2000) 162 Can. Medical Assn. J. 787.

[7]   See, Y.H. Azuelos *et al.*, "A Review of Ice Hockey Injuries: Location, Diagnosis, Mechanism" in D.J. Pearsall & A.B. Ashare (eds.), *Safety in Ice Hockey: Fourth Volume* (West Conshohocken: American Society for Testing and Materials International (ASTM International), 2004) at 59, 63. On body checking in minor hockey, see Chapter 6, "Play Safe: On the Ice", section A, 2.

[8]   Y.H. Azuelos *et al.*, "A Review of Ice Hockey Injuries: Location, Diagnosis, Mechanism" in D.J. Pearsall & A.B. Ashare (eds.), *Safety in Ice Hockey: Fourth Volume* (West Conshohocken: American Society for Testing and Materials International (ASTM International), 2004) at 66 (study of junior level and higher).

[9]   See, P.F. Vinger, "Is the Face Mask Good for Ice Hockey?" in A.B. Ashare (ed.), *Safety in Ice Hockey: Third Volume* (West Conshohocken: American Society for Testing and Materials (ASTM), 2000) at 63. On the obligation to provide helmets in indoor cricket, see, *Woods v. Multi-Sport Holdings Pty. Ltd.* (2002), 208 C.L.R. 460 (H.C. of Aust.).

[10]  See, R.W. Dick, "Injuries in Collegiate Ice Hockey" in C.R. Castaldi, P.J. Bishop & E.F. Hoerner (eds.), *Safety in Ice Hockey: Second Volume* (Philadelphia: American Society for Testing and Materials (ASTM), 1993) at 21, 24-25.

[11]  On rink configuration, see, M. Keating & R. Norris, "Design of Hockey Rinks and the Development of Standards" in C.R. Castaldi & E.F. Hoerner (eds.), *Safety in Ice Hockey* (Philadelphia: American Society for Testing and Materials (ASTM), 1989) at 187. On rink size, see: R.C. Watson, M. Nystrom & E. Buckholz, "Safety in Canadian Junior Ice Hockey: The Association Between Ice Surface Size and Injuries and Aggressive Penalties in the Ontario Hockey League" (1997) 7 Clinical J. of Sport Medicine 192; R. Wennberg, "Effect of Ice Surface Size on Collision Rates and Head Impacts at the World Junior Hockey Championships, 2002-2004" (2005) 15 Clinical J. of Sport Medicine 67; R. Wennberg, "Collision Frequency in Elite Hockey on North American versus International Size Rinks" (2004) 31 Can. J. of Neurological Sciences 373.

indicates that injuries are more prevalent among players born earlier in the year, possibly because of a reckless tendency to throw their weight around.[12]

In response to the risk, rate and pattern of injury, it has been necessary to adopt a range of measures involving equipment, rules and human behaviour. Player safety calls for programs and action in at least seven areas:

1. facilities;

2. players' equipment and clothing;

3. rule systems and officiating;

4. training and conditioning;

5. coaching and supervision;

6. fair play and values; and

7. medical response and treatment.

1. *Facilities*: A rink must be properly constructed and maintained to avoid unnecessary risks from the ice, boards, glass, goals and other standing plant and equipment.[13]

2. *Players' equipment and clothing*: There must be adequate "protective quality" in players' gear through the use of reputable and properly fitted helmets, facial protectors, pads, skates, sticks and other equipment.[14] At the same time, equipment must not become a weapon or a source of new risks.

3. *Rule systems and officiating*: The adequacy of rules turns on both the terms of the text[15] and the actual enforcement by referees and other officials responsible for discipline.[16] Where there is evidence that particular actions or styles of play present unreasonable risks, they must be prohibited by functioning rule systems.

---

[12] See, N. Wattie *et al.*, "Injuries in Canadian Youth Ice Hockey: The Influence of Relative Age" (2007) 120 Pediatrics 142.

[13] See: Chapter 4, "Build Safe: Rink Management and Risk Management", section A, 3 (occupiers' liability), section B (protection of spectators); Chapter 6, "Play Safe: On the Ice", section C, 3 (liability of facility operators).

[14] See: C.R. Castaldi & E.F. Hoerner (eds.), *Safety in Ice Hockey* (Philadelphia: American Society for Testing and Materials (ASTM), 1989) at 117-83, 207-73; C.R. Castaldi, P.J. Bishop & E.F. Hoerner (eds.), *Safety in Ice Hockey: Second Volume* (Philadelphia: American Society for Testing and Materials (ASTM), 1993) at 159-212; A.B. Ashare (ed.), *Safety in Ice Hockey: Third Volume* (West Conshohocken: American Society for Testing and Materials (ASTM), 2000) at 63-129; Hockey Canada, *Safety Requires Teamwork & Safety For All* (2009-2010) at 70-95 ("Equipment Tips"). See also, Chapter 6, "Play Safe: On the Ice", sections A, 3 (legal standards); C, 7 (products liability).

[15] See, R.C. Watson & G.D. Rickwood, "'Stewards of Ice Hockey': A Historical Review of Safety Rules in Canadian Amateur Ice Hockey" (1999) 30 Sport History Review 27.

[16] See, L. Livingston & S. Forbes, "Rule Modification and Strict Rule Enforcement as a Means of Reducing Injury in Invasion Games" (2003) 8 Avante 12 (hockey has many proscriptive rules but comparatively few statements about enforcement).

4. *Training and conditioning*: Many injuries are prevented by general conditioning and by warming-up.[17]

5. *Coaching and supervision*: Coaches must be qualified and competent as instructors and well-informed in matters of health and safety.[18] They must also lead by example in promoting good sportsmanship.

6. *Fair play and values*: Coaches, spectators and players[19] must be committed to fair play and must avoid resort to violence, intimidation or other detrimental tactics.[20]

7. *Medical response and treatment*: Personnel must be trained to implement the emergency action plan and respond with suitable first aid and other treatment.[21] Special precautions are required in relation to spinal injuries[22] and concussions.[23]

Criminal liability[24] may follow from deliberate acts of violence and other threats to public order, and there can be civil liability when injury results from the failure to maintain reasonable standards of safety in any one of these seven areas. In Canadian civil litigation arising from injuries to hockey players, the usual defendants are players or facility operators, but liability is not restricted to those who are in direct contact with the victim or who have a role in putting on particular events. Liability can also be traced to organizations that have an overall responsibility for the safe playing of the sport. A sports governing body can, for example, be held responsible for mandating particular rules or tolerating known risks[25] or for failing to provide adequate medical care.[26] A

---

[17] See, K.A. Gilder & J. Grogan, "Prevention of Ice Hockey Injuries by Strength and Conditioning" in C.R. Castaldi, P.J. Bishop & E.F. Hoerner (eds.), *Safety in Ice Hockey: Second Volume* (Philadelphia: American Society for Testing and Materials (ASTM), 1993) at 56.

[18] See Chapter 6, "Play Safe: On the Ice", section C, 4 (liability of instructors and supervisors).

[19] See: Chapter 5, "Be Safe: Off the Ice", section B, 1 ("rink rage"); Chapter 6, "Play Safe: On the Ice", section B (criminal liability of players); section C, 2 (civil liability of players).

[20] See, D.J. Pearsall & A.B. Ashare (eds.), *Safety in Ice Hockey: Fourth Volume* (West Conshohocken: American Society for Testing and Materials International (ASTM), 2004) at 26-39, 135-79.

[21] See Chapter 6, "Play Safe: On the Ice", sections C, 3-6.

[22] See, R.F. LaPrade *et al.*, "Care and Transport of Injured Participants with Potential Spine Injuries from Ice Rinks" in A.B. Ashare (ed.), *Safety in Ice Hockey: Third Volume* (West Conshohocken: American Society for Testing and Materials (ASTM), 2000) at 173.

[23] See: R.L. Bednarz, "Concussions in Youth Ice Hockey Players" in A.B. Ashare (ed.), *Safety in Ice Hockey: Third Volume* (West Conshohocken: American Society for Testing and Materials (ASTM), 2000) at 133; Hockey Canada, *Safety Requires Teamwork & Safety For All* (2009-2010) at 58-61 ("Concussion Awareness"). See further, Chapter 6, "Play Safe: On the Ice", section A, 4 (concussions in the NHL).

[24] On the criminal liability of organizations, see Chapter 6, "Play Safe: On the Ice", section B, 5.

[25] See: G.M. Kelly, "Prospective Liabilities of Sport Supervisors" (1989) 63 Aus. L.J. 669 at 679-85; *Agar v. Hyde* (2000), 201 C.L.R. 552 (H.C. of Aust.) (International Rugby Football Board did not owe a duty of care to players, but court recognised circumstances when a governing body could be held liable); *Haymes v. Prowse*, [2001] NSWCA 328 (N.S.W.C.A.) (duty of baseball association); *Woods v. Multi-Sport Holdings Pty. Ltd.* (2002), 208 C.L.R. 460 (H.C. of Aust.); *Watson v. Haynes* (1987), Aust. Torts Reports ¶80-094 (N.S.W.S.C.) (duty of government department to advise of risk of neck injury). For a claim based on the risk of collision un-

sports organization is required to show that it has taken positive steps to reduce unnecessary risks and has addressed the various sources and causes of injury. One aspect of minor hockey has caused particular concern.

## 2.    Body Checking

Hockey Canada defines body checking as,

> an individual defensive tactic designed to legally separate the puck carrier from the puck. The tactic is the result of a defensive player applying physical extension of the body toward the puck carrier moving in an opposite or parallel direction. The action of the defensive player is deliberate and forceful in an opposite direction to which the offensive player is moving.[27]

In November 2007, Hockey Canada affirmed the playing rule that permits body checking at or above the Pee Wee age level (11-12). The age group adopted by Hockey Quebec is Bantam (13-14). Hockey Canada's decision followed an experimental study at the Atom level (9-10) involving the Saskatchewan Hockey Association and the Ontario Hockey Federation.[28]

Hockey Canada's present[29] position dates from 2003 and followed a controversy over the reliability of research used to justify a more general authorisation of body checking for nine-year-olds.[30] The effects of body checking have subsequently been the subject of detailed study as analysts have considered the associated risks and the appropriate age for introducing the technique. The presentations at hospital emergency departments in 2002-03 indicated that body checks accounted for a major portion of the injuries,[31] and a further study in

---

der "touch icing" rules, see, *Mohney v. USA Hockey, Inc.*, 77 F.Supp. 2d 859 (N.D. Ohio, 1999), vard 5 Fed. Appx. 450 (6th Cir., 2001).

[26] *Watson v. British Boxing Board of Control*, [2001] Q.B. 1150 (C.A.) (failure to provide ringside resuscitation services).

[27] See online: <http://www.hockeycanada.ca> "Checking FAQs" (2007).

[28] See online: <http://www.hockeycanada.ca> "Background on Checking" (2007). For a study of body checking under a strictly controlled system at the atom age level, see, W.J. Montelpare & M.N. McPherson, "Measuring the Effects of Initiating Body Checking at the Atom Age Level" in D.J. Pearsall & A.B. Ashare (eds.), *Safety in Ice Hockey: Fourth Volume* (West Conshohocken: American Society for Testing and Materials International (ASTM), 2004) at 70 (injury rates did not differ between the control group in the ODMHA and the body checking "treatment group" in the OHF).

[29] On changes to age categories in 1985, see: G. Régnier *et al.*, "Effects of Body-Checking in the Pee-Wee (12-13 Years Old) Division in the Province of Quebec" in C.R. Castaldi & E.F. Hoerner (eds.), *Safety in Ice Hockey* (Philadelphia: American Society for Testing and Materials (ASTM), 1989) at 84; "The case against peewee body checks" *The Globe and Mail* (Toronto: March 17, 1989) at A18.

[30] See: "CHA bungled over bodychecking for young players" *The Globe and Mail* (Toronto: January 22, 2003) at S1, S2; M. Robidoux & P. Trudel, "Hockey Canada and the Bodychecking Debate in Minor Hockey" in D. Whitson & R. Gruneau (eds.), *Artificial Ice: Hockey, Culture, and Commerce* (Peterborough, ON: Broadview Press, 2006) at 101, 107-13.

[31] Canadian Institute for Health Information ("CIHI"), "Hockey injuries in Ontario" (July 28, 2003). See also, "Facts say bodychecks, not pucks, harming young hockey players" *The Globe and Mail* (Toronto: July 30, 2003) at A1, A4.

2003 concluded that body checking was not necessary in minor league play, especially in age groups where there are pronounced variations in the size of players.[32] This study included the following data:

> Bodychecking, the most common cause of trauma in hockey, accounts for 86% of all injuries among players 9-15 years old. Players in contact leagues are 4 times as likely to be injured (among those 9-15 years old) and 12 times as likely to receive a fracture (among those 12-13 years old) as players in non-contact leagues. Of reported injuries among players 9-15 years old, 45% are caused by legal bodychecks and 8% by illegal checks, without a significant difference in the injury profiles between the 2 types of checking.[33]

A comparison of injury rates in Ontario and Quebec between 1995 to 2002 concluded that players aged 10 to 13 had significantly greater odds of suffering a checking injury where checking was allowed,[34] and a study of 11-year-old players in Alberta revealed that rates of injury at Pee Wee level (with body checking) increased significantly compared with those playing Atom hockey, the rate of severe injuries being twice as great.[35] Besides being a cause of direct injury, it has been suggested that body checking contributes to an atmosphere of heightened aggression and so increases the probability of injuries from other forms of contact.[36]

Given the risk factors involved, commentators and medical associations have suggested that body checking should be reserved for higher age groups, and the president of the Canada Safety Council has recommended that 17 is the

---

[32]  A. Marchie & M.D. Cusimano, "Bodychecking and Concussions in Ice Hockey: Should Our Youth Pay the Price?" (2003) 169 Can. Medical Assn. J. 124. On size variation, see also, G. Régnier *et al.*, "Effects of Body-Checking in the Pee-Wee (12-13 Years Old) Division in the Province of Quebec" in C.R. Castaldi & E.F. Hoerner (eds.), *Safety in Ice Hockey* (Philadelphia: American Society for Testing and Materials (ASTM), 1989) at 84.

[33]  A. Marchie & M.D. Cusimano, "Bodychecking and Concussions in Ice Hockey: Should Our Youth Pay the Price?" (2003) 169 Can. Medical Assn. J. 124. The greater risks in contact hockey are noted in *Martino c. Hockey région Laval*, [2006] J.Q. no 14158, 2006 QCCS 5737 (Que. S.C.).

[34]  A. Macpherson, L. Rothman & A. Howard, "Body-Checking Rules and Childhood Injuries in Ice Hockey" (2006) 117 Pediatrics 143.

[35]  B.E. Hagel *et al.*, "Effect of Bodychecking on Injury Rates among Minor Ice Hockey Players" (2006) 175 Can. Medical Assn. J. 155. See also, C.A. Emery & W.H. Meeuwisse, "Injury Rates, Risk Factors, and Mechanisms of Injury in Minor Hockey" (2006) 34 Am. J. of Sports Medicine 1960.

[36]  See: W.N. Widmeyer & E.J. McGuire, "Reducing Injury in Ice Hockey by Reducing Player Aggression" in C.R. Castaldi, P.J. Bishop & E.F. Hoerner, *Safety in Ice Hockey: Second Volume* (Philadelphia: American Society for Testing and Materials (ASTM), 1993) at 109; P. Trudel *et al.*, "Effects of an Intervention Strategy on Body Checking, Penalties, and Injuries in Ice Hockey" in A.B. Ashare (ed.), *Safety in Ice Hockey: Third Volume* (West Conshohocken: American Society for Testing and Materials (ASTM), 2000) at 237.

appropriate age.[37] (From a legal defence perspective, the age of majority (18 or 19) would be the best time since this allows for the use of waivers.[38]) Hockey Canada[39] has noted that the sudden introduction at age 17 might cause an "abnormal spike in injuries" and maintains that players and parents appreciate a choice in the style of play. The problem comes down to how and when to implement a period of adjustment,[40] bearing in mind that there is serious potential for legal liability when injuries result from dangerous disparities in the size of players.[41] Hockey Canada argues that the most appropriate approach is to develop educational programs and instructional models that focus on body checking as a game skill[42] to be learned at a relatively early age. The ability to deliver and take the hit is certainly useful to the fraction of players who advance to professional careers, but the risks of body checking require that a safer model also be available in the high-participation age groups that precede the drop-off around the mid-teens. Hockey Canada seeks to protect itself by close study of the effects of body checking and by offering the choice of contact or no-contact hockey. An organization can show reasonable care by offering proper instruction at a suitable age, by requiring good protective equipment and by conducting games in an atmosphere of fair play. It is, however, unclear from the studies that the proper teaching of body checking affects injury rates. Players currently learn the technique at 11, and it continues to be a major cause of injury for the next four years, with consequential effects on insurance rates. Hockey Canada acknowledges that there "are no easy answers" in the quest for the safest form of

---

[37]  See: "Official calls for ban" *The Globe and Mail* (Toronto: July 31, 2003) at S1; "Why hesitate to make game safer, official asks" *The Globe and Mail* (Toronto: December 5, 2003) at S3 (interviews with Émile Thérien). See also online: <http://www.safety-council.org>.

[38]  On difficulties in enforcing waivers, see Chapter 4, "Build Safe: Rink Management and Risk Management", section C.

[39]  See online: <http://www.hockeycanada.ca> "Checking FAQs" (2007).

[40]  See, B. Willer *et al.*, "Injury Rates in House League, Select, and Representative Youth Ice Hockey" (2005) 37 Medicine & Science in Sports & Exercise 1658.

[41]  An activity must be "suitable to [the plaintiff's] age and condition (mental and physical)"; see, *Thornton v. Board of School Trustees of School Dist. No. 57 (Prince George)*, [1976] B.C.J. No. 1390, [1976] 5 W.W.R. 240, 73 D.L.R. (3d) 35 (B.C.C.A.), varg [1975] B.C.J. No. 1116, [1975] 3 W.W.R. 622, 57 D.L.R. (3d) 438 (B.C.S.C.), vard [1978] S.C.J. No. 7, [1978] 2 S.C.R. 267 (S.C.C.). On liability for mismatching, see: *Châtelain c. Prémont*, [1985] C.P. 120 (breach of weight regulations in football; coach and school liable when 90 pound player injured trying to stop opponent who weighed 174 pounds); *Hamstra (Guardian ad litem of) v. B.C. Rugby Union*, [1989] B.C.J. No. 1521, 1 C.C.L.T. (2d) 78 (B.C.S.C.), revd on other grounds, [1995] B.C.J. No. 633, 123 D.L.R. (4th) 693 (B.C.C.A.), revd [1997] S.C.J. No. 43, [1997] 1 S.C.R. 1092 (S.C.C.) (no mismatch in scrum). On instructors' liability, see Chapter 6, "Play Safe: On the Ice", section C, 4, a.

[42]  For "Key Instructional Points" in relation to body checking and protection in body checking, see, Hockey Canada, *Skills Development Manual* (PeeWee) at 122. See also, M.S. Juhn, "Body Checking and Injury in Ice Hockey: A Technical and Behavioral Assessment" in D.J. Pearsall & A.B. Ashare (eds.), *Safety in Ice Hockey: Fourth Volume* (West Conshohocken: American Society for Testing Materials International (ASTM), 2004) at 180.

phase-in,[43] and the full legal dimensions of body checking in minor hockey are yet to be explored.

## 3.    Legal Standards and Regulation

Safety in hockey is promoted by regulatory standards required by federal and provincial legislation.[44] Under the federal *Hazardous Products Act*,[45] helmets and face protectors must meet standards established by the Canadian Standards Association ("CSA").[46] The Act classifies equipment not meeting the standard as a "prohibited product" that may not be advertised, sold or imported.[47] Hockey Canada requires the use of helmets certified by the CSA and requires all minor and female players to wear full facial protectors certified by the CSA and properly attached to the helmet.[48]

In Quebec, the *Act respecting safety in sports*[49] designates the Minister of Education, Recreation and Sports as "responsible for supervising personal safety and integrity in the practice of sports". "Sport" is defined to mean,

a physical activity engaged in at the beginner or expert level, for competition or recreation and involving a form of training, the observance of rules of practice, supervision, technical content or a period of practice.[50]

The Act does not apply to professional sport except in relation to combat sports (see, s. 2). By section 21 of the Act, the Minister may "approve, with or without amendment, the safety regulations of a sports federation" and may "make regulations to ensure the safety of sports participants and spectators". In accordance with the legislative regulations, any person "participating in an ice

---

[43]   See online: <http://www.hockeycanada.ca> "Checking FAQs" (2007).

[44]   On recommended standards for boards and glass, see Chapter 4, "Build Safe: Rink Management and Risk Management", section B. On international standards for equipment, see: J.L. Dixon & I.K.R. Brodie, "The New ISO Standards for Ice Hockey Helmets and Face Protectors: Moving Toward International Standards Harmonization and Conformity Assessment" in C.R. Castaldi, P.J. Bishop & E.F. Hoerner (eds.), *Safety in Ice Hockey: Second Volume* (Philadelphia: American Society for Testing and Materials (ASTM), 1993) at 192; C.A. Morehouse, "The Certification of Protective Equipment for Ice Hockey in the United States" in A.B. Ashare (ed.), *Safety in Ice Hockey: Third Volume* (West Conshohocken: American Society for Testing and Materials (ASTM), 2000) at 72. For comparative studies of the performance of equipment, see, A.B. Ashare, *Safety in Ice Hockey: Third Volume* (West Conshohocken: American Society for Testing and Materials (ASTM), 2000) at 78-129.

[45]   R.S.C. 1985, c. H-3, Schedule I, Part I, ss. 19-20. See also, *Hazardous Products (Ice Hockey Helmets) Regulations*, S.O.R./89-257.

[46]   The CSA standards are: CAN/CSA-Z262.1-M90, *Ice Hockey Helmets*; CAN 3-Z262.2-M78, *Face Protectors for Ice Hockey and Box Lacrosse Players.*

[47]   *Hazardous Products Act*, R.S.C. 1985, c. H-3, s. 4(1).

[48]   See, Hockey Canada, *Safety Requires Teamwork & Safety For All* (2009-2010) at 82-86.

[49]   R.S.Q., c. S-3.1, s. 20. Besides hockey, the Act and Regulations include special provisions dealing with combat sports, alpine skiing and diving.

[50]   *An Act respecting safety in sports*, R.S.Q., c. S-3.1, s. 1(5).

hockey activity...carried out on a game surface reserved for that purpose" must wear a helmet and full face protector complying with CSA standards and must wear a neck protector complying with the standard of the Bureau de normalisation du Québec.[51] Partial visors in conjunction with mouthguards are permitted in the Quebec Major Junior Hockey League, the Ligue de hockey junior AAA du Québec and in certain leagues involving players 18 years or older where the Minister has approved safety regulations (see, reg., s. 2). The requirement to wear CSA-certified helmets and full face protectors does not apply to players on teams from outside of Canada; the requirement to wear CSA-certified full face protectors does not apply to players on Canadian teams from outside of Quebec; and the requirement to wear approved neck protectors does not apply to players on teams from outside Quebec.[52] It is, therefore, a legal requirement in Quebec that players on visiting Canadian amateur teams wear CSA-certified helmets.

Provincial legislation dealing with safe working conditions offers a further potential source of standards for the benefit of professional players.[53] In Ontario, s. 25(2)(h) of the *Occupational Health and Safety Act* requires employers to "take every precaution reasonable in the circumstances for the protection of the worker" and provides protection against disciplinary reprisals where employees comply with the Act or seek to enforce rights (see, s. 50). The Act authorizes making regulations to promote health and safety in the workplace (see, s. 70) and requires employers to provide any prescribed equipment and to carry out any prescribed measures or procedures (see, s. 25(1)). Although the Act is available as a means of promoting safer play in professional games in the Province, it has not been applied to require specific protective equipment or otherwise regulate safety standards in hockey. The Act does, however, grant a general right to refuse to work where employees have reason to believe that they may be endangered by equipment or the physical condition of the workplace (see, s. 43(3)). Where professional players' anxiety comes from the presence on the ice of a salaried goon or "penalty leader", it is not clear that the Ontario legislation is applicable. In other Provinces, there are specific regulations dealing with violence in the workplace, and employers are subject to obligations to report incidents and to inform workers of the risks.[54] There is, however, a general reluctance to apply ordinary occupational safety standards to professional sport. In determining to exempt professional sports competitors from the statutory compensation scheme, the Workers' Compensation Board of

---

[51] See, *Protective equipment for the practice of ice hockey, Regulation respecting,* R.Q. c. S-3.1, r.0.1.01, s. 1 (O.C. 36-92). The standard for the neck protector (protège-cou) is, NQ9415-370.

[52] *For the exclusion from the application of the Regulation respecting protective equipment for the practice of ice hockey, Regulation,* R.Q. c. S-3.1, r.0.1.1 (O.C. 214-90, O.C. 37-92).

[53] See, for example: *Workers Compensation Act,* R.S.B.C. 1996, c. 492, Part 3 (ss. 106-230); *Occupational Health and Safety Act,* R.S.A. 2000, c. O-2; *Occupational Health and Safety Act,* R.S.O. 1990, c. O.1; *An Act respecting occupational health and safety,* R.S.Q., c. S-2.1.

[54] See, for example, *Occupational Health and Safety Regulation,* B.C. Reg. 296/97, ss. 4.24-4.31 (made under *Workers Compensation Act*). In Ontario, see now, *Occupational Health and Safety Amendment Act (Violence and Harassment in the Workplace), 2009,* S.O. 2009, c. 23.

British Columbia has stated that it would be inappropriate to alter the "aim of the business":

> Sports are governed by rules prescribing how they are played. The rules often involve violence or other risks as an essential part of the sport's normal conduct. The risk is part of the product marketed to the public. Outside the sport, the actions in question might be inappropriate or unlawful. To regulate a sport, it would be necessary to eliminate or minimize the risks by changing the rules. This would change the method of play and therefore the game itself.[55]

## 4.    Injuries in the National Hockey League

The NHL maintains injury recording systems and since 1997 has operated a testing and review program in relation to concussions. Injury information is a staple of sports news and betting sites, and the player is also entitled to know how beaten up he is. Under the collective bargaining agreement ("CBA"),[56] the team or team physician must provide the player with a complete copy of his medical records at the end of the season, and the annual "exit physical" must document all injuries requiring medical or dental treatment (see, article 23.10). Attention has focussed on the incidence of concussions and eye injuries, although other injuries and their relation to equipment are also of concern.[57] In 2007, hits to the head became the particular focus of disciplinary sanctions.

Canadian amateur hockey organizations began to mandate CSA-certified helmets for minor players in the late 1970s and the requirements subsequently extended to the use of helmets, visors and face masks in different categories of play. The NHL required helmets to be worn by new players entering the league in the 1979-80 season, but granted an exemption for existing players. It took until 1996-97 before all players adopted head gear, although the impact standard of the skull caps remained variable.[58] As of 2008, the NHL did not require its players to wear visors or neck guards,[59] and the position of the NHL Players' Association ("NHLPA") is that protection is a matter of individual choice for players; by 2004, about 35 per cent of players opted for some form of face shield.

---

[55] (April 1994) 10(2) *Workers Compensation Reporter* 167 at 174 (Workers' Compensation Board of B.C.; Decision of Governors, No. 60, Appendix D, exemption for "Professional Sports Competitors" under s. 2(1) of the *Workers' Compensation Act*).

[56] NHL, Collective Bargaining Agreement ("CBA") (2005), available online: <http://www.nhlpa.com>. See Chapter 9, "National Hockey League", section C.

[57] On the throat injury to Trent McCleary of the Montreal Canadiens, see: "McCleary out of danger" *The Globe and Mail* (Toronto: January 31, 2000) at S1; "Injury risk renders shot blocking lost hockey art" *The Globe and Mail* (February 1, 2000) at S3.

[58] See, "Hard heads shun safer helmets" *The Globe and Mail* (Toronto: December 6, 1997) at A28, A30.

[59] In February 2008, a teammate's skate accidentally severed the carotid artery of Richard Zednik during a game in Buffalo; see, "Zednik in stable condition" *The Globe and Mail* (Toronto: February 12, 2008) at R8. On comments by Don Cherry about the wearing of visors, see Chapter 2, "Legal Fundamentals and Equality Rights", section E, 6.

The wearing of standardized helmets and facial protection reduces the risk of fatalities from blows to the head, but even with protective equipment there is a persistent high rate of concussions.[60] Concussion occurs when violent shock or trauma to the head, face or chin causes a rapid acceleration or rotation of the brain. The injury involves bruising of the jello inside the head, and the symptoms include headache, fatigue, mental disorientation, loss of coordination, unconsciousness and memory loss. Any form of concussion is a serious injury, and the risk of permanent damage is increased by repeated trauma since the effects of concussion are cumulative. A study based on NHL injury reports from 1986-87 to 2001-02 indicated a marked rise in concussions after 1997 and hypothesized that "bigger, faster players, new equipment and harder boards and glass have all theoretically increased the risk of concussion in the NHL in recent years".[61] The study concluded that the rise was primarily attributable to increased recognition and reporting of concussions, especially in light of cases involving prominent players[62] and retirements brought on by head injuries.[63]

Rule changes and protective equipment have significantly reduced the incidence of eye injuries caused by contact with the stick or puck. This risk does, however, continue to cut short careers:

> Since 1972, forty NHLers have been forced into retirement because of eye injuries. In the year 2000 alone, twelve players in the NHL sustained eye injuries, including Bryan Berard of the Leafs...[64]

To reduce the possibility of total blindness, a long-standing eligibility rule of the NHL excludes players who have already lost one eye.[65]

---

[60] See: N. Biasca & H-P. Simmen, "Minor Traumatic Brain Injury 'MTBI' in Ice Hockey and Other Contact Sports: Injury Mechanisms at the Macro and Histological Levels and Prevention Strategies" in D.J. Pearsall & A.B. Ashare (eds.), *Safety in Ice Hockey: Fourth Volume* (West Conshohocken: American Society for Testing and Materials International (ASTM), 2004) at 98; 2110 IIHF Medical Regulations, I, at 27 (Return to Play Guidelines).

[61] See, R.A. Wennberg & C.H. Tator, "National Hockey League Reported Concussions, 1986-87 to 2001-02" (2003) 30 Can. J. of Neurological Sciences 206 (reporting 30 concussions for every 1000 games in some seasons). Data presented at a symposium in New York in November 2008, indicated that 759 NHL players had been diagnosed with a concussion since 1997.

[62] See, *Boston Mutual Insurance Co. v. New York Islanders Hockey Club, L.P.*, 165 F.3d 93 (1st Cir., 1999) (insurer rescinded disability policy because of failure to disclose three prior concussions suffered by Brett Lindros); "Lindros sidelined up to six weeks" *The Globe and Mail* (Toronto: March 23, 2000) at S1 (fourth concussion suffered by Eric Lindros in two years; by 2004, Eric Lindros had suffered his eighth concussion); A.N. Hecht, "Legal and Ethical Aspects of Sports-Related Concussions: The Merril Hoge Story" (2002) 12 Seton Hall J. of Sport L. 17 at 43.

[63] The retirements precipitated by concussions include: Michel Goulet (1994), Brett Lindros (1996), Pat LaFontaine (1998), Jim Johnson (1998), Nick Kypreos (1998), Geoff Courtnall (1999), Jeff Beukeboom (1999), Adam Deadmarsh (2005) and Keith Primeau (2006).

[64] L. Scanlan, *Grace Under Fire: The State of Our Sweet and Savage Game* (Toronto: Penguin Canada, 2002) at 65. See also, "Berard's career could be over" *The Globe and Mail* (Toronto: March 13, 2000) at S1, S3.

[65] See, NHL By-Laws, sec. 12.7. See also: *Neeld v. American Hockey League*, 439 F.Supp. 459 (W.D.N.Y., 1977); *Neeld v. National Hockey League*, 439 F.Supp. 446 (W.D.N.Y., 1977);

NHL players who suffer serious injury have the benefit of insurance coverage established by the CBA (see, article 23). The CBA requires the teams and the NHLPA to maintain group life insurance and accidental death and dismemberment policies (see, articles 23.1, 23.2) and requires the teams to pay the cost of a hospital, major medical and dental plan administered through a trust (see, article 23.5). The teams and the NHLPA must also maintain disability policies (see, article 23.3). The "career ending disability policy" pays a scale of benefits according to the age of the player who is permanently prevented from playing professional hockey. The "serious disability policy" provides for payment of USD $375,000 for the loss of one eye and USD $750,000 in the event of blindness, dismemberment, paralysis or brain damage. A player who is disabled in the course of his employment is entitled to receive his salary for the remaining fixed term of the standard player contract (see, article 23.4). Where a claim is made under the career ending disability insurance, the player must execute releases of liability in relation to the league, the teams, the NHLPA and their employees (see, article 23.4; exhibits 10-12). The purpose of the release is to exclude additional obligations or civil liability arising from the claim and the injury. Civil liability is also excluded under American workers' compensation laws, and article 31.5 of the CBA requires teams to obtain workers' compensation coverage in any state where it is not compulsory for professional athletes.

## 5.  Costs: Masculinity Revisited

As noted in the previous chapter, aggressive or reckless behaviour is a male trait that is reinforced by the environment of men's sport. The off-field consequences then include rink rage, sexual abuse and other forms of criminal activity. On the field of play, the culture of masculinity[66] shows itself in the preference for robust contact sports, fisticuffs and the disregard of pain. The odd concussion or fracture is seen as a rite of passage, and "real men" often try to show their toughness by not adopting necessary safety precautions. It is hardly surprising that male participants account for the major share of the increasing global costs of sports injuries of which the Canadian medical and economic burden is probably in excess of CDN $2 billion a year.[67] These costs will only rise if women follow the male example.[68]

---

*Neeld v. National Hockey League* 594 F.2d 1297 (9th Cir., 1979) (no anti-competitive purpose in rule).

[66] See, R. Gruneau & D. Whitson, *Hockey Night in Canada: Sport, Identities, and Cultural Politics* (Toronto: Garamond Press, 1993) at 175-96.

[67] See, P. White, "The Costs of Injury from Sport, Exercise and Physical Activity: A Review of the Evidence" in K. Young (ed.), *Sporting Bodies, Damaged Selves: Sociological Studies of Sports-Related Injury* (Amsterdam: Elsevier Ltd., 2004) at 309, esp. at 21-22 (estimated economic cost in Ontario in 1995 of CDN $637 million). A report in 2006 found that 5.2 million Australians suffer sports-related injuries each year at an approximate cost of AUD $2 billion; see, *Safe Sports Report 2006* (Melbourne: Medibank Private, 2006).

[68] On "physicality" in women's hockey, see, N. Theberge, *Higher Goals: Women's Ice Hockey and the Politics of Gender* (Albany: State University of New York Press, 2000) at 113-37.

Besides playing hurt and accumulating wounds, the macho warrior is not averse to inflicting pain on opponents because the "code" requires retribution and the willingness to fight when challenged or instructed.[69] There are, however, limits to the violence that is permitted, and the ice surface offers no immunity from criminal law. The criminal prosecution of players for on-ice conduct is in fact the distinctive Canadian contribution to the law of sports.

## B. PLAYER VIOLENCE AND CRIMINAL LAW

To effectually stop the existing brutality in hockey the penalties of the *Criminal Code* must be administered to the offending player as principal and the members of the executive of his club as accessories.[70]

When Marty McSorley[71] and Todd Bertuzzi[72] were sentenced for criminal assault in 2000 and 2004, they joined a long heritage of players tried or convicted for offences committed during play.[73] Criminal prosecution dates back to the earliest years of organized hockey,[74] when notions of masculinity made for particularly brutal encounters,[75] and the years 1905 and 1907 produced two cases of hockey homicide.[76] Although there was nothing gentle about the game in the middle years of the twentieth century,[77] criminal sanctions for on-ice misconduct seemed

---

[69] See: L. Scanlan, *Grace Under Fire: The State of Our Sweet and Savage Game* (Toronto: Penguin Canada, 2002) at 25-51 ("The Code") at 204 (Paul Mulvey's refusal to fight in 1982); Scanlan notes (at 112-13) the medical team attending "hockey warrior" Marty McSorley and his eight major surgeries. See also, R. Bernstein, *The Code: The Unwritten Rules of Fighting and Retaliation in the NHL* (Chicago: Triumph Books, 2006).

[70] "Mr. Harry Brophy's Idea" *The Montreal Daily Star* (March 18, 1905) at 18.

[71] See, *R. v. McSorley*, [2000] B.C.J. No. 1993, 2000 BCPC 116 (conviction), [2000] B.C.J. No. 1994, 2000 BCPC 117 (sentencing) (B.C. Prov. Ct.).

[72] See, *R. v. Bertuzzi*, [2004] B.C.J. No. 2692, 26 C.R. (6th) 71 (B.C. Prov. Ct.).

[73] See: L. Scanlan, *Grace Under Fire: The State of Our Sweet and Savage Game* (Toronto: Penguin Canada, 2002), esp. at 53-70; R.C. Watson & J.G. MacLellan, "Smitting to Spitting: 80 Years of Ice-Hockey in Canadian Courts" (1986) 17(2) Can. J. of History of Sport 10.

[74] On the evolution of associations and leagues, see Chapter 1, "Lord Stanley and the Wednesday Nighters", section B. On the emerging problem of *brutalité* between 1875 and 1917, see, D. Guay, *L'histoire du Hockey au Québec: Origine et développement d'un phénomène culturel avant 1917* (Chicoutimi: Les Éditions JCL Inc., 1990) at 200-18.

[75] A game between the Ottawa Silver Seven and the Montreal Wanderers on January 12, 1907 led to convictions for assault against the Ottawa players, Charlie Spittal and Alf Smith; see: J. Barnes, *Two Cases of Hockey Homicide: The Crisis of a Moral Ideal* (Paper presented to the North American Society for Sport History, 1990) at 15-16; S.L. Lorenz & G.B. Osborne, "'Talk About Strenuous Hockey': Violence, Manhood, and the 1907 Ottawa Silver Seven-Montreal Wanderer Rivalry" (2006) 40 J. Can. Studies 125.

[76] See, Appendix I. There were four cases of accidental death in 1904; see, S.F. Wise & D. Fisher, *Canada's Sporting Heroes* (Don Mills, ON: General Publishing, 1974) at 48-49.

[77] See, L. Scanlan, *Grace Under Fire: The State of Our Sweet and Savage Game* (Toronto: Penguin Canada, 2002) at 26-51, 199-202, 265-66 ("Atrocities on Ice"). In *Gagné v. Hébert* (1932), 70 C.S. 454 (Que. S.C.), Archambault J. condemned the violence in the professional game and its condonation by the press and league management. It was the view of the judge that, "il est grand temps que

largely to go into hibernation until the 1970s.[78] Faced with the mayhem offered by the likes of the Big Bad Bruins (Boston) and the Broad Street Bullies (Philadelphia), public authorities were again forced to act.[79] The violent spectacles of professional hockey in the 1970s were commercially inspired and offered an unhealthy model for the wider game, and criminal law continues to be available as the ultimate remedy against violent excess.

## 1.    Criminal Law and the Legality of Sports

The Fathers of Confederation wisely decided that federal politicians are the experts in criminal matters. Under the Canadian constitutional system, Parliament has the power to enact laws relating to criminal law and criminal procedure, although the main responsibility for enforcement and for the administration of justice belongs to the Provinces.[80] Crimes have chiefly been created within the framework of the modified but unreformed *Criminal Code*[81] of 1892.

The *Criminal Code* forbids certain acts that have been held to be contrary to public order or morals or that threaten personal safety or security. These wrongful acts are thought to be of concern to society at large and are prohibited under threat of punishment or "just sanctions"(see, s. 718). The criminal trial calls for personal accountability through a public morality play in which society asserts its basic values. These values include the presumed innocence of the accused and the accused's liberty, so that the Crown bears the burden of establishing all defined elements of the crime and must prove guilt beyond reasonable doubt. Criminal prosecution and trial are, therefore, cumbersome and difficult processes best reserved as the social control of last resort. Where the accused is found guilty, sentencing is largely at the discretion of the trial judge since most crimes are subject only to maximum penalties. A wide range of sanctions and dispositions is usually available to take account of the circumstances of the particular case, the harm done and the character of the accused. The *Criminal Code* does, however, state the general purposes of sentencing and the principles to be applied. The purposes include denunciation, deterrence, the separation of offenders from society, rehabilitation, reparation of harm and the promotion of a sense of responsibility in offenders (see, s. 718). By

---

les tribunaux s'interviennent et s'élèvent contre ces spectacles révoltants, servis pour satisfaire l'appétit bestial de certains spectateurs" (at 458).

[78]    In "Smitting to Spitting: 80 Years of Ice-Hockey in Canadian Courts" (1986) 17(2) Can. J. History of Sport 10, R.C. Watson & J.G. MacLellan identify only four criminal cases between 1912 and 1969. The authors note Sprague Cleghorn's conviction for aggravated assault in 1912. Cleghorn is also reputed to have been convicted of assault on an opposing player in 1923.

[79]    See further, Chapter 6, "Play Safe: On the Ice", section B, 5.

[80]    *Constitution Act, 1867*, (U.K.) 30 & 31 Vict., c. 3; R.S.C. 1985, App. II, No. 5, ss. 91 (27), 92 (14). See also, Chapter 2, "Legal Fundamentals and Equality Rights", section B, 2.

[81]    R.S.C. 1985, c. C-46. By s. 8 of the *Criminal Code*, criminal law is primarily the product of Acts of Parliament. Common law defences are, however, preserved "except in so far as they are altered by or are inconsistent with" federal legislation (see, s. 8(3)). See also, *R. v. Jobidon*, [1991] S.C.J. No. 65, [1991] 2 S.C.R. 714 (S.C.C.).

s. 718.1, "A sentence must be proportionate to the gravity of the offence and the degree of responsibility of the offender." It is also a principle of sentencing that penalties "should be similar to sentences imposed on similar offenders for similar offences committed in similar circumstances" (see, s. 718.2(b)).

Criminal law interacts with the physical and disorderly dimensions of sport in a number of ways:

i. Teams and organizations may be the site for abusive behaviour, and games may be accompanied by rioting or fisticuffs by spectators.

ii. Some life-threatening or exploitive activities are declared unlawful so that it is an offence to organize events or participate in them. Under the *Criminal Code*, these illegal sports[82] include duelling (see, s. 71) and "prize fights" (see, s. 83). A "prize fight" is an "encounter or fight with fists or hands between two persons who have met for that purpose by previous arrangement" (see, s. 83(2)),[83] but boxing contests between amateur sportsmen and other bouts authorized by provincial athletic commissions are excluded from the prohibition.[84] The *Criminal Code* also bans certain contests or exhibitions involving cruelty to animals (see, ss. 445.1, 447), including the fighting or baiting of animals (see, s. 445.1(b)).[85]

iii. In the case of games such as hockey, the event itself is not prohibited, but participants may be guilty of particular illegal acts toward playing opponents or officials. Illegal violence is, however, not the sole problem since many serious injuries arise from the inherent action of contact sports and the ordinary run of play.

Criminal law therefore condemns off-ice misconduct and prohibits certain events, but largely tolerates the aggressive robustness on the rink and the consequent burden of broken bones and other costs.[86] We may well ask why it is that we applaud an injury-inducing check during a game, but deplore a similar blow between pedestrians on the sidewalk. The players may be consenting to the risks, but the law discounts the willingness of the participants in many harmful activities. Public fist fighting between adults[87] and sado-masochistic[88] practices

---

[82]  See: G. Létourneau and A. Manganas, "La légalité des sports violents et le Code criminel" (1977) 55 Can. Bar Rev. 256; J. Anderson, *The Legality of Boxing: A Punch Drunk Love?* (Abingdon: Birkbeck Law Press, 2007).

[83]  A "spontaneous, *ad hoc* event" does not qualify; see, *R. v. Jobidon*, [1991] S.C.J. No. 65, [1991] 2 S.C.R. 714 at 765 (S.C.C.).

[84]  See also, *R. v. M.A.F.A. Inc.*, [2000] O.J. No. 899, 31 C.R. (5th) 384 (Ont. C.J.) (unlicensed Thai kickboxing event).

[85]  From 1999, a series of Bills proposed to reform the status of animals in the *Criminal Code*; see, for example, Bill C-50, an Act to amend the *Criminal Code* in respect of cruelty to animals (2005). Amendments to ss. 444-47 of the *Criminal Code* were enacted by S.C. 2008, c. 12.

[86]  See, G. Létourneau & A. Manganas, "La tolérance des droits pénal et sportif: source de violence dans les sports" (1976) 17 C. de D. 741; the authors note (at 761) that involuntarily causing injury is a crime under the *French Penal Code*.

[87]  See, *R. v. Jobidon*, [1991] S.C.J. No. 65, [1991] 2 S.C.R. 714 (S.C.C.).

[88]  See, *R. v. Brown*, [1994] 1 A.C. 212 (H.L.). On homoerotic and sado-masochistic elements in sport, see, V. Burstyn, *The Rites of Men: Manhood, Politics, and the Culture of Sport* (Toronto: University of Toronto Press, 1999).

have, for example, been held to be illegal. The answer lies in the favoured status enjoyed by "manly sports" since the mid-Victorian period.[89] Robust games are pragmatically accepted because of their social utility[90] in providing exercise and entertainment, and rough team sports have been especially prized for offering a rule-controlled environment in which to teach the hard-knock lessons of life. In spite of their toll of injuries, the established sports are not banned because society has faith in their value and has invested heavily in their diversionary and educational functions. Particular blows or shots may, nevertheless, bring criminal prosecution.

## 2.    Crimes On Ice

Players' conduct is subject to different systems of disciplinary control: the playing rules of the game that allow officials to call penalties; punishment imposed by a league, association or commission in the case of more serious infractions; and the general standards of civil or criminal law. Most misconduct is dealt with by the internal procedures, but the ultimate sanction of criminal liability is also available even when a league takes disciplinary action of its own. In *R. v. Prénoveau*,[91] a hockey player was convicted of assault after he broke the referee's nose by striking him in the face with his stick. The criminal court refused to accept that it would lack jurisdiction if a player had already been punished under league rules and stated that it would be illegal for a sports organization, by contract or regulation, to try to prevent a player or official from exercising legal rights.

Violent encounters between players usually bring charges of assault, but various other offences against public order or offences against the person are also be applicable. By section 175(1)(a) of the *Criminal Code*, it is a summary conviction offence[92] to cause a disturbance in or near a public place "by fighting, screaming, shouting, swearing, singing or using insulting or obscene language".[93] By section 221, it is an indictable offence to cause bodily harm to another person by criminal negligence, which consists of showing "wanton or reckless disregard for the lives or safety of other persons" (see, s. 219(1)). This charge has been

---

[89]   In *R. v. Bradshaw* (1878), 14 Cox C.C. 84 (Assize Court), involving a death in Association Football, Bramwell L.J. said (at 85) that "he was unwilling to decry the manly sports of this country, all of which were no doubt attended with more or less danger". See further, Chapter 6, "Play Safe: On the Ice", section B, 2.

[90]   See further, *R. v. Jobidon*, [1991] S.C.J. No. 65, [1991] 2 S.C.R. 714 (S.C.C.), discussed at Chapter 6, "Play Safe: On the Ice", section B, 3.

[91]   [1971] R.L. 21 (Qué. C.S.P.). On the absence of any immunity for players, see: *R. v. Maki*, [1970] O.J. No. 1607, [1970] 3 O.R. 780 at 783, 14 D.L.R. (3d) 164 at 167 (Ont. Prov. Ct. (Crim. Div.)); *R. v. Gray*, [1981] S.J. No. 1429, [1981] 6 W.W.R. 654 (Sask. Prov. Ct.).

[92]   The maximum general penalty for an offence punishable on summary conviction is a fine of CDN $5000 and six months' imprisonment: *Criminal Code*, s. 787(1).

[93]   On obscenities during hockey, see: *R. v. Peters*, [1980] A.J. No. 993, 14 Alta. L.R. (2d) 17 (Alta. Prov. Ct.); *R. v. Gallant*, [1992] P.E.I.J. No. 136, 101 Nfld. & P.E.I.R. 232 (P.E.I.S.C.T.D.).

used against skiers who caused collisions[94] and is potentially available in hockey.[95] By section 88(1), it is an indictable offence to carry a weapon or imitation of a weapon "for a purpose dangerous to the public peace or for the purpose of committing an offence". A "weapon" is defined in section 2 as anything used, designed or intended for killing, injuring or threatening.[96] Since the offence in section 88(1) requires proof of a prior or specific intent to use the weapon for a dangerous purpose,[97] it is unlikely that it is committed by a player who reacts by striking an opponent.[98]

Fatal attacks may constitute culpable homicide, which the *Criminal Code* classifies to include murder and manslaughter (see, ss. 222, 234). A person commits murder who kills a human being when meaning to cause death or when meaning to cause bodily harm known to be likely to cause death (see, s. 229). Culpable homicide that is not murder (or infanticide) is manslaughter:

A person commits culpable homicide when he causes the death of a human being,

(a) by means of an unlawful act;

(b) by criminal negligence;

(c) by causing that human being, by threats or fear of violence...to do anything that causes his death....[99]

Manslaughter includes killing by criminal negligence or by an objectively dangerous "unlawful act" that contributes to the cause of death.[100] Such acts include blows struck during illegal contests such as duels (see, s. 71) or prize fights (see, s. 83). More typically, the "unlawful act' is an assault, which now includes intentional blows causing bodily harm struck in consensual fights.[101] Culpable homicide that would otherwise be murder may be reduced to manslaughter if the person who committed it did so in the heat of passion caused by sudden provocation (see, s. 232). Reasonable self-defence (see, ss. 34, 35, 37), even to the point of causing death may justify the accused's action. No

---

[94] See, *R. v. S.(M.)*, [1992] A.J. No. 193, 5 Alta. L.R. (3d) 29 (Alta. Prov. Ct.).

[95] See, *R. v. Jobidon*, [1991] S.C.J. No. 65, [1991] 2 S.C.R. 714 at 770 (S.C.C.) (failing to lower the stick).

[96] See also, *R. v. Lamy*, [2002] S.C.J. No. 11, [2002] 1 S.C.R. 860 (S.C.C.) (dildo used in sexual assault).

[97] See, *R. v. Kerr*, [2004] S.C.J. No. 39, [2004] 2 S.C.R. 371 (S.C.C.) (prison inmate had to carry knife for self-defence against credible threats of imminent danger).

[98] See, "Williams acquitted of assault charges on Penguin player" *The Globe and Mail* (Toronto: November 5, 1977) at 54 (Tiger Williams acquitted of assault causing bodily harm and possession of a dangerous weapon; injuries suffered by Dennis Owchar).

[99] *Criminal Code*, R.S.C. 1985, c. C-46, s. 222(5).

[100] See, *R. v. Smithers*, [1977] S.C.J. No. 58, [1978] 1 S.C.R. 506 (S.C.C.) (post-game fight in arena parking lot). See also, "Teen rugby player guilty in game death" *The Globe and Mail* (Toronto: May 29, 2009) at A9 (15-year-old driven head-first into ground at end of high school rugby game; player subsequently sentenced to one year's probation and 100 hours of community service).

[101] See, *R. v. Jobidon*, [1991] S.C.J. No. 65, [1991] 2 S.C.R. 714 (S.C.C.). See further, Chapter 6, "Play Safe: On the Ice", section B, 3.

person can consent to death and so absolve from criminal responsibility the person inflicting the death (see, s. 14).

The leading case on death occurring in a lawful game is the British decision, *R. v. Bradshaw*,[102] where a player died from a rupture of the intestines after a collision with an opponent during a soccer match. The deceased was dribbling the ball along when the accused charged at him and jumped in the air, striking his knee into the deceased's stomach. There was conflicting testimony as to whether the deceased still had the ball when the accused charged, which would have justified a tackle under the rules. The witnesses agreed that a charge with the knee protruding would be unfair, and one umpire stated that nothing unfair had been done. In summing up the case for the jury, Bramwell L.J. stated the relevant law as follows:

> No rules or practice of any game whatever can make that lawful which is unlawful by the law of the land; and the law of the land says you shall not do that which is likely to cause the death of another. For instance, no persons can by agreement go out to fight with deadly weapons, doing by agreement what the law says shall not be done, and thus shelter themselves from the consequences of their acts. Therefore, in one way you need not concern yourselves with the rules of football. But, on the other hand, if a man is playing according to the rules and practice of the game and not going beyond it, it may be reasonable to infer that he is not actuated by any malicious motive or intention, and that he is not acting in a manner which he knows will be likely to be productive of death or injury. But, independent of the rules, if the prisoner intended to cause serious hurt to the deceased, or if he knew that, in charging as he did, he might produce serious injury and was indifferent and reckless as to whether he would produce serious injury or not, then the act would be unlawful.[103]

This direction holds that private rules cannot prevail over public law and calls on the jury to determine the accused's intention in the particular case: the act is unlawful if there is an intentional or reckless causing of serious injury. On the facts, the jury found the accused not guilty.

There are Canadian examples of prosecutions for hockey homicide,[104] and convictions have been recorded in other jurisdictions.[105] In *Re Duchesneau*,[106] a

---

[102] (1878), 14 Cox C.C. 84 (Assize Court).

[103] *Ibid.*, at 84-85. See also, *R. v. Moore* (1898), 14 T.L.R. 229 (Assize Ct.).

[104] See, Appendix I. On a trial for manslaughter in 1953 following the death of Bob Gillies of the Collingwood Greenshirts, see, "For those left behind, a lifelong penalty" *The Globe and Mail* (Toronto: February 2, 2009) at A7. See also, *R. v. Smithers*, [1977] S.C.J. No. 58, [1978] 1 S.C.R. 506 (S.C.C.).

[105] See, "Boni fined $1,800" *The Toronto Star* (February 17, 1994) at D1, D8; "Sun shines at last on big Jim Boni" *The Toronto Star* (February 18, 1994) at A25 (death of Miran Schrott from cardiac arrest after Jim Boni of Toronto struck him in the chest with his stick; plea of guilty to reduced charge of manslaughter in Aosta, Italy). See also, A.N. Wise & B.S. Meyer, *International Sports Law and Business*, Volume 2 (The Hague: Kluwer Law International, 1997) at 1307-08 (charge of *omicidio preterintenzionale* reduced to *omicidio colposo*).

17-year-old was charged with causing the death of an opponent in a Quebec "no-contact" league. The accused either punched or collided with the deceased after taking the puck across the blue line and after play was halted for an offside. This uncertain initial clash caused the deceased to fall and become unconscious. The accused was then clearly seen to punch the deceased in the back of the head as he lay on the ice. Faced with contradictory accounts of the first encounter, the court acquitted the accused of manslaughter because it was unclear that it was the second blow that caused the concussion and haemorrhage that led to the death. The court did, however, convict the accused of assault in respect of the blow struck while the victim was prostrate.

One commentator has noted that, "For all its violence hockey has not had a long death roll".[107] The list of victims was, however, extended in 2009 when a 21-year-old senior AAA player lost his helmet during a fight and struck his head when falling to the ice.[108] Although the death in this case was accidental, it would not have occurred but for the exchange of punches, and the fatality renewed the debate about mutual combat during play and the fighting "code". It also prompted a review of rules and standards relating to helmets.

## 3.   Assaults Between Players: The Limits of Consent

The charge most often used against players is assault.[109] The *Criminal Code*,[110] in sections 266-270, includes a basic offence of assault and various more serious forms carrying heavier penalties.[111] A related offence is unlawfully causing bodily harm (see, s. 269), which is an indictable offence punishable with ten years imprisonment.[112] "Bodily harm" means any hurt or injury that interferes with health or comfort and is more than merely transient or trifling (see, s. 2).

Ordinary assault ("common assault") and the offence of assaulting a peace officer are punishable on summary conviction or may be punished on indictment with a term of five years imprisonment (see, ss. 266, 270). Assault with a weapon or assault causing bodily harm[113] carry a maximum penalty of ten years

---

[106] [1978] J.Q. no 228, 7 C.R. (3d) 70 (T.J. Qué.).

[107] I. Gitler, *Blood on the Ice* (Chicago: Henry Regnery Co., 1974) at 30. The close calls include Eddie Shore's blow to Ace Bailey in 1933, Ted Kennedy's collision with Gordie Howe in 1950 and the stick-swinging duel between Wayne Maki and Ted Green in 1969. On the Shore-Bailey incident, see, L. Scanlan, *Grace Under Fire: The State of Our Sweet and Savage Game* (Toronto: Penguin Canada, 2002) at 97-103. On Eddie Shore, see, D. Cruise & A. Griffiths, *Net Worth: Exploding the Myths of Pro Hockey* (Toronto: Viking, 1991) at 166-92.

[108] See, "Hockey player's death prompts police probe" *The Globe and Mail* (Toronto: January 3, 2009) at A3 (death of Don Sanderson of the Whitby Dunlops).

[109] See, R.C. Watson & J.C. MacLellan, "Smitting to Spitting: 80 Years of Ice-Hockey in Canadian Courts" (1986) 17(2) Can. J. of History of Sport 10.

[110] R.S.C. 1985, c. C-46.

[111] See, A. Husa & S. Thiele, "In the Name of the Game: Hockey Violence and the Criminal Justice System" (2002) 45 Crim. L. Q. 509.

[112] See, *R. v. DeSousa*, [1992] S.C.J. No. 77, [1992] 2 S.C.R. 944 (S.C.C.).

[113] On the mental elements of assault causing bodily harm, see: *R. v. Vandergraaf*, [1994] M.J. No. 503, 34 C.R. (4th) 266, 93 C.C.C. (3d) 286 (Man. C.A.) (spectator intended jar to hit ice and not

imprisonment as indictable offences and are punishable on summary conviction with a term not exceeding 18 months (see, s. 267). Aggravated assault, an indictable offence punishable with 14 years imprisonment, is committed when the accused "wounds, maims, disfigures or endangers the life" of the victim (see, s. 268).[114]

The various crimes of assault are subject to the definitional and general provisions in section 265(1) of the *Criminal Code*:

(1) A person commits an assault when

(a) without the consent of another person, he applies force intentionally to that other person, directly or indirectly;

(b) he attempts or threatens, by an act or a gesture, to apply force to another person, if he has, or causes that other person to believe on reasonable grounds that he has, present ability to effect his purpose...[115]

Assault, therefore, consists of attempting or threatening immediate bodily contact or, more normally, intentionally making contact without the victim's consent. Mere words without any threatening gesture do not constitute assault,[116] although they may constitute the crime of uttering threats under section 264.1 of the *Criminal Code*. Assault requires proof of a general intent,[117] and there need not be a specific intent to harm the actual victim.[118] The action must be performed in an intentional manner, so that a reflex action[119] or mere carelessness[120] are insufficient. Recklessness in relation to the action (as opposed to the consequences) probably does not constitute assault. Assault consists of an unlawful resort to force, so that no offence is committed where the accused makes a lawful arrest, acts in self-defence or applies reasonable corporal punishment (see, s. 43).[121]

Assault is typically committed only where physical force is applied without the victim's consent. No consent is obtained where the victim submits by reason of force, threats, fraud or the exercise of authority (see, s. 265(3)). An honest belief in consent can excuse an assault, but the judge of fact may consider

---

front row spectator); *R. v. E.(A.)*, [2000] O.J. No. 2984, 35 C.R. (5th) 386, 146 C.C.C. (3d) 449 (Ont. C.A.) (recklessness as to whether harm is caused).

[114] On the mental elements of aggravated assault, see: *R. v. Williams*, [2004] 2 S.C.R. 134 (S.C.C.) (foresight of consequences).

[115] *Criminal Code*, R.S.C. 1985, c. C-46, s. 265(1).

[116] See, *R. v. Byrne*, [1968] B.C.J. No. 106, [1968] 3 C.C.C. 179 (B.C.C.A.).

[117] See, *R. v. George*, [1960] S.C.J. No. 53, [1960] S.C.R. 871 (S.C.C.).

[118] See, *R. v. Deakin*, [1974] M.J. No. 8, 16 C.C.C. (2d) 1 (Man. C.A.).

[119] See: *R. v. Wolfe*, [1974] O.J. No. 868, 20 C.C.C. (2d) 382 (Ont. C.A.); *R. v. Leclerc*, [1991] O.J. No. 1533, 4 O.R. (3d) 788, 67 C.C.C. (3d) 563 (Ont. C.A.). For the contrary view, see, *R. v. Tardy*, [1986] R.J.Q. 2607 (C.S.P.).

[120] See: *R. v. Deakin*, [1974] M.J. No. 8, 16 C.C.C. (2d) 1 (Man. C.A.); *R. v. Vandergraaf*, [1994] M.J. No. 503, 34 C.R. (4th) 266, 93 C.C.C. (3d) 286 (Man. C.A.); *R. v. François*, [1995] M.J. No. 648, 107 Man.R. (2d) 223 (Man. C.A.).

[121] See, for example: *R. v. Kanhai*, [1981] S.J. No. 1353, 60 C.C.C. (2d) 71 (Sask. Dist. Ct.) (assault by physical education teacher); *Canadian Foundation for Children, Youth and the Law v. Canada (Attorney General)*, [2004] S.C.J. No. 6, [2004] 1 S.C.R. 76 (S.C.C.) (s. 43 is constitutional).

whether there were reasonable grounds for the belief (see, s. 265(4)).[122] The relevant consent in contact sports is usually an implied consent. The participant is taken to accept the forms and levels of rough treatment or physicality associated with the game, and the issue of authorised limits also arises in relation to fights.

The wording of the *Criminal Code* suggests that the accused can be convicted of assault only where the prosecution proves, as essential elements, that the victim did not consent and that the accused did not believe that the victim was consenting.[123] The *Code* disallows consent to death in section 14, but does not clearly impose any further limit on the freedom willingly to suffer blows or injuries. Until the 1990s, case law recognized that combatants could lawfully consent to engage in fair fist fights, even to the point of inflicting bodily harm.[124] Assault would, however, be committed if the victim ceased to consent[125] or if the accused exceeded the agreement and resorted to kicking[126] or biting;[127] the victim's consent was also no excuse where the accused intended to cause serious injury[128] or used a weapon.[129] This approach contrasted with British case law declaring more generally that it is against public policy to allow the intentional infliction of actual bodily harm.[130]

Canadian criminal law then took a paternalistic turn in 1991 with the decision in *R. v. Jobidon*,[131] dealing with a charge of manslaughter arising from a consensual fist fight outside a Sudbury hotel: the deceased died after receiving repeated blows to the head. In determining that the accused acted unlawfully, the Supreme Court of Canada placed specific limits on the effect of a victim's consent:

---

[122] On consent and belief in consent in relation to sexual assaults, see: *Criminal Code*, ss. 273.1, 273.2, 276. See further, Chapter 5, "Be Safe: Off the Ice", section C, 2. On sex at the rink, see, *R. v. R.J.S.*, [1994] P.E.I.J. No. 109, 123 Nfld. & P.E.I.R. 317 (P.E.I.S.C.T.D.).

[123] See: *R. v. Ciccarelli*, [1989] O.J. No. 2388, 54 C.C.C. (3d) 121 (Ont. Dist. Ct.) (evidence relating to Ciccarelli's belief that Luke Richardson was consenting to stick blows).

[124] See: *R. v. Dix*, [1972] O.J. No. 914, 10 C.C.C. (2d) 324 (Ont. C.A.); *R. c. Abraham*, [1974] J.Q. no 53, 30 C.C.C. (2d) 332 (Que. C.A.); *R. v. Setrum*, [1976] S.J. No. 417, 32 C.C.C. (2d) 109 (Sask. C.A.); *R. v. Bergner*, [1987] A.J. No. 539, 36 C.C.C. (3d) 25 (Alta. C.A.), leave to appeal to S.C.C. refd, [1987] S.C.C.A. No. 302 (S.C.C.).

[125] See, *R. v. Thomas* (1984), 13 W.C.B. 268 (B.C. Co. Ct.).

[126] See: *R. v. MacTavish*, [1972] N.B.J. No. 88, 8 C.C.C. (2d) 206 (N.B.C.A.); *R. v. Turner*, [1983] B.C.J. No. 2331 (B.C.C.A.); *R. v. Maher*, [1987] N.J. No. 126, 63 Nfld. & P.E.I.R. 30 (Nfld. C.A.) (use of karate skills).

[127] See, *R. v. Loonskin*, [1990] A.J. No. 23, 103 A.R. 193 (Alta. C.A.).

[128] See: *R. v. Maloney*, [1976] O.J. No. 2447, 28 C.C.C. (2d) 323 (Ont. Co. Ct.); *R. v. Kusyj*, [1983] N.W.T.J. No. 42, 51 A.R. 243 (N.W.T.S.C.).

[129] See: *R. v. Gur*, [1986] N.S.J. No. 175, 27 C.C.C. (3d) 511 (N.S.C.A.); *R. v. Carriere*, [1987] A.J. No. 105, 56 C.R. (3d) 257, 35 C.C.C. (3d) 276 (Alta. C.A.).

[130] See: *R. v. Coney* (1882), 8 Q.B.D. 534 (C.C.R.) (prize fight); *R. v. Donovan*, [1934] 2 K.B. 498 (C.C.A.) (caning for sexual gratification); *A.G.'s Reference (No. 6 of 1980)*, [1981] 1 Q.B. 715 (C.A.) (street fight); *R. v. Brown*, [1994] 1 A.C. 212 (H.L.) (sado-masochistic activity).

[131] [1991] S.C.J. No. 65, [1991] 2 S.C.R. 714 (S.C.C.). See: J. Barnes, "Recent Developments in Canadian Sports Law" (1991) 23 Ottawa L. Rev. 623 at 680-89; S.J. Usprich, Annotation, [1991] S.C.J. No. 65, 7 C.R. (4th) 233 at 235-36.

The limitation demanded by s. 265 as it applies in the circumstances of this appeal is one which *vitiates consent between adults intentionally to apply force causing serious hurt or non-trivial bodily harm to each other in the course of a fist fight or brawl.* (This test entails that a minor's apparent consent to an adult's intentional application of force in a fight would also be negated.)[132]

The Court declared a policy to disallow consent in these circumstances because fist fighting is a socially useless activity that tends to lead to larger brawls and breaches of the peace. Consent would not be nullified in the case of "risky sparring or daredevil activities" performed by stuntmen "in the creation of a valuable cultural product". Consent would also apply to the "'ordinary' school-yard scuffle", but the Court left open the case where persons under 18 "truly intend to harm one another, and ultimately cause more than trivial bodily harm".[133]

*Jobidon* effectively created a new common-law crime applying to adults who intentionally cause bodily harm in fist fights: combatants commit assault when they intend to cause bodily harm to their opponent and when it actually results.[134] Assault cases must now undergo a preliminary classification to see if the context is analogous to a street brawl so that similar policy considerations apply. Assaults must be categorized according to the setting, the age of the participants and the perceived utility of the activity. Criminal liability will sometimes turn on the social or economic value that the judge places on a particular recreation or entertainment.[135]

The Supreme Court in *Jobidon* recognized that special considerations apply to participants in contact sports:

> ...the policy of the common law will not affect the validity or effectiveness of freely given consent to participate in rough sporting activities, so long as the intentional applications of force to which one consents are within the customary norms and rules of the game. Unlike fist fights, sporting activities and games usually have significant social value; they are worthwhile.[136]

---

[132] *R. v. Jobidon*, [1991] S.C.J. No. 65, [1991] 2 S.C.R. 714 at 766 (S.C.C.), *per* Gonthier J.

[133] See: *R. v. Cantin*, [1993] A.J. No. 710, 144 A.R. 237 (Alta. Prov. Ct.); *R. v. W.(G.)*, [1994] O.J. No. 898, 18 O.R. (3d) 321, 90 C.C.C. (3d) 139 (Ont. C.A.); *R. v. M.(S.)*, [1995] O.J. No. 836, 22 O.R. (3d) 605, 97 C.C.C. (3d) 281 (Ont. C.A.).

[134] See, *R. v. Paice*, [2005] S.C.J. No. 21, [2005] 1 S.C.R. 339 (S.C.C.). A person is not criminally responsible for bodily harm accidentally caused to another "during the course of play" (at 346 *per* Charron J.).

[135] Sopinka J., in a pointed dissent in *R. v. Jobidon*, [1991] S.C.J. No. 65, [1991] 2 S.C.R. 714 (S.C.C.), asked (at 774), "Where does one search to determine the social utility of a fight during a hockey game to take one example? There are those that would argue that it is an important part of the attraction".

[136] *R. v. Jobidon*, [1991] S.C.J. No. 65, [1991] 2 S.C.R. 714 at 766-67 (S.C.C.), *per* Gonthier J. See also, *R. v. Anderson*, [2000] B.C.J. No. 2398, 40 C.R. (5th) 329 at 335 (B.C.S.C.) (social utility of recreational softball for recovering alcoholics).

The Court then specifically approved the analysis provided by the Saskatchewan Court of Appeal in 1989 in *R. v. Cey*.[137] That decision provided a framework for determining the scope of players' implied consent and is now the primary authority in respect of assaults between participants.

*Cey* noted[138] the following cases reported since 1970 that had considered the limits of the implied consent: *R. v. Maki*,[139] *R. v. Green*,[140] *R. v. Leyte*,[141] *R. v. Langton*,[142] *R. v. Watson*,[143] *R. v. Maloney*,[144] *R. v. Henderson*,[145] *R. v. Lecuyer*,[146] *R. v. St. Croix*,[147] *R. v. Côté*,[148] *R. v. Gray*,[149] *R. v. Milligan*,[150] *R. v. Thiel*[151] and *R. v. Tardy*.[152] (Other reported cases[153] decided before *Cey* included *R. v. Kelly*[154]

---

[137] [1989] S.J. No. 264, 48 C.C.C. (3d) 480 (Sask. C.A.).

[138] The judgment quotes the synthesis of case law in J. Barnes, *Sports and the Law in Canada*, 2d ed. (Toronto: Butterworths, 1988) at 92-94.

[139] [1970] O.J. No. 1607, [1970] 3 O.R. 780, 14 D.L.R. (3d) 164 (Ont. Prov. Ct.) (vertical chopping blow with stick to opponent's head; accused acquitted; self-defence; NHL exhibition).

[140] [1970] O.J. No. 1699, [1971] 1 O.R. 591, 16 D.L.R. (3d) 137 (Ont. Prov. Ct.) (push or punch to face with glove; accused acquitted; implied consent; NHL exhibition).

[141] [1973] O.J. No. 2345, 13 C.C.C. (2d) 458 (Ont. Prov. Ct.) (punch to nose; accused acquitted; school handball).

[142] (1976), 32 C.R.N.S. 121 (Sask. C.A.) (slashing stick across leg; accused convicted and given absolute discharge after appeal; Junior A hockey).

[143] [1975] O.J. No. 2681, 26 C.C.C. (2d) 150 (Ont. Prov. Ct.) (armlock to throat; accused convicted and given absolute discharge; juvenile hockey).

[144] [1976] O.J. No. 2447, 28 C.C.C. (2d) 323 (Ont. Co. Ct.) (blow to head; dazed opponent then hauled up and down on the ice; accused acquitted by jury; NHL regular season game).

[145] [1976] B.C.J. No. 1211, [1976] 5 W.W.R. 119 (B.C. Co. Ct.) (punch to head; accused convicted and given discharge conditional on not playing regular league hockey for about one month; junior hockey).

[146] [1978] A.J. No. 755, 11 A.R. 239 (Alta. Dist. Ct.) (spearing and striking; accused convicted; CDN $200 fine; junior hockey).

[147] [1979] O.J. No. 4556, 47 C.C.C. (2d) 122 (Ont. Dist. Ct.) (cross-check to mouth; accused convicted and given discharge conditional on making monetary restitution; neighbourhood hockey).

[148] [1981] J.Q. no 167, 22 C.R. (3d) 97 (Que. Prov. Ct.) (violent punch to face; accused convicted; CDN $200 fine; amateur non-contact hockey).

[149] [1981] S.J. No. 1429, [1981] 6 W.W.R. 654 (Sask. Prov. Ct.) (stoppage in play; unsuspecting player knocked unconscious by straight-arm; accused convicted; absolute discharge; senior amateur hockey).

[150] [1982] N.B.J. No. 62, 7 W.C.B. 135 (Sask. Prov. Ct.) (knee to face; contradictory evidence as to intention; accused acquitted; rugby).

[151] (1982), 8 W.C.B. 154 (Ont. Co. Ct.) (unintentional slash to face; accused acquitted; accepted risk; senior hockey).

[152] [1986] R.J.Q. 2607 (C.S.P.) (blow with stick to face; accused convicted of aggravated assault; broomball).

[153] For further unreported cases, see: R.C. Watson & J.G. MacLellan, "Smitting to Spitting: 80 Years of Ice-Hockey in Canadian Courts" (1986) 17(2) Can. J. of History of Sport 10; R.C. Watson, "Athletes Beware: Legal Reasons to Play Fair" (1991) 3 Educ. & L.J. 167, esp. at 181-91 (convictions and sentencing).

[154] (1980), 4 W.C.B. 103 (B.C. Co. Ct.) (use of stick in serious fight that led to charges against seven players; discharge conditional on not participating in organized hockey for three months; junior hockey).

and *R. v. Mayer*.[155]) These cases recognized that participants agreed to the risk of blows provided they were unintentional, instinctive or reasonably incidental to the game.[156] The vigour of the contact would vary according to the level of competition:

> I would think that professionally trained and professionally employed hockey players in the National Hockey League consent to more assaultive type behaviour than in a purely amateur (in the full sense of the word) friendly neighbourhood hockey game. I do not accept that the players in a neighbourhood match, where no protective equipment is worn, no officials are present and the puck is not to be raised off the ice, consent to being struck in the mouth by a hockey stick, that is, fore-checking of the type involved in this case.[157]

It was also held that the victim's consent would not apply to deliberate, violent attacks outside the run of play, especially when a player was in a helpless position or suffered serious injury from blows from a stick or other equipment.[158]

Gerwing J.A. in *Cey* noted from the previous case law that it is difficult to state the scope of the implied consent since the determination is a matter of degree. In *Cey*, an amateur player had caused injuries to an opponent's face and mouth by cross-checking him from behind into the boards; the incident occurred in the "Wild Goose Hockey League" which played contact hockey. At first instance, Cey was acquitted on a charge of assault causing bodily harm when the judge directed his mind to three issues: did the accused intend to cause serious injury?; did he exceed long-standing standards in hockey?; and, was the victim willing to play hockey again? In ordering a new trial, Gerwing J.A. held that the trial judge ought to have considered, "whether there was express or implied consent to this type of contact and whether the contact was of such a nature that in any event no true consent could be given".[159] On the facts, the judge had to determine whether cross-checking "in such close proximity to the boards, and with such force as was employed, was so violent and inherently dangerous as to have been excluded from the implied consent".[160]

Gerwing J.A. held that the scope of the implied consent calls primarily for an objective analysis. In determining intention and possible belief in the victim's

---

[155] [1985] M.J. No. 503, 41 Man.R. (2d) 73 (Man. Prov. Ct.) (sucker punch to face; accused convicted; conditional discharge; Junior A hockey).

[156] See: *R. v. Leyte*, [1973] O.J. No. 2345, 13 C.C.C. (2d) 458 at 459 (Ont. Prov. Ct.); *R. v. Maloney*, [1976] O.J. No. 2447, 28 C.C.C. (2d) 323 at 326 (Ont. Co. Ct.); *R. v. Henderson*, [1976] B.C.J. No. 1211, [1976] 5 W.W.R. 119 at 122, 124 (B.C. Co. Ct.).

[157] *R. v. St. Croix*, [1979] O.J. No. 4556, 47 C.C.C. (2d) 122 at 124 (Ont. Dist. Ct.), *per* Stortini D.C.J.

[158] See: *R. v. Maki*, [1970] O.J. No. 1607, [1970] 3 O.R. 780 at 783, 14 D.L.R. (3d) 164 at 167 (Ont. Prov. Ct.) ("no athlete should be presumed to accept malicious, unprovoked or violent attack" *per* Carter Prov. Ct. J.); *R. v. Leyte*, [1973] O.J. No. 2345, 13 C.C.C. (2d) 458 at 459 (Ont. Prov. Ct.); *R. v. Henderson*, [1976] B.C.J. No. 1211, [1976] 5 W.W.R. 119 at 124 (B.C. Co. Ct.) at 124.

[159] *R. v. Cey*, [1989] S.J. No. 264, 48 C.C.C. (3d) 480 at 493 (Sask. C.A.).

[160] *R. v. Cey*, [1989] S.J. No. 264, 48 C.C.C. (3d) 480 at 491-92 (Sask. C.A.), *per* Gerwing J.A.

consent, the court does consider the subjective factor of the accused's state of mind; individual factors and "specific consents" may also be relevant where there is a fight between players. However, in determining consent to contact during play, the subjective attitude of accused and victim are not the sole considerations because a uniform standard should apply to all players at a particular level. The implied consent is to be fixed by objective criteria that take account of playing conditions, such as the setting of the game, the league and the age level. The court must consider the accused's conduct "qualitatively and quantitatively" and look at the nature of the act and the degree of force used. In determining whether the Crown has negatived consent, the accused's state of mind is just one of many considerations. The court must consider all the circumstances, including:

> The conditions under which the game in question is played, the nature of the act which forms the subject-matter of the charge, the extent of the force employed, the degree of risk of injury, and the probabilities of serious harm....[161]

In cases since 1989,[162] *Cey* has often been cited and followed and was particularly recognized in *R. v. Ciccarelli*,[163] where the court stated that the objective criteria for determining the scope of the implied consent include:

a)   the nature of the game played; whether amateur or professional league and so on;

b)   nature of the particular act or acts and their surrounding circumstances;

c)   the degree of force employed;

---

[161] *R. v. Cey*, [1989] S.J. No. 264, 48 C.C.C. (3d) 480 at 490-91 (Sask. C.A.), *per* Gerwing J.A.

[162] Subsequent cases include: *R. v. Paul*, [1989] M.J. No. 243, 7 W.C.B. (2d) 207 (Man. Prov. Ct.), vard October 6, 1989, [1989] M.J. No. 497 (Man. C.A.) (vicious stick swing to face; CDN $2000 fine; case suitable for incarceration but Crown sought only fine; recreational hockey); *R. v. Francis*, [1989] N.B.J. No. 1187, 100 N.B.R. (2d) 34 (N.B.P.C.) (cross-check to back of neck; CDN $300 fine and one day in jail; city hockey league); *R. v. Holt*, [1992] A.J. No. 1447, 126 A.R. 269 (Alta. Q.B.) (former NHL player; two counts of assault causing bodily harm for cross-checking and punching; CDN $1000 fine on each charge and one day in jail; accused acquitted of using a weapon to commit assault; oldtimers hockey); *R. v. Krzysztofik*, [1992] M.J. No. 185, 79 Man.R. (2d) 234 (Man. Q.B.) (cross-check into boards causing face lacerations; accused convicted of aggravated assault; non-contact hockey); *R. v. Aussem* (1997), 36 W.C.B. (2d) 335 (Ont. Prov. Div.) (cross-check during hockey warm-up, which is "integral to the game"; accused convicted of assault with a weapon); *R. v. Anderson*, [2000] B.C.J. No. 2398, 40 C.R. (5th) 329 (B.C.S.C.) (collision in softball; accused acquitted); *R. v. Owen*, [2004] O.J. No. 1410, 2004 ONSC 10895, 61 W.C.B. (2d) 258 (Ont. S.C.J.) ("motivated" tackle from behind causing broken leg; accused convicted of assault causing bodily harm; recreational soccer); *R. v. O'Grady*, [2006] O.J. No. 1957, 2006 ONSC 13136 (Ont. S.C.J.) (uncertain evidence regarding slashing incident; accused acquitted; recreational, non-contact hockey); *R. v. Chu*, [2006] B.C.J. No. 3398, 2006 BCPC 587 (B.C. Prov. Ct.) (evidence inconsistent as to collision in non-contact recreational hockey); *R. v. Faith*, [2006] A.J. No. 846 (Alta. Prov. Ct.) (punch to jaw held to be incidental to play in Junior B league). See also, cases at note 177, below (fighting cases) and Chapter 6, "Play Safe: On the Ice", section B, 4 (sentencing).

[163] [1989] O.J. No. 2388, 54 C.C.C. (3d) 121 (Ont. Dist. Ct.), affg 5 W.C.B. (2d) 310 (Ont. Prov. Ct.) (three stick blows to head; CDN $1000 fine and one day in jail; NHL hockey).

d)    the degree of risk of injury; and

e)    the state of mind of the accused.[164]

In *R. v. Leclerc*,[165] the Ontario Court of Appeal added that it was important to consider "whether the rules of the game contemplate contact"[166] and emphasised that it was not necessary to prove an intent to injure:

> Conduct which evinces a deliberate purpose to inflict injury will generally be held to be outside of the immunity provided by the scope of the implied consent in a sports arena. This is not to be taken to mean...that in order to negative implied consent, the prosecution has the burden of proving a deliberate purpose or resolve to inflict injury.[167]

The brief formulation in *R. v. Jobidon*[168] limits players' consent to applications of force that are "within the customary norms and rules of the game". In professional hockey,[169] a player expects conduct that is contrary to the official rules, so that serious disciplinary consequences and criminal liability only kick in for egregious acts or breach of the customary "code".

In 2000, the precedents of *Cey* and *Jobidon* formed the basis of the well-publicised decision in *R. v. McSorley*,[170] after "policeman"[171] Marty McSorley of the Boston Bruins had taken his stick to the head of Donald Brashear of the Vancouver Canucks.[172] Besides being suspended by the league,[173] McSorley was

---

[164] *R. v. Ciccarelli*, [1989] O.J. No. 2388, 54 C.C.C. (3d) 121 at 126 (Ont. Dist. Ct.), *per* Corbett D.C.J.

[165] [1991] O.J. No. 1533, 4 O.R. (3d) 788, 67 C.C.C. (3d) 563 (Ont. C.A.) (cross-check into boards causing paralysis; accused acquitted; instinctive reflex action; non-contact recreational hockey).

[166] *Ibid.*, at O.R. 796, C.C.C. 571, *per* Lacourcière J.A. The "ideal of non-contact rules was frequently breached in a spirited game" (at O.R. 797, C.C.C. 572). On the importance of judicial reinforcement of safety rules, see, R.C. Watson, "Safety Rule Gets a Shot in the Arm" (1992) 4 Educ. & L.J. 217.

[167] *Ibid.*, at O.R. 797, C.C.C. 572, *per* Lacourcière J.A.

[168] [1991] S.C.J. No. 65, [1991] 2 S.C.R. 714 at 766-67 (S.C.C.).

[169] See, A. Baxter, "Hockey Violence: The Canadian Criminal Code and Professional Hockey" (2005) 31 Man. L.J. 281.

[170] [2000] B.C.J. No. 1993, 2000 BCPC 116 (conviction for assault with a weapon), [2000] B.C.J. No. 1994, 2000 BCPC 117 (sentence of conditional discharge) (B.C. Prov. Ct.). See: A. Husa & S. Thiele, "In the Name of the Game: Hockey Violence and the Criminal Justice System" (2002) 45 Crim. L.Q. 509; J.C.H. Jones & K.G. Stewart, "Hit Somebody: Hockey Violence, Economics, the Law, and the *Twist* and *McSorley* Decisions" (2002) 12 Seton Hall J. of Sport L. 165; D. Rosenberg, "The Banality of Violence in Sport and the McSorley Affair" (2003) 9 Avante 30.

[171] McSorley referred to himself as a "policeman" (see, *R. v. McSorley*, [2000] B.C.J. No. 1993, 2000 BCPC 116 at 13 (B.C. Prov. Ct.) and in 2000 was the third most penalized player in NHL history. The term "policeman" incurred the displeasure of Edmondson Prov. Ct. J. in *R. v. Watson*, [1975] O.J. No. 2681, 26 C.C.C. (2d) 150 at 154 (Ont. Prov. Ct.) ("a euphemism for a ... bully-boy ... [bringing] into disrepute a noble calling").

[172] See, "'Bad enough to kill someone'" *The Globe and Mail* (Toronto: February 23, 2000) at S1, S2. For the 2006-07 season, Donald Brashear (Washington Capitals) was in sixth place among penalty leaders with 156 minutes from 77 games.

tried in the Provincial Court of British Columbia on a charge of assault with a weapon. The game in Vancouver had featured an early fight between McSorley and Brashear that ended with Brashear skating past the Boston bench "dusting off" his hands to suggest that he had made short work of McSorley. Both players were involved in further incidents, and at the very end of the game the Boston assistant coach effectively directed McSorley to go and deal with Brashear. McSorley left the bench, made a play on the puck and then skated out to come up behind Brashear at the Vancouver blue line. At this point, he took a "baseball swing" with his stick so that the heel of the blade impacted against the side of Brashear's head. The blow dislodged the helmet of Brashear who collapsed unconscious on the ice and suffered a grade three concussion. In determining McSorley's criminal responsibility, Kitchen J. considered the "unwritten code" agreed to by players and officials that may allow some strategic slashing and fights between consenting players.[174] With respect to McSorley's action, the judge observed,

> If the slash was intended for the shoulder, delivered with the intention of starting a fight, my conclusion would be that it was within the common practices and norms of the game.[175]

However, following *Cey* and *Jobidon*, a question would arise whether it was worth the risk and contrary to public policy as an overly dangerous act. In the end, the judge found that Brashear was the focus of McSorley's frustrations and that the intention was to land a blow on the head:

> He slashed for the head. A child, swinging as at a Tee ball, would not miss. A housekeeper swinging a carpetbeater would not miss. An NHL player would never, ever miss. Brashear was struck as intended.[176]

Such a blow exceeded the implied and permitted consent so that McSorley was guilty as charged.

The *Cey* decision offers authoritative guidelines for evaluating blows that are related to play, but the status of fighting between players remains ambiguous.[177]

---

[173] See, Chapter 6, "Play Safe: On the Ice", sections B, 4, 5.

[174] *R. v. McSorley*, [2000] B.C.J. No. 1993, 2000 BCPC 116 at 4-5 (B.C. Prov. Ct.); see also, [2000] B.C.J. No. 1994, 2000 BCPC 117 at 1 (the rules were "indefinite").

[175] *R. v. McSorley*, [2000] B.C.J. No. 1993, 2000 BCPC 116 at 9 (B.C. Prov. Ct.), *per* Kitchen Ct. Prov. J.

[176] *R. v. McSorley*, [2000] B.C.J. No. 1993, 2000 BCPC 116 at 16 (B.C. Prov. Ct.), *per* Kitchen Prov. Ct. J.

[177] Recent cases involving fights in sports include: *Protection de la jeunesse - 819*, C.Q. 520-03-000141-953, J.E. 96-1407 (fight in school floor hockey; player guilty of assault causing bodily harm); *R. v. T.(G.)*, [1996] O.J. No. 4424, 33 W.C.B. (2d) 140 (Ont. Fam. Ct.) (fight in hockey; accused removed opponent's headgear and showed intention to cause serious injury; accused guilty of assault causing bodily harm). For a fight after a "chippy" game, see, *R. v. M.(J.)*, [2001] O.J. No. 5566, 53 W.C.B. (2d) 71 (Ont. C.J. (Youth Ct.)). See, further, Chapter 6, "Play Safe: On the Ice", section B, 5.

(There was no mutual combat in *McSorley* since the effect of the blow from behind was immediately to put Brashear out of action.) *Cey* expressly declined to pursue the scope of consent in fights, and the Supreme Court in *Jobidon* drew a clear distinction between the social value of brawling and that of sporting activities or games. Fighting is nevertheless clearly recognized in the "customary norms and rules" of hockey at some levels, so that players' consent may not be automatically disallowed when there is intentional infliction of bodily harm. The policy-based restrictions in *Jobidon* possibly do not apply to "worthwhile" fisticuffs that give value for money. Given that some fights are part of the "code", courts will probably continue with the traditional Canadian approach that investigates the reality and scope of the consent in the particular circumstances of the fight, including whether both skilled sluggers were in a position to defend themselves.

Combatants generally consent to contact that is harsher than the ordinary run of play, but courts have carefully investigated whether both fighters actually consented and have placed limits on the permissible blows. Accidentally hitting an opponent or dropping a stick and gloves in anticipation of an attack will not necessarily be taken to indicate agreement to fight.[178] A combatant may also not have consented to a particular type of blow. In *R. v. MacTavish*,[179] two boys agreed to fight (not in the course of sport) but without laying down precise rules for the combat. It was held that the agreement permitted a limited use of force, but it was not reasonable for the accused to believe he was licensed to inflict bodily harm by kicking. The victim "admitted he agreed to a 'fair fight' but not having his 'head kicked in'".[180] Even where players are voluntarily exchanging types of blows, the infliction of serious harm has been disallowed. In *R. v. Maki*,[181] Wayne Maki became involved in a brief stick-swinging duel that ended with him inflicting serious head injuries on Ted Green. The court expressly commented that there could be no consent to such a blow, although in the circumstances Maki was acquitted on the basis of self-defence.

Reasonable and necessary force may be used in self-defence or defence of others,[182] including the protection of teammates.[183] In *R. v. Maki*,[184] it was held

---

[178] See, *R. v. Watson*, [1975] O.J. No. 2681, 26 C.C.C. (2d) 150 (Ont. Prov. Ct.). But see, *R. v. Faith*, [2006] A.J. No. 846 (Alta. Prov. Ct.) (pulling stick away interpreted as invitation to fight).

[179] [1972] N.B.J. No. 88, 8 C.C.C. (2d) 206 (N.B.C.A.).

[180] *R. v. MacTavish*, [1972] N.B.J. No. 88, 8 C.C.C. (2d) 206 at 208 (N.B.C.A.), *per* Hughes C.J.N.B.

[181] [1970] O.J. No. 1607, [1970] 3 O.R. 780, 14 D.L.R. (3d) 164 (Ont. Prov. Ct.).

[182] See: *Criminal Code*, R.S.C. 1985, c. C-46, ss. 34, 35, 37; *R. v. Goudey*, [2007] N.S.J. No. 287, 258 N.S.R. (2d) 201 (N.S.S.C.) (use of force against fans). See also, *R. v. Paice*, [2005] S.C.J. No. 21, [2005] 1 S.C.R. 339 (S.C.C.) (self defence under s. 34(1) not available to combatants in consensual fist fights).

[183] In relation to rugby, see: *R. v. Tevaga*, [1991] 1 N.Z.L.R. 296 (C.A.) (jaw-breaking blow was excessive); *Babiuk v. Trann*, [2005] S.J. No. 41, [2005] 9 W.W.R. 274, 248 D.L.R. (4th) 530 (Sask. C.A.) (civil action; player used reasonable force against opponent who was stepping on teammate).

[184] [1970] O.J. No. 1607, [1970] 3 O.R. 780, 14 D.L.R. (3d) 164 (Ont. Prov. Ct.).

that the Crown had failed to prove beyond a reasonable doubt that the accused did not feel himself under reasonable apprehension of bodily harm or that he had used excessive force in the circumstances. Up to the point of the accused's blow, the victim had been the aggressor. In *R. v. Green*,[185] it was found that Ted Green struck Maki "a sort of half chop on the shoulder" because Maki had just speared him in the testicles. The court did not consider that Green "was doing anything more in the circumstances than protecting himself".[186] However, in *R. v. Watson*,[187] it was held that the accused, who began throttling an opponent at some time and distance from being accidentally hit by him, could not rely on self-defence since the victim was not offering any resistance.

A further category of player violence involves assaults on the officiating crew.[188] The on-ice officials take the risk of accidental blows and collisions, but there is usually no issue of implied consent in relation to deliberate attacks.[189] Timekeepers normally enjoy a quiet shift, but they too occasionally get the wrong end of the stick.[190] Given that issues of consent and self-defence are not applicable, players who take out their frustrations on the officials can expect to be convicted. The "Battle of Charlottetown" in 1996 duly resulted in guilty pleas by four players and an assistant coach after the referee was swarmed following his decision to allow the game-winning goal in an inter-university semi-final.[191]

Although violent acts by players may result in assault charges, some commentators suggest that judges have shown undue tolerance in applying the law,[192] and public sympathy for the accused can also be seen in the few jury

---

[185] [1970] O.J. No. 1699, [1971] 1 O.R. 591, 16 D.L.R. (3d) 137 (Ont. Prov. Ct.).

[186] *Ibid.*, at O.R. 596, D.L.R. 142 (Prov. Ct. J.), *per* Fitzpatrick. See also, *R. v. Jacques*, [1998] O.J. No. 5505, 40 W.C.B. (2d) 422 (Ont. Prov. Ct.) (reflexive self-defence in oldtimers hockey).

[187] [1975] O.J. No. 2681, 26 C.C.C. (2d) 150 (Ont. Prov. Ct.).

[188] See, R. Watson, "Canadian Courts on Ice: 'Bench Penalties' for Player Assaults on Officials in Ice Hockey" (2002) 12 Educ. & L.J. 23. On "rink rage", including attacks on officials by spectators, see, Chapter 5, "Be Safe: Off the Ice", section B, 1.

[189] See: *R. v. Prénoveau*, [1971] R.L. 21 (Que. C.S.P.); *R. v. Opekokew*, [1994] S.J. No. 310, 120 Sask.R. 159 (Sask. C.A.) (appeal court increased sentence to 90 days in jail); *R. v. Bosien*, [1998] N.B.J. No. 254, 200 N.B.R. (2d) 197 (N.B.Q.B.) ("minor assault" on referee; accused given conditional discharge and six months probation); *R. v. Regimbald*, unreported, Fournier J.C.M., November 27, 2003 (Cour municipale, Laval) (CDN $300 fine, CDN $400 restitution and six months probation). See also, *Sarvian v. Pereira*, [1999] O.J. No. 4833, 93 A.C.W.S. (3d) 650 (Ont. S.C.J.) (civil action by soccer referee; defendant had previously been convicted for the assault and sentenced to 30 days in jail).

[190] See, *R. v. Smalldon*, [2000] O.J. No. 3401, 47 W.C.B. (2d) 323 (Ont. C.J.) (player attempting to hit another player hit timekeeper; absolute discharge).

[191] See: "Hockey program faces suspension" *The Globe and Mail* (Toronto: February 27, 1996) at D10; "Hockey hotheads face charges after referee roughed up" *The Globe and Mail* (Toronto: February 28, 1996) at C8; "Moncton suspends four players, fires coach" *The Globe and Mail* (Toronto: March 2, 1996) at A18. In the criminal proceedings, all of the accused received conditional discharges. The University of Moncton retained Ken Dryden to study the incident and make recommendations with respect to its hockey program.

[192] See: G. Létourneau & A. Manganas, "La tolérance des droits pénal et sportif, source de violence dans les sports" (1976) 17 C. de D. 741 at 759-66; G.E. Néron, *Rapport final du Comité d'étude*

verdicts.[193] Judicial leniency is particularly evident at the sentencing stage. Few players have been jailed, even when the on-ice victim was a referee or other official, and the author of a comprehensive study has concluded that "the courts have shown little evidence that they view attacks on officials any differently than attacks on players".[194] The issue of appropriate sanctions is addressed in the next section, and the discussion of criminal liability concludes with consideration of alternative means of dealing with violent acts on the ice.

## 4.   Sentencing

In Britain, rugby or soccer players who assault and injure opponents in "off-the-ball" incidents can expect imprisonment for between three and 18 months.[195] In Canada, it has been suggested that a serious attack following a hockey game merits punishment through a deterrent sentence,[196] but the general practice in cases of in-play violence has been to impose non-custodial sanctions. The recurring sentences and dispositions include fines, probation and conditional discharges,[197] sometimes accompanied by a one-day jail visit.[198] The longest

---

*sur la violence au hockey amateur au Québec* (Gouvernement du Québec, Haut-Commissariat à la jeunesse, aux loisirs et aux sports, novembre 1977) at 118-46.

[193] See: *R. v. Maloney*, [1976] O.J. No. 2447, 28 C.C.C. (2d) 323 (Ont. Co. Ct.) (jury acquitted Dan Maloney but commented that it did not condone his actions); R. Kennedy, "A Nondecision Begs the Question" *Sports Illustrated*, July 28, 1975 (hung jury in prosecution of Dave Forbes in Minnesota; spearing of Henry Boucha). See also, Appendix I (cases in 1905 and 1907).

[194] R. Watson, "Canadian Courts on Ice: 'Bench Penalties' for Player Assaults on Officials in Ice Hockey" (2002) 12 Educ. & L.J. 23 at 47. Watson identifies seven cases of imprisonment, including, *R. v. Opekokew*, [1994] S.J. No. 310, 120 Sask.R. 159 (Sask. C.A.). See also, "Ex-hockey player jailed for attacking linesman" *The Globe and Mail* (Toronto: July 31, 2008) (ejected player came out of stands; 30 days in jail).

[195] See, for example: *R. v. Johnson* (1986), 8 Cr.App.R.(S.) 343 (C.A.); *R. v. Lloyd* (1989), 11 Cr.App.R.(S.) 36 (C.A.); *R. v. Chapman* (1989), 11 Cr.App.R.(S.) 93 (C.A.); *R. v. Rogers* (1993), 15 Cr.App.R.(S.) 393 (C.A.); *R. v. Calton*, [1998] EWCA Crim 3263, [1999] 2 Cr.App.R.(S.) 64 (C.A.); "Defender jailed for four months over on-field punch" *Guardian* (London: January 11, 2007) (James Cotterill pleaded guilty to fracturing opponent's jaw during FA Cup match); "Rugby player jailed for stamping" *BBC News*, November 12, 2007 (stamping on opponent's head caused 10cm wound; Rhys Garfield sentenced to 15 months imprisonment). On substantive liability in English law, see, *R. v. Barnes*, [2004] EWCA Crim 3246, [2005] 2 All E.R. 113 (C.A. (Crim. Div.)) (tackle in soccer).

[196] See, *R. v. Verner*, [1968] O.J. No. 1043, [1968] 1 O.R. 467 (Ont. C.A.) (sentence of three months definite for 16-year-old who kicked fellow student causing loss of an eye). More recently, see, "Tiger Williams guilty of assault" *The Globe and Mail* (Toronto: June 25, 1998) at A9 (retired player punched player in the eye in post-game scuffle; CDN $300 fine and one year's probation).

[197] Except in specified cases, the accused may be discharged absolutely or on conditions prescribed in a probation order, where the court "considers it to be in the best interests of the accused and not contrary to the public interest"; see, *Criminal Code*, R.S.C. 1985, c. C-46, ss. 730-31. On conditional sentences of imprisonment, see, *Criminal Code*, s. 742.1.

[198] See cases listed above at notes 142, 143, 145, 146, 147, 148, 149, 154, 162, and 163. See also: *R. v. Entwistle* (1984), 12 W.C.B. 267 (Ont. Prov. Ct.); *R. c. Savenco*, [1988] J.Q. no 2105, 26 Q.A.C. 291 (Que. C.A.); *R. v. Hrehirchuk*, [1992] M.J. No. 430, 81 Man.R. (2d) 257 (Man.

incarceration for an on-ice attack seems to be 89 days, with some players receiving 30 days.[199] The Canadian reluctance to imprison does not necessarily reflect a favoured status for hockey players since the general principles of sentencing in the *Criminal Code* now specify that "an offender should not be deprived of liberty if less restrictive sanctions may be appropriate" and "all available sanctions other than imprisonment that are reasonable in the circumstances should be considered" (see, s. 718.2(d)(e)). In relation to all assaults occurring in different settings, absolute or conditional discharges are given in 26 per cent of cases of "major assault" and in 47 per cent of cases of "common assault",[200] and the hockey context increases the likelihood that the sanction will not be jail. Players are usually young and with clean records in off-ice life, in spite of the general problem of athlete criminality.[201] Misconduct during play is easily represented as an out-of-character lapse brought on by the pressures of the game. In other cases, the players were simply doing their job.

The sentences given to professional players include a CDN $3000 fine for Rick Jodzio in 1977,[202] a CDN $500 fine for Jimmy Mann in 1982,[203] a CDN

---

C.A.); *R. v. Thompson*, [1994] N.J. No. 110, 116 Nfld. & P.E.I.R. 84 (Nfld. T.D.); *R. v. Carroll*, [1995] B.C.J. No. 365, 38 C.R. (4th) 238 (B.C.C.A.); *R. v. Vargas* (1999), 44 W.C.B. (2d) 145 (Ont. Gen. Div.) (conditional sentence and probation); *R. v. Neeld*, unreported, April 11, 2000 (B.C. Prov. Ct., Coquitlam); *R. v. Stewart*, [2005] A.J. No. 1942 (Alta. Q.B.) (51-year-old goalie swung stick into player's face; conditional sentence and community service); *R. v. Tropea*, [2007] O.J. No. 2122, 2007 ONCJ 241 (Ont. C.J.) (kicking in women's hockey not suitable for discharge; suspended sentence, probation, community service and suspension from organized hockey). In October 2009, Jonathan Roy received an absolute discharge after pleading guilty to assault in relation to a fight during a QMJHL game in March 2008.

[199] See: "Nepean man given 89-day sentence, sports ban for assault during game" *The Ottawa Citizen* (November 1, 1991) at C3 (Senior-A player, Neil Sandilands, with previous hockey-related convictions broke opponent's jaw; aggravated assault); *R. v. Kammerer*, unreported, B. Smith J., October 24, 1986 (Ont. Dist. Ct., Whitby) (kick to throat while opponent lying on ice; 30 days in jail and one-year probation with ban from organized hockey); *R. v. Heeg*, [1986] S.J. No. 760, 52 Sask.R. 159 (Sask. C.A.) (27-year-old used stick to strike opponent in face during amateur game; sentence increased from one day to 30 days in jail).

[200] See, Statistics Canada, "Cases in adult criminal court by type of sentence; fine, restitution, absolute or conditional discharge, other sentence, by province and Yukon Territory". In 2003, of the 13,007 convictions for "major assaults", 5730 (44 per cent) resulted in jail; of the 25,607 convictions for "common assaults", 6128 (24 per cent) resulted in jail.

[201] On crimes by athletes, see Chapter 5, "Be Safe: Off the Ice", section D.

[202] See, "Struck rival, hockey player fined $3000" *The Globe and Mail* (Toronto: August 18, 1977) at 40. During a game in the World Hockey Association on April 11, 1976, Jodzio, of the Calgary Cowboys, had repeatedly punched Marc Tardif, of the Quebec Nordiques, while Tardif lay motionless on the ice. Jodzio was originally charged with assault with intent to injure and pleaded guilty to causing bodily harm.

[203] See, "Record unlikely to impede Mann" *The Globe and Mail* (Toronto: May 20, 1982) at 17; "Mann pays painful price for delivering a sucker punch" *The Globe and Mail* (Toronto: March 13, 2004) at S2. During a game on January 13, 1982, Mann, of the Winnipeg Jets, had broken the jaw of Paul Gardner of the Pittsburgh Penguins. Mann was convicted of assault, and the judge in Winnipeg declined to grant a conditional discharge.

$1000 fine and one day in jail for Dino Ciccarelli in 1989,[204] and a conditional discharge and one year's probation for Alexander Perezhogin in 2005.[205] In February 2000, the career of 37-year-old enforcer, Marty McSorley, was essentially brought to an end when the NHL imposed its longest suspension to-date for violent play. The league initially suspended McSorley for the remaining 23 games of the regular season and for the play-offs,[206] and this was later extended to run for one year from the date of his attack on Brashear.[207] Following McSorley's criminal conviction, Kitchen J., of the British Columbia Provincial Court, found that the player had already suffered "considerable expense... [and] embarrassing publicity"[208] and would carry the stigma of the incident. The judge was conscious that McSorley had acted under pressure from his employer and was impressed by the player's dedication and remorse. The sentence imposed was a conditional discharge for 18 months, the conditions being that McSorley keep the peace, be of good behaviour and "not engage in any sporting event where Donald Brashear is on the opposition".[209]

The decision in *McSorley* stood as the obvious precedent when it came to sentencing Todd Bertuzzi,[210] after the hulking star with the Vancouver Canucks' pleaded guilty to assaulting Steve Moore, of the Colorado Avalanche. Bertuzzi's violent attack occurred during a game in Vancouver on March 8, 2004[211] and was in retaliation for an unpenalized check by Moore three weeks earlier that resulted in injuries to the Canucks' captain, Markus Naslund. A close game between the two divisional rivals on March 3, 2004 was accompanied by some Canucks' players making threats of retribution against Moore, and there were further "comments" before the game on March 8. That game turned out to be one-sided in favour of Colorado, and Canucks' players made various attempts to goad Moore into fights. Bertuzzi took up the pursuit of "payback" in the third period and launched his assault after "talking at" Moore:

---

[204] See, *R. v. Ciccarelli*, [1989] O.J. No. 2388, 54 C.C.C. (3d) 121 (Ont. Dist. Ct.), affg [1988] O.J. No. 2547, 5 W.C.B. (2d) 310 (Ont. Prov. Ct.). Ciccarelli, of the Minnesota North Stars, used his stick to deliver three blows to the head of Luke Richardson, of the Toronto Maple Leafs.

[205] See, *R. v. Perezhogin*, [2005] O.J. No. 3205 (Ont. C.J.); "Player pleads guilty to assault" *The Globe and Mail* (Toronto: June 8, 2005) at R11. During an American Hockey League game on April 30, 2004, Perezhogin, of the Hamilton Bulldogs, had swung his stick at the face of Garrett Stafford, of the Cleveland Barons, causing concussion and severe cutting. Perezhogin was required to pay CDN $5000 to charity and CDN $2500 to cover Stafford's medical expenses.

[206] See, "NHL hits McSorley with stiff suspension" *The Globe and Mail* (Toronto: February 24, 2000) at A1, A6.

[207] See, "Bettman ends McSorley circus" *The Globe and Mail* (Toronto: November 8, 2000) at S1, S3. NHL Commissioner Gary Bettman made this decision after the criminal trial and after McSorley decided not to appeal the conviction.

[208] See, *R. v. McSorley*, [2000] B.C.J. No. 1994 at para. 17, 2000 BCPC 117 (B.C. Prov. Ct. (Crim. Div.)). On McSorley's conviction for assault with a weapon, see Chapter 6, "Play Safe: On the Ice", section B, 3.

[209] *R. v. McSorley*, [2000] B.C.J. No. 1994 at para. 21, 2000 BCPC 117 (B.C. Prov. Ct. (Crim. Div.)).

[210] *R. v. Bertuzzi*, [2004] B.C.J. No. 2692, 26 C.R. (6th) 71 (B.C. Prov. Ct.).

[211] See, "Canada's troubled game suffers yet another blow" and "Nightmare in the family living room" *The Globe and Mail* (Toronto: March 10, 2004) at A1, A8, S3.

Bertuzzi reached out with his left hand and dropped his stick from his right hand and struck Moore very hard from behind and on the side, landing the blow, it looks like, in the right temple of Moore...After the punch lands, Moore falls, with Bertuzzi falling on top of him. Very quickly thereafter members of both teams join on to what is really a dog pile. After the referees become involved and pull the others off, it is clear that Mr. Moore is lying in a prone position on his chest. There is blood on the ice, and he is in obvious severe discomfort and pain.[212]

As a result of the punch and fall, Steve Moore suffered lacerations, concussion and hairline fractures to two bones associated with vertebrae in the neck. Nine months later at Bertuzzi's sentencing, Moore's prognosis was uncertain as he continued to experience neurological effects in the form of post-concussion symptoms. It was particularly uncertain whether he would play hockey again, and as of 2009 he had not played again.

The NHL responded by fining the Canucks USD $250,000 and suspending Bertuzzi for the remaining 13 games of the regular season and for the playoffs, which cost Bertuzzi USD $500,000 in lost salary.[213] (Bertuzzi was barred from employment in other hockey leagues during the 2004-05 NHL lockout and was finally reinstated by NHL Commissioner Gary Bettman in August 2005.[214] At this time, he was also invited to join the Canadian hockey team preparing for the 2006 Winter Olympics in Turin.) The decision to charge Bertuzzi with assault causing bodily harm was not taken until late June 2004, and Bertuzzi entered a plea of not guilty on August 26, 2004. The trial on summary procedure was scheduled for January 2005, but a prolonged media event was avoided on December 22, 2004 when negotiations between the crown prosecutor and defence counsel resulted in a joint recommendation that the appropriate sanction was a conditional discharge. Bertuzzi agreed to plead guilty to the charge and faced only a sentencing hearing at which Steve Moore's experience was narrated in the form of a victim impact statement.[215] Weitzel J. addressed whether the discharge would be in Bertuzzi's interest and "not contrary to the public interest" and considered Bertuzzi's character and the presence of aggravating and mitigating factors. The judge recognized Bertuzzi as a public-spirited, family man, whose style of play was that of a rough "power forward" rather than an "enforcer"; his character was good and was supported by references. The

---

[212] *R. v. Bertuzzi*, [2004] B.C.J. No. 2692, 26 C.R. (6th) 71 at 75 (B.C. Prov. Ct.), *per* Weitzel Prov. Ct. J.

[213] See, "Canucks share blame game" and "No more frontier justice" *Ottawa Citizen* (March 12, 2004) at B1, B2; "Canucks fuming over fine" *The Globe and Mail* (Toronto: March 12, 2004) at S1, S5.

[214] See, "4:29 p.m. EDT" and "Relieved Bertuzzi goes back to work" *The Globe and Mail* (Toronto: August 9, 2004) at R6, R7, R9. For the "Partial text of Gary Bettman's ruling" see online: <http://sports.espn.go.com/nhl/news/story?id=2129039>; the ruling notes the effects of the suspension over 17 months and the costs incurred by Bertuzzi in defending civil actions.

[215] See, "I made a terrible mistake" *The Globe and Mail* (Toronto: December 23, 2004) at A1, A6, and "Steve Moore" (victim impact statement online at: <http://www.theglobeandmail.com>). The reading in court of the impact statement is required by s. 722(2.1) of the *Criminal Code*.

aggravating factors were the prolonged pursuit of the victim and Moore's serious injuries. The mitigating factors included Bertuzzi's guilty plea, his remorse, his financial losses and his continuing suspension. Weitzel J. considered that there was sufficient deterrence in the public notoriety and disruption associated with the trial process and found that a conditional discharge was consistent with previous decisions in similar cases. The judge therefore granted the discharge in association with a one-year probation order requiring Bertuzzi to keep the peace and be of good behaviour, appear before the court when required and not play in any game involving Steve Moore. He was also required to perform 80 hours of community service work and pay a victim surcharge of CDN $500, the judge being satisfied that Bertuzzi had the funds to pay.

The league suspension and criminal prosecution were not the end of the matter since Steve Moore initiated civil actions for compensation and so compounded Bertuzzi's potential losses.[216] On Moore's side, the losses were outlined in his victim impact statement:

> ...after playing through the comparatively low entry-level contracts of my first few years, this summer was to be my first chance at a contract of even average compensation. That chance has been lost. I now sit, without a contract, without an effort by the Avalanche to sign me, and without any contract offers at all. Even if I am somehow to make a recovery, and get back to game-playing condition, I still face the possibility that teams will see me as damaged goods, and avoid the perceived risk of signing me.[217]

Civil actions represent additional means of holding parties to account and controlling violence. The criminal sanctions applied in Canada may not have been severe, but it is an open question whether criminal prosecution and heavy sentences are the road to reform.

## 5.   Control and Reform

> ...there exists a market for "goons", and...aggressiveness and intimidation are financially rewarded.[218]

In the early 1970s, as league franchises proliferated across North America, professional hockey sought to sell itself through a brutal style of play involving strategic violence and intimidation. The hired "goon"[219] or "enforcer"[220] found a

---

[216] See Chapter 6, "Play Safe: On the Ice", sections C, 1, 2, 5.

[217] "Steve Moore", victim impact statement, *The Globe and Mail* (Toronto: December 23, 2004).

[218] M. Lavoie & G. Grenier, "Discrimination and Salary Determination in the National Hockey League: 1977 and 1989 Compared" in G.W. Scully (ed.), *Advances in the Economics of Sport* (Greenwich: Jai Press, 1992) at 163-64. See also, J.C.H. Jones, S. Nadeau & W.D. Walsh, "The Wages of Sin: Employment and Salary Effects of Violence in the National Hockey League" (1997) 25 Atlantic Econ. J. 191.

[219] For judicial consideration of the image of the "goon", see: *National Hockey League v. Pepsi-Cola Canada Ltd.*, [1992] B.C.J. No. 1221, 92 D.L.R. (4th) 349 at 357, 372 (B.C.S.C.); *Na-*

place on teams, all players were under pressure to fight and scenes of prolonged mayhem became available for public consumption. Younger players then inevitably adopted the style of the professional antiheroes, and there were deaths in fights on[221] and off[222] the ice. Particular incidents and the new model of play led to a series of official inquiries during the 1970s and 1980s,[223] including research by the Commission for Fair Play which was established in 1986.[224]

Faced with widespread (although far from unanimous) condemnation of violent games, the Attorney-General of Ontario, the Honourable Roy McMurtry, in October 1975 announced a policy calling on police and prosecutors to watch for and take action against criminal conduct at sporting events.[225] Mr. McMurtry did not anticipate prosecution for ordinary fist fights between players, but saw no reason why charges should not be laid where, for example, a stick is deliberately used to cause serious injury. This policy was later endorsed by other Provincial Attorneys General, and the prosecution of players surged during 1976.[226] Among

---

*tional Hockey League v. Pepsi-Cola Canada Ltd.*, [1993] B.C.J. No. 1301, 102 D.L.R. (4th) 80 at 90-91 (B.C.S.C.).

[220] An "enforcer" has been judicially defined as, "a person whose sole task when being on the ice is to either settle scores or to focus on the physical aspect of the play"; see, *R. v. Bertuzzi*, [2004] B.C.J. No. 2692, 26 C.R. (6th) 71 at 77 (B.C. Prov. Ct.), *per* Weitzel Prov. Ct. J.

[221] See, *Re Duchesneau*, [1978] J.Q. no 228, 7 C.R. (3d) 70 (T.J. Qué). See Chapter 6, "Play Safe: On the Ice", section B, 2.

[222] See, *R. v. Smithers*, [1978] 1 S.C.R. 506 (S.C.C.). Paul Smithers had suffered racial insults during a game in 1973 and kicked an opponent in the stomach during a fight in the arena parking lot. One commentator noted that had the attack occurred during the game, there would have been a five-minute penalty, whereas off the ice Smithers was liable to a jail term; see, R.T. Runfola, "He is a Hockey Player, 17, Black and Convicted of Manslaughter" *New York Times* (October 27, 1974) at S2.

[223] See: W.R. McMurtry, *Investigation and Inquiry into Violence in Amateur Hockey* (Toronto: Ministry of Community and Social Services, 1974) (inquiry following game between Hamilton and Bramalea); G.E. Néron, *Rapport final du Comité d'étude sur la violence au hockey amateur au Québec* (Gouvernement du Québec, Haut-Commissariat à la jeunesse, aux loisirs et aux sports, novembre 1977); *Play it Safe - Report from the Hearings on Hockey Safety and Development* (Ontario NDP Caucus, June 1984); Law Reform Commission of Canada, Working Paper 38, Assault (1984) at 30-36, 52-53. On general studies of the organization of amateur hockey, see Chapter 3, "Organizations and Regulations", section A.

[224] See: M.D. Smith, *Violence in Canadian Amateur Sport: A Review of Literature* (Commission for Fair Play, August 1987); M.D. Smith & K. Young, *Violence in Amateur Sport: An Annotated Bibliography* (Commission for Fair Play, August 1987). In 1996, the Commission merged with the Canadian Centre for Ethics in Sport; see online: <http://www.cces.ca>.

[225] See: "Police ordered to act on hockey violence" *The Globe and Mail* (Toronto: October 29, 1975) at 1; "Crackdown extended to all sports" and "No sanctuary on the ice" *The Globe and Mail* (Toronto: October 30, 1975) at 1, 4, 6. The immediate outcome of the "purge" was the prosecution of Dan Maloney, of the Detroit Red Wings, with respect to blows struck to Brian Glennie, of the Toronto Maple Leafs, during a game on November 5, 1975; see, *R. v. Maloney*, [1976] O.J. No. 2447, 28 C.C.C. (2d) 323 (Ont. Co. Ct.).

[226] See, J.G. MacLellan, *Player versus Player Hockey Assaults Adjudicated in Canadian Courts* (M.A. thesis, Faculty of Graduate Studies, University of Western Ontario, 1984) at 163; 14 cases have been identified from 1976, compared to the usual average of four between 1973 and 1982. See also, R.C. Watson & J.G. MacLellan, "Smitting to Spitting: 80 Years of Ice-Hockey in Canadian Courts" (1986) 17(2) Can. J. History of Sport 10.

those charged, were four members of the Philadelphia Flyers who were involved in a crowd brawl and other incidents during a violent play-off series against the Toronto Maple Leafs.[227] The proliferation of the Canadian case law was so marked that it even drew the interest of an American law journal.[228]

The use of the criminal sanction as a control device[229] of last resort can be justified on two main grounds:

1. equality before the law, and

2. particular need for prosecution.

1. *Equality before the law*: Sports participants are not exempt from legal standards. It is not in the public interest to delegate all disciplinary authority to internal tribunals, especially where leagues have a financial self-interest in promoting a violent style of play that has paid dividends in the past. The commissioner of a professional league is not an independent figure, and exclusive league authority would establish a two-tier justice system by which ordinary citizens go before the judge, while players enjoy the privilege of in-house discipline.[230] We no longer have "benefit of clergy", and there is no reason to have benefit of Bettman (or clemency of Campbell).

2. *Particular need for prosecution*: Public control through criminal law is particularly required because of the violent nature of some games, the opportunities that powerful players have to cause serious injury and the visibility of the violence. Prosecutions can serve as a deterrent and warning, encouraging renewed emphasis on clean play and technical skills. Public control of professional leagues is required because their model of play influences minor leagues and the development of the game.

---

[227] See: "Three Flyers face charges" *The Globe and Mail* (Toronto: April 17, 1976) at 1, 2; "Flyer, fan charged with assault" *The Globe and Mail* (Toronto: April 24, 1976) at 1, 2; "Flyers' Watson, Kelly fined for '76 hockey assaults" *The Globe and Mail* (Toronto: April 16, 1977) at 49. Some members of the Flyers had been involved in a previous crowd brawl at a game in Vancouver on December 29, 1972; see, "Swinging Flyers are fined CDN $500 in Vancouver" *The Globe and Mail* (Toronto: June 9, 1973) at 46.

[228] See, D.V. White, "Sports Violence as Criminal Assault: Development of the Doctrine by Canadian Courts", [1986] Duke L. J. 1030.

[229] On the various control systems, see: W. Kuhlman, "Violence in Professional Sports", [1975] Wis. L. Rev. 771; E.W. Vaz, "Institutionalized Rule Violation in Professional Hockey: Perspectives and Control Systems"(1977) 43(3) CAHPER J. 6; R.B. Horrow, *Sports Violence: The Interaction Between Private Law Making and Criminal Law* (Arlington: Carrollton Press, 1980); G. Létourneau, "Sports, Violence and Criminal Law in Canada" (1981) 22 C.R. (3d) 103; R.B. Horrow, "Violence in Professional Sports: Is It Part of the Game?" (1982) 9 J. Legis. 1; G. Létourneau, "Problématique de la violence dans les loisirs et moyens d'action corrective et préventive: l'expérience québécoise et canadienne" (1988) 19 R.G.D. 653; A. Husa & S. Thiele, "In the Name of the Game: Hockey Violence and the Criminal Justice System" (2002) 45 Crim L. Q. 509; J.C.H. Jones & K.G. Stewart, "Hit Somebody: Hockey Violence, Economics, the Law, and the *Twist* and *McSorley* Decisions" (2002) 12 Seton Hall J. of Sport L. 165.

[230] On equality before the law, see Chapter 2, "Legal Fundamentals and Equality Rights", sections D, E. The criminal law recognizes two-tier justice by allowing more fighting and violence in the professional game; see Chapter 6, "Play Safe: On the Ice", section B, 3.

The contrary position holds that criminal prosecution is problematic for two main reasons:

1. part of the structure, and

2. who really understands *Jobidon* and *Cey*?

1. *Part of the structure*: Vigorous contact sports are encouraged by society and valued for their robust style. Professional players are a sub-group in a continuing relationship where the working culture promotes an apparent willing acceptance of risks.[231] The show is inherently violent, and the whole object of the enterprise is to assert the survival of the fittest and "beat" the opposition in a "dogfight". Given that the public wants it and the participants agree to it, the violence of the gladiators is not "real crime", and it is unjust and hypocritical to single out the occasional player who is merely fulfilling the expectations of the coach, teammates and fans. Players who protect teammates and brawl with a hated enemy are particularly likely to receive public and official support.[232] A society that pays top dollar to encourage and promote fierce competition[233] can hardly be heard to complain, and it would be more consistent to praise enforcers for their desire, team loyalty and work ethic. As in the case of doping,[234] the only thing that can be said against "offenders" is that they may have taken their admirable will to win a bit too far.

2. *Who really understands Jobidon and Cey?*: The scope of the implied consent is vaguely defined and dependent on the level of play.[235] The uncertainty of the law is unfair to the accused and may lead to wide variations in prosecutorial policy. Charges occur at random according to the vagaries of reporting and publicity and are usually laid against visiting or neutral players rather than home-town heroes.[236]

---

[231] On occupational safety, legal recourse and the construction of the culture of "consent", see, K. Young, "Violence, Risk, and Liability in Male Sports Culture" (1993), 10 Soc. of Sport J. 373.

[232] On the Canadian junior team's bench-clearing brawl with the Soviets at the 1987 world championships (the "Punch-Up in Piestany"), see: "Canadian kids did right thing" *The Ottawa Citizen* (January 5, 1987) at B1; "Soviet actions, not Canadian, led to disgrace" *The Globe and Mail* (Toronto: January 5, 1987) at A10; "Soviets' action cost Canada any chance of gold" *The Globe and Mail* (Toronto: January 7, 1987) at A13; "IIHF ruling is appealed by Canada" *The Globe and Mail* (Toronto: January 16, 1987) at A12; G. Joyce, *When the Lights Went Out: How One Brawl Ended Hockey's Cold War and Changed the Game* (Scarborough, ON: Doubleday Canada, 2006).

[233] See, *People v. Schacker*, 670 N.Y.S. 2d 308 (Dist.Ct., 1998) (blow struck after the whistle in a non-checking league; "If cross checking, tripping and punching were criminal acts, the game of hockey could not continue in its present form ... The idea that a hockey player should be prosecuted runs afoul of the policy to encourage free and fierce competition in athletic events" *per* Judge L. Donohue, at 309, 310).

[234] See Chapter 3, "Organizations and Regulations", section D.

[235] See Chapter 6, "Play Safe: On the Ice", section B, 3. Besides working through *Jobidon* and *Cey*, the law-abiding player may also need to interpret and apply, *R. v. Paice*, [2005] S.C.J. No. 21, [2005] 1 S.C.R. 339 (S.C.C.).

[236] The prosecution of Todd Bertuzzi in 2004 was a rare example of proceeding against the home side.

The criminal process is, furthermore, a cumbersome means of control because of the difficulty of proving each element of the offence. This difficulty may be compounded by evidentiary[237] problems when an incident is sudden and confused[238] or seen differently according to the team loyalties of observers. (The prosecution's task is, however, aided where police are able to seize film or videotape.[239] Film is admissible in evidence where it is a fair and true reproduction of events. In *R. v. Maloney (No. 2)*,[240] the court admitted silent film and videotapes showing incidents at normal speed but rejected a slow-motion sequence. The Crown had sought to use the sequence to clarify events, but the court accepted the defence argument that it was essential to show the ordinary spontaneous behaviour of players; slow-motion might introduce a false appearance of deliberateness into the accused's conduct.)

In spite of the drawbacks of the process, criminal charges have served as a short-term remedy and can claim some success in suppressing the worst excesses of the 1970s. If prosecution is to be used, the process might be strengthened by creating specific criminal offences dealing with sports violence,[241] and it has also been suggested that criminal charges should be brought against league organizers and team officers as the promoters and instigators of violence.[242] Teams would feel a new incentive to exercise control if the costs of the violence also fell on them. Liability could be based on a theory of conspiracy, aiding or counselling,[243] and the

---

[237] See, G. Létourneau & A. Manganas, "Violence in Sports: Evidentiary Problems in Criminal Prosecutions" (1978) 16 Osgoode Hall L.J. 577.

[238] See: *R. v. Sharpley*, unreported, Fitzpatrick J., June 9, 1977 (Ont. Prov. Ct., Cornwall); *R. v. A.W.*, (1987), 4 W.C.B. (2d) 25 (Ont. Prov. Ct.).

[239] See, "Hockey Night staff asked to find tapes investigators missed" *The Globe and Mail* (Toronto: May 6, 1976) at 2 (tapes from Flyers-Leafs game). A film made by a member of the public was used in: *R. v. Hutchison*, unreported, Sherwood Prov. Ct. J., August 2, 1972 (Ont. Prov. Ct., Ottawa-Carleton) (issue of protection of a teammate; accused convicted of assault causing bodily harm and fined CDN $500). See also: "Owner of 67's admits holding film of brawl" *The Ottawa Citizen* (July 25) at 1, 3; "Linseman fined CDN $300 for assault" *The Globe and Mail* (Toronto: September 6, 1978) at 31 (kick to head during Major Junior game).

[240] [1976] O.J. No. 2446, 29 C.C.C. (2d) 431 (Ont. Co. Ct.). See also, *R. v. Williams*, [1977] O.J. No. 2556, 35 C.C.C. (2d) 103 (Ont. Co. Ct.) (slow-motion film ruled inadmissible; admissibility of similar fact evidence considered).

[241] See: *Sports Violence Act, 1980*, H.R. 7903, 96th Cong., 2d Sess., 126 Cong. Rec. 6946 (crime of using "excessive physical force" in a professional sports event); *Sports Violence Act, 1981*, H.R. 2263, 97 Cong., 1st Sess., 127 Cong. Rec. H760; "A Proposed Legislative Solution to the Problem of Violent Acts by Participants During Professional Sporting Events: The Sports Violence Act of 1980" (1981) 7 U. Dayton L. Rev. 91.

[242] On the directions given to Marty McSorley, see Chapter 6, "Play Safe: On the Ice", section B, 3. In the 1972 Canada-Soviet Summit Series, Bobby Clarke famously broke the ankle of Valeri Kharlamov at the hint of coach John Ferguson. See also: "Refusal to fight led to waivers, Mulvey says" *The Globe and Mail* (Toronto: February 2, 1982) at 13; "NHL suspends Kings' coach" and "Ziegler informs Kings by letter" *The Globe and Mail* (Toronto: February 4, 1982) at 19.

[243] See: *Criminal Code*, R.S.C. 1985, c. C-46, ss. 21-22; Law Reform Commission of Canada, Working Paper 38, Assault (1984) at 36; W. Hechter, "The Criminal Law and Violence in Sports" (1977) 19 Crim. L.Q. 425, at 435. According to the decision in *Wilcox v. Jeffrey*, [1951] 1 All E.R. 464 (K.B.D.), a journalist is also guilty of aiding and abetting by deliberately attending and encouraging an event and describing illegal acts for profit.

criminal liability of organizations is now also subject to section 22.2 of the *Criminal Code*, dealing with parties to offences. This special provision is in the following terms:

> In respect of an offence that requires the prosecution to prove fault — other than negligence — an organization is a party to the offence if, with the intent at least in part to benefit the organization, one of its senior officers
>
> (a) acting within the scope of their authority, is a party to the offence;
>
> (b) having the mental state required to be a party to the offence and acting within the scope of their authority, directs the work of other representatives of the organization so that they do the act or make the omission specified in the offence; or
>
> (c) knowing that a representative of the organization is about to be a party to the offence, does not take all reasonable measures to stop them from being a party to the offence.[244]

There is, therefore, the potential to extend liability beyond the individual player and hold the organization to account where a "senior officer" directs an assault or fails to stop it; the term "senior officer" includes a representative who "is responsible for managing an important aspect of the organization's activities" (see, s. 2). The best strategy for teams is to have a junior assistant coach on the bench when the nod is given.

Rather than relying on criminal law, some commentators suggest the use of alternative legal strategies focussing on regulation and compensation. Violent sports could be placed under the supervision of a public commission,[245] and it may be appropriate to legislate to control the broadcasting or display of violence both as a penalty and as a limit on the exposure of a harmful model.[246] To hold organizations accountable, a particular recommendation involves creating a process to arbitrate compensation claims where a professional team loses a player through violence.[247] The goals here are restitution and deterrence since the team that employs the assailant would be required to compensate both the injured player and the other team that has suffered financial losses and competitive disadvantage because of the incapacitation of its employee. In professional hockey, violence presents issues of occupational safety, so that it is also open to players' associations to negotiate for safer working conditions and

---

[244] *Criminal Code*, R.S.C. 1985, c. C-46, s. 22.2.

[245] See: G.E. Néron, *Rapport final du Comité d'étude sur la violence au hockey amateur au Québec* (Gouvernement du Québec, Haut-Commissariat à la jeunesse, aux loisirs et aux sports, novembre 1977) at 190-91; *Act respecting safety in sports*, R.S.Q. c. S-3.1 (see Chapter 6, "Play Safe: On the Ice", section A, 3).

[246] See: J. Barnes (ed.), *Sports Violence and Law Reform* (Ottawa: Institute for Studies in Policy, Ethics and Law, Carleton University, 1984) at 27; M.D. Smith, *Violence and Sport* (Toronto: Butterworths, 1983) at 109-30.

[247] See: "The Sports Court: A Private System to Deter Violence in Professional Sports" (1982) 55 S. Cal. L. Rev. 399; *Sports Violence Arbitration Act, 1981*, H.R. 5079, 97th Cong. 1st Sess., 127 Cong.Rec. H8759; *Sports Violence Arbitration Act, 1983*, H.R. 4495, 98th Cong., 1st Sess., 129 Cong.Rec. H10,579.

improved insurance benefits.[248] While regulation on the basis of employment law has the potential to improve safety standards, it is not clear that the players' association acts for the public good. A disciplinary case places the association in a conflict of interest because both the victim and the assailant can claim fair representation, and it is the natural inclination of the union to reject heavy sanctions.[249] The players' association is part of the wider problem since it has a vested interest in maintaining a commercially-appealing model of play and may wish to preserve the jobs of the enforcers and policemen. When player compensation is based on a percentage of league revenue, the players, as much as the league, will be attracted by the principle that "violence sells". There is evidence that the prospect of violence gives a boost to attendance, especially in American cities,[250] although the financial benefit falls mainly to team owners since the style of play is likely to cut short playing careers.

Although the league is not an independent authority and has little incentive to reduce "popular violence", the primary responsibility to maintain law and order will continue to fall to the organizations that are closest to the game and have the technical knowledge to determine what conduct is unacceptable. The NHL has addressed violence and safety through rule changes[251] and disciplinary decisions and has made progress in areas such as bench-clearing brawls, "instigation", hits to the head and hits from behind. The penalties for interference also now give the advantage to players with speed and skill. The league's disciplinary system has the potential to inflict serious financial pain, and the league is often encouraged to show more consistency in suspensions and to put a sharper bite on offending players and teams. More imaginative forms of sanction might also be used. Rather than suspending unskilled enforcers, it is commonly suggested that teams should be required to play them; a team would soon feel the pinch in its results and revenue if its lumbering goon had to clock 25 minutes of ice time for 25 home games. If the Commissioner's justice in the NHL[252] and other leagues[253] is

---

[248] See Chapter 6, "Play Safe: On the Ice", sections A, 3-4. See also, K. Young, "Violence, Risk, and Liability in Male Sports Culture" (1993) 10 Soc. of Sport J. 373.

[249] In the NHL, "Commissioner Discipline" is subject to article 18 of the Collective Bargaining Agreement ("CBA") (2005), article 6 of the Constitution, By-Law 17, and Rule 33a (Supplementary Discipline); see further, Chapter 9, "National Hockey League", section D. Where a player is subject to criminal investigation or civil action, he may seek a reasonable delay in league disciplinary proceedings; see, CBA of NHL (2005), article 18.6 and Exhibit 8.

[250] See: J.C.H. Jones, D.G. Ferguson & K.G. Stewart, "Blood Sports and Cherry Pie: Some Economics of Violence in the National Hockey League" (1993) 52 Am. J. of Econ. and Soc. 63; J.C.H. Jones, K.G. Stewart & R. Sunderman, "From the Arena Into the Streets: Hockey Violence, Economic Incentives and Public Policy" (1996) 55 Am. J. of Econ. and Soc. 231; M. Lavoie, *Avantage numérique: l'argent et la Ligue nationale de hockey* (Hull: Éditions Vents d'Ouest, 1997) at 33-38.

[251] See, in particular, from the *Official Rules* of the NHL: Rule 44 (Checking from Behind); Rule 47 (Fighting), dealing with "instigators", "aggressors" and "third man in" intervention; see online: <http://www.nhl.com/league/ext/rules>.

[252] Besides the suspensions of Marty McSorley and Todd Bertuzzi (see Chapter 6, "Play Safe: On the Ice", section B, 4), recent suspensions in the NHL include: Scott Niedermayer (10 games in March 2000 for stick blow to head of Peter Worrell); Brad May (20 games in November 2000 for slash to face of Steve Heinze); Owen Nolan (11 games in February 2001 for hit to head of

seen to be severe and effective, there is less likelihood of violence and less need to call for intervention by other keepers of the game.

Discussion has focussed on the form of violence that involves aiming fists at the head. It is a peculiarity of hockey at some levels that fighting is tolerated as a traditional part of the game since throwing a punch does not result in automatic expulsion and suspension.[254] In the two seasons following the lockout of 2004-05, there were fewer fights in the NHL, but by 2007-08 the figures were returning to the previous levels. Fighting is a source of injuries, but is also claimed to serve a safety function by holding abusers to account. Attempts have been made to categorize fights as "retaliatory" (both justified and unjustified), "spontaneous", "inspirational" or "staged", although it would be difficult to draft rules and maintain a disciplinary system that effectively reflects the context and subtleties of the particular fisticuffs. The game can clearly be played without fights, and majority public opinion now follows medical opinion in favouring a ban. The more probable approach in the NHL is some modification of the rules of engagement to limit the role of heavyweights, guarantee that protective equipment is in place and otherwise keep the boxing reasonably safe. The issue could, however, be quickly resolved if a criminal court were to determine that under *Jobidon* the victim's consent is no defence when blows are struck between NHL players.

To achieve more general long-term change and safer playing conditions for children, many Canadian commentators have called for general educational measures to reform the values of the playing environment[255] and the sporting

---

Grant Marshall); Tie Domi (11 games, including playoffs, in May 2001 for elbow to Scott Nied-ermayer); Wade Belak (eight games in March 2004 for stick blow to head of Ossi Vaananen); Chris Simon (25 games, including playoffs, in March 2007 for slash to head of Ryan Hollweg); Steve Downie (20 games in September 2007 for hit to head of Dean McAmmond); Jesse Boul-erice (25 games in October 2007 for cross-check to face of Ryan Kesler); and Chris Simon (30 games in December 2007 for stepping on Jarkko Ruutu).

[253] In November 1998, the OHL initially imposed a "lifetime" ban on Jeff Kugel of the Windsor Spitfires after he left the bench in a game against the Owen Sound Players, punched an opponent and wildly challenged and pursued other players. In March 2008, the QMJHL suspended coach Patrick Roy for five games and goalkeeper Jonathan Roy for seven games following a brawl be-tween the Québec Remparts and the Chicoutimi Saguenéens. In November 2009, the OHL sus-pended Michael Liambas for the season and playoffs for a boarding hit that caused serious injuries. The QMJHL gave the same suspension to Patrice Cormier in January 2010 for a blow with the elbow.

[254] On fighting and league rules, see: B. Kidd & J. Macfarlane, *The Death of Hockey* (Toronto: New Press, 1972) at 41-43; R. Gruneau & D. Whitson, *Hockey Night in Canada: Sport, Identities, and Cultural Politics* (Toronto: Garamond Press, 1993) at 182-86. For a proposal to mandate rule changes, see, R.A. DiNicola & S. Mendeloff, "Controlling Violence in Professional Sports: Rule Reform and the Federal Professional Sports Violence Commission" (1983) 21 Duquesne L. Rev. 843.

[255] See: E.W. Vaz, "Institutionalized Rule Violation in Professional Hockey: Perspectives and Control Systems" (1977) 43(3) CAHPER J. 6; W.R. McMurtry, *Investigation and Inquiry into Violence in Amateur Hockey* (Toronto: Ministry of Community and Social Services, 1974) at 36-46; G. Létour-neau & A. Manganas, "La tolérance des droit pénal et sportif, source de violence dans les sports" (1976) 17 C. de D. 741 at 766-76; G.E. Néron, *Rapport final du Comité d'étude sur la violence au hockey amateur au Québec* (Gouvernement du Québec, Haut-Commissariat à la jeunesse, aux

culture in which players are raised.[256] The goals and organization of minor and junior hockey have been the subject of frequent study,[257] and both government[258] and Hockey Canada[259] have developed policies to promote fair play, safety and ethical conduct.[260] Suitable playing rules and domestic discipline[261] are part of the solution, and a special study in 2000 recommended "positive behaviour" and "attitude shifts"[262] by players, parents, coaches, media[263] and other influential members of the hockey community to bring about a new emphasis on skill development, safety and enjoyment. Programs will continue to try to realise this long-projected ideal for the kids, although it may be a long time before we can dispense with the need for a police presence among the parents and in the professional game. Since the skaters sometimes need the law to protect them from fellow skaters, the *Official Rules* of the NHL are wise to require in Rule 41.8 that, "All clubs shall provide adequate police or other protection for all players, goalkeepers and officials at all times".

---

loisirs et aux sports, novembre 1977) at 187-206; B.D. McPherson & L. Davidson, *Minor Hockey in Ontario: Toward a Positive Learning Environment for Children in the 1980s* (Ministry of Culture and Recreation/Ontario Hockey Council, 1980); L. Scanlan, *Grace Under Fire: The State of Our Sweet and Savage Game* (Toronto: Penguin Canada, 2002) at 254-78.

[256] See, M.D. Smith, *Violence and Sport* (Toronto: Butterworths, 1983) at 40-46 (violent subcultures) at 75-107 (interpersonal influences).

[257] See Chapter 3, "Organizations and Regulations", section A. On safety programs: see Chapter 5, "Be Safe: Off the Ice", section B; Chapter 6, "Play Safe: On the Ice", sections A, 1-3.

[258] See, "Canadian Strategy for Ethical Conduct in Sport: Policy Framework", May 24, 2002, online: <http://www.pch.gc.ca> "Sport Canada". See Chapter 2, "Legal Fundamentals and Equality Rights", section B.

[259] See, "Safe and Fun Hockey" and "It's a New Game", online: <http://www.hockeycanada.ca>. The "Open Ice Summit" in 1999 played an important role in developing programs.

[260] On Fair Play programs, see also: Canadian Centre for Ethics in Sport, online: <http://www.cces.ca>; True Sport Foundation, online: <http://www.truesportpur.ca>, including "Fair Play in Minor Hockey".

[261] See: *Lecuyer v. Alberta Junior "A" Hockey League*, [1977] A.J. No. 580, 3 A.R. 213 (Alta. T.D.) (player suspended for spearing); *Trudelle (Litigation Guardian of) v. Saskatchewan Hockey Assn. Inc.*, [2003] S.J. No. 207, 233 Sask.R. 51 (Sask. Q.B.) (player suspended for head butting linesman). On fairness in association proceedings, see: Chapter 3, "Organizations and Regulations", sections C, 1, 5; Chapter 9, "National Hockey League", section D. See also: "Quebec blows whistle on minor league hockey fights" *The Globe and Mail* (Toronto: August 21, 2008) at A7B; "QMJHL cracks down on fighting" *The Globe and Mail* (Toronto: September 11, 2008) at R9 (new system of penalties and suspensions); "OHL institutes suspension for removing helmet to fight" *The Globe and Mail* (Toronto: January 15, 2009) at R7.

[262] See, B. Pascall, *Eliminating Violence in Hockey* (British Columbia Ministry of Small Business, Tourism and Culture, May 2000) at 56. See also, Commission de l'aménagement du territoire, *La problématique de la violence dans le hockey mineur, Rapport final* (Québec: Assemblée nationale, octobre 2001).

[263] On the image and influence of Don Cherry, see, *National Hockey League v. Pepsi-Cola Canada Ltd.*, [1992] B.C.J. No. 1221, 92 D.L.R. (4th) 349 at 354 (B.C.S.C.) ("a very distinctive public character ... [who] projects a 'tough guy' image and appears to favour a violent brand of hockey" *per* Hardinge J.).

## C.    INJURIES TO PLAYERS AND CIVIL LIABILITY[264]

## 1.    Actions for Damages

As noted in the preceding chapters, the purpose of a civil action in tort is to hold the defendant responsible for injuries caused and compensate the plaintiff through an award of damages. Deliberate violence can be remedied by an action for civil assault, and the defendant who fails to exercise due care may also be liable in negligence. Given that the goal is restitution, the civil process holds particular appeal for victims in that the outcome may be a financial settlement between the parties or a judicial assessment of the appropriate cash figure.

In assessing compensatory damages, the court makes an informed estimate of what it will take to cover actual and anticipate losses and so restore the victim to his or her condition prior to the injury.[265] The categories of damages include pre-trial pecuniary losses ("special damages") and a general award for future pecuniary losses and all non-pecuniary losses. General damages assess aspects such as pain and suffering, loss of expectation of life, lost earning capacity, and future medical, health care and other expenses. The award may also include a small sum for loss of "amenities" or "enjoyment of life" in the form of diminished capacity to engage in pleasant activities such as sport or recreation. Although the injuries suffered in hockey sometimes require substantial awards,[266] judgments in Canada do not approach the gargantuan dimensions of the American system.[267] Significant compensation for lost earnings may, however, be required where the victim is an established professional or high performance athlete[268] or talented draftee[269] whose career has been cut short or

---

[264] See: J. Barnes, *Sports and the Law in Canada*, 3d ed. (Toronto: Butterworths, 1996) at 269-318; S. Bird & J. Zauhar, *Recreation and the Law*, 2d ed. (Scarborough, ON: Carswell, 1997).

[265] See, K.D. Cooper-Stephenson, *Personal Injuries Damages in Canada*, 2d ed. (Scarborough, ON: Carswell, 1995).

[266] See, for example: *Unruh (Guardian ad litem of) v. Webber*, [1994] B.C.J. No. 467, [1994] 5 W.W.R. 270, 112 D.L.R. (4th) 83 (B.C.C.A.) (CDN $3.7 million; cross-check into boards caused quadriplegia); *Stein v. Sandwich West (Township)*, [1995] O.J. No. 423, 25 M.P.L.R. (2d) 170 (Ont. C.A.) (CDN $8.5 million; fall on rink caused quadriplegia).

[267] In a game in 1978, Wilf Paiement, of the Colorado Rockies, broke the nose of Dennis Polonowich, of the Detroit Red Wings. Polonowich won the lottery in 1982 when a U.S. federal court jury awarded him USD $850,000. See: "850,000 damages for hockey player" *The Globe and Mail* (Toronto: August 18, 1982) at 1; "Another black eye for hockey's image" *Maclean's* (August 30, 1982) at 40-41.

[268] See, *Mellanby v. Chapple*, [1995] O.J. No. 1299, 54 A.C.W.S. (3d) 1307 (Ont. Gen. Div.) (Scott Mellanby slashed on forearm when intervening in fight in bar; judgment for CDN $826,000, including lost differential between actual earnings and other salaries); see also: *Renaissance Leisure Group Inc. v. Frazer*, [2004] O.J. No. 3486, 242 D.L.R. (4th) 229 (Ont. C.A.) (tavern had been held partially responsible; action for contribution and indemnity); *Bonham v. Smith*, [1998] B.C.J. No. 98, [1998] 9 W.W.R. 673, 41 C.C.L.T. (2d) 1 (B.C.S.C.) (CDN $1.1 million; lost earnings of champion Australian Ironwoman triathlete).

[269] See, *Morrow v. Outerbridge*, [2009] B.C.J. No. 640, 2009 BCSC 433 (B.C.S.C.) (Joshua Morrow selected in seventh round of NHL draft in 2002; total wage loss of approximately CDN $1.2 million).

diminished and who loses lucrative payments in the form of salary or commercial contracts. There is no equality before the law in the capitalist torts system, which recognizes elite status and richly rewards the famous and talented. Unproven athletes and those with a mere hope of fortune can expect much less.[270] In evaluating a player's skill and potential, the court may hear expert testimony from witnesses such as experienced professional scouts.[271]

Where the defendant's conduct has been particularly reprehensible, it is possible to supplement the award through aggravated and exemplary damages, which are available in relation to both intentional torts[272] and negligence.[273] Aggravated damages provide augmented compensation for injury to the plaintiff's feelings caused by the defendant's behaviour. Exemplary damages serve a punitive function and are designed to deter similar conduct. For example, in *Karpow v. Shave*,[274] the schoolboy plaintiff was involved in an altercation with the defendant's brother while playing in a hockey game; the plaintiff suffered a broken nose when the defendant, a spectator, punched him in the face at the end of the game. Such inexcusable conduct was punished by the inclusion of an award for exemplary damages.

Injuries to players bring potential liability in various types of defendant standing in different relationships towards the participant. Players may sue fellow participants or parties who have contributed to the injuries through their role as organizers, instructors or providers of products or services. Liability is usually based on negligence, although intentional torts are also relevant,[275]

---

[270] See: *Clark v. Kereiff*, [1983] B.C.J. No. 1586, 43 B.C.L.R. 157 (B.C.C.A.) (university hockey player; CDN $10,000 for loss of prospect of playing professionally); *Mori v. Weeks*, [2001] B.C.J. No. 1688, 2001 BCSC 1094 (B.C.S.C.) (junior goaltender; CDN $15,000 for chance of a career in the minors).

[271] See, *Vigoren v. Nystuen*, [2006] S.J. No. 293, [2006] 10 W.W.R. 223, 266 D.L.R. (4th) 634 (Sask. C.A.).

[272] See: *Pettis v. McNeil*, [1979] N.S.J. No. 560, 8 C.C.L.T. 299 (N.S.S.C.) (player struck across mouth with stick; CDN $3,850, including CDN $200 in punitive damages); *Deshaies c. Asnong*, [2003] J.Q. no 150, [2003] R.R.A. 697 (C.Q.) (parent assaulted referee; CDN $3,000, including CDN $2,500 in punitive damages); *Reddemann v. McEachnie*, [2005] B.C.J. No. 1374, 2005 BCSC 915 (B.C.S.C.) (coach assaulted mascot; CDN $35,000, including CDN $10,000 in punitive damages); *Leonard v. Dunn*, [2006] O.J. No. 3941, 151 A.C.W.S. (3d) 1172 (Ont. S.C.J.), affd [2008] O.J. No. 2051, 167 A.C.W.S. (3d) 227 (Ont. Div. Ct.) (punch to player's face; CDN $13,500, including CDN $3,000 in punitive damages).

[273] See, *Robitaille v. Vancouver Hockey Club Ltd.*, [1979] B.C.J. No. 887, 19 B.C.L.R. 158 (B.C.S.C.), vard [1981] B.C.J. No. 555, [1981] 3 W.W.R. 481, 124 D.L.R. (3d) 228, 16 C.C.L.T. 225 (B.C.C.A.) (humiliating treatment of injured professional player); see further: Chapter 6, "Play Safe: On the Ice", section C, 5; *Morrow v. Outerbridge*, [2009] B.C.J. No. 640, 2009 BCSC 433 (B.C.S.C.) (negligence in operation for shoulder injury; aggravated damages).

[274] [1974] A.J. No. 215, [1975] 2 W.W.R. 159 (Alta. S.C.) (CDN $2000 for the nose and CDN $500 exemplary damages). See also, *Hodgins v. Barnes*, [2007] O.J. No. 2072, 157 A.C.W.S. (3d) 964 (Ont. S.C.J.) (assault on coach; player punished in other forums; punitive damages not awarded).

[275] See, for example, *Butrimas (Litigation Guardian of) v. Applewood Hockey Assn.*, [2006] O.J. No. 3494, 147 A.C.W.S. (3d) 144 (Ont. S.C.J., Small Claims Ct.) (alleged intentional infliction of emotional harm when 8-year-old dismissed from novice team).

especially in cases of "rink rage"[276] or violence by playing opponents. Where a player is following orders or acting in an authorized capacity, the team risks vicarious liability for the consequences.

## 2.    Player Sues Player[277]

### a.    *Intentional Torts: Assault and Battery*

An act is intentional or deliberate when it has a desired purpose or is consciously performed knowing that a consequence is substantially certain. Battery and assault are torts involving deliberate interference with other people's bodily integrity or security.[278] A person commits battery who intentionally makes direct or indirect physical contact, however slight, with the person of another, the offensiveness being in the eyes of the recipient. For example, a kick or punch delivered on purpose is a battery, and it does not matter if the victim is someone other than the person targeted. The illegal intent and the final contact are what count. Battery is based on the protection of rights:

> The tort of battery is aimed at protecting the personal autonomy of the individual. Its purpose is to recognize the right of each person to control his or her body and who touches it, and to permit damages where this right is violated. The compensation stems from the violation of the right to autonomy, not fault.[279]

Assault involves the physical threatening of contact through actions that make a victim reasonably apprehensive that harm will follow. Shaking a fist in front of someone or swinging and missing are, therefore, civil assaults. Battery and assault usually occur together, and it is the final contact that accounts for most of the damage. Deliberate threatening, attempting and striking — assault and battery — are invariably referred to collectively as "assault". This private civil

---

[276] See Chapter 5, "Be Safe: Off the Ice", section B, 2.

[277] See: S.A. Thiele, "Sports and Torts: Injuring a Fellow Participant Can Be Costly" (2000) 23 Adv.Q. 348; N. Cox, "Civil Liability for Foul Play in Sport" (2003) 54 N.I.L.Q. 351; J.A. Citron & M. Ableman, "Civil Liability in the Arena of Professional Sports" (2003) 36 U.B.C.L. Rev. 193; T.E. Fenton, "Actionable Violence or 'Just Part of the Game'? Applying Standard Trespass and Negligence Principles to Sports Violence in Canada" (2005) 13 Tort L. Rev. 122.

[278] Under rules relating to trespass, where the plaintiff proves a direct blow or direct interference, the burden shifts to the defendant to show the absence of intent or negligence. This reversal of onus helps the plaintiff where the circumstances are best known to the defendant or where it is unclear which of a number of defendants applied the force. See: *Cook v. Lewis*, [1951] S.C.J. No. 28, [1951] S.C.R. 830 (S.C.C.) (hunting accident); *Ellison v. Rogers*, [1967] O.J. No. 1151, [1968] 1 O.R. 501, 67 D.L.R. (2d) 21 (Ont. H.C.J.) (golfer hit by ball); *Goshen v. Larin*, [1974] N.S.J. No. 248, 56 D.L.R. (3d) 719 (N.S.C.A.) (spectator at wrestling match knocked over by referee).

[279] *Non-Marine Underwriters, Lloyd's of London v. Scalera*, [2000] S.C.J. No. 26, [2001] 1 S.C.R. 551 at 565 (S.C.C.), *per* McLachlin J. See also, *Reibl v. Hughes*, [1980] S.C.J. No. 105, [1980] 2 S.C.R. 880 (S.C.C.). ("The tort [of battery] is an intentional one, consisting of an unprivileged and unconsented to invasion of one's bodily security" *per* Laskin C.J.C. at 890).

action for compensation provides a concurrent remedy with criminal prosecution as a response to undue violence.[280]

There is a defence[281] in assault if the defendant proves that the action occurred with the plaintiff's consent. Once the plaintiff shows that physical interference occurred, the defendant is called upon to explain and bears the burden of proving that the plaintiff was willing.[282] Consent may be express (*e.g.*, a formal agreement to undergo surgery) or it may be implied from conduct, including voluntarily engaging in a fair fight.[283] Participation in contact sports is taken to involve consent to the ordinary blows and collisions incidental to play, including contact that is in breach of the game rules. Decisions have sought to define the limits of this implied consent by distinguishing the ordinary and expected checks and bodily contact from actions that are deliberately and unnecessarily harmful.[284] The leading civil judgment is *Agar v. Canning*,[285] where the defendant amateur hockey player, in response to a hooking blow to the neck, knocked the plaintiff unconscious by bringing his stick down with a two-handed blow onto the plaintiff's face. Bastin J. first referred to the types of contact and the risk of injury that are accepted in hockey:

> Hockey necessarily involves violent bodily contact and blows from the puck and hockey sticks. A person who engages in this sport must be assumed to accept the risk of accidental harm...in return for enjoying a corresponding immunity with

---

[280] See, for example, *Proulx v. Viens*, [1994] R.J.Q. 1130 (C.Q. (C.C.)) (assault during "sponge hockey"; defendant had previously been convicted by criminal court). On proceedings involving Marc Tardif and Rick Jodzio, see, note 202, above, note 292, below.

[281] A further important defence is reasonable self-defence or defence of others in response to threatened harm. See: *Tremblay c. Deblois*, [1998] J.Q. no 353, 78 A.C.W.S. 836 (Que. C.A.) (defendant's punch during skirmish in hockey game was excessive); *Babiuk v. Trann*, [2005] S.J. No. 41, [2005] 9 W.W.R. 274, 248 D.L.R. (4th) 530 (Sask. C.A.) (rugby player used reasonable force in defending teammate).

[282] *Non-Marine Underwriters, Lloyd's of London v. Scalera*, [2000] S.C.J. No. 26, [2000] 1 S.C.R. 551 (S.C.C.).

[283] See: *Wade v. Martin*, [1955] N.J. No. 9, [1955] 3 D.L.R. 635 (Nfld. S.C.) (plaintiff's participation in fist fight was voluntary and illegal and he had no cause to complain); *Wright v. McLean*, [1956] B.C.J. No. 177, 7 D.L.R. (2d) 253 (B.C.S.C.) (boy was willing participant in mudball fight). On excessive force in general fights outside of sport, see: *Fillipowich v. Nahachewsky*, [1969] S.J. No. 5, 3 D.L.R. (3d) 544 (Sask. Q.B.) (fight ceased to be fair when defendant used a stone); *Lane v. Holloway*, [1968] 1 Q.B. 379 (C.A.) (older man received severe punch after younger man's wife had been told, "Shut up, you monkey-faced tart"); *Walsh v. Buchanan*, [1995] O.J. No. 64, 52 A.C.W.S. (3d) 800 (Ont. Gen. Div.) (excessive force in fight between students).

[284] For an early decision holding a player liable for a blow with the stick to the face, see, *Gagné v. Hébert* (1932), 70 C.S. 454 (Que. S.C.). Archambault J. noted that amateur clubs were following the violent example of the professional game and was not surprised that, "beaucoup de parents sages ne permettent plus à leurs enfants de participer à ces joutes, de crainte qu'ils ne soient estropiés pour la vie"(at 458).

[285] [1965] M.J. No. 24, 54 W.W.R. 302 (Man. Q.B.), affd [1966] M.J. No. 10, 55 W.W.R. 384 (Man. C.A.).

respect to other players...the leave and licence will include an unintentional injury resulting from one of the frequent infractions of the rules of the game.[286]

There are, however, limits to the player's immunity:

But injuries inflicted in circumstances which show a definite resolve to cause serious injury to another, even when there is provocation and in the heat of the game, should not fall within the scope of the implied consent.[287]

The defendant's deliberate retaliatory blow was held to exceed the limit, so that he was found liable for assault; but since the plaintiff had provoked the attack, damages were reduced by one third.[288] Subsequent cases have similarly found hockey[289] and other players[290] liable for intentional violent blows to playing opponents. No liability has been found where the player's action was accidental or instinctive.[291]

Civil actions for assault have been commonly used by amateur or community players injured by deliberate acts that exceeded the implied risk of the game. Among professional players, Marc Tardif sued Rick Jodzio in 1977 with respect to Jodzio's violent attack during a World Hockey Association game in April 1976. Tardif initially sought CDN $150,000 in compensation and settled the case in 1981.[292]

---

[286] *Agar v. Canning*, [1965] M.J. No. 24 at para. 6, 54 W.W.R. 302 (Man. Q.B.).

[287] *Agar v. Canning*, [1965] M.J. No. 24 at para. 8, 54 W.W.R. 302 (Man. C.A.), *per* Bastin J.

[288] There is now authority that provocation mitigates only exemplary and not compensatory damages: *Lane v. Holloway*, [1968] 1 Q.B. 379 (C.A.); *Shaw v. Gorter*, [1977] O.J. No. 2243, 16 O.R. (2d) 19, 2 C.C.L.T. 111 (Ont. C.A.); *Landry v. Patterson*, [1978] O.J. No. 3647, 22 O.R. (2d) 335, 7 C.C.L.T. 202 (Ont. C.A.).

[289] See: *Martin v. Daigle*, [1969] N.B.J. No. 109, 6 D.L.R. (3d) 634 (N.B.C.A.) (punch to mouth); *Pettis v. McNeil*, [1979] N.S.J. No. 560, 8 C.C.L.T. 299 (N.S.S.C.); *Holt v. Verbruggen*, [1981] B.C.J. No. 1427, 20 C.C.L.T. 29 (B.C.S.C.) (arm broken by retaliatory blow with stick; *Leonard v. Dunn*, [2006] O.J. No. 3941, 151 A.C.W.S. (3d) 1172 (Ont. S.C.J.), affd [2008] O.J. No. 2051, 167 A.C.W.S. (3d) 227 (Ont. Div. Ct.); *Leighton v. Best*, [2009] O.J. No. 2145 (Ont. S.C.J.).

[290] See: *Colby v. Schmidt*, [1986] B.C.J. No. 3248, [1986] 6 W.W.R. 65, 37 C.C.L.T. 1 (B.C.S.C.) (late hit in rugby); *Conger v. Gianoli*, [1991] S.J. No. 17, 88 Sask.R. 299 (Sask. Q.B.) (intentional collision in softball); *Dunn v. University of Ottawa*, [1995] O.J. No. 2856, 58 A.C.W.S. (3d) 712 (Ont. Gen. Div.) (hit on punt returner in university football; claim based on intentional infliction of injury and negligence).

[291] See: *Gaudet v. Sullivan*, [1992] N.B.J. No. 503, 128 N.B.R. (2d) 409 (N.B.Q.B.) (blow with stick to mouth not delivered in "deliberate violation of the rules of the game with the intent to injure"); *Knockwood v. Cormier*, [1995] N.B.J. No. 411, 167 N.B.R. (2d) 147 (N.B.Q.B.) (defendant raised stick instinctively without "premeditated intention to cause bodily harm"); *Johnson v. Webb*, [2002] M.J. No. 478, [2003] 1 W.W.R. 415 (Man. C.A.), affg [2002] M.J. No. 54, [2002] 5 W.W.R. 671 (Man. Q.B.) (student did not intentionally body check teacher during recreational no-contact game); *Scott v. Patenaude*, [2009] S.J. No. 309, 2009 SKQB 181 (Sask. Q.B.) (insufficient evidence that stomping in rugby was intentional).

[292] See, "Tardif settles" *The Globe and Mail* (Toronto: May 22, 1981) at 53. On Jodzio's criminal conviction, see, "Struck rival, hockey player fined $3000" *The Globe and Mail* (Toronto: August 18, 1977) at 40.

## b.   *Negligence*

Sports participants agree to the ordinary hazards of the activity, including the risk of stray blows, inadvertence by opponents and expected rule infractions. This acceptance of risk applies to those who take part in organized games and does not extend to uninvolved bystanders. It is, for example, negligent to fire slap shots on a public rink when they are likely to strike unsuspecting skaters standing near the goal.[293] Although the participants impliedly consent to the normal or inherent risks, they are subject to a duty of care towards fellow players and may be liable in negligence for injury-causing conduct that in all the circumstances is unreasonable.

Negligence is a flexible tool capable of embracing the action in different sports.[294] Negligence by players may take the form of serious foul play, dangerous hits or other misconduct in breach of rules or customs that shows unreasonable disregard for safety. The duty of care begins prior to the game, although a player may be able to show that an incident was merely an unfortunate accident involving no negligence. In *King v. Redlich*,[295] the defendant was found not liable for hitting an opponent with a puck that deflected off an empty goal during a warm-up in recreational hockey. The plaintiff was struck in the temple, having taken to the ice without his helmet. Pre-game practice shots were customary in the league, and it was held that there had been no breach of the standard of care appropriate to this level of play. The defendant did not deliberately shoot at the plaintiff and had allowed him to skate away from the goal before the puck took its random deflection off the post.

Compared to more sedate activities that allow time to consider and room to manoeuvre, hockey presents difficulties in defining the standard of due care. The speed of play may also make it hard to prove negligence in a particular case. Hockey necessarily involves vigorous banging around with sticks and pucks in the confines of the rink, so that players cannot be expected to show the measured courtesy of the golf course or croquet lawn:

---

[293]  See, *Daigneault c. Gallant*, [2009] J.Q. no 621, 2009 QCCS 297 (Que. S.C.) (*lancer frappé* by 15-year-old struck 9-year-old in the face; award of CDN $44,000 in damages).

[294]  See, for example: *Ratcliffe v. Whitehead*, [1933] M.J. No. 49, [1933] 3 W.W.R. 447 (Man. Q.B.) (golf); *Ellison v. Rogers*, [1967] O.J. No. 1151, [1968] 1 O.R. 501, 67 D.L.R. (2d) 21 (Ont. H.C.J.) (golf); *Rootes v. Shelton* (1967), 116 C.L.R. 383 (H.C. of Aust.) (waterskiing); *Fink v. Greeniaus*, [1973] O.J. No. 2283, 2 O.R. (2d) 541, 43 D.L.R. (3d) 485 (Ont. H.C.J.) (skiing); *Ryan v. Hickson*, [1974] O.J. No. 2251, 7 O.R. (2d) 352, 55 D.L.R. (3d) 196 (Ont. H.C.J.) (snowmobiling); *Condon v. Basi*, [1985] 2 All E.R. 453, [1985] 1 W.L.R. 866 (C.A.) (soccer); *Johnston v. Frazer* (1990), 21 N.S.W.L.R. 89 (C.A.) (horse race); *Dyck v. Laidlaw*, [2000] A.J. No. 730, [2000] 9 W.W.R. 517, 82 Alta. L.R. (3d) 60 (Alta. Q.B.) (skydiving). On risk and assumption of risk in sport, see Chapter 4, "Build Safe: Rink Management and Risk Management", sections A, 1, 2.

[295]  [1984] B.C.J. No. 2793, [1984] 6 W.W.R. 705, 30 C.C.L.T. 247 (B.C.S.C.), affd [1985] B.C.J. No. 2489, [1986] 4 W.W.R. 567, 24 D.L.R. (4th) 636, 35 C.C.L.T. 201 (B.C.C.A.) (defendant perceived the risk, delayed the shot and could not foresee the ricochet). On negligence in the dressing room, see, *Williams v. Froese*, [1984] S.J. No. 839, 36 Sask.R. 275 (Sask. Q.B.) (14-year-old lost eye in tape ball fight at hockey school; defendant negligent in throwing tape).

The conduct of a [hockey] player in the heat of the game is instinctive and unpremeditated and should not be judged by standards suited to polite social intercourse.[296]

While an overly scrupulous standard might destroy the nature of the game, it is possible to envisage want of due care: an obvious form of fault is for the player to take to the ice with dangerous or defective equipment that is likely to injure other skaters. Canadian courts recognize that there can be negligence on the rink, but there are conflicting opinions about the degree of carelessness required and the mental element associated with the defendant's conduct. (American courts have also grappled with the problem.[297]) The judicial altercation over the standard of care comes from cases involving blows or collisions during the action of the game.[298] Players in British Columbia accept the risk of minor body contact in breach of the rules,[299] but may sue for unintended injuries under a general standard of negligence.[300] Life is rougher east of the Rockies, so that hockey plaintiffs in other Provinces have to show that they were on the receiving end of a bit extra.[301]

The west coast standard was spelled out in two cases from the 1990s involving catastrophic injuries to young players. In *Unruh v. Webber*,[302] the defendant Midget AA player was found liable for an intentional hit from behind that propelled the 17-year-old plaintiff into the boards breaking his

---

[296] *Agar v. Canning*, [1965] M.J. No. 24 at para. 7, 54 W.W.R. 302 (Man. Q.B.), *per* Bastin J.

[297] See: *Nabozny v. Barnhill*, 334 N.E.2d 258 (App.Ct. Ill.,1975) (kick to head in soccer; liability requires conduct that is "deliberate, wilful or with a reckless disregard for the safety of the other player"(at 261)); *Hackbart v. Cincinnati Bengals, Inc.*, 601 F.2d 516 (10th Cir., 1979) (hit to head in professional football; "recklessness is the appropriate standard" (at 524)); *Gauvin v. Clark*, 537 N.E.2d 94 (Mass. 1989) (butt-end in hockey; liability requires reckless misconduct); *Babych v. McRae*, 567 A. 2d 1269 (Sup.Ct. Conn., 1989) (blow with stick in professional hockey; liability in negligence is actionable); *McKichan v. St. Louis Hockey Club, L.P.*, 967 S.W. 2d 209 (C.A. Mo., 1998) ("a severe body check is a part of professional hockey ... [and] not actionable" (at 213)). See also, R. Yasser, "In the Heat of Competition: Tort Liability of One Participant to Another; Why Can't Participants Be Required to Be Reasonable?" (1995) 5 Seton Hall J. of Sport *L.* 253.

[298] See: G.M. Moore, "Has Hockey Been 'Checked from Behind' North of the Border? *Unruh, Zapf*, and Canada's Participant Liability Standard" (1996) 18 Loy.L.A. Int'l. & Comp. L.J. 641; J.A. Citron & M. Ableman, "Civil Liability in the Arena of Professional Sports" (2003) 36 U.B.C.L. Rev. 193 at 201-09.

[299] See, *Roy v. Canadian Oldtimers' Hockey Assn.* [1997] B.C.J. No. 262, 68 A.C.W.S. (3d) 1185 (B.C.C.A.), affg [1994] B.C.J. No. 1644, 49 A.C.W.S. (3d) 413 (B.C.S.C.) (player not liable for injuries caused by deliberate minor body check in non-contact tournament).

[300] See, *Herok v. Wegrzanowski*, [1985] B.C.J. No. 1778 (B.C.C.A.) (plaintiff suffered facial injuries in "fun league"; defendant liable for swing of stick).

[301] In Quebec, see, for example, *Canuel c. Sauvageau*, [1991] J.Q. no 57, 25 A.C.W.S. (3d) 386 (Que. C.A.) (defendant not liable for injury caused by collision in ball game on ice), leave to appeal refused, [1991] C.S.C.R. no 123 (S.C.C.).

[302] [1994] B.C.J. No. 467, [1994] 5 W.W.R. 270, 112 D.L.R. (4th) 83 (B.C.C.A.), affg [1992] B.C.J. No. 2336, 98 D.L.R. (4th) 294 (B.C.S.C.).

neck and rendering him a quadriplegic. The trial judge found that the defendant did not mean to inflict injury but was well aware that the check was illegal under the rules and might well have disastrous results; the defendant was "reckless" in running the substantial risk of injury. The British Columbia Court of Appeal confirmed that the principles of negligence applied and approved the following statement as to the applicable standard:

> The standard of care test is — *what would a reasonable competitor, in his place, do or not do.* The words "in his place" imply the need to consider the speed, the amount of body contact and the stresses in the sport, as well as the risks the players might reasonably be expected to take during the game, acting within the spirit of the game and according to standards of fair play. A breach of the rules may be one element in that issue but not necessarily definitive of the issue.[303]

*Unruh v. Webber* was followed in *Zapf v. Muckalt,*[304] where a Junior A player suffered quadriplegia after being checked from behind and propelled head first into the end boards. The British Columbia Court of Appeal again held that liability in negligence did not require proof that the injury was inflicted intentionally or recklessly. The test to be applied was whether the conduct exceeded the assumed risks and whether it failed to conform to what a "reasonable competitor" would do in the circumstances.

In cases decided in Manitoba, Ontario and Nova Scotia,[305] courts have adapted the standard in *Agar v. Canning*[306] and have held that negligence between players requires proof of an intention to injure[307] or "reckless disregard for the consequences...in an uncontrolled and undisciplined manner".[308] The plaintiff

---

[303] *Ibid.,* at W.W.R. 285, 112 D.L.R. 96.

[304] [1996] B.C.J. No. 2402, [1997] 1 W.W.R. 617, [1997] 2 W.W.R. 645, 142 D.L.R. (4th) 438, 31 C.C.L.T. (2d) 201 (B.C.C.A.), affg [1995] B.C.J. No. 1882, [1996] 1 W.W.R. 175, 26 C.C.L.T. (2d) 61 (B.C.S.C.); leave to appeal refused [1997] S.C.C.A. No. 76 (S.C.C.). See also, *Wilson v. Haddock,* [1999] B.C.J. No. 2198, 1999 BCCA 552 (B.C.C.A.), revg [1998] B.C.J. No. 1036, [1998] 10 W.W.R. 660, 50 B.C.L.R. (3d) 325 (B.C.S.C.) (collision in softball).

[305] See, *Matheson v. Dalhousie University and College,* [1983] N.S.J. No. 86, 25 C.C.L.T. 91, 57 N.S.R. (2d) 56 (N.S.T.D.) (wrestler with knee injury suffered broken ankle in warm-up game of borden ball; coach not liable for heel trip).

[306] [1965] M.J. No. 24, 54 W.W.R. 302 (Man. Q.B.), affd [1966] M.J. No. 10, 55 W.W.R. 384 (Man. C.A.).

[307] See: *Temple v. Hallem,* [1989] M.J. No. 203, [1989] 5 W.W.R. 669, 58 D.L.R. (4th) 541 (Man. C.A.) (collision in softball; no breach of the rules and risk accepted); *Champagne v. Cummings,* [1999] O.J. No. 3081, 90 A.C.W.S. (3d) 503 (Ont. S.C.J.) (injury in recreational hockey; hit was not a "retaliatory blow, struck in anger" (at para. 7) and defendant did not intend "to strike the plaintiff with his stick or to injure him" (at para. 10)). See also, *Johnson v. Webb,* [2002] M.J. No. 478, [2003] 1 W.W.R. 415, 170 Man.R. (2d) 58 (Man. C.A.), affg [2002] M.J. No. 54, [2002] 5 W.W.R. 671, 162 Man.R. (2d) 48 (Man. Q.B.).

[308] *Dunn v. University of Ottawa,* [1995] O.J. No. 2856 at para. 36, 58 A.C.W.S. (3d) 712 (Ont. Gen. Div.), *per* Cunningham J. The punt returner in football who is looking up for the ball does not "consent to being headbutted or speared in the face by an on-rushing 225 pound linebacker

must, therefore, show elements beyond ordinary negligence, and no liability has been found in cases involving injuries from a body check[309] and batting a player away with the stick.[310] One case in Ontario has applied the "reasonable competitor" standard, while holding that a stick check is a legitimate tactic in a recreational game:

> The no-contact nature of the match does not eliminate the inherent dangers of the sport of ice hockey. Players will inevitably collide, sticks will inevitably clash, pucks will fly in unforeseen directions.[311]

The more tolerant standard of Manitoba[312] and points east reflects legitimate concerns about inhibiting robust play, discouraging participation and increasing the incidence and costs of liability. It does, however, involve a mingling of negligence with concepts that belong to the realm of intentional torts. Conceptual purity and safety considerations make the general negligence standard preferable, and there is no reason to anticipate that the ice will be strewn with torts. The negligence standard recognizes that players accept inherent risks, and the care required can take account of the general context of rough, physical play. A requirement of reasonable care in the circumstances best serves the goals of injury prevention and the promotion of fair play.

### c.    Liability of Teams and Vicarious Liability

Players[313] injured by deliberate acts of violence have often attempted to hold organizations such as teams responsible for the conduct of their employee.[314] The plaintiff may allege complicity in the assault in that a coach directed, encouraged or condoned it[315] or may claim that a team was negligent in failing to supervise a

---

while in that vulnerable position" (at para. 40). See also, *Seaton v. Gagnon,* [1997] O.J. No. 3982, 74 A.C.W.S. (3d) 399 (Ont. Gen. Div.) (collision in soccer).

[309] See, *Sexton v. Sutherland,* [1991] O.J. No. 624, 26 A.C.W.S. (3d) 472 (Ont. Gen. Div.).

[310] See, *St. Laurent v. Bartley,* [1998] M.J. No. 159, [1998] 8 W.W.R. 373 (Man. Q.B.) (plaintiff lost an eye in industrial league where play was aggressive and competitive; liability requires proof of intention, recklessness or negligence; standard of a "reasonable competitor in his place" also noted ).

[311] *Nichols v. Sibbick,* [2005] O.J. No. 2873 at para. 18, 140 A.C.W.S. (3d) 768 (Ont. S.C.J.), *per* Milanetti J. (plaintiff lost an eye when struck by stick in recreational league).

[312] See, P.H. Osborne, "A Review of Tort Decisions in Manitoba, 1989" (1990) 19 Man. L. J. 419 at 432-41, discussing *Temple v. Hallem,* [1989] M.J. No. 203, [1989] 5 W.W.R. 669, 58 D.L.R. (4th) 541 (Man. C.A.), leave to appeal to S.C.C. refused [1989] S.C.C.A. No. 450 (S.C.C).

[313] On allegations brought by persons associated with an adult entertainment lounge see, *Cimpean v. Payton,* [2008] O.J. No. 2665, 168 A.C.W.S. (3d) 445 (Ont. S.C.J.) (claims against players, the Milwaukee Bucks and the NBA).

[314] See: *Lachance v. Bonsant,* [1983] C.S. 596 (team and coach not liable when broomball player attacked opponent); *Gaudet v. Sullivan,* [1992] N.B.J. No. 503, 128 N.B.R. (2d) 409 (N.B.Q.B.) (coach and team sponsor not liable for cross-check); *McKichan v. St. Louis Hockey Club, L.P.,* 967 S.W. 2d 209 (C.A.Mo., 1998) (team owner not liable for body check).

[315] See, *Canterbury Bankstown Rugby League Football Club Ltd. v. Rogers* (1993) Aust. Torts Reports ¶81-246 (N.S.W.C.A.), where Mahoney J. considered the "Influence of the Coach" (at 62, 543-44), including the possibility that the coach might instruct players to use illegal tactics or might have them "revved up" so as to make blows to the head likely.

player of known violent tendencies.[316] This form of liability serves the useful purpose of extending responsibility to the controlling organization and improves the plaintiff's prospects of financial recovery in that the corporate defendant may have a deeper pocket.

Even though there was no precise instruction to deliver a blow or hit, a team can be vicariously liable for violent play that was closely related to the employee's duties so as to be within the scope of the employment.[317] As noted in Chapter 5, "Be Safe: Off the Ice", the Supreme Court of Canada has held that an organization can be strictly liable for sexual abuse when the employee's position and empowerment in the enterprise materially increase the risk of assault.[318] The team that puts a designated enforcer on the ice is certainly enhancing opportunities for violence, and the assaults are committed on behalf of and for the benefit of the team enterprise. Marty McSorley was, for example, doing his job for the Boston Bruins when he made his ill-fated attempt to engage Donald Brashear.[319] It is open to the injured player to seek compensation from the opposing team "where the wrongful act is *sufficiently related* to conduct authorized by the employer...and may have furthered the employer's aims".[320] The strategic attack is a clear case, but vicarious liability may also extend to spontaneous assaults on behalf of the team or even negligent acts that help the cause by disabling a troublesome opponent.

### d.    *Moore v. Bertuzzi et al.*

Steve Moore has launched civil proceedings against Todd Bertuzzi and other defendants with respect to Bertuzzi's assault during the game in Vancouver on

---

[316] See, A.J. Turro, "Tort Liability in Professional Sports" (1980) 44 Albany L. Rev. 696, at 706-18, discussing *Tomjanowich v. California Sports Inc.* See also: *Olinski v. Johnson*, [1997] O.J. No. 926, 32 O.R. (3d) 653 (Ont. C.A.) (occupiers and coach liable for attacks on lacrosse referees); *Dunn v. University of Ottawa*, [1995] O.J. No. 2856, 58 A.C.W.S. (3d) 712 (Ont. Gen. Div.) (football coach not negligent); *Johnson v. Webb*, [2002] M.J. No. 478, [2003] 1 W.W.R. 415, 170 Man.R. (2d) 58 (Man. C.A.), affg [2002] M.J. No. 54, [2002] 5 W.W.R. 671, 162 Man.R. (2d) 48 (Man. Q.B.) (school not liable).

[317] See: *Canterbury Bankstown Rugby League Football Club Ltd. v. Rogers* (1993), Aust. Torts Reports ¶81-246 (N.S.W.C.A.) (team vicariously liable for blow and head-high tackle; such tackle assisted the team and was a "well recognized" event and "not infrequent" (at 62,551)); *Gravil v. Carroll*, [2008] EWCA Civ 689 (C.A.) (punch in rugby).

[318] See Chapter 5, "Be Safe: Off the Ice", section C, 2, referring to *Bazley v. Curry*, [1999] S.C.J. No. 35, [1999] 2 S.C.R. 534 (S.C.C.) and *Jacobi v. Griffiths*, [1999] S.C.J. No. 36, [1999] 2 S.C.R. 570 (S.C.C.).

[319] See, *R. v. McSorley*, [2000] B.C.J. No. 1993, 2000 BCPC 116 (B.C. Prov. Ct.); [2000] B.C.J. No. 1994, 2000 BCPC 117 (B.C. Prov. Ct.), discussed at Chapter 6, "Play Safe: On the Ice", sections B, 3, 4.

[320] *Bazley v. Curry*, [1999] S.C.J. No. 35, [1999] 2 S.C.R. 534 at 559-60 (S.C.C.), *per* McLachlin J. See, *Reddemann v. McEachnie*, [2005] B.C.J. No. 1374, 2005 BCSC 915 (B.C.S.C.) (coach's attack on mascot was not related to authorized conduct).

March 8, 2004.[321] Moore's ability to participate in hockey was effectively terminated when he suffered injuries that included fractures to two bones associated with vertebrae in the neck. The case is potentially an important precedent in relation to the liability of professional players and their employers and offers the opportunity to assess the substantial loss of income when a career ends prematurely.

Moore initially brought suit in Colorado, claiming that the state had jurisdiction because of his residence as a player with the Avalanche and because the animosity against him had its origins in the game in Denver when Markus Naslund was injured. This action was dismissed in 2005 when a court in Colorado held that British Columbia bears the most significant relationship to Moore's claims.[322] Moore then filed suit in the Ontario Superior Court[323] and the British Columbia Supreme Court[324] claiming CDN $15 million in lost wages, CDN $1 million in aggravated damages, CDN $2 million in punitive damages and CDN $1.5 million for mental distress caused to his parents. The action has proceeded in Ontario against Bertuzzi and Orca Bay Hockey LP, the former owners of the Vancouver Canucks, and the claim has been amended to ask for CDN $38 million. Bertuzzi has named the Canucks' head coach Marc Crawford as a third party who should share responsibility because of an alleged direction that Moore should "pay the price". To avoid further adverse publicity, the NHL has arranged meetings with representatives of the parties in an attempt to reach a settlement.[325]

As an accompaniment to this litigation, Brian Burke, the former general manager of the Canucks, has brought an action in defamation against the *New York Post*, denying the suggestions that on March 8, 2004 he "personally challenged" his players to "get" Moore and that he was a participant "in the plot to retaliate". The British Columbia Supreme Court has held that the Province has jurisdiction to hear this case and is the convenient forum.[326]

---

[321] See, *R. v. Bertuzzi*, [2004] B.C.J. No. 2692, 26 C.R. (6th) 71 (B.C. Prov. Ct.), discussed at Chapter 6, "Play Safe: On the Ice", section B, 4. See also, P.K. Thornton, "Rewriting Hockey's Unwritten Rules: *Moore v. Bertuzzi*" (2009) 61 Maine L. Rev. 206.

[322] See, "US court won't hear Moore's lawsuit against Bertuzzi" *The Globe and Mail* (Toronto: October 14, 2005) at R7 (decision of Denver District Judge Shelley Gilman).

[323] See: "Moore files lawsuit against Bertuzzi" *The Globe and Mail* (Toronto: February 16, 2006) at R6; "He must pay the price" *The Globe and Mail* (Toronto: December 6, 2007) at A1, A8; "Crawford brought into Moore lawsuit" *The Globe and Mail* (Toronto: March 29, 2008) at S3; *Moore v. Bertuzzi*, [2007] O.J. No. 5113, 88 O.R. (3d) 499 (Ont. S.C.J.) (access to discovery transcripts); *Moore v. Bertuzzi*, [2008] O.J. No. 347, 164 A.C.W.S. (3d) 609 (Ont. S.C.J.) (motion to amend statement of claim).

[324] See: "Moore fires another legal salvo at Bertuzzi" *The Globe and Mail* (Toronto: March 8, 2006); "Bertuzzi's lawyers to ask for change of venue in Moore lawsuit" *The Globe and Mail* (Toronto: April 26, 2006).

[325] See, "Bettman to try to get out-of-court settlement in Moore's lawsuit" *The Globe and Mail* (Toronto: December 15, 2006) at R6. The initial offer was CDN $350,000.

[326] See, *Burke v. NYP Holdings, Inc.*, [2005] B.C.J. No. 1993, 48 B.C.L.R. (4th) 363 (B.C.S.C.) (plaintiff could sue in British Columbia because newspaper was available on website).

## 3.    Liability of Facility Operators

Where it is alleged that a player's injury was caused by the defective condition of
the rink or some other failure to exercise due care in the operation of a program, the
player may bring action under the law of occupiers' liability or in negligence. As
noted in Chapter 4, "Build Safe: Rink Management and Risk Management",
occupiers' liability relates to the duties owed to persons entering premises, whether
playing participants, spectators or other visitors.[327] Occupiers' liability is subject to
special legislation in most Provinces, while Saskatchewan retains the common law
rules. In Ontario, section 3(1) of the *Occupiers' Liability Act*[328] requires the person
or organization in control of premises to exercise reasonable care in the
circumstances for the safety of visitors. This duty applies to both the condition of
the premises and to the activity carried on (see, s. 3(2)), but does not apply to risks
that are "willingly assumed" (see, s. 4(1)). In *Christie v. Toronto (City)*,[329] it was
held that there was an assumption of risk when an experienced player knew of
dangerous ice conditions but willingly continued to play. It may, however, be
doubted whether the player accepted the legal risk and absolved the defendant by
waiving legal rights. It has now been held that the defence in section 4(1) requires
the defendant to show that the plaintiff fully accepted the known risks and agreed to
give up any cause of action.[330]

The participant at a facility is entitled to a reasonable standard of safety[331]
with respect to the physical condition of the premises and the organization of
activities.[332] The player accepts the inherent risks of hockey and has no cause
for complaint because ice is slippery, wet[333] or affected by minor cuts or
blemishes.[334] There may, however, be liability with respect to serious defects
in the rink such as holes in the ice surface,[335] insufficient thickness of the ice[336]

---

[327] See Chapter 4, "Build Safe: Rink Management and Risk Management", sections A, 3, 4; B.

[328] R.S.O. 1990, c. O.2.

[329] [1983] O.J. No. 2443, 20 M.P.L.R. 145 (Ont. Co. Ct.).

[330] See, *Waldick v. Malcolm*, [1991] S.C.J. No. 55, [1991] 2 S.C.R. 456 (S.C.C.).

[331] Perfection is not required; see, *Buis v. Centennial Arena Commission*, [1994] N.S.J. No. 589,
136 N.S.R. (2d) 33 (N.S.S.C.) (contractual visitor; player alleged that he hit protrusion at exit
gate at boards; action dismissed).

[332] On the general responsibilities of program operators, see, J. Barnes, *Sports and the Law in Canada*, 3d ed. (Toronto: Butterworths, 1996) at 292-95.

[333] See, *Tobin v. Avalon Consolidated School Board of Education*, [1992] N.J. No. 197, 98 Nfld. &
P.E.I.R. 331 (Nfld. T.D.) (contractual visitor; ice was soft and wet but reasonably fit for the purpose; others continued to play after plaintiff fell). In *Drodge v. St. John's Young Men's and
Young Women's Christian Assn.*, [1987] N.J. No. 357, 67 Nfld. & P.E.I.R. 57 (Nfld. T.D.), the
defendant was found liable when a player fell in a pool of water on a gymnasium floor used for
floor hockey.

[334] See, *Quenville v. Ratter (Township)* (1984), 28 A.C.W.S. (2d) 464 (Ont. Dist. Ct.).

[335] See: *Stein v. Sandwich West (Township)*, [1995] O.J. No. 423, 25 M.P.L.R. (2d) 170 (Ont. C.A.)
(fall head first into boards resulted in quadriplegia; CDN $8.5 million in damages); *Brinco v.
Milton (Town)*, [2000] O.J. No. 4474, 101 A.C.W.S. (3d) 651 (Ont. S.C.J.) (skate caught in
gouge in ice; inferior maintenance for pick-up games). See also, *Blondeau (Litigation guardian*

or dangerous boards or other standing equipment.[337] Ice should be prepared and maintained[338] according to an acceptable business standard, and the rink should operate a reasonable system of inspection and cleaning.[339] The skater is entitled to a smoother glide at a modern indoor facility, as compared to the rougher surface to be expected at a natural outdoor rink offered by a public authority. The obligation to maintain reasonable safety extends to floors, structures and equipment in accessible areas of the facility such as locker rooms and walkways.[340]

Besides maintaining its physical plant, a facility has the responsibility to supervise activities[341] and prevent participation by those who are a danger to themselves or others.[342] Particular dangers may arise from conflicting uses of the ice surface. In *Moran v. Sault Ste. Marie (City)*,[343] the city failed to enforce a notice and schedule that prescribed "no hockey during free skating" and was held liable when a puck shot by a youth hit a small child on the head. Where a facility hires out skates or other equipment, it should ensure that the equipment is reasonably safe in accordance with business practice.[344] The facility may also be required to give appropriate instructions about use.[345]

---

*of) v. Peterborough (City)*, [1998] O.J. No. 3428, 82 A.C.W.S. (3d) 207 (Ont. Gen. Div.) (figure skater fell in depression left by goal post hole).

[336] See, *Stein v. Sandwich West (Township)*, [1995] O.J. No. 423, 25 M.P.L.R. (2d) 170 (Ont. C.A.) (need for separate flooding of the goal crease areas to counteract thinning caused by Zamboni).

[337] See, *Bilawchuk v. Prince George (City)*, [2000] B.C.J. No. 2053, 100 A.C.W.S. (3d) 175 (B.C.C.A.), affg [1998] B.C.J. No. 2934, 85 A.C.W.S. (3d) 205 (B.C.S.C.) (player's hand caught in wire mesh fence and poorly secured supporting pipes).

[338] See: *Christie v. Toronto (City)*, [1983] O.J. No. 2443, 20 M.P.L.R. 145 (Ont. Co. Ct.) (plaintiff hit rut in snow-covered ice; heavily used ice was in deplorable condition since Zamboni had broken down); *Herman v. London (City)*, [1996] O.J. No. 3097, 34 M.P.L.R. (2d) 222 (Ont. Gen. Div.) (defendant had systematic maintenance procedures).

[339] See: *Potozny v. Burnaby (City)*, [2001] B.C.J. No. 1224, 23 M.P.L.R. (3d) 100 (B.C.S.C.) (skater fell in "winter wonderland"; failure to clean tree debris from ice surface); *Roper v. Nanaimo (City)*, [2006] B.C.J. No. 3099, 28 M.P.L.R. (4th) 213 (B.C.S.C.) (claim that roller rink was littered with candies; rink was properly patrolled).

[340] On injuries suffered by spectators and other visitors, see Chapter 4, "Build Safe: Rink Management and Risk Management", section B.

[341] On collisions between skaters, see: *Mar v. Tokaryk* (1982), 14 A.C.W.S. (2d) 123 (B.C.S.C.) (figure skaters); *Rampersaud v. 386697 Ontario Ltd.* (1987), 8 A.C.W.S. (3d) 189 (Ont. H.C.J.) (roller rink); *Leslie v. Mississauga (City)*, [2006] O.J. No. 2927, 81 O.R. (3d) 415 (Ont. Div. Ct.), revg [2003] O.J. No. 4410, 43 M.P.L.R. (3d) 274 (Ont. S.C.J.), affg [2003] O.J. No. 1188, 37 M.P.L.R. (3d) 211 (Ont. S.C.J.) (collision with patroller).

[342] See, *Crocker v. Sundance Northwest Resorts Ltd.*, [1988] S.C.J. No. 60, [1988] 1 S.C.R. 1186 (S.C.C.) (organizers had duty to exclude drunken competitor from tubing race at ski hill).

[343] [1967] O.J. No. 979, [1967] 2 O.R. 105, 62 D.L.R. (2d) 452 (Ont. C.A.). See also, *Blondeau (Litigation guardian of) v. Peterborough (City)*, [1998] O.J. No. 3428, 82 A.C.W.S. (3d) 207 (Ont. Gen. Div.).

[344] See, *MacLeod v. Roe*, [1947] S.C.J. No. 20, [1947] S.C.R. 420 (S.C.C.) (roller-skates were in good condition and made by well-known manufacturer).

[345] See, *Rozenhart v. Skier's Sport Shop (Edmonton) Ltd.*, [2002] A.J. No. 1063, [2003] 5 W.W.R. 534, 15 C.C.L.T. (3d) 239 (Alta. Q.B.), affd [2004] A.J. No. 582, [2004] 9 W.W.R. 527, 26 C.C.L.T. (3d) 109 (Alta. C.A.) (shop renting in-line skates negligently represented that in-line skating was "very similar" to ice skating).

The responsibility to maintain safe conditions falls primarily to the owner or operator, rather than to individuals or groups who temporarily hire the rink. The person who arranges the rental on behalf of a group of adults does not normally have a contractual obligation to fellow players to inspect the facility, supervise play or check the thickness of the ice by drilling holes in it.[346]

## 4. Liability of Instructors and Supervisors

### a. *Teachers and Coaches*

It is the common law duty of a school[347] teacher to supervise in the manner of a careful or prudent parent.[348] This standard applies to the organization and control of general school activities and sports programs, although the gymnastics teacher is bound to show "supraparental expertise."[349] The careful parent standard is flexible and requires reasonable care in the circumstances:

> Its application will vary from case to case and will depend upon the number of students being supervised at any given time, the nature of the exercise or activity in progress, the age and the degree of skill and training which the students may have received in connection with such activity, the nature and condition of the equipment in use at the time, the competency and capacity of the students involved, and a host of other matters which may be widely varied but which, in any given case, may affect the application of the prudent parent-standard to the conduct of the school authority in the circumstances.[350]

One responsibility of the school is to try to prevent fights between students and promptly break up any fisticuffs that do occur. In *Walsh v. Buchanan*,[351] a school was found to have exercised proper supervision and control when an altercation that began in a non-contact floor hockey game was later resumed in

---

[346] See, *Griffiths v. New Westminster (City)*, [2001] B.C.J. No. 2274, 25 M.P.L.R. (3d) 31 (B.C.S.C.).

[347] On the liability of school boards and teachers, see: J. Barnes, *Sports and the Law in Canada*, 3d ed. (Toronto: Butterworths, 1996) at 296-302; A.F. Brown & M.A. Zuker, *Education Law*, 3d ed. (Toronto: Carswell, 2002) at 77-148; A.W. McKay & L. Sutherland, *Teachers and the Law*, 2d ed. (Toronto: Emond Montgomery, 2006) at 1-41.

[348] See, *Myers v. Peel County Board of Education*, [1981] S.C.J. No. 61, [1981] 2 S.C.R. 21 (S.C.C.).

[349] See, *Thornton v. Prince George Board of Education*, [1976] B.C.J. No. 1390, [1976] 5 W.W.R. 240 at 265, 73 D.L.R. (3d) 35 at 57 (B.C.C.A.), *per* Carrothers J.A. On injuries in gymnastics, see also, *MacCabe v. Westlock Roman Catholic Separate School District No. 110*, [2001] A.J. No. 1278, [2002] 1 W.W.R. 610, 9 C.C.L.T. (3d) 259 (Alta. C.A.).

[350] *Myers v. Peel County Board of Education*, [1981] S.C.J. No. 61, [1981] 2 S.C.R. 21 at 32 (S.C.C.), *per* McIntyre J. A parent is also subject to supervisory responsibilities and may be liable for injuries that are attributable to a lack of care and control. See also, *Daigneault c. Gallant*, [2009] J.Q. no 621, 2009 QCCS 297 (Que. S.C.) (15-year-old struck 9-year-old with a slap shot on a public rink; parent was not in breach of duty in article 1459 of the *Code civil du Québec*).

[351] [1995] O.J. No. 64, 52 A.C.W.S. (3d) 800 (Ont. Gen. Div.).

a hallway outside a classroom. The court found that the floor hockey league was "prudently and carefully organized" and found no negligence by staff members in relation to the further outbreak of violence that resulted in injuries to the student.

In *Thornton v. Prince George Board of Education*,[352] dealing with somersaulting from a springboard in a Grade X physical education class, Carrothers J.A. formulated four tests for reviewing whether the teacher and school exercised reasonable care in selecting and supervising an activity.[353] The tests are SPES: Suitability, Progression, Equipment and Supervision. Liability follows if there is a negative answer to any one of the following questions:

i. Was the attempted exercise suitable to the student's age and condition (mental and physical)?

ii. Was the student progressively trained and coached to do this exercise properly and avoid the danger?

iii. Was the equipment adequate and suitably arranged?

iv. Was the performance properly supervised?

The standard developed in the cases against school teachers and school boards has been applied to instruction provided to adults in recreational or commercial programs.[354] In any context where the participant relies on the experience and expertise of the instructor, there is an obligation to maintain reasonable safety according to the known risks of the activity. In the case of a volunteer coach assisting in a selection match in rugby, it has been held that the standard is not as exacting as the "careful or prudent parent", but the coach is required to show "ordinary skill and care", which involves following the laws of the game and observing safety guidelines.[355] Teachers and coaches must, in particular, maintain current knowledge about the risk of injury in the sport, including the circumstances that may lead to spinal injury.[356]

Although the duties of instructors have been considered in relation to other sports, there are relatively few cases brought against hockey coaches alleging

---

[352] [1976] B.C.J. No. 1390, [1976] 5 W.W.R. 240, 73 D.L.R. (3d) 35 (B.C.C.A.), vard [1978] S.C.J. No. 7, [1978] 2 S.C.R. 267 (S.C.C.).

[353] See, *Thornton v. Prince George Board of Education*, [1976] B.C.J. No. 1390, [1976] 5 W.W.R. 240 at 265-70, 73 D.L.R. (3d) 35 at 58-61 (B.C.C.A.), vard [1978] S.C.J. No. 7, [1978] 2 S.C.R. 267 (S.C.C.).

[354] See, for example, *Smith v. Horizon Aero Sports Ltd.*, [1981] B.C.J. No. 1861, 19 C.C.L.T. 89, 130 D.L.R. (3d) 91 (B.C.S.C.) (sport parachute jumping).

[355] See, *Hamstra v. British Columbia Rugby Union*, [1989] B.C.J. No. 1521, 1 C.C.L.T. (2d) 78 (B.C.S.C.), revd on other grounds [1995] B.C.J. No. 633, 123 D.L.R. (4th) 693 (B.C.C.A.), revd [1997] S.C.J. No. 43, [1997] 1 S.C.R. 1092 (S.C.C.) (alleged mismatching of players in scrum; sole cause of collapse was plaintiff's loss of balance).

[356] See, *Hamstra v. British Columbia Rugby Union*, [1989] B.C.J. No. 1521, 1 C.C.L.T. (2d) 78 at 85 (B.C.S.C.). See also, *Watson v. Haynes* (1987), Aust. Torts Reports ¶80-094 (N.S.W.C.A.) (duty of government department to advise of risk of neck injury).

negligence in teaching or supervision. Various reasons may go to explain this gap in the litigation. There has been a generous acceptance of risk in hockey, the coach is likely to be a volunteer, and claims can be settled under the Hockey Canada insurance policy.[357] Furthermore, games are usually organized by associations rather than schools. Except for *Walsh v. Buchanan*, an injury to a teacher[358] and cases relating to field hockey,[359] there is no pattern of reported decisions involving the liability of school boards. The characteristic sources of hockey injuries also tend to explain the shortage. Hockey injuries usually occur in the course of games, as opposed to practice drills where the coach has a clear responsibility to select safe routines and to provide proper organization and supervision.[360] During games, matters are largely out of the coach's hands, and the direct cause of injury is likely to be a hit, a collision or the state of the rink. The typical defendant is the opposing player or the facility, although coaches might be implicated where it is alleged that they incited violence. Other common sources of liability include hothead behaviour by spectators and cases of harassment or abuse.[361] The hockey coach has recognized duties in relation to fair play and ethical conduct, but there is a lack of decisions discussing responsibilities as a teacher of playing technique.

In spite of this absence of direct authority, the principles in *Thornton* can be applied to hockey instructors. The precise responsibilities will vary according to the circumstances and the age and experience of the group being supervised. Practice drills, playing techniques and other demands must be suitable to the age, skill level and medical condition of the players. Proper conditioning and medical check-ups are advisable, and players must not be forced to continue when injured, exhausted or otherwise incapable. The premature teaching of body checking is one potential source of liability,[362] as is excessive playing time caused by an overly demanding schedule or the limited availability of players caused by a "short bench". The competition is also "unsuitable" when players are up against opponents who are twice their size.[363] Careful progression is required in the acquisition of skills and safety techniques, so that players should

---

[357] See Chapter 4, "Build Safe: Rink Management and Risk Management", section D.

[358] See, *Johnson v. Webb*, [2002] M.J. No. 478, [2003] 1 W.W.R. 415, 170 Man.R. (2d) 58 (Man. C.A.), affg [2002] M.J. No. 54, [2002] 5 W.W.R. 671, 162 Man.R. (2d) 48 (Man. Q.B.).

[359] See: *Gard v. Duncan Board of School Trustees*, [1946] B.C.J. No. 8, [1946] 1 W.W.R. 305, [1946] 2 D.L.R. 441 (B.C.C.A.) (school not liable when 11-year-old injured by high-sticking during unsupervised game after school); *Hussack v. Chilliwack School Dist. No. 33*, [2009] B.C.J. No. 1271, 2009 BCSC 852 (B.C.S.C.) (school liable for allowing participation by 13-year-old student who had missed all prior field hockey class units; ice hockey experience enhanced risk when checking from behind).

[360] For an action against a player based on warm-up shots, see, *King v. Redlich*, [1984] B.C.J. No. 2793, [1984] 6 W.W.R. 705, 30 C.C.L.T. 247 (B.C.S.C.), affd [1985] B.C.J. No. 2489, [1986] 4 W.W.R. 567, 24 D.L.R. (4th) 636, 35 C.C.L.T. 201 (B.C.C.A.). See further, Chapter 6, "Play Safe: On the Ice", section C, 2.

[361] See Chapter 5, "Be Safe: Off the Ice", sections B; C.

[362] See Chapter 6, "Play Safe: On the Ice", sections A, 1, 2.

[363] See: *Châtelain c. Prémont*, [1985] C.P. 120 (breach of weight regulations in football; coach and school liable when 90-pound player injured trying to stop opponent who weighed 174 pounds).

not be thrown into a rough environment for which they are unprepared.[364] Progression is best achieved through demonstration of the skill and repeated practice with accompanying safety precautions. The *Thornton* obligations in relation to satisfactory equipment and proper supervision are particularly relevant. The coach should inspect ice conditions[365] and standing equipment and ensure that players' equipment and clothing are in accordance with regulations and safety standards. Full protective equipment must be worn during both practices and games. The coach must also oversee activities to avoid dangerous drills, control play and respond to emergencies. Besides the responsibilities in relation to on-ice activities, the coach has a general supervisory role to promote safety when children are on the premises of a facility or during team travel.[366]

Hockey Canada regulations require one team coach to be qualified in the Hockey Canada Safety Program,[367] and it is the particular responsibility of team officials to arrange for medical attention in the event of injury and to secure transportation. In *Poulton v. Notre Dame College*,[368] a residential school was held liable for failing to arrange prompt treatment for a student who developed a severe hip infection as a result of injuries sustained in hockey. The coach responsible for the player's residence was found to be in breach of the duty of a careful parent in not letting the player see a physician and in refusing to let him leave the school to go to hospital.

A further source of potential liability relates to physically or emotionally abusive coaching methods that may lead to illness or psychological problems. Such methods are forbidden by Hockey Canada policies, which treat the humiliation of athletes as a form of abuse of power.[369] Besides condemning sexual abuse, the policies prohibit bullying and actions such as grabbing, striking or imposing excessive exercise as a form of punishment.[370] The "committed"

---

[364] See, for example, *Kern v. Camp Robinson Ltd.*, [1980] C.S. 611 (rough basketball game at summer camp; insufficient instruction).

[365] See, *Blondeau (Litigation guardian of) v. Peterborough (City)*, [1998] O.J. No. 3428, 82 A.C.W.S. (3d) 207 (Ont. Gen. Div.) (injury during figure skating lesson; coaches failed to inspect ice around goal post hole areas).

[366] On "prevention guidelines" and "supervisory responsibilities", see, *Participant's Workbook: Speak Out! It's more than just a game*, 3d ed. (Canadian Red Cross RespectED/Hockey Canada, 2005) at 52-61, 75-79.

[367] See, Hockey Canada, Regulations (amended to June 2008), Regulation E, 1(a) (definition of "team").

[368] [1975] S.J. No. 214, 60 D.L.R. (3d) 501 (Sask. Q.B.). See also: *Freer (Guardian ad Litem of) v. School District No. 67 (Okanagan/Skaha)*, [2002] B.C.J. No. 2739, 2002 BCSC 1682, 120 A.C.W.S. (3d) 73 (B.C.S.C.) (student walked back to school unassisted after re-breaking leg at soccer field); *Wright (Litigation Guardian of) v. Moosomin First Nation*, [2003] S.J. No. 138, 2003 SKPC 32, 120 A.C.W.S. (3d) 978 (Sask. Prov. Ct.). On medical negligence, see Chapter 6, "Play Safe: On the Ice", section C, 6.

[369] See, "Recognition and Prevention of Abuse Policy" (revised, May 2008) and "Bullying and Harassment Policy" (revised, May 2008), online: <http://www.hockeycanada.ca>. See further, Chapter 5, "Be Safe: Off the Ice", section C, 2.

[370] On "Prevention Guidelines for Training", see, *Participant's Workbook: Speak Out! It's more than just a game*, 3d ed. (Canadian Red Cross RespectED/Hockey Canada, 2005) at 77-79. See

atmosphere of high-performance centres in some sports has been characterized as a form of child labour or child abuse[371] as young athletes are subject to strict regimes of discipline, drug use and dietary control.[372] The coach and responsible organization[373] may be liable where injury or illness are attributable to abusive or exploitive training. "Intense" methods may yield athletic results in the short term, but risk damage to the health and stability of the child in the long run.

When defining and applying the necessary standard of care, reference may be made to recommended procedures and approved techniques developed through Hockey Canada's Coaching Program.[374] The qualifications of a coach can be assessed according to the National Coaching Certification Program ("NCCP") which distinguishes "training" from "certification" and is divided into three "streams" serving different goals and contexts.[375] The Hockey Canada Program offers a "Community" or recreational stream that emphasises fitness, fun and participation. The "Developmental" and "High Performance" streams focus on teaching skills, tactics and strategy appropriate to increasingly higher levels of performance. The methods used by a coach can be evaluated according to the relevant training environment and according to approved models for players of a particular age and skill level. A failure to comply with directives in the Hockey Canada skills development coaching manuals[376] does not automatically constitute negligence, but professional guidelines are admissible evidence as to what is a reasonable technique.[377] Hockey Canada documentation might, for example, be used to evaluate whether a practice session was well designed, well supervised and properly suited to the players. The coaching manuals outline lessons and drills for different categories of minor play and can serve to show that a coach was exercising reasonable care in the chosen methods. The manuals also include general "Safety Tips for Practice".

---

also, "Toronto coach charged for allegedly hitting teen players with hockey stick" *The Globe and Mail* (Toronto: January 26, 2008).

[371] See: R. Propson, "A Call for Statutory Regulation of Elite Child Athletes" (1995) 41 Wayne L. Rev. 1773; P. Donnelly, "Child Labour, Sport Labour: Applying Child Labour Laws to Sport" (1997) 32 Int. Rev. for the Soc. of Sport 389.

[372] See: J. Ryan, *Little Girls in Pretty Boxes: The Making and Breaking of Elite Gymnasts and Figure Skaters* (New York: Doubleday, 1995); L. Robinson, *Black Tights: Women, Sport, and Sexuality* (Toronto: HarperCollins Publishers, 2002) at 119-47.

[373] See, B. Bickford, "The Legal Duty of a College Athletics Department to Athletes with Eating Disorders: A Risk Management Perspective" (1999) 10 Marquette Sports L. Rev. 87.

[374] See, "Coaching Program" online: <http://www.hockeycanada.ca>.

[375] The new NCCP model of the Coaching Association of Canada is made up of "community", "competition" and "instruction" streams; see online: <http://www.coach.ca>. On liability based on lack of qualifications, see, *Cudmore Estate v. Deep Three Enterprises Ltd.*, [1991] O.J. No. 1453, 28 A.C.W.S. (3d) 985 (Ont. Gen. Div.) (defendant unqualified to conduct scuba dive).

[376] See, "Hockey Canada Skills Development Coaching Manual" in "Coaching Program" online at: <http://www.hockeycanada.ca>. See also, IIHF Coach Development Program, *Level 1 Coaching Manual*, esp. at Part 10 "Safety and Risk Management" online: <http://www.iihf.com>.

[377] See, for example, *Hamstra v. British Columbia Rugby Union*, [1989] B.C.J. No. 1521, 1 C.C.L.T. (2d) 78 (B.C.S.C.), revd on other grounds [1995] B.C.J. No. 633, 123 D.L.R. (4th) 693 (B.C.C.A.), affd [1997] S.C.J. No. 43, [1997] 1 S.C.R. 1092 (S.C.C.).

## b. Sue the Ref: Liability of Officials

Every player and coach harbours a secret desire to sue the ref and hold him or her responsible for the bad calls that cost the game. Courts rarely sympathize with attempts to reverse technical decisions or amend scores,[378] but there are cases in which sports referees, umpires or other officials have been found liable for negligent supervision that resulted in injury to players.[379] The referee is responsible for overseeing play, enforcing rules and maintaining discipline, and there is the potential for liability when it can be shown that a player's injury was causally linked to acts or omissions by the official. The appropriate number of officials may also be in issue. In *Walsh v. Buchanan*,[380] it was found that floor hockey involving ten players could be properly supervised by one physical education teacher acting as referee.

The duties of a hockey referee include inspecting the condition of the rink, checking players' equipment, supervising play and calling penalties. It is also the referee's responsibility to halt play when a participant is down on the ice with an injury or otherwise seriously crocked or hampered. Hockey Canada states that the general role of an official is to:

> apply the rules of the game as fairly and as accurately as possible at all time...uphold...the rights of all hockey participants to fair play and penalize accordingly all violent acts...raise the standard of play in each game they officiate.[381]

The official is unlikely to be held responsible for an unexpected incident in a well-regulated game, but becomes a possible defendant when there has been a consistent pattern of tolerating illegal or dangerous play and not enforcing safety rules.[382] Where fighting is permitted, the referee and linesmen have established roles in ensuring that players are able to defend themselves and do not suffer undue punishment. If a player is abandoned to his fate, the officials may share some responsibility for the beating inflicted.

---

[378] See Chapter 3, "Organizations and Regulations", sections C, 1, 4.

[379] See: *Carabba v. Anacortes School District No. 103*, 435 P. 2d 936 (Wash., 1967) (high school wrestler paralysed by full nelson while referee's attention directed to closing gap in mats); *Smolden v. Whitworth*, unreported, April 19, 1996 (Q.B.D.), affirmed December 17, 1996 (Eng. C.A.) (failure to prevent scrums collapsing in rugby); *Vowles v. Evans*, [2003] 1 W.L.R. 1607 (C.A.) (enforcement of safety rules in rugby). See also: H. Opie, "Referee Liability in Sport: Negligent Rule Enforcement and *Smolden v. Whitworth*" (1997) 5 Torts L.J. 17; R.J. Hunter, "An 'Insider's Guide to the Legal Liability of Sports Contest Officials" (2005) 15 Marq. Sports L. Rev. 369; *Brown v. National Football League*, 219 F.Supp. 372 (S.D.N.Y., 2002) (player hit in eye by referee's flag); *Patton v. United States of America Rugby Football, Union. Ltd.*, 851 A.2d 566 (C.A. Md., 2004) (lightning strike).

[380] [1995] O.J. No. 64, 52 A.C.W.S. (3d) 800 (Ont. Gen. Div.).

[381] See, "Officiating Program - My Role as an Official" online: <http://www.hockeycanada.ca>.

[382] On injury to a spectator in softball, see, *Santopietro v. City of New Haven*, 682 A.2d 106 (S.C. Conn., 1996).

Just as the performance of coaches may be tested against approved standards, the actions of officials in controlling games or intervening in particular incidents are subject to evaluation according to the Officiating Program or other rules or guidelines of leagues and associations. Hockey Canada maintains six levels of certification for officials and requires candidates to attend instructional clinics, pass examinations at specified percentage scores and pass on-ice evaluations.[383] Fitness and skating tests also apply to officials certified at Levels V and VI, which relate to elite playoffs and national and international championships. Individual Branches set minimum age guidelines for Level I officials, and an official certified at Level II must be at least 16 years of age. An official cannot attain two Levels in one year, although persons 17 years of age or older can obtain certification at Levels I and II in one year based on ability. Certification is maintained through annual attendance at clinics and annual examination, and it may be determined through supervision that an official should be re-certified at a lower level. The age, qualifications and performance record of a official may be relevant to determining whether there was negligence in a particular case, and actions or decisions can be compared with recommended policies and procedures.

## 5.    Liability of Organizations

### a.    *Clubs and Associations*

A club is a continuous private association of persons voluntarily engaged in a social or recreational purpose; the only obligation of the membership, which changes continually, is to pay subscriptions and abide by club rules.[384] A club, therefore, differs from a business partnership or a trading or profit-making association. Incorporated or proprietary clubs may be sued in their own name, but an unincorporated members' club has no legal existence apart from the individuals who compose it.[385] The constitution and rules of such a club are a contract between members who pay fees to meet expenses. Club property is usually owned equally among members, and business is conducted through general meetings or committees; the property is normally vested in trustees who manage it for the benefit of members. In suing an unincorporated club, it is usual to name as defendants all the individuals who were members at the time of the alleged wrong; where there is a trust fund, action may be allowed against trustees as representatives of the club and its assets.[386] The substantive liability of associations

---

[383] See, "Officiating Program - How to Get Started - Level System" online: <http://www.hockey canada.ca>.

[384] See, *Wise v. Perpetual Trustee Co.*, [1903] A.C. 139 (P.C.).

[385] See, *Stephen v. Stewart*, [1943] B.C.J. No. 61, [1943] 3 W.W.R. 580, [1944] 1 D.L.R. 305 (B.C.C.A.).

[386] See also, *Class Proceedings Act*, S.O. 1992, c. 6 (appointment of representative plaintiff or defendant).

is an evolving area of law that recognizes that clubs and their members may be bound by obligations in contract or tort or subject to fiduciary duties.[387]

Unincorporated sports clubs have been held liable to both members[388] and non-members[389] who were injured while watching events, and a lodge has been required to pay damages in consequence of a rough initiation ritual.[390] However, in *Dodd v. Cook*[391] it was held that a 12-year-old member of an unincorporated skating club could not succeed against the management committee when she fell on the rope used to divide the rink leased by the club. The court held that the club did not have the supervisory responsibilities of a school. Furthermore, all club members, including the plaintiff, were engaged in occupying the rink and organizing the activities, so that no duty was owed to her in spite of her youth. Similarly, the members of a group who arrange a rink rental[392] or organize a tournament[393] do not normally owe duties of care to fellow players in their capacity as social organizers. Membership alone does not attract liability for injuries suffered by club members, although "liability may arise directly for members who are negligent, and vicariously for those who control".[394]

Sports governing bodies are usually incorporated entities that may be sued in their own name. As noted earlier,[395] a sports association or federation can be held responsible for maintaining unsafe rules or systems of play, although liability is restricted to organizations that are in a position to mandate standards and that exercise control over the playing of games.[396] It is also recognized that in supervising the operations of member clubs, a national association cannot be expected to attend every instructional session.[397] However, where an association

---

[387] See, R. Flannigan, "The Liability Structure of Nonprofit Associations: Tort and Fiduciary Assignments" (1998) 77 Can. Bar Rev. 73.

[388] See, *Reese v. Coleman*, [1976] S.J. No. 72, [1976] 3 W.W.R. 739 (Sask. Q.B.), affd [1979] S.J. No. 535, [1979] 4 W.W.R. 58 (Sask. C.A.) (snowmobile races).

[389] See, *Brown v. Lewis* (1896), 12 T.L.R. 455 (Div. Ct.) (committee of soccer club employed incompetent person to repair stand).

[390] See, *Kinver v. Phoenix Lodge, I.O.O.F.*, [1885] O.J. No. 335, 7 O.R. 377 (Ont. H.C.J.). On hazing, see Chapter 5, "Be Safe: Off the Ice", section E.

[391] [1956] O.J. No. 546, [1956] O.R. 470, 4 D.L.R. (2d) 43 (Ont. C.A.).

[392] See, *Griffiths v. New Westminster (City)*, [2001] B.C.J. No. 2274, 25 M.P.L.R. (3d) 31 (B.C.S.C.) (defendant was merely agent of players for collecting funds).

[393] See, *Calliou Estate v. Calliou Estate*, [2002] A.J. No. 74, 99 Alta L.R. (3d) 390 (Alta. Q.B.) (motor vehicle accident; host hockey team not liable for supply of beer).

[394] R. Flannigan, "The Liability Structure of Nonprofit Associations: Tort and Fiduciary Assignments" (1998) 77 Can. Bar Rev. 73 at 86.

[395] See Chapter 6, "Play Safe: On the Ice", sections A, 1, 2.

[396] See, in particular: *Agar v. Hyde* (2000), 201 C.L.R. 552 (H.C. of Aust.); J. Kirk & A. Trichardt, "Sports, Policy and Liability of Sporting Administrators" (2001) 75 Aus. L.J. 504; H. Opie, "The Sport Administrator's Charter: *Agar v. Hyde*" (2001) 9 Torts L. J. 131 and (2002) 12 Seton Hall J. of Sport L. 199; S. Yeo, "The Infallibility of Rule-Making Bodies" (2001) 9 Tort L. Rev. 104.

[397] See, *Smith v. Horizon Aero Sports Ltd.*, [1981] B.C.J. No. 1861, 19 C.C.L.T. 89, 130 D.L.R. (3d) 91 (B.C.S.C.) (responsibilities and standard of care to be expected of the Canadian Sport Parachuting Association with respect to supervision of teaching methods and personnel).

is directly involved in putting on events, it carries the status of occupier or operator and is bound by the responsibilities that accompany those roles.[398]

## b.    Professional Teams

The professional player who suffers injury or disability through service with the team is entitled to various contractual benefits such as salary and insurance payments.[399] A tort action may also be possible where it is alleged that injury was caused by the negligence of team staff, although the action may be barred by American workers' compensation legislation[400] or through contractual waiver.[401] Players have sued Canadian professional teams alleging indiscriminate use of stimulants, medications and pain killers,[402] and there have been actions in various jurisdictions relating to the failure to disclose injuries or to provide proper treatment.[403] Teams have a general responsibility for the health and safety of players and are potentially liable when an injured player is coerced into service or given medical treatment or advice that disregards long-term effects. The issues are closely linked to liability for medical negligence[404] and present the question whether a team doctor was an independent contractor or a team

---

[398] See Chapter 6, "Play Safe: On the Ice", section C, 3.

[399] See Chapter 6, "Play Safe: On the Ice", section A, 4. See also: *Boston Mutual Insurance Co. v. New York Islanders Hockey Club, L.P.*, 165 F.3d 93 (1st Cir., 1999) (failure to disclose concussions suffered by Brett Lindros); *Dubinsky v. St. Louis Blues Hockey Club*, 229 S.W. 3d 126 (C.A. Mo., 2007) (compensation claim; employer's credit for wages and benefits paid).

[400] Under state workers' compensation legislation, injured employees are entitled to benefits in exchange for renouncing the right to sue the employer; see, for example, *Brinkman v. Buffalo Bills Football Club*, 433 F.Supp. 699 (W.D.N.Y., 1977) (player's exclusive remedy was claim for workers' compensation). The immunity from civil action usually extends to co-employees, except where the injury was intentional or resulted from gross negligence; see, for example, *Stringer v. Minnesota Vikings Football Club, LLC*, 705 N.W. 2d 746 (Minn. S.C., 2005), varg 686 N.W. 2d 545 (Minn. App., 2004) (death of Korey Stringer from heat stroke during training camp; immunity of medical staff working in the course of their employment). See also, *Stringer v. National Football League*, 474 F.Supp. 2d 894 (S.D. Ohio, 2007) (actions against league and manufacturer of equipment).

[401] See, CBA of NHL, art. 23.4, Exhibits 11, 12 (release of liability on receiving disability payments). American workers' compensation coverage is required under article 31.5.

[402] See, for example, "Argos settle pep-pill case out of court" *The Globe and Mail* (Toronto: November 16, 1977) at 5 (action by Joe Vijuk against Ottawa Rough Riders and Toronto Argonauts based on supply of amphetamines). On the abuse of pain killers and therapeutic drugs in football, see, L. Barnes, *The Plastic Orgasm* (Richmond Hill, ON: Pocket Book, 1973) at 154-85.

[403] See: *Krueger v. San Francisco Forty Niners*, 234 Cal. Rptr. 579 (C.A., 1987) (intentional and fraudulent concealment of football player's knee injury; injection of novocain and cortisone and encouragement to use amphetamines); "Martin triumphant in malpractice suit" *The Hockey News* (February 4, 1994) at 5 (USD $2.5 million awarded to Rick Martin in action against team doctor of Buffalo Sabres; treatment of knee injury); *Belanger v. Pittsburgh Penguins Inc.*, [1998] O.J. No. 427, 17 C.P.C. (4th) 245 (Ont. Gen. Div.) (claims by Roger Belanger; allegations of negligence were not subject to arbitration procedures; "Ontario is the appropriate forum to litigate the 'hockey' issues" *per* Gans J. at 251).

[404] See Chapter 6, "Play Safe: On the Ice", section C, 6.

employee. Where action is barred against the team, it may still be possible to maintain the claim against the medic.[405]

The leading Canadian decision dealing with the duty of care of a professional team is *Robitaille v. Vancouver Hockey Club Ltd.*,[406] where the management and medical staff of the Vancouver Canucks had formed the opinion that plaintiff Michael Robitaille's complaints of physical injury and pain were "all in his head"[407] — the result of the player's imagination and emotional difficulties. During a road trip in January 1977, Robitaille experienced pain in the neck and shoulder area, symptoms of spinal cord disorder; this was given only cursory attention by team doctors and management. In a game shortly afterwards, Robitaille suffered a spinal cord contusion that resulted in weakness and loss of co-ordination; in spite of these apparent symptoms, Robitaille was ignored by the team doctor and received no treatment. After a slight improvement in his condition, Robitaille continued to play and did not consult his own doctor nor report his symptoms to the defendant club. In doing so, "he was influenced by his knowledge that his complaints were not being taken seriously and his fear of doing anything which would tend to enhance his reputation as a malingerer."[408] During a subsequent game, Robitaille received a heavy check that caused permanent spinal damage and permanent disability. Esson J. found that a proper earlier examination would have discovered the cord contusion, and Robitaille would not then have been exposed to potential aggravation of the injury.

Esson J. held that the defendant team was under a general duty to exercise reasonable care for the safety, fitness and health of its players; this duty arose from the close proximity in the relationship between the plaintiff and the defendant. Esson J. found the defendant in breach of this duty, "in failing to react reasonably to the plaintiff's complaints and symptoms, in failing to provide appropriate medical care and in putting pressure on him to ignore his injuries".[409] The team's system of medical care failed Robitaille partly because of the club doctors' lack of independence and objectivity:

> The failure to act objectively, the plaintiff argues, is a direct result of the close relationship between the club and the doctors. There is some truth in that. The doctors, by their terms of employment, have a responsibility to the club. That creates a tendency for them to resolve doubts in favour of keeping players in the line-up. The same tendency results from their interest as fans.[410]

---

[405] On Dave Babych's action against the Philadelphia Flyers and their team doctor, see, "Babych wins $1.37-million judgment" *The Globe and Mail* (Toronto: November 1, 2002) at S3. See also, J.D. Young, "Liability for Team Physician Malpractice: A New Burden Shifting Approach" (2003) 27 Rutgers L. Record 4.

[406] [1979] B.C.J. No. 887, 19 B.C.L.R. 158 (B.C.S.C.), vard [1981] B.C.J. No. 555, [1981] 3 W.W.R. 481, 16 C.C.L.T. 225, 124 D.L.R. (3d) 228 (B.C.C.A.).

[407] *Ibid.*, at 19 B.C.L.R. 164, *per* Esson J. Robitaille had previously used tranquilizers to control acute anxiety.

[408] *Ibid.*, at 19 B.C.L.R. 164, *per* Esson J.

[409] *Ibid.*, at 19 B.C.L.R. 176.

[410] *Ibid.*, *per* Esson J.

Besides receiving compensatory damages, Robitaille was awarded substantial exemplary damages because he had been singled out for mistreatment in a callous and wrongheaded course of action and aggravated damages because of the injury to his honour, dignity and self-respect. The compensatory damages of CDN $400,000 were reduced by 20 per cent because Robitaille was guilty of contributory negligence in failing to act reasonably to protect his own health and well-being.

In allowing Robitaille's claim, the trial court rejected various arguments that sought to exclude any responsibility in the team. Esson J. held that a duty of care in tort was neither superseded by the parties' contractual relationship nor excluded by provisions in the NHL's collective bargaining agreement or standard player contract. He also found that the team doctors were not independent contractors but team employees, so the defendant was vicariously liable for their negligence:

> The defendant had the power of selecting, of controlling and of dismissing. The doctors were supplied as part of the services rendered to the plaintiffs. That service was supplied to further the defendant's business purposes. The measure of control asserted by the defendant over the doctors in carrying out their work was substantial. The degree of control exercised need not be complete in order to establish vicarious liability. In the case of a professional person, the absence of control and direction over the manner of doing the work is of little significance.[411]

## 6.   Medical Negligence[412]

Where a participant is injured while under the supervision of a sports organization,[413] there is a responsibility to provide adequate medical services and arrange further treatment through effective communications and transportation.[414]

---

[411] *Ibid.*, at 19 B.C.L.R. 175. In *Wilson v. Vancouver Hockey Club*, [1983] B.C.J. No. 2016, 5 D.L.R. (4th) 282 (B.C.S.C.), affd [1985] B.C.J. No. 2450, 22 D.L.R. (4th) 516 (B.C.C.A.), a doctor was found negligent in not ordering an immediate biopsy for a player suspected of having a small skin cancer. The court distinguished *Robitaille* and held that the doctor was an independent contractor serving the players and was not subject to control by team management. See also, *Bryant v. Fox*, 515 N.E. 2d 775 (Ill. C.A., 1987) (doctor not an employee of the Chicago Bears).

[412] On general legal-medical issues, see: E.I. Picard & G.B. Robertson, *Legal Liability of Doctors and Hospitals in Canada*, 4th ed. (Toronto: Thomson Carswell, 2007); J. Downie *et al.* (eds.), *Canadian Health Law and Policy* (Markham, ON: LexisNexis Butterworths, 2002); B. Sneiderman, *et al.*, *Canadian Medical Law: An Introduction for Physicians, Nurses, and Other Health Care Professionals* (Scarborough, ON: Carswell, 2003).

[413] On sports medicine, see: R.T. Ball, "Legal Responsibilities and Problems" in A.J. Ryan & F.L. Allman (eds.), *Sports Medicine*, 2d ed. (San Diego: Academic Press, 1989) at 447; H. Opie, "Legal Requirements" in M. Zuluaga *et al.* (eds.), *Sports Physiotherapy: Applied Science and Practice* (Melbourne: Churchill Livingstone, 1995) at 739; M.J. Mitten, "Emerging Legal Issues in Sports Medicine: A Synthesis, Summary, and Analysis" (2002) 76 St. John's L. Rev. 5.

[414] See: *Gies v. Gunwall*, [1982] B.C.J. No. 99, 143 D.L.R. (3d) 126 (B.C.S.C.) (absence of radio at isolated hunting camp); *Procureur Général de la Province de Québec v. Ski Secours Québec Inc.*, [1983] C.A. 625 (delay in assisting member of ski patrol); *Heaslip Estate v. Mansfield Ski*

The obligation to provide medical care has been recognized in cases involving a student at a school,[415] a client receiving instruction,[416] a professional player employed by a team[417] and a correctional inmate.[418] The operator of a sports facility or event is also bound to arrange for reasonably prompt and satisfactory care, which includes allowing convenient access for emergency vehicles and personnel:

> The persons and organizations in charge of sports activities will have a duty to secure or provide reasonable medical assistance to injured participants or spectators as soon as possible under the circumstances.[419]

The required standard of medical services varies according to the resources reasonably available to the facility and the risks of the activity. Few community rinks can afford resident physicians and intensive care facilities, so that obligations will often be discharged by providing competent first aid and calling for para-medical assistance. Superior personnel and equipment may, however, be required at professional games and other elite events. The IIHF *Medical Care Guide*[420] incorporates operational recommendations for host organizers and suggests standards in relation to the emergency action plan, pharmaceutical supplies and the response to life-threatening cases such as airway injuries, thoracic trauma and cardiac arrest.

The treatment of sports injuries usually involves a sequence of interventions by different personnel and may eventually reach the level of consultation with a specialist. Before professional attention can be given, there should be suitable interim care, provided the injured party consents.[421] A layperson such as a coach

---

*Club Inc. and Ontario*, [2009] O.J. No. 3185, 2009 ONCA 594 (Ont. C.A.) (duty of Province to provide air ambulance).

[415] See, *Poulton v. Notre Dame College*, [1975] S.J. No. 214, 60 D.L.R. (3d) 501 (Sask. Q.B.).

[416] See, *Mile v. Club Med Inc.*, [1988] B.C.J. No. 710, 10 A.C.W.S. (3d) 50 (Ont. H.C.J.) (scuba training; failure to provide functioning oxygen equipment or medical help).

[417] See, *Robitaille v. Vancouver Hockey Club Ltd.*, [1979] B.C.J. No. 887, 19 B.C.L.R. 158 (B.C.S.C.), vard [1981] B.C.J. No. 555, [1981] 3 W.W.R. 481, 16 C.C.L.T. 225, 124 D.L.R. (3d) 228 (B.C.C.A.).

[418] See, *Kandola v. British Columbia*, [1991] B.C.J. No. 813, 26 A.C.W.S. (3d) 304 (B.C.S.C.) (proper treatment of hockey injury).

[419] J.C. Weistart & C.M. Lowell, *The Law of Sports* (Indianapolis: The Bobbs-Merrill Co., 1979) at 982. See, for example: *Clark v. State*, 89 N.Y.S. 2d 132 (Ct.Cl., 1949), affd 93 N.Y.S. 2d 28 (App.Div., 1949), affd 99 N.E.2d 300 (N.Y.C.A., 1951) (treatment of injuries after bobsled crash); *Classen v. State*, 500 N.Y.S. 2d 460 (Ct.Cl., 1985), *Classen v. Izquierdo*, 520 N.Y.S. 2d 999 (S.C., 1987) (medical services at boxing match); *Watson v. British Boxing Board of Control*, [2001] Q.B. 1150 (Eng. C.A.) (Board liable for failing to provide ring-side resuscitation to assist fighter who suffered sub-dural haemorrhage).

[420] See, *IIHF Medical Care Guide: Operational Recommendations for Host Organisers of IIHF Championships and Events* (July 1, 2005), online at: <http://www.iihf.com> "Medical Development"; see also, 2010 IIHF Medical Regulations. See also, "Russian's death sends chill through hockey world" *The Globe and Mail* (Toronto: October 15, 2008) at R6, R9 (death of Alexei Cherepanov on bench during KHL game; undetected heart problem; need for functioning defibrillator).

[421] See, *Clayton v. New Dreamland Roller Skating Rink*, 82 A.2d 458 (N.J.App.Div., 1951) (rink patron protested at unqualified treatment by prize fight manager; battery committed).

or trainer who gives immediate attention must meet the standard of a competent person of similar experience, and the first aid requirements associated with coaching certification would be relevant in evaluating what was done. The standard is higher than that required of the ordinary citizen who has no experience of sports injuries, but is less demanding than the knowledge expected of a qualified physician. The common law does not, in general, impose a duty to give medical assistance to strangers,[422] but a person who is in a special relationship of care must provide reasonable first aid and summon further assistance. The layperson, ambulance attendant or doctor who volunteers first aid or provides interim care may be liable for unsuitable treatment that worsens injuries.[423] Actions such as moving a player with a suspected neck injury[424] or providing inappropriate treatment for heat exhaustion[425] have been found to constitute unreasonable medical care that aggravated the player's condition. Where assistance is given in an emergency, legislation in a number of Provinces now provides that the doctor or other person rendering treatment will be liable for worsening the condition only on proof of "gross" negligence.[426] This protection of the "Good Samaritan" applies only to voluntary treatment given at the immediate scene of the accident outside a hospital or other medically equipped facility.

A qualified physician who provides medical services or treats injuries is bound to exercise a professional standard of care. The doctor does not guarantee cure and is not liable for reasonable errors of judgment, but is required to exercise the skill of "a normal, prudent practitioner of the same experience and standing".[427] The doctor undertakes with the patient that "he possesses the skill, knowledge and judgment of the generality or average of the special group or class of technicians to which he belongs and will faithfully exercise them".[428] The specialist is bound to a higher standard of care than the general practitioner and

---

[422] See, A.M. Linden & B. Feldthusen, *Canadian Tort Law*, 8th ed. (Markham, ON: LexisNexis Butterworths, 2006) at 314-32. On the duty in civil law, see, *Charter of Human Rights and Freedoms*, R.S.Q. c. C-12, s. 2 (aiding person whose life is in peril).

[423] See: *Fraser v. Kelowna Motorcycle Club*, [1988] B.C.J. No. 350, 9 A.C.W.S. (3d) 56 (B.C.S.C.) (appropriate treatment by ambulance attendants); *Thomas v. Hamilton (City) Board of Education*, [1990] O.J. No. 147, 19 A.C.W.S. (3d) 602 (Ont. H.C.J.), affd [1994] O.J. No. 2444, 20 O.R. (3d) 598 (Ont. C.A.) (proper first aid services in treatment of football neck injury); *Stevenson v. Clearview Riverside Resort*, [2000] O.J. No. 4863, 101 A.C.W.S. (3d) 1212 (Ont. S.C.J.) (diving accident; "textbook" transfer to traction board by ambulance attendants).

[424] See, *Welch v. Dunsmuir Joint Union High School District*, 326 P. 2d 633 (Cal.App., 1958).

[425] See, *Mogabgab v. Orleans Parish School Board*, 239 So. 2d 456 (La.App., 1970).

[426] See: *Good Samaritan Act*, R.S.B.C. 1996, c. 172; *Emergency Medical Aid Act*, R.S.A. 1980, c. E-9; *Emergency Medical Aid Act*, R.S.S. 1978, c. E-8; *Good Samaritan Act, 2001*, S.O. 2001, c. 2; *Medical Act*, R.S.P.E.I. 1988, c. M-5, s. 50 (standard for physicians); *Volunteer Services Act*, R.S.N.S. 1989, c. 497; *Emergency Medical Aid Act*, R.S.N. 1990, c. E-9.

[427] *Crits v. Sylvester*, [1956] O.J. No. 526, [1956] O.R. 132 at 143 (Ont. C.A.), *per* Schroeder J.A., affd [1956] S.C.J. No. 71, [1956] S.C.R. 991 (S.C.C.). See, A.M. Linden & B. Feldthusen, *Canadian Tort Law*, 8th ed. (Markham, ON: LexisNexis Butterworths, 2006) at 170-96.

[428] *Wilson v. Swanson*, [1956] S.C.J. No. 58, [1956] S.C.R. 804 at 811 (S.C.C.), *per* Rand J. See, for example, *Morrow v. Outerbridge*, [2009] B.C.J. No. 640, 2009 BCSC 433 (B.C.S.C.) (operation on player's shoulder; orthopaedic surgeon negligent in leaving metal anchors sticking up).

must exercise the skill of an average specialist in the field. The physician can avoid liability by showing that treatment was conducted in accordance with a reasonable and approved medical practice. The patient must consent to the treatment, otherwise battery is committed.[429] It is, furthermore, negligence not to disclose to the patient adequately the risks involved in the procedure; the subject must be informed of side effects, consequences and alternatives to the extent that a reasonable patient would require.[430]

Most sports injuries are treated by team trainers or general practitioners. The trainer must show the level of modern knowledge or technique to be expected of an ordinary competent athletic therapist, as evidenced by the standards of certification programs of governing associations.[431] The general practitioner is bound by the ordinary professional standard of a doctor.[432] Doctors who hold themselves out as specialists, either in a recognized discipline such as orthopaedics or in the emerging field of "sports medicine", are required to show a higher standard of care. The duty of care owed by a consultant is to the patient-player, rather than to the employer-team that has a stake in the player's services and market value.[433]

Team doctors occupy unusual positions in that they are retained by the employer. Players are then bound by contract to submit to examination by a medic who is not of their own choosing, and the team is entitled to receive information about the player's condition that would ordinarily be confidential. The apparent split loyalty of the team doctor has the potential to create conflicts of interest,[434] since the team owner or coach may exert pressure to use the quick

---

[429] No express consent is needed in emergencies or where the patient is unconscious. A valid consent may be given by someone over the age of majority or who understands the nature of the treatment; see, *Johnston v. Wellesley Hospital*, [1970] O.J. No. 1741, [1971] 2 O.R. 103, 17 D.L.R. (3d) 139 (Ont. H.C.J.). See, A.M. Linden & B. Feldthusen, *Canadian Tort Law*, 8th ed. (Markham, ON: LexisNexis Butterworths, 2006) at 78-87; L.E. Rozovsky, *Canadian Law of Consent to Treatment*, 3d ed. (Markham, ON: LexisNexis Butterworths, 2003). On "mature" children under 16 and "best interests" decisions, see, *A.C. v. Manitoba (Director of Child and Family Services)*, [2009] S.C.J. No. 30, 2009 SCC 30 (S.C.C.).

[430] See, *Reibl v. Hughes*, [1980] S.C.J. No. 105, [1980] 2 S.C.R. 880 (S.C.C.); *Arndt v. Smith*, [1997] S.C.J. No. 65, [1997] 2 S.C.R. 539 (S.C.C.).

[431] See, L. Barnes, "Beloved 'Outlaws' – Trainers Look at Liability" (1978) 6(9) The Physician and Sports Medicine 121.

[432] See, for example: *Price v. Milawski*, [1977] O.J. No. 2477, 18 O.R. (2d) 113, 82 D.L.R. (3d) 130 (Ont. C.A.) (negligent treatment of ankle broken at soccer); *Ryan v. Avenue Animal Hospital Ltd.*, [1989] N.B.J. No. 118, 95 N.B.R. (2d) 405 (N.B.Q.B. (T.D.)) (negligent cryosurgery on race horse; athlete had to be put down); *Duquette c. Gauthier*, [2007] J.Q. no 6229, 2007 QCCA 863 (Que. C.A.) (treatment of international level athletes; disciplinary proceedings).

[433] See, *West Bromwich Albion Football Club Ltd. v. El-Safty*, [2006] EWCA Civ. 1299 (Eng. C.A.), affg [2005] EWHC 2866 (Q.B.) (consultant surgeon recommended knee surgery that proved unsuccessful; ligament tear should have been treated conservatively). See also, *Appleton v. El Safty*, [2007] EWHC 631 (Q.B.) (assessment of damages).

[434] See: L.L. Balbi, "The Liability of Professional Team Sport Physicians" (1984) 22 Alta. L. Rev. 247, (1984) 5 Health L. in Canada 20 and 41; M.J. Mitten, "Team Physicians and Competitive Athletics" (1993) 55 U. Pitt. L. Rev. 129; T. Keim, "Physicians for Professional Sports Teams: Health Care Under the Pressure of Economic and Commercial Interests" (1999) 9 Seton Hall J.

fix or running repairs to keep a player in the active line-up. Similarly, the player may be overly eager to keep a place on the team. It is, however, negligent not to have primary regard to the well-being and long-term health of the patient-player. Where team physicians can reasonably infer that the player is unfit or suffering from a condition, it is their duty so to inform both the player and the team and to ensure that medications[435] are taken and the required course of treatment followed. Team doctors have been found liable for failing to disclose long-term risks associated with injuries or with the painkilling shots,[436] and particular precautions are now required where the player suffers concussion.[437] There has also been liability where doctors failed to detect or diagnose a condition, so that the player's career was cut short through the aggravation of an injury.[438] Since awards or settlements in favour of highly-paid athletes are likely to be substantial, there have been difficulties in obtaining affordable malpractice insurance for doctors serving professional players.[439]

Given the high rates of injury in sport in general and hockey in particular, medical negligence is likely to be a developing field of liability. The potential for litigation is also increased by the improved standards expected of trainers, physiotherapists and other medics. Future liability is unlikely to be restricted to cases of traumatic injury and may also be based on the cumulative long-term effects of body-pounding. Retired NHL players are largely precluded from bringing action, but at least are now in a position to lay aside savings for the best painkillers and arthritis drugs that money can buy. Other players may choose to seek compensation based on the lingering effects or undisclosed risks of the robust play of their early days, as aggravated by short-sighted medical treatment.

---

Sport L. 196; B.R. Furrow, "The Problem of the Sports Doctor: Serving Two (or Is It Three or Four?) Masters" (2005) 50 Saint Louis U. L. Rev. 165.

[435] On the death of Hank Gathers of Loyola Marymount, see: B.J. Lorence, "The University's Role Toward Student-Athletes: A Moral or Legal Obligation?" (1991) 29 Duquesne L. Rev. 343; C.J. Jones, "College Athletes: Illness or Injury and the Decision to Return to Play" (1992) 40 Buffalo L. Rev. 113.

[436] See: *Krueger v. San Francisco Forty Niners*, 234 Cal. Rptr. 579 (C.A., 1987) (playing with "profoundly damaged" knee and treatment with steroid injections); J.D. Young, "Liability for Team Physician Malpractice: A New Burden Shifting Approach" (2003) 27 Rutgers L. Record 4 (action based on foot fracture suffered by Wayne Babych).

[437] See, A.N. Hecht, "Legal and Ethical Aspects of Sports-Related Concussions: The Merril Hoge Story" (2002) 12 Seton Hall J. of Sport L. 19. See further, Chapter 6, "Play Safe: On the Ice", section A, 4.

[438] See, *Robitaille v. Vancouver Hockey Club Ltd.*, [1979] B.C.J. No. 887, 19 B.C.L.R. 158 (B.C.S.C.), vard [1981] B.C.J. No. 555, [1981] 3 W.W.R. 481, 16 C.C.L.T. 225, 124 D.L.R. (3d) 228 (B.C.C.A.), discussed at Chapter 6, "Play Safe: On the Ice", section C, 5, b.

[439] See: "Doctors worry about lost coverage" *The Globe and Mail* (Toronto: October 22, 2002) at S1; "Clubs ponder higher cost of insurance" *The Globe and Mail* (Toronto: October 23, 2002) at S2 (decision by Canadian Medical Protective Association to discontinue coverage).

## 7.    Products Liability[440]

Previous sections have noted that program operators, coaches or other supervisors may be liable for supplying or permitting the use of dangerous or defective equipment. Further actions based specifically on products liability may also occur. These include actions in contract by the person who buys or leases equipment and actions in tort by the ultimate user who is injured as a result of the condition of the product. (Although there are few cases of sports products liability in Canada, this type of litigation has occurred frequently in the United States where the injured user may base the action on negligence, on breach of the seller's warranties or on strict liability when the injury is caused by a defective condition that is unreasonably dangerous to the user.[441])

A contractual action may be brought against the seller for breach of the implied warranties that the goods are fit for the purpose and of merchantable quality.[442] Such liability is strict,[443] so that the exercise of reasonable care to discover a defect is no defence. The injured consumer may also bring an action in negligence alleging failure to deliver the required product, defective design, improper installation or adjustment, or failure to warn of dangers.[444] Negligence actions may involve manufacturers,[445] suppliers, retailers, renters, testers, repairers, inspectors or other parties responsible for circulating the product.

Equipment such as a hockey helmet[446] does not guarantee safety in all circumstances, and the manufacturer or retailer will not be liable for a failure of protective qualities that were never claimed. In *Moore v. Cooper Canada Ltd.*,[447] it was held that the helmet was intended only to reduce the risk of head injury, so

---

[440] See: S.M. Waddams, *Products Liability*, 4th ed. (Scarborough, ON: Carswell, 2002); D.F. Edgell, *Product Liability Law in Canada* (Markham, ON: LexisNexis Butterworths, 2000).

[441] See, J.C. Weistart & C.M. Lowell, *The Law of Sports* (Indianapolis: The Bobbs-Merrill Co., 1979) at 996-1007. See, for example, *Everett v. Bucky Warren, Inc.*, 380 N.E. 2d 653 (Mass., 1978) (manufacturer should have known that puck could penetrate helmet consisting of three head pieces; liability based on negligence and strict liability).

[442] See, *Sale of Goods Act*, R.S.O. 1990, c. S.1, s. 15. See, for example, *Leitz v. Saskatoon Drug & Stationery Co. Ltd.*, [1980] S.J. No. 197, 112 D.L.R. (3d) 106 (Sask. Q.B.) (lenses were not strengthened and hardened as advertised).

[443] See: *Matheson v. Watt*, [1956] B.C.J. No. 150, 19 W.W.R. 424, 5 D.L.R. (2d) 437 (B.C.C.A.) (wheel detached from skate rented at roller rink); *Moore v. Cooper Canada Ltd.*, [1990] O.J. No. 66, 2 C.C.L.T. (2d) 57 at 77-79 (Ont. H.C.J.) (purpose of hockey helmet).

[444] See, for example: *Dunsmore v. Deshield*, [1977] S.J. No. 342, 80 D.L.R. (3d) 386 (Sask. Q.B.) (lenses were not hardened and impact resistant); *Walford (Litigation Guardian of) v. Jacuzzi Canada Inc.*, [2007] O.J. No. 4053, 87 O.R. (3d) 281 (Ont. C.A.) (store failed to warn of risks in installing pool slide).

[445] See, *Resurfice Corp. v. Hanke*, [2007] S.C.J. No. 7, [2007] 1 S.C.R. 333 (S.C.C.) (action against manufacturer and distributor of ice-resurfacing machine).

[446] On regulatory standards in relation to import, sale and wearing of helmets, see Chapter 6, "Play Safe: On the Ice", sections A, 3, 4.

[447] [1990] O.J. No. 66, 2 C.C.L.T. (2d) 57 (Ont. H.C.J.). See also: *Everett v. Bucky Warren Inc.*, 380 N.E. 2d 653 (Mass., 1978); *Durkee v. Cooper of Canada, Ltd.*, 298 N.W. 2d 620 (Mich., 1980); *Mohney v. USA Hockey, Inc.*, 138 Fed. Appx. 804 (6th Cir., 2005).

that there was no liability when an amateur player broke his neck sliding into the boards.

## D.  CONCLUSION: SAFETY PROCESSES

This chapter and the two preceding chapters have explored the wide range of hazards in hockey and the evolution of systems to prevent injuries, manage risks and avoid the costs of liability. While there is no absolute guarantee of safety or security, the ongoing efforts aim to limit the risks to those that are "inherent in and reasonably incidental to the normal playing of the game of hockey".[448] As discussed, safety is a function of facilities and equipment, rules of play and the ethical and cultural climate of the game. There are roles for engineers, associations, coaches, medics and others, and the consuming public also plays its part in determining what is a worthy spectacle. Safety is primarily maintained by "hockey insiders" through the rules, policies and codes of conduct of leagues and associations: the governing bodies set goals and standards, and the locals have the job of seeing that all works out in practice. Public institutions also have a role. Some standards are established by formal legal regulations, and the possibility of criminal or civil liability hovers in the background to deter dangerous or exploitive conduct and offer a reminder of the responsibilities of individuals and organizations. The role of the courts is to encourage the healthy and robust dimensions of hockey, while applying principles of liability that clearly condemn conduct that is destructive and to the detriment of the game.

The final safety process is on-going research, evaluation and review. The standard of "reasonable care in the circumstances" is checked against the current state of knowledge, so that the playing and organization of the game must conform to recognized best practices. Safety and security in hockey call for constant development and improvement so that the avoidable tragedies of the past are not repeated.

---

[448] *R. v. Maloney*, [1976] O.J. No. 2447, 28 C.C.C. (2d) 323 at 326 (Ont. Co. Ct.), *per* Lesage Co. Ct. J.

# Chapter 7

# THE BUSINESS OF HOCKEY

The amount of these gross receipts depends upon the fancy of the public and its interest in these matches....The essentials to the enterprise are: first, a team; secondly, ice to play on; and, thirdly, other teams with whom to arrange a series of matches. I should add that the members of the team are professionals.[1]

## A. MONEY MATTERS AND PROPERTY RIGHTS

### 1. The Ice Industry

In 2004, the "fancy of the public" extended to CDN $15.8 billion in household spending on sport, which constituted 1.2 per cent of the Canada's gross domestic product; at the same time, sport supported 2 per cent of jobs.[2] In 2006, teams and organizations offering spectator sports generated revenue of CDN $2.2 billion, representing a CDN $600 million increase from the previous year when there was a decline attributable to the lockout in the National Hockey League ("NHL").[3] By the 2007-08 season, "hockey-related revenue" in the NHL as a whole had reached USD $2.575 billion, of which 56 per cent was destined for the NHL Players' Association ("NHLPA").

The games offered by the NHL and the NHLPA are a visible part of the service sector of hockey, but represent only one dimension of the wider industry where the "clusters" and "streams" of production include primary extraction, construction, manufacture and the marketing of goods and services.[4] To take one example, the licensed or autographed stick has followed a value-added journey from the forestry industry, to finished product, to specially endorsed property. The elements of the business may be grouped as follows:

1. infrastructure;

2. manufacture of products; and

---

[1]  *Toronto Hockey Club Ltd. v. Arena Gardens of Toronto Ltd.*, [1925] O.J. No. 88, [1925] 4 D.L.R. 546 at 546-47 (Ont. C.A.), *per* Masten J.A.

[2]  See, *Strengthening Canada: The Socio-economic Benefits of Sport Participation in Canada* (Conference Board of Canada, August 2005). See also, "The Canadian Sport Policy" (May 24, 2002) at 6, available online: Canadian Heritage <http://www.pch.gc.ca> "Sport Canada".

[3]  See, Statistics Canada, "Spectator Sports, Event Promoters, Artists and Related Industries" (Catalogue No. 63-246-X, 2006).

[4]  See, J. Harvey & M. Saint-Germain, "L'industrie et la politique canadiennes du sport en contexte de mondialisation" (1995) 25:1 Sociologie et sociétés 33.

3. services.

1. *Infrastructure*: There are about 3,000 ice arenas in Canada. This infrastructure is largely owned by public authorities, although the major field of construction and maintenance falls to the private sector. One census has identified and analysed 2,486 arenas, of which 86 per cent are owned and operated by municipalities.[5] The largest construction boom occurred in the 1970s, and 73 per cent of the arenas were built before 1980. The renovation of facilities is a significant area of economic activity, requiring CDN $535 million for buildings by 2010 and CDN $335 million for refrigeration systems by 2015.

2. *Manufacture of Products*: General sporting goods are manufactured in 200 establishments employing 10,000 people and producing CDN $1.1 billion worth of equipment.[6] Exports of skating and hockey equipment reached CDN $111.6 million in 2000 as markets recognize the innovations developed by the Canadian industry.

3. *Services*: Services are provided by commercial enterprises, public agencies and private associations. The various services include:

- wholesale and retail of sporting goods (which accounts for 50,000 jobs),[7] clothing, collectibles and novelties;

- wholesale and retail of video and computer games;

- management of arenas;[8]

- teaching, coaching and officiating;

- hockey tours, camps and schools;[9]

---

[5]   See, "National Arena Census" (Canadian Recreation Facilities Council/Hockey Canada, 2005).

[6]   See, Industry Canada, "Industrial Sector — Canadian Sporting Goods Industry", available online: <http://www.ic.gc.ca>.

[7]   See, Standing Committee on Canadian Heritage, Sub-Committee on the Study of Sport in Canada (Chair, Dennis Mills), *Sport in Canada: Leadership, Partnership and Accountability, Everybody's Business* (House of Commons Canada, November 1998) at 14. The report notes (at 17) that there are 59,000 people whose primary occupation is coach, referee or athlete in different sports.

[8]   See, *Hastings Minor Hockey Assn. v. Pacific National Exhibition*, [1981] B.C.J. No. 1970, [1981] 6 W.W.R. 514 (B.C.S.C.) (established use of rink; order requiring defendants to continue to make it available).

[9]   See: *Gold in the Net Hockey School Inc. v. Netpower Inc.*, [2007] A.J. No. 1526, 430 A.R. 38 (Alta. Q.B.) (plaintiffs denied injunction to restrain defendants from operating competing school; no breach of confidence by former employee and shareholder); *Charlie Bourgeois Hockey School Inc. v. Cormier*, [2008] N.B.J. No. 361, 336 N.B.R. (2d) 389 (N.B.Q.B. (T.D.)) (former employee now coaching son's team; injunction denied); *Collin-Knoblauch v. Oakville Skating Club*, [2008] O.J. No. 4579, 70 C.C.E.L. (3d) 88 (Ont. S.C.J.) (issues related to contract of employment and operation of skating school); *Symonds v. All Canadian Hockey School Inc. (c.o.b. St. Peter's A.C.H.S. College School)*, [2009] O.J. No. 3688 (Ont. S.C.J.) (refund of tuition fees). See also, "Fraud charges laid over hockey hopefuls' 'dream' trip" *The Globe and Mail* (Toronto: October 16, 2009) at A2.

- administration of teams, leagues and associations;

- public administration and regulation by government agencies;

- production of tournaments and championships involving amateur or minor participants;

- production of major international events involving national-level athletes;

- production of minor-pro and major league games involving professional players;

- publishing and media; and

- betting and gambling systems.

The consumers of the different services include players, parents, associations, fans and punters. Besides the services directly related to participation and games, there are major associated services such as transport, accommodation, hospitality and sports medicine. Although not all betting systems involve sports events, the quantities of cash invested by punters are particularly impressive.[10]

Facilities, goods and services are, therefore, supplied by both the for-profit and the not-for-profit sectors. In either case, the game presents no shortage of opportunity for expenditures, and a deep pocket is a particular requirement of the hockey parent. In the rare event of a child advancing to a playing career, one family's estimate of the cost of the 12-year journey from minor hockey to the pros is USD $144,000.[11] The poor kid who rises to stardom is part of hockey's mythology, but the NHL player is more likely to be solidly middle class and from free-spending suburbia.

The scale of the various economic activities is enhanced by the large population group that is engaged in the winter game. The total amounts to,

> 4.2 million Canadians involved in organized hockey, including 500,000 players, 75,000 coaches, 30,000 officials, 100,000 volunteers and 300,000 involved parents.[12]

The manufacturing and service sectors of this strong domestic market are also linked to worldwide enterprises. Hockey Canada affiliates with the International Ice Hockey Federation ("IIHF"),[13] and the industrial aspects of the game reflect the full force of the business version of "globalization". Besides the well-

---

[10]   See Chapter 7, "The Business of Hockey", section A, 5.

[11]   See, "The Two Hundred Thousand Dollar Question" *The Hockey News* (September 2, 2008) at 19 (family of Patrick Kane).

[12]   Hockey Canada, *Safety Requires Teamwork & Safety For All* (2009–2010) at 23. In 2005, hockey drew 1.3 million participants; see, Statistics Canada, *Sport Participation in Canada, 2005* (February 2008).

[13]   See Chapter 3, "Organizations and Regulations", sections A; B.

established import[14] and export of equipment, many media systems are transnational, teams are subject to ownership by conglomerates, and global brands actively engage in sponsorship and advertising.[15] The North American labour market is especially cosmopolitan since European talent features prominently in the professional ranks. "Globalization" has the potential to celebrate cultural diversity and bring an international approach to world problems, but the business model is more one of bringing uniformity to the money-making and idealizing "an expensive international culture in which differences are smoothed over and standardized, in which North Americans, Europeans and Japanese follow the same sports in similar 'world class' facilities".[16] The ultimate goal in the industrial capitalism of sport is to sustain growth by developing markets and reaching the consuming public, and the corporate objective in "globalization" is to see international convergence in lifestyle and consumption.

**Figure 1: Canada — US$ Exchange Rate, 1951-2007**

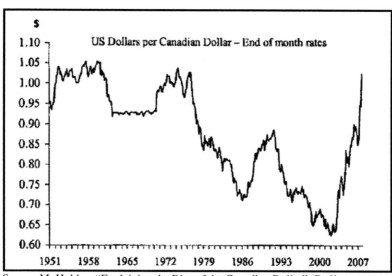

*Source*: M. Holden, "Explaining the Rise of the Canadian Dollar" (Parliamentary Information and Research Service, Library of Parliament, November 22, 2007).

---

[14]  On the remission of duties, see, *Customs Tariff*, S.C. 1997, c. 36, Schedule; *Customs Duties Accelerated Reduction Order, No. 6*, SOR/92-514. See also, *Re Rubber Hockey Pucks* (1986), 11 C.E.R. 142 (Can. Import Trib.) (anti-dumping legislation). On duty-free import into the United States, see, *Bauer Nike Hockey USA, Inc. v. United States*, 393 F.3d 1246 (Fed. Cir., 2004).

[15]  See, "Special report, The Business of Sport, Sponsorship form" *The Economist* (July 31, 2008) (USD $38 billion in sponsorship and USD $449 billion in advertising in 2007).

[16]  R. Gruneau & D. Whitson, *Hockey Night in Canada: Sport, Identities and Cultural Politics* (Toronto: Garamond Press, 1993) at 245.

## 2. The Business of Amateur Hockey

This section notes the commercial dimensions of two leading organizations. Hockey Canada is primarily involved in the administration of the amateur game, but derives substantial revenue from commercial sources. This business orientation applies particularly to the teams of the Canadian Hockey League and the associated junior tournaments.

### a. *Hockey Canada Enterprises*

Hockey Canada operates programs in conjunction with its Branches and associates and is supported by a membership that in 2009 included 585,000 registered players. The programs, services and operations are partly financed by grants from government and funding agencies, but 83 per cent of Hockey Canada's revenue derives from private and commercial sources, including sponsorship (27 per cent), events (24 per cent), goods and services (10 per cent), Branch assessments (8 per cent), interest and other sources (7 per cent), and fundraising (7 per cent).[17] In 2006-07, over 130,000 fans attended national championships and domestic events, and over 120,000 attended the IIHF world women's championship held in Winnipeg in 2007; the 2006 IIHF world junior championship in Vancouver contributed over CDN \$8.6 million.[18] The popularity and profitability of the junior tournament make Canada the favoured site, so that the host cities include Ottawa (2009), Saskatoon and Regina (2010) and Calgary and Edmonton (2012). Major events offer particular opportunities for the sale of licensed products and official merchandise bearing the Team Canada brand, and Hockey Canada was particularly concerned to retain the right to display its logo on team jerseys during the 2010 Winter Olympics. Hockey Canada maintains partnerships with 56 licensees specializing in different categories of product such as clothing, equipment and accessories. Official merchandise is available through 1500 retail storefronts and through mail-order and Internet operators; the value of retail sales in 2007-08 was CDN \$29 million.

Many of the national and international championships are broadcast on The Sports Network ("TSN") and Le Réseau des sports ("RDS"). Given the popularity and exposure of the game, programs and events are of interest to leading corporate sponsors and official suppliers. Hockey Canada's "Premier" marketing partners are Esso, Nike, Royal Bank Financial Group ("RBC") and Telus. The "International" partners include Air Canada, Pepsi, McDonald's, Samsung and Chevrolet, and the fundamental link between hockey and beer is confirmed by the presence of Molson.

---

[17] See, Hockey Canada, *2009 Annual Report*, at 24-25 (operating profit of CDN \$2.7 million in 2008). On finances and rights fees, see, Hockey Canada, By-Law Nine (amended to June 2008).

[18] See, Hockey Canada, *2007 Annual Report*, at 26, 32-33.

The sponsors and corporate partners are subject to taxation on their revenue, although the costs of sponsorship and advertising are a recognized deduction.[19] Hockey Canada itself is subject to a special tax regime. To encourage tax-deductible gifts to national sports organizations,[20] the *Income Tax Act* recognizes a "registered Canadian amateur athletic association"[21] ("RCAAA"), which is defined in section 248(1) as,

> an association that was created under any law in force in Canada, that is resident in Canada, and that
>
> (a)  is a person described in paragraph 149(1)(l), and
>
> (b)  has, as its primary purpose and its primary function, the promotion of amateur athletics in Canada on a nation-wide basis,
>
> that has applied to the Minister in prescribed form for registration, that has been registered and whose registration has not been revoked under subsection 168(2). [22]

The "person" referred to in section 149(1)(l) is a non-profit organization, which means,

> a club, society or association that, in the opinion of the Minister, was not a charity within the meaning assigned by subsection 149.1(1) and that was organized and operated exclusively for social welfare, civic improvement, pleasure or recreation or for any other purpose except profit, no part of the income of which was payable to, or was otherwise available for the personal benefit of, any proprietor, member or shareholder thereof unless the proprietor, member or shareholder was a club, society or association the primary purpose and function of which was the promotion of amateur athletics in Canada.[23]

Hockey Canada qualifies as a RCAAA and a non-profit organization. As such, it is able to issue receipts for donations to its programs and is exempt from income tax on its revenue. Since Hockey Canada is involved in "amateur athletics", it is also able to distribute income to member associations.

Further exemptions apply in relation to the federal goods and services tax ("GST") and provincial retail sales tax. The *Excise Tax Act* recognizes exemptions for goods and services supplied by "public sector bodies",[24] which

---

[19]  See, *Income Tax Act*, R.S.C. 1985 (5th Supp.), c. 1, ss. 18(1)(a), 19.1 (limitation for broadcasting advertising expenses).

[20]  Contributions to RCAAAs are not a significant source of revenue. See also, "Taxman sacks Football Canada" *The Globe and Mail* (Toronto: September 5, 2008) at R6, R11 (Canada Revenue Agency revoked status when associations participated in tax shelter).

[21]  See, *Income Tax* Act, R.S.C. 1985, c. 1 (5th Supp.), ss. 110.1(1)(a)(ii), 118.1(1)(b).

[22]  *Ibid.*, s. 248(1).

[23]  *Ibid.*, s. 149(1)(l).

[24]  See, *Excise Tax Act*, R.S.C. 1985, c. E-15, s. 123 (interpretation), s. 135 (sponsorship of public sector bodies), Schedule V (exempt supplies), Part VI (public sector bodies).

include non-profit organizations and municipalities.[25] In particular, no GST is payable on tickets to attend amateur events in which no remuneration is paid to performers.[26] In Ontario, there is a 10 per cent tax on tickets to "places of amusement", which includes a place where an "athletic contest" or other performance is held.[27] Exemption is provided for events in which the performers receive no remuneration and for events held,

> under the auspices or sponsorship of, (a) a registered Canadian amateur athletic association, as defined by subsection 248(1) of the *Income Tax Act* (Canada), including a branch or affiliate association to which the registration under that Act of the Canadian amateur association of which it is as branch or affiliate has been extended.[28]

In spite of the business orientation of Major Junior competitions, the exemption applies to tickets for games in the Ontario Hockey League ("OHL") since the league offers a form of amateur event under the "auspices" of provincial Branches and Hockey Canada.

### b. Canadian Hockey League

The Canadian Hockey League ("CHL")[29] is the coordinating organization for the three regional Major Junior leagues: the Western Hockey League ("WHL"), the Ontario Hockey League ("OHL") and the Quebec Major Junior League ("QMJHL"). By 2007-08, the leagues had expanded to 60 franchises,[30] including both private companies and community-owned teams.[31] Total regular season attendance was close to 9 million, compared to the 4.7 million fans who attended games of the Canadian NHL teams.[32] In 2007-08, 10 CHL teams had average

---

[25] See: *Metropolitan Toronto Hockey League v. Canada*, [1995] F.C.J. No. 944, [1995] G.S.T.C. 31, 184 N.R. 371 (F.C.A.) (rental of ice time from municipal and school arenas); *Quesnel and District Minor Hockey Assn. v. Canada*, [1997] T.C.J. No. 442, [1997] 3 C.T.C. 2260 (T.C.C.) (association's small food concession operated by volunteers was not subject to GST).

[26] See, *Excise Tax Act*, R.S.C. 1985, c. E-15, Sch. V, Part VI, s. 11; *Club de hockey Les Seigneurs du Kamouraska Inc. v. Canada*, [2003] T.C.J. No. 642, 2003 TCC 786 (T.C.C.) (mistaken collection of GST where no remuneration paid to players).

[27] See, *Retail Sales Tax Act*, R.S.O. 1990, c. R.31, ss. 1, 2(5).

[28] *Retail Sales Tax Act*, R.S.O. 1990, c. R.31, s. 9(2)(a).

[29] See further, Chapter 3, "Organizations and Regulations", sections A, 1, 2; B, 3.

[30] The WHL consists of 22 teams, of which 17 are in the Western provinces and five are in the United States. The OHL consists of 20 teams, of which three are in the United States. The QMJHL consists of 18 teams located in Quebec and the Maritime provinces, with one in the state of Maine.

[31] See also, *River City Hockey, Inc. v. Kamloops Blazers Sports Society*, [2007] B.C.J. No. 2054, 2007 BCSC 1401 (B.C.S.C.) (sale of team owned by society did not require amendment to society's constitution).

[32] See online: <http://www.mib.org/~lennier/hockey/leagueatt.cgi>. See also, Standing Committee on Canadian Heritage, Sub-Committee on the Study of Sport in Canada (Chair, Dennis Mills), *Sport in Canada: Leadership, Partnership and Accountability, Everybody's Business* (House

attendance over 6,000, including the Québec Remparts (11,000), the London Knights (9,000) and the Calgary Hitmen (9,000). The CHL asserts that its teams are "the premiere sports/entertainment attraction in 44 of the 50 Canadian markets."[33]

CHL games are broadcast through national and regional packages with Rogers Sportsnet, RDS and other systems, and games are also available through Internet broadcasting. The "Title Sponsors" of the CHL are ADT, Home Hardware and MasterCard, and the league also maintains the categories of "Associate Sponsor", "Affiliate Sponsor" and "Partner" (*e.g.*, Molson). The product licensees include Reebok/CCM. The regional leagues and individual teams also benefit from associations with international brands and local and national companies.

Given this commercial focus, the franchises are truly in the business of hockey and their players are in insurable and pensionable employment, in spite of the program of university scholarships[34] and the amateur affiliations. With their modest obligations to pay salaries and allowances, CHL teams are valuable assets that have regularly sold for over CDN $3 million since 2004.[35] The business arrangements are illustrated in *Guelph Centre Partners Inc. v. Guelph Storm Ltd.*,[36] where Guelph Centre Partners ("GCP") leased land from the city and built the Guelph Sports and Entertainment Centre, with the city guaranteeing CDN $21 million in loans secured by the building. Guelph Storm Ltd. ("GSL"), owners of the Guelph Storm team, entered into a facility licence agreement with GCP providing for a division of revenue from concessions and advertising and guaranteeing a stated level of revenue from ticket sales. If revenue fell below the guaranteed amount, GSL could demand the difference from GCP, but such a demand for a "Deficiency Payment" entitled GCP to buy the team for CDN $3.25 million. The litigation revolved around GSL's reluctance to satisfy its obligation to provide due diligence information to GCP to enable it to make its decision. Hambly J. concluded that. "The only reasonable inference is that the Due Diligence Materials will show that the hockey team is doing very well. GSL may have agreed to sell the team too cheaply. That is irrelevant....Valid commercial agreements must be upheld."[37]

---

of Commons Canada, November 1998) at 24, 33-36 (CHL attendance "is more than any major league sport in Canada").

[33]  See online: <http://www.chl.ca> at "CHL Fast Facts" (March 2008).

[34]  See, *McCrimmon Holdings Ltd. v. Canada (Minister of National Revenue - M.N.R.)*, [2000] T.C.J. No. 823 (T.C.C.) (player arrangements of Brandon Wheat Kings held not to be "a form of private education").

[35]  See, "Franchise values a good indication of a rosy future" *The Globe and Mail* (Toronto: May 20, 2005) at R7.

[36]  [2005] O.J. No. 457 (Ont. S.C.J.), affd [2005] O.J. No. 5345 (Ont. C.A.) (on basis of settlement, no third party appeared to buy Centre and team; no binding offer for GSL to buy Centre). On costs for taxpayers, see also, *Dolan v. Moose Jaw (City)*, [2008] S.J. No. 813, 52 M.P.L.R. (4th) 25 (Sask. C.A.) (construction of "Multiplex").

[37]  *Guelph Centre Partners Inc. v. Guelph Storm Ltd.*, [2005] O.J. No. 458 at para. 11 (Ont. S.C.J.) (application to enforce judgment).

## 3. Rights, Properties and the Fear of Ambush

Sports organizations and their associated partners look to promote and market their enterprises and "properties". Legal remedies are available against unauthorized promotions that directly infringe recognized rights, but the subtle "ambush" hinting at a business connection is always a possibility in a free market. Besides the problem of the free rider, there is the risk of conflicting sponsorships, especially when individual athletes seek to capitalize on their names and reputations through product endorsements and other commercial ventures.[38] The sponsor of an event seeks a "clean venue" and finds the value of the investment diminished when the name of a corporate rival features prominently in an arena or on the players. Fans wearing the wrong beer advertisement may also be required to remove the offending garment.[39]

"Sports marketing"[40] has the dual senses of "marketing of sports" and "marketing through sports". Marketing is a co-ordinated process to generate revenue and realize goals by identifying demand and maintaining consumer satisfaction. It involves researching wants and needs and then promoting and delivering a program, product or service through suitable public relations, selling techniques and schedules of price and payment.[41] Marketing *of* sports refers to techniques used by sports organizations to promote their own products and services. Given fans' love of team clothing and gear, this includes merchandising agreements[42] with manufacturers by which the organization takes a share of revenue ("royalties") from the sale of licensed goods bearing the organization's name or marks. In marketing *through* sports, wider business enterprises associate themselves with organizations or events and use the publicity, appeal and celebrity of sport to reach a target audience. Although companies are free to make unacknowledged, benevolent donations, their preferred association is one that has the potential for exposure and revenue. In a leading decision involving MasterCard, the court noted:

> MasterCard utilizes sports sponsorships around the world to increase public awareness of, preference for and usage of its brand...Through advertising rights associated with a given sponsorship, MasterCard is able to promote its brand to target audiences. Furthermore, through the development and execution of

---

[38] On players' personality rights, see Chapter 7, "The Business of Hockey", section A, 4.

[39] See, "The new World Cup rule: Take off your trousers, they're offending the sponsor" *The Guardian* (London: June 19, 2006) (Dutch fans forced to remove garish "Bavaria" trousers; official sponsors included Budweiser, Yahoo and McDonald's). On conditions of entry to premises, see Chapter 4, "Build Safe: Rink Management and Risk Management", section A, 4.

[40] See: C.M. Brooks, *Sports Marketing: Competitive Business Strategies for Sports* (Englewood Cliffs: Prentice-Hall, 1994); B.J. Mullin, S. Hardy & W.A. Sutton, *Sport Marketing*, 3d ed. (Champaign: Human Kinetics Publishers, 2007).

[41] On legal standards in promotions, advertising and labelling, see, B. Pritchard & S. Vogt, *Advertising and Marketing Law in Canada*, 3d ed. (Markham, ON: LexisNexis Canada, 2009).

[42] See, R. Verow, C. Lawrence & P. McCormick, *Sports Business: Law, Practice and Precedents*, 2d ed. (Bristol: Jordan Publishing, 2005) at 257-72, 406-19.

marketing programs tied to the sponsorship, MasterCard and its member institutions are further able to leverage the sponsorship directly into increased card issuances and usage. Sponsorships also provide MasterCard with content for many of its advertising campaigns.[43]

When general commercial enterprises or industrial sectors buy into sports performances, there should be a symbiotic exchange of interests as sports organizations, media and sponsoring companies engage in mutual promotion. The challenge for sports organizations is to make deals that contribute to the financing of programs without entirely abandoning their interests to the corporate sector.

Companies seek access to consumers through mechanisms such as space advertising, television advertising[44] or sponsorship. Besides traditional means of display, the exposure can involve websites and the use of other outlets based on the Internet or telecommunications systems.[45] The medium, "platform" or gadget can be as attractive as the product or service on offer, and delivery via the Internet is particularly effective in reaching a young audience. An advertisement is a display, announcement or sales pitch directly promoting a company's wares or services. The available techniques now include "virtual advertising" by which the image visible on television differs from what is in the arena.[46] Sponsorship[47] is a right of public association designed to publicize the name of the sponsor and enhance its image or reputation by sharing in the goodwill of an event, program or other activity. Through the contract, the sponsor and the sports organization obtain designated rights to use each other's names, logos or other properties.

Advertisers and sponsors look for certainty in their acquired rights and seek value for money through some guarantee of exposure and exclusivity. By way of preliminary precaution, they should ensure that they negotiate with the body that actually holds the desired rights,[48] and the promotion should not be contrary to association regulations or general law.[49] Official sponsors (as opposed to ambush merchants) buy the right of association by entering into a promotional licence

---

[43]    *MasterCard International Inc. v. Fédération Internationale de Football Assn.*, 464 F. Supp. 2d 246 at 251 (S.D.N.Y., 2006), *per* Preska Dist. J.

[44]    See, *Coca-Cola Ltd. v. The Sports Network*, [1992] O.J. No. 2010, 44 C.P.R. (3d) 478 (Ont. Gen. Div.) (non-renewal of Coke's advertising contract for Blue Jays' games; TSN entered into new contract with Pepsi).

[45]    On "new media" revenue in the NHL, see Chapter 7, "The Business of Hockey", section B, 2.

[46]    See, H.Y. Mendez, "Virtual Signage: The Pitfalls of 'Now You See It, Now You Don't'" (1999) 8:4 Sport Marketing Q. 15.

[47]    See: S. Townley & E. Grayson, *Sponsorship of Sport, Arts and Leisure: Law, Tax and Business Relationships* (London: Sweet & Maxwell, 1984); J. Amis & T.B. Cornwell, eds., *Global Sport Sponsorship* (Oxford: Berg, 2005).

[48]    See, for example: Hockey Canada, By-Law 905 (amended to June 2008) (broadcasting and television fees); IIHF Statutes and Bylaws, 2008–2012 (July 2008), Statute 13, Bylaw 410 (commercial and other rights).

[49]    On advertising and sponsorship involving tobacco products, see: *Tobacco Act*, S.C. 1997, c. 13, ss. 20, 22, 24; *Canada (Attorney General) v. JTI-Macdonald Corp.*, [2007] S.C.J. No. 30, [2007] 2 S.C.R. 610 (S.C.C.).

agreement linking them to the sports organization as a whole or to some aspect of its programs. The sponsorship contract[50] should specify the rights granted (including entitlements to tickets and hospitality facilities) and deal with matters such as the payment of fees or benefits, the territorial scope of the rights, the duration of the agreement and grounds for termination. The right to renew the contract is an important element as sponsors may claim option powers or rights such as "first offer", "right to match" or "first right to acquire".[51] The contract must provide particular detail as to how the sponsor's name or logo will be acknowledged, whether on signs, tickets, publications or background sets used for press conferences or other sessions with media. The anticipated coverage through broadcasting or on-line systems is of fundamental concern to sponsors, and the sports organization may be obliged to ensure that its third-party contracts with media ensure due exposure. Special rights are usually given to leading sponsors such as those who purchase naming rights attached to an event, trophy or award. The name sponsor of a league or arena[52] qualifies as a principal player who has paid handsomely for the privilege. Leading sponsors and "official suppliers" usually claim the right to approve minor sponsors or to veto business rivals whose presence would undermine their exclusive status. The careful categorization of sponsors is one way of keeping competitors apart. Where an agreement grants advertising rights, precision is required as to the size and location of the advertisement. The allocation of space may involve arena signage,[53] the scoreboard, players' uniforms or some other billboard.

Various types of action serve to protect the exclusive rights of owners and licensees.[54] An arena and its tenant team are entitled to prevent the distribution of a rival magazine on their lands,[55] and remedies are sometimes available against scalpers selling tickets above the issue price.[56] The "secondary sales" business is

---

[50]   See, R. Verow, C. Lawrence & P. McCormick, *Sports Business: Law, Practice and Precedents*, 2d ed. (Bristol: Jordan Publishing, 2005) at 235-56, 396-405.

[51]   See, *MasterCard International Inc. v. Fédération Internationale de Football Assn.*, 464 F. Supp. 2d 246 (S.D.N.Y., 2006), remanded 239 Fed. App'x. 625 (2nd Cir., 2007) (MasterCard granted injunction after FIFA sold sponsorship rights to VISA).

[52]   See, for example, *Ice Gardens at York University Inc. v. Parmalat Dairy and Bakery Inc.*, [2004] O.J. No. 1083 (Ont. S.C.J.) (arena's entitlement to payment under five-year contract for sponsorship and naming rights).

[53]   See: *Oland Breweries Ltd. v. Trade Centre Ltd.*, [1984] N.S.J. No. 441, 65 N.S.R. (2d) 204 (N.S.T.D.) (renewal of contract to display advertisements in arena; injunction to prevent display of rival signs refused); *Magellan Entertainment Group (Ontario) Inc. v. Global Media Corp.* (1999), 90 A.C.W.S. (3d) 702 (Ont. S.C.J.) (breach of contract and duress by race promoter; promoter not entitled to additional funds from advertisers and sponsors).

[54]   On unfair competition and business practices, see also: *Competition Act*, R.S.C. 1985, c. C-34, s. 52 (misleading advertising), s. 53 (testimonials), s. 60 (defence); *Consumer Protection Act, 2002*, S.O. 2002, c. 30, Sch. A.

[55]   See, *Gameday Publication(s) Ltd. v. Keystone Agricultural and Recreational Centre Inc.*, [1999] M.J. No. 57, 170 D.L.R. (4th) 617 (Man. C.A.) (magazine was in direct competition with Brandon Wheat Kings' program).

[56]   See, *Ticket Speculation Act*, R.S.O. 1990, c. T.7 (prohibition and penalties). See also: *R. v. Cacciatore*, [2002] O.J. No. 2366, 161 O.A.C. 132 (Ont. C.A.) (scalper ticketed as unlicensed

operated both by street dealers[57] and established agencies[58] offering online reservation services. Further causes of action relate to intellectual property, including the statutory rights associated with trademarks, patents and copyright.[59] The common law action for passing-off is also available where one trader pretends that goods are those of someone else.[60] The owner of the business goodwill then brings action for damage caused by a confusing and false representation as to the origin or identity of the wares or services.[61]

Sports organizations now regularly register distinguishing names and insignia and defend them by trademark opposition proceedings and actions alleging infringement or confusion.[62] The Baltimore team in the Canadian Football League duly found itself in conflict with the National Football League over the use of the name "Colts".[63] Marks should also be registered for the purpose of websites and domain names to supplement the special protections and dispute resolution processes that apply to cyber-addresses.[64] In 1982, the Canadian Olympic Association (now, Canadian Olympic Committee ("COC")) was held to be a "public authority"[65] for the purpose of s. 9(1)(n)(iii) of the *Trade-marks*

---

pedlar of "goods"); *R. v. Wassilyn*, [2006] O.J. No. 2900, 25 M.P.L.R. (4th) 277 (Ont. C.J.) (sale of event tickets contrary to municipal code).

[57]   See, *Toronto Blue Jays Baseball Club v. John Doe*, [1992] O.J. No. 1086, 9 O.R. (3d) 622 (Ont. Gen. Div.) (order for return of tickets refused). See also, B.M. Pukier, "Exiled on Main Street: A Ticket Scalper's Dilemma" (1992) 50 U.T. Fac. L. Rev. 282.

[58]   See, *Toronto Blue Jays Baseball Club v. Tri-Tickets Inc.*, [1991] O.J. No. 2002, 85 D.L.R. (4th) 422 (Ont. Gen. Div.) (injunction refused). See also, J. Gibson, "Hot tickets" *The Lawyers Weekly* (May 9, 2008) at 7.

[59]   On criminal prosecution for the sale of counterfeit merchandise, see, *R. v. AFC Soccer*, [2002] M.J. No. 441, 22 C.P.R. (4th) 369 (Man. Prov. Ct.), revd [2004] M.J. No. 194, [2005] 1 W.W.R. 666 (Man. C.A.).

[60]   See: *Centre Ice Ltd. v. National Hockey League*, [1994] F.C.J. No. 68, 53 C.P.R. (3d) 34 (F.C.A.) ("Centre Ice" goods); *Sport Maska inc. c. Canstar Sports Group inc.*, [1994] J.Q. no 2044, 57 C.P.R. (3d) 323 (Que. S.C.) (action in relation to hockey helmets dismissed); *Hillerich & Bradsby Co. v. Christian Brothers, Inc.*, 943 F.Supp. 1136 (D. Minn., 1996) (injunction to prevent sale of "Marc Messier" blades). See also, *Trade-marks Act*, R.S.C. 1985, c. T-13, s. 7.

[61]   On the guarantee of origin, see, *Arsenal Football Club PLC v. Reed*, [2003] EWCA Civ 696 (C.A.) (vendor sold merchandise carrying club's marks).

[62]   See: for example, *Boston Professional Hockey Assn., Inc. v. Dallas Cap & Emblem MFG., Inc.*, 510 F.2d 1004 (5th Cir., 1975) (cloth emblems showing plaintiffs' marks); *Leaf Confections Ltd. v. Maple Leaf Gardens Ltd.*, [1986] F.C.J. No. 766, 12 C.P.R. (3d) 511 (F.C.T.D.), affd [1988] F.C.J. No. 176, 19 C.P.R. (3d) 331 (F.C.A.) ("Leaf" and design in association with bubble gum; resemblance and confusion with well-known Toronto mark); *Hockey Canada v. Hofbauer Associates*, [1999] F.C.J. No. 1571 (F.C.). See also, *Canadian Tire Corp. v. Accessoires d'autos Nordiques Inc.*, [2007] F.C.J. No. 1555, 2007 FCA 367 (F.C.A.) (survey evidence; "Nordiques" evokes nostalgic images of the hockey team).

[63]   *Indianapolis Colts, Inc. v. Metropolitan Baltimore Football Club*, 34 F.3d 410 (7th Cir., 1994).

[64]   Arbitration procedures are available through the World Intellectual Property Organization, in accordance with the Uniform Domain Name Dispute Resolution Policy; see, <http://arbiter.wipo.int>. See also, *Anticybersquatting Consumer Protection Act*, 15 U.S.C. s.1129 (2001).

[65]   *Registrar of Trade Marks v. Canadian Olympic Assn.*, [1982] F.C.J. No. 174, [1983] 1 F.C. 692 (F.C.A.).

*Act*[66] and gained the right to object to marks "resembling" its own. The COC has since been zealous in enjoining unapproved use of over 100 words, numbers and pictograms, but was unsuccessful in a case relating to fundraising campaigns where there was no evidence that phrases had been used by the Olympic movement.[67] The *Olympic and Paralympic Marks Act*[68] grants special protection for words or phrases associated with the Olympic movement and with the 2010 Vancouver and Whistler Winter Olympics. Subject to "excepted uses" (see, s. 3(4)) and references in news reports (see, s. 3(5)), no person may use designated marks "in connection with a business" (see, s. 3(1)). Businesses are also prohibited from directing attention to themselves through a misleading implication that they are approved by an Olympic organization or are associated with the Olympics (see, s. 4(1)).

New and useful inventions may be granted patents.[69] Patents apply particularly to technological innovations and improvements in equipment,[70] although an invention may also relate to an "art" or "process". There is, therefore, some possibility of patenting a novel athletic move or playing technique.[71] Works of literary creation and other forms of original expression are protected by copyright.[72] A league or association may, for example, claim rights in a fixture list[73] or database,[74] and an artist may claim that the design of a logo is his creation.[75] Copyright is less certain with respect to sporting information such as game scores since sports events are not "authored",[76] although the action might be allowed where a competitor free-rides on

---

[66] R.S.C. 1985, c. T-13.

[67] *See You In - Canadian Athletes Fund Corp. v. Canadian Olympic Committee*, [2007] F.C.J. No. 541, 57 C.P.R. (4th) 287 (F.C.), affd [2008] F.C.J. No. 580, 65 C.P.R. (4th) 421 (F.C.A.).

[68] S.C. 2007, c. 25. See, T. Scassa, "Faster, Higher, Stronger: The Protection of Olympic and Paralympic Marks Leading up to Vancouver 2010" (2008) 41 U.B.C. L. Rev. 31.

[69] See, *Patent Act*, R.S.C. 1985, c. P-4.

[70] See, for example: *Puckhandler Inc. v. BADS Industries Inc.* (1998), 81 C.P.R. (3d) 261 (Pat. App. Bd. and Commr. of Pat.) (licence for hockey stick training device); *Giffin v. Canstar Sports Group Inc.*, [1990] F.C.J. No. 233, 30 C.P.R. (3d) 238 (F.C.T.D.) (skate); *Bauer Nike Hockey Inc. v. Easton Sports Canada Inc.*, [2006] F.C.J. No. 1362, 54 C.P.R. (4th) 182 (F.C.) (skate boot).

[71] See, J.A. Smith, "It's Your Move - No It's Not! The Application of Patent Law to Sports Moves" (1999) 70 U. Colo. L. Rev. 1051. On copyright protection, see, H.M. Abromson, "The Copyrightability of Sports Celebration Moves: Dance Fever or Just Plain Sick" (2004) 14 Marq. Sports L.J. 571.

[72] See, *Copyright Act*, R.S.C. 1985, c. C-42. On copyright in broadcasts, see Chapter 7, "The Business of Hockey", section B, 4.

[73] *Football League Ltd. v. Littlewoods Pools Ltd.*, [1959] 2 All E.R. 546 (Ch. Div.).

[74] *British Horseracing Board Ltd. v. William Hill Organization Ltd.*, [2005] 1 C.M.L.R. 15 (E.C.J.); *British Horseracing Board Ltd. v. William Hill Organization Ltd.*, [2005] EWCA Civ 863 (C.A.).

[75] *Robb v. Orca Bay Sports and Entertainment*, [1999] B.C.J. No. 34, 1 C.P.R. (4th) 49 (B.C.S.C.) (action dismissed; logo of Vancouver Canucks did not imitate plaintiff's work).

[76] *National Basketball Assn. v. Motorola, Inc.*, 105 F.3d 841 (2nd Cir., 1997) (pager displaying information on games in progress).

information produced by a league.[77] A musical composition is a fixed work and subject to copyright. Signature music for the CBC's "Hockey Night in Canada" was composed in 1968 by Dolores Claman, who originally received a one-time creative fee, while retaining property rights in the anthem; she later became entitled to "theme" licence payments and other fees-for-use.[78] After the public network conducted unsuccessful negotiations to buy the composition during 2007-08, ownership passed to the CTV, which apparently paid well over CDN $1 million to obtain perpetual rights to Ms Claman's tune. The iconic notes then served to introduce hockey broadcasts by the CTV and its affiliated channels, and the CBC launched a contest to find a new theme for "Hockey Night in Canada".[79] Through the formal purchase of rights, the CTV was guilty of neither "poaching" nor "ambush", although it was able to benefit from the music's cultural associations.

The term "ambush marketing"[80] is sometimes applied to the unauthorized use of trademarks and other properties, but is best reserved for intrusive promotions that piggyback on an organization or event without obviously misappropriating legal rights.[81] The ambush challenges the exclusivity in sponsorship arrangements by implying a link or relationship. It relies on rights of free speech and often shows imagination, although the creativity is not appreciated by official sponsors and suppliers. An ambushing Telecom advertisement has been characterized as "adventurous", while the complaining organizations were regarded as "a little paranoid".[82] One strategy is to present images of athletes and sporting activity at times when there is likely to be a general association with an upcoming event. Other techniques include expressions of support to athletes, congratulatory announcements and the offer of prizes and rewards. Sometimes a company has no official link to the Games or tournament as a whole but is able to exploit its tie-in with a participating player or team. A company may also get exposure through an established minor sponsorship or through advertising rights held with a broadcaster. Although official sponsors object to the alleged ambush

---

[77] *Morris Communications Corp. v. PGA Tour, Inc.*, 235 F.Supp. 2d 1269 (M.D. Fla., 2002), affd 364 F.3d 1288 (11th Cir., 2004) (property right in golf scores before they are in the public domain; Tour had right to control access to information).

[78] See, "Hockey theme 'wasn't hard to do'" *The Globe and Mail* (Toronto: June 12, 2008) at A1, A10.

[79] See, "CTV's going to be calling the tune now after composer sells Hockey Night song" *The Globe and Mail* (Toronto: June 10, 2008) at A1, A9. In October 2008, "Canadian Gold" by Colin Oberst was selected as the new theme for CBC broadcasts. Oberst was awarded CDN $100,000 and 50 per cent of royalties.

[80] See: L.L. Bean, "Ambush Marketing: Sport Sponsorship Confusion and the Lanham Act" (1995) 75 B.U.L. Rev. 1099; A.M. Wall, "The Game Behind the Games" (2002) 12 Marq. Sports L.J. 557 (protection of Olympic sponsors); S. McKelvey & J. Grady, "Sponsorship Program Protection Strategies for Special Sport Events: Are Event Organizers Outmaneuvering Ambush Marketers?" (2006) 22 J. of Sport Management 550.

[81] See, J. Hoek, "Ambush Marketing: Research and Management Implications" in J. Amis & T.B. Cornwell, eds., *Global Sport Sponsorship* (Oxford: Berg, 2005) at 207.

[82] *New Zealand Olympic and Commonwealth Games Assn. Inc. v. Telecom New Zealand Ltd.* (1996), 35 I.P.R. 55 at 61-62 (N.Z.H.C.), *per* McGechen J.

as unfair dealing, corporate competitors cannot be expected to abandon sports themes or withdraw from their promotional activities for the duration of an event. If rights have been infringed, official sponsors enjoy extensive common law and statutory remedies, and further protection can be achieved through contractual provisions and the comprehensive coordination of sponsorships.

In the leading decision on "ambush marketing", the court determined that an advertising campaign did not create a false impression of authorization and endorsement by the NHL. In *National Hockey League v. Pepsi-Cola Canada Ltd.*,[83] the league objected to a Pepsi promotional contest and to CBC advertisements that showed Don Cherry, "dressed in his own inimitable style", explaining the contest to three hockey players of goonish demeanour. For USD $2.6 million, NHL Services Ltd. had licensed Coca-Cola as the "official Soft Drink of the NHL", giving Coke the right to use league and team symbols. The NHL had, however, sold broadcast rights to Molson Breweries, which granted Pepsi the exclusive right to advertise soft drinks during the CBC's "Hockey Night in Canada". Pepsi had, therefore, acquired some lawful connection with NHL games. Pepsi's contest used scratch cards and bottle caps referring to NHL cities and the outcome of play-off series (*e.g.*, "Calgary in Six"). The bottle tags and television advertisements contained a disclaimer stating that the "Pro Hockey Playoff Pool is neither associated with nor sponsored by the National Hockey League". Hardinge J. found nothing illegal in the contest and held that Pepsi had not interfered with performance of the contract between Coke and NHL Services Ltd. There had been no use of trademarks, and it was quite proper to refer to the league by its correct name in the disclaimer. Hardinge J. dismissed an action for passing-off, finding no false representation of league approval of the contest. The reasonable viewer would regard Cherry's Pepsi-talks as "amusing but obvious spoofs".[84]

## 4.   Personality Rights

Besides the recognized properties of organizations, rights of privacy, personality and publicity attach to individuals.[85] Prominent celebrities in sports and entertainment[86] regularly license their names or images for use in authorised

---

[83]   [1992] B.C.J. No. 1221, 92 D.L.R. (4th) 349 (B.C.S.C.), affd [1995] B.C.J. No. 310, 122 D.L.R. (4th) 412 (B.C.C.A.). See also, *National Hockey League v. Pepsi-Cola Canada Ltd.*, [1993] B.C.J. No. 1301, 48 C.P.R. (3d) 149 (B.C.S.C.), affd [1995] B.C.J. No. 311, 59 C.P.R. (3d) 225 (B.C.C.A.). (Pepsi awarded increased costs).

[84]   *Ibid.*, at 92 D.L.R. (4th) 349 at 372, *per* Hardinge J. See also: *Cardtoons, L.C. v. Major League Baseball Players Assn.*, 868 F.Supp. 1266 (N.D. Okla., 1994), affd 95 F.3d 959 (10th Cir., 1996) (caricature cards; parody defence); *New Zealand Olympic and Commonwealth Games Assn. Inc. v. Telecom New Zealand Ltd.* (1996), 35 I.P.R. 55 (N.Z.H.C.) (injunction refused against advertisement using the word "ring" five times).

[85]   B. Pritchard & S. Vogt, *Advertising and Marketing Law in Canada*, 3d ed. (Markham, ON: LexisNexis, 2009) at 313-27.

[86]   See: *Heath v. Weist-Barron School of Television Canada Ltd.*, [1981] O.J. No. 3109, 34 O.R. (2d) 126 (Ont. H.C.J.) (photograph of child actor); *Gould Estate v. Stoddart Publishing Co.*, [1996] O.J. No. 3288, 30 O.R. (3d) 520 (Ont. Gen. Div.), affd [1998] O.J. No. 1894, 39 O.R.

promotions and may take action where their identity has been misappropriated.[87] In various proceedings brought by Tony Twist, the former "enforcer" with the Quebec Nordiques and St. Louis Blues objected to the use of his name in association with a comic book and action figures.[88] Rights may be protected by common law actions,[89] and further rights and remedies are recognized under provincial legislation.[90] The right to privacy enjoys particular protection under the legal system of Quebec.[91] A further accepted right relates to good reputation, which may be protected in defamation proceedings[92] or other actions alleging that the individual's public standing was diminished.[93]

Celebrities are able to exploit their fame by agreeing to speaking engagements or other public appearances and have opportunities to enter into personal endorsement, sponsorship and licensing contracts.[94] For a chosen few, the income from these sources can vastly exceed the salaries paid under contracts of employment. Maurice Richard famously endorsed Grecian Formula, and the corporate Wayne Gretzky realised substantial commercial revenue during the 1980s and 1990s. Endorsement is a technique of promotion and marketing by

---

(3d) 545 (Ont. C.A.) (photographer held copyright for the purpose of a book about Glenn Gould).

[87] But see: *Krouse v. Chrysler Canada Ltd.*, [1973] O.J. No. 2157, 1 O.R. (2d) 225 (Ont. C.A.) (no specific exploitation of player's personality in automobile advertisement); *Joseph v. Daniels (Brent Daniels Photography)*, [1986] B.C.J. No. 3231, 4 B.C.L.R. (2d) 239 (B.C.S.C.) (bodybuilder was not recognizable); *Horton v. Tim Donut Ltd.*, [1997] O.J. No. 390, 75 C.P.R. (3d) 451 (Ont. Gen. Div.), affd [1997] O.J. No. 4154, 75 C.P.R. (3d) 467 (Ont. C.A.) (rights had been licensed to company and purpose was charitable).

[88] *Doe a/k/a Tony Twist v. TCI Cablevision*, 110 S.W.3d 363 (S.C. Mo., 2003); *Doe a/k/a Tony Twist v. McFarlane*, 207 S.W.3d 52 (C.A. Mo., 2006).

[89] See: *Athans v. Canadian Adventure Camps Ltd.*, [1977] O.J. No. 2417, 17 O.R. (2d) 425 (Ont. H.C.J.) (wrongful use of photograph of water-skier in advertisement); D. Gibson, "Comment on *Athans v. Canadian Adventure Camps Ltd.*" (1978) 4 C.C.L.T. 37; *Salé v. Barr*, [2003] A.J. No. 595, [2003] 10 W.W.R. 720 (Alta. Q.B.) (injunction against use of photographs of professional figure skaters).

[90] See: *Privacy Act*, R.S.B.C. 1996, c. 373; *The Privacy Act*, R.S.S. 1978, c. P-24; *Privacy Act*, C.C.S.M. c. P125; *Privacy Act*, R.S.N.L. 1990, c. P-22; D. Vaver, "What's Mine Is Not Yours: Commercial Appropriation of Personality under the Privacy Acts of British Columbia, Manitoba and Saskatchewan" (1981) 15 U.B.C. L. Rev. 241; *Joseph v. Daniels (Brent Daniels Photography)*, [1986] B.C.J. No. 3231, 4 B.C.L.R. (2d) 239 (B.C.S.C.).

[91] See: *Charter of human rights and freedoms*, R.S.Q. c. C-12, s. 5; *Aubry v. Éditions Vice-Versa inc.*, [1998] S.C.J. No. 30, [1998] 1 S.C.R. 591 (S.C.C.) (photograph taken without consent); *Marquis c. Journal de Québec, division de Communications Québécor inc.*, [2002] J.Q. no 3813, 219 D.L.R. (4th) 305 (Que. C.A.) (no breach of privacy); S.H. Abramovitch, "Publicity Exploitation of Celebrities: Protection of a Star's Style in Quebec Civil Law" (1991) 32 C. de D. 301.

[92] Some libel actions are noted at, Chapter 4, "Build Safe: Rink Management and Risk Management", section A, 2.

[93] On actions for wrongful dismissal in relation to broadcasting, see: *Racine v. C.J.R.C. Radio capitale ltée*, [1977] O.J. No. 2407, 17 O.R. (2d) 370 (Ont. Co. Ct.); *Cranston v. Canadian Broadcasting Corp.*, [1994] O.J. No. 605, 2 C.C.E.L. (2d) 301 (Ont. Gen. Div.) (loss of publicity for retired skater).

[94] See, R. Verow, C. Lawrence & P. McCormick, *Sports Business: Law, Practice and Precedents*, 2d ed. (Bristol: Jordan Publishing, 2005) at 206-12, 381-87.

which companies rely on the association with the celebrity: it is a form of sponsorship or advertising in which the celebrity is seen to use and recommend a product or service. The endorsement contract usually obliges the celebrity to make specified personal appearances in promotions and grants to the company rights to use the name, personality or image of the celebrity.[95] The company seeks exclusivity, so that the celebrity is prohibited from endorsing a rival product within the same category. A "morals" or "Tiger" clause is also advisable to allow the company to terminate the contract should the celebrity bring disgrace or disrepute through particular types of misconduct.

A player's fame is usually based on the connection with a team, and there is the potential for conflict between personal endorsement deals and the sponsorship arrangements of the team or league. The commercial rights of individual NHL players and of the NHLPA are subject to the collective bargaining agreement ("CBA") and the standard player contract ("SPC"),[96] which include provision for "performance rights" where players' skills are caught in film or television footage.[97] By article 25.3 of the CBA, the league or team may use "game action" images in their sponsorships, provided the focus is not on an individual player. The SPC recognizes that the player owns exclusive rights to his individual personality, although the written consent of the team is required for the player to make public appearances or to sponsor commercial products.

The NHLPA licenses companies that provide services to hockey pools and has been concerned about the use of the names and images of players in the pools.[98] The use of games in gambling systems has also drawn the attention of the leagues.

## 5.  Betting and Gambling

> The gaming industry is one of the largest entertainment industries in Canada. It is larger than television and movie rentals and it is larger than the combined revenues generated by magazines and book sales, drinking places, spectator sports, movie theatres and performing arts.[99]

Sports betting is one sector of the general gambling business conducted by authorized agencies of provincial governments such as the Ontario Lottery and Gaming Corporation ("OLG").[100] Services are also offered by casinos and book-

---

[95]   See, for example, *Hillerich & Bradsby Co. v. Christian Brothers, Inc.*, 943 F.Supp. 1136 (D. Minn., 1996) (Mark Messier stick blades).

[96]   See, Collective Bargaining Agreement of NHL (2005), article 25; Standard Player Contract of NHL (2005), para. 8. See further, Chapter 9, "National Hockey League", sections B; C; E.

[97]   But see, *Baltimore Orioles, Inc. v. Major League Baseball Players' Assn.*, 805 F.2d 663 (7th Cir., 1986) (players' publicity rights pre-empted by copyright law).

[98]   See, "NHLPA expects piece of pool pie" *The Ottawa Citizen* (September 5, 1998) at F7.

[99]   Canadian Gaming Association, *Economic Impact of the Canadian Gaming Industry* (January 2008) at v; see online: Canadian Gaming Association <http://www.canadiangaming.ca> and <http://cga.bristolnet.ca>.

[100]  See, *Ontario Lottery and Gaming Corporation Act, 1999*, S.O. 1999, c. 12, Sched. L; online: Ontario Lottery and Gaming Corporation <http://www.olg.ca>. See also, *Gaming Control Act, 1992*, S.O. 1992, c. 24.

makers in states and countries that permit betting and by illegal bookmaking operations. One area of rapid growth for the business has been online betting.

Although punters represent a committed group of fans, professional leagues express formal opposition to betting as a threat to the integrity of contests and impose disciplinary sanctions on players or officials who are implicated in inappropriate betting schemes.[101] The leagues also object to the use of their games, names and trade-marks in betting systems,[102] especially when they receive no share of the substantial revenue.[103] In 1992, the Ontario Lottery Corporation introduced "Sport Select Pro-Line" which involved predicting the outcome of major league games.[104] In 1994, as a condition of granting the Toronto Raptors franchise, the National Basketball Association insisted that its games be removed from "Pro-Line". The Ontario government agreed to this in exchange for the league and the Raptors making payments for medical research and other public and charitable projects.[105]

The *Criminal Code*[106] prohibits commercial betting, gaming, pool-selling, bookmaking and lotteries (see, ss. 201-203, 206), but provides exemptions for "lottery schemes" operated by provincial governments or by organizations licensed by provincial governments (see, s. 207).[107] By section 207(4)(b), a "lottery scheme" does not include betting on a single sport event. The *Criminal Code* also recognizes the pari-mutuel system of wagering on horse races which is maintained through regulations issued by the federal Minister of Agriculture (see, s. 204). No offence in relation to sections 201 or 202 is committed where a person is the stakeholder for money to be paid to the winner of a lawful race or game, or for money to be paid to "the winner of any bets between not more than ten individuals (see, s. 204(1)(a)). Similarly, no crime is committed in relation to "a private bet between individuals not engaged in any way in the business of betting" (see, s. 204(1)(b)).

The substantial provincial control of the operation of betting and lotteries dates from 1985 when the federal government withdrew from the business in exchange for a lump sum and an annual indexed payment based on lottery

---

[101]  See Chapter 9, "National Hockey League", section D, 2.

[102]  See, *National Hockey League v. Quebec (Société des Loteries et courses)*, [1993] F.C.J. No. 824, 50 C.P.R. (3d) 481 (F.C.T.D.) (infringement action withdrawn). See also, *Professional and Amateur Sports Protections Act*, P.L. 102-559, 102nd Cong., 2nd Sess.; *Legislation Prohibiting State Lotteries from Misappropriating Professional Sports Service Marks*, Hearings before Senate Subcommittee on Patents, Copyrights and Trade Marks (101st Cong., 2nd Sess., June 26, 1990).

[103]  On the subsidy of professional teams, see Chapter 7, "The Business of Hockey", section B, 3.

[104]  O. Reg. 630/92, s. 2(2) made under *Ontario Lottery Corporation Act*, R.S.O. 1990, c. 0.25 (lotteries based on the outcome of events).

[105]  See, "Big-league basketball coming to Toronto" *The Globe and Mail* (Toronto: February 11, 1994) at A1, A7.

[106]  R.S.C. 1985, c. C-46.

[107]  See, *R. v. Furtney*, [1991] S.C.J. No. 70, [1991] 3 S.C.R. 89 (S.C.C.) (provincial licensing of lottery schemes is constitutionally valid).

sales.[108] The forms of authorized play now include electronic gaming machines and casinos, so that in 2008,

> Net revenue from government-run lotteries, video lottery terminals (VLTs), casinos and slot machines not in casinos...[was] $13.67 billion...Net revenue from pari-mutuel betting (horse racing)...[was] $378 million...[109]

In 2007, 52 per cent of households engaged in one gambling activity, at an average annual expenditure of CDN $646.00.[110] As noted in Chapter 2, "Legal Fundamentals and Equality Rights", revenue from the various gambling systems is one source of funding for sports, fitness and recreation programs.[111]

"Sport Select" betting operated by the authorised provincial gaming corporations[112] is lawful where it involves picking a series of winning results or scores. The various games are a form of parlay betting in which wagers are placed on at least three matches identified by general reference to the sport and the city of the home team. The cumulative nature of the bet gives a heavy advantage to the house, so that the "Sport Select" punter is unlikely to profit in the long run. Betting based on picking winners is also offered by the underworld fraternity:

> Sport Select, with a 35% house edge, does not compete well with illegal bookmaking operations for serious bettors. In addition to providing a far better pay out percentage, illegal bookmakers offer client-friendly services such as extended hours of operation, more extensive betting menus, telephone betting, credit and higher betting limits that Sport Select cannot match.[113]

With their improved odds and higher stakes, the illegal bookmakers therefore find a heavy demand for their formats and services. From 1997 to 2001, investigations of the different types of illegal gambling in Ontario,

> recorded 1,370 illegal gambling occurrences, 2,069 persons charged, 3,517 charges laid, and 2,034 machines seized at a value of $6,016,505. In addition, $1,233,763 in cash was seized and $2,839,533 worth of fines and forfeitures was imposed.[114]

---

[108]  See: J. Barnes, *Sports and the Law in Canada*, 3d ed. (Toronto: Butterworths Canada, 1996) at 27-30; C.S. Campbell, T.F. Hartnagel & G.J. Smith, *The Legalization of Gambling in Canada (What is a Crime?)* (Law Commission of Canada, July 2005) at III, "The Federal-Provincial Struggle Over Gambling".

[109]  Statistics Canada, *Perspectives on Labour and Income* (July 2009), "Gambling". See also, Canadian Gaming Association, *Economic Impact of the Canadian Gaming Industry: Key Findings Report* (January 2008).

[110]  Statistics Canada, *Perspectives on Labour and Income* (July 2009), "Household expenditures on gambling activities".

[111]  See Chapter 2, "Legal Fundamentals and Equality Rights", section B, 4.

[112]  See, *Canada (A.G.) v. Loto Québec*, [1983] J.Q. no 475, 9 C.C.C. (3d) 508 (Que. C.A.) ("Hockey Select" held to be permitted scheme).

[113]  C.S. Campbell, T.F. Hartnagel & G.J. Smith, *The Legalization of Gambling in Canada (What is a Crime?)* (Law Commission of Canada, July 2005), at IX, "Accounting for Illegal Gambling".

[114]  C.S. Campbell, T.F. Hartnagel & G.J. Smith, *The Legalization of Gambling in Canada (What is a Crime?)* (Law Commission of Canada, July 2005), at VII, "Illegal Gambling".

In 2002, a court in Ontario imposed fines and forfeitures on the leader of one interprovincial sports betting syndicate and heard evidence that the ring had handled CDN $20 million in five months.[115] Prosecutors were determined to crack down because the operation constituted a clear threat to the rackets run by the government of the Province.

## B.   THE BUSINESS OF PROFESSIONAL HOCKEY

## 1.   Owners of NHL Teams

**Figure 2** lists the teams of the National Hockey League and their principal owners and associated businesses. The foundations of the NHL include real estate, leisure industries, investment services, food and drugs. The teams are presented in order of franchise value as reported by *Forbes* magazine in October 2008.[116] In 2008, most of the six Canadian teams were valued above the median position. This relative economic strength contrasted with the mid-1990s when the Quebec Nordiques and Winnipeg Jets departed for Colorado and Phoenix in search of more favourable conditions. Based on the rankings for 2008, one of these moves was a success. In November 2009, *Forbes* valued the Canadian franchises as follows: 1. Toronto Maple Leafs (USD $470m.); 3. Montreal Canadiens (USD $339m.); 9. Vancouver Canucks (USD $239m.); 16. Calgary Flames (USD $200m.); 17. Ottawa Senators (USD $197m.); and 24. Edmonton Oilers (USD $166m.). In 2009, 14 of the 30 teams decreased in value.

Various structures are available for the ownership of professional teams, including sole proprietorship, the public non-profit corporation (community ownership) or public trading on the stock market.[117] In the NHL, teams are held privately through partnerships or incorporated companies as the league prefers to deal with identifiable entrepreneurs or chief shareholders and avoid the regulation and disclosure associated with public equity markets. League rules place restrictions on ownership and deal with the transfer of interests.[118] Public companies do, however, maintain a presence when a team falls within the network of a conglomerate or parent corporation maintaining diversified

---

[115]  See, "Ontario judge levies record gambling fine" *The Globe and Mail* (Toronto: November 9, 2002) at A10.

[116]  See, M. Ozanian & K. Badenhausen, "Special Report: The Business of Hockey" *Forbes* (October 29, 2008). On team revenue, see Chapter 7, "The Business of Hockey", section B, 2.

[117]  See, B.R. Cheffins, "Sports Teams and the Stock Market: A Winning Match?" (1998) 32 U.B.C. L. Rev. 271.

[118]  Under NHL By-Law 34.3, no more than 49 per cent of equity ownership may be sold to the public. To control the ownership of franchises, league approval is required for the acquisition of a 5 per cent interest or further multiples of 5 per cent (see, By-Law 34.5; see also, article 3.5). On transfers of ownership and relocation, see further, Chapter 8, "Competition Law and Labour Law", sections A, 4; C, 4.

interests. Professional teams are commonly held by media corporations[119] which have been attracted by the opportunities for cross-promotion and the use of the games for program content. This model of "alliance" or "convergence" sometimes loses favour in particular cases, so that AOL Time Warner sold the Atlanta Thrashers in 2004, Disney (ABC, ESPN) relinquished the "Mighty Ducks of Anaheim" in 2005, and CTVglobemedia Inc. sold its interest in Maple Leafs Sports and Entertainment in 2009.

The corporate elite who own professional teams have a variety of motivations. Some enter the business as a public service to provide a focal point for entertainment within a particular community. Others are motivated by athletic success and wish to maximize wins and emerge victorious in championships. The individual entrepreneur is often a *Fortune 500* magnate, with a distinguished record in other ventures, who then wishes to satisfy a craving for achievement in sport. In other cases, the goals are all business. The reasons then include maximizing the profits of the team or league, increasing the profits or public profile of the holding company or realizing tax advantages. A mixture of motivations is also common, so that the owner finds reward in community status, playing success and a positive financial return. Where a team is in conglomerate ownership or associated with media interests, the primary concern is the profitability of the enterprise as a whole, which may be unrelated to the business of the team or successful runs in the playoffs. The two NHL teams with the highest cash valuations have been strangers to the Stanley Cup in recent decades.

## Figure 2: NHL Teams (2008)

| Team | Principal Owner (interests and holdings) | USD$ Value million | (2007) |
|---|---|---|---|
| 1. *Toronto Maple Leafs* | Maple Leaf Sports and Entertainment Ltd. | 448 | (413) |
| 2. New York Rangers | Cablevision Systems, Madison Square Garden | 411 | (365) |
| 3. *Montreal Canadiens* | G. Gillett (Ski resorts, food products)* | 334 | (283) |
| 4. Detroit Red Wings | M. Ilitch (Little Caesars Pizza, Ilitch Holdings Inc.) | 303 | (293) |
| 5. Philadelphia Flyers | Comcast-Spectator (cable media) | 275 | (244) |
| 6. Dallas Stars | T. Hicks (investments, Hicks Holdings Inc.) | 273 | (254) |
| 7. Boston Bruins | J. Jacobs (Delaware North, hospitality, sports) | 263 | (243) |

---

[119] See, J. Harvey, A. Law & M. Cantelon, "North American Professional Sport Franchise Ownership Patterns and Global Entertainment Conglomerates" (2001) 18 Soc. of Sport J. 435 (31 per cent of franchises are part of media empires).

| 8. *Vancouver Canucks* | Aquilini Investment Group (real estate, hotels) | 236 | (211) |
|---|---|---|---|
| 9. Colorado Avalanche | S. Kroenke (real estate, sports, media) | 231 | (214) |
| 10. New Jersey Devils | J. Vanderbeek (investments) | 222 | (195) |
| 11. Minnesota Wild | C. Leipold (hockey franchises) | 217 | (180) |
| 12. Los Angeles Kings | P. Anschutz, E. Roski (AEG – sports, entertainment) | 210 | (209) |
| 13. *Ottawa Senators* | E. Melnyk (pharmaceuticals) | 207 | (186) |
| 14. Chicago Blackhawks | R. Wirtz (liquor distribution, Comcast SportsNet) | 205 | (179) |
| 15. *Calgary Flames* | Limited Partnership, M. Edwards, H. Hotchkiss | 203 | (164) |
| 16. Anaheim Ducks | H. and S. Samueli (Broadcom Corporation)** | 202 | (197) |
| 17. Tampa Bay Lightning | OK Hockey LLC, O. Koules (film), L. Barrie (resorts)*** | 200 | (199) |
| 18. Pittsburgh Penguins | M. Lemieux, R. Burkle (food and other investments) | 195 | (155) |
| 19. San Jose Sharks | San Jose Sports and Entertainment Enterprises | 179 | (165) |
| 20. *Edmonton Oilers* | D. Katz (Rexall and other pharmacies) | 175 | (157) |
| 21. Buffalo Sabres | T. Golisano (Paychex) | 169 | (162) |
| 22. Carolina Hurricanes | P. Karmanos (Compuware Corp., hockey franchises) | 168 | (156) |
| 23. Nashville Predators | D. Freeman, H. Fritch (health care) | 164 | (143) |
| 24. Florida Panthers | A. Cohen (pharmaceuticals), B. Kosar **** | 163 | (151) |
| 25. St. Louis Blues | D. Checketts, SCP Worldwide (investment services) | 162 | (144) |
| 26. Washington Capitals | T. Leonsis (AOL, Lincoln Holdings LLC) | 160 | (145) |
| 27. Atlanta Thrashers | Atlanta Spirit LLC | 158 | (148) |
| 28. Columbus Blue Jackets | J.P. McConnell (steel industries) | 157 | (150) |
| 29. New York Islanders | C. Wang (Computer Associates) | 154 | (149) |
| 30. Phoenix Coyotes***** | J. Moyes (trucking), W. Gretzky | 142 | (147) |

* In 2009, the Canadiens were purchased by members of the Molson family.

** The NHL suspended Henry Samueli as team owner from June 2008 to November 2009 after he pleaded guilty to making a false statement to the US Securities and Exchange Commission.

*** In February 2010, the Lightning were purchased by asset manager Jeffrey Vinik for USD $170 million.

**** In 2009, the general partnership controlling the Panthers was led by Cliff Viner of AVM financial services and S. Siegel.

***** The Coyotes were in bankruptcy proceeding from May 2009 and were purchased by the NHL in November 2009. The Ice Edge Holdings partnership then emerged as a likely future owner.

The ownership of the Canadian franchises and their arenas offers a colourful history generated by some forceful entrepreneurs and the occasional idiosyncratic character.[120] The boardroom dealings and financial arrangements have sometimes been a little involved, litigation has been common and there is the odd instance of bankruptcy and incarceration.

### a.    *Toronto Maple Leafs (Air Canada Centre)*

In the mid-1920s, the Toronto franchise was the St. Patricks, which played at the 8000-seat Arena Gardens on Mutual Street. During this period of NHL expansion into the United States, a group in Philadelphia offered to take the St. Pats off the city's hands, but the franchise was preserved in 1927 when it was bought by Conn Smythe[121] and other business associates. The team was later renamed as the Maple Leafs. Smythe was a player, coach and army officer who had established a sand and gravel company in Toronto and who pursued various business interests that included horse racing. Recognizing the need for higher revenue from a larger arena, in 1930 Smythe and a consortium of investors incorporated Maple Leaf Gardens Ltd. ("MLG") and with the assistance of over CDN $2 million in loans purchased land from the Eaton Company and succeeded in completing construction of the new facility on Carlton Street in November 1931.[122] Smythe increased his share holdings in MLG in 1947 and became president of the company during a period of increased profitability and playing success for the Leafs. His tenure in various management positions represented an earlier model that combined experience of the game with concerns for lucrative investment and the financial stability of the league as whole.[123]

Conn Smythe yielded majority control in 1961 when he sold his shares for CDN $2 million to a group consisting of his son Stafford, media magnate John Bassett, and Harold E. Ballard. In 1971-72, ownership passed to Ballard's holding company[124] just as the man himself received a three-year prison sentence

---

[120]    See, R.B. Beamish, "The Impact of Corporate Ownership on Labor-Management Relations in Hockey" in P.D. Staudohar & J.A. Mangan, eds., *The Business of Professional Sports* (Urbana: University of Illinois Press, 1991) at 202. On general league history, see further, Chapter 1, "Lord Stanley and the Wednesday Nighters", section B; Chapter 9, "National Hockey League", section A, 1.

[121]    See: J. Batten, *Hockey Dynasty: The Inside Story of Conn Smythe's Hockey Dynasty* (Toronto: Pagurian Press, 1969); C. Smythe with S. Young, *If You Can't Beat 'Em in the Alley: The Memoirs of the Late Conn Smythe* (Toronto: McClelland & Stewart, 1981).

[122]    See, B. Kidd, *The Struggle for Canadian Sport* (Toronto: University of Toronto Press, 1996) at 216-23.

[123]    See, D. Mills, "The Blue Line and the Bottom Line: Entrepreneurs and the Business of Hockey in Canada, 1927-1990" in P.D. Staudohar & J.A. Mangan, eds., *The Business of Professional Sports* (Urbana: University of Illinois Press, 1991) 175 at 179-86.

[124]    See, *820099 Ontario Inc. v. Harold E. Ballard Ltd.*, [1991] O.J. No. 1082, 3 B.L.R. (2d) 113 at 122 (Ont. Div. Ct.) and [1991] O.J. No. 266, 3 B.L.R. (2d) 113 at 123 (Ont. Gen. Div.) (action by minority shareholders relating to transactions in the late 1980s).

for tax evasion and stealing money and securities from MLG.[125] Ballard attached various sports subsidiaries to MLG and in the mid-1980s realised annual revenue over CDN $30 million in spite of the Leafs' poor playing record. Ballard's periodic ill health usually caused step jumps in the price of MLG shares.[126] Ballard died in 1990[127] leaving his shares in trust for the eventual benefit of a group of charities. In 1994, grocery magnate Steve Stavro, who was serving as chairman of MLG and executor of the will, attempted to gain private control of MLG by exercising an option to buy shares at a price based on valuation reports; the purchase was to be made Stavro's companies, Knob Hill Farms Ltd. and its subsidiaries.[128] Minority shareholders and the Public Trustee, acting on behalf of the charities, then alleged that open bidding would have yielded a higher market price and obtained an order to delay the takeover.[129] Stavro's control was confirmed in April 1996 when he agreed to pay CDN $49.50 a share for Ballard's interest rather than the original offer of CDN $34. The Leafs and the Gardens were duly acquired for around CDN $175 million, and MLG later became a private company.

By 1997, the Toronto Raptors of the National Basketball Association ("NBA") had begun construction of the Air Canada Centre at a time when MLG was pursuing sites for a new arena for the Leafs. Consolidated ownership was then established in February 1998 when Steve Stavro and MLG acquired the Raptors and the Air Canada Centre for an estimated purchase price of CDN $400 million.[130] The various sports operations came to be owned by Maple Leaf Sports and Entertainment Ltd. ("MLSE"), which in turn was owned by the Ontario Teachers Pension Plan (49 per cent) and by MLG Holdings (51 per cent) shared between Stavro (55 per cent), Larry Tanenbaum (25 per cent) and the TD Bank (20 per cent). Stavro began to dissolve the Knob Hill Farms grocery empire in 2000 and in February 2003 he sold his interest in MLSE, which by 2008 had a combined value of CDN $1.2 billion and was partly owned by CTVglobemedia

---

[125] See, W. Houston, *Ballard: A Portrait of Canada's Most Controversial Sports Figure* (Toronto: Seal Books, 1985) at 98-122.

[126] See, "Ballard making millions as investors await his death" *The Globe and Mail* (Toronto: November 1, 1986) at A1.

[127] See, *Ballard Estate v. Ballard Estate*, [1991] O.J. No. 574, 3 O.R. (3d) 65 (Ont. C.A.) (powers of trustees under will; repayment of debt to Molson through loan from Knob Hill freeing pledge of common shares; Knob Hill received option to purchase shares).

[128] See, T. Tedesco, *Offside: The Battle for Control of Maple Leaf Gardens* (Toronto: Viking, 1996). See also, *Re Maple Leaf Sports & Entertainment Ltd.* (1999), 22 OSCB 2015 (Ont. Sec. Comm.).

[129] See, *Re Ballard Estate*, [1994] O.J. No. 1898, 20 O.R. (3d) 189 (Ont. Gen. Div.). The valuators were not aware of an approach by the Raptors of the NBA to consider a joint-use stadium.

[130] See, "Leafs buy Raptors, solve arena problem" *The Globe and Mail* (Toronto: February 13, 1998) at A14.

Inc.[131] By August 2009, the controlling interests were: Ontario Teachers Pension Plan (66 per cent), Tanenbaum (20.5 per cent) and TD Capital (13.5 per cent).

The Leafs are, therefore, one unit of a private sports and entertainment conglomerate that includes the Leafs and Raptors, their associated television systems and the Air Canada Centre. Additional holdings include Toronto FC of Major League Soccer and the Toronto Marlies of the American Hockey League.

### b.   Montreal Canadiens (Bell Centre)

The Canadiens were established by the O'Brien industrialists in 1909 as a franchise of the National Hockey Association[132] and subsequently purchased by George Kennedy. The team became a founding member of the NHL in 1917 when it adopted the name, Club de Hockey Canadien. Following Kennedy's death, the Canadiens were purchased for CDN $11,000 in 1921 by L. Dandurand, J. Cattarinich and L.A. Létourneau and began regular play at the Montreal Forum in 1926[133] after the opening of the arena in 1924. The team passed into the ownership of the Canadian Arena Company and Senator Donat Raymond in 1935 and from 1957 was held by different members of the Molson family. In 1971, this group sold the arena and the team to a consortium led by the Bronfman family.

Molson Breweries of Canada Ltd. purchased the Canadiens in 1978 and operated the team at the Forum until 1996 when the new Molson Centre arena was opened. By 2000, Molson had resolved to return its focus to beer and eliminate the costs of its sports holdings. In January 2001, Canadian institutions passed into American hands when the ski resort owner, George Gillett, paid CDN $250 million for 80 per cent of the Canadiens and 100 per cent of the Molson Centre (now, the Bell Centre).[134] Molson retained a 20 per cent interest in the team. In 2007, Gillett extended his international holdings in professional sport by buying a 50 per cent share of Liverpool FC, but by 2009 needed to reduce the debts carried by that team and by his other businesses. Gillett duly invited offers for the assets in Montreal and received expressions of interest from various corporate groups in Quebec. In June 2009, it was announced that the Canadiens and the Bell Centre would return to members of the Molson family for a purchase price around USD $550 million. The value of the Canadiens was incorporated into this overall figure which took account of debts and liabilities of

---

[131] See: "MLSE to shoot for more assets and TV" *The Globe and Mail* (Toronto: February 12, 2003) at B1, B10; "A true blue investment" *The Globe and Mail* (Toronto: August 21, 2009) at B1-B2.

[132] See: Chapter 1, "Lord Stanley and the Wednesday Nighters", section B; Chapter 9, "National Hockey League", section A, 1. On the history of the Canadiens, see, D. Jenish, *The Montreal Canadiens: 100 Years of Glory* (Scarborough, ON: Doubleday Canada, 2008).

[133] On the Canadiens' obligation to play games in their previous arena, see, *Canadian Hockey Club, Inc. v. Arena Amusements Ltd.*, [1930] 1 D.L.R. 127 (S.C.C.).

[134] See, "Gillett strikes $250-million deal, tells anxious fans team will stay", "Gillett seen as sharp guy" *The Globe and Mail* (Toronto: February 1, 2001) at A1, A5, S1.

the arena and the value of the associated entertainment company. The NHL approved the purchase in December 2009.

### c.   Vancouver Canucks (GM Place)

The Canucks entered the NHL in the league expansion of 1970 when the cost of a new franchise was USD $6 million. The original purchasing group was led by Thomas Scallen of the Medicor Corporation of Minneapolis, but by 1974 ownership had passed to the Griffiths family, including the radio and television magnate, Frank A. Griffiths, who died in 1994. In 1993, the Griffiths holding company, Northwest Sports Enterprises Ltd., and Arthur Griffiths initiated construction of GM Place as a replacement for the Pacific Coliseum arena, and the following year they secured the Vancouver Grizzlies as an expansion franchise in the NBA for a fee of USD $125 million. A proposed reorganization and takeover by Griffiths with a view to placing the NBA franchise and arena in a private company then gave rise to a petition by minority shareholders in Northwest alleging the taking of a corporate opportunity.[135] The financing of the projects was assisted by investments by John and Bruce McCaw, of the McCaw Cellular Communications company of Seattle, and by 1995 control of the Canucks, Grizzlies and GM Place passed to John McCaw through the parent company, Orca Bay Sports and Entertainment.

Facing losses in all spheres of operation, in 1999 Orca Bay initiated the sale of the Grizzlies and in 2000 succeeded in disposing of the team for USD $160 million to Michael Heisley, who subsequently relocated the franchise to Memphis. In November 2004, the Aquilini Investment Group purchased 50 per cent of Orca Bay and acquired all remaining shares from McCaw in 2006. Original negotiations to buy the Canucks and GM Place had been conducted by Francesco Aquilini in association with Tom Gaglardi and Ryan Beedie. When Aquilini purchased his holding independently, Gaglardi and Beedie alleged that there was breach of a partnership or joint venture agreement. In *Blue Line Hockey Acquisition Co. v. Orca Bay Hockey Limited Partnership*,[136] Wedge J. found that Aquilini was free to leave the group and that there was no breach of fiduciary obligations or unfair dealing. The association was merely an informal exploration of the prospect of a partnership with McCaw, and Gaglardi and Beedie did not object to Aquilini's departure. The Aquilini Investment Group, including brothers Francesco, Roberto and Paolo, were therefore confirmed in their ownership of the Canucks.

---

[135]   *Primex Investments Ltd. v. Northwest Sports Enterprises Ltd.*, [1995] B.C.J. No. 2262, [1996] 4 W.W.R. 54 (B.C.S.C. (In Chambers)), revd [1996] B.C.J. No. 2309, [1997] 2 W.W.R. 129 (B.C.C.A.). See also, *Primex Investments Ltd. v. Northwest Sports Enterprises Ltd.*, [1998] B.C.J. No. 220, 77 A.C.W.S. (3d) 751 (B.C.S.C. (In Chambers)) (injunction to prevent rights offering; claim that ownership of NBA franchise would have offset Northwest's losses).

[136]   [2008] B.C.J. No. 24, 40 B.L.R. (4th) 83 (B.C.S.C.), affd [2009] B.C.J. No. 136, 2009 BCCA 34 (B.C.C.A.).

### d. Ottawa Senators (Scotiabank Place)

The Senators were revived after a 56-year absence through the conditional award of a franchise in December 1990 and began play at the Ottawa Civic Centre in 1992. The new incarnation was realised by Bruce Firestone, of Terrace Investments Ltd., who proposed to incorporate the team and the Palladium arena in a real estate project in Kanata in the west end of Ottawa.[137] Rod Bryden was hired by Terrace in 1991 to assist in obtaining investors and loans to finance the USD $50 million franchise fee and the costs of constructing the new arena. The team was originally held by Terrace as general partner, together with 67 limited partners, while a separate partnership controlled by Terrace owned the development site. (Some well-publicized litigation related to Paul Anka's involvement as an investor.[138]) In August 1993, Firestone sold his remaining share in Terrace to Bryden, who subsequently operated through Stormont Capital Corporation.[139] Financing for the construction of the CDN $217 million arena was obtained from lenders that included the Government of Ontario, a consortium of Canadian and international banks and the Ogden Corporation (Covanta Energy). The Palladium opened in January 1996, being almost immediately renamed as the Corel Centre (and subsequently becoming Scotiabank Place). By 1999, the team was "mired in serious financial difficulties",[140] and the campaign to "save the Senators" became a central issue in the debate over the public subsidy and retention of Canadian professional teams.[141]

Rod Bryden proposed a series of tax shelters and limited partnership plans during 2001-02 designed to attract new investors, but the Senators faced cash flow problems following the bankruptcy of their principal creditor, Covanta Energy.[142] (In December 2002, *Forbes* valued the Senators in 27th position at USD $95 million.) The team was declared bankrupt and subject to the *Companies' Creditors Arrangement Act*[143] in January 2003,[144] when total debts of

---

[137] In reviewing the project for planning and zoning purposes, the Ontario Municipal Board reduced the size of the Palladium to 18,500 seats and required Terrace to pay capital costs for roads and infrastructure: *Re Ottawa-Carleton (Regional Municipality) Official Plan Amendment 8* (1991), 26 O.M.B.R. 132.

[138] See, "Anka opens second round in Terrace fight" *Ottawa Citizen* (May 20, 1992) at A1; *Anka v. Ottawa Senators Hockey Club Ltd. Partnership*, [1992] O.J. No. 2564 (Ont. Gen. Div.) and [1992] O.J. No. 2491 (Ont. Gen. Div.) (pleadings alleging damage to reputation).

[139] See, "Showdown for Senators" *The Globe and Mail* (Toronto: January 15, 1996) at B1, B7.

[140] *Re Ottawa Senators Hockey Club Corp.*, [2005] O.J. No. 9, 73 O.R. (3d) 737 at 740 (Ont. C.A.), *per* MacPherson J.A.

[141] See Chapter 7, "The Business of Hockey", section B, 3.

[142] See, "Senators forced to borrow from NHL" *The Globe and Mail* (Toronto: November 28, 2002) at S1, S6.

[143] R.S.C. 1985, c. C-36.

[144] *Re Ottawa Senators Hockey Club Corp.*, [2005] O.J. No. 9, 73 O.R. (3d) 737 (Ont. C.A.), revg [2003] O.J. No. 5201, 68 O.R. (3d) 603 (Ont. S.C.J.).

the Senators and the Corel Centre exceeded CDN $350 million.[145] After further attempts by Bryden to assemble a partnership scheme, in August 2003 the Senators and the arena were bought for CDN $130 million by Eugene Melnyk of Biovail pharmaceuticals through Capital Sports & Entertainment Inc.

### e.    Calgary Flames (Pengrowth Saddledome)

The Calgary team began life as the Atlanta Flames, which relocated to Southern Alberta in 1980 when purchased for USD $16 million by sports entrepreneur, Nelson Skalbania.[146] The Flames passed into the ownership of local business partners in 1981 and began play at the publicly financed Saddledome arena in 1983. The owners have maintained a relatively low public profile and may be characterised as "boosters" concerned to promote local sport and the economic development of the city.[147] The partnership has usually had about eight members and includes Harley Hotchkiss as governor.

### f.    Edmonton Oilers (Rexall Place)

The Oilers were founding members of the World Hockey Association ("WHA") which operated from 1972 to 1979. The original owner was the amateur hockey promoter, Bill Hunter, who was later joined by Nelson Skalbania. In 1974, the team benefited from the city's construction of the Edmonton Coliseum (subsequently renamed as the Northlands Coliseum, Skyreach Centre and Rexall Place). In 1976, ownership of the team passed to Peter Pocklington, who in 1978 acquired Wayne Gretzky and three other players for USD $700,000 in a trade from the Indianapolis Racers, which were then owned by Skalbania. Gretzky's existing personal services contract was succeeded by a similar contract with Pocklington for CDN $3 million over 10 years. Together with three other WHA teams, the Oilers joined the NHL for the 1979-80 season on paying the franchise fee of USD $6 million.

Peter Pocklington remained as the prominent figure controlling the Oilers during the 1980s and 1990s, although he gradually acquired the status of "not a popular person...in some circles",[148] especially following his business

---

[145]   See: "Senators banking on bailout" *The Globe and Mail* (Ottawa: January 4, 2003) at S1, S2; "Ottawa faces sale of NHL's Senators" *The Globe and Mail* (Toronto: January 8, 2003) at A1, A4.

[146]   On Skalbania's previous ownership of the Indianapolis Racers, see, *Skalbania v. Simmons*, 443 N.E.2d 352 (C.A. Ind., 1982) (class action by season ticket holders after collapse of team). See also: *R. v. Skalbania*, [1997] S.C.J. No. 97, [1997] 3 S.C.R. 995 (S.C.C.) (investment funds received under direction; accused convicted of misappropriation even though funds were repaid); *R. v. Skalbania*, [1998] B.C.J. No. 2872, 131 C.C.C. (3d) 166 (B.C.C.A.) (sentencing).

[147]   See, D. Mills, "The Blue Line and the Bottom Line: Entrepreneurs and the Business of Hockey in Canada, 1927-90" in P.D. Staudohar & J.A. Mangan, eds., *The Business of Professional Sports* (Urbana: University of Illinois Press, 1991) 175 at 198.

[148]   *Pocklington Foods Inc. v. Alberta (Provincial Treasurer)*, [1998] A.J. No. 354, [1998] 10 W.W.R. 244 at 269 (Alta. Q.B.), *per* Ritter J.

decision in August 1988 to trade Wayne Gretzky to the Los Angeles Kings. After starting up as a car dealer, Pocklington had relied on borrowed capital and tax shelters to expand into real estate, meat-packing (Gainers), the Fidelity Trust company, minor league sports teams and oil drilling (Capri).[149] Many of these enterprises collapsed in the early 1980s, but Pocklington was able to reconstruct his food-processing empire and continued various enterprises through his main holding company, Pocklington Financial Corporation ("PFC"). The business difficulties resumed in 1989 when two companies controlled by Pocklington defaulted on a loan from the Alberta Treasury Branches ("ATB"), which then took action to enforce its security.[150] In 1993-94, Pocklington threatened to relocate the Oilers during negotiations to obtain a more advantageous arena lease, and there was the prospect of purchase by an American buyer in 1997 when Pocklington put the Oilers up for sale to assist in paying down debts owed to ATB.[151]

The debt load on PFC was reduced by about CDN $100 million in March 1998[152] when the Oilers passed into the hands of the Edmonton Investors Group, consisting of local individuals and companies.[153] This group retained control until 2008 when they sold the team for CDN $200 million to Daryl Katz, the owner of the Rexall chain of pharmacies.

In summary, the ownership of the Canadian teams has followed a variety of models and has seen high financial dealing as facilitated by corporate law, tax law and different forms of public subsidy. Controlling interests have been held by individual sports entrepreneurs, families or partnerships, and teams are sometimes acquired by successful magnates as hobby enterprises. Teams have also formed parts of diversified conglomerates engaged in mixed business activities. The NHL has been based in both Canada and the United States since the 1920s and is now integrated into other global patterns of ownership and operation. Franchises have the status of marketable business units and are subject to relocation in the hope of more stable returns. Given the material motivations and the complex structures of corporate ownership, it is a miracle of sports marketing that fans still identify with their team as part of the community.

---

[149] See, D. Mills, "The Blue Line and the Bottom Line: Entrepreneurs and the Business of Hockey in Canada, 1927-90" in P.D. Staudohar & J.A. Mangan, eds., *The Business of Professional Sports* (Urbana: University of Illinois Press, 1991) 175 at 186-89.

[150] *Pocklington Foods Inc. v. Alberta (Provincial Treasurer)*, [1998] A.J. No. 354, [1998] 10 W.W.R. 244 (Alta. Q.B.), affd [2000] A.J. No. 16, 184 D.L.R. (4th) 152 (Alta. C.A.) (valuation of shares in Gainers companies).

[151] See, "Edmonton Oilers go on the block today" *The Globe and Mail* (Toronto: June 6, 1997) at A11. See further, Chapter 7, "The Business of Hockey", section B, 3.

[152] See, *Alberta (Treasury Branches) v. Pocklington*, [1998] A.J. No. 1091, 68 Alta. L.R. (3d) 52 (Alta. Q.B.); *Alberta (Treasury Branches) v. Pocklington Financial Corp.*, [1998] A.J. No. 830, 222 A.R. 243 (Alta. Q.B.), affd [1998] A.J. No. 1238, 228 A.R. 119 (Alta. C.A.). The purchase price for the Oilers was USD $70 million.

[153] See: "Deal keeps Oilers in Edmonton" *The Globe and Mail* (Toronto: March 14, 1998) at A29, A30; D. Hamilton & P. Pelletier, "The Puck Stops Here" *CA Magazine* (October 1999) at 24.

## 2.   Assets, Revenue and Taxation

The profitability of NHL teams has been contested in the debate over public subsidy[154] and in labour conflicts focussing on the cost of players' salaries.[155] The failure to secure substantial media contracts might also suggest weakness in the business when compared to other major leagues.[156] The history of the Canadian franchises does, however, reveal that new investors are always willing to step forward, and there has been a similarly active market in the United States both before and after 2005 when the CBA introduced the payroll range system and linked salaries to revenue. Purchasers have been drawn by the relatively modest franchise valuations and have also seen the potential for revenue and favourable tax treatment. This interest may, however, be tested in relation to teams in the "Sunbelt".

On buying a team, the owner receives a franchise in the league and rights associated with league membership, including the right to share in the distribution of revenue. The assets of the team consist of its trade name and business goodwill, together with intellectual property such as trademarks, websites, business information and customer lists. Further acquired assets may include the arena or rights to use the arena, team equipment and affiliated minor league teams. The particular acquisition by the purchaser is the rights and obligations under players' employment contracts as the franchise looks to continue to engage in the entertainment business and ice a competitive team.

The various business structures used in team ownership offer benefits and drawbacks in relation to administration, investment, financial liability and rates of taxation.[157] The corporation offers the advantages of separate identity and limited liability, but involves elements of double taxation when the organization is subject to corporate tax and shareholders are liable to tax on dividends received. Furthermore, where the corporation operates at a loss, there is normally no "flow through" to shareholders. Operating losses may, however, be written off against other income where the team is held as a partnership[158] or is owned by entities that enjoy partnership status for tax purposes. Additional deductions have also derived from an understanding with the Canada Revenue Agency that has also allowed partners to allocate 60 per cent of the franchise's purchase price to players' contracts and amortize this over four years.[159] A traditional advantage in American tax law was the ability to annualize intangible assets as expenses in

---

[154]   See Chapter 7, "The Business of Hockey", section B, 3.

[155]   See Chapter 9, "National Hockey League", sections B; C.

[156]   See Chapter 7, "The Business of Hockey", section B, 4.

[157]   In American law, the structures include sole proprietorship, general partnership, limited partnership, "S-Corporation", "C-Corporation", limited liability corporation (LCC) and limited liability partnership (LLP); see, L.K. Miller, *Sport Business Management* (Gaithersburg: Aspen Publishers, 1997) at 61-89.

[158]   See, *Income Tax Act*, R.S.C. 1985 (5th Supp.), c. 1, s. 96.

[159]   See, D. Hamilton & P. Pelletier, "The Puck Stops Here" *CA Magazine* (October 1999) 24 at 29. See also, "MPs question tax breaks for Senators" *The Globe and Mail* (Toronto: February 14, 2003) at S2 (write-off of "player rights" over two years).

the manner of capital costs.[160] On buying and re-incorporating a franchise, a purchaser would assign at least 90 percent of the purchase to players' contracts and then depreciate these over the average playing career period of five years; the incentive then arose to sell the team.[161] From 1976 to 2004, there was a presumption that no more than 50 per cent of the price of the franchise was allocable to contracts and the purchaser normally could not exceed the value basis assigned by the previous owner. The *Internal Revenue Code* now requires that the "transferee and transferor agree in writing as to the allocation of any consideration"; this allocation must be "appropriate" and binds both sides.[162]

Revenue can be affected by the allowable deduction for companies that use sport in public and client relations. A reasonable amount spent in sponsoring a team may be written off as an advertising expense.[163] Where companies incur reasonable entertainment expenses through hospitality services such as supplying tickets or renting luxury suites, 50 per cent of the cost may be deducted.[164]

The NHL experienced significant growth in revenue from the 1990s to 2008. In 1994-95, the total annual revenue of the 26 franchises was USD $816 million; the team average was USD $31 million, of which an average of USD $13 million was allocated to the players' payroll.[165] In 2003-04, at a time of disputed losses and player costs, the total annual revenue of the 30 teams in the NHL was USD $2.1 billion. By the 2006-07 season, this had risen to USD $2.4 billion, of which the

---

[160] *Income Tax Act*, R.S.C. 1985 (5th Supp.), c. 1, s. 20(1)(a), (b) (capital cost allowance); *Income Tax Regulations*, Schedule II, Class 14. See further, Chapter 7, "The Business of Hockey", section B, 3.

[161] See: J. Quirk & R.D. Fort, *Pay Dirt: The Business of Professional Team Sports* (Princeton: Princeton University Press, 1992) at 88-124; *Laird v. United States*, 391 F.Supp. 656 (N.D. Ga., 1975), affd 556 F.2d 1224 (5th Cir., 1977).

[162] See, *Internal Revenue Code*, 26 U.S.C., ss. 1056 [repealed], 1060. By article 3.5 of James Balsillie's "Asset Purchase Agreement" (May 5, 2009) with the Phoenix Coyotes, the "Buyer and Seller" agreed to allocate 85 per cent of the purchase price and "Assumed Liabilities" to "Assumed Player Contracts"; on the sale and relocation of the Coyotes, see, Chapter 8, "Competition Law and Labour Law", sections A, 4; C, 4.

[163] See, for example: *No. 511 v. M.N.R.*, 58 D.T.C. 307 (I.T.A.B.) (lumber company sponsored professional baseball team); *No. 608 v. M.N.R.*, 59 D.T.C. 190 (I.T.A.B.) (brewery sponsored baseball team); *Browning Harvey Ltd. v. M.N.R.*, [1983] C.T.C. 2341, 83 D.T.C. 311 (T.R.B.) (scoreboards were a capital expense); *Derome v. Canada (Minister of National Revenue - M.N.R.)*, [1991] T.C.J. No. 1111, [1992] 1 C.T.C. 2693 (T.C.C.) (chiropractic clinic; costs of minor hockey team not deductible).

[164] *Income Tax Act*, R.S.C. 1985, c. 1 (5th Supp.), s. 67.1. See, *Stapley v. Canada*, [2006] F.C.J. No. 130, [2006] 3 C.T.C. 188 (F.C.A.) (certificates and tickets provided by real estate agent to clients).

[165] See, M.K. Ozanian *et al.*, "Suite Deals" *Financial World* (May 9, 1995) 42 at 48. The Quebec Nordiques had revenues of USD $18.9 million and operating expenses, including player costs, of USD $17.7 million. The Winnipeg Jets had revenues of USD $14.2 million and operating expenses, including player costs, of USD $17.8 million.

Canadian teams accounted for USD $584 million.[166] The team revenues and payrolls[167] in 2006-07 were as follows:

|                      | **Revenue**        | **Payroll**          |
| -------------------- | ------------------ | -------------------- |
| Toronto Maple Leafs  | USD $138 million   | USD $43.5 million    |
| Montreal Canadiens   | USD $109 million   | USD $43 million      |
| Vancouver Canucks    | USD $96 million    | USD $44 million      |
| Ottawa Senators      | USD $93 million    | USD $42 million      |
| Calgary Flames       | USD $77 million    | USD $42 million      |
| Edmonton Oilers      | USD $71 million    | USD $41 million      |

In 2007-08, the league took in USD $1.1 billion in ticket revenue, of which the six Canadian franchises, benefiting from the rise in value of the Canadian dollar (see, **Figure 1**), accounted for 31 per cent.[168] With 4.7 million people attending regular season games in Canada, ticket revenues and game averages for the 41 home games in 2007-08 were as follows:[169]

|                      | **Ticket Revenue** | **Game Average**   | **Attendance** |
| -------------------- | ------------------ | ------------------ | -------------- |
| Toronto Maple Leafs  | USD $78 million    | USD $1.9 million   | 796,803        |
| Montreal Canadiens   | USD $69 million    | USD $1.7 million   | 872,193        |
| Vancouver Canucks    | USD $57 million    | USD $1.4 million   | 763,830        |
| Ottawa Senators      | USD $49 million    | USD $1.2 million   | 812,665        |
| Calgary Flames       | USD $54 million    | USD $1.3 million   | 789,849        |
| Edmonton Oilers      | USD $49 million    | USD $1.2 million   | 690,399        |

Besides the USD $78 million from tickets, the Leafs received USD $24 million from local television rights, USD $1.5 million from radio rights, USD $6.5

---

[166] See, M.K. Ozanian & K. Badenhausen, "Special Report: The Business of Hockey" *Forbes* (November 8, 2007).

[167] "Why did fans have to endure a lockout" *The Globe and Mail* (Toronto: December 16, 2006) at S5 (total league payroll of USD $1.2 billion).

[168] See, "The Bettman era: An unequivocal failure" *The Globe and Mail* (Toronto: May 31, 2008) at S7.

[169] See, "$1.6 billion? Really?" *The Globe and Mail* (Toronto: November 1, 2008) S1 at S2. For attendance figures, see online: <http://www.mib.org/~lennier/hockey/leagueatt.cgi>, recording total regular season attendance in the league for 2007–2008 of 21.2 million.

million from league television rights, USD $3 million from merchandising, and additional revenue from concessions, luxury suite rentals and other sources.[170]

The potential revenue sources for the league and its teams are indicated by article 50 of the 2005 Collective Bargaining Agreement ("CBA"), which establishes "a fixed relationship between League-wide Player Compensation and Hockey Related Revenues" ("HRR"). The designated sources sometimes include revenue of affiliated entities, and "Club Affiliated Entity" is defined to mean,

> its parent company, subsidiary company, sister company, or any other entity which shares common or family operating control with that Club, or which is controlled by a member of that Club's senior management...[171]

Article 50.1(a) of the CBA prescribes that HRR includes revenues from:

- Regular season and play-off gate receipts, including (1) season tickets (2) single game tickets (3) group sales, and (4) the face ticket value of luxury box seats and club or premium seats;
- Pre-season games;
- Special games;
- National, international and digital broadcasts, including rights fees, license fees, advertising revenues (net of agency fees paid) and allocated cable subscriber fees;
- NHL networks;
- Local cable television broadcasts;
- Local over-the-air television broadcasts;
- Local pay-for-view, satellite and other broadcasts;
- Local radio broadcasts;
- Club Internet;
- Publications;
- In-arena novelty sales;
- Non-arena novelty sales;
- Concessions;
- Luxury boxes or suites;
- Club or premium seats;
- Fixed signage and arena sponsorships;
- Temporary signage and club sponsorships;
- Dasher boards;
- Parking; and

---

[170]   See, "$1.6 billion? Really?" *The Globe and Mail* (Toronto: November 1, 2008) S1 at S2.
[171]   Collective Bargaining Agreement, article 50.1(c).

- Other sources such as: sponsored events, promotions or camps; sales of equipment worn by players; product placement rights; and dedicated subsidies such as lotteries.

Article 50.1(b) of the CBA recognizes other potential sources, receipts, assets or credits that are not classified as HRR:

- Revenues from the assignment of contracts through waivers;
- Revenues from the relocation or sale of teams or from the grant of new franchises;
- Revenues from the operation of non-NHL teams;
- Revenues from the sale of certain personal property;
- Proceeds from loans or other financing;
- Advances or contributions from owners, shareholders, members or partners;
- Amounts collected by the league from fines;
- Compensation Cost Redistribution paid by the league;
- Interest income;
- Proceeds from investments;
- Insurance recoveries;
- Proceeds of legal proceedings in excess of lost revenues;
- Revenues from real estate;
- Certain revenues raised for charities;
- Certain benefits or value associated with title to property, improvements or tax credits;
- Certain payments made to induce teams to remain in their location or relocate; and
- Reimbursements from the Escrow Account.[172]

These types of revenue include both recurrent sources and occasional payments. During the 1990s, the league was sustained by a total of USD $570 million in non-recurrent fees received for the grant of nine new franchises.[173]

The ongoing revenue in the NHL is largely attributable to live attendance at venues and the consequent takings from ticket sales, concessions, parking and other services. Since the mid-1990s, the average "announced attendance" at NHL games has been around 16,000, with an official average of 17,468 in 2008-09. Attendance increases following the opening of a new arena.[174] The spectators' contributions are now supplemented by increased revenue from

---

[172] See Chapter 9, "National Hockey League", section C.

[173] From 1991 to 1993, the league added the Sharks, Senators, Lightning, Ducks and Panthers for fees of USD $50 million. From 1998 to 2000, USD $80 million was the entry price for the Predators, Thrashers, Blue Jackets and Wild.

[174] See, J.C. Leadley & Z.X. Zygmont, "When is the Honeymoon Over? National Hockey League Attendance, 1970-2003" (2006) 32 Can. Pub. Pol'y 213.

merchandising and sponsorship, including proceeds from the sale of naming rights to arenas. In 2002, BCE reportedly paid CDN $100 million for a 20-year association with the Canadiens' Bell Centre.

Revenues such as fees for national broadcasting rights or the admission of new franchises are generated centrally by the league, while other sources are developed through the marketing programs of the individual teams. The league has the authority to use or license team trade marks[175] and since 2000 has operated an integrated network for the purpose of promotions through the Internet. In 2005, the NHL resolved to establish a "new media strategy" that would project its "national brand" and generate interest in the league as a whole. Although teams remained free to place their own content on their websites, the league's "common technology platform" provided a standardized layout and connections across the network. This centralized system was resisted in 2007 by the New York Rangers, which faced the threat of fines by the NHL after they maintained an independent site and made modified Internet broadcasts of their games. In *Madison Square Garden, L.P. v. National Hockey League*,[176] the Rangers unsuccessfully argued that the common platform was anti-competitive and contrary to antitrust law. In refusing an injunction against the league, Preska D.J. noted that the uniform exposure of the NHL's network provided efficient access for sponsors and advertisers and had the potential to improve the league's position when competing with other providers of sports entertainment.

A traditional characteristic of the NHL has been the low percentage of revenue that is shared between teams and the disparity in resources between franchises located in large and small markets. Before the lockout in 2004, team payrolls ranged from the USD $83 million paid by the Detroit Red Wings to the USD $22 million paid by the Pittsburgh Penguins. In order to improve the financial and competitive balance, the CBA of 2005 introduced the "Team Payroll Range System" (see, art. 50) and the "Player Compensation Cost Redistribution System" ("PCCR") (see, art. 49).[177] The latter system,

> ...is designed to cause certain high-revenue Clubs to contribute even more of their revenues toward the payment of Player Compensation - albeit indirectly - by redistributing a certain portion of the revenues of such Clubs to the lower-grossing, small market Clubs...[178]

---

[175] Centralized or cooperative licensing does not normally involve any violation of antitrust law: *Major League Baseball Properties, Inc. v. Salvino, Inc.*, 542 F.3d 290 (2nd Cir., 2008), affg 420 F.Supp. 2d 212 (S.D.N.Y., 2005); *American Needle, Inc. v. National Football League*, 538 F.3d 736 (7th Cir., 2008), affg *American Needle, Inc. v. New Orleans Louisiana Saints*, 496 F.Supp. 2d 941, 533 F.Supp. 2d 790 (N.D. Ill., 2007). See Chapter 8, "Competition Law and Labour Law", section C.

[176] No. 07 CV 8455 (LAP) (S.D.N.Y., November 2, 2007), affd 270 Fed. Appx. 56 (2nd Cir., 2008); 2008 WL 4547518 (S.D.N.Y., October 10, 2008). See also, M. Huntowski, "Blades of Steal? The Fight for Control of Sports Clubs' Websites and Media Rights in *Madison Square Garden, L.P. v. National Hockey League*" (2009) 16 Vill. Sports & Ent. L.J. 123.

[177] See Chapter 9, "National Hockey League", section C.

[178] Collective Bargaining Agreement of NHL (2005), article 49, Preamble.

By 2007-08, the Canadian teams were in the "high-revenue" category and were redistributing a total of USD $41 million as follows:[179]

|                        | **PCCR Payments**   |
| ---------------------- | ------------------- |
| Toronto Maple Leafs    | USD $12 million     |
| Montreal Canadiens     | USD $11.5 million   |
| Vancouver Canucks      | USD $10 million     |
| Calgary Flames         | USD $6 million      |
| Ottawa Senators        | USD $1 million      |
| Edmonton Oilers        | USD $0.8 million    |

The growth in their revenue stabilized the "small market" Canadian franchises, while increasing the profits of teams such as the Leafs that were restricted in the amount they could allocate to salaries. The overall rise in revenue caused difficulties for weaker American franchises that were obliged to meet the increased minimum payroll. The payroll ranges were of little assistance to teams that were unable to increase their revenue, and their profitability was not greatly aided by the systems of revenue sharing, especially when their performance in the local market did not entitle them to a full share. The economic crisis beginning in the Fall of 2008 initially had little effect on the league since revenue from broadcasting rights, sponsorship and season tickets had already been collected. The crisis did, however, compound the instability of some franchises, including "Sunbelt" teams relying on the novelty of hockey and the continued playing success of the team. The Phoenix Coyotes and the transportation firm of team owner Jerry Moyes were operating under a heavy debt load, and the team incurred total losses of USD $391 million from 2004 to 2008. During the 2008-09 season, the Coyotes were sustained by USD $45 million in cash advances and loans from the NHL which gained certain voting rights in the management of the franchise. The team then declared bankruptcy in May 2009 on receiving an offer of purchase from James Balsillie. Seeing no future for the team at its current location, Balsillie's plan was to relocate the team to Hamilton, Ontario.[180] Among the opponents of this move was the City of Glendale which from 2001 to 2003 had provided USD $183 million to construct a new arena. Glendale also held an "Arena Management, Use and Lease Agreement" in which the Coyotes covenanted to play at the facility for 30 years.

---

[179] See, "The giant sucking sound" *The Globe and Mail* (Toronto: October 11, 2008) at S1, S4.

[180] See, *In re Dewey Ranch Hockey, LLC*, 2009 WL 1702767, 406 B.R. 30 (Bkrtcy. D. Ariz., June 15, 2009); *In re Dewey Ranch Hockey, LLC*, 2009 WL 3170452, 414 B.R. 577 (Bkrtcy. D. Ariz., September 30, 2009). See further, Chapter 8, "Competition Law and Labour Law", sections A, 4; C, 4.

## 3.    Public Subsidy

Professional teams and leagues in North America benefit from tax exemptions and deductions, special treatment in competition law[181] and public funding of facilities and athlete training programs. The generous allocation of taxpayers' money is particularly associated with the construction of arenas and stadia, where the leading examples of massive losses include the Olympic Stadium in Montreal and the SkyDome (now, Rogers Centre) in Toronto.[182] The current trend is for the private sector to have a greater role in developing facilities, although the proportion invested by government authorities remains substantial.[183] (There is also a blurring of the line between private and public through partnership arrangements and "municipal capitalism".[184]) While the stimulation of business development is a common feature of public policy, "corporate welfare" for profit-oriented sports enterprises does not enjoy universal approval because of the well-heeled condition of the primary beneficiaries. Subsidies or development projects have been questioned as misplaced priorities that lack clear benefits for society at large and can be challenged on legal grounds as the unauthorized use of public funds[185] or as contrary to planning objectives.[186] Community protest and democratic evaluation through municipal referenda serve the useful purpose of addressing the value of the scheme, although "stadium advocates" tend to have the edge in referenda by virtue of well-funded campaigns and the support of the political establishment.[187]

---

[181]   See Chapter 7, "The Business of Hockey", section B, 4; Chapter 8, "Competition Law and Labour Law", sections A-C; E.

[182]   See, M.S. Rosentraub, *Major League Losers: The Real Cost of Sports and Who's Paying for It* (New York: Basic Books, 1997) at 321-67 (R. Whelan co-author).

[183]   On the various historical eras in stadium construction, see: J. Quirk & R.D. Fort, *Pay Dirt: The Business of Professional Team Sports* (Princeton: Princeton University Press, 1992) at 126-37, 154-63 (public construction from 1960); J.L. Crompton, D.R. Howard & T. Var, "Financing Major League Facilities: Status, Evolution and Conflicting Forces" (2003) 17 J. of Sport Management 156.

[184]   See, T. Chapin, "Beyond the Entrepreneurial City: Municipal Capitalism in San Diego" (2002), 24 J. of Urban Affairs 565.

[185]   See, *Gilbert v. Toronto (Metropolitan)*, [1985] O.J. No. 2526, 50 O.R. (2d) 654 (Ont. Div. Ct.) (power to make grants for domed stadium). See also: P. Edwards, "How Much Does That $8 Yankee Ticket Really Cost?" (1991) 18 Fordham Urb. L.J. 695 (investment by Dunedin, FL in a new stadium for the Toronto Blue Jays; D.F. Rubin, "Public Aid to Professional Sports Teams — A Constitutional Disgrace: The Battle to Revive Judicial Rulings and State Constitutional Enactments Prohibiting Public Subsidies to Private Corporations" (1999), 30 U. Tol. L. Rev. 393.

[186]   See, *Re Ottawa-Carleton (Regional Municipality) Official Plan Amendment 8* (1991), 26 O.M.B.R. 132 (O.M.B.).

[187]   See, C. Brown & D.M. Paul, "The Political Scorecard of Professional Sports Facility Referendums in the United States, 1984-2000" (2002) 26 J. of Sport & Social Issues 248. On the obligation to hold a further referendum when costs increase, see, *Dolan v. Moose Jaw (City)*, [2008] S.J. No. 813, 52 M.P.L.R. (4th) 25 (Sask. C.A.) (course of action is to apply to quash resolution of city council).

In professional hockey, the claim to public relief is mainly associated with teams' requests for assistance in times of business or competitive difficulty. Faced with a declining Canadian dollar (see, **Figure 1**), a small local market, increasing costs of players' salaries and variations in rates of taxation, teams have relocated to the United States or have threatened that their cash-strapped condition makes departure imminent. This opportunistic mobility follows from the scarcity of teams and from their status as commercial franchises rather than community institutions. By limiting membership, the major league monopolies ensure that alternative and apparently viable urban locations are available and so establish competition between cities to offer the most advantageous terms.[188] The inducements include tax concessions, improvements to facilities, favourable rents and the generous allocation of revenue from arenas. To avoid losing the franchise, these benefits must be matched by the current facility and different levels of government; the theme of "buy-or-else" is also used in periodic campaigns to sell season tickets. In 1995, there were offers of assistance to save the Quebec Nordiques and the Winnipeg Jets prior to their respective departures for Denver and Phoenix. The government of Quebec proposed to buy shares in the Nordiques and cover part of their deficit for three seasons.[189] The City of Winnipeg, the Province of Manitoba and the federal government promised CDN $120 million to build a new arena that would be leased to the team at a free rent.[190]

During the 1990s, the Calgary Flames and the Edmonton Oilers raised the prospect of franchise migration, although in the case of the Oilers the terms of the stadium lease assisted in retaining the franchise. In *Edmonton Northlands v. Edmonton Oilers Hockey Corp.*,[191] the Oilers initiated negotiations for more favourable terms in their long-term licence agreement and at different times announced the intention to move to Hamilton or Minneapolis. The city obtained an interim injunction to prevent the exit from Alberta's jurisdiction and successfully argued that the Northlands Coliseum would suffer irreparable loss through damage to goodwill and termination of sponsorship and advertising contracts. New leasing arrangements in 1994 created a shared responsibility for renovating the arena and included a "location agreement" requiring the Oilers to stay in Edmonton until 2004, provided local buyers were prepared to pay USD $70 million for the team.[192] After the various crises in Alberta, attention turned to

---

[188] See, for example, *Hamilton County Board of Commissioners v. National Football League*, 491 F.3d 310 (6th Cir., 2007) (alleged use of monopoly power by Cincinnati Bengals and NFL to obtain subsidized lease). On antitrust aspects of the control of franchises, see Chapter 8, "Competition Law and Labour Law", section C, 4.

[189] See, "Offer by Quebec rejected by Nordiques" *The Globe and Mail* (Toronto: May 17, 1995) at A11.

[190] See, "Jets revived in Winnipeg" *The Globe and Mail* (Toronto: June 15, 1995) at A15. See also, J. Silver, *Thin Ice: Money, Politics and the Demise of an NHL Franchise* (Halifax: Fernwood Publishing, 1996).

[191] [1993] A.J. No. 1001, 23 C.P.C. (3d) 49 (Alta. Q.B.), affd [1994] A.J. No. 138, 23 C.P.C. (3d) 72 and [1994] A.J. No. 203, 23 C.P.C. (3d) 83 (Alta. C.A.). See also, *Metropolitan Sports Facilities Commission v. Minnesota Twins Partnership*, 638 N.W.2d 214 (Minn. C.A., 2002) (injunction to maintain stadium Use Agreement).

[192] See, "Location agreement roadblock to Edmonton Oilers sale" *The Globe and Mail* (Toronto: November 5, 1997) at A23.

the financial condition of the Ottawa Senators.[193] A peculiarity of this case was that both the arena and the team were in private ownership, so that any departure by the Senators involved the owners depriving themselves of their main tenant and source of revenue. The construction of the Palladium (now, Scotiabank Place) was authorized in August 1991 after the Ontario Municipal Board limited the size of the arena and the associated development and accepted the applicants' offer to pay for public infrastructure such as a highway interchange.[194] This additional responsibility added CDN $38 million to the cost of the project, but was largely financed by a loan of CDN $28 million from the Government of Ontario; the arena project also received a federal infrastructure grant of CDN $6 million. After construction was completed in 1996, the companies associated with the Senators became heavily indebted through the costs of the franchise fee, the real estate development and the ongoing operations of the team. Some government assistance arrived in 1998-99 when the Senators obtained relief from federal income tax in relation to borrowing costs and a reduced rate of provincial property tax. The Government of Ontario did, however, disallow a scheme by which games would be sponsored by a charitable foundation as a means of avoiding payment of amusement tax.[195]

During 1997-98, a House of Commons Sub-Committee chaired by Dennis Mills studied general aspects of the Canadian sport system and considered the disadvantaged condition of Canadian professional teams when compared to franchises located in the United States.[196] In their report of November 1998, the parliamentarians outlined the differential effects of municipal subsidies, currency exchange and rates of provincial and federal taxation[197] and observed that:

> The six Canadian hockey teams pay more than five times the amount of municipal taxes paid by the 20 American teams. The Montreal Canadiens pay more than twice what is paid by all American hockey teams.[198]

The committee noted that the disadvantages had been addressed by two programs operated by the NHL: the "Group 2 Equalization Plan" established a

---

[193] On the ownership of the Flames, Oilers and Senators, see Chapter 7, "The Business of Hockey", section B, 1.

[194] *Re Ottawa-Carleton (Regional Municipality) Official Plan Amendment 8* (1991), 26 O.M.B.R. 132 (O.M.B.).

[195] See, "Ontario won't entertain Senators' charity ploy" *The Globe and Mail* (Toronto: December 1, 1999) at S4.

[196] See: D. Whitson, J. Harvey & M. Lavoie, "The Mills Report, the Manley Subsidy Proposals, and the Business of Major-League Sport" (2000) 43 Can. Public Admin. 127; G. Rail, "Contextualizing the Mills Report: Pro Sport, Corporate Welfare and the Canadian State" (2000) 6 Avante 1.

[197] See, Standing Committee on Canadian Heritage, Sub-Committee on the Study of Sport in Canada, *Sport in Canada: Leadership, Partnership and Accountability - Everybody's Business* (House of Commons Canada, November 1998) at 90-100.

[198] See, Standing Committee on Canadian Heritage, Sub-Committee on the Study of Sport in Canada, *Sport in Canada: Leadership, Partnership and Accountability - Everybody's Business* (House of Commons Canada, November 1998) at 99 (referring to brief submitted by NHL).

fund to enable Canadian teams to match offers made to that group of restricted free agents, and the "Supplementary Currency Assistance Plan" subsidized teams whose revenue fell below the league's median. To further stabilize the Canadian franchises, the Mills Report proposed a "Sport Pact"[199] involving income tax harmonization for professional players and enhanced tax deductions. Teams would benefit from full deduction of entertainment expenses by small businesses, an income tax credit and transferable capital cost allowance for investment in facilities. This "stabilization program" was to operate for two years and was conditional on the NHL maintaining the currency assistance plan and exploring new forms of revenue sharing. To be eligible for the program, franchises would have to show long-term viability, contributions to local employment and community activity and efforts to control the salaries of players and the prices of tickets. The initial response of the federal government to the "Sport Pact" was to recognize "professional sport as an industry of importance to Canadians" and examine the issue further.[200]

The task of devising an acceptable assistance formula was assigned to the federal Industry Minister, John Manley, who as the MP for a riding in Ottawa was close to the debate about the fate of the Senators. The issues were addressed at a "hockey summit" in June 1999 attended by representatives of the federal government, affected provincial and municipal governments, the NHL and its six Canadian franchises and the NHLPA. The federal government then appeared to be offering a contribution of CDN $15 million a year,[201] but Ontario was not prepared to direct funds from lottery revenues. By October 1999, a report by the Public Policy Forum found little prospect of a shared solution.[202] The process climaxed in January 2000 when Minister Manley proposed a "temporary, modest package" capped at 25 per cent of total contributions.[203] The Canadian teams could each receive up to CDN $3 million, provided there was participation by the league and the relevant provincial and municipal governments. Faced with intense public protest[204] and non-cooperation by the other levels of government, this program was then withdrawn after three days.[205]

---

[199] See, Standing Committee on Canadian Heritage, Sub-Committee on the Study of Sport in Canada, *Sport in Canada: Leadership, Partnership and Accountability - Everybody's Business* (House of Commons Canada, November 1998) at 101-105. In a "Supplemental Submission" (July 22, 1998) to the committee, the NBA had addressed the payment of Canadian income tax by players based on "duty days".

[200] "Elaboration of the Government Response to the Sixth Report of the Standing Committee on Canadian Heritage" (1999), response to Recommendation #36.

[201] See, "Ottawa offering hockey bailout" *The Globe and Mail* (Toronto: June 28, 1999) at A1, A5.

[202] Public Policy Forum, "The National Hockey League in Canada" (October 1999).

[203] See, "NHL's Bryden gets bailout amid howls of outrage" *The Globe and Mail* (Toronto: January 19, 2000) at A1, A2.

[204] See, J. Scherer & S.J. Jackson, "From Corporate Welfare to National Interest: Newspaper Analysis of the Public Subsidization of NHL Hockey Debate in Canada" (2004) 21 Sociology of Sport J. 36.

[205] See, "This proposal is dead" *The Globe and Mail* (Toronto: January 22, 2000) at A1; "Canada kills subsidy plan for 6 N.H.L. teams" *The New York Times* (January 22, 2000) at D1.

The collapse of the Manley proposals did not result in any further departures by the small market franchises, even as the Government of Ontario showed reluctance to grant further concessions to professional teams.[206] The Senators raised ticket prices for the 2000-01 season and launched a successful campaign to increase corporate support. From 2001, the Government of Alberta assisted the Oilers and the Flames through allocations from a special lottery and from 2002 to 2006 operated an income tax on visiting players for the benefit of the two teams.[207] (This tax was unsuccessfully challenged by the NHLPA in grievance arbitration proceedings where the players maintained that the teams lobbied to implement a payroll tax in contravention of the collective agreement of 1995.[208]) The Canadian teams continued to benefit from the public concessions received, but their "stabilization" largely resulted from increases in the value of the Canadian dollar and the arrival of well-funded owners. The NHL also moved to put the league house in order when the CBA of 2005 attempted to constrain payrolls and related players' salaries to revenue received.

Supporters of public assistance for professional franchises or major international Games draw heavily on emotional appeal and on the cultural value of sports. Teams or events are seen to enhance civic pride and identity and "put the city on the map" by declaring it "major league" or "world class".[209] (These designations can be linked to economic development through the supposed effect of making the location more desirable to residents and businesses.) The city that loses a franchise suffers a blow to the soul since the team is an amenity of entertainment that serves to focus community spirit,[210] and the loss of a hockey team from Canada affects national sentiment because of the apparent diminishing of the sporting heritage. The feel-good factors are initially threatened when the

---

[206] See, *Toronto Blue Jays Baseball Club v. Ontario (Minister of Finance)*, [2005] O.J. No. 485, 250 D.L.R. (4th) 63 (Ont. C.A.) (team required to pay employer health tax on full amount of players' remuneration, including salaries paid for away games). On the reluctance of British Columbia to guarantee a loan for the construction of an arena, see, *Victoria Sports/Entertainment Associates v. Toronto-Dominion Bank*, [2006] B.C.J. No. 2172, 2006 BCSC 1441 (B.C.S.C.).

[207] See: *NHL Tax Regulation*, Alta. Reg. 171/2002 (rate of 12.5 per cent for each "game day"); D.J.S. Brean & A. Forgione, "Missing the Net: The Law and Economics of Alberta's NHL Players Tax" (2003) 41 Alta. L. Rev. 425; M. Lavitt, "The Alberta NHL Players Tax: The Jock Tax Comes to Alberta - or Does It?" (2004) 52 Can. Tax J. 514; A. Pogroszewski, "Is Canada Overstepping its Borders? The Alberta Province Tax Specifically Targets Professional Hockey Players in order to Help Finance its Professional Franchises" (2004) 14 Marq. Sports L.J. 509.

[208] See, "NHL wins Alberta tax case" (online) *The Globe and Mail* (Toronto: March 5, 2003). See now, Collective Bargaining Agreement of NHL (2005), article 26.16 (payroll taxes returned to teams must be returned to the taxed players).

[209] See: D. Whitson & D. Macintosh, "Becoming a World-Class: Hallmark Events and Sport Franchises in the Growth Strategies of Western Canadian Cities" (1993) 10 Soc. of Sport J. 221; R. Gruneau & D. Whitson, *Hockey Night in Canada: Sport, Identities, and Cultural Politics* (Toronto: Garamond Press, 1993) at 234-46.

[210] On the departure of the Dodgers from Brooklyn to Los Angeles in 1957, see, N.J. Sullivan, *The Dodgers Move West* (New York: Oxford University Press, 1987).

team ceases to be a playing success, so that the rationale for subsidies is also related to the need for competitive balance in a league.[211]

There is cultural value in high-quality contests, but the spectacle is not exempt from issues of price and priority. Proposed subsidies must, therefore, respond to economic questions relating to the financial or fiscal benefits that follow from the presence of a team, arena or mega-event. In its submission to the Mills Committee in 1998, the NHL argued that the Canadian teams generated substantial economic benefits in the form of "jobs...wages...infrastructure development...taxes...indirect spin-offs...lottery revenues...and minor league farm teams".[212] For 1997, the submission placed the total product at CDN $437 million, including direct employment in 8,689 full- and part-time jobs and direct wages and benefits at CDN $300 million; the direct taxes paid were CDN $211 million.[213] The positive economic effect of professional teams was, however, questioned in an academic brief,[214] and the size of the NHL's contribution was open to evaluation during the 2004-05 lockout when it was estimated that the shutdown caused a 2.1 per cent drop in the output of Canada's entertainment industries. The gross domestic product was reduced by CDN $170 million out of a total economy of CDN $1.05 trillion.[215] While the presence of a team generates some business activity, a leading objection to public subsidy is that there is a regressive effect when taxes on the general population, including lottery revenues, are applied for the benefit of elites:

> Initial construction provides good jobs when buildings and infrastructure are put in place, but it usually involves a large debt load for the government involved. After construction is complete, most of the jobs the stadiums provide are low-paid and low-skilled. Despite spill-offs for sport tourism, most of the huge revenues go directly into the private pockets of team and stadium owners and players, not back into the local economy or tax base to support the continuing public debt and operating infrastructure costs.[216]

---

[211] See further, Chapter 7, "The Business of Hockey", section C, 1.

[212] Submission Presented to the Sub-Committee on the Study of Sport in Canada (April 28, 1998), Executive Summary, at 3-4.

[213] See, Submission Presented to the Sub-Committee on the Study of Sport in Canada (April 28, 1998) at 12-22.

[214] J. Harvey, M. Lavoie & M. Saint-Germain, "Sport in Canada: Its Economic Importance and Impact and the Role of Government" (January 27, 1998). See also: M. Lavoie, *Avantage numérique: l'argent et la Ligue nationale de hockey* (Hull: Éditions d'Ouest, 1997) at 118-36; M. Lavoie, "Les équipes professionnelles n'ont pas d'impact économique significatif: le cas des Expos" (2000) 6 Avante 33.

[215] See: "Hockey lockout slashes GDP, economic growth put on ice" *The Globe and Mail* (Toronto: December 24, 2004) at A2 (study by Statistics Canada); M. Leeds & P. von Allmen, *The Economics of Sports*, 3d ed. (Boston: Pearson/Addison Wesley, 2008) at 324. Following the lockout, the revenues of the spectator sport industry increased by CDN $600 million.

[216] V. Burstyn, *The Rites of Men: Manhood, Politics and the Culture of Sport* (Toronto: University of Toronto Press, 1999) at 256.

The favoured elites also include the corporate elements enjoying luxury suites in gentrified arenas. The infrastructure costs represent a particular burden when public authorities are left with white elephant facilities after the circus has left town.

Various American studies have cast doubt on the economic impact and benefit of professional sport,[217] and it has been suggested that Congress should prevent local governments from using general taxes to offer inducements to team owners.[218] (Such assistance may also be in breach of the North American Free Trade Agreement,[219] although the preference of Canadian team owners is to receive equivalent largesse rather than have the American subsidies disallowed under NAFTA.) Critical analysis of sports development[220] takes account of the tax burden and costs of public subsidy, including the opportunity costs of failing to assist other projects that are more likely to bring on-going benefits to ordinary mortals and retain funds within the community. A professional team may in fact constitute a drain on a city's economy because so much revenue is allocated to the salaries of players, who are then likely to lodge or spend the funds elsewhere. Claimed spin-off effects are subject to exaggeration,[221] especially because "discretionary substitution" by consumers means that money will still be spent on some form of leisure pursuit, whether amateur sport, the arts or the local *maison de tolérance*.[222] The effect of the 2004-05 lockout was to increase attendance at junior games in the area of NHL teams.[223] Out-of-town visitors[224] create some additional expenditures, although most tickets for professional games are bought by local residents such as season-ticket holders. Any extra

---

[217] See, for example: M.S. Rosentraub, *Major League Losers: The Real Costs of Sports and Who's Paying for It* (New York: Basic Books, 1997); R.G. Noll & A. Zimbalist, *Sports, Jobs, and Taxes: The Economic Impact of Sports and Stadiums* (Washington: Brookings Institution Press, 1997).

[218] See, P.C. Weiler, *Leveling the Playing Field: How the Law Can Make Sports Better for Fans* (Cambridge: Harvard University Press, 2000) at 263-77, 338-39. On tax-free bonds, see also, P.C. Weiler & G.R. Roberts, *Sports and the Law: Text, Cases and Problems*, 2d ed. (St. Paul, MN: West Group, 1998) at 545-46.

[219] See: Appleton and Associates, "NAFTA & Sports", Submission to the House of Commons Standing Committee on Canadian Heritage, Sub-Committee on the Study of Sport in Canada (May 12, 1998); T. Wu & N. Longley, "The Applicability of NAFTA to the Subsidization of US-based NHL Teams: Legal and Economic Perspectives" (2003) 9 L. and Business Rev. of the Americas 571; R.A. Schmoll, "NAFTA Chapter 11 and Professional Sports in Canada" (2003) 36 Vand. J. Transnat'l L. 1027.

[220] See: "Symposium: Sports Facilities and Development" (2000) 10 Marq. Sports L.J. 173-460; M.J. Greenberg, "Sports Facility Financing and Development Trends in the United States" (2004) 15 Marq. Sports L.J. 93.

[221] See, J.L. Crompton, "Economic Impact Analysis of Sports Facilities and Events: Eleven Sources of Misapplication" (1995) 9 J. of Sport Management 14.

[222] It must, however, be recognized that professional athletes constitute an important clientele for the city's adult entertainment establishments; see, *Cimpean v. Payton*, [2008] O.J. No. 2665 (Ont. S.C.J.), leave to appeal granted [2008] O.J. No. 4713 (Ont. S.C.J.).

[223] See, J.A. Winfree & R. Fort, "Fan Substitution and the 2004-05 NHL Lockout" (2008) 9 J. of Sports Economics 425.

[224] On the uncertain benefits of major events, see, H.A. Solberg & H. Preuss, "Major Sports Events and Long-Term Tourism Impacts" (2007) 21 J. of Sport Management 213.

consumption is only to the credit of the team or stadium when attending the game is the sole reason for the tourist's trip.

In spite of the almost unanimous scepticism of independent economists, the Mills Report favoured additional assistance for professional franchises because "if a National Hockey League...team currently located in a Canadian city moves to another city, that city will be in the United States...[and] infrastructures used by professional sports can be used to attract other major sport events".[225] The committee feared a loss to the national economy and accepted the cultural value of Canadian teams because the broadcasting of their games reduced American program content. The Report therefore continued the tradition of identifying the Canadian game with its NHL version. The greatest public aid to the league dates from the 1930s when NHL games came to dominate the airwaves as access to radio commentary was extended through the Canadian Broadcasting Corporation ("CBC").[226] Though called "Hockey Night in Canada", for most listeners the program "was really 'A Night of NHL Hockey from Maple Leaf Gardens in Toronto'".[227]

## 4.   Television Contracts

Broadcasters are prepared to pay rights fees because sports properties are a means of attracting cable subscribers and advertisers.[228] The expense of the fee sometimes exceeds the revenue, but the broadcasts serve the useful purpose of increasing overall viewership. The leading exponent of the lucrative television contract is the National Football League ("NFL") which earns a total annual fee of USD $3.7 billion, giving each franchise in the 32-team league in excess of USD $100 million a year. By April 2005, the NFL had renewed its agreements with American networks for the following years and looked to receive USD $4.3 billion over six years from Fox, USD $3.7 billion over six years from CBS, USD $1.1 billion over eight years from ESPN and USD $600 million over six years from NBC. At this time, the National Hockey League was scheduled to receive USD $60 million from ESPN for the 2004-05 season, but realised nothing because of the lockout. The NHL's current American and Canadian contracts are outlined in **Figure 3**.

Previous broadcasting arrangements in the United States included early network contracts with CBS and NBC, contracts with Fox (1994-99) and

---

[225]  Standing Committee on Canadian Heritage, Sub-Committee on the Study of Sport in Canada, *Sport in Canada: Leadership, Partnership and Accountability - Everybody's Business* (House of Commons Canada, November 1998) at 94-95.

[226]  On the radio broadcasting from the 1920s, see, B. Kidd, *The Struggle for Canadian Sport* (Toronto: University of Toronto Press, 1996) at 222-28, 254-61 (state assistance in consolidating the NHL monopoly).

[227]  B. Kidd, *The Struggle for Canadian Sport* (Toronto: University of Toronto Press, 1996) at 254.

[228]  See, for example, *Coca-Cola Ltd. v. The Sports Network*, [1992] O.J. No. 2010, 44 C.P.R. (3d) 478 (Ont. Gen. Div.) (TSN entered into a new contract with Pepsi for advertising during Blue Jays games; Coke claimed first refusal and incumbency rights; mandatory order refused).

ABC-ESPN (1999-2004), and cable distribution by SportsChannel America and ESPN-ESPN2. The development of broadcasting revenue continues to be a leading business goal of the NHL, although the bouncing between systems hardly makes for a happy relationship with the television partner or for holding the attention of a loyal following of viewers. The location of new franchises has been driven by the desire to be represented throughout the United States, especially in growing metropolitan areas that constitute important media markets.[229] The strategy is, however, yet to bear fruit as hockey lacks cultural significance in many parts of America and is lost in the fragmented clutter of modern media. In the absence of lucrative contracts with national systems in the United States, the NHL is also faced with the unequal distribution of revenue resulting from teams' individual contracts for local and regional rights.

### Figure 3: NHL Television Contracts (2009)

| League/Team | Network/Contract | Years | Approximate Fee |
| --- | --- | --- | --- |
| NHL | CBC – National | 2008-14 | CDN $100 million a year |
| NHL | TSN – National | 2008-14 | CDN $40 million a year |
| NHL | RDS – National (and Réseau Info-Sports) | 2007-13 | CDN $30 million a year |
| NHL | NBC – USA National | 2009-11 | Since 2005-06: no rights fee, share of revenue |
| NHL | Versus (formerly OLN (Comcast)) - USA cable | 2008-11 | USD $72.5 million a year (2007-08) |
| NHL | The NHL Network | – | – |
| NHL | North America Sports Network (NASN) /ESPN America - Europe | – | – |
| NHL | All Sports Network (ASN) - Asia | – | – |
| Leafs | Leafs TV | – | CDN $450,000 a game (2007) |
| | TSN – Regional | | |
| | Sportsnet Ontario | 2007-15 | CDN $700,000 a game |

---

[229] See, R. Bellamy & K. Schultz, "Hockey Night in the United States? The NHL, Major League Sports, and the Evolving Television/Media Market Place" and D. Mason, "Expanding the Footprint? Questioning the NHL's Expansion and Relocation Strategy", in D. Whitson & R. Gruneau, eds., *Artificial Ice: Hockey, Culture, and Commerce* (Peterborough, ON: Broadview Press, 2006) at 163 and 181.

| Canadiens | RDS – Regional | – | CDN $275,000 a game (2007) |
| Canucks | Sportsnet Pacific | – | CDN $300,000 a game (2007) |
| Senators | Sportsnet East RDS Regional | – | – |
| Flames | Sportsnet West | – | – |
| Oilers | Sportsnet West | – | – |

In Canada, the general principles of broadcasting policy are declared in the *Broadcasting Act*,[230] and the system is subject to regulation and licensing by the Canadian Radio-televison and Telecommunications Commission ("CRTC").[231] By section 3 of the *Broadcasting Act*, the system is to be "effectively owned and controlled by Canadians" and programming is to be of a high standard "that reflects Canadian attitudes, opinions, ideas, values and artistic creativity" (see, s. 3(1) (a), (d)(ii), (g)). As the national public broadcaster, the Canadian Broadcasting Corporation (see, ss. 35-71) bears the special responsibility to "be predominantly and distinctively Canadian" and to offer "a wide range of programming that informs, enlightens and entertains" (see, s. 3 (1)(l)(m)). The CBC is required to include amateur and high-performance sport in its program content,[232] but also carries professional sport. CBC's television broadcasts of "Hockey Night in Canada"[233] date from 1952 and at different periods have been sponsored by Imperial Oil, Molson[234] and Labatt. *La Soirée du hockey* was similarly a fixture on Société Radio-Canada ("SRC") from 1952 to 2002 when broadcasts passed to the Réseau des Sports ("RDS") and so limited access to French-language programming featuring the Canadiens.

Besides the publicly-funded CBC, the broadcasting system includes private networks offering general programming. It also includes specialty channels that normally deliver their services through cable subscription, and since 2001 cable companies may own specialty channels and pay-for-view services.[235] The sports specialty channels include Sportsnet, The Sports Network ("TSN") and RDS, The Score[236] and The NHL Network. Sportsnet was originally licensed as a regional service and TSN as a national service, but a change in regulatory policy

---

[230]  S.C. 1991, c. 11.

[231]  See, *Broadcasting Act*, S.C. 1991, c. 11, ss. 5-34; *Canadian Radio-television and Telecommunications Commission Act*, R.S.C. 1985, c. C-22. See online: <http://www.crtc.gc.ca>. See, in particular, Broadcasting Regulatory Policy CRTC 2009-562 (September 4, 2009) (conditions of licence and Canadian content for specialty services in mainstream sports).

[232]  Decision CRTC 2000-1 (January 6, 2000) at para. 51 (CBC licence renewal).

[233]  See, S. Young, *The Boys of Saturday Night: Inside Hockey Night in Canada* (Toronto: Macmillan, 1990).

[234]  See, *Jets Hockey Ventures v. Molson Breweries of Canada Ltd.*, [1989] M.J. No. 523, 63 D.L.R. (4th) 119 (Man. Q.B.), affd [1990] M.J. No. 47, 66 D.L.R. (4th) 767 (Man. C.A.) (blackout rights of teams).

[235]  Public Notices CRTC 2001-66 (June 7, 2001) and CRTC 2001-66-1 (August 24, 2001).

[236]  See, Broadcasting Decision CRTC 2004-10 (January 21, 2004) (licence renewal).

in 2008 introduced competition between providers of mainstream sports services.[237] Sportsnet was established in 1998 and passed into the full ownership of Rogers Communications Inc. in 2004; in 2006, Sportsnet had 8.2 million subscribers and revenues of CDN $141.5 million. The leading channel is TSN which was originally licensed in 1984 and in 2006 had 8.4 million subscribers and revenues of CDN $201 million.[238] Since 2001, TSN has been owned by CTVglobemedia Inc. (80 per cent) and ESPN (20 per cent).

Both Sportsnet and TSN/RDS therefore form part of the private media oligopolies.[239] By way of example, the sports specialty holdings of CTVglobemedia Inc. in 2009 are set out in **Figure 4**. In December 2008, CTVglobemedia Inc. reduced its stake in Maple Leaf Sports and Entertainment Ltd. to 7.7 per cent and sold all of its holding to the Ontario Teachers' Pension Plan in August 2009. Prior to this time, a game between the Leafs and Canadiens was firmly within the CTV family, even when broadcast on the CBC.

Although "television rights"[240] are regularly bought and sold, there is in fact no direct property interest in a sports event; the only impediments to making an independent recording are access to the action and contractual conditions imposed by a stadium or arena. There could, for example, be no exclusive rights to a marathon run in public streets,[241] although organisers may be able to block off areas and reserve prime camera locations for a chosen broadcaster. Physical contests or games are not subject to copyright because they are fluid and unpredictable. They are fleeting spectacles rather than fixed works[242] and may be described by anyone who witnesses them. Remedies against misappropriation

---

[237] Broadcasting Public Notice CRTC 2008-100 (October 30, 2008) at paras. 266-276 (competition in genre of mainstream sports).

[238] On the "financial performance" of the different specialty services, see, CRTC, "Broadcasting Policy Monitoring Report 2007" at 47-51, available online: <http://www.crtc.gc.ca>.

[239] See, J. Harvey & A. Law, "'Resisting' the Global Media Oligopoly? The Canada Inc. Response" in M.L. Silk, D.L. Andrews & C.L. Cole, eds., *Sport and Corporate Nationalisms* (Oxford: Berg, 2005) 187.

[240] See: J.-P. Blais, "The Protection of Exclusive Television Rights to Sporting Events held in Public Venues: An Overview of the Law in Australia and Canada" (1992) 18 Melbourne U.L. Rev. 503; R. Verow, C. Lawrence & P. McCormick, *Sports Business: Law, Practice and Precedents*, 2d ed. (Bristol: Jordan Publishing, 2005) at 321-47.

[241] See, *WCVB-TV v. Boston Athletic Assn.*, 926 F.2d 42 (1st Cir., 1991) (no likelihood of trademark confusion).

[242] See, *Copyright Act*, R.S.C. 1985, c. C-42, s. 3(1)(f) (copyright in telecommunication of any "literary, dramatic, musical or artistic work"). On the need for sports to be "fixed", see: *Canadian Admiral Corp. Ltd. v. Rediffusion Inc.*, [1954] Ex. Ct. R. 382 (live telecast of Alouettes game; "you can't control your subject at all; you have no authority over a football player" at 395); *Re Retransmission of Distant Radio and Television Signals*, [1990] C.B.D. No. 3, 32 C.P.R. (3d) 97 at 137-38 (Canada Copyright Board); *FWS Joint Sports Claimants v. (Copyright Board)*, [1991] F.C.J. No. 501, 36 C.P.R. (3d) 483 at 489-90 (F.C.A.) ("No one bets on the outcome of a performance of Swan Lake" at 490, *per* Linden J.A.).

must be based on other recognized properties of the promoter or on athletes' personality rights.[243]

**Figure 4: CTVglobemedia, CTV Specialty Television Corporate Structure (2009)**

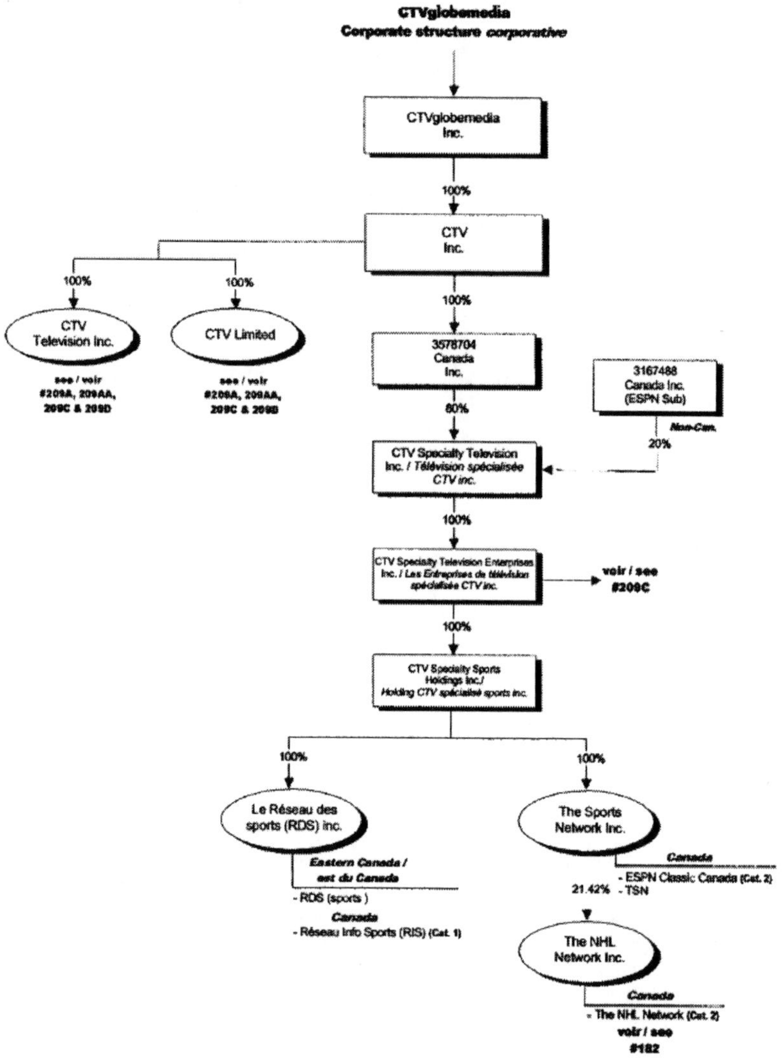

*Source*: Online: <http://www.crtc.gc.ca/ownership/cht209b.pdf>, last accessed January 19, 2010.

---

[243] See Chapter 7, "The Business of Hockey", section A, 4. See also, *Baltimore Orioles, Inc. v. Major League Baseball Players Assn.*, 805 F.2d 663 (7th Cir., 1986) (players' publicity rights preempted by copyright law).

Copyright protection applies to the unauthorized taking of a particular recording or television production since there is the power to control the rebroadcast, re-transmission or use[244] of images recorded in material form. Copyright crystallizes once images are fixed by film, videotape or simultaneous recording.[245] In *Titan Sports Inc. v. Mansion House (Toronto) Ltd.*,[246] the producer of World Wrestling Federation matches shown on closed circuit television obtained injunctions against unauthorized taverns that pirated the simultaneously recorded satellite signal. The court noted the planning and expense that went into the production, including the acquisition of music rights, and noted the steps taken to protect copyright, including scrambling the signal and warning against unauthorized broadcasts. Although remedies have been granted against commercial premises[247] that engage in the unauthorized interception of signals,[248] technological develop-ments have introduced the further problem of piracy based on streaming on the Internet.[249]

The collective sale and pooling of television rights is permitted under an exemption from American antitrust law[250] that enables leagues to control output and set terms for advertising on the national systems. The exemption is, however, read "narrowly, with beady eyes and green eyeshades" and did not extend to attempts by the NBA to limit the exposure of the Chicago Bulls on "superstations".[251] Under section 1 of the *Sports Broadcasting Act of 1961*,[252]

---

[244] On fair dealing, see, *Copyright Act*, R.S.C. 1985, c. C-42, s. 29.2 (news reporting). See also, *British Broadcasting Corp. v. British Satellite Broadcasting Ltd.*, [1992] Ch. 141, [1991] 3 All E.R. 833 (Ch. Div.) (use of short excerpts in newscasts).

[245] *Copyright Act*, R.S.C. 1985, c. C-42, s. 3(1.1). See also, s. 21 (copyright in "communication signals" originating from certain countries).

[246] [1989] F.C.J. No. 805, [1990] 1 F.C. 448 (F.C.T.D.). See also: *National Football League v. McBee & Bruno's, Inc.*, 792 F.2d 726 (8th Cir., 1986) (injunction against restaurant using sat-ellite dish to show black-out games); *NFL Enterprises L.P. v. 1019491 Ontario Ltd. (c.o.b. Wrigley's Field Sports Bar & Grill)*, [1998] F.C.J. No. 1063, 229 N.R. 231 (F.C.A.) (injunction against three taverns); *Interbox Promotion Corp. v. 9012-4314 Québec Inc. (Hippo Club)*, [2003] F.C.J. No. 1581, 253 F.T.R. 1 (F.C.) (promoter of boxing match awarded damages); *1395047 Ontario Inc. (c.o.b. FPTV – Festival Portuguese Television) v. 1548951 Ontario Ltd. (c.o.b. O Bola Sports Bar)*, [2006] F.C.J. No. 1098, 56 C.P.R. (4th) 58 (F.C.) (contempt pro-ceedings); *Setana Sport Ltd. v. 2049630 Ontario Inc. (c.o.b. Verde Minho Tapas & Lounge)*, [2007] F.C.J. No. 1167, 2007 FC 899 (F.C.) (evidence of copyright defective).

[247] See, A. Bleau, "To see or not to see: A primer on sports blackouts" *The Lawyers Weekly* (June 22, 2001) at 17.

[248] See: *Radiocommunication Act*, R.S.C. 1985, c. R-2; *NFL Enterprises L.P. v. Sotirios and Peter Restaurant Co. (c.o.b. J.J. Kapps Pasta Bar & Grill)*, [1999] F.C.J. No. 1209 (F.C.) (assess-ment of damages). On decoding equipment, see also, *Bell ExpressVu Limited Partnership v. Rex*, [2002] S.C.J. No. 43, [2002] 2 S.C.R. 559 (S.C.C.).

[249] See, for example, *National Football League v. PrimeTime 24 Joint Venture*, 211 F.3d 10 (2nd Cir., 2000). See also, M.J. Mellis, "Internet Piracy of Live Sports Telecasts" (2008) 18 Marq. Sports L.J. 259.

[250] See Chapter 8, "Competition Law and Labour Law", section C.

[251] See: *Chicago Professional Sports Limited Partnership v. National Basketball Assn.*, 961 F.2d 667 (7th Cir., 1992); *Chicago Professional Sports Limited Partnership v. National Basketball Assn.*, 95 F.3d 593 (7th Cir., 1996) (antitrust laws apply but NBA is closer to single firm in

professional football, baseball, basketball or hockey teams may sell rights to "sponsored telecasting" of their games through joint agreements negotiated by their leagues. Section 2 of the Act allows the local blackout of games when the professional team is playing at home. The exemption is limited to the four professional sports and does not apply to joint contracts arranged by intercollegiate associations.[253] "Sponsored telecasting" refers to broadcasts supported by commercial advertising and does not include satellite distribution paid for by subscription.[254]

The centralized sale of rights to network television continues as a means of providing exposure because the time-outs in North American sports allow frequent opportunities for advertising. This form of delivery is, however, only one source of revenue in an increasingly diverse media environment,[255] and programming is likely to continue to stray from "free" television as leagues and team owners look to use cable and pay systems to sell electronic admissions by the millions. Broadcasts can also be viewed by subscribing to cellphone services. Since 2009, NHL Mobile in association with Bell Mobility Inc. has allowed access to games except where local blackout restrictions apply.

## 5.    Coaches' Contracts

Revenue is sometimes related to winning games, and it is the coach's responsibility to get the results. Making the playoffs is particularly important in the NHL where ticket sales during the "second season" are an important source of a team's finances. An unproductive run regularly results in a changing of the guard behind the bench, although the parting of the ways can occur for any number of reasons as higher management chooses to "restructure the coaching staff".[256] Coaches' contracts represent a significant part of team expenses, especially when there are continuing obligations to former personnel. When the Toronto Maple Leafs fired Pat Quinn in April 2006, the successful coach remained entitled to receive his salary of USD $2 million through the following season.[257] In 2009, the average annual salary of a head coach in the NHL was USD $1 million. As a celebrity figure in Phoenix, Wayne Gretzky was receiving USD $8 million.

---

broadcasting market; remand for further proceedings or agreement among parties). The Bulls, the NBA and WGN subsequently agreed on the number of games that could go on national cable as "superstation" broadcasts.

[252]    15 U.S.C. ss. 1291-95 (2001). See, L.S. Sobel, *Professional Sports and the Law* (New York: Law-Arts Publishers, 1977) at 575-634.

[253]    See, *National Collegiate Athletic Assn. v. University of Oklahoma*, 468 U.S. 85 (1984) (package agreement controlling network broadcasting was unlawful restriction on competition over price, consumer choice and output).

[254]    See, *Shaw v. Dallas Cowboys Football Club, Ltd.*, 172 F.3d 299 (3rd Cir., 1999).

[255]    On the NHL's "new media strategy", see Chapter 7, "The Business of Hockey", section B, 2.

[256]    See, *Murray v. Jets Hockey Ventures (c.o.b. Winnipeg Jets Hockey Club)*, [1996] M.J. No. 277, 109 Man.R. (2d) 215 (Man. Q.B.) (oral agreement to extend two-year contract by another year; assignment to work as scout was constructive dismissal; general damages of CDN $140,000).

[257]    See, "In the boardroom Leafs fire Quinn" *The Globe and Mail* (Toronto: April 21, 2006) at R6.

Coaches' contracts take a variety of forms, whether informal arrangements, letter agreements or fully negotiated contracts detailing the duties, conditions and duration of the employment.[258] Although interests can be protected by contract, the only certainty in the job is that one day it will come to an end by non-renewal, outright firing or constructive dismissal through the assignment of other duties or the loss of essential responsibilities. (The coach too may suddenly choose to leave for pastures new.[259]) Where the contract is for ongoing employment or where there is time remaining on a fixed term, issues arise as to the appropriate settlement, and the disgruntled departing coach has the option of bringing action for wrongful dismissal.[260] In assessing damages, there is divided opinion as to whether there is any great stigma in a coach being selected for external career development.[261] In a case involving a "normal termination", the "accepted practice" in the employment and disposal of coaches has been described as follows:

> ...in the coaching world and particularly in the NHL the coaches' job security is uncertain, and ...the coaching role itself is dependent on many variables that can result in change or termination of responsibility with little warning or notice...a change of position or replacement of a coach is not particularly surprising and does not necessarily generate adverse publicity or embarrassment or humiliation or loss of reputation...[262]

Adverse publicity may, however, follow from a coach signing with a competitor while still under contract with a current team.[263] Such a move raises issues relating to the structures of a league and the integrity of its competition.

---

[258] On college coaches' contracts, see, M.J. Greenberg, *Sports Law Practice*, vol. 1 (Charlottesville: The Michie Company, 1993) at 445-535. See also: *Loranger v. Mount Allison University*, [1998] N.B.J. No. 473, 206 N.B.R. (2d) 96 (N.B.Q.B.) (wrongful dismissal of football coach employed for unlimited term); *McGarrigle v. Canadian Interuniversity Sport*, [2003] O.J. No. 1842, 2003 ONSC 10719 (Ont. S.C.J.) (unauthorized suspension). On coaches' contracts in the NFL, see, R.H. Lattinville & R.A. Boland, "Coaching in the National Football League: A Market Survey and Legal Review" (2006) 17 Marq. Sports L.J. 109.

[259] In July 1994, one month after leading the New York Rangers to the Stanley Cup, Mike Keenan left the team for the St. Louis Blues, claiming that the Rangers had failed to pay required bonuses. See: "Rangers seek NHL intervention" *The Globe and Mail* (Toronto: July 19, 1994) at A10; M.A. Conrad, "Mike Keenan's Power Play - A Slap Shot Against the Rangers and a Slap on the Wrist by the NHL" (1995) 5 Seton Hall J. Sport L. 637.

[260] See: *Neilson v. Vancouver Hockey Club Ltd.*, [1988] B.C.J. No. 584, 51 D.L.R. (4th) 40 (B.C.C.A.) (team terminated "guaranteed" fixed term contract; damages mitigated by earnings from employment with other teams; award reduced to CDN $64,364); *Boutin c. Club Hockey Caron et Guay inc.*, [2006] J.Q. no 11054, 2006 QCCQ 8326 (C.Q.) (semi-professional league; award of CDN $4,100).

[261] For the view that the dismissal involves "detrimental consequences" and "loss of public reputation and esteem", see, *Neilson v. Vancouver Hockey Club Ltd.*, [1988] B.C.J. No. 584, 51 D.L.R. (4th) 40 (B.C.C.A.) at 46, 49 *per* Carrothers J.A. (dissenting).

[262] *Murray v. Jets Hockey Ventures (c.o.b. Winnipeg Jets Hockey Club)*, [1996] M.J. No. 277, 109 Man.R. (2d) 215 at 222 (Man. Q.B.), *per* Wright J.

[263] See, *Vancouver Hockey Club Ltd. v. 8 Hockey Ventures Inc.*, [1987] B.C.J. No. 2074, 47 D.L.R. (4th) 51 (B.C.S.C.) (while coach of the L.A. Kings, Pat Quinn signed a contract for fu-

## C.  ECONOMICS OF PROFESSIONAL LEAGUES

## 1.  General

This section notes the peculiar economics of leagues in both the supply of the product and the control of the labour market.[264] Although competition prevails in the general entertainment market and in the on-field contests, the business organization of sports reveals various monopolistic features.[265] A single major league usually emerges as the exclusive source of superior events in a particular sport, and one member team is usually the sole supplier of the league's product in a particular territory. In the labour market, free agency has modified restraints on employees, but historically teams have held monopsony power (monopoly on the demand side) through league rules granting exclusive rights to purchase and reserve particular players. Salaries exceeded non-sporting alternatives so that players willingly accepted the reservation wage,[266] but they could not receive competing offers from other teams that might recognize in a player a greater potential to improve performance and increase revenue. Under reservation, there was no bidding up of the salary as far as the player's value to another team; the highest "marginal revenue product" was not achieved.

By restricting output and controlling wages, leagues realized attractive profits that were envied by competitors. Rival operators have periodically challenged the dominant position of major leagues[267] and caused sharp increases in players' salaries through open-market bidding.[268] The business then claims that it is over-extended, and competitive balance in the established league can be affected when the weaker teams lose their best players to the new operation. The exclusive position of one league is soon re-established by a general merger, by absorbing selected franchises or by the total failure of the rival circuit. It may even be suggested that major leagues are "natural monopolies" and that the overall product is improved when the best talent faces-off under one structure. Normally, government regulation is the means of control over monopoly

---

        ture services with the Canucks; fine and suspension imposed by league president were support-
        able, but particular fine was unauthorised by league bylaws).

[264]   See: J. Cairns, N. Jennett & P.J. Sloane, "The Economics of Professional Team Sports: A Sur-
        vey of Theory and Evidence" (1986) 13 J. of Econ. Studies 3; M. Leeds & P. von Allmen, *The
        Economics of Sports*, 3d ed. (Boston: Pearson/Addison Wesley, 2008); S. Syzmanski, *Play-
        books and Checkbooks: An Introduction to the Economics of Modern Sport* (Princeton: Prince-
        ton University Press, 2009).

[265]   See, J. Quirk & R. Fort, *Hard Ball: The Abuse of Power in Pro Team Sports* (Princeton: Prince-
        ton University Press, 1999).

[266]   In the 1950s, the average NHL salary was about 2.5 times the average industrial wage; see, M.
        Lavoie, *Avantage numérique: L'argent et la Ligue nationale de hockey* (Hull: Éditions Vents
        d'Ouest, 1997) at 189-90. By 2001, it was 80 times the earnings of the average employee.

[267]   See, J. Quirk & R.D. Fort, *Pay Dirt: The Business of Professional Team Sports* (Princeton:
        Princeton University Press, 1992) at 294-361.

[268]   During the operation of the rival World Hockey Association, average player salaries in major
        league hockey increased from USD $37,000 to USD $101,000; see, M. Lavoie, *Avantage numéri-
        que: L'argent et la Ligue nationale de hockey* (Hull: Éditions Vents d'Ouest, 1997) at 186.

enterprises.[269] This method has not, however, been applied to leagues which are either subject to the ordinary standards and prohibitions of competition law or enjoy exemption from such scrutiny.[270]

Professional leagues operate as cartels or co-operative unions of member teams seeking to maximize joint profits.[271] The North American structure involves a closed circuit of established franchises that do not run the risk of losing their place through relegation to a lower division. The teams are separate entities but are economically interdependent because general revenue and reputation can be affected by the legitimacy and performance of each member. Teams require viable playing opponents because the contest is usually worthwhile for the paying public only if the outcome is uncertain. It is possible for a league to be sustained by media contracts based on the fame and perennial domination of a few powerhouse franchises, but the preferred model is to maintain relative equality in both finances and on-field results. Although teams have an interest in the competitiveness of the league's product, they are also concerned about their own success since revenue and player benefits are usually increased by reaching the play-offs and winning the championship. The fans, in particular, have a decided preference for the home-town win rather than "balanced competition". The pursuit of victory at any price can, however, destroy the cartel.

Play is organized as league competition for the benefit of members and so as to improve performance and provide entertainment. To facilitate orderly competition, leagues make internal arrangements of three different types:[272] game scheduling and playing rules to standardize the product; disciplinary regulations; and devices to equalize the playing strength and financial condition of teams. Members of North American leagues are usually subject to supervision by a president or commissioner selected by team owners;[273] the co-operative confederation is maintained by league rules and by-laws that control the business operations of teams. Some rules primarily affect ownership or management and deal with matters such as revenue sharing, the admission and qualifications of franchise holders and the location or movement of teams.[274] Other economic

---

[269]   See: B. Kidd, *The Political Economy of Sport* (Ottawa: CAHPER Monograph/ University of Calgary, 1979) at 48; J.C.H. Jones & D.K. Davies, "Not Even Semitough: Professional Sport and Canadian Antitrust" (1978) 23 Antitrust Bull. 713 at 740. See also, S.F. Ross, "Monopoly Sports Leagues" (1989) 73 Minn. L. Rev. 643.

[270]   See Chapter 8, "Competition Law and Labour Law", sections A-C.

[271]   On the motivation of team owners and collective financial health, see, W. Vamplew, *Pay Up and Play the Game: Professional Sport in Britain, 1875-1914* (Cambridge: Cambridge University Press, 1988) at 75-153, 174-80. For an ideal view of the owner's fiduciary duty, see, *Professional Hockey Corp. v. World Hockey Assn.*, 143 Cal. App. 3d 410, 191 Cal. Rptr. 773 (C.A., 1983) (duty to benefit league and not act in self-interest).

[272]   See, H.G. Demmert, *The Economics of Professional Team Sport* (Lexington: D.C. Heath, 1973) at 15-16.

[273]   See, *Lysko v. Braley*, [2006] O.J. No. 1137, 79 O.R. (3d) 721 (Ont. C.A.) (action for wrongful dismissal by former commissioner of the Canadian Football League; amendment of statement of claim).

[274]   See Chapter 8, "Competition Law and Labour Law", sections A, 4; C, 4.

devices relate to the labour market for players.[275] The freedom of players to negotiate with any team in the league has been restricted by entry systems such as territorial rights, negotiation lists or draft claims on graduating juniors. Salary caps place limits on overall compensation paid by teams, and the mobility of players signed with a team has been restricted by the standard player contract, the prohibition on "tampering" that prevents negotiations for future services and by the "waivers" process that allows a priority of claims to released players. The most famous restraint is the reservation system in its various forms. The reserve clause in hockey and major league baseball formerly allowed a team to renew a player's contract in perpetuity. Free agency is now limited by eligibility periods, rights of first refusal and by the compensation that must be paid to a players' former team.

Reservation and other restraints were defended by team owners as necessary for the integrity of the game and the economic survival of the majority of teams in the league.[276] The moral threat supposedly came from players negotiating with current opponents, but this could be solved by long-term contracts and a "tampering" rule. The death threat can also be discounted, both as a matter of theory and on the evidence of recent history. Reservation, it was argued, averted economic collapse by ensuring player continuity and equal competitive opportunities for teams in small population centres. Reservation did, however, allow for the trading of players, and the only difference from free agency was that the property right or value in the players' services (the "rent") accrued to teams.[277] In either system, the player moves to the team that most values the services, and that team may be one in a richer market. Historically, reservation never achieved parity since some teams dominated the winning of championships, and profitability was similarly limited to a few franchises. The real effect of reservation was to reduce operating costs for the also-rans, while increasing the profits of the perennial winners. Economists have shown that a less restrictive allocation of talent according to team need and player preference would be equally effective in balancing competition.[278] The era of free agency has not brought any significant change in the spread of teams' win-loss

---

[275]  See Chapter 8, "Competition Law and Labour Law", sections A, 2, 3; B; C, 2, 3.

[276]  See, M. Lavoie, *Avantage numérique: L'argent et la Ligue nationale de hockey* (Hull: Éditions Vents d'Ouest, 1997) at 49-51.

[277]  See, S. Rottenberg, "The Baseball Players' Labor Market" (1956) 64 J. of Pol. Econ. 242 at 247, 255-56. See also, A.C. Krautmann, "Qualifications to the Rottenberg Invariance Theorem" (2008) 9 J. of Sports Econ. 88.

[278]  See: H.G. Demmert, *The Economics of Professional Team Sport* (Lexington: D.C. Heath, 1973); M. El-Hodiri & J. Quirk, "The Economic Theory of a Professional Sport League" in R.G. Noll, ed., *Government and the Sports Business* (Washington, D.C.: The Brookings Institution, 1974) at 33; T.N. Daymont, "The Effects of Monopsonistic Procedures on Equality of Competition in Professional Sport Leagues" (1975) 10:2 Int. Rev. of Sport Soc. 83; J.C. Jones, "The Economics of the National Hockey League" in R.S. Gruneau & J.G. Albinson, eds., *Canadian Sports: Sociological Perspectives* (Don Mills, ON: Addison Wesley Canada, 1976) at 225, 249. See also, M. Boucher, "Le marché des joueurs de la ligue nationale de hockey: Une approche économique" (1983) 59 L'Actualité économique 753.

percentages[279] or in the turnover of teams vying for championships or participating in play-offs.

While oppressive restraints proved to be both unnecessary and illegal,[280] some control mechanisms and limits on player mobility may contribute to parity and so enhance the league's product. Although the draft cannot be a panacea,[281] there is evidence that the long-term accumulation of high first-round picks eventually has the effect of improving a team.[282] First-round selection rights, in combination with delayed eligibility for unrestricted free agency, may therefore give a team a fighting chance. A particular threat to competitive balance occurs when large-market teams seek to maximize wins, and there has been a positive correlation between the size of the payroll and the winning percentage.[283] In an attempt to restore balance, the favoured control mechanisms are now the team salary cap and revenue sharing.[284] "Taxing" payments above a certain point in teams' payrolls is also available in an attempt to deter big spenders from indulging their natural tendency to accumulate players at any price. A system of "payroll standards"[285] must also include a salary floor to ensure that small-market teams use the redistributed revenue for the purpose of acquiring talented players.

The details of the controls on expenditure are hammered out in collective bargaining with the players' association[286] so that the restrictions apply to the labour market for playing talent. These limitations would seem to be counter-productive in the case of the high-revenue team that has a poor record of playing performance: such a "large-market loser" seems to be denied the chance to spend its way out of the basement. A team is, however, free to allocate resources to its scouting system, its minor league teams and its coaching staff. The upper limit for players' salaries does not preclude improvements in the development system, in management or in services for long-suffering fans, although corporate owners may simply prefer to pocket the enhanced profits that follow from a cap on players' salaries. Where a team does invest in the identification and development

---

[279] On standard deviation in winning percentage (SDWP), see: J. Quirk & R.D. Fort, *Pay Dirt: The Business of Professional Team Sports* (Princeton: Princeton University Press, 1992) at 284-93; J. Maxcy & M. Mondello, "The Impact of Free Agency on Competitive Balance in North American Professional Team Sports Leagues" (2006) 20 J. of Sport Management 345 ("The NHL shows the most improvement in SDWP as labor market restrictions are relaxed" at 363).

[280] See Chapter 8, "Competition Law and Labour Law", sections A-C; E; Chapter 9, "National Hockey League", section A, 2.

[281] See Chapter 8, "Competition Law and Labour Law", section A, 3.

[282] See: M. Lavoie, *Avantage numérique: L'argent et la Ligue nationale de hockey* (Hull: Éditions Vents d'Ouest, 1997) at 72-73; D.H. Richardson, "Pay, Performance and Competitive Balance in the National Hockey League" (2000) 26 Eastern Economic J. 393. On the effects of different mechanisms, see, Lavoie, M. Lavoie, *Avantage numérique: L'argent et la Ligue nationale de hockey* (Hull: Éditions Vents d'Ouest, 1997) at 59-82.

[283] See, M. Lavoie & D. Whitson, "The Economics of Sport" in J. Crossman, ed., *Canadian Sport Sociology* (Scarborough, ON: Thomson Nelson, 2003) 139 at 148.

[284] See, S. Kesenne, "Competitive Balance in Team Sports and the Impact of Revenue Sharing" (2006) 20 J. of Sport Management 39.

[285] See, P.C. Weiler, *Leveling the Playing Field: How the Law Can Make Sports Better for Fans* (Cambridge: Harvard University Press, 2001) at 186-97.

[286] See Chapter 9, "National Hockey League", sections B; C.

of talent, this is unlikely to create a dynasty or disturb competitive balance in the long term because the relative equality in payrolls means that players will eventually migrate through free agency.

## 2.   NHL Constitution and By-Laws

The co-operative union of the NHL is defined in the articles of its Constitution and the sections of its by-laws which establish rights of membership and powers and procedures for the operation of the league. A unanimous vote is required to amend the Constitution in relation to the main articles dealing with members' rights (see, Article 12).

The NHL is an unincorporated, not-for-profit association organized to promote the common interests of members and promulgate rules of play and rules governing relationships between members (see, Article 2.1). The NHL is managed through meetings of its Board of Governors, which consists of one governor or alternate appointed by each member team (see, Article 5). There are now 30 "Member Clubs" holding franchises in the league (see, Article 3.1). Members are prohibited from exercising control over other franchises or having interests in them (see, Articles 8, 13). Candidates for admission must meet eligibility criteria and receive a favourable vote from three-fourths of the members (see, Articles 3.2, 3.3; By-Law 37). The Board of Governors by majority vote determines the price of entry and any indemnification fee. On admission, candidates subscribe to and agree to be bound by the Constitution and by-laws and other resolutions, agreements and rules of the league. The transfer of ownership requires the consent of three-fourths of the members (see, Article 3.5), who must consider whether the potential new owner has "sufficient financial resources to provide for the financial stability of the franchise" and whether the person is "of good character and integrity" (see, By-Law 35.1). Article 4 of the Constitution and By-Law 36 address the "Territorial Rights" of the league and its members and deal with the relocation of franchises.[287]

The Commissioner (formerly "President") of the league is elected through a majority vote of the Board (see, Article 6.1) and normally presides at meetings (see, Article 5.10). The Commissioner serves as the chief executive officer and public spokesman of the league and has "responsibility for the general supervision and direction of all business and affairs of the League" (see, Article 6.3(a)). The current Commissioner, Gary Bettman, was first appointed in 1993 and has subsequently led collective bargaining on behalf of management. His annual salary at the time of the lockout in 2004-05 was USD $3.7 million, and his earnings and benefits in 2007-08 were USD $7.1 million (considerably less than payments received by the commissioners of the other three major leagues in North America).[288]

---

[287]   See Chapter 8, "Competition Law and Labour Law", sections A, 4; C, 4.

[288]   See, "Bettman's salary in 2007-08: $7.1 million" *The Globe and Mail* (Toronto: July 14, 2009) at R6 (report in *SportsBusiness Journal*).

The powers and duties of the Commissioner include resolving disputes involving teams, players or employees, interpreting league rules, entering into contracts on behalf of the league (subject to financial limits), preparing the schedule and supervising league officials (see, Article 6.3). The Commissioner holds disciplinary authority[289] in relation to "conduct...detrimental to the League or the game of hockey (see, Article 6.3(j)), "tampering" with personnel (see, By-Law 15) and "prejudicial" conduct or remarks, including public comments by team officers relating to expansion or collective bargaining (see, By-Law 17). Under By-Law 14, a NHL team may be held responsible for actions taken by an affiliated club in another league. The Commissioner's powers in relation to the players are recognized in the collective bargaining agreement.[290]

The by-laws assign further responsibilities to the Commissioner in relation to eligibility under player allocation systems and incorporate rules dealing with players' contracts, registration and team lists. Besides the rules relating to the ownership of teams, the by-laws also address the administration of league competition through divisional alignments, the playing schedule and the obligations of host teams.

---

[289] See Chapter 9, "National Hockey League", section D.
[290] Collective Bargaining Agreement (2005), articles 10.2(b)(iv), 18.2, 18.4, exhibit 8.

# Chapter 8

# COMPETITION LAW AND LABOUR LAW

It is certainly no secret to these parties, to this Court, or to the average eight-year-old sports fan that antitrust issues exist in professional sports.[1]

As noted in the preceding chapter, league regulations control the commercial operations of franchises and the allocation of players between teams. The restrictions may, for example, prevent free movement or create a monopsony power granting one team exclusive rights to negotiate with a player. Besides the controls maintained by North American organizations, transfer and mobility are also subject to international regulations and agreements.[2] This chapter considers how restraints on either franchises or players may be challenged under laws that promote free and fair commercial competition. It also addresses the legal framework of collective bargaining, which is a further means of modifying players' employment conditions, and particular difficulties arise in reconciling remedies under competition law with the labour relations system.[3] Restrictive rules and practices are subject to standards and prohibitions in federal, provincial, American and European law. The most important federal legislation is the *Competition Act*,[4] the renamed and revised successor to the *Combines Investigation Act*.[5] In provincial law, restrictions in contracts or regulations may be challenged under the common law restraint of trade doctrine. In the case of American-based leagues, the antitrust laws have frequently served to eliminate or modify anti-competitive or monopolistic league arrangements, and the law of the European Union is relevant to international transfers.

---

[1]  *National Hockey League v. National Hockey League Players' Assn.*, 789 F.Supp. 288 (D. Minn., 1992), at 295 *per* Rosenbaum, D.J.

[2]  See Chapter 3, "Organizations and Regulations", section C, 2, a; Chapter 8, "Competition Law and Labour Law", section E.

[3]  See Chapter 8, "Competition Law and Labour Law", sections A, 3; C, 3; D; Chapter 9, "National Hockey League", sections B; C.

[4]  R.S.C. 1985, c. C-34. See Chapter 8, "Competition Law and Labour Law", section A.

[5]  R.S.C. 1970, c. C-23.

## A. *COMPETITION ACT*

## 1. General

The *Competition Act* seeks "to maintain and encourage competition in Canada in order to promote the efficiency and adaptability of the Canadian economy ... [and] provide consumers with competitive prices and product choices".[6] The Act preserves common law rights of action (see, s. 62), while creating criminal and civil remedies[7] and establishing the office of Commissioner of Competition. The Commissioner leads the Competition Bureau[8] and is responsible for the administration and enforcement of the Act (see, s. 7). Persons alleging non-compliance with the Act may apply to the Commissioner to inquire into the matter (see, s. 9). The Act also establishes an adjudicative process before the Competition Tribunal,[9] which may review market restrictions, refusals to deal and mergers likely to lessen competition (see, ss. 75-107). By sections 78-79,[10] the Tribunal may on application by the Commissioner issue prohibition orders in respect of "Abuse of Dominant Position" or an "anti-competitive act" where the Tribunal finds that,

    (a)   one or more persons substantially or completely control, throughout Canada or any area thereof, a class or species of business,

    (b)   that person or those persons have engaged in or are engaging in a practice of anti-competitive acts, and

    (c)   the practice has had, is having or is likely to have the effect of preventing or lessening competition substantially in a market...[11]

---

[6]   *Competition Act*, R.S.C. 1985, c. C-34, s. 1.1. See, B.A. Facey, D.H. Assaf & R.J. Roberts, *Competition and Antitrust Law: Canada and the United States*, 3d ed. (Markham, ON : LexisNexis Butterworths, 2006).

[7]   *Competition Act*, R.S.C. 1985, c. C-34, s. 36 (private action for damages by person suffering loss); *General Motors of Canada Ltd. v. City National Leasing Ltd.*, [1989] S.C.J. No. 28, [1989] 1 S.C.R. 641 (S.C.C.) (civil remedy is constitutionally valid). On sports-related actions, see: *R.D. Belanger & Associates Ltd. v. Stadium Corp. of Ontario Ltd.*, [1991] O.J. No. 1962, 5 O.R. (3d) 778 (Ont. C.A.) (Skybox licence agreements; cost of food and beverage services); *Oz Merchandising Inc. v. Canadian Professional Soccer League Inc.*, [2006] O.J. No. 2882, 150 A.C.W.S. (3d) 31 (Ont. S.C.J.) (action based on revocation of Ottawa Wizards' franchise; pleadings not specific or tenable).

[8]   See online: <http://www.competitionbureau.gc.ca>. See, for example, "Enforcement Guidelines on the Abuse of Dominance Provisions" (July 2001).

[9]   See, *Competition Tribunal Act*, R.S.C. 1985, c. 19 (2nd Supp.).

[10]  See, in particular, *Competition Act*, R.S.C. 1985, c. C-34, s. 78(e), "pre-emption of scarce facilities or resources required by a competitor". *Cf.: International Boxing Club of N.Y. v. U.S.*, 358 U.S. 242 (1959) (monopoly control of boxing arenas); *Hecht v. Pro Football, Inc.*, 570 F.2d 982 (D.C. Cir., 1977) (restrictive covenant in stadium lease; stadium unavailable to franchise holder in rival league); *Fishman v. Wirtz Estate*, 807 F.2d 520 (7th Cir., 1986) (antitrust violation in denial of arena lease preventing purchase of Chicago Bulls).

[11]  *Competition Act*, R.S.C. 1985, c. C-34, s. 79.

Part VI of the *Competition Act* includes various criminal conspiracy offences that may be prosecuted as an alternative[12] to the use of remedial orders issued by the Tribunal. Collective combinations of employees "for their own reasonable protection" are, however, specifically exempted from the prohibitions (see, s. 4(1)(a)).[13] Section 45 of the *Competition Act* creates the general offence of forming conspiracies or agreements that limit competition "unduly". Undue limitation refers to serious restraints that are detrimental to the public and that arise from a combination of behaviour and market power.[14] In proving that a restraint is undue it is not necessary to show that the object or effect was "to eliminate completely or virtually competition in the market" (see, s. 45(2)). The reference in section 45 to undue restrictions contrasts with the common-law restraint of trade doctrine that prohibits "unreasonable" limitations. In determining reasonableness, courts consider business interests or advantages of the parties as well as the public interest, and the restraint will be struck down only where it is wider than required.

Until 1976, the prohibitions in the *Competition Act* applied only to "articles" of commerce. In 1969, a report by the Economic Council of Canada noted the growing importance of business, professional and financial services and recommended that the Act cover both products and services; the report anticipated that "all recreational services, including professional sports"[15] would be subject to supervision. The early 1970s brought a series of abortive Bills as interest group lobbying delayed the reform process, but amendments dealing with services were eventually enacted in 1976.[16] At this time, a special section (now, s. 48) was introduced into the *Competition Act* relating to limitations in professional sport. This provision recognizes the peculiar economics of professional leagues, but was also a response to the critique of employment conditions in the National Hockey League and the concern about the NHL's control of amateur hockey.[17]

## 2.  Sections 6 and 48

In earlier Bills,[18] the sports provisions in the *Competition Act* applied equally to amateur and professional organizations,[19] but the finally enacted

---

[12]  *Competition Act*, R.S.C. 1985, c. C-34, ss. 45.1, 79(7) (proceedings under s. 45(1) as an alternative to an abuse of dominant position or merger order).

[13]  On "labour exemptions", see further, Chapter 8, "Competition Law and Labour Law", sections A, 3; C, 3.

[14]  *R. v. Nova Scotia Pharmaceutical Society*, [1992] S.C.J. No. 67, [1992] 2 S.C.R. 606 (S.C.C.) (s. 45(1)(c) "does not permit a full-blown discussion of the economic advantages and disadvantages of the agreement" at 650 *per* Gonthier J.).

[15]  Economic Council of Canada, *Interim Report on Competition Policy* (Ottawa: Information Canada, 1969) at 148.

[16]  See: C. Backhouse, "Labour Unions and Anti-Combines Policy" (1976) 14 Osgoode Hall L.J. 113; G. Kaiser, "The Stage I Amendments: An Overview" in R.J. Prichard *et al.* (eds.), *Canadian Competition Policy: Essays in Law and Economics* (Toronto: Butterworths, 1979) at 25; W.T. Stanbury, *Business Interests and the Reform of Canadian Competition Policy, 1971-1975* (Toronto: Carswell/Methuen, 1977).

[17]  See Chapter 3, "Organizations and Regulations", section A.

[18]  Bills: C-256 (1971); C-227 (1973); C-7 (March 1974); C-2 (October 1974).

version refers only to professional participation. Section 48 is a special exemption that declares in subsection 3 that the legality of certain internal arrangements made by teams or officers of professional leagues is to be determined by applying that section and not the ordinary conspiracy section (s. 45) of the *Competition Act*. Section 48 makes it an indictable offence:

1.   to limit unreasonably the opportunities of a player to participate in professional sport or to impose unreasonable terms or conditions;

2.   to limit unreasonably the opportunities of a competitor to participate in professional sport or to impose unreasonable terms or conditions;

3.   to limit unreasonably opportunities to negotiate with and play for a team of the player's choice.

Section 48(3) also declares that the section "applies" to "the granting and operation of franchises in the league". In determining whether an arrangement violates subsection (1), courts are directed in section 48(2) to have regard to:

*(a)*   whether the sport in relation to which the contravention is alleged is organized on an international basis and, if so, whether any limitations, terms or conditions alleged should, for that reason, be accepted in Canada; and

*(b)*   the desirability of maintaining a reasonable balance among the teams or clubs participating in the same league.[20]

On its face, subsection (1) prohibits restrictive conspiracies by any party or individual. Subsection (3), however, indicates that the section applies only to arrangements between members of the "same league" that relate exclusively to playing or competitive opportunities or to franchise operations. Where an agreement is formed between separate organizations, involves non-league members or relates to other matters, section 45 is applicable. The Act gives no definition of "league", so that interpretative difficulties may occur where one organization operates through some affiliation with another body.

The main aim of section 48 is to protect freedom of employment for players; the provisions apply more naturally to the labour market, particularly with regard to the justificatory factors (internationalism and balance) in subsection (2). The use of the term "competitor" may, however, indicate that section 48 also applies to external business operators in the product market, so that it is an offence to maintain unreasonable anti-competitive arrangements that limit opportunities for rival organizations. A competing league might, for example, be hindered by lack of access to players or facilities held under monopoly control. However, the denial of a franchise to an outside applicant is probably not an offence under section 48(1) since subsection (3) distinguishes the matters in subsection (1) from the "granting

[19]   J. Barnes, *Sports and the Law in Canada*, 2d ed. (Toronto: Butterworths, 1988) at 108-10.

[20]   *Competition Act*, R.S.C. 1985, c. C-34, s. 48(2).

and operation of franchises". The offence is also for that reason inapplicable to restrictions on teams in the league.[21]

Section 6, which exempts amateur sport from the Act, is in the following terms:

(1) This Act does not apply in respect of agreements or arrangements between or among teams, clubs and leagues pertaining to participation in amateur sport.

(2) For the purposes of this section, "amateur sport" means sport in which the participants receive no remuneration for their services as participants.[22]

The exemption is limited therefore to agreements between teams or leagues and does not apply to restraints maintained by individuals; neither does it apply to agreements with amateur organizations for the supply of players to professional leagues. Under the definition of "amateur sport", it is clear that Major Junior hockey leagues are regarded as professional organizations.[23] Section 48 and other provisions of the *Competition Act* apply to any league in which there is widespread payment to players of salary for services.[24] This may now include the traditionally "amateur" sports organizations whose high-performance competitors receive various forms of payment.

Section 48(2)(a) directs the court to consider the international organization of the sport when assessing the legality of an arrangement. This provision recognizes that Canadian participation may depend on accepting an international regulation and recognizes that most professional franchises are located in the United States so that the major leagues are subject to American law. On one interpretation of section 48(2)(a), Canadian courts will automatically allow restraints that have been approved in the numerous American antitrust decisions.[25] The section does, however, merely direct the Canadian court to "have regard to" the international aspect, so that a limitation might still be disallowed. (American case law and commentary do, furthermore, show some lack of unanimity on leading issues.) Under section 48(2)(b), the court is directed to consider the "desirability of maintaining a reasonable balance among the teams". The need for parity has been the

---

[21] See further, Chapter 8, "Competition Law and Labour Law", section A, 4. The language of s. 48 distinguishes a "franchise" from a "competitor", so that it would seem that a team is not a competitor; but see further, Chapter 8, "Competition Law and Labour Law", section C, 4.

[22] *Competition Act*, R.S.C. 1985, c. C-34, s. 6.

[23] Senate Committee on Banking, Trade and Commerce, Issue no. 61 (November 19, 1975) at 18. See also, Chapter 3, "Organizations and Regulations", section B, 3; Chapter 7, "The Business of Hockey", section A, 2 (business aspects).

[24] Committee on Finance, Trade and Economic Affairs, Issue no. 39 (April 22, 1974) at 31-34.

[25] See, R.M. Sedgewick, "The Combines Investigation Act", replying to G.D. Finlayson, "Personal Service Contracts" in *Special Lectures of the Law Society of Upper Canada: Current Problems in the Law of Contracts* (Toronto: Richard De Boo, 1975) 383 at 385. See also, J.C.H. Jones & D.K. Davis, "Not Even Semitough: Professional Sport and Canadian Antitrust" (1978) 23 The Antitrust Bulletin 713 at 740.

standard management justification for market restrictions,[26] but courts need not accept that the traditional restraints are the only way to achieve it.[27]

## 3.   Player Restraints

Section 48 refers to three types of limitation on players:

i.   Unreasonable limits on opportunities to participate (see, s. 48(1)(a)): This category would apply to the exclusion of a player through oppressive eligibility rules, refusals to deal, boycotts or blacklisting. It would be particularly relevant where a player has been suspended under an ill-defined disciplinary power[28] that is not clearly related to legitimate interests of the team or league. The category might also be used to impugn "protective" regulations of professional leagues such as those that require a minimum age[29] or period of amateur experience,[30] or the hockey rule that excludes players who have already lost one eye.[31]

ii.   Unreasonable terms or conditions imposed on participants (see, s. 48(1)(a)): This category would apply to contractual provisions, salary limitations and reservation systems as prescribed in league by-laws and the standard player contract and modified by collective bargaining. When section 48 was originally introduced in Bill C-227 of 1973, the accompanying memorandum noted that, "of particular concern are contracts imposed upon players which are self-repeating and bind a player indefinitely to any team to which he may be, from time to time, assigned". Similarly, "a contract which binds the individual to a single

---

[26]   See Chapter 7, "The Business of Hockey", section C, 1.

[27]   See, D.I. Shapiro, "The Professional Athlete: Liberty or Peonage?" (1975) 13 Alberta L. Rev. 212 at 231-34.

[28]   *Cf. Willey v. McLaughlin*, [1976] B.C.J. No. 1018, 49 C.P.R. (2d) 86 (B.C.S.C.) (suspension by professional golfers' association; restraints on supply of equipment).

[29]   *Goulet c. National Hockey League*, [1980] R.P. 122 (Que. S.C.) (no discrimination and no breach of the Act). In the context of American antitrust law, see: *Linseman v. World Hockey Assn.*, 439 F.Supp. 1315 (D. Conn., 1977) (age rule of 20 years contrary to antitrust law); *National Hockey League Players' Assn. v. Plymouth Whalers Hockey Club*, 325 F.3d 712 (6th Cir., 2003), *National Hockey League Players' Assn. v. Plymouth Whalers Hockey Club*, 419 F.3d 462 (6th Cir., 2005) (limit on "overage" players).

[30]   In the context of American antitrust law, see: *Denver Rockets v. All-Pro Management, Inc.*, 325 F.Supp. 1049 (C.D.Cal., 1971); *Haywood v. National Basketball Assn.*, 401 U.S. 1204 (1971) (rule requiring four years since graduation from high school); *Clarett v. National Football League*, 369 F.3d 124 (2nd Cir., 2004, revg 306 F.Supp 2d 379 (S.D.N.Y., 2004) (labour exemption applied).

[31]   In the context of American antitrust law, see: *Neeld v. American Hockey League*, 439 F.Supp. 459 (W.D.N.Y., 1977); *Neeld v. National Hockey League*, 439 F.Supp. 446 (W.D.N.Y., 1977); *Neeld v. National Hockey League*, 594 F.(2d) 1297 (9th Cir., 1979) (no anticompetitive purpose); NHL By-Law 12.7.

club for a whole playing career"[32] would be unreasonable. Less extreme restraints on player movement may also be suspect. The one-year option clause has been held to be enforceable under the common-law restraint of trade doctrine,[33] but free agency may also be inhibited by collusive agreements or by compensation payable to a player's former team.

iii. Unreasonable limits on the opportunity to negotiate with and play for the team of the player's choice (see, s. 48(1)(b)): This category would apply to amateur or free agent drafts or to waiver systems that give teams prior or exclusive negotiating rights to selected players. The entry draft operates by giving first claim on the best incoming amateur or junior player to the professional team that finished last during the previous season; selections in each draft round then continue in reverse order of league standing. The draft is widely defended as essential for spreading talent and maintaining competitive balance,[34] but in both its theory and practice it cannot achieve this: the first round is the only significant one[35] and the draft actually limits access by weaker teams to this pool; star amateurs may not excel in professional play; much depends on teams' skill in scouting, selecting and developing players; and teams vary the order of the draft by trading picks. A draft may be particularly unreasonable where it ties up rights to a large number of players and grants exclusive rights to draftees over a long period.

In the thirty years since enactment, there has been no criminal prosecution under section 48, but players have taken advantage of the possibility of civil remedies, including the right to bring action for damages under section 36. Restraints operating in Canada have also been the subject of investigation by the Competition Bureau and its predecessors, and section 48 is periodically cited in actions to prevent the enforcement of league regulations.[36] In the leading example, investigations and litigation persuaded the Canadian Football League ("CFL") to repeal a by-law that had originally been challenged by the CFL

---

[32] R.M. Sedgewick, "The Combines Investigation Act", replying to G.D. Finlayson, "Personal Service Contracts" in *Special Lectures of the Law Society of Upper Canada: Current Problems in the Law of Contract* (Toronto: Richard De Boo, 1975) at 385.

[33] *Detroit Football Co. v. Dublinski*, [1955] O.J. No. 619, 7 D.L.R. (2d) 9 (Ont. C.A.), revg [1956] O.J. No. 561, 4 D.L.R. (2d) 688 (Ont. H.C.J.). See also, *Watson v. Prager*, [1991] 3 All E.R. 487, [1991] 1 W.L.R. 726 (Ch. Div.) (three-year renewal option in boxer's management and promotion contract held to be unreasonable).

[34] *Greenlaw v. Ontario Major Junior Hockey League*, [1984] O.J. No. 3373, 48 O.R. (2d) 371 (Ont. H.C.J.) (need for OHL draft).

[35] In a pure draft in a 20-team league, the chump takes players, 1, 21, 41, 61, *etc.*, while the champ has numbers, 20, 40, 60, *etc.* There are few sports where one untried newcomer can transform the team.

[36] *Sheddon v. Ontario Major Junior Hockey League*, [1978] O.J. No. 3273, 19 O.R. (2d) 1, 83 D.L.R. (3d) 734 (Ont. H.C.J.) (injunction to allow transfer); *Goulet c. National Hockey League*, [1980] R.P. 122 (Que. S.C.).

Players' Association ("CFLPA"). In *Reed v. Canadian Football League*,[37] the association, on behalf of John Mandarich, obtained an interim injunction against enforcement of a rule that delayed a player's return after he had been cut by a team in another league. The CFL had unilaterally amended the by-law to discourage players from playing out their option, trying out in the National Football League and then resuming with a CFL team in the same season. The CFLPA successfully argued that the rule was contrary to the *Competition Act*, the restraint of trade doctrine and the article in the collective bargaining agreement ("CBA") that protected the negotiating rights of free agents.[38] In 1990, the Bureau of Competition Policy investigated reports that CFL teams had agreed not to sign free agents or had agreed to pay compensation for their loss. The complaints followed criticism by other teams of a series of free agent signings by the Ottawa Rough Riders, but the Bureau found no evidence of conspiracy.[39]

The text of the *Competition Act* presents particular difficulties where a labour market restraint has been subject to bargaining with the players' association or is maintained through the CBA or its incorporated contracts or regulations.[40] Although a wide "labour exemption" from antitrust liability is recognized in American law,[41] the Canadian legislation does not clearly exclude litigation and liability in relation to professional sport and there is no guarantee that a Canadian court would adopt American decisions dealing with the application, scope or duration of the exemption. It may, in particular, be necessary to draw a distinction between restraints affecting current members of the bargaining unit and exclusions or limitations imposed on outsiders. These third parties include amateur players selected as draftees or other players subject to "entry level" restrictions.[42] The NHL entry draft is recognized in article 8 of the CBA, but the established professional players agreeing to it are no longer subject to the draft process and may be inclined to join with the employers in limiting the leverage of the entering cohort. The possibility of a major challenge arose in 1991 when Eric Lindros refused to sign with the Quebec Nordiques after they had selected

---

[37]  [1988] A.J. No. 1236, 62 Alta. L.R. (2d) 347 (Alta. Q.B.). *Cf.* CBA of NFL, art. 32(1) (prohibition on signing CFL players in the same year).

[38]  CBA of CFL, art. 14.3.

[39]  See: "CFL rivals give Ottawa a rough ride" *The Globe and Mail* (Toronto: March 29, 1990) at A15; "Competition watchdog investigates CFL" *The Globe and Mail* (Toronto: June 20, 1990) at A12; "Feds rule out a free-agent conspiracy in CFL" *The Globe and Mail* (Toronto: July 26, 1990) at A12.

[40]  See: S.F. Ross, "The NHL Labour Dispute and the Common Law, The *Competition Act* and Public Policy" (2004) 37 U.B.C. L. Rev. 343 at 378-84; B.A. Facey, D.H. Assaf & R.J. Roberts, *Competition and Antitrust Law: Canada and the United States* (Markham, ON: LexisNexis Butterworths, 2006) at 446-51. On collective bargaining in the NHL, see Chapter 9, "National Hockey League", sections B-G.

[41]  See Chapter 8, "Competition Law and Labour Law", section C, 3.

[42]  In 2008, the NHL rejected the standard contract of 28-year-old Jonas Frogren who signed with the Toronto Maple Leafs after several years of professional experience in Europe. The league took the position that Frogren was a first-year player who should be signed to an entry-level contract.

him as the first overall choice.[43] Lindros had declared his opposition to playing in *la vieille capitale*, but found himself the unwilling property of the team: the Nordiques would have held exclusive rights for two years, at which point Lindros would have been subject to a second draft selection. The issue was resolved when the Nordiques accepted an offer from the Philadelphia Flyers and traded Lindros' rights in exchange for five players and USD $15 million.[44] Although the Flyers gave Lindros a six-year, USD $21 million contract, his case may suggest that open market bargaining would have recognized in him a higher economic value and yielded even greater earnings. The draft might, therefore, have been suspect under the *Competition Act* as an unreasonable limitation on the opportunity to negotiate.

When section 48 of the *Competition Act* was adopted in 1976, collective bargaining was established in professional leagues, so that it is arguable that the purpose of the provision was to provide players with additional recourse beyond the labour relations process. Litigation under the Act also serves the useful purpose of avoiding the disruption of play associated with strikes or lockouts.[45] Section 48 must, however, be reconciled with general provisions that authorize trade union activity and joint arrangements between employers relating to collective bargaining.[46] By section 4(1),

> Nothing in this Act applies in respect of
> (a) combinations or activities or workmen or employees for their own reasonable protection as such workmen or employees;
>
> ...
>
> (c) contracts, agreements or arrangements between or among two or more employers in a trade, industry or profession, whether effected directly between or among the employers or through the instrumentality of a corporation or association of which the employers are members, pertaining to collective bargaining with their employees in respect of salary or wages and terms or conditions of employment.[47]

Contrary to one judicial afterthought,[48] neither paragraph (a) nor paragraph (c) creates a "labour exemption" that could be relied on by team owners in professional sport and there is no general exemption for restraints incorporated into CBAs. Subsection 4(1)(a) merely declares that organization and "activities"

---

[43] See, D. Cruise & A. Griffiths, *Net Worth; Exploding the Myths of Pro Hockey* (Toronto: Viking, 1991) at 339-56.

[44] *In the Matter of...Philadelphia Flyers and Quebec Nordiques and New York Rangers* (June 30, 1992, L. Bertuzzi, arb.).

[45] In the absence of antitrust remedies before 1998, major league baseball experienced regular interruptions; see, J. Barnes, *Sports and the Law in Canada*, 3d ed. (Toronto: Butterworths, 1996) at 193-205.

[46] See, C. Backhouse, "Labour Unions and Anti-Combines Policy" (1976) 14 Osgoode Hall L.J. 113 at 144-60.

[47] *Competition Act*, R.S.C. 1985, c. C-34, s. 4(1).

[48] See, *Yashin v. National Hockey League*, [2000] O.J. No. 3306, 192 D.L.R. (4th) 747 at 763 (Ont. S.C.J.) (dictum of Cunningham J.; issues not argued).

by labour groups are not an illegal conspiracy, provided the activity is "reasonable" and for the protection of employees. Similarly, subsection 4(1)(c) relates to agreements between employers and is inapplicable to a CBA which is an agreement between employers and employee players. Subsection 4(1)(c) might have the paradoxical effect of affording greater protection to agreements forged between team owners rather than those that involve the players' association, but the general terms of the subsection are overridden by the specific prohibitions in relation to professional sport in section 48. Any "labour exemption" in Canada is best found in the text of section 48 and in the general policy of favouring collective bargaining. Subject to the reservation about restraints affecting third parties, if a restraint has been accepted by the players' association, it would seem that the majority do not find it "unreasonable", and agreed terms or conditions are hardly "imposed",[49] as required by the language of section 48(1)(a). Furthermore, section 48(2)(a) directs the court to have regard to the international organization of the sport, so that a restraint accepted in accordance with American case law might be upheld in the interests of uniformity or out of a practical need to defer to the system applying to most teams. The absence of definitive decisions does, however, leave doubt as to the application of section 48, which will continue to stand in uneasy relation with provisions of collective agreements.

## 4.    Franchise Restraints

Franchise restraints relate to the product market or business operations of teams, rather than the labour market for players. Section 48(3) of the *Competition Act* states that the section as a whole applies to "the granting and operation of franchises in the league", but section 48(1) creates no offence in relation to restraints on franchises.[50] Since section 48(3) also excludes the application of the "undue" standard in section 45, franchise arrangements must be assessed under other provisions of the *Competition Act*. These arrangements include the contracts, procedures and decisions of leagues relating to the ownership and relocation of teams.

The transfer of ownership of a NHL team is subject to Articles 3.5 of the NHL Constitution[51] and By-Law 35, which require a three-fourths majority vote following consideration of the applicant's "financial resources" and "good character and integrity". Under article 4 of the Constitution, teams possess a

---

[49]    But see, *Brown v. Pro Football, Inc.*, 50 F.3d 1041 (D.C. Cir., 1995) ("the nonstatutory labor exemption waives antitrust liability for restraints on competition imposed through the collective bargaining process" (at 1056)); affd 518 U.S. 231 (1996).

[50]    In June 1983, a Bill to bring franchise arrangements under what is now s. 45 was introduced by Ray Hnatyshyn, M.P. for Saskatoon West. See: Bill C-690 (1983); House of Commons Debates, 1st Sess., 32nd Parl., pp. 27553-59; Committee on Justice and Legal Affairs, Issue no. 133 (October 20, 1983) at 5-28.

[51]    See Chapter 7, "The Business of Hockey", section C, 2.

"home territory" consisting of the city of their location and 50 miles (80 km) beyond the city's limits (see, article 4.1(c)). Articles 4.2 and 4.3 grant teams exclusive territorial rights for controlling the playing of hockey games, and a franchise may be suspended or terminated if there is an attempt to transfer it in breach of territorial rights (see, article 3.9(b)(x)). Article 4.3 declares that, "No franchise shall be granted for a home territory within the home territory of a member, without the written consent of such member". By granting a right of veto, this article seems to require the unanimous consent of members where a team will intrude on existing territory. Articles 4.2 and 4.3 are, however, subject to modification by NHL By-Law 36.4(c) where the league receives the opinion of counsel that the prohibition of a transfer is unlawful.[52] The league will then consent to a "proposed transfer of location receiving the affirmative votes of a majority of Member Clubs present and voting". Under By-Law 36, a committee of the league investigates the merits of a proposed transfer, and the applicant must be given the opportunity to make a presentation to the Board of Governors. When voting on the transfer, member clubs must consider prescribed factors relating to the business operation of the league and the team. These "considerations" include fan support, revenue and market exposure in the relevant locations, the receipt of subsidies from public authorities, the effect on rivalries between teams and potential liability to third parties (see, By-Law 36.5). When consenting to a transfer, the league may impose "reasonable and appropriate conditions" and charge a "transfer fee" to reflect the "goodwill" developed by the league in the new location and an "indemnification fee" to reflect the "goodwill" developed by neighbouring teams (see, By-Law 36.6).

The NHL takes the position that relocation is a last resort when a team is no longer financially viable and it encourages prospective owners to stay put by sometimes requiring a covenant that the team will not relocate for seven years.[53] In recent decades, the league has approved the migration of teams from Canada, but has refused or circumvented the journey north. In the process, it has attracted the attention of the Competition Bureau and its predecessors.

In May 1983, the NHL board of governors voted to disallow the sale of the St. Louis Blues to business interests in Saskatoon.[54] This refusal gave rise to an antitrust action in St. Louis by the team's owners, and an investigation in Canada of a possible breach of section 33 of the *Combines Investigation Act*,[55] which made it an offence to form a monopoly. The inquiry was conducted by the Bureau of Competition Policy of the federal Department of Consumer and

---

[52]    On franchise restraints under American antitrust law, see Chapter 8, "Competition Law and Labour Law", section C, 4.

[53]    See, Competition Bureau Canada, "Competition Bureau Concludes Examination into National Hockey League Franchise Ownership Transfer and Relocation Policies" (March 31, 2008) at 3; online at: <http://www.competitionbureau.gc.ca>.

[54]    See: "NHL rejects plan for Saskatoon club" *The Globe and Mail* (Toronto: May 19, 1983) at 1, 2; "Disappointment in Saskatoon" *The Globe and Mail* (Toronto: May 20, 1983) at 18.

[55]    R.S.C. 1970, c. C-23. See now, *Competition Act*, R.S.C. 1985, c. C-34, ss. 78-79 (civil review of abuse of dominant position).

Corporate Affairs and took the form of closed hearings before one member of the Restrictive Trade Practices Commission.[56] The league made various unsuccessful applications to the Federal Court seeking to suspend the hearings[57] and to resist orders from the Commission and the Director of Investigation that it produce documents relating to changes in the location and ownership of NHL franchises;[58] the league was also required to produce financial statements of individual teams.[59] The inquiry continued in private until December 1985, when the Director of Investigation announced that no evidence of league wrongdoing had been found.[60] Throughout the controversy, the NHL argued that it had a responsibility to keep the franchise in St. Louis in recognition of the support given by fans there. NHL president John Ziegler asserted that the league was historically opposed to franchise moves and indicated that it would be appropriate to take similar action to prevent a Canadian team moving to the United States.[61] In 1995, efforts were duly made to extract provincial government funding[62] for the Quebec Nordiques, but in this instance the league accepted the sale of the franchise to new owners in Denver. The Winnipeg Jets were also soon lost to Phoenix.

Neither the Nordiques nor the Jets relocated to Hamilton, Ontario, where the city had constructed the Copps Coliseum in 1985 on the theory of "build it and they will come". Hamilton has a long-standing interest in regaining a NHL franchise[63] and was a leading candidate during league expansion in 1991. On that occasion, the league opted for more northerly Ottawa rather than the hockey heartland of the Golden Horseshoe and avoided creating local competition for the Toronto Maple Leafs and the Buffalo Sabres. A potential relocation to southwest Ontario arose in 2006 when James Balsillie, the BlackBerry device

---

[56] See: "Anti-combines officials to probe NHL decision" *The Globe and Mail* (Toronto: May 20, 1983) at 16; "Ottawa's might could sway NHL" *The Globe and Mail* (Toronto: June 29, 1983) at 17; "Ottawa playing 'chicken' with NHL" *The Globe and Mail* (Toronto: July 8, 1983) at 14; "NHL will ask court to block Ottawa probe" *The Globe and Mail* (Toronto: February 2, 1984) at 16.

[57] *Ziegler v. Hunter, Director of Investigation and Research* (1983), 75 C.P.R. (2d) 163 (Fed. C.T.D.), affd (1983), 75 C.P.R. (2d) 246 (C.A.).

[58] *Ziegler v. Hunter*, [1984] 1 F.C. 138, 75 C.P.R. (2d) 222 (F.C.T.D.), affd (sub nom., *Director of Investigation and Research v. Ziegler*), [1983] F.C.J. No. 176, 51 N.R. 1, 81 C.P.R. (2d) 1 (F.C.A.) (subpoena powers held not to infringe the Charter).

[59] *Director of Investigation and Research v. Restrictive Trade Practices Commission*, [1985] F.C.J. No. 232, 60 N.R. 376 (F.C.A.) ("unified reports of operations" insufficient; confidentiality protected by statutory requirement of private hearings).

[60] See, "NHL brass finds trophy is remedy" *The Globe and Mail* (Toronto: December 11, 1985) at A14.

[61] See, "Ziegler defends NHL stand in confidential letter to PM" *The Globe and Mail* (Toronto: July 14, 1983) at 13 (letter by Ziegler to Prime Minister Pierre Trudeau).

[62] On public subsidy programs, see Chapter 7, "The Business of Hockey", section B, 3.

[63] See: "NHL continues to give Hamilton cold shoulder" *The Globe and Mail* (Toronto: January 11, 1996) at C10; "Toronto said to stand between Hamilton and NHL team" *The Globe and Mail* (Toronto: January 12, 1996) at C12, C10. On the Hamilton team of 1920-1925, see: J.C. Wong, *Lords of the Rinks: The Emergence of the National Hockey League, 1875-1936* (Toronto: University of Toronto Press, 2005) at 79-87; S. & D. Wesley, *Hamilton's Hockey Tigers* (Toronto: James Lorimer & Co., 2005).

magnate and chairman of Research in Motion Inc., offered USD $175 million for the purchase of the financially troubled Pittsburgh Penguins. This offer was withdrawn when the NHL attached conditions relating to the control of the franchise and the conduct of negotiations for financing a new arena and apparently limited Balsillie's ability to move the team.[64] In 2007, Balsillie focussed his attention on acquiring the Nashville Predators and offered a generous purchase price estimated between USD $220 million and USD $238 million.[65] The Predators' lease allowed the team to leave Nashville after the 2007-08 season if attendance fell below 14,000, and Balsillie immediately conducted negotiations for the use of the Copps Coliseum while running a successful season ticket campaign in Hamilton for the imminent franchise. Some league governors were unimpressed by this manouevre, and Craig Leopold, the owner of the Predators, unexpectedly requested the league to discontinue the review of Balsillie's application.[66] Leopold eventually accepted an offer of USD $193 million from local investors[67] after promotional campaigns generated sufficient interest to keep the Predators in Nashville and the team benefitted from assistance and loans from the city. The NHL was able to resist Balsillie's plan while avoiding any formal disallowance of a move to Hamilton, and the market in southwest Ontario remained safe for the Leafs and Sabres.

James Balsillie's attempts to acquire the Penguins and the Predators were the subject of investigation by the Competition Bureau which assessed whether there was evidence of abuse of dominant position involving anti-competitive acts contrary to section 79 of the *Competition Act*. In March 2008, in a "Technical Backgrounder" not binding on the Commissioner of Competition, the Bureau found that "in the present circumstances, the NHL policies were not applied in furtherance of a predatory, exclusionary or disciplinary purpose."[68] Citing decisions under American antitrust law, the Bureau noted that properly circumscribed

---

[64] See: "Balsillie pulls plug on bid for franchise" *The Globe and Mail* (Toronto: December 16, 2006) at S1; "Balsillie leaves Lemieux fuming" *The Globe and Mail* (Toronto: December 19, 2006) at R9; "Bettman, Balsillie discussed Hamilton NHL team" *The Globe and Mail* (Toronto: December 22, 2006) at R6. Balsillie withdrew his offer prior to a decision by the Pennsylvania gaming board that denied a casino licence to a company that proposed to build a new arena in Pittsburgh.

[65] See: "Balsillie makes Predators his latest prey" *The Globe and Mail* (Toronto: May 24, 2007) at R6; "Predators staying put, Bettman says" *The Globe and Mail* (Toronto: May 29, 2007) at R7.

[66] See: "RIM boss hit by delay of game" *The Globe and Mail* (Toronto: June 23, 2007) at A1, A5; "Never in Hamilton" *The Globe and Mail* (Toronto: July 14, 2007) at S1, S7. On the league's further review of Balsillie's candidacy in 2009, see, *In re Dewey Ranch Hockey, LLC*, 2009 WL 3170452, 414 B.R. 577 (Bkrtcy. D.Ariz., September 15, 2009); see Chapter 8, "Competition Law and Labour Law", section C, 4.

[67] The investors also included William Del Biaggio who was originally interested in buying the Predators outright with a view to moving the team to the Sprint Centre in Kansas City. Del Biaggio acquired a 27 per cent share of the team, but went into bankruptcy in June 2008. In September 2009, he was sentenced to eight years imprisonment for forging financial documents to obtain loans.

[68] Competition Bureau Canada, "Competition Bureau Concludes Examination into National Hockey League Franchise Ownership Transfer and Relocation Policies" (March 31, 2008) at 3.

restrictions on the location of franchises promote stability and goodwill and serve legitimate interests, including,

> creating and enhancing spectator interest by preserving traditional team rivalries ...; encouraging investment by private parties and municipalities in arena construction and related infrastructure; ... [and] attracting spectators and corporate sponsors by showing a strong commitment to a local market ...[69]

The Bureau was satisfied that the NHL had a legitimate interest in ensuring that the Predators were successful in Nashville and found no anti-competitive conduct for the purpose of section 79. The Bureau did, however, note that fostering new team rivalries is also a legitimate league object and expressed concerns "if a single team were entitled to exercise a veto to prevent a franchise from entering its local region within Canada".[70] The Bureau analyzed a professional league as a collaborative enterprise in which the members have a shared interest in the quality and revenue of each franchise, although it did not engage in an explicit comparison of the commercial viability of Nashville and Hamilton. In the end, consumer choice in southwest Ontario suffered as both the *Competition Act* and antitrust law gave priority to the league's right to choose its membership and determine the location of teams.

Since 2007, the Canadian franchises have emerged as prime generators of league revenue that must be shared with the players' association in accordance with the CBA of 2005. The suspicion remains that team owners in the NHL fear that a Hamilton franchise will be too competitive, too successful and a threat to weaker entities. The desire to protect the *status quo* was seen again in 2009 when James Balsillie made his third bid for a team by offering USD $212.5 million (subsequently increased to USD $242.5 million) for the Phoenix Coyotes. Since he sought to buy the team out of bankruptcy, the case presented the problem of the relation between the priorities of bankruptcy proceedings, the league's power to control its franchises and the standards of American antitrust law. Once again, the process and legal regime were of no assistance to Hamilton.[71]

## B.   RESTRAINT OF TRADE DOCTRINE[72]

The common law restraint of trade doctrine protects the right of individuals to dispose freely of their knowledge or skill in pursuit of employment or commercial opportunities. Unreasonable restraints on the freedom to work or to

---

[69] Competition Bureau Canada, "Competition Bureau Concludes Examination into National Hockey League Franchise Ownership Transfer and Relocation Policies" (March 31, 2008) at 2.

[70] Competition Bureau Canada, "Competition Bureau Concludes Examination into National Hockey League Franchise Ownership Transfer and Relocation Policies" (March 31, 2008) at 4.

[71] See Chapter 8, "Competition Law and Labour Law", section C, 4.

[72] See: M.J. Trebilcock, *The Common Law of Restraint of Trade; A Legal and Economic Analysis* (Toronto: Carswell, 1986); J.D. Heydon, *The Restraint of Trade Doctrine*, 2d ed. (Sydney: Butterworths, 1999); S.F. Ross, "The NHL Labour Dispute and the Common Law, the *Competition Act*, and Public Policy" (2004) 37 U.B.C.L. Rev. 343 at 346-68.

compete may be held to be illegal and unenforceable; a restraint is justifiable only if it is reasonable as between the parties, reasonable in the public interest, and in protection of legitimate proprietary or commercial interests.[73] This public policy doctrine complements statutory remedies and extends to contracts or regulations in amateur sport where competitors have direct opportunities for financial reward:

> ... in a sport which allows competitors to exploit their ability in the sport for financial gain and which allows that gain to be a direct consequence of participation in competition, a ban on competition is, in my judgment, a restraint of trade.[74]

The doctrine clearly applies to professional sport, although a challenge based on restraint of trade may have to yield to decisional processes established through the labour relations system.[75]

The various types of restraint in sport include outright exclusions, limitations on the freedom to choose one's employer or caps on available salary or other payments. Some restraints operate through terms[76] or covenants[77] in a player's contract, but the more significant limitations are "extra-contractual" regulations maintained by member teams in a league or association.[78] Where employment opportunities are unreasonably prejudiced by an employers' "ring", a plaintiff may obtain a declaration that the system is invalid, or an injunction[79] to prevent enforcement, but cannot recover damages unless it is proved that a conspiracy was formed with the intent to harm the individual.[80]

---

[73] See: *Nordenfelt v. Maxim Nordenfelt Guns and Ammunition Co. Ltd.*, [1894] A.C. 535 (H.L.); *Johnson v. Athletics Canada*, [1997] O.J. No. 3201, 41 O.T.C. 95 (Ont. Gen. Div.) (lifetime ban for second doping infraction was reasonable).

[74] *Gasser v. Stinson*, unreported, Ch.Div., CH-88-G-2191, June 15, 1988, at 37, *per* Scott J. (doping suspension). See also, *Chambers v. British Olympic Assn.*, [2008] EWHC 2028 (Q.B.D.) (sprinter's financial prospects from participation in Olympics were speculative).

[75] *Yashin v. National Hockey League*, [2000] O.J. No. 3306, 192 D.L.R. (4th) 747 (Ont. S.C.J.) (arbitrator's interpretation of free agency rights did not impose a perpetual limitation).

[76] *Watson v. Prager*, [1991] 3 All E.R. 487, [1991] 1 W.L.R. 726 (Ch. Div.).

[77] *Adler v. Moore*, [1961] 2 Q.B. 57 (soccer player required to repay disability payment when he began playing again). Promises not to compete operating after a period of service are subject to strict tests regarding the scope and duration of the limit. Restrictions during employment are normally valid since the employer has a recognized interest in loyalty and exclusive service.

[78] See: J. Sopinka, "Extra-Contractual Aspects of Canadian Professional Football" (1958) 16 U. of T. Faculty L. Rev. 38; *Figure Skating Coaches of Canada v. Canadian Figure Skating Assn.*, [1983] O.J. No. 3314, 71 C.P.R. (2d) 41 (Ont. H.C.J.).

[79] *Nagle v. Feilden*, [1966] 2 Q.B. 633 (C.A.) (Jockey Club rule denying trainers licences to women; arbitrary denial of the right to work). See also, *Newport Assn. Football Club Ltd. v. Football Assn. of Wales*, [1995] 2 All E.R. 87 (Ch. Div.) (teams wished to play in English FA).

[80] *Mogul S.S. Co. v. McGregor Gow and Co.*, [1892] A.C. 25 (H.L.). See also: J. Sopinka, "Extra-Contractual Aspects of Canadian Professional Football" (1958) 16 U. of T. Faculty L. Rev. 38 at 50; *Cranmer v. B.C. Lions Football Club*, [1979] O.J. No. 149, 1 A.C.W.S. 209 (Ont. H.C.J.) (no conspiracy).

In applying the common law doctrine, courts have recognized the unusual collaborative structure of professional leagues and their need to regulate operations to protect legitimate business or moral interests.[81] The primary accepted interest is the goal of equalizing the playing strength of teams and maintaining competitive balance. Leagues have, however, had difficulty in showing that particular restraints properly contributed to the claimed goal. Less restrictive alternatives have been available, and the challenged system is usually found to offend the players' countervailing interest in freedom of movement. In *Eastham v. Newcastle United Football Club*,[82] the player obtained declarations against his former team and against the Football League and Football Association, declaring that the "retain and transfer" system was in restraint of trade. Under this system (which was characterized as a medieval relic involving the sale of human chattels), a player could be retained indefinitely by his team through the offer of a one-year contract at reasonable salary. A player's consent was required for a transfer, but a player registered with one team could only move to another if the teams agreed to a sale price; the contract and transfer systems were subject to review by a league management committee. Eastham refused to sign again with Newcastle and was only transferred (one year after his initial request) after bringing legal action. Wilberforce J. recognized the league's interest in preventing the richer teams from buying the best players, but held that the system failed to achieve this and went beyond what was necessary. If a team was interested in retaining a player, it could prevent "poaching" by offering a long-term contract and so recover any development costs it might have incurred.[83] Other "employers' systems" or association rules that limit transfer or team selection by a player who is not under contract have similarly been held to be in restraint of trade.[84] These include: a retain and transfer system in rugby league;[85] denying clearance for play overseas;[86] residence rules binding a player to one team;[87] and refusing to clear a zoned player to an interested team after the original team moved to another city.[88] In *Adamson v. New South Wales Rugby League Ltd. (N.S.W.R.L. Draft Case)*,[89] an "internal draft" of players whose contracts had expired was found to be an unreasonable limit on players' choice of employment that did little to protect the financial and other interests of the league.

---

[81] On disciplinary powers and public relations, see Chapter 9, "National Hockey League", section D.

[82] [1964] 1 Ch. 413. See also, *Johnston v. Cliftonville Football and Athletic Club Ltd.*, [1984] N.I. 9 (Ch. Div.) (maximum wage rule).

[83] See, *Eastham v. Newcastle United Football Club Ltd.*, [1964] 1 Ch. 413 at 432-38.

[84] See, G.M. Kelly, *Sport and the Law* (North Ryde, N.S.W.: The Law Book Company, 1987) at 267-95.

[85] *Buckley v. Tutty* (1971), 125 C.L.R. 353 (H.C. of Aust.), affg 92 W.N. (N.S.W.) 329 (S.C.); overruling *Elford v. Buckley*, [1970] 2 N.S.W.R. 170 (S.C.).

[86] *Blackler v. New Zealand Rugby Football League, Inc.*, [1968] N.Z.L.R. 547 (C.A.); *Kemp v. New Zealand Rugby Football League Inc.*, [1989] 3 N.Z.L.R. 463 (H.C.). See also, *Adamson v. West Perth Football Club Inc.* (1979), 27 A.L.R. 475 (Fed.C. of Aust.).

[87] *Hall v. Victorian Football League* (1977), [1982] V.R. 64 (S.C.).

[88] *Foschini v. Victorian Football League*, unreported, Vict. S.C., April 15, 1983, Crockett J.

[89] (1991), 31 F.C.R. 242 (Fed.C. of Aust., Full Ct.), revg (1991), 27 F.C.R. 535 (Fed.C. of Aust.).

The mere protection of an employer against competition or the preservation of the established order are not legitimate interests, although an association may be able to show that a system contributes to the wider development and financing of the game. In *Greig v. Insole*,[90] the traditional international cricket governing body resolved to ban players who participated in a new commercial league that was planning games in Australia during the off-season of the English winter.[91] The domestic county cricket board also proposed a ban which would have prevented earning a living from the game. No contract of employment existed between the players and the governing bodies when the players signed to join the new operation; they were not in breach of any legal obligation and were held not to have any moral duty of loyalty requiring them to avoid joining the private promoter. Slade J. found that the governing bodies had a legitimate interest in protecting the finances of international matches, but held that the ban was not reasonable and justifiable: it deprived players of the opportunity to make a living and deprived the public of the chance to watch them. The players and the promoter were entitled to declarations that the rules imposing the ban were illegal and in restraint of trade. The promoter was also held to have grounds of action in tort since the ban induced the players to breach their employment contracts with the promoter.[92]

## C. AMERICAN ANTITRUST LAW — THE NATIONAL FOOTBALL LEAGUE (NFL) CASES

### 1. General

Challenges to restrictive systems in North American leagues have usually been brought under the antitrust laws of the United States, which have been used to attack both monopsony powers in the labour market and restraints and monopolies in the product market. Such actions are usually based on federal law, although antitrust laws have also been enacted by the individual states. Contracts or combinations restraining interstate trade or commerce are illegal under section 1 of the *Sherman Antitrust Act, 1890*,[93] monopolization of any part of such trade or commerce is prohibited under section 2. Section 1 requires joint action by at least two parties; section 2 refers rather to a market condition — the misuse of monopoly power. The *Clayton Act, 1914*,[94] prohibits various restrictive arrangements, such as price discrimination and exclusive dealing contracts. This

---

[90] [1978] 1 W.L.R. 302 (Ch. Div.). See also: *Hughes v. Western Australian Cricket Assn. Ltd.* (1986), 19 F.C.R. 10 (Fed.C. of Aust.) (rule banning player after he participated in tour of South Africa held to be in restraint of trade); *Barnard v. Australian Soccer Federation* (1988), 81 A.L.R. 51 (Fed.C. of Aust.) (order restraining ban required by FIFA).

[91] See, H. Blofeld, *The Packer Affair* (London: Collins, 1978), esp. at 104-23.

[92] See Chapter 9, "National Hockey League", section E, 3.

[93] 15 U.S.C. ss. 1-7 (2001).

[94] 15 U.S.C. ss. 12-27; 29 U.S.C. ss. 52-53 (2001).

Act also provides for the remedy of treble damages for persons injured "by reason of anything forbidden in the antitrust laws".[95]

On its face, section 1 of the *Sherman Act* is wide-ranging in its prohibitions, declaring illegal "Every contract ... in restraint of trade", but judicial interpretations have limited the scope to combinations that restrain competition "unreasonably":

> Under the rule of reason, a restraint must be evaluated to determine whether it is significantly anticompetitive in purpose or effect. In making this evaluation, a court generally will be required to analyze "the facts peculiar to the business, the history of the restraint, and the reasons why it was imposed". If, on analysis, the restraint is found to have legitimate business purposes whose realization serves to promote competition, the "anticompetitive evils" of the challenged practice must be carefully balanced against its "procompetitive virtues" to ascertain whether the former outweigh the latter. A restraint is unreasonable if it has the "net effect" of substantially impeding competition.[96]

A limited category of business practices will not be justifiable as reasonable since they are viewed as *per se* violations of the *Sherman Act* "entirely void of redeeming competitive rationales".[97] These include price-fixing, territorial divisions of the market and boycotts. Arrangements that clearly seem to be anticompetitive may also be subject to the "quick look" standard which requires only truncated analysis because justification of the restraint is highly unlikely.

The federal antitrust laws apply to the organization of professional and intercollegiate sports in the United States,[98] except that there is residual exclusion of baseball based on an anomalous, judge-made exemption.[99]

---

[95]  15 U.S.C. s. 15 (2001).

[96]  *Smith v. Pro Football Inc.*, 593 F.2d 1173, at 1183 (D.C. Cir., 1978), *per* Wilkey J., varg 420 F.Supp. 738 (D.D.C., 1976). See also: *Law v. National Collegiate Athletic Assn.*, 134 F.3d 1010 (10th Cir., 1998), affg 902 F.Supp. 1394 (D.Kan., 1995) (salary cap for entry level coaches should be analyzed under the rule of reason); *Fraser v. Major League Soccer*, 7 F.Supp.2d 73 (D. Mass., 1998) (transfer fees for out-of-contract players).

[97]  *Law v. National Collegiate Athletic Assn.*, 134 F.3d 1010, at 1016 (10th Cir., 1998).

[98]  See: J.C. Weistart & C.H. Lowell, The Law of Sports (Indianapolis: The Bobbs-Merrill Co., 1979) at 477-776; (Supplement 1985) at 81-190; M.J. Greenberg & J.T. Gray, *Sports Law Practice*, 2d ed. (Charlottesville: Lexis Law Pub., 1998). On various sports, see: *U.S. v. International Boxing Club of New York Inc.*, 348 U.S. 236 (1955) (promotion of championships); *Gunter Harz Sports, Inc. v. U.S. Tennis Assn.*, 511 F.Supp. 1103 (D.Neb., 1981), affd 665 F.2d 222 (8th Cir., 1981) (approval of rackets); *Volvo North American Corp. v. Men's Int. Professional Tennis Council*, 857 F.2d 55 (2nd Cir., 1988) (commercial restraints operated by tour); *Gilder v. PGA Tour, Inc.*, 936 F.2d 417 (9th Cir., 1991) (ban on "U-groove" clubs); *Toscano v. Professional Golfers Assn.*, 258 F.3d 978 (9th Cir., 2001) (sponsorship agreements).

[99]  *Federal Baseball Club of Baltimore Inc. v. National League of Professional Baseball Clubs*, 259 U.S. 200 (1922), affg 269 F. 681 (D.C. Cir., 1921); *Flood v. Kuhn*, 407 U.S. 258 (1972). On the scope of the exemption, see: J. Barnes, *Sports and the Law in Canada*, 3d ed. (Toronto: Butterworths, 1996) at 195-98; *Major League Baseball v. Crist*, 331 F.3d 1177 (11th Cir.,

Baseball's status was modified by the *Curt Flood Act of 1998* so that conduct or agreements by persons "in the business of organized professional major league baseball directly relating to or affecting employment of major league baseball players" are subject to the antitrust laws to the same extent as "any other professional sports business affecting interstate commerce".[100] The labour market in MLB is, therefore, now subject to antitrust law, although collective bargaining activities enjoy substantial immunity under the "labour exemption".[101] Limited statutory exemptions also apply to agreements between professional teams for the joint sale of television rights by their leagues[102] and to merger agreements between professional football leagues that serve to increase the number of operating teams.[103] Apart from these important exclusions, actions by leagues may be reviewed as either "section 1 restraints" or as "section 2 monopolization" under the *Sherman Act*. The standard of review is usually the rule of reason rather than *per se* illegality.

Antitrust action may concern the labour market for players, involving challenges to player allocation systems, contractual provisions or restrictions on participation and rights of free agency.[104] Or the case may concern the product market, which relates to franchise operations and the production and exhibition of games. A challenge to employment conditions might brought by a player or by the players' association. A challenge relating to the product market might be brought by a franchise holder, a franchise applicant, or by a rival league claiming to have been damaged in its business operations. In 1986, the United States Football League ("USFL") was unsuccessful in a USD $1.69 billion suit against the NFL alleging that the league monopolized essential television coverage through contracts with all three major networks. The jury agreed that the NFL held a general monopoly in the professional football market but awarded the USFL only USD $1 damages on the point.[105]

---

2003) (league contraction and decisions relating to the number of operating teams), affg *Major League Baseball v. Butterworth*, 181 F.Supp.2d 1316 (N.D. Fla., 2001).

[100] *Curt Flood Act of 1998*, Pub.L. 105-297, 112 Stat. 2824, s. 3. MLB players now "have the same rights under the antitrust laws as do other professional athletes" (s. 2).

[101] See Chapter 8, "Competition Law and Labour Law", section C, 3. See, in particular, *Brown v. Pro Football*, 518 U.S. 231 (1996).

[102] 15 U.S.C. ss. 1291-95 (2001); *Mid-South Grizzlies v. National Football League*, 720 F.2d 772 (3rd Cir., 1983). See Chapter 7, "The Business of Hockey", section B, 4.

[103] 15 U.S.C. ss. 1291, 1294 (2001). This provision was enacted in 1966 to authorize the merger between the AFL and NFL.

[104] See, for example: *National Hockey League Players' Assn. v. Plymouth Whalers Hockey Club*, 419 F.3d 462 (6th Cir., 2005) ("Van Ryn" rule excluding ex-NCAA 20-year-old players from the OHL did not have anti-competitive effects; relevant market was pool of 16 to 20-year-olds playing in different leagues); *National Hockey League Players' Assn. v. Plymouth Whalers Hockey Club*, 325 F.3d 712 (6th Cir., 2003) (rule merely substitutes an arguably less skilled player). See further, Chapter 3, "Organizations and Regulations", section B, 3.

[105] *U.S. Football League v. National Football League*, 634 F.Supp. 1155, 644 F.Supp. 1040 (S.D.N.Y., 1986), affd 842 F.2d 1335 (2nd Cir., 1988). See also, *Independent Entertainment Group, Inc. v. National Basketball Assn.*, 853 F.Supp. 333 (C.D.Cal., 1994) (proper refusal by NBA to allow its players to participate in one-on-one event); *News Ltd. v. Australian Rugby Football League Ltd.* (1996), 64 F.C.R. 410 (Fed.C. of Aust., Full Ct.), revg 58 F.C.R. 447 (Fed.C. of Aust.) (Super League versus ARL).

Liability under section 1 of the *Sherman Act* requires a combination by separate units, so that a "single entity" is incapable of the necessary multi-party action. In 1984, the U.S. Supreme Court in *Copperweld Corp. v. Independence Tube Corp.*[106] held that a parent company and its wholly owned subsidiary had a unity of interest and were incapable of conspiring for the purpose of section 1. A sports league necessarily operates as a joint or cooperative venture, but the member teams are in independent ownership and have been known to secede to join new leagues. Besides the organizational separation, franchises have their own business interests in relation to revenue, fan support and location. In decisions both before and after *Copperweld*, various Circuit courts in cases relating to the financing or location of franchises held that the main major leagues were not single entities.[107] The separation of units and interests is clear in the labour markets,[108] where collective bargaining with the players is conducted on a multi-employer basis and teams are supposed to compete with one another to hire personnel under individual service contracts. From the point of view of the players, the protection afforded by section 1 is an essential remedy against restraints on free agency or collusion by cost-cutting team owners. The "multi unit" characterization of a league has, however, been questioned in decisions that suggest that the application of section 1 requires a case-by-case approach that considers the structure of the particular league and the commercial activity in question. In central marketing activities such as the sale of media rights and the licensing of properties, it has been found that a league is closer to a unified operation or single firm.[109] In this context, the league is looking to promote its general product in the wider entertainment market, where teams have a common interest in outperforming the competition offered by other sports. The shared central revenue also enables teams to compete against their playing opponents. The nature of the league "entity" may, therefore, vary according to the particular

---

[106]   467 U.S. 752 (1984). In the early decision in *San Francisco Seals Ltd. v. National Hockey League*, 379 F.Supp. 966 (C.D.Cal., 1974), the NHL was held to be a "single entity".

[107]   *North American Soccer League v. National Football League*, 670 F.2d 1249 (2nd Cir., 1982), revg 505 F.Supp. 659 (S.D.N.Y., 1980), *cert.* denied 459 U.S. 1074 (1982); *Mid-South Grizzlies v. National Football League*, 720 F.2d 772 (3rd Cir., 1983); *Los Angeles Memorial Coliseum Comm. v. National Football League*, 726 F.2d 1381 (9th Cir., 1984), affg 519 F.Supp. 581 (C.D.Cal., 1981); *Sullivan v. National Football League*, 34 F.3d 1091 (1st Cir., 1994). See, Chapter 8, "Competition Law and Labour Law", section C, 4.

[108]   See: *Mackey v. National Football League*, 543 F.2d 606 (8th Cir., 1976); *Smith v. Pro Football, Inc.*, 593 F.2d 1173 (D.C. Cir., 1978); *Fraser v. Major League Soccer*, 284 F.3d 47 (1st Cir., 2002). See Chapter 8, "Competition Law and Labour Law", section C, 2.

[109]   See: *Chicago Professional Sports Limited Partnership v. National Basketball Assn.*, 95 F.3d 593 (7th Cir., 1996) ("when acting in the broadcast market the NBA is closer to a single firm", at 600, *per* Easterbrook, C.J.); *American Needle Inc. v. National Football League*, 538 F.3d 736 (7th Cir., 2008) ("the NFL teams are best described as a single source of economic power when promoting NFL football through licensing the teams' intellectual property" at 744 *per* Kanne, C.J.). See also: *Major League Baseball Properties, Inc. v. Salvino, Inc.*, 542 F.3d 290 (2nd Cir., 2008), affg 420 F.Supp.2d 212 (S.D.N.Y., 2005) (interdependence of teams and centralized trademark licensing; *Madison Square Garden, L.P. v. National Hockey League*, No. 07 CV 8455, S.D.N.Y. November 2, 2007, affd 270 Fed. Appx. 56 (2nd Cir., 2008); 2008 WL 4547518, S.D.N.Y. October 10, 2008 (centralized league website).

enterprise and the various markets affected, and it is unlikely that there is a definitive characterization applying to all facets of all leagues. On June 29, 2009 in *American Needle, Inc. v. National Football League*, the U.S. Supreme Court agreed to address the conflicting theories of league economics in a case dealing with an exclusive licensing agreement.

Unlike the Canadian *Competition Act*, the *Sherman Act* contains no special prohibitions relating to sport, so that league arrangements must be assessed under the general antitrust theory of promoting competition and curbing excess market power. Courts take account of leagues' need for co-operative structures, but many traditional controls have been found not to have the claimed economic effects in the appropriate market, so that leagues have a poor playing record in resisting allegations of restraint of trade or monopolization. Unnecessary restrictions on the grant of franchises or on broadcasting may also be seen to impede output and consumer choice and are contrary to the consumer welfare goals of antitrust law. Consumer welfare may, however, be a more problematic *rationale* for greater labour market freedom and higher salaries.[110] The direct beneficiaries here are the players, and the outcome for consumers may be higher prices, lack of identification with the playing mercenaries, more television advertising and other commercialization, and the concentration of successful franchises in the largest urban markets. Courts have, however, accommodated players' employment interests and have not accepted the theory that antitrust law serves to maintain a supply of cheap and unfairly constrained labour. Player restraints have, however, been recognized where they are the result of free collective bargaining and so are consistent with labour law policy.

## 2. Player Restraints

Antitrust litigation has served to liberalize players' employment conditions in sports other than MLB, where contractual freedom was achieved through the labour relations and arbitration processes.[111] In *Radovich v. National Football League*,[112] the U.S. Supreme Court specifically limited the antitrust exemption to "the business of organized baseball", so that a player who had been blacklisted for playing in a rival league could bring action under the *Sherman Act*. The 1970s brought a series of successful antitrust challenges to player restraints and eligibility rules, including litigation between the National Hockey League and

---

[110] The case can, nevertheless, be made. The recent history of leagues suggests that a free, highly rewarded labour market for players improves the product for fans by enabling each team to improve itself, by enhancing competition, and by providing financial incentives for improved play or athletic "output".

[111] See: J. Barnes, *Sports and the Law in Canada*, 3d ed. (Toronto: Butterworths, 1996) at 198-205; *Los Angeles Club and Montreal Club v. Messersmith and McNally* (Decision No. 29, December 23, 1975, Seitz, arb.), reported as *Re Professional Baseball Clubs* (1975), 66 L.A. 101; *Kansas City Royals Baseball Corp. v. Major League Baseball Players' Assn.*, 409 F.Supp. 233 (W.D. Mo., 1976), affd 532 F.2d 615 (8th Cir., 1976).

[112] 352 U.S. 445 (1957). See also, *Toolson v. New York Yankees*, 346 U.S. 356 (1953); *Flood v. Kuhn*, 407 U.S. 258 (1972) (antitrust exemption is limited to baseball).

the World Hockey Association as the NHL sought to enforce its reserve clause. Injunctions were denied to NHL teams when the league's systems of reservation and league affiliation were found to be monopolistic.[113]

The most important litigation involved the NFL as players strategically attacked different forms of restraint. The traditional football contract included a one-year option clause, rather than a perpetual reserve clause. If a player failed to sign an entirely new contract, the team could exercise the option and prolong the existing contract by one year; contract terms during the "option year" would be the same as the previous year except that salary could be reduced by 10 per cent. Once the player "played out his option", he was a free agent at liberty to negotiate with other teams. Mobility was, however, severely curtailed by the "Rozelle Rule" by which the league commissioner (failing agreement between the two teams) could order the signing team to pay compensation to the player's former team; the award could take the form of money, future draft picks or the forced trade of an existing player. Since the compensation was indeterminate and potentially high, teams were deterred from signing agents, so that players invariably remained with their original team.

Leagues have defended free agent compensation as necessary to preserve team equality and as just reimbursement for recruiting and training the player, but the "Rozelle Rule" failed to survive substantive antitrust scrutiny. In *Kapp v. National Football League*,[114] the player claimed to have been the victim of an illegal boycott when dismissed from an NFL team for refusing to sign a standard player contract. Kapp challenged the contract requirement, the option and free agent compensation rules and the prohibition on tampering, claiming that these constituted a combination by the defendant teams in the nature of a refusal to deal amounting to *per se* violations of antitrust law. The court apparently supported this contention on the facts alleged, but indicated that ordinarily player restraints would be subject to the test of reasonableness. (In a subsequent jury assessment of Kapp's actual loss, the player failed to recover any award.[115]) The fullest consideration of the effects of the "Rozelle Rule" occurred in *Mackey v. National Football League*,[116] a suit by a group of former and current NFL players who alleged that the compensation system amounted to an illegal restraint of trade. After a lengthy trial, a federal district court held that the effect of the rule was to limit the free agent's ability to negotiate in an open market; as such it amounted to a group boycott and refusal to deal similar to lifetime reservation, so was improper *per se*. On appeal, the court agreed that the restraint was illegal but found that the appropriate test was one of reasonableness. The appellate court recognized the NFL's interest in securing competitive balance and indicated that some player restraints might be reasonable. The "Rozelle Rule" was, however, so unfair and onerous that it could not withstand antitrust challenge: the rule applied to all players regardless of ability, operated as a perpetual restriction on players' ability to sell their

---

[113]  See, Chapter 9, "National Hockey League", section A, 2.
[114]  390 F.Supp. 73 (N.D.Cal., 1974).
[115]  *Kapp v. National Football League*, 586 F.2d 644 (9th Cir., 1978).
[116]  407 F.Supp. 1000 (D.Minn., 1975), vard 543 F.2d 606 (8th Cir., 1976).

services, and lacked adequate procedural safeguards. Players affected by the system received a financial settlement,[117] and reform of free agent compensation became the subject of collective bargaining.

The NFL amateur draft was considered in *Smith v. Pro Football Inc.*[118] The annual draft gives teams selections of qualifying college players in reverse order of league standing; the team with the worst record from the previous season takes first pick in each round. Until modified by collective agreement in 1977, the draft operated for 17 rounds and granted teams exclusive and perpetual negotiating rights:

> Even though the draft was justified primarily by the need to disperse the *best* players, it applied to all graduating seniors, including average players who were, in a sense, fungible commodities. It permitted college players to negotiate *with only one team*. If a player could not contract with that team, *he could not play at all.*[119]

Smith was drafted by the Washington Redskins in 1968; he was an outstanding prospect whose career ended prematurely in his first season when he suffered a neck injury. Smith claimed that the draft operated to deny him the level of compensation he would have been able to receive from free competition for his services. At trial, the court held the draft to be *per se* illegal as a group boycott in restraint of trade serving only to eliminate competition. The court also considered the draft under the rule of reason and found it unnecessarily restrictive and not productive of balance between teams. On appeal, the majority held that the co-operative nature of a sports league made it inappropriate to characterize the draft as a group boycott illegal *per se*: Smith was not in competition with the league and had not been excluded from the market. Applying the rule of reason, the majority did, however, agree that the draft was anti-competitive in purpose and effect. They noted that the alleged pro-competitive effect related to the league's product of athletic exhibitions, whereas the anti-competitive effect related to the market for players' services. Since the effects were not comparable, the court took the position that they could not be balanced under the rule of reason.[120] On this view, there was no pro-competitive virtue in the draft to weigh against its severely restrictive effects. As it existed in 1968, the draft unreasonably restrained trade in violation of section 1 of the *Sherman Act*, and Smith was entitled to treble damages.

Armed with the decisions in *Kapp*, *Mackey* and *Smith*, the NFL Players' Association ("NFLPA") was in a position to bargain for a substantially less

---

[117] *Reynolds v. National Football League*, 584 F.2d 280 (8th Cir., 1978) (objections to the "Alex-ander Settlement" and the 1977 CBA).

[118] 593 F.2d 1173 (D.C.Cir., 1978), varg 420 F.Supp. 738 (D.D.C., 1976).

[119] *Ibid.*, at 1187, *per* Wilkey J. The alternative of playing in the CFL was not regarded as very attractive (*ibid.*, at 1185). For suggested modifications to the draft, see, *ibid.*, at 1188.

[120] *Ibid.*, at 1186. For criticism of this analysis, see J.C. Weistart & C.H. Lowell, *The Law of Sports* (Indianapolis: The Bobbs-Merrill Co., 1979), at 1985 Supplement, at 114-18. See also, *Brown v. Pro Football, Inc.*, 812 F.Supp. 237 (D.D.C., 1992) (salary scale for players on devel-opment squad).

restrictive player market. Paradoxically, the five-year collective agreements of 1977 and 1982 came to barely modify the traditional restraints. Option clauses were required in first-year players' one-year contracts and could be included in veterans' contracts; "option year" salary had to be 110 per cent of the previous year's salary. Free agent compensation persisted in the form of highly valued draft selections, varying according to salary offers. The original team also had a right of first refusal and could retain the free agent by matching any bids received. The amateur draft continued with 12 rounds of selections and so still affected most of the available talent. The drafting team held exclusive rights for one year; an unsigned player was then subject to the next draft and only had complete freedom of negotiation after sitting out two years. If a drafted player played outside the NFL, the team retained exclusive rights for four years; this period was fixed at two years in 1977, but increased in 1982, thereby limiting the leverage of players temporarily "defecting" to the CFL or to the United States Football League.

By 1987, when the second collective agreement expired, hardly any NFL "free agents" had received offers from other teams, and the players' association had unsuccessfully relied on two avenues of reform. In 1980, a grievance arbitration held that the language of the collective agreement did not clearly grant unrestricted free agency after the option year or place any general limit on how often a team could exercise the right of first refusal.[121] In 1982, the NFLPA proposed to eliminate the negotiation of individual player contracts by seeking a fixed percentage of league income that would then be shared between players according to their experience and playing performance; after a 57-day strike, the players settled for the traditional contract system in exchange for benefits of USD $1.6 billion over five years.[122] Negotiations to liberalize free agency duly resumed in 1987, and the NFLPA called another strike in September of that year. The teams resorted to the tactic of hiring replacement players, and the stoppage ended after 24 days. The regular players returned to work without a new collective agreement and revived the antitrust action as the means of challenging the system of free agent compensation and right of first refusal. This litigation and other cases from this period focus on the scope and duration of the labour exemption.

## 3.   The Labour Exemption

The labour exemption from antitrust law addresses the apparent conflict between the *Sherman Act* and activities of organized labour: antitrust policy promotes competition and prohibits "combination", yet it is the policy of American labour

---

[121] *NFL Players' Assn. v. NFL Management Council*, (May 14, 1980, Luskin, arb.) (John Dutton received no offers at contract expiry or after option year; agreement provided for 120 per cent salary after option year).

[122] See, R.C. Berry, W.B. Gould & P.D. Staudohar, *Labor Relations in Professional Sports* (Dover: Auburn House Publishing, 1986) at 123-52.

law[123] to encourage union organization and collective bargaining, which involve concerted economic action and the standardization of working conditions. This conflict has been accommodated by "statutory" and "non-statutory" exemptions from antitrust law. The historic purpose of the exemptions was to protect union organization and contract terms benefitting employees, but protection does extend to some joint action by employers. The statutory exemption immunizes the co-ordinated organization and economic tactics associated with labour disputes, provided unions act in their own self-interest and do not combine with non-labour groups.[124] The non-statutory exemption extends the immunity to the contents of collective agreements, provided there is no intent to harm outsiders and the union is seeking to protect the immediate interests of its members in matters relating to working conditions and employment opportunities.[125] Although there would be no immunity for agreements imposing external restraints in the product market,[126] the exemption may apply where agreed terms primarily relate to the labour market. The non-statutory exemption also extends to reasonable practices closely linked to collective bargaining. In *Brown v. Pro Football, Inc.*,[127] dealing with the league's unilateral implementation of a salary scale for players on the "developmental squad", the U.S. Supreme Court applied the exemption to the conduct of the employers:

> That conduct took place during and immediately after a collective-bargaining negotiation. It grew out of, and was directly related to, the lawful operation of the bargaining process. It involved a matter that the parties were required to negotiate collectively. And it concerned only the parties to the collective-bargaining relationship.[128]

---

[123] See Chapter 8, "Competition Law and Labour Law", section D, 2. See also, M.S. Jacobs & R.K. Winter, "Antitrust Principles and Collective Bargaining by Athletes: Of Superstars in Peonage" (1971) 81 Yale L. J. 1.

[124] *Clayton Act*, 15 U.S.C. s. 17; 29 U.S.C. ss. 52-53 (2001); *Norris-LaGuardia Act*, 29 U.S.C. ss. 101-15 (2001); *U.S. v. Hutcheson*, 312 U.S. 219 (1941).

[125] *Allen Bradley Co. v. Local Union No. 3, IBEW*, 325 U.S. 797 (1945); *United Mine Wkrs. v. Pennington*, 381 U.S. 657 (1965); *Local Union No. 189, Amalgamated Meat Cutters v. Jewel Tea Co.*, 381 U.S. 676 (1965); *Connell Construction Co. v. Plumbers and Steamfitters Local No. 100*, 421 U.S. 616 (1975).

[126] In *Clarett v. National Football League*, 369 F.3d 124 (2nd Cir., 2004), Sotomayor C.J. observed (at 143), "This is simply not a case in which the NFL is alleged to have conspired with its players union to drive its competitors out of the market for professional football". See also, *Collins v. National Basketball Players Assn.*, 850 F.Supp. 1468 (D.Colo., 1991) (labour exemption applies to programs of players' associations to regulate agents); see further, Chapter 9, "National Hockey League", section G, 3.

[127] *Brown v. Pro Football, Inc.*, 518 U.S. 231 (1996), affg 50 F.3d 1041 (D.C.Cir., 1995) (multi-employer bargaining; agreement among employers to implement last good faith offer after impasse).

[128] *Ibid.*, at 250 *per* Breyer J.

The imposition of terms would not, however, be exempt if it was "distant in time and in circumstances from the collective-bargaining process".

In sports cases, employers and league management have relied on the non-statutory exemption to maintain restraints once collective bargaining has been established. Teams are here resisting the effort of players to stack antitrust remedies onto the labour relations process since "primary responsibility for policing the collective-bargaining process" belongs to the National Labor Relations Board ("NLRB") and not to "antitrust courts".[129] In attempting to reconcile antitrust and labour law policy, cases have grappled with three general questions: does the exemption turn on specific union consent to the restraint? which players are bound by negotiated restraints? and, when does the exemption expire?

League immunity was denied in the earliest decisions when courts recognized that unions were in their infancy and players had not participated in creating the basic restraints, which had been imposed unilaterally by management. For example, in *Philadelphia World Hockey Club, Inc. v. Philadelphia Hockey Club, Inc.*,[130] the NHL was unable to rely on the exemption to resist a challenge to its reservation system brought by the WHA because there had been no serious bargaining over the reserve clause. Furthermore, the restraint affected interests beyond those of the NHL and its players' association: it harmed the competing league by limiting access to playing talent.

Two leading cases from later in the 1970s then addressed the process of incorporating restraints in collective agreements. *Mackey v. National Football League*[131] occurred at a time of collective bargaining for a new agreement and involved general union objection to the "Rozelle Rule" system of free agent compensation. The appeal court of the Eighth Circuit proceeded on the assumption that the "Rozelle Rule" had been recognized in previous agreements and addressed the case from the point of view of the non-statutory exemption. The court formulated three tests for the application of that exemption:

> the restraint must primarily affect the parties to the collective agreement;
> it must concern a mandatory subject of bargaining;[132] and the restraint must be the product of *bona fide* arm's length negotiations.

The "Rozelle Rule" was found to have little effect on outsiders, and was held to be a mandatory subject of bargaining because it affected players' salaries and mobility. The exemption was, however, denied because the court found that reference to the rule in the collective agreements of 1968 and 1970 was not the result of *bona fide* bargaining. The players had received no specific trade-off or benefit in exchange for acquiescing in the system, and there had been little or no

---

[129]   *Ibid.*, at 240, 242.
[130]   351 F.Supp. 462 (E.D.Pa., 1972). See Chapter 9, "National Hockey League", section A, 2.
[131]   543 F.2d 606 (8th Cir., 1976), varg 407 F.Supp. 1000 (D.Minn., 1975).
[132]   Wages, hours and other terms or conditions of employment are mandatory subjects of bargaining; see, *National Labour Relations Act*, July 5, 1935, c. 372, s. 8(d); 29 U.S.C. s. 158(d) (2001) (NLRA).

discussion of it. The court was, therefore, prepared to investigate the details of the negotiation process and whether specific gains were made. A modified approach was taken in *McCourt v. California Sports, Inc.*,[133] involving one player's objection to the system of free agent compensation in the NHL. In this case, the plaintiff's team, the Detroit Red Wings, had signed star goaltender, Rogatien Vachon, as a free agent from the Los Angeles Kings; Dale McCourt then found himself the subject of a forced trade to Los Angeles when the league's arbitrator awarded his contract to that team as compensation for the loss of Vachon. McCourt initially obtained a preliminary injunction from a federal district court halting the transfer when the compensation system was found to be a probable breach of antitrust law because of its restraint on the signing of free agents. Applying the standards in *Mackey*, the court found that there had been no *bona fide* bargaining over compensation, the system having been unilaterally imposed on the players. The majority of the court of appeal disagreed with this interpretation, applied the labour exemption and vacated the injunction. (McCourt eventually stayed in Detroit when the teams agreed to other compensation.) The appellate court found that reservation and compensation had been discussed through a process involving alternative proposals, a strike threat, threatened litigation and the yielding of ground on other issues. The owners had been obdurate and the players did not succeed in amending the system, but a process of *bona fide*, arm's length bargaining had occurred.

The non-statutory labour exemption may, therefore, serve to uphold limits on player mobility or freedom of negotiation. Decisions since *Mackey* have formulated a general non-statutory exemption based on the policy of favouring collective bargaining and the system of labour law:

> The nonstatutory labor exemption waives antitrust liability for restraints on competition imposed through the collective bargaining process, so long as such restraints operate primarily in a labor market characterized by collective bargaining.[134]

In *Zimmerman v. National Football League*, the court held that "potential future players for a professional sports league are parties to the bargaining relationship",[135] and it is an inevitable feature of collective bargaining that future employees will be subject to the agreed terms. The exemption may, therefore, extend to negotiated restraints that primarily affect incoming players. Although

---

[133]  600 F.2d 1193 (6th Cir., 1979), revg 460 F.Supp. 904 (E.D. Mich., 1978).

[134]  *Brown v. Pro Football*, 50 F.3d 1041, at 1056 (D.C. Cir., 1995), *per* Edwards C.J., affd 518 U.S. 231 (1996).

[135]  *Zimmerman v. National Football League*, 632 F.Supp. 398 (D.D.C., 1986), at 405 *per* Parker S.D.J. In *Brown v. Pro Football*, 518 U.S. 231 (1996), the U.S. Supreme Court noted (at 250) that it is an important element of the non-statutory labour exemption that conduct concern "only the parties to the collective-bargaining relationship".

draft systems[136] or age rules[137] are suspect in the absence of a CBA, restrictive eligibility rules,[138] entry drafts,[139] or caps on the salaries of rookie players[140] have now been upheld when the labour exemption was available. In *Clarett v. National Football League*, dealing with the NFL's requirement that players wait "three full college seasons" since graduation from high school, it was stated:

> In the context of this collective bargaining relationship, the NFL and its players union can agree that an employee will not be hired or considered for employment for nearly any reason whatsoever so long as they do not violate federal laws such as those prohibiting unfair labor practices ... federal labor policy permits the NFL teams to act collectively as a multi-employer bargaining unit in structuring the rules of play and setting the criteria for player employment.[141]

In *Clarett*, the Second Circuit declined to recognize the tests in *Mackey* as "appropriate" and followed the decision of the U.S. Supreme Court in *Brown v. Pro Football, Inc.*[142] in affording a wide exemption for the collective bargaining process. The key feature in *Brown* was, however, that there had been meaningful negotiation over salaries to the point of *impasse* prior to the teams' unilateral

---

[136] See, *Smith v. Pro Football Inc.*, 593 F.2d 1173 (D.C. Cir., 1978), varg 420 F.Supp. 738 (D.D.C., 1976).

[137] See: *Denver Rockets v. All-Pro Management, Inc.*, 325 F.Supp. 1049 (C.D. Cal., 1971); *Haywood v. National Basketball Assn.*, 401 U.S. 1204 (1971) (rule requiring four years since graduation from high school); *Linseman v. World Hockey Assn.*, 439 F.Supp. 1315 (D. Conn., 1977) (age rule of 20).

[138] *Clarett v. National Football League*, 369 F.3d 124 (2nd Cir., 2004), revg 306 F.Supp.2d 379 (S.D.N.Y., 2004) (three years since high school graduation). See also, *National Hockey League Players' Assn. v. Plymouth Whalers Hockey Club*, 419 F.3d 462 (6th Cir., 2005) ("Van Ryn rule" excluding ex-NCAA 20-year-olds from OHL; elimination of path to free agency is caused by CBA).

[139] *Zimmerman v. National Football League*, 632 F.Supp. 398 (D.D.C., 1986) (USFL player held bound by NFL's supplemental draft of defecting players). See also, *Powell v. National Football League*, 711 F.Supp. 959 (D.Minn., 1989) (college draft).

[140] *Wood v. National Basketball Assn.*, 809 F.2d 954 (2nd Cir., 1987), affg 602 F.Supp. 525 (S.D.N.Y., 1984) (draftee bound by terms of collective agreement; individual negotiation would subvert national labour policy).

[141] 369 F.3d 124, at 141 (2nd Cir., 2004), *per* Sotomayor C.J., revg 306 F.Supp.2d 379 (S.D.N.Y., 2004). The decision of the Circuit Court in *Clarett* has had mixed reviews; see, for example: Note, "Antitrust Law-Nonstatutory Labor Exemption-Second Circuit Exempts NFL Eligibility Rules from Antitrust Scrutiny" (2005), 118 Harv.L.Rev. 1379 (*Clarett* is persuasive and *Mackey's* third prong is "pernicious"; proof of bargaining over particular terms is contrary to labour policy); J.R. Gerba, "Instant Replay: A Review of the Case of Maurice Clarett, the Application of the Non-Statutory Labor Exemption, and its Protection of the NFL Draft Eligibility Rule" (2005), 73 Fordham L. Rev. 2383 (*Clarett* is wrong because the eligibility rule is not a mandatory subject of collective bargaining); T. Pensyl, "Let Clarett Play: Why the Nonstatutory Labor Exemption Should not Exempt the NFL's Draft Eligibility Rule from Antitrust Law" (2006), 37 U. Toledo L. Rev. 523 (eligibility rule fails two of the *Mackey* prongs).

[142] 518 U.S. 231 (1996). Breyer J. noted (at 235) "we do not interpret the exemption as broadly as did the Appeals Court".

imposition of standard terms. The tests in *Mackey* and a continued threat of antitrust liability are preferable where the restraints are not a mandatory subject of bargaining or victimize outsiders such as prospective employees. *Mackey* is unusual in demanding "arm's length" negotiation and *quid pro quo*, but it at least ensures that the agreed restraints primarily affect players' working conditions and are the result of genuine give-and-take between players and owners. Eligibility requirements such as age rules have more to do with maintaining favourable relations with amateur organizations and they hardly affect working conditions since the number of positions in the professional league remains the same; so far as the excluded player is concerned, the rule is in fact a denial of work. As to draft systems, they certainly affect wages but only by depressing the salaries of the rookies through the allocation of exclusive rights of negotiation or the imposition of limits at the "entry level". With both eligibility rules and draft systems, there is considerable unity of interests between the senior players and the owners so that adversarial bargaining is illusory. Eligibility rules requiring fixed formative periods make some contribution to superior maturity and athletic performance and so benefit both the playing personnel and the team owners; veteran players may equally appreciate a limit on the entering cohort since it might reduce the chance of one of their own being displaced. At the same time, the veterans join with owners in restricting the mobility and compensation of the rookies since maxima at the "entry level" preserve a larger share for the old guard. While benefits based on seniority are a common feature of industrial agreements, professional sport offers the double peculiarity of retaining negotiation of individual service contracts and severely constraining the bargaining position of newcomers. Although players' associations have historically tried to reduce the number of rounds in the draft, neither eligibility rules nor draft systems seem to hold serious points of difference between management and established players. Excluded amateur players or draftees might be able to pursue labour remedies by complaining that the union has failed in its duty of fair representation, but antitrust liability is the more potent weapon and the three-pronged attack of *Mackey* provides more ammunition than the blanket exclusion of *Clarett*.

Although labour relations and labour law are now the primary processes for establishing the conditions of players' employment, the negotiation of a collective agreement does not permanently extinguish antitrust remedies. The issue of the duration of the labour exemption[143] was central to the actions brought by the NFLPA after the 1987 strike and has also been addressed in the National Basketball Association ("NBA"). The primary authority on the subject is the series of cases known as *Powell v. National Football League*.[144]

Various tests have been suggested for the life of the exemption. The end of the collective agreement would provide, "a bright line for the parties to take into

---

[143]  See: Note, (1982) 57 N.Y.U.L. Rev. 164; Lock, [1989] Duke L.J. 339; Roman, (1990) 67 Denver U.L. Rev. 111; Note, (1991) 104 Harv. L. Rev. 874; St. Louis, [1993] Detroit C.L. Rev. 1221.

[144]  678 F.Supp. 777 (D. Minn., 1988).

the bargaining room",[145] but labour law policy suggests that the exemption survive formal expiry since the prospect of instant antitrust liability might inhibit free bargaining. Parties are obliged to maintain the *status quo* while negotiations are continuing and it is only when *impasse* has been reached that employers may unilaterally implement material changes. The prospect of parties eventually agreeing to renew a restraint caused one court to suggest that the exemption for that restraint,

> survives only as long as the employer continues to impose that restriction unchanged, and reasonably believes that the practice or a close variant of it will be incorporated in the next collective agreement.[146]

The more commonly suggested test has been that the exemption survives only until *impasse* on the issue. This was the position originally taken by the District Court in *Powell v. National Football League*,[147] dealing with the challenge to free agent compensation and the right of first refusal previously incorporated in collective agreements. On appeal, however, it was held in *Powell* (1989) that the non-statutory exemption "protects agreements conceived in an ongoing collective bargaining relationship".[148] An antitrust suit could not be maintained so long as there was the prospect of a solution through bargaining, resort to economic force, or a final order of the National Labour Relations Board. The exemption therefore survived *impasse*.

Twelve years of fruitless negotiation now induced the NFLPA to secure a vote from a majority of the players that the association cease to be the recognized bargaining representative. Eight players whose contracts had expired then initiated an antitrust suit in respect of the "Plan B" system of player allocation unilaterally imposed by NFL teams in 1989. Under this system, teams could "protect" 37 of their 55 roster players through compensation and first refusal; the remainder were not so constrained and had two months to sign a better deal with another team. In *McNeil v. National Football League*,[149] the District Court held that the bargaining relationship and the labour exemption had ceased with the players' majority vote and it was not necessary to have a formal

---

[145] *Brown v. Pro Football, Inc.*, 782 F.Supp. 125 (D.D.C., 1991), at 134 *per* Lamberth D.J. (exemption ends at expiry or impasse; system of uniform salaries for development squad had never been included in collective agreement), revd 50 F.3d 1041 (D.C.Cir., 1995), 518 U.S. 231 (1996).

[146] *Bridgeman v. National Basketball Assn.*, 675 F.Supp. 960 (D.N.J., 1987), at 967 *per* Debevoise D.J. (challenge to college player draft, salary cap and right of first refusal).

[147] 678 F.Supp. 777 (D.Minn., 1988). See also, *Powell v. National Football League*, 690 F.Supp. 812 (D. Minn., 1988) (injunction against free agent compensation system refused while labour dispute was in progress).

[148] *Powell v. National Football League*, 930 F.2d 1293 (8th Cir., 1989), at 1303 *per* Gibson C.J. See also, *Brown v. Pro Football, Inc.*, 518 U.S. 231 (1996), affg 50 F.3d 1041 (D.C.Cir., 1995) (unilateral implementation of uniform salaries).

[149] 764 F.Supp. 1351 (D.Minn., 1991). See also: 773 F.Supp. 1250 (D.Minn., 1991); 790 F.Supp. 871 (D.Minn., 1992).

decertification of the NFLPA. The action in *McNeil* then proceeded to trial, and in September 1992 a jury held that "Plan B" had a substantially harmful effect on competition for players' services. The jury found that four of the eight plaintiffs had suffered losses totalling USD $540,000, so that the treble damages under antitrust law were USD $1.6 million.[150]

Peace returned to the NFL in 1993 when further litigation by players affected by "Plan B" was settled[151] for USD $195 million and the reconstituted NFLPA signed an initial seven-year collective agreement with the league. This highly complex document prohibited the automatic inclusion of option clauses in players' contracts and allowed veterans unrestricted free agency after five years of service or after four years if a salary cap was in operation.[152] The CBA was subsequently extended, although by 2008 team owners had initiated the process for negotiating a new agreement.

The influence of the NFL's experience began to be seen in 1994 when the six-year collective agreement in the National Basketball Association expired. In *National Basketball Assn. v. Williams*,[153] NBA teams obtained declarations that there was no antitrust violation in the continued implementation of the college draft, right of first refusal and salary cap. After both sides agreed to abstain from industrial action during the 1994-95 season, the league and the players' association worked out a new collective agreement in June 1995, but some prominent players (and their agents) delayed full ratification declaring that they were dissatisfied with the negotiation process and the agreed terms. The league responded with a lockout and threats to cancel the upcoming season. The dissident player group initiated an antitrust suit while applying to the NLRB for an election to decertify the union. Further bargaining resulted in a modified collective agreement, so that the formal vote in September 1995 impliedly involved ratification. In the result, a clear majority of players voted to retain the association as their bargaining representative.

Players in professional leagues now face a choice between litigation and negotiation since the result of *Powell* (1989) and *Brown* (1996) is that "unions in all sports were deprived of the tactic of antitrust liability unless they were willing

---

[150]   See, "N.F.L.'s Free-Agency System Is Found Unfair by U.S. Jury" *The New York Times*, September 11, 1992, at A1, B15. See also, *Jackson v. National Football League*, 802 F.Supp. 226 (D. Minn., 1992) (four players granted temporary restraining order against enforcement of "Plan B").

[151]   *White v. National Football League*, 822 F.Supp. 1389 (D. Minn., 1993); 836 F.Supp. 1458 (D. Minn., 1993); 836 F.Supp. 1508 (D. Minn., 1993), affd 41 F.3d 402 (8th Cir., 1994) (approval of settlement; actions by objectors).

[152]   CBA of NFL (1993-2000), art. 15 (any option clause must be negotiated as a separate addendum), art. 19 (veteran free agency), art. 24 (salary cap at 62 per cent to 64 per cent is triggered if teams' "Player Costs" reach 67 per cent of "actual Defined Gross Revenues"). At least 58 per cent of league revenues must go to player compensation. The college draft (art. 16) was reduced to seven rounds.

[153]   45 F.3d 684 (2nd Cir., 1995; affg 857 F.Supp. 1069 (S.D.N.Y., 1994) (following *Powell*, 930 F.2d 1293 (8th Cir., 1989)) *Cf. National Hockey League v. National Hockey League Players Assn.*, 789 F.Supp. 288 (D. Minn., 1992) (league refused declaration as to antitrust status of free agent equalization plan).

to decertify themselves or could produce evidence that would establish a moribund bargaining process".[154] An active players' association serves the ironic function of shielding the league and team management, so that in 2000 "arena football owners ... fearing antitrust liability...threatened a lockout unless their employees *joined* a union!".[155] The antitrust action nevertheless retains its role in sports and organizations unaffected by collective bargaining, and debate will continue about the remedies available to prospective employees. Antitrust liability also remains relevant to commercial agreements and franchise operations.

## 4.    Franchise Restraints[156]

League controls on franchises relate to the product market or the output of exhibitions rather than the labour market for players. The constitutions and other rules of leagues prescribe procedures for the admission of new members and include restrictions on the location, ownership and operation of teams.[157] There are also formal controls on relocation, although the bidding to host professional sport commonly causes cities to lose franchises (and occasionally get them back).[158] The restraints reflect teams' interdependence and seek to guarantee that each member is economically viable as a playing opponent, and attempts are sometimes made to reduce operations by eliminating weaker entities.[159] Franchise restraints have prompted antitrust actions by league members and by external parties who claim that league rules or practices are anticompetitive. Both sections 1 and 2 of the *Sherman Act* are applicable: the claim may relate to a joint agreement in restraint of trade or to monopolization.

An action by an outsider may claim that a league is monopolizing the market by expanding into new locations with the intention of precluding

---

[154]  W.B. Gould, "Labor Issues in Professional Sports: Reflections on Baseball, Labor, and Antitrust Law" (2004) 15 Stan. L. & Policy Rev. 61 at 82.

[155]  W.B. Gould, "Labor Issues in Professional Sports: Reflections on Baseball, Labor, and Antitrust Law" (2004) 15 Stan. L. & Policy Rev. 61 at 82.

[156]  See, J.C. Weistart & C.H. Lowell, *The Law of Sports* (Indianapolis: The Bobbs-Merrill Co., 1979) at 687-759; (Supplement 1985) at 131-70.

[157]  See, for example: *Sullivan v. National Football League*, 34 F.3d 1091 (1st Cir., 1994) (restriction on sale of franchise through public stock offering); *Madison Square Garden, L.P. v. National Hockey League*, No. 07 CV 8455 (LAP), S.D.N.Y., November 2, 2007 (integration of team websites). On the Constitution and By-Laws of the NHL, see Chapter 7, "The Business of Hockey", sections B, 1; C, 2; Chapter 8, "Competition Law and Labour Law", section A, 4.

[158]  See Chapter 7, "The Business of Hockey", section B, 3. See also, *City of Oakland v. Oakland Raiders*, 220 Cal. Rptr. 153 (1985) (eminent domain action).

[159]  On contraction in baseball, see, *Major League Baseball v. Crist*, 331 F.3d 1177 (11th Cir., 2003). See also, *News Ltd. v. South Sydney District Rugby League Football Club Ltd.* (2003) 215 C.L.R. 563 (H.C. of Aust.) (decision to cut South Sydney Rabbitohs was not an "exclusionary provision" with the purpose of limiting the supply of services).

opportunities for a rival league[160] or for a franchise holder[161] in that league. Or the claim may be by an unsuccessful applicant who has been refused admission to the league.[162] In *North American Soccer League v. National Football League*,[163] the soccer league successfully attacked the NFL's cross-ownership ban by which franchise holders were prevented from having interests in other sports teams. Cross-ownership within a league is commonly prohibited to preserve the integrity of the competition, but the NFL rule precluded external holdings in other leagues. The court considered the need for inter-team co-operation and league loyalty but held that the ban exceeded legitimate interests and interfered with the NASL's ability to obtain capital investors. The court characterized the NFL as a multiple entity capable of joint action under section 1 of the *Sherman Act*. League practices adversely affecting market rivals or other third parties such as stadium operators[164] may, therefore, involve liability as restraints of trade.

The "multi unit" or "separate competitor" analysis has also been applied in actions by league members. Earlier decisions dealing with review of franchise candidates[165] and franchise relocation[166] indicated that a professional league is a single venture of integrated parties incapable of combined action for the purposes of section 1. However, in *Los Angeles Memorial Coliseum Comm. v. National Football League*,[167] it was held that a league consists of distinct and competing entities; although much league revenue is shared, each team is an

---

[160] *American Football League v. National Football League*, 205 F.Supp. 60 (D.Md., 1962); affd 323 F.2d 124 (4th Cir., 1963) (action dismissed). Only the harmed league has standing to allege that franchise decisions are designed to injure the rival organization: *San Francisco Seals, Ltd. v. National Hockey League*, 379 F.Supp. 966 (C.D.Cal., 1974) (NHL team refused right to move to Vancouver; league planned to sell expansion franchise there; team could not allege monopolistic intent to cover lucrative areas and prevent formation of rival league). See also, *News Ltd. v. Australian Rugby Football League Ltd.* (1996), 64 F.C.R. 410 (Fed.C. of Aust., Full Ct.), revg (1996), 58 F.C.R. 447 (Fed.C. of Aust.) (Super League versus ARL).

[161] *Shayne v. National Hockey League*, 504 F.Supp. 1023 (E.D.N.Y., 1980) (WHA option holder; action dismissed).

[162] *Mid-South Grizzlies v. National Football League*, 720 F.2d 772 (3rd Cir., 1983) (no obligation to admit applicant; no harm to external competition). See also, *Seattle Totems Hockey Club, Inc. v. National Hockey League*, 783 F.2d 1347 (9th Cir., 1986).

[163] 670 F.2d 1249 (2nd Cir., 1982), revg 505 F.Supp. 659 (S.D.N.Y., 1980); cert. denied 459 U.S. 1074 (1982).

[164] *Los Angeles Memorial Coliseum Comm. v. National Football League*, 468 F.Supp. 154 (C.D.Cal., 1979); *Los Angeles Memorial Coliseum Comm. v. National Football League*, 484 F.Supp. 1274 (C.D.Cal., 1980), revd 634 F.2d 1197 (9th Cir., 1980) (NFL rule requiring three-fourths majority vote by team owners to allow transfer).

[165] *Levin v. National Basketball Assn.*, 385 F.Supp. 149 (S.D.N.Y., 1974) (league refusal to allow transfer of ownership; teams held to be partners not competitors).

[166] *San Francisco Seals, Ltd. v. National Hockey League*, 379 F.Supp. 966 (C.D.Cal., 1974). In the wake of decisions in the 1980s, there was conflicting analysis of league structures and the control of franchise moves, see: Grauer, (1983) 82 Mich. L. Rev. 1, (1989) 64 Tulane L. Rev. 71; Lazaroff, (1984) 53 Ford. L. Rev. 157, (1988) 20 Ariz.St. L. J. 953; Roberts, (1984) 32 U.C.L.A. L. Rev. 219, (1985) 52 U.Chi. L. Rev. 999, (1986) 60 Tulane L. Rev. 562, (1989) 64 Tulane L. Rev. 117. On legislative proposals in Congress, see (1987) 38 Hastings L.J. 345.

[167] 726 F.2d 1381 (9th Cir., 1984), affg 519 F.Supp. 581 (C.D.Cal., 1981).

independent business capable of making profits or losses according to its management policies. In this case, the Oakland Raiders (and the L.A. Coliseum) objected to the NFL rule that required an affirmative three-fourths majority vote by team owners before a franchise could move into another team's territory. Such a rule reinforced teams' local monopolies and restrained competition between stadia and between teams (intrabrand competition). In this case, it would have prevented the Raiders moving into the vast Los Angeles area and acting as a local rival for the Rams. Outside of sports, a horizontal or territorial market allocation would constitute an illegal cartel, but the NFL argued that a league required regional balance and separation to promote the stability and continuity of its franchises and to strengthen its position against other forms of entertainment (interbrand competition). The league's voting requirement was, however, held to be arbitrary and unnecessarily restrictive of intrabrand competition between teams. The practice infringed the rule of reason because it made no reference to relevant standards and provided no protections for the team wanting to move:

> To withstand antitrust scrutiny, restrictions on team movement should be more closely tailored to serve the needs inherent in producing the NFL "product" and competing with other forms of entertainment. An express recognition and consideration of those objective factors espoused by the NFL as important, such as population, economic projections, facilities, regional balance, etc., would be well advised. ... Fan loyalty and location continuity could also be considered. ... Some sort of procedural mechanism to ensure consideration of all the above factors may also be necessary, including an opportunity for the team proposing the move to present its case. ... Their vote against the Raiders' move could have been motivated by animosity [against team owner Al Davis] rather than business judgment.[168]

The first Raiders' trial ended in a hung jury, but the second jury found the NFL rule an unreasonable restraint of trade, and the NFL was enjoined from interfering with the franchise move. The damages trial resulted in awards of USD $4.86 million to the L.A. Coliseum and USD $11.55 million to the Raiders; these figures were then trebled under the *Clayton Act*. On appeal,[169] the Raiders' damages were ordered to be reassessed to take account of what the NFL could have charged the team for moving into the Los Angeles area and thereby precluding the sale of an expansion franchise there.

---

[168]　*Ibid.*, at 1397-98 *per* Anderson C.J. On required transfer procedures in the NHL, including "considerations" when voting, see NHL By-Law 36.

[169]　*Los Angeles Memorial Coliseum Comm. v. National Football League*, 791 F.2d 1356 (9th Cir., 1986). The damages were ordered reduced by "the value of the NFL's Los Angeles expansion opportunity in 1980, prior to the NFL's illegal conduct, less the value of the Oakland opportunity returned to the league". *Ibid.*, at 1372, *per* Williams D.C.J.

The *Oakland Raiders* decisions[170] denied leagues absolute control of team moves and allowed for further "free agency" by franchises; the Baltimore Colts took advantage of this in 1984 to do a nocturnal flit to Indianapolis,[171] a move that detracted from the competition previously existing in the Washington area. The National Hockey League faced the problem in 1983 when the owners of the St. Louis Blues (Ralston Purina) attempted to sell the franchise to interests in Saskatoon.[172] A vote by NHL owners disapproved of the sale, and the league subsequently took possession of the franchise and sold it to another business group in St. Louis. Ralston Purina then brought an antitrust suit against the NHL for preventing the Saskatoon sale;[173] this case was settled in 1985 after 10 days of trial.[174] The *Oakland Raiders* decisions do, however, recognize that relocation into a particular area is a valuable right belonging to a league. A reasonable fee for relocation or "indemnification"[175] may also be chargeable, provided it is reduced by the value of any territory that is being freed up and returned. Leagues may maintain approval processes and reasonable rules to control team movement,[176] provided the restraints promote competition within the league and in the wider entertainment market. These criteria are not easily applied, and a league's decision to create a new local rivalry might be challenged because it eliminated an old one. Leagues must, however, approve an owner's decision to relocate where the clear effect is to strengthen the franchise and the league.

---

[170] The Raiders returned to Oakland in 1995 and launched a series of unsuccessful actions against the NFL based on the league's alleged failure to support them in obtaining a new stadium in Los Angeles; see, *Oakland Raiders v. National Football League*, 161 P. 3d 151, 61 Cal.Rptr. 3d 634 (Cal. S.C., 2007), affg 32 Cal.Rptr. 3d 266 (Cal. C.A., 2005).

[171] See, "12 Vans to Indianapolis" "Lease on Stadium Approved for Colts By Indianapolis" *The New York Times* (April 1, 1984) at S3. See also, *Mayor of Baltimore v. Baltimore Football Club, Inc.*, 624 F.Supp. 278 (D.Md., 1985).

[172] See also, Chapter 8, "Competition Law and Labour Law", section A, 4 (inquiry under the *Combines Investigation Act*).

[173] See: "$20 million lawsuit filed by Blues" *The Globe and Mail* (Toronto: May 25, 1983) at 14; "NHL sues Blues' owner" *The Globe and Mail* (Toronto: June 1, 1983) at 16; "Saskatoon blues: The life and death of 'fantasy'" *The Globe and Mail* (Toronto: August 18, 1984) at S3; "Depositions stack up four feet as NHL battles $70 million suit" *The Globe and Mail* (Toronto: February 5, 1985) at 16.

[174] See, "NHL, Ralston settle suits over blocked Blues sale" *The Globe and Mail* (Toronto: June 28, 1985) at 16.

[175] The move from Colorado cost the New Jersey Devils USD $30 million in NHL transfer fees and indemnities to local teams; see, "Rockies sold; NHL approves move to N.J." *The Globe and Mail* (Toronto: May 28, 1982) at 15. In 1993, the Disney Company paid only the expansion franchise fee for the Anaheim Ducks, which were in the "territory" of the Los Angeles Kings.

[176] *National Basketball Assn. v. SDC Basketball Club, Inc.*, 815 F.2d 562 (9th Cir., 1987). See also: *St. Louis Convention & Visitors Commission v. National Football League*, 154 F.3d 851 (8th Cir., 1998) (Rams were sole candidate for stadium and league charged USD $29 million relocation fee; no concerted action by NFL to restrain moves); *VKK Corp. v. National Football League*, 244 F.3d 114 (2nd Cir., 2001) (release of antitrust claims relating to relocation of New England Patriots).

The commercial viability of a particular location was a central issue in 2009 when Jerry Moyes took the Phoenix Coyotes into bankruptcy after receiving an offer of purchase from James Balsillie.[177] The offer was conditional on moving the team to Hamilton, Ontario and was supported by antitrust claims seeking to prevent the league from prohibiting the relocation. Balsillie made his offer in the name of "PSE Sports & Entertainment, LP", which had been approved to become a member of the NHL in 2006 when Balsillie was interested in buying the Pittsburgh Penguins. In *Re Dewey Ranch Hockey, LLC* (June 15, 2009), Bankruptcy Judge Baum recognized the right of leagues to maintain territorial restrictions and to control the ownership of teams, but was sceptical that unapproved relocations would "wreak havoc" because of the frequency of past flits. Justice Baum accepted that the case presented novel issues as to the relation between bankruptcy and antitrust law since the interests of some creditors came into conflict with those of the NHL and of the City of Glendale, which held a long-term agreement for the lease of its arena. He therefore declined to follow an accelerated timetable for the sale and possible relocation of the team and anticipated that the validity of league rules and their enforcement in bankruptcy proceedings would eventually be determined in accordance with the "rule of law". The anticipated determinations include clarification of when and how leagues function as multiple or single entities. Any authoritative ruling on this and other antitrust issues was carefully avoided in the Coyotes' case.

In protracted proceedings during 2009, Baum J. first ordered an auction involving purchasers who wished to keep the team in Phoenix, to be followed by offers from parties proposing to move the franchise, although in the end the process came down to one auction. The offers from cities and investors outside Phoenix were more likely to satisfy some of the creditors and so maximize their recovery. The creditors included SOF Investments Ltd., which was owed USD $80 million, and Moyes claimed that a contribution of USD $104 million to the team was in the nature of a loan rather than an equity investment. The outside bidders would need to know their obligation to pay reasonable and appropriate relocation fees to the league, and they were not helped by "economics experts" whose opinions ranged from USD $11 million to USD $195 million. One reason for the variation was that the figures would differ depending on whether the move was the result of bankruptcy proceedings or was in accordance with NHL By-Law 36. In the case of a forced move to Hamilton, the fees would reflect the value of the franchise in southwest Ontario, less the value of the Phoenix territory returned to the league. Under a relocation supervised by the league, By-Law 36.6 requires that the "transfer fee" reflect the "goodwill" developed by the league in

---

[177] See: *In re Dewey Ranch Hockey, LLC*, 2009 WL 1702767, 406 B.R. 30 (Bkrtcy. D. Ariz., June 15, 2009); *In re Dewey Ranch Hockey, LLC*, 2009 WL 31704552, 414 B.R. 577 (Bkrtcy. D. Ariz., September 30, 2009). The NHL's position in relation to the control of franchises was supported by briefs from the NBA, NFL and MLB. On the financial condition of the Coyotes and previous attempts to move teams to Hamilton, see Chapter 7, "The Business of Hockey", section B, 2; Chapter 8, "Competition Law and Labour Law", section A, 4.

Hamilton and the "indemnification fee" reflect the "goodwill" developed by the Leafs and the Sabres. The fees would, therefore, be minimal in the case of a relocation under By-Law 36.

Prior to the auction, the NHL rejected Balsillie's formal application for ownership on the basis that he had now become an unsuitable candidate or person lacking "good character and integrity" under By-Law 35.1(b). This decision was taken at a meeting on July 29, 2009 where the Board of Governors considered a memorandum reciting Balsillie's previous applications to purchase the Penguins and the Predators and his conduct in the current litigation. Justice Baum nevertheless permitted Balsillie to remain in the game, where he was opposed by "local" offers from sports entrepreneur Jerry Reinsdorf and from Ice Edge Holdings, LLC, with Reinsdorf's candidacy enjoying the approval of the league. Conditional on a new lease and negotiated arrangements with creditors, Reinsdorf offered USD $148 million and Ice Edge offered USD $150 million. The purchase price initially proposed by PSE and Balsillie was USD $212.5 million, including USD $22.5 million in potential payments to minority owner Wayne Gretzky in his capacity as head coach and managing partner. The three candidates and the league made extensive filings before Baum J. challenging the actions of the parties and the validity of the offers. An advantage seemed to fall to Reinsdorf in August 2009 when he negotiated an agreement for repayment with the SOF creditor but he soon withdrew from the bidding on failing to secure a more favourable lease and other subsidies from the City of Glendale. At this point, the NHL entered an offer of USD $140 million also conditional on a renegotiated lease. The league's intention was to operate the Coyotes in Glendale during 2009-10 and eventually sell the team to an acceptable third party. If no "local" purchaser emerged, the league was prepared to organize a sale involving the relocation of the franchise. By making an offer, the NHL claimed the dual roles of purchaser and controller of bidders.

At the auction on September 11, 2009, the only operative bids were from Balsillie and the NHL. Balsillie increased his offer to USD $242.2 million to provide further compensation to the City of Glendale and included a payment of USD $62.5 million to Moyes. Out of the NHL's offer of USD $140 million, the compensation for Moyes was up to USD $29 million. Fearing an appeal and further litigation if Balsillie was successful, the main creditors preferred the immediate cash of the NHL's bid. Wayne Gretzky, meanwhile, resigned as head coach.

In *Re Dewey Ranch Hockey, LLC* (September 30, 2009), Baum J. held that Balsillie could not force a sale and relocation through the bankruptcy process because this would fail to protect the NHL's "claimed rights" to select its members and control the location of teams: permitting the move to Hamilton would effectively predetermine issues as to the legality of the league's review processes. The original bid by the NHL was also rejected because it sought to select which unsecured creditors would be paid in full. In particular, Baum J. held that Moyes and Gretzky were entitled to be heard as to the legitimacy of their claims as creditors. Judge Baum did not call for an increase in the league's offer but stated that "the court is passing the puck to the NHL who can decide to take another shot".

This decision in *Dewey Ranch Hockey, LLC* terminated Balsillie's bid while leaving the NHL to restructure its offer and deal with the continuing business problem of hockey in the desert. The NHL duly acquired the franchise in November 2009 after offering a total package of USD $140 million and agreeing to reduce Moyes' debt to the league. The NHL was successful in avoiding a summary declaration that its constitutional rules on relocation were illegal, and bankruptcy proceedings largely emerged as an unsuitable forum through which to litigate antitrust issues and relocate teams. The decision did not include a full review of the legality of league rules, including the apparent veto power in article 4 of the NHL constitution dealing with territorial rights. Neither did Baum J. rule on the good faith of the league's change-of-heart over Balsillie or on the appropriate relocation fee. Throughout the proceedings, Baum J. was anxious to leave any final decision on the merits to higher powers. These determinations may be made in the antitrust suit filed by Jerry Moyes at the time of the application for bankruptcy.

## D. LABOUR LAW

This section notes the general legal framework of labour relations in the United States and Canada. Together with antitrust litigation, collective bargaining and other labour remedies are the main processes for modifying players' employment conditions. The various leagues each have their own distinctive history of employment relations and economic conflict,[178] but a general "labour law of sports" is evolving as traditional industrial remedies are applied to the unusual context of professional sport. The labour relations process is regulated by public agencies but also includes private systems of dispute resolution as parties establish grievance procedures and agree to refer cases to various forms of arbitration.[179] The final determination of disputes over the interpretation of collective agreements or players' contracts is usually in the hands of an arbitrator. **Figure 5** illustrates the positions and roles of the different agencies and participants.

---

[178] On labour organization and collective bargaining in the NHL, see, Chapter 9, "National Hockey League", sections B; C.

[179] See, Chapter 9, "National Hockey League", sections C-E.

**Figure 5: Labour Relations in Professional Leagues**

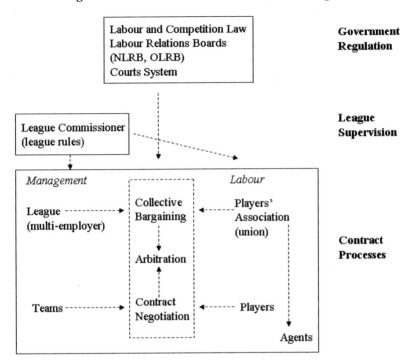

## 1.    General

Modern players' associations began to be organized during the 1950s, but it was only in the late 1960s and in the 1970s that substantial collective agreements were negotiated. This slow development reflects cultural ambivalence about "sports unions" and other difficulties in labour organization.[180] Resistance to the mode of production continues to be particularly weak in junior and minor leagues where the culture is one of playing along in the remote hope of receiving lucrative reward.[181]

Professional players form an elite group of entertainers fragmented between the various teams that hold their immediate loyalty; they are young and enjoy only brief professional careers. High turnover occurs as players are released outright or join the floating membership of free agents and players sent down to the minors. This unstable and individualistic membership obviously does not enhance solidarity or long-term commitment to collective rights. Associations

---

[180]    *Cf.* B. Dabscheck, "Player Associations and Sports Unions in Australia" in R.C. Wilcox (ed.), *Sport in the Global Village* (Morgantown: Fitness Information Technology, Inc., 1994), at 125-36.

[181]    See, M.A. Robidoux, *Men at Play: A Working Understanding of Professional Hockey* (Montreal & Kingston: McGill-Queens University Press, 2001).

also face difficulties in representing a workforce that ranges from the stars, to the established players, to the more fungible utility performers. Associations are obliged to represent fairly the interests of future,[182] present and retired players.[183] Finances have derived from the check-off of fees from members of the bargaining unit,[184] but this has often been insufficient to support operations, especially where the association has been weakened by the expenses of litigation. More recently, associations can rely on substantial income from central licensing and have increased their independence and bargaining resources.[185] During the negotiations and strike in the NHL in 1992, the NHLPA insisted that the collective agreement explicitly recognize its group program in player images, and the teams released claims to revenue from the licensing of photographs and hockey cards.[186]

The bargaining process reveals a number of unusual characteristics. Players' associations bargain on behalf of players throughout the league and deal with representatives of all teams. On the management side, the bargaining structure is an example of multi-employer bargaining that fixes common terms and conditions for all franchises. The collective agreements differ from ordinary industrial pacts in that players' salaries are not negotiated and no attempt is made to standardize payments through job classification. Players or their agents negotiate salaries individually[187] so that distinctions according to skill, experience and star status are preserved. Associations fix only minimum salary levels and concern themselves more with aspects such as player allocation and free agency, the standard player contract, "fringe benefits", and disciplinary or dispute processes. Collective agreements also recognize the authority of players' associations to certify agents and regulate standards in contract negotiations.

One recent peculiarity of the system in major league sport is the exclusive status and commercial orientation of both labour and management. The class war is now notably lacking from the periodic disputes and conflicts, which are best

---

[182]  *Wood v. National Basketball Assn.*, 809 F.2d 954 (2nd Cir., 1987).

[183]  See also, *Bathgate v. National Hockey League Pension Society*, [1992] O.J. No. 2168, 11 O.R. (3d) 449, 98 D.L.R. (4th) 326 (Ont. Gen. Div.), affd [1994] O.J. No. 265, 16 O.R. (3d) 761, 110 D.L.R. (4th) 609 (Ont. C.A.). See further, Chapter 9, "National Hockey League", section B, 2.

[184]  But see, *National Football League Players' Assn. v. Pro-Football, Inc.*, 849 F.Supp. 1 (D.D.C., 1993); 857 F.Supp. 71 (D.D.C., 1994) (jobsite of Washington Redskins is in Virginia; players relied on right-to-work law and refused to pay service fee; arbitrator's award vacated); 56 F.3d 1525 (D.C. Cir., 1995) (case dismissed as moot; season over). See also, NLRA, ss. 8(a)(3), 8(b)(2).

[185]  See: J. Helyar, *Lords of the Realm; The Real History of Baseball* (New York: Ballantine Books, 1995) at 89-91; *Topps Chewing Gum, Inc. v. Major League Baseball Players Assn.*, 641 F.Supp. 1179 (S.D.N.Y., 1986).

[186]  See now, CBA of NHL (2005), art. 25. See also, Chapter 9, "National Hockey League", section B, 3.

[187]  On individual service contracts in the arts, see: *National Ballet of Canada and Canadian Actors' Equity Assn. (Glasco) (Re)*, [2000] O.L.A.A. No. 209, 87 L.A.C. (4th) 1 (Ont., C. Albertyn, arbitrator); *National Ballet of Canada v. Glasco*, [2000] O.J. No. 1071, 49 O.R. (3d) 223, 185 D.L.R. (4th) 372 (Ont. Div. Ct.); *National Ballet of Canada v. Glasco*, [2000] O.J. No. 2083, 49 O.R. (3d) 230, 186 D.L.R. (4th) 347 (Ont. S.C.J.).

understood as two capitalist units fighting over the division of the spoils. Teams are typically owned by deep-pocketed individuals or diversified corporations.[188] The "workers" too are not without coin, since "player unions ... now share significantly in the monopoly superprofits enjoyed by the industry".[189] Anticipating future conflict, by 2000 the "war chest" of the NHLPA was estimated to have reached USD $100 million,[190] and as a "labour organization" it was exempt from tax under section 149(1)(k) of the *Income Tax Act*.[191] At the time of the lockout in 2004, the average salary of a player in the NHL was USD $1.7 million. In collective bargaining, the players typically assume the role of competitive entrepreneurs favouring freedom of negotiation. The owners also have business goals, but they are in the camp of controls, restraints and public assistance. As the free-market millionaire workers take on the regulation-loving billionaire owners, the negotiations become a mere parody of labour relations. The system is nevertheless subject to the general framework of labour law.

## 2.    *National Labor Relations Act*

The "labour law of sports" is largely the product of rights and processes recognized in the *National Labor Relations Act* ("NLRA")[192] of the United States.[193] This federal legislation establishes the National Labor Relations Board ("NLRB"), whose jurisdiction relates to American-based leagues that affect interstate commerce.[194] The functions of the Board and of its subordinate agents include conducting elections by employees for joining unions, deciding the appropriate bargaining unit (see, NLRA, s. 9(b)) and hearing charges of unfair labour practices. The Board assumed particular prominence in 1995 when it issued a complaint against team owners in Major League Baseball ("MLB") alleging that they had unilaterally eliminated the salary arbitration and anti-collusion provisions of the expired collective agreement.[195] By obtaining a preliminary injunction from a federal court (see, NLRA, s. 10(j)),[196] the Board

---

[188]  See, Chapter 7, "The Business of Hockey", section B, 1.

[189]  B. Kidd, *The Struggle for Canadian Sport* (Toronto: University of Toronto Press, 1996) at 269.

[190]  See, "At what price cost certainty?" *The Ottawa Citizen* (March 4, 2000) at F1, F2. On learning in 1998 that the NHLPA had a strike fund of USD $80 million, the league resolved to put aside USD $300 million; see, "NHL kitty to counter players' strike pot" *The Globe and Mail* (Toronto: December 8, 1998) at A25.

[191]  R.S.C. 1985, c. 1 (5th Supp.).

[192]  July 5, 1935, c. 372, ss. 1-19; 29 U.S.C., ss. 151-69 (2001).

[193]  See further, W.B. Gould, *A Primer of American Labor Law*, 4th ed. (Cambridge: The MIT Press, 2004).

[194]  *American League of Professional Baseball Clubs*, 180 N.L.R.B. 189 (1969) (umpires).

[195]  See: J.J. Lippner, "Replacement Players for the Toronto Blue Jays?: Striking the Appropriate Balance Between Replacement Worker Law in Ontario, Canada and the United States" (1995) 18 Fordham Int.L.J. 2026 at 2041-45; W.B. Gould, "The 1994-'95 Baseball Strike and National Labor Relations Board: To the Precipice and Back Again" (2008) 110 West Virginia L. Rev. 983.

[196]  *Silverman v. Major League Baseball Player Relations Comm., Inc.*, 880 F.Supp. 246 (S.D.N.Y., 1995), affd 67 F.3d 1054 (2nd Cir., 1995).

accelerated the end of the eight-month baseball strike after the players agreed to resume play under the terms of the old agreement.

Section 7 of the NLRA confers on employees the right to form labour organizations, to bargain collectively through chosen representatives and to promote their interests through "concerted activities" such as the strike.[197] By section 8(a) it is an unfair labour practice for an employer to interfere with these rights or to discriminate against an employee on the basis of union activity or membership in an employee organization; there is also protection for employees who do not wish to engage in union activities (see, ss. 7, 8(b)). Employers must meet with representatives of employees, and both sides must "confer in good faith with respect to wages, hours, and other terms and conditions of employment" (see, s. 8(d)) which constitute "mandatory" subjects of bargaining. The general legislative scheme seeks to promote free collective bargaining and to protect members' rights. It would, for example, be an unfair labour practice to cut,[198] trade or otherwise coerce players because of union activity. Similarly, teams may not engage in conduct calculated to frustrate any collective negotiation.[199] American labour law does, however, grant employers important economic weapons. As a general principle, replacements may be hired during a strike, and "temporary workers" may be used during a multi-employer lockout.[200]

The appropriate players' bargaining unit has usually been held to be players throughout the league, excluding those who have become free agents without any reasonable prospect of re-employment.[201] Independent negotiation by separately identified "special craft" players (*e.g.*, hockey goalies) or by superstars is unlikely to be permitted because their functions are integrated with the activities of teammates. On the management side, disputes have occurred as to whether the multi-employer unit (which must be agreed to by the union) should include the

---

[197] On the USD $30 million in back pay awarded to striking NFL veterans who were denied the opportunity to play in the first game after the 1987 strike, see: *National Football League Management Council and National Football League Players' Assn.*, 309 N.L.R.B. No. 10 (1992), affg Schlesinger, Admin.L.J., March 21, 1991 (unfair labour practice in discriminating against strikers).

[198] *Nordstrom, dba Seattle Seahawks and National Football League Players Assn.*, 292 N.L.R.B. No. 110 (1989), affg Ries, Admin.L.J., November 23, 1983 (player representative Sam McCullum cut by team during lead-up to 1982 strike); see also, 304 N.L.R.B. No. 78 (1991); 984 F.2d 479 (D.C. Cir., 1993). See, "Discriminatory Discharge in a Sports Context: A Reassessment of the Burden of Proof and Remedies under the National Labour Relations Act" (1984) 53 Ford. L. Rev. 613. See also, *Caldwell v. American Basketball Assn., Inc.*, 66 F.3d 523 (2nd Cir., 1995); affg 825 F. Supp. 558 (S.D.N.Y., 1993) (antitrust claim refused).

[199] In 1980, a collective agreement was established in the now defunct North American Soccer League after protracted resistance by team owners: *North American Soccer League*, 241 N.L.R.B. 1225 (No. 199) (1979); *North American Soccer League v. N.L.R.B.*, 613 F.2d 1379 (5th Cir., 1980); *Morio v. North American Soccer League*, 501 F.Supp. 633 (S.D.N.Y., 1980), affd 632 F.2d 217 (2nd Cir., 1980).

[200] See, W.B. Gould, *A Primer of American Labor Law*, 4th ed. (Cambridge: The MIT Press, 2004) at 106-113.

[201] *Major League Rodeo, Inc.*, 246 N.L.R.B. 743 (No. 113) (1979).

league or commissioner.[202] In *North American Soccer League*,[203] the appropriate unit of joint employers was found to be the league and the teams; the NLRB found that the league and commissioner exercised considerable control over players' working conditions and contractual relations. The Board directed a representation election for players on teams located in the United States. Players based in Canada were excluded from the unit because the NLRB concluded that its jurisdiction did not extend to those employers.

By section 8(d) of the *NLRA*, the mandatory issues must be the subject of good faith bargaining, although neither side is obliged to agree to a proposal or to make a concession. Other "permissive" (but not illegal) topics may also be raised. The obligation to bargain over "terms and conditions" carries with it duties to disclose needed information[204] and not to make unilateral changes to matters under discussion until *impasse* has been reached. Controversy may occur over the scope of the duty to bargain and the subjects that must be placed on the table, and players may in future assert an interest in wider aspects of the league's product. Management has traditionally claimed the prerogative to make decisions about playing rules or matters of league organization such as marketing programs and the ownership and location of franchises. Where, however, changes directly affect work opportunities (*e.g.*, roster size) or employment conditions (*e.g.*, playing time or the schedule) they should more properly be settled by collective bargaining. In disputes filed by the NFLPA, it has been held that management actions that affect compensation or that increase the chances of injury are mandatory subjects of bargaining. The power to fine[205] and the use of artificial turf[206] have, therefore, been found to be subjects requiring joint negotiation. Case law has also recognized that restrictions on player mobility through devices such as the draft,[207] free agent compensation[208] and right of first refusal[209] are mandatory subjects of bargaining (and subject to preservation through the labour exemption).[210]

---

[202] *Cf.: National Football League Players' Assn. v. N.L.R.B.*, 503 F.2d 12 (8th Cir., 1974) (owners and commissioner unilaterally promulgated bench fine rule); *Silverman v. Major League Baseball Player Relations Comm., Inc.*, 516 F.Supp. 588 (S.D.N.Y., 1981) (baseball commissioner made statements about teams' ability to pay; union requested disclosure of financial information; held that statements could not be attributed to the bargaining committee).

[203] 236 N.L.R.B. 1317 (No. 181) (1978), affd 613 F.2d 1379 (5th Cir., 1980); see also, *U.S. Football League Players Assn., AFL-CIO v. U.S. Football League*, 650 F.Supp. 12 (D.Or., 1986) (league not liable for salary). On the certification application in Ontario, see *North American Soccer League Players Assn. v. Toronto Blizzard Soccer Club*, [1979] OLRB REP. 449.

[204] *Silverman v. Major League Baseball Player Relations Comm., Inc.*, 516 F.Supp. 588 (S.D.N.Y., 1981).

[205] *National Football League Players' Assn. v. N.L.R.B.*, 503 F.2d 12 (8th Cir., 1974).

[206] *National Football League Management Council*, 203 N.L.R.B. 958 (No. 165) (1973) (no breach of duty to bargain on issue found).

[207] *Smith v. Pro-Football Inc.*, 420 F.Supp. 738 (D.D.C., 1976); *Wood v. National Basketball Assn.*, 809 F.2d 954 (2nd Cir., 1987).

[208] *Mackey v. National Football League*, 543 F.2d 606 (8th Cir., 1976).

[209] *Powell v. National Football League*, 930 F.2d 1293 (8th Cir., 1989). See also, *Silverman v. Major League Baseball Player Relations Comm., Inc.*, 880 F.Supp. 246 (S.D.N.Y., 1995), affd

Particular labour law difficulties may be caused by the co-existence with collective agreements of individual service contracts.[211] Once a union is certified, it becomes the exclusive bargaining representative for all unit members (see, NLRA, section 9(a)) and is under a duty to provide fair representation;[212] the negotiated benefits must not unreasonably discriminate against particular employee groups. Management is bound to negotiate with the employees' chosen agent and may be prohibited from direct dealing with individual employees since this could disrupt the collective activities of the union and undermine its authority. Negotiation of individual service contracts cannot be used as a device to frustrate the general statutory policy of promoting collective bargaining.[213] Collective agreements may, however, authorize individuals to negotiate contract terms that exceed and do not derogate from benefits in the collective agreement, and the union can agree that certain contract topics can be the subject of direct individual negotiation by the employee. The allowable modification of the collective agreement has been considered in arbitration decisions in MLB,[214] where there is a widespread practice of including special clauses in contracts. Article 2 of MLB's Basic Agreement allows "special Covenants to be included in the individual Uniform Player's Contract, which actually or potentially provide additional benefits to the Player". This provision has been interpreted to permit negotiation of accelerated free agency entitlement, provided procedures affecting other teams' interests (*e.g.*, the re-entry draft and quota[215] and free agent compensation[216]) are observed. Equally, a special option right in the team that is accepted by the player in exchange for consideration can validly have the effect of delaying free agent mobility.[217] There is, therefore, some potential to modify general arrangements. Arbitrators have indicated, however, that teams

---

67 F.3d 1054 (2nd Cir., 1995) (NLRB had reasonable cause to believe that free agency, reservation and salary arbitration are mandatory issues).

[210] See, Chapter 8, "Competition Law and Labour Law", section C, 3.

[211] See, S. Handman, "The juridical status of an individual work contract in relation to a collective agreement and recourses of an employee" (1979) 39 R. du B. 995. See also, CBA of NHL (2005), article 2.1 (recognition of NHLPA, but players may bargain on an individual basis with respect to salary and bonuses).

[212] On failures to process injury grievances, see: *Chuy v. National Football League Players' Assn.*, 495 F.Supp. 137 (E.D.Penn., 1980); *Peterson v. Kennedy*, 771 F.2d 1244 (9th Cir., 1985); *Sharpe v. National Football League Players' Assn.*, 941 F.Supp. 8 (D.D.C., 1996).

[213] *J.I. Case Co. v. N.L.R.B.*, 321 U.S. 332, 64 S.Ct. 576 (1944); *Morio v. North American Soccer League*, 501 F.Supp. 633 (S.D.N.Y., 1980), affd 632 F.2d 217 (2nd Cir., 1980); *Wood v. National Basketball Assn.*, 809 F.2d 954 (2nd Cir., 1987).

[214] See: R.C. Berry & G.M. Wong, *Law and Business of the Sports Industries, Vol.1, Professional Sports Leagues* (Dover: Auburn House Publishing, 1986) at 429-36, 447-60; G.M. Wong, "A Survey of Grievance Arbitration Cases in Major League Baseball" (1986) 41 Arb. J. 42 at 45-47; R.C. Berry, W.B. Gould & P.D. Staudohar, *Labour Relations in Professional Sports* (Dover: Auburn House Publishing, 1986) at 241-46.

[215] *Moore v. Atlanta Braves* (September 7, 1977, Porter, arb.).

[216] *Marshall v. Minnesota Twins* (October 25, 1978, Porter, arb.) (cost to signing team cannot normally be waived).

[217] *Tidrow v. Chicago Cubs* (November 4, 1980, Goetz, arb.) (benefit must attach to option clause; in circumstances player was estopped from repudiating the option as inconsistent with the collective agreement).

cannot use contract terms to systematically override collectively agreed conditions and benefits.

Although the NLRB declined to assert jurisdiction over Canadian teams in *North American Soccer League*,[218] the Board has subsequently asserted a more general jurisdiction extending to all teams in North American leagues.[219] At the same time, Canadian labour Boards have had a role.

## 3. Canadian Labour Law[220]

The cross-border operation of the major leagues presents developing issues as to how local law may apply to Canadian-based teams. The United States and Canada share a similar model of labour relations[221] except that in Canada primary constitutional jurisdiction in labour law belongs to the Provinces,[222] and federal law applies only to certain employees in the public sector or in federally regulated industries. The federal presence is felt mainly through immigration regulations that consider "whether the employment of a foreign national is likely to adversely affect the settlement of any labour dispute in progress or the employment of any person involved in the dispute."[223] The Montreal Expos did, however, receive a waiver of an earlier rule barring foreign workers when it appeared that replacement players would be used during MLB's 1995 season.[224]

In Ontario, the *Labour Relations Act, 1995*[225] ("OLRA") seeks to encourage collective bargaining and the settlement of differences and requires disputes over the interpretation or application of a collective agreement to be resolved by arbitration (see, s. 48). The establishment of a collective regime normally

---

[218]  236 N.L.R.B. 1317 (No. 181) (1978), affd 613 F.2d 1379 (5th Cir., 1980). See also, *Orca Bay Hockey Limited Partnership v. British Columbia Chapter of the National Hockey League Players' Assn.*, [2005] B.C.L.R.B.D. No. 125, BCLRB No. B127/2005 (B.C.L.R.B.) (NHL conceded that NLRB had no jurisdiction to make an order against certification application in Canada).

[219]  See: *Silverman v. Major League Baseball Player Relations Committee, Inc.*, 880 F.Supp. 246 (S.D.N.Y.), affd 67 F.3d 1054 (2nd Cir., 1995); *National Basketball Assn.*, Case No. 2-RD-1354 (July 26, 1996). See further, W.B. Gould, "Globalization in Collective Bargaining, Baseball, and Matsuzaka: Labor and Antitrust Law on the Diamond" (2007) 28 Comp. Lab.L. & Policy J. 283 at 301-06.

[220]  See, G.W. Adams, *Canadian Labour Law*, 2d ed. (Aurora, ON: Canada Law Book Inc., 1993 - supplements, 2008).

[221]  *North American Soccer League*, 236 N.L.R.B. 1317 (No. 181) (1978) at 1322-25.

[222]  *Toronto Electricity Commissioners v. Snider*, [1925] A.C. 396, [1925] 2 D.L.R. 5 (P.C.). On a complaint to the Alberta Labour Relations Board alleging collusion in collective bargaining, see, *Forbes v. Eagleson*, 228 F.3d 471, at 476 (3rd Cir., 2000), affg 19 F.Supp.2d 352 (E.D.Penn., 1998).

[223]  *Immigration and Refugee Protection Regulations*, S.O.R./2002-227, s. 203(3)(f).

[224]  See, "Expos can use replacements" *The Globe and Mail* (Toronto: March 2, 1995) at C8 (non-enforcement of S.O.R./78-172, s. 20(1)(b)(i)).

[225]  S.O. 1995, c. 1, Sch. A. On a dispute related to terminations, see, *National Hockey League v. National Hockey League Officials' Assn. (Ernst Grievance)*, [2000] O.L.A.A. No. 838 (Ont., Kaplan, arb.).

precludes individual negotiations,[226] and once recognized as the exclusive bargaining agent only the union or association has standing to apply for judicial review of an arbitrator's decision. Individual employees may, however, challenge a decision in cases or unfair representation or where the interests of the employee and union are in conflict.[227] The jurisdiction of the Ontario Labour Relations Board ("OLRB") applies to grievances arising from employment that has a substantial connection with Ontario; the Board lacks jurisdiction where a player is employed by an American team and makes only occasional visits to the Province for the purpose of away games.[228]

By section 17 of the OLRA, it is the duty of employers to bargain in good faith with a certified union. The attempted organization by NHL players in 1957 included a certification application to the OLRB on behalf of players with the Toronto Maple Leafs,[229] and during the 2004-05 lockout there were applications to the labour Boards in Quebec[230] and British Columbia. Normally, however, bargaining proceeds on a league-wide basis after associations such as the CFLPA and NHLPA have been recognized voluntarily by teams. In *Orca Bay Hockey Limited Partnership v. National Hockey League*,[231] the British Columbia Labour Relations Board ("BCLRB") declined to certify players on the Vancouver Canucks as a separate unit to be known as the BC-NHLPA. The BCLRB distinguished the case of a branch plant company and held that the established system of league-wide bargaining was the appropriate structure because both the employing team and the employees were integrated into the wider operations of the league. The statutory duties of the Board included encouraging cooperation and fostering "the employment of workers in economically viable businesses",[232] and it was persuaded that the league-wide settlement in 2005 and the new CBA would enhance competitiveness.

---

[226] See, for example, *Loyalist College of Applied Arts and Technology v. Ontario Public Service Union*, [2003] O.J. No. 743, 63 O.R. (3d) 641, 225 D.L.R. (4th) 123 (Ont. C.A.).

[227] See, *Yashin v. National Hockey League*, [2000] O.J. No. 3306, 192 D.L.R. (4th) 747 (Ont. S.C.J.) (interests of NHLPA were not averse to those of Alexei Yashin). See, Chapter 9, "National Hockey League", section B, 3.

[228] *Riendeau v. National Hockey League Players' Assn.*, [2001] O.L.R.D. No. 4832 (Ont.L.R.B.) (Vincent Riendeau apparently retired and lost guaranteed contract with the Boston Bruins; "The fact that the NHLPA has its head office in Ontario does not give this Board a nexus". (at para. 11)).

[229] See: "NHL Refuses Players' Demands" *The Globe and Mail* (Toronto: September 24, 1957) at 17; "Lawyer Mound Scoffs at Report 'Union' Wavering" *The Globe and Mail* (Toronto: November 20, 1957) at 17; "OLRB Opens Hearings As Leaf Players Seek Ruling on Certification" *The Globe and Mail* (Toronto: November 22, 1957) at 14; D. Cruise & A. Griffiths, *Net Worth: Exploding the Myths of Pro Hockey* (Toronto: Viking, 1991) at 107-12. See further, Chapter 9, "National Hockey League", section B, 1.

[230] See, *Association des joueurs de la Ligue nationale de Hockey c. Club de hockey Canadien inc.*, [2005] D.C.R.T.Q. no 354, 2005 QCCRT 354 (Comm. des relations du travail).

[231] [2007] B.C.L.R.B.D. No. 172, BCLRB No. B172/2007 (B.C.L.R.B.), reconsidering [2006] B.C.L.R.B.D. No. 138, BCLRB No. 138/2006 (B.C.L.R.B.). See also, *Orca Bay Hockey Limited Partnership v. British Columbia Chapter of the National Hockey League Players' Assn.*, [2005] B.C.L.R.B.D. No. 125, BCLRB No. B127/2005 (B.C.L.R.B.) (adjournment denied).

[232] *Labour Relations Code*, R.S.B.C. 1996, c. 244, s. 2(b), (d).

Provincial labour laws occasionally modify economic tactics available to particular teams. In 1995, the NHL teams in Ontario[233] and Alberta[234] were obliged to maintain the existing agreement and could not immediately implement the Commissioner's provocative roll-back of training camp benefits.[235] The tactic of bringing in replacement workers is also subject to local variations. Section 73.1 of the OLRA formerly banned the use of replacements[236] during any lockout or during a strike approved by 60 per cent of voting employees, and the Toronto Blue Jays duly planned in 1995 to play regular-season "home" games in Dunedin, Florida. The applications for certification in 2005 by the players of the Montreal Canadiens and the Vancouver Canucks were designed to preclude replacements since their use is prohibited under the labour codes of Quebec[237] and British Columbia[238] where the union is certified and where a lawful strike or lockout is in progress. Fragmented provincial jurisdiction can, however, have little overall effect in resolving league-wide disputes. For example, a lawful shut-down in the United States might be illegal in Ontario because of the failure to follow the mandatory conciliation process required by section 79 of the OLRA. The OLRB could not, however, grant a remedy relating to games or pre-season training camps located in the United States, and even if a team was required to stay in operation in Ontario it would be deprived of American-based opponents.

Game officials do not have quite the same need for a playing opposition. At the end of MLB's player strike in 1995, attention turned to the four-month old lock-out of the umpires, and the umpires' association invoked Ontario law to prevent the use of replacement officials in games to be played at the SkyDome. In *Assn. of Major League Umpires v. American League*,[239] the OLRB denied a bizarre claim by the umpires that they were Blue Jays employees but held that working relations between the umpires' association and the American and National Leagues were under provincial jurisdiction, so that the lockout was unlawful in the absence of the conciliation process required by the OLRA. The

---

[233] See, *Labour Relations Act*, R.S.O. 1990, c. L.2, ss. 53(2), 54, 81 (now, *Labour Relations Act*, S.O. 1995, c. 1, Sch. A, ss. 58(2), 59, 86).

[234] See, *Labour Relations Code*, S.A. 1988, c. L-1.2, s. 128 (now, *Labour Relations Code*, R.S.A. 2000, c. L-1, s. 130).

[235] See: "NHLPA furious at league" *The Globe and Mail* (Toronto: August 9, 1994) at C6; "Angry NHL players await Bettman's word" *The Globe and Mail* (Toronto: August 18, 1994) at F5; "Lockout delayed as NHL gives green light to open camps" *The Globe and Mail* (Toronto: September 1, 1994) at C6; "NHL rollbacks face uneven application" *The Globe and Mail* (Toronto: September 3, 1994) at A15. See Chapter 9, "National Hockey League", section B, 3.

[236] *Labour Relations Act*, R.S.O. 1990, c. L.2, am. 1992, c. 21, s. 32. See, J.J. Lippner, "Replacement Players for the Toronto Blue Jays?: Striking the Appropriate Balance Between Replacement Worker Law in Ontario, Canada and the United States" (1995) 18 Fordham Int. L. J. 2026.

[237] *Labour Code*, R.S.Q., c. C-27, s. 109.1. But see, *I.A.T.S.E., Stage Local 56 v. Société de la Place des Arts de Montréal*, [2004] S.C.J. No. 4, [2004] 1 S.C.R. 43 (S.C.C.) (company shut down services which were then provided by others).

[238] *Labour Relations Code*, R.S.B.C. 1996, c. 244, s. 68.

[239] [1995] OLRB REP. April, 540 (effect of declaration postponed to allow further negotiation before the Jays' next home series). See also, *National Basketball Assn.*, [1995] OLRB REP. November, 1389 (lockout of NBA referees held unlawful; league required to use NBRA members).

engagement of replacement umpires was likewise unlawful, and the Leagues and Blue Jays were required to "conduct business as usual". The parties then quickly settled on a new five-year agreement, although the OLRB's decision was just one of many factors hastening a solution throughout MLB.

## E.   INTERNATIONAL TRANSFER AGREEMENTS

The IIHF recognises that without compensation being paid for players trained by a club who move to a new club before the old club has recovered its investment, development of the sport will be severely curtailed. The IIHF is working with its advisors and intends to replace the current system for compensation for players moving out of contract and replace it with a new system with worldwide applicability.[240]

As outlined in Chapter 3, "Organizations and Regulations",[241] transfers of players are subject to IIHF Bylaws and to the International Transfer Regulations (IT Reg.). Entry into the NHL has also been subject to the various versions of the "Memorandum of Agreement" between the NHL and the IIHF. Where agreements or arrangements limit international transfer, the restraint may be challenged as a breach of the applicable system of law. Given hockey's important base in Europe, the relevant standards include the fundamental laws of the European Union ("EU")[242] relating to mobility rights and competition policy. Countries such as Sweden, Finland and the Czech Republic are members of the EU.

The European Economic Community ("EEC") was founded by six original Member States following the signing of the Treaty of Rome in 1957. The EU was established when the Maastricht Treaty came into force in 1993, and by 2008 full membership had risen to 27 countries. Since the Treaty of Amsterdam in 1997, Member States now subscribe to the European Community ("EC") Treaty, which incorporated new provisions and a renumbering of previous articles. Further integration and reform are now in progress as a result of the Treaty of Lisbon in 2007. In relation to sport, significant decisions have been rendered by the ECJ — the Court of Justice of the European Communities (or European Union).

By article 39 of the EC Treaty (formerly, article 48),

1. Freedom of movement for workers shall be secured within the Community.
2. Such freedom of movement shall entail the abolition of any discrimination based on nationality between workers of the Member States as regards employment, remuneration and other conditions of work and employment.

---

[240]   IIHF International Transfer Regulations (July 2008), 12. See now, IIHF International Transfer Regulations (May 2009).

[241]   See Chapter 3, "Organizations and Regulations", section C, 2, a.

[242]   See, J. Steiner, L. Woods & C. Twigg-Flesner, *EU Law*, 9th ed. (Oxford: Oxford University Press, 2006).

Articles 81 and 82 (formerly 85, 86) deal with anti-competitive behaviour. Article 81 prohibits,

> all agreements between undertakings, decisions by associations of undertakings and concerted practices which may affect trade between Member States and which have as their object or effect the prevention, restriction or distortion of competition within the common market.

Article 82 provides that,

> Any abuse by one or more undertakings of a dominant position within the common market or in a substantial part of it shall be prohibited as incompatible with the common market insofar as it may affect trade between Member States.

Article 81 requires agreement between different parties; the abuse of dominant position in article 82 may be satisfied by unilateral action.

The EC Treaty applies to economic aspects of sport organization in the EU,[243] although the ECJ and other institutions recognize that some dispensation is needed for sport because of the specific characteristics of the activities and competitions.[244] The ECJ did, however, hold in 2006 that,

> the mere fact that a rule is purely sporting in nature does not have the effect of removing from the scope of the Treaty the person engaging in the activity governed by that rule or the body which has laid it down.[245]

A decade earlier, treaty rights had been famously upheld in a decision that transformed association football.

In 1995, in *Union Royale Belge des Sociétés de Football Association ASBL v. Bosman*,[246] the ECJ addressed the status of a Belgian soccer player who was unable to move from the Belgian to the French football association because his former team, RC Liège, did not request a transfer certificate. After Jean-Marc

---

[243] See: *Walgrave and Koch v. Association Union Cycliste Internationale*, [1974] E.C.R. 1405 (nationality rules); *Donà v. Mantero*, [1976] E.C.R. 1333 (nationality rules in football); *Deliège v. Ligue Francophone de Judo et Disciplines Associées*, [2000] E.C.R. I-2549 (team selection); *Meca-Medina and Majcen v. Commission (Competition)*, [2006] E.C.R. I-6991 (anti-doping rules). Under article 2 of the EC Treaty, the "task" of the Community includes developing "economic activities". The freedom to provide services is protected in article 49.

[244] See: R. Parrish, *Sports Law and Policy in the European Union* (Manchester: Manchester University Press, 2003); S. Weatherill, *European Sports Law: Collected Papers* (The Hague: TMC Asser Press, 2007); R. Parrish & S. Miettinen, *The Sporting Exception in European Law* (The Hague: TMC Asser Press, 2008).

[245] *Meca-Medina and Majcen v. Commission (Competition)*, [2006] E.C.R. I-6991, at para. 27.

[246] [1996] 1 C.M.L.R. 645 (E.C.J.). See: R. Blanpain & R. Inston, *The Bosman Case: The End of the Transfer System?* (London: Sweet & Maxwell, 1996); A. Caiger & S. Gardiner (eds.), *Professional Sport in the EU: Regulation and Re-regulation* (The Hague: The Asser Press, 2000); D. McArdle, *From Boot Money to Bosman: Football, Society and the Law* (London: Cavendish Publishing, 2000); J-J. Gouguet (ed.), *Le sport professionnel après l'arrêt Bosman: Une analyse économique internationale* (Limoges: Presses Universitaires de Limoges, 2004).

Bosman's contract with RC Liège had expired, he was placed on their transfer list and then signed with US Dunkerque of the French second division. A compensation fee was concluded between the two teams, but RC Liège developed doubts about Dunkerque's ability to pay and declined to initiate the transfer through the national associations. Bosman found himself suspended by RC Liège, unable to work for the team of his choice and effectively boycotted by other European teams. The ECJ determined that payments restraining transfers between Member States by players who were no longer under contract were contrary to article 48(1) of the Treaty of Rome (now, article 39 of the EC Treaty) in that they limited freedom of movement by workers. Rules limiting the employment of players who were nationals of other Member States were also found to be contrary to the former article 48(2) in that they constituted discrimination based on nationality.[247] Having decided the case on this basis, the court found it unnecessary to consider the transfer restrictions from the point of view of competition law.

The ECJ in *Bosman* acknowledged that an alternative compensation system might be justifiable by "the need to maintain financial and competitive balance between clubs and to support the search for talent":

> In view of the considerable social importance of sporting activities and in particular football in the Community, the aims of maintaining a balance between clubs by preserving a certain degree of equality and uncertainty as to results and of encouraging the recruitment and training of young players must be accepted as legitimate.[248]

The existing transfer system was not, however, an adequate means of achieving these aims. It did not preclude the richest teams from securing the best players, and fees based on the uncertain prospect of a successful future career were unrelated to the actual costs of player development.

The effect of *Bosman* was to liberalize the migration of players at the club-level of competition. Following the decision, there was a period of consultation with institutions of the EU, and in 2001 and 2005 the Fédération Internationale de Football Association ("FIFA") and the Union Européenne de Football Association ("UEFA") developed new transfer rules in an attempt to comply with EU standards.[249] One prominent critic was not impressed, finding the new system incompatible with laws and Conventions dealing with,

---

[247] On limitations based on nationality, see also: *Lehtonen v. Fédération Royale Belge des Sociétés de Basket-ball ASBL*, [2000] E.C.R. I-2681 (transfer deadlines); *Deutscher Handballbund v. Kolpak*, [2003] E.C.R. I-4135 (registration as non-EU player); *Simutenkov v. Ministerio de Educación y Cultura and Real Federación Española Fútbol*, [2005] E.C.R. I-2579 (registration as non-EU player).

[248] *Union Royale Belge des Sociétés de Football Association ASBL v. Bosman*, [1996] 1 C.M.L.R. 645 (E.C.J.), at paras. 105-06.

[249] See: FIFA Regulations for the Status and Transfer of Players (2005); S. Van den Bogaert, *Practical Regulation of the Mobility of Sportsmen in the EU Post Bosman* (The Hague: Kluwer Law International, 2005); S. Gardiner et al. (eds.), *Sports Law*, 3d ed. (London: Cavendish Publish-

human trafficking ... freedom of labour ... the Rights of the Child ... free movement of workers ... [and] competition law.[250]

Under the system, disputes relating to transfer and compensation are referred to the FIFA Dispute Resolution Chamber ("DRC")[251] and the Court of Arbitration for Sport ("CAS"),[252] and a particular feature of the regulations is that compensation is payable to teams that contributed to a player's training where the player signed a first professional contract before the age of 23.[253] Since *Bosman* disallows compensation where the player's employment contract has expired, many European teams responded by signing players for longer terms and incorporated option clauses allowing the unilateral renewal of contracts. The length of contracts and the compensation payable in cases of premature termination are now subject to FIFA regulations and the dispute resolution processes.[254] *Bosman* therefore initiated a preliminary phase of revisions to the labour market and transfer rules. Some commentators anticipate that professional soccer players in Europe will eventually follow the North American model and negotiate comprehensive collective bargaining agreements ("CBA") through "Social Dialogue".[255] In the EU, there is ongoing re-regulation of the labour and other markets as sports are required to comply with the European legal order.[256]

In hockey, the IT Regulations (2009) on the transfer of professionals mainly relate to players who are under contract. IT Reg. II 4.4 provides that,

> The transfer of a player during the term of his contract will not be subject to any restrictive regulations, provided that an agreement is reached between all three parties concerned (the former club, the player and the new club).

Where a player transfers to another jurisdiction, disputes and litigation commonly focus on alleged continuing obligations of the player and the validity

---

ing, 2006) at 368-72, 500-19, 576-88; J-C. Drolet, "Extra Time: Are the New FIFA Transfer Rules Doomed?" [2006] (1-2) Int. Sports L.J. 66.

[250] R. Blanpain, *The Legal Status of Sportsmen and Sportswomen under International, European and Belgian National and Regional Law* (The Hague: Kluwer Law International, 2003) at 60. See also, R. Blanpain, *European Labour Law*, 10th Revised ed. (The Hague: Kluwer Law International, 2006) at 325-31.

[251] See, F. de Weger, *The Jurisprudence of the FIFA Dispute Resolution Chamber* (The Hague: TMC Asser Press, 2008).

[252] See Chapter 2, "Legal Fundamentals and Equality Rights", sections A; C.

[253] See, M. Bakker, "The Training Compensation System" [2008] (1-2) Int.Sports L.J. 29.

[254] See, for example, *Wigan Athletic AFC, Ltd. v. Heart of Midlothian, P.L.C.*, CAS 2007/A/1298, 1299, 1300, January 30, 2008 (Andy Webster case).

[255] See: H.E. Meier, "From Bosman to Collective Bargaining Agreements? The Regulation of the Market for Professional Soccer Players" [2004] (3-4) Int. Sports L.J. 4; R.B. Martins, "Social Dialogue in the European Professional Football Sector: A European Legal Football Match Heading for Extra Time" [2004] (3-4) Int. Sports L.J. 17.

[256] See, S. Gardiner, R. Parrish & R. Siekmann (eds.), *EU, Sport, Law and Policy: Regulation, Re-regulation and Representation* (The Hague: TMC Asser Press, 2009).

of the original contract.[257] The agreements between the NHL and leading countries in the IIHF[258] have sought to avoid the problem of out-of-contract payments by providing general systems of compensation for player development, but this top-down structure is open to challenge under the competition law of the EU because it may not allow sufficient input from the affected teams.[259] Similar claims may also be based on the competition laws of North America. European teams may allege that the NHL agreements are anti-competitive in that they prevent individual deals,[260] and one player has brought an antitrust action complaining that an agreement with Sweden limited his right to negotiate with different teams.[261] International transfer agreements[262] present issues as to the extraterritorial application of antitrust and labour law. The involvement of the players' association is also important since the league will claim the labour exemption when the CBA incorporates rules about the import of foreign players.

---

[257]  See, Chapter 3, "Organizations and Regulations", section C, 2, a.

[258]  See, A.N. Wise & B.S. Meyer, *International Sports Law and Business* (The Hague: Kluwer Law International, 1997), Vol. 1 at 655-59. On transfers with "Non-Member Organizations", see now, IIHF International Transfer Regulations, I 5 (May 2009).

[259]  See, S. Weatherill, "Is the Pyramid Compatible with EC Law?" [2005] (3-4) Int. Sports L.J. 3.

[260]  See, C. Miller, "Hockey's Cold War - Russia's Defiance of the IIHF and the Evgeny Malkin Saga" (2007) 17.1 Seton Hall J. of Sports and Ent. L. 163 at 194-95.

[261]  On the action brought by Markus Naslund in 1993-94, see, A.N. Wise & B.S. Meyer, *International Sports Law and Business* (The Hague: Kluwer Law International, 1997), Vol. 1 at 668-9, Vol. 3 at 1162-65 (NHL agreement with Sweden prevented player from negotiating with NHL teams as a free agent). On the European hockey market, see, A.E. Reitz, "The NHL Lockout: The Trickle-Down Effect on European Hockey" (2006) 13 Sports Lawyers J. 179.

[262]  See: W.B. Gould, "Globalization in Collective Bargaining, Baseball and Matsuzaka: Labor and Antitrust Law on the Diamond" (2007) 28 Comp. Labor L. & Policy J. 283; J.P. Gleason, "From Russia with Love: The Legal Repercussions of the Recruitment and Contracting of Foreign Players in the National Hockey League" (2008) 56 Buffalo L. Rev. 599.

# Chapter 9

# NATIONAL HOCKEY LEAGUE

The plaintiff club's success was contingent on securing additional skilled men, and such men were scarce and difficult to secure. Further financial success is contingent on good management and on successful co-operation between the manager, the players, and the other clubs. It is also contingent on the whim of the public and their attitude towards hockey for that season.[1]

## A.  LEGAL HISTORY

### 1.  Origins: Rubbing Out the Competition

The NHL was born out of money troubles, clashes of personality and litigation. The undoubted founding father was Edward J. Livingstone (1884-1945),[2] who brought the team owners together and consolidated powers in the hands of the league president. This unusual unity came from a fierce determination that Livingstone would play no part in the league.

As noted in Chapter 1, "Lord Stanley and the Wednesday Nighters", from 1910 the dominant professional league in eastern Canada was the National Hockey Association ("NHA") which included teams in Ottawa, Montreal and Quebec.[3] The NHA added two franchises in Toronto for 1912 of which one was bought by the quarrelsome Livingstone in 1914. Livingstone was an experienced team manager in football and hockey who acquired the NHA's "Ontarios", subsequently renamed the "Shamrocks", and made use of the rink operated by the Arena Gardens Company. During 1914-15, the NHA faced operating difficulties and labour shortages associated with the Great War and suffered further losses of players as they were signed to the Pacific Coast Hockey Association ("PCHA"). In 1915, Livingstone resolved to consolidate operations in Toronto by also buying the "Blueshirts". By this time, he was in conflict with other teams in the league and with Arena Gardens, and the NHA had no intention of allowing him two votes at league meetings. The decision was then made to transfer his Shamrocks franchise to a military team, the 228th Battalion. When that unit was ordered overseas, the NHA met on February 11, 1917 and

---

[1]  *Toronto Hockey Club Ltd. v. Arena Gardens of Toronto Ltd.*, [1925] O.J. No. 88, [1925] 4 D.L.R. 546 at 550-51 (Ont. C.A.), *per* Masten J.A.

[2]  See, M. Holzman & J. Nieforth, *Deceptions and Doublecross: How the NHL Conquered Hockey* (Toronto: Dundurn Press, 2002).

[3]  See, J.C. Wong, *Lords of the Rinks: The Emergence of the National Hockey League, 1875-1936* (Toronto: University of Toronto Press, 2005) at 58-78, 160-68 (NHA constitution).

established a new schedule that also left out the Blueshirts.[4] In one of many court actions, Livingstone challenged this exclusion as a form of wrongful interference with his players' contracts. The decision of the trial judge to dismiss this action was confirmed on appeal, where it was noted that the scheduling rules of the NHA's constitution made no provision for one of the six members going out of business. The Divisional Court declined to issue an injunction and held that,

> the members of the association had power, acting honestly, to adopt a schedule leaving out one of their number...this was the only arrangement that could be carried out, with any reasonable hope of avoiding financial loss to the majority of the members and players.[5]

The NHL was formed at meetings beginning on November 22, 1917 at the Windsor Hotel in Montreal when four NHA teams met to reconstitute the association and formally abandon Livingstone's team. Frank Calder, the former treasurer and secretary of the NHA, was then elected as the first president of the NHL. The teams represented at the meeting were the Ottawa Senators, Montreal Wanderers, Montreal Canadiens and Quebec Bulldogs. The Quebec team withdrew before the inaugural season as the new league recognized the importance of retaining a stake in the Toronto market. A franchise was given to the Toronto Hockey Club of the Arena Gardens company (later, "Toronto Arenas") as one of the NHL's "original four". Livingstone now found himself with the sole team in the NHA and failed in an attempt to form a new association when the ice facilities in Toronto and Ottawa opted to go with the NHL.[6] He was, however, able to maintain a link with the NHL by entering into an agreement to transfer his players' contracts to Arena Gardens and receive a percentage of net profits. When the Arenas organization refused to return the players after the 1917-18 season, Livingstone brought actions for delivery of the contracts and for the loss of the services of seven players.[7] Both claims were upheld, with an award of CDN $20,000 for the first claim and further references to the Master to ascertain damages. These were originally assessed at CDN $100,000 based on an allowance of CDN $20,000 in profits over five years. A series of appeals resulted in this sum being reduced to CDN $10,000 as the appellate courts noted a recent suggested purchase price or capital value for Livingstone's franchise and questioned whether the profits made by the new

---

4   See, *Toronto Hockey Club Ltd. v. Ottawa Hockey Assn. Ltd.*, [1918] O.J. No. 293, 15 O.W.N. 145 (Ont. C.A.).

5   *Toronto Hockey Club Ltd. v. Ottawa Hockey Assn. Ltd.*, [1918] O.J. No. 293, 15 O.W.N. 145 at 145-46 (Ont. C.A.), *per* Ferguson J.A.

6   See, J.C. Wong, *Lords of the Rinks: The Emergence of the National Hockey League, 1875-1936* (Toronto: University of Toronto Press, 2005) at 77 (plan to create the "Canadian Hockey Association"and final meeting of the NHA).

7   *Toronto Hockey Club Ltd. v. Arena Gardens Ltd.*, [1920] O.J. No. 592, 17 O.W.N. 370 (Ont. H.C.J.), affd [1920] O.J. No. 227, 19 O.W.N. 119 (Ont. Div. Ct.). See, M. Holzman & J. Nieforth, *Deceptions and Doublecross: How the NHL Conquered Hockey* (Toronto: Dundurn Press, 2002) at 214-29.

team in Toronto were the appropriate basis of assessment.[8] Any success or venture by Livingstone was "speculative and contingent", and while his company had "7 good players, it had no ice and no league".[9] The Ontario Court of Appeal found the Arenas' conduct "utterly dishonest and despicable"[10] but was unable to find a legitimate basis for increasing the CDN $10,000 in damages. Both the Court of Appeal and the Privy Council[11] were prepared to accept that leagues could eliminate franchises at will and use their influence to exclude Livingstone from playing facilities.

The NHL was reduced to three teams in its opening season when fire destroyed the Montreal Arena in January 1918, forcing the withdrawal of the Wanderers. President Calder realized the need for a four-team operation, so that a Quebec franchise was re-established for the 1919-20 season. By 1920, the Toronto franchise was renamed the St. Patricks and was in danger of losing access to the Arena Gardens facility after it came under the management of an ally of Livingstone, Percy Quinn. There was also the prospect of Livingstone and Quinn organizing a new association that would include Hamilton. The NHL preempted the threat by dropping Quebec from the schedule and accepting a new franchise in the steel city. The Hamilton Tigers duly formed part of the league from 1920 to 1925.[12] Livingstone continued as a thorn in the side of the NHL for many years by attempting to start new leagues and launching further actions against team owners. His challenges eventually petered out as the NHL expanded, achieved greater economic power and rose to a dominant position in the hockey hierarchy.

By the mid-1920s, the NHL recognized the business potential of the northeastern United States where there was a flourishing consumer market and a demand for commercial entertainment.[13] For the 1924-25 season, the league added the Boston Bruins, together with the Montreal Maroons as the new team of that city's English community.[14] The Pittsburgh Pirates and New York Americans followed in 1925, the Americans being purchased by bootlegger "Big Bill" Dwyer who acquired the suspended Hamilton players.[15] An amendment to the NHL constitution in 1926 allowed new teams to be admitted

---

[8]    *Toronto Hockey Club Ltd. v. Arena Gardens of Toronto Ltd.*, [1924] O.J. No. 53, [1924] 4 D.L.R. 384 (Ont. H.C.J.), affd [1925] O.J. No. 88, [1925] 4 D.L.R. 546 (Ont. C.A.), affd [1926] 4 D.L.R. 1 (J.C.P.C.).

[9]    *Toronto Hockey Club Ltd. v. Arena Gardens of Toronto Ltd.*, [1925] O.J. No. 88, [1925] 4 D.L.R. 546 at 550-51 (Ont. C.A.), *per* Masten J.A.

[10]   *Toronto Hockey Club Ltd. v. Arena Gardens of Toronto Ltd.*, [1925] O.J. No. 88, [1925] 4 D.L.R. 546 at 554 (Ont. C.A.).

[11]   *Toronto Hockey Club Ltd. v. Arena Gardens of Toronto Ltd.*, [1926] 4 D.L.R. 1 (J.C.P.C.).

[12]   See, S. Wesley with D. Wesley, *Hamilton's Hockey Tigers* (Toronto: James Lorimer & Co., 2005). On recent attempts to place a team in Hamilton, see Chapter 8, "Competition Law and Labour Law", sections A, 4; C, 4.

[13]   See, R. Gruneau & D. Whitson, *Hockey Night in Canada: Sport, Identities, and Cultural Politics* (Toronto: Garamond Press, 1993) at 92-103.

[14]   See, W. Brown, *The Montreal Maroons: The Forgotten Stanley Cup Champions* (Montreal: Véhicule Press, 1999).

[15]   See Chapter 9, "National Hockey League", section B, 1.

on a two-thirds majority vote, so that by 1926-27 the league operated with 10 teams, including the New York Rangers, Detroit Cougars and Chicago Blackhawks. At the same time, the NHL assumed a monopoly position in major league hockey with the collapse of the Western Canada Hockey League, and the league's product was enhanced when it had the choice of the best playing talent from the western teams. Since 1927, the Stanley Cup championship has been determined by the playoffs of the NHL.[16]

The NHL further consolidated its controlling position through its sponsorship agreements with amateur hockey[17] and affiliation agreements with minor professional leagues.[18] The strategy of bringing professional organizations into the fold finally saw off Edward J. Livingstone after he had acquired the Chicago Cardinals of the American Hockey Association ("AHA"). In 1927, the NHL insisted that its recognition of the AHA was conditional on Livingstone's absence, and his franchise was duly terminated. When four of his players were assigned to the NHL's Blackhawks, Livingstone sued team owner Frederick McLaughlin and two of his associates alleging interference with the players' contracts.[19] Three years later, this case foundered in allegations of jury tampering and declarations of mistrial, and Livingstone uncharacteristically withdrew the action. With no record of a settlement, the leading commentators have asked whether, "Instead of cash, could he have been on the receiving end of threats from Chicagoland gangsters?"[20] (The AHA (later, AHL) was promoted by the transplanted Canadian entrepreneur, James E. Norris, who held the Chicago Shamrocks. Norris subsequently gained entry into the NHL which he turned into a fiefdom of his friends and associates as the "Norris House League".[21] The Norris family held interests in the teams or arenas in Chicago, Detroit and New York and made particular use of the facilities for professional boxing, where the entourage of J.D. Norris Jr. was especially dubious.[22])

The expanded NHL was unable to sustain the economic effects of the Great Depression and the Second World War, so that it lost the Pittsburgh-Philadelphia team in 1931, the Montreal Maroons in 1938 and the New York Americans in 1942. The Ottawa Senators suspended operations for the 1931-32 season,

---

[16]   On the NHL's claim to the Stanley Cup, see Chapter 1, "Lord Stanley and the Wednesday Nighters".

[17]   See Chapter 3, "Organizations and Regulations", section A, 1.

[18]   See, J.C. Wong, *Lords of the Rinks: The Emergence of the National Hockey League, 1875-1936* (Toronto: University of Toronto Press, 2005) at 102-20.

[19]   *Livingstone v. McLaughlin, Foster and Keough*, U.S. District Court, Chicago, Case No. 36839 (1927).

[20]   M. Holzman & J. Nieforth, *Deceptions and Doublecross: How the NHL Conquered Hockey* (Toronto: Dundurn Press, 2002) at 309.

[21]   See, D. Cruise & A. Griffiths, *Net Worth: Exploding the Myths of Pro Hockey* (Toronto: Viking, 1991) at 26-77.

[22]   See, D. Cruise & A. Griffiths, *Net Worth: Exploding the Myths of Pro Hockey* (Toronto: Viking, 1991) at 43-51.

finished last in the standings in 1933 and 1934 and then expired in 1935 after relocating to St. Louis.[23] In 1932, the league governors,

> took steps to counter the Depression's effects by cutting roster sizes and instituting a team salary cap of $70,000. Moreover, they agreed to limit an individual player's salary to no more than $7500.[24]

At this period, the league's problems lay in the dire decline in revenue rather than player costs, since the labour market was now well under control. Exclusive rights to playing talent were held through the affiliation agreements and waiver and contract systems, including the power to loan players to the minors. Players submitted to autocratic rule in the workplace while playing a schedule that expanded to 70 games in 1950. Teams held unfettered disciplinary authority, limited players in their commercial opportunities, exercised discretion in the grant of injury benefits and maintained a system of perpetual reservation that denied players any leverage or choice of team. The standard player's contract incorporated an annual undertaking by the team to offer a new contract, which the player agreed to accept subject to negotiation of salary or salary arbitration determined by the league president.[25] When concerted efforts occurred in 1957[26] to emancipate players, the average salary was CDN $7700, no more than 2.5 times that of the ordinary worker.[27]

Frank Calder served as league president until his death in 1943, having been well rewarded[28] by team owners for his efficiency in defeating Edward Livingstone. After a brief presidency by Mervyn (Red) Dutton, the position was given to Clarence Campbell who had experience as a referee, lawyer and army officer. From 1946 to 1977, Campbell faithfully served the team bosses, while presenting an image of unity and rationality in the league:

> Stately and dignified, Campbell personified integrity, wisdom and leadership, an image that has survived to this day. But as far as hockey was concerned, Campbell functioned as a servant...Campbell had no illusions about his position. He carefully described himself as the manager or the executive officer who didn't formulate policy but carried out the wishes of the owners.[29]

---

[23] See, J.C. Wong, *Lords of the Rinks: The Emergence of the National Hockey League, 1875-1936* (Toronto: University of Toronto Press, 2005) at 121-32.

[24] J.C. Wong, *Lords of the Rinks: The Emergence of the National Hockey League, 1875-1936* (Toronto: University of Toronto Press, 2005) at 131.

[25] See, *Philadelphia World Hockey Club, Inc. v. Philadelphia Hockey Club, Inc.*, 351 F. Supp. 462 at 474-76, 482 (E.D. Pa., 1972). See further, Chapter 9, "National Hockey League", section A, 2.

[26] See Chapter 9, "National Hockey League", section B, 1.

[27] See, M. Lavoie, *Avantage numérique: L'argent et la Ligue nationale de hockey* (Hull: Éditions Vents d'Ouest, 1997) at 189-90.

[28] See, J.C. Wong, *Lords of the Rinks: The Emergence of the National Hockey League, 1875-1936* (Toronto: University of Toronto Press, 2005) at 75, 81.

[29] D. Cruise & A. Griffiths, *Net Worth: Exploding the Myths of Pro Hockey* (Toronto: Viking, 1991) at 41-42.

From 1943 to 1967, the NHL operated with its surviving core of six teams: Montreal Canadiens, Toronto Maple Leafs, Boston Bruins, New York Rangers, Chicago Blackhawks and Detroit Red Wings. The Leafs and the Canadiens began to enhance their wealth with television money during the 1950s, and the league held contracts with CBS from 1956 to 1958. The new medium could best be exploited by further expansion into the United States, but the league resisted occasional applications for new teams in Cleveland, Los Angeles and San Francisco. In 1967, the prospect of competition from a rival league eventually induced the addition of six American franchises which formed a western division. Each new team was permitted to draft 20 established players, and the sponsorship system was replaced by the amateur draft with entry set at age 20. A further four franchises, including the Vancouver Canucks, followed in 1970 and 1971, raising the total haul from expansion fees to USD $40 million and significantly reducing the attractive locations available to an impending rival league.[30]

## 2. World Hockey Association

The NHL's monopoly was disturbed in 1972 when the World Hockey Association ("WHA") was established with 12 franchises.[31] The inter-league competition saw salaries rise from an average of CDN $26,000 in 1971 to CDN $96,000 in 1977 as players enjoyed "the greatest boon to [their] well-being since the invention of the protective aluminium cup".[32] When players jumped to the WHA, NHL teams were usually denied preliminary injunctions because they could show neither "irreparable harm" nor any likelihood that NHL regulations and the standard player's contract ("SPC") were valid under antitrust law:

> ...the record establishes that this integrated group of contracts, constitutions, by-laws and agreements, all of which are in evidence, and which in their totality run to hundreds of pages of legal verbiage, effectively and totally control the careers of any hockey player in the United States or Canada...it would be unrealistic to rule that the Bruins have sustained their legal burden of showing that there is a probability that this tangled web of legal instruments will not be found to restrain trade in professional hockey.[33]

---

[30] The expansion of the NHL and formation of the WHA hastened the end for the minor professional WHL; see, J.C. Stott, *Ice Warriors: The Pacific Coast/ Western Hockey League, 1948-1974* (Surrey: Heritage House Publishing, 2008).

[31] See: G. Davidson & B. Libby, *Breaking the Game Wide Open* (New York: Atheneum, 1974) at 117-241; R.A. Eagleson & S. Young, *Power Play: The Memoirs of Hockey Czar Alan Eagleson* (Toronto: McClelland & Stewart, 1991) at 132-44; E. Willes, *The Rebel League: The Short and Unruly Life of the World Hockey Association* (Toronto: McClelland & Stewart, 2004).

[32] D. Cruise & A. Griffiths, *Net Worth: Exploding the Myths of Pro Hockey* (Toronto: Viking, 1991) at 268; on the WHA and the 1979 merger, see, 268-92.

[33] *Boston Professional Hockey Assn., Inc. v. Gerry Cheevers Boston Professional Hockey Assn., Inc.*, 348 F.Supp. 261 at 267 (D. Mass. 1972), *per* Caffrey C.J.; remanded 472 F.2d 127 (1st

Only the New York Islanders had a minor success when their selection in the 1972 expansion draft was prevented from playing in the WHA for one year. Garry Peters was found to have raised "the antitrust question only when it appears to be no longer in his economic interest to comply with his agreement".[34] Peters could elect to play the option year obtained by the Islanders but was not obliged to sign a contract allowing further renewal.

The most detailed analysis of the NHL's affiliation structures occurred in *Philadelphia World Hockey Club, Inc. v. Philadelphia Hockey Club, Inc.*,[35] a consolidation of actions[36] arising from the signings in the WHA, including Winnipeg's acquisition of Bobby Hull after teams in the league agreed to provide pro-rata shares of his USD $1 million salary. Higginbotham D.J. found that the reserve clause, by-laws and agreements had the effect of monopolizing and controlling the market for major league players contrary to section 2 of the *Sherman Antitrust Act*. He was not satisfied that the league's practices were a combination in restraint of trade under section 1 and recognized the commercial need to offer competitive games between competent playing opponents;[37] he did, however, note that the reserve clause had failed in its supposed purpose of maintaining parity in the winning of championships.[38] The league could not rely on antitrust immunity through the "labour exemption" because the reserve clause had been "fathered" by the NHL rather than established through collective bargaining with the players' association; the league was, furthermore, seeking to enforce restraints against outside competitors.[39]

The WHA, on posting a bond of USD $2.5 million, was granted a preliminary injunction to restrain teams in the NHL from taking action to enforce the reserve clause. Higginbotham D.J. held that the WHA would suffer irreparable damage if it was uncertain that superstars such as Hull could remain with the new operation. The potential loss to the established league was less serious:

> The NHL is no shaky institution which will collapse if it loses a few superstars or even many average players during the pendency of this preliminary injunction. The NHL is merely sustaining the fate which monopolists must face when they can no longer continue their prior total dominance of the market. For the reality of today

---

Cir., 1972). See also, *Nassau Sports v. Hampson*, 355 F.Supp. 733 (D. Minn., 1972). On antitrust law, see Chapter 8, "Competition Law and Labour Law", section C.

[34] *Nassau Sports v. Peters*, 352 F.Supp. 870 at 881 (E.D.N.Y., 1972), *per* Neaher D.J. The Islanders paid a USD $6 million franchise fee that included the right to draft NHL players.

[35] 351 F.Supp. 462 (E.D. Pa., 1972).

[36] See, *In re Professional Hockey Antitrust Litigation*, 352 F.Supp. 1405 (J.P.M.L., 1973), revd 531 F.2d 1188 (3rd Cir., 1976), revd (*sub nom. National Hockey League v. Metropolitan Hockey Club, Inc.*) 427 U.S. 639, 96 S. Ct. 2778 (1976).

[37] *Philadelphia World Hockey Club, Inc. v. Philadelphia Hockey Club, Inc.*, 351 F.Supp. 462 at 503-504 (E.D. Pa., 1972).

[38] *Philadelphia World Hockey Club, Inc. v. Philadelphia Hockey Club, Inc.*, 351 F.Supp. 462 at 486 (E.D. Pa., 1972).

[39] *Philadelphia World Hockey Club, Inc. v. Philadelphia Hockey Club, Inc.*, 351 F.Supp. 462 at 498-500 (E.D. Pa., 1972). Higginbotham D.J. noted (at 485) that "there does not appear to have been any 'collective bargaining' on the reserve clause except as to arbitration of salary".

is that the federal antitrust laws preclude the continued implementation of NHL President Campbell's fondest dream that it remain the *only* major professional hockey league operating from coast-to-coast in the United States and Canada.[40]

The WHA subsequently settled its antitrust claims and agreed not to challenge the one-year option and free agent compensation systems that the NHL inserted into the 1974 version of the SPC. By agreement between the two leagues, the WHA could contract with minor professional leagues, free agents could move between leagues, inter-league exhibition games were planned, and each side agreed to allow freer access to arenas.[41] The settlement required the NHL to reimburse the WHA's legal costs of USD $1.75 million.

Players now had the advantage of a competing league, but the WHA operated in perpetual crisis as teams floundered where they stood or migrated to new sites.[42] The financial malaise also began to be felt by NHL teams, and there were periodic attempts to arrange a merger.[43] The independent existence of the WHA finally ended in March 1979[44] when the NHL voted for "expansion" and accepted four teams at an entry fee of USD $6 million each: Edmonton Oilers, Winnipeg Jets, Quebec Nordiques and New England (Hartford) Whalers. The NHL players' association ("NHLPA") then asserted a power under the collective agreement to re-open bargaining in the event of a "merger"[45] and initially sought half of the expansion fees and a less restrictive system of free agent compensation.[46] Although apparently bargaining from strength, the association then made a mysterious turn-around and accepted a three-year extension of the original agreement in exchange for increased pension contributions and other benefits.[47] This decision renewed

---

[40]   *Philadelphia World Hockey Club, Inc. v. Philadelphia Hockey Club, Inc.*, 351 F.Supp. 462 at 516-17 (E.D. Pa., 1972).

[41]   See, G. Davidson & B. Libby, *Breaking the Game Wide Open* (New York: Atheneum, 1974) at 228-29.

[42]   Of the WHA's total of 32 teams, the Cincinnati Stingers and Birmingham Bulls remained in operation in 1979 and were indemnified by the four other survivors. On franchise sales and owners' duties, see, *Professional Hockey Corp. v. World Hockey Assn.*, 143 Cal. App. 3d 410, 191 Cal. Rptr. 773 (C.A., 1983). See also, *Skalbania v. Simmons*, 443 N.E.2d 352 (C.A. Ind., 1982) (class action; holders of season tickets with Indianapolis Racers).

[43]   See: "Financial crisis hits 7 NHL clubs" *The Globe and Mail* (Toronto: December 8, 1976) at S1; "NHL agrees to take 6 from WHA" *The Globe and Mail* (Toronto: June 25, 1977) at 43.

[44]   See, *The Globe and Mail* (Toronto: March 31, 1979) at S2-S4, S12-13. On the draft of WHA players under the "Plan of Fifth Expansion", see, *Goulet v. National Hockey League*, [1980] R.P. 122 (Que. S.C.).

[45]   See, CBA of NHL, 1975–1980 (May 4, 1976), article 9.03(c).

[46]   See: "Deadline of July 1 will halt expansion, Eagleson suggests" *The Globe and Mail* (Toronto: June 6, 1977) at S3; "NHL players plan law suit over merger" *The Globe and Mail* (Toronto: March 27, 1979) at 35; "NHL and players far apart in talks on agreement" *The Globe and Mail* (Toronto: May 10, 1979) at 47; "Stormy talks loom at NHL meetings" *The Globe and Mail* (Toronto: June 2, 1979). See also, D. Clayton, *Eagle: The Life and Times of R. Alan Eagleson* (Toronto: Lester & Orpen Dennys, 1982) at 203-208.

[47]   See, "Owners, players settle" *The Globe and Mail* (Toronto: June 7, 1979). For conflicting accounts of the value of the new benefits, see: R.A. Eagleson & S. Young, *Power Play: The Memoirs of Hockey Czar Alan Eagleson* (Toronto: McClelland & Stewart, 1991) at 144; D.

concerns about the effectiveness of the NHLPA and initiated an early attempt to challenge its leader, R. Alan Eagleson.

## B.  PLAYERS' ASSOCIATION

## 1.  To Form a More Perfect Union

Faced with a controlled labour market and limits on their earning power, players made occasional early attempts to improve working conditions. A union had been considered in the National Hockey Association to resist the salary cap and other collusive agreements,[48] and the Hamilton Tigers players of the NHL refused their services during the playoffs in 1925 in protest at not receiving extra money for an increased schedule.[49] The Tigers were fined and suspended but increased their earnings on the profits of Prohibition when re-hired for 1925-26 as the New York Americans. A pension or savings scheme began in the NHL in 1947 requiring players to contribute $900 a year from their salaries; the league contributed two-thirds of the proceeds of the annual all-star game and 25 cents for each admission to playoff games. Concern over the administration of the Pension Society and other financial issues prompted Ted Lindsay's famous attempt to organize in 1957.[50]

Lindsay announced the formation of the association in February 1957[51] and set the particular goal of sharing in recent television revenue of the league.[52] Nearly all players at first agreed to join in spite of intimidation[53] by teams, including the tactic of wholesale trading: Lindsay's reward was to be shifted from Detroit to Chicago. When the league refused to recognize the association or deal with its lawyers, certification proceedings were begun before provincial labour boards and the National Labor Relations Board.[54] After initially declaring

Cruise & A. Griffiths, *Net Worth: Exploding the Myths of Pro Hockey* (Toronto: Viking, 1991) at 286.

[48] See: C.L. Coleman, *The Trail of the Stanley, Vol. I, 1893-1926* (National Hockey League, 1966) at 202-205 (salary limit in 1910); D. Guay, *L'histoire du Hockey au Québec* (Chicoutimi: Les Éditions JCL, 1990) at 124 (inter-league agreements in 1913).

[49] See: M. Semiatycki, "The Stanley Cup Strike of 1925" in D. Diamond, ed., *The Official Stanley Cup Centennial Book* (Toronto: McClelland & Stewart, 1992) 60; M. Holzman & J. Nieforth, *Deceptions and Doublecross: How the NHL Conquered Hockey* (Toronto: Dundurn Press, 2002) at 241-58.

[50] See, D. Cruise & A. Griffiths, *Net Worth: Exploding the Myths of Pro Hockey* (Toronto: Viking, 1991) at 59-62, 74-112.

[51] See, "NHL players' association formed, Wings' Ted Lindsay is president" *The Globe and Mail* (Toronto: February 12, 1957) at 21.

[52] See: "Better Pension Sought" *The New York Times* (April 23, 1957) at 36; D. Parker, "The Hockey Rebellion" *Sports Illustrated* (October 28, 1957) at 19.

[53] See, "Intimidation by Smythe is charged" *The Globe and Mail* (Toronto: November 5, 1957) at 16.

[54] See: "NHL refuses players' demands" *The Globe and Mail* (Toronto: September 24, 1957) at 17; "NHL players' association threatening court action" *The Globe and Mail* (Toronto: September 25, 1957) at 17; "OLRB hearings open as Leaf players seek ruling on certification" *The Globe and Mail* (Toronto: November 22, 1957) at 14; "Unfair labor practice charge withdrawn

goodwill towards the league, the players filed a promising USD $3 million antitrust action claiming that the league had "monopolized and obtained complete domination and control and dictatorship" of professional hockey.[55] The campaign received a set-back in November 1957 when the Detroit players withdrew,[56] and the movement eventually collapsed in February 1958.[57] Team owners offered some minor improvements in benefits and agreed to form an Owner-Player Council on condition that the players discontinue the lawsuit and certification proceedings. The minimum salary was guaranteed at $7000, and there were increases in team pension contributions, playoff winnings and hospitalization and moving expenses; a player also received the theoretical right to judge his own fitness following injury. In general, players resumed their role as "underpaid serfs, hired to play hockey and keep [their] mouths shut".[58]

The NHLPA was finally recognized by the league in June 1967 after players were successfully recruited[59] by Alan Eagleson, a Toronto real estate lawyer and Conservative MLA who established initial contact with professional hockey by providing legal services to players. The "Eagle" then achieved fame by negotiating Bobby Orr's first contract and assisted players at Springfield in their protest against the unconventional working conditions maintained by Eddie Shore.[60] The formation of the NHLPA gave Eagleson the base to operate Sports Management Ltd. and other agency services, so that by 1979 his companies represented around 150 players.[61] The league did not resist the organizing effort for fear that more radical union leadership might take up the players' cause. Co-operative relations were first established with Clarence Campbell and then with John Ziegler who served as league president from 1977 to 1992 after Eagleson declined an offer of the position.

Eagleson's leadership of the NHLPA lasted until 1991 when he was succeeded by Robert Goodenow. The Eagleson years were marked by a conciliatory form of labour relations that maintained restrictions on free agency through successive uncontested renewals of the collective agreement.[62] The players and the Canadian sports media deferred to Eagleson's power, and outside

---

by hockey players" *The New York Times* (November 20, 1957) at 47. See also, Chapter 8, "Competition Law and Labour Law", section D.

[55]  See, "Hockey clubs hit in antitrust suit" *The New York Times* (October 11, 1957) at 38.

[56]  See, "Red Wings' squad quits association" *The New York Times* (November 13, 1957) at 45.

[57]  See: "Stanley Cup champs may each get $4,000 as result of meeting" *The Globe and Mail* (Toronto: February 6, 1958) at 26; "Hockey players win concessions" *The New York Times* (February 6, 1958) at 35.

[58]  D. Clayton, *Eagle: The Life and Times of R. Alan Eagleson* (Toronto: Lester & Orpen Dennys, 1982) at 69, quoting Ted Lindsay.

[59]  See: D. Clayton, *Eagle: The Life and Times of R. Alan Eagleson* (Toronto: Lester & Orpen Dennys, 1982) at 63-75; D. Cruise & A. Griffiths, *Net Worth: Exploding the Myths of Pro Hockey* (Toronto: Viking, 1991) at 203-11.

[60]  See: D. Clayton, *Eagle: The Life and Times of R. Alan Eagleson* (Toronto: Lester & Orpen Dennys, 1982) at 52-62; D. Cruise & A. Griffiths, *Net Worth: Exploding the Myths of Pro Hockey* (Toronto: Viking, 1991) at 160-65, 174-203.

[61]  On the representation of individual players by agents, see Chapter 9, "National Hockey League", section G.

[62]  See Chapter 9, "National Hockey League", section B, 3.

investigators provided only muted criticism of his autocratic style and thriving network of business interests.[63] Critics did, however, note the bitter separation from Bobby Orr.[64] Eagleson was usually depicted as a powerful entrepreneur openly functioning as leader of the association, agent, lawyer and organizer of the Canada Cup tournaments through joint ventures with the league and Hockey Canada. The merger agreement with the WHA prompted dissent by some players in 1980, but serious discontent developed after the round of bargaining in 1986 when the collective agreement limited free agency in exchange for "security" payments at age 55 to current players who accumulated 400 games during their careers. As noted in Chapter 3, "Organizations and Regulations", players initiated a report on Eagleson's activities in 1989,[65] and investigations by various agencies eventually led to criminal convictions in 1998.[66]

In 1995, labour relations during the 1970s and 1980s were the subject of a class action in the United States as a group of players relied on the *Racketeer Influenced and Corrupt Organizations Act* ("RICO")[67] and the *Labor Management Relations Act*.[68] This action was brought against Eagleson, various of his associates and the league. The civil complaint[69] in *Forbes v. Eagleson*[70] alleged that there had been private profiteering from the management of the Canada Cup with consequent losses of revenue for the players' association. It was further alleged that the arrangements led to the league exercising control and influence over the leadership of the association so that it failed to bargain for a free labour market, improved compensation and other benefits:

> In return for the NHL defendants' facilitation of and acquiescence in his self-enriching schemes, Eagleson allegedly betrayed the interests of players in collective bargaining. Without attempting to gain concessions in return or marshal the players' collective leverage, he agreed to the 1979 merger of the NHL and the World Hockey Association (WHA), lack of free agency, supplemental drafts, equalization rules, and non-disclosure of players' salaries; he acquiesced in the removal of player representatives from the board of the players' pension funds and in the owners' practice of offsetting pension contributions by the amount the player contributed via international hockey; and he agreed to inadequate minimum

---

[63]  See: D. Clayton, *Eagle: The Life and Times of R. Alan Eagleson* (Toronto: Lester & Orpen Dennys, 1982); J. Papanek & B. Brubaker, "The Man Who Rules Hockey" *Sports Illustrated* (July 2, 1984) at 60.

[64]  For later accounts, see: W. Houston & D. Shoalts, *Eagleson: The Fall of a Hockey Czar* (Toronto: McGraw-Hill Ryerson, 1993) at 53-72; R.A. Eagleson & S. Young, *Power Play: The Memoirs of Hockey Czar Alan Eagleson* (Toronto: McClelland & Stewart, 1991) at 186-96, 233-53.

[65]  See, R. Conway, *Game Misconduct: Alan Eagleson and the Corruption of Hockey* (Toronto: Macfarlane Walter & Ross, 1995, revised edition 1997) at 18-23, 35-42, 198-204.

[66]  See Chapter 3, "Organizations and Regulations", sections A, 3-4.

[67]  18 U.S.C. s. 1961 *et seq.* (2001).

[68]  29 U.S.C. s. 186 (2001).

[69]  See, A.N. Wise & B.S. Meyer, *International Sports Law and Business, vol. I* (The Hague: Kluwer International, 1997) at 98-102.

[70]  19 F.Supp. 2d 352 (E.D. Pa., 1998), affd 228 F.3d 471 (3rd Cir., 2000).

salaries. As a result, the players' compensation was substantially suppressed from what it would have been had they been represented by an un-compromised and aggressive union negotiator.[71]

This case was dismissed when the federal courts held that the players knew of the allegations against Eagleson by 1989 so that the action was barred under the applicable four-year statute of limitation.

Although *Forbes v. Eagleson* did not proceed on the substantive issues, a further action was litigated to a conclusion. In the first of the pension cases — *Bathgate v. National Hockey League Pension Society* — the NHLPA was again not a defendant, but the judgment found "moral shortcoming"[72] and clearly revealed the financial hardship of retired players.

## 2.   The Pension Cases

In response to the players' own proposal for a savings plan, the league formally constituted the NHL Pension Society in 1948 and originally included two player representatives on the five-person board of directors. To provide benefits, the contributions from the players and teams were invested with Manufacturers Life in a group annuity contract that provided for declarations of premium discounts or "experience rate credits" when a surplus was achieved in accumulated interest earnings. The plan was re-organized for tax purposes in 1966 through trust documents that affirmed vested benefits and prohibited any amendment providing for the use of funds "other than for the benefit of the Participants".[73]

In 1967, the league began negotiations with the NHLPA as the representative of current or active players, and in 1969 it was agreed that contributions to the plan would be made solely by the teams; the players then withdrew from the board of directors. When sizeable surpluses arose in 1970 and 1971, they were used to purchase additional annuity benefits for participants. In the first formal collective agreement in 1975, teams were required to raise their contribution so that a player's benefit at age 45 increased from $500 to $750 for each year of service.[74] The NHLPA agreed to pay half the increase from its share of revenue from international tournaments, although the teams were ultimately responsible if these proceeds were insufficient. The Canada Cup therefore served merely to reduce the liability of the teams, which enjoyed the further tax advantage of

---

[71]   *Forbes v. Eagleson*, 19 F.Supp. 2d 352 at 360 (E.D. Pa., 1998), *per* O'Neill D.J.; see also, 228 F.3d 471 at 476 (3rd Cir., 2000).

[72]   *Bathgate v. National Hockey League Pension Society*, [1992] O.J. No. 2168, 11 O.R. (3d) 449 at 530, 98 D.L.R. (4th) 326 (Ont. Gen. Div.), *per* Adams J., affd [1994] O.J. No. 265, 16 O.R. (3d) 761, 110 D.L.R. (4th) 609 (Ont. C.A.), leave to appeal refused [1994] S.C.C.A. No. 170, 114 D.L.R. (4th) vii (S.C.C.).

[73]   *Bathgate v. National Hockey League Pension Society*, [1992] O.J. No. 2168, 11 O.R. (3d) 449 at 467, 98 D.L.R. (4th) 326 at 344 (Ont. Gen. Div.).

[74]   See, CBA of NHL, 1975-80 (May 4, 1976), article 13.

deducting contributions to the Pension Society in full and then recovering reimbursement from the NHLPA.[75]

The claim by the retired players was based on allocations and trust amendments made in 1982-83 after interest earnings rose sharply. Without notifying the participants, the Pension Society and the NHL allocated surpluses to the teams, except for funds allocated to participants based on their own contributions.[76] Out of CDN $2.9 million in "experience rate credits", CDN $900,000 went to improve pensions and the remainder was distributed to the teams or used to service current contributions. By 1986-87, the total surplus in the plan was CDN $26 million, of which about CDN $4 million went to provide benefits to retired participants. The NHLPA was now aware of the available credits and negotiated a CDN $250,000 "security package" at age 55 for current players who went on to play 400 games. This benefit was funded by CDN $10.8 million from the plan, together with CDN $1.3 million attributable to the NHLPA's proceeds from international hockey.[77] The league and the NHLPA jointly notified retired players of some improvement in their pensions in late 1988.

Seven retired players took action in Ontario[78] in 1991 seeking to recover the pension surplus on behalf of about 1400 alumni.[79] These players included Gordie Howe, who after 26 seasons received a pension of CDN $13,000 a year, and Carl Brewer, whose 12 seasons merited CDN $6,200. In *Bathgate v. National Hockey League Pension Society*,[80] Adams J. found that there had been a misallocation of over CDN $21 million. After an unsuccessful appeal in 1994, the league's liability grew to over CDN $41 million as interest accumulated and dispute continued over the precise calculation.[81] (A subsequent settlement also resulted in agreed compensation for various groups of non-playing personnel.[82])

[75] See, W. Houston & D. Shoalts, *Eagleson: The Fall of a Hockey Czar* (Toronto: McGraw-Hill Ryerson, 1993) at 98-99.

[76] See, *Bathgate v. National Hockey League Pension Society*, [1992] O.J. No. 2168, 11 O.R. (3d) 449 at 478-85, 98 D.L.R. (4th) 326 at 355-62 (Ont. Gen. Div.).

[77] *Bathgate v. National Hockey League Pension Society*, [1992] O.J. No. 2168, 11 O.R. (3d) 449 at 484, 98 D.L.R. (4th) 326 at 361 (Ont. Gen. Div.).

[78] This suit precluded action in the American federal court system; see, *Dailey v. National Hockey League*, 987 F.2d 172 (3rd Cir., 1993), *cert.* denied 114 S.Ct. 67 (1993).

[79] See: D. Cruise & A. Griffiths, *Net Worth: Exploding the Myths of Pro Hockey* (Toronto: Viking, 1991) at 1-25, 298-300; B. Dowbiggin, *The Defense Never Rests* (Toronto: HarperCollins Canada, 1993); W. Houston & D. Shoalts, *Eagleson: The Fall of a Hockey Czar* (Toronto: McGraw-Hill Ryerson, 1993) at 144-65; R. Conway, *Game Misconduct: Alan Eagleson and the Corruption of Hockey* (Toronto: Macfarlane Walter & Ross, 1995, revised edition 1997) at 106-28.

[80] [1992] O.J. No. 2168, 11 O.R. (3d) 449, 98 D.L.R. (4th) 326 (Ont. Gen. Div.), affd [1994] O.J. No. 265, 16 O.R. (3d) 761, 110 D.L.R. (4th) 609 (Ont. C.A.), leave to appeal refused [1994] S.C.C.A. No. 170, 114 D.L.R. (4th) vii (S.C.C.).

[81] See, *Bathgate v. National Hockey League Pension Society* (1995), 10 C.C.P.B. 210 (Ont. Gen. Div.) (simple interest on reimbursable amounts at plan rate of return).

[82] See, "Ex-NHL employees get $20-million" *The Globe and Mail* (Toronto: July 23, 1997) at A17.

Adams J. held that the plan created a trust "whereby the defined contributions of both the players and clubs were irrevocable and held by the Pension Society as trustee for the exclusive benefit of the participant players".[83] The trust could not be altered by an undocumented "deal" in 1969, and the Society was not authorised to re-allocate the surplus derived from contributions before 1982. The collective bargaining in 1986 could not justify the allocation since the NHLPA did not represent the retired players:

> Not only did the NHLPA represent only active players on that occasion, the Pension Society had trust, contractual and fiduciary duties to ensure that the beneficial interest of former players in these funds was protected. Obviously, no one else was concerned about these people.[84]

Player representation on the Pension Society resumed in 1993 when the Ontario government revoked an exemption that had been continued in 1999 after Alan Eagleson wrote to support it.[85] The retired players duly received their shares of the surplus funds[86] and had to face the tax consequences of the payouts.[87]

In a later dispute, in 2008 NHLPA representatives on the Board of Trustees applied to the Ontario Superior Court of Justice for directions in relation to death benefits payable to the beneficiaries of players who died before they started collecting their pensions. On the applicants' interpretation, one member of the plan would be entitled to CDN $668,659, while the trustees appointed by the NHL claimed that the benefit should be CDN $214,300. In *Healy v. Gregory*,[88] Perell J. held that since 1966 the terms of the plan clearly called for the beneficiary to receive the "greater" amount. The benefits should be "pension-based" and calculated according to the "commuted" or present value of the investment contracts, as opposed to a methodology based on contributions.

---

[83] *Bathgate v. National Hockey League Pension Society*, [1992] O.J. No. 2168, 11 O.R. (3d) 449 at 517, 98 D.L.R. (4th) 326 at 394 (Ont. Gen. Div.).

[84] *Bathgate v. National Hockey League Pension Society*, [1992] O.J. No. 2168, 11 O.R. (3d) 449 at 529, 98 D.L.R. (4th) 326 at 406 (Ont. Gen. Div.), *per* Adams J.

[85] See: "Players likely to get say on pension plan" *The Globe and Mail* (Toronto: March 2, 1993) at A12; R. Conway, *Game Misconduct: Alan Eagleson and the Corruption of Hockey* (Toronto: Macfarlane Walter & Ross, 1995, revised edition 1997) at 119-20, 125-27. The exemption related to representation of plan members under the *Pension Benefits Act*, R.S.O. 1990, c. P.8.

[86] For a list of the approximate final awards over CDN $5,000, see, "NHL Pension settlements" *The Globe and Mail* (Toronto: November 6, 1996) at A20. According to this information, 57 players were owed more than CDN $100,000, with Gordie Howe receiving the highest amount at CDN $205,005.

[87] See, *Nanne v. R.*, [1999] T.C.J. No. 871, [2000] 1 C.T.C. 2776 (T.C.C.) (*Income Tax Act*, s. 212(1)(h); exemption for players on American teams "only occasionally employed" in Canada).

[88] [2009] O.J. No. 2562 (Ont. S.C.J.).

## 3. Collective Bargaining: 1967-1997

The first twenty years of collective bargaining by the NHLPA realised only modest increases in salaries and other benefits[89] so that the payments fell well behind those enjoyed in other professional leagues:

> By 1988 the average salary in hockey had fallen to 38 per cent of the average basketball salary. This relative decline in NHL salaries occurred during a time when the NHL was experiencing a period of significant economic prosperity.[90]

Salary increases occurred during the period of external competition from the World Hockey Association ("WHA") and resulted from individual negotiations. The position of the players in negotiating contracts was, however, improved in 1989-90 when the NHLPA resolved to disclose salary figures.[91] A more adversarial style of collective labour relations developed after 1991 when the leadership of the NHLPA passed from Alan Eagleson to Robert Goodenow. The first strike in modern major league hockey duly occurred in April 1992 and was followed by the longer lockout at the start of the 1994-95 season, which at the time seemed like a serious disruption. Prior to these stoppages, the NHLPA mounted only modest claims to a greater share of league revenue and did not achieve fundamental changes to the restrictions on free agency.

Following the litigation involving teams in the WHA, the NHL adopted contract systems allowing for a one-year option and free agent compensation. Under the 1974 version of the standard player's contract ("SPC"), these provisions were incorporated in section 17 of the contract. By section 17(a), in the final year of a player's contract the team could tender a one-year "Player's Termination Contract" on the same terms but allowing for "unconditional release" after the additional season; if the player did not execute this contract, he received automatic release. If the team did not offer a termination contract, by section 17(b) it had to offer a new SPC, including section 17, with the possibility of a different salary and term of service. Regardless of the team's actions, by section 17(c) the player could give notice that he wished to sign a one-year Player's Option Contract allowing for restricted free agency at the end of the season. If the team failed to offer a termination contract and the player did not request an option contract, by section 17(d) the parties had to enter a new SPC[92] by mutual agreement; failing agreement, the SPC was for

---

[89] See, D. Cruise & A. Griffiths, *Net Worth: Exploding the Myths of Pro Hockey* (Toronto: Viking, 1991) at 255-300.

[90] R. Gruneau & D. Whitson, *Hockey Night in Canada: Sport, Identities, and Cultural Politics* (Toronto: Garamond Press, 1993) at 127, referring to D. Cruise & A. Griffiths, *Net Worth: Exploding the Myths of Pro Hockey* (Toronto: Viking, 1991) at 287.

[91] See, M. Edge, *Red Line, Blue Line, Bottom Line: How Push Came to Shove Between the National Hockey League and its Players* (Vancouver: New Star Books, 2004) at 107-28.

[92] On the negotiation of a new contract following the exercise of the option in subsection (d) (later, s. 18(d)), see, *Newport Sports Management Inc. v. Reichel*, [2000] O.J. No. 177 (Ont. S.C.J.).

one year on the same terms, including section 17, but with salary "determined by neutral arbitration under the applicable collective bargaining agreement". The player who played out the option was subject to the free agent compensation system in league by-law 9A, which declared that the purpose of "equalization" was to "compensate a player's Prior Club fairly for loss of the right to his services". Under this system, teams first negotiated the compensation. Failing agreement, the issue was referred to Judge Edward Houston of Ottawa for final offer selection: the arbitrator could choose either team's proposed compensation package, which might involve the assignment of professional players' contracts,[93] draft choices or cash.

The 1974 version of the SPC was recognized in the first comprehensive collective bargaining agreement ("CBA") signed in May 1976, covering the period 1975 to 1980. By articles 9.03(b) and 9.03(e) of the CBA, the NHLPA represented that it was authorized to agree to the option and free agency provisions, and both parties to the CBA expressed the good faith belief that they were lawful subjects of bargaining. The NHLPA acquiesced in the system in 1979 at the time of the merger with the WHA even though it greatly inhibited the signing of free agents and applied to every level of player:

> Between 1976 and 1980, 137 players declared their intention to move to another club, but only 23 actually did so. In essence, the players were as restricted as they had been under the reserve clause.[94]

Arbitrated equalization was also open to the criticism that it failed to protect the interests of the player who was subject to a forced trade as a result of the award.[95]

The CBA of 1976 dealt with a range of benefits, rights and procedures. For example, articles 9 and 19 of the original text prescribed a minimum annual salary of $12,500, a $15,000 award for players winning the Stanley Cup, and a meal allowance for away games of $24. Amendments resulting from ongoing negotiations were then incorporated in the second formal printing of the CBA dated August 1, 1981, so that by 1982 the minimum salary was $25,000, Stanley Cup winners received $20,000 and the allowance was $31. By the time of the fourth formal printing in June 1988, the minimum salary remained at $25,000 ($18,000 in the minors), Stanley Cup winners received $25,000 and the allowance was $45. From 1980 to 1990, the average annual salary for NHL players saw a modest increase from CDN $118,000 to CDN $233,000, and these

---

[93]  See, *McCourt v. California Sports, Inc.*, 600 F.2d 1193 (6th Cir., 1979) (labour exemption); see Chapter 8, "Competition Law and Labour Law", section C, 3.

[94]  D. Cruise & A. Griffiths, *Net Worth: Exploding the Myths of Pro Hockey* (Toronto: Viking, 1991) at 271.

[95]  See, D.L. Steinberg, "The National Hockey League Reserve System: A Restraint of Trade" (1979) 56 U. Detroit J. of Urban L. 467 at 513-14.

gains were minimal when expressed in real dollars adjusted according to the consumer price index and the rate of inflation.[96]

Under article 2.02 of the amended agreement, the NHLPA could give notice of termination of the equalization provisions in 1981. Negotiations in 1982[97] then resulted in the abolition of compensation for free agents over age 33 (Group III). Arbitrated awards were retained for players under 24 or with less than five years of professional experience (Group I). Other free agents offered salaries over $85,000 were subject to a fixed schedule of compensation involving draft picks or professional players (Group II). After further negotiations in 1986, the parties incorporated changes in the form of a five-year CBA.[98] The age level for Group III was set at 31 and the player was allowed to choose whether his former team would have a right of first refusal or arbitrated compensation in the form of draft picks or cash. The salary scale for Group II was increased and the compensation schedule now excluded professional contracts. The agreement retained the Group I category, subject to the former team making a minimum contract offer according to a rising scale. The heavy and disruptive nature of arbitrated compensation was seen in 1991 when Judge Houston awarded all-star defenseman Scott Stevens to the New Jersey Devils after St. Louis had signed Brendan Shanahan from the Devils.[99] Stevens had recently been acquired as a Group II free agent from the Washington Capitals, and St. Louis still owed draft picks for that move. The Stevens-Shanahan award inspired new efforts to liberalize free agency as the players sought to reduce the deterrent effect of compensation.

The NHLPA issued notice of termination of the CBA in May 1991[100] and took the opening position that the league would benefit from eliminating the amateur draft and free agency restrictions.[101] The negotiations were now led by Robert Goodenow, who subsequently assumed the position of executive director of the NHLPA. The association received a strike mandate from the players in March 1992 just as final cheques were being issued for the regular season. The players were now better informed and determined to realize gains, while the owners failed to appreciate the discontent and put themselves at the tactical disadvantage

---

[96] See, M. Lavoie, *Avantage numérique: L'argent et la Ligue nationale de hockey* (Hull: Éditions Vents d'Ouest, 1997) at 188-92.

[97] See: "NHL agreement may lead to overtime" *The Globe and Mail* (Toronto: August 18, 1982) at 11; NHL/NHLPA, Collective Bargaining Agreement (Third Formal Printing, November 1, 1984).

[98] See: NHLPA, "NHL/NHLPA Agreement – July 25, 1986"; "NHL's new labor pact restricts 18-year-old draft" *The Globe and Mail* (Toronto: July 26, 1986) at D1, D4; NHL/NHLPA, Collective Bargaining Agreement (Fourth Formal Printing, June 1, 1988). See also, I.C. Pulver, "A Face Off between the National Hockey League and the National Hockey League Players' Association: The Goal of a More Competitively Balanced League" (1991) 2 Marq. Sports L.J. 39.

[99] See, "Stevens deal provides ammunition for NHL free agency" *The Globe and Mail* (Toronto: September 4, 1991) at A12.

[100] See, *National Hockey League v. National Hockey League Players' Assn.*, 789 F.Supp. 288 (D. Minn., 1992) (league refused declaration of labour exemption for equalization rules; NHLPA was not an appropriate defendant and there was no concrete dispute). See also, Chapter 8, "Competition Law and Labour Law", section C, 3.

[101] NHLPA, "Players' Position on Free Agency Issues" (June 1991).

of dealing with fully paid opponents. Negotiations addressed free agency, financial benefits and the salary arbitration system.[102] The players were particularly concerned to protect the right to license "likeness"[103] and retain a share of revenue from hockey cards. When the players rejected an offer in early April and voted 560 - 4 to go on strike,[104] the team owners risked losing their lucrative haul of playoff revenue. After a ten-day stoppage, the parties settled on a short-term retroactive CBA covering only 1991-93.[105] This agreement included minor changes to the draft and financial benefits and made some amendments to by-law 9A,[106] including the addition of unrestricted free agency for ten-year professionals who were not earning the average league salary (Group V).[107] The players retained the right to market personal image and achieved changes in the salary arbitration process. The parties also agreed to a number of joint studies relating to economic development and safety.

The NHLPA issued a termination notice under the CBA in May 1993, but only sporadic negotiation occurred during the 1993-94 season. The players were experiencing a period of rapid growth in earnings so that average salaries rose from CDN $360,000 during the 1991-92 season to CDN $510,000 in 1992-93, CDN $709,000 in 1993-94 and CDN $900,000 in 1994-95.[108] The owners were now led by Gary Bettman who assumed the role of NHL Commissioner in February 1993 having previously worked as an executive with the National Basketball Association. In January 1994, the owners proposed a team payroll pyramid fixing percentage shares for individuals or groups of players.[109] Bettman was determined to establish a new CBA for the 1994-95 season and gave negotiations a jolt in August by imagining an *impasse* and unilaterally eliminating 16 benefits.[110] Management took the further initiative by locking the players out on October 1, 1994 and threatened to cancel the season if the regular schedule fell below 50 games. The owners bargained from financial security bolstered by franchise sales and licensing revenue, and the league could look forward to January 1995 when its new schedule of broadcasts on the Fox

---

[102]  See Chapter 9, "National Hockey League", section F, 2.

[103]  See Chapter 7, "The Business of Hockey", section A, 4.

[104]  See, "Strike hits NHL with both sides losing optimism", "Strike a show of solidarity" *The Globe and Mail* (Toronto: April 2, 1992) at A1, A2, A11.

[105]  See: "Even after overtime, strike ends in tie" *The New York Times* (April 12, 1992) at S1, S4; "Here's what the NHL, NHLPA agreed upon" *The Hockey News* (April 24, 1992) at 4.

[106]  On By-Laws 9A and 9B and Group IV "defected players", see, A.N. Wise & B.S. Meyer, *International Sports Law and Business* (The Hague: Kluwer Law International, 1997), vol. 1, at 668-69, vol. 3, at 1162-65 (antitrust action by Markus Naslund against NHL in 1993).

[107]  In *National Hockey League Players' Assn. v. National Hockey League Member Clubs: "Average League Salary"* (August 14, 1992, St. Antoine), the arbitrator held that signing bonuses and deferred salary should be included and the calculation should be weighted to take account of the number of games played. See, CBA of NHL (1993–2004), arts. 1, 10.

[108]  See, M. Lavoie, *Avantage numérique: L'argent et la Ligue nationale de hockey* (Hull: Éditions Vents d'Ouest, 1997) at 190.

[109]  See, "Dunce cap fits NHL owners better than players" *The Globe and Mail* (Toronto: January 28, 1994) at A12.

[110]  See, "NHLPA furious at league" *The Globe and Mail* (Toronto: August 9, 1994) at C6.

network was due to begin. Terms were agreed on January 11, 1995 after a lockout lasting 103 days.[111] The new CBA was originally scheduled to cover 1993-2000 and allowed either side to reopen the agreement in 1998. This power was waived in September 1995 when the league and the association participated in negotiations to make NHL players available for the 1998 Winter Olympic Games in Nagano.[112] After further negotiations in 1997 relating to league expansion[113] and the 2002 Salt Lake City Olympics, the CBA was extended until 2004.[114]

In the negotiations in 1994-95, the players conceded points in areas such as free agency and salary arbitration but succeeded in resisting proposals by the team owners to "tax" payrolls that exceeded the league average. Revenue sharing arrangements and aid to "small market" teams also did not feature in the CBA, although the league later established the Group 2 Equalization Plan and a revenue pool to assist Canadian teams disadvantaged by the low value of the Canadian dollar. Since the owners had failed to achieve a payroll "tax" plan through collective bargaining, the NHLPA filed a grievance in 2002 when Alberta adopted a 12.5 per cent "game days" tax on visiting and home players for the benefit of the Edmonton Oilers and the Calgary Flames.[115] The players' association argued that the league was using the provincial government to transfer money out of the pockets of the players, but the arbitrator found no breach of the CBA.[116]

A particular feature of the CBA for 1993-2004 was the "compensation limits" imposed on rookies. By article 9.3 of the CBA, maximum annual compensation for players at the entry level was fixed at USD $850,000 in 1995, rising to USD $1.295 million in 2004. These maxima soon became the contract standard, and the CBA permitted the payment of performance bonuses based on play during the regular season.[117] Some young stars duly negotiated clauses that realised additional annual payments of around USD $3 million.

The CBA recognized five classes of free agency normally operating when the player's contract had expired.[118] Groups III, V and VI were "unrestricted" and consisted of players over age 31 with sufficient "accrued seasons" (Group III), ten-year professionals not earning the average league salary ("ALS") (Group V)

---

[111] See, "The Contract", "Players outmuscled in NHL war of attrition" *The Globe and Mail* (Toronto: January 12, 1995) at C6, C8.

[112] On international participation, see Chapter 3, "Organizations and Regulations", section A, 3.

[113] See, "Leafs lose short term in new alignment" *The Globe and Mail* (Toronto: June 18, 1997) at A16, A17.

[114] See, NHLPA/NHL, Collective Bargaining Agreement (June 25, 1997).

[115] On the public subsidy of teams, see Chapter 7, "The Business of Hockey", section B, 3.

[116] See: "Alberta tax on players contested" *The Globe and Mail* (Toronto: October 23, 2002) at S3; "NHL wins Alberta tax case" *The Globe and Mail* (Toronto: March 5, 2003) (online).

[117] See, CBA of NHL (1993–2004), article 9.6; Exhibit 5 (bonuses based on league awards and ranking, individual play and winning the Stanley Cup).

[118] See, CBA of NHL (1993–2004), article 1 (definitions), article 9 (entry level compensation), article 10 (free agency). See also: J. Barnes, *Sports and the Law in Canada*, 3d ed. (Toronto: Butterworths, 1996) at 185-88; M. Lavoie, *Avantage numérique: L'argent et la Ligue nationale de hockey* (Hull: Éditions Vents d'Ouest, 1997) at 160-68.

and three-year professionals over age 25 who had played less than 80 NHL games (Group VI). Group II "restricted" free agents were those in the early years of their careers and were subject to the right of first refusal or draft choice compensation, provided their present team tendered a "qualifying offer" at the required level of salary. The offer had to consist of a one-year contract at 110 per cent of the previous year's major league salary where the player was receiving less than the ALS or at equal salary where the player exceeded the ALS. Where the "restricted" free agent received an offer from another team that he intended to accept, the previous team had to be notified of its "principal terms" and then had seven days to exercise the right of refusal.[119] Failing such exercise, the previous team was entitled to a scale of draft choices related to the average annual value of the "principal terms" of the new team's offer sheet. The further category of "restricted" free agents involved Group IV "defected players" which gave rise to a series of disputes relating to the definition of affiliated and unaffiliated leagues.[120]

The player's obligation to serve the full term of the contract was considered in 2000 when Alexei Yashin, of the Ottawa Senators, resorted to arbitration and court proceedings in an attempt to be declared a "restricted" free agent. Yashin was dissatisfied with the USD $3.6 million payable in 1999-2000 and was looking for future payments of USD $23 million over two seasons. The Senators declined to renegotiate the contract or to trade Yashin and suspended him in November 1999 when he failed to report to the team. Yashin then sat-out the 1999-2000 season in the hope of being declared a "restricted" free agent at the end of his five-year contract. The Senators responded with an action for damages, initially claiming that the hold-out had caused USD $7 million in losses. Yashin's status and the expiry point of his contract were addressed in arbitration proceedings, where the NHLPA argued that there was no language in the CBA requiring a player to serve every year of the contract in order to become a free agent. Such a rule is declared in other major league sports, but the NHL had been unsuccessful in negotiating to include a similar provision. The arbitrator considered parol evidence relating to the collective bargaining in 1995 and determined that it had been both sides' intention to maintain the "existing policy" on a player's obligation to provide full performance. The *status quo* was then fixed from testimony and correspondence involving earlier administrations of the league and the NHLPA. Based on this dubious material from a period of union compliance, the arbitrator was persuaded that a player was bound to perform the full contractual obligation. He therefore held that:

---

[119]  On the Carolina Hurricanes' offer of USD $38 million over six years to Sergei Federov, see, "Wings win Federov with offer" *The Globe and Mail* (Toronto: February 27, 1998) at A15, A16.

[120]  See: *National Hockey League Players' Assn. v. National Hockey League*, 30 F.Supp. 1025 (N.D. Ill., 1998), 30 F.Supp. 1029 (N.D. Ill., 2000) (signing with team in International Hockey league; systems issues raised by Kevyn Adams grievance); *In the Matter of the Arbitration between the National Hockey League Players' Assn. and the National Hockey League, Grievances Concerning Ben Clymer and Mike Van Ryn* (June 22, 2000, Lawrence T. Holden, arbitrator) (players were not "defected players" since Canadian Hockey League is an affiliated league). See further, Chapter 3, "Organizations and Regulations", section 3.

Mr. Yashin's contract has been tolled by virtue of the fact that he withheld his services for the entire playing season, 1999-2000, and that his SPC does not expire until he provides one additional season of service to the Club.[121]

The NHLPA was dissatisfied with this decision but adhered to its practice of not challenging the outcome. Yashin was, however, anxious to have a determination before the start of the 2000-01 season and applied for judicial review. This application was denied in *Yashin v. National Hockey League*[122] when Cunningham J. held that only the association had standing to make the application. Cunningham J. decided that the interests of Yashin and the NHLPA were not adverse and held that the individual negotiation of the SPC did not affect the association's status as the exclusive bargaining agent. The role of the NHLPA was more extensive than that of associations representing performers in the arts[123]:

> The CBA in the present case does far more than set minimum terms of employment for professional hockey players. Not only does the NHLPA negotiate the CBA but with the exception of compensation, the terms of the SPC as well. Without any question, the NHLPA is the exclusive bargaining agent which apparently is significantly different from the relationship between Actors Equity and its ballet dancers. The SPC is 11 pages long and contains 20 clauses. The only portion of that agreement which the applicant, through his agent in the present case, negotiated, is compensation which is found as an addendum to the SPC.[124]

Cunningham J. also addressed the merits of further arguments raised by Yashin. He found that the arbitrator had not exceeded his jurisdiction, but "simply interpreted the meaning of the term 'contract expiration' in the context of restricted free agency status as defined by the CBA".[125] Yashin was not condemned to "perpetual servitude", was not being forced into specific performance of a service contract,[126] and was not the victim of a restraint of trade.[127] The only alternative for Alexei Yashin was to report to the Ottawa

---

[121] *In the Matter of the Arbitration between the National Hockey League Players' Assn. and the National Hockey League (Ottawa Senators); Grievance of Alexei Yashin* (Lawrence T. Holden, arbitrator, June 28, 2000) at 18.

[122] [2000] O.J. No. 3306, 192 D.L.R. (4th) 747 (Ont. S.C.J.).

[123] See, *National Ballet of Canada v. Canadian Actors' Equity Assn. (Glasco Grievance)*, [2000] O.L.A.A. No. 209, 87 L.A.C. (4th) 1 (Ont. Lab. Arb.), C. Albertyn, arbitrator; *National Ballet of Canada v. Glasco*, [2000] O.J. No. 1071, 49 O.R. (3d) 223, 185 D.L.R. (4th) 372 (Ont. Div. Ct.); *National Ballet of Canada v. Glasco*, [2000] O.J. No. 2083, 49 O.R. (3d) 230, 186 D.L.R. (4th) 347 (Ont. S.C.J.).

[124] *Yashin v. National Hockey League*, [2000] O.J. No. 3306, 192 D.L.R. (4th) 747 at 755-56 (Ont. S.C.J.), *per* Cunningham J.

[125] *Yashin v. National Hockey League*, [2000] O.J. No. 3306, 192 D.L.R. (4th) 747 at 760 (Ont. S.C.J.).

[126] See Chapter 9, "National Hockey League", section E, 5.

[127] See Chapter 8, "Competition Law and Labour Law", sections A; B.

Senators for the 2000-01 campaign. His troubled reign in the capital[128] came to an end in June 2001 when he was traded to the New York Islanders where he signed a 10-year contract for USD $87.5 million.

## 4.    Leadership and Structure of the NHLPA

In 2002, the NHLPA renewed the employment of Robert Goodenow for six years at an annual salary of USD $2.5 million: the players were evidently appreciative of his services since their own salaries had advanced from an average of USD $248,000 in 1991 to USD $1.6 million in 2002. Goodenow remained as executive director throughout the lockout of 2004-05,[129] having taken the initial bargaining position that the new CBA should not include a team salary cap linked to league revenue. After the 2004-05 season was cancelled, many players began to lean towards compromise and did not want to see the stoppage extend into a second year. The authority to fashion a deal then appeared to shift to the president of the association, Trevor Linden, and senior director, Ted Saskin.[130] The new CBA was finalized on July 13, 2005, and Robert Goodenow resigned two weeks later indicating that it was a case of a "jump aided by a push".[131]

After Goodenow's departure, the executive committee of the NHLPA promoted Ted Saskin to the position of executive director. The committee and the player representatives of the thirty teams then considered this hiring in a conference call in late August 2005 and voted by a majority to confirm it, so that Saskin received a four-to-six year contract at USD $2.1 million a-year.[132] Following protests that NHLPA by-laws required a secret ballot, a formal vote was eventually completed in December 2005 when 28 of the eligible 37 ballots were received and 24 votes favoured Saskin's appointment.[133] A dissident group of about 60 players had previously challenged the ratification of the CBA and the hiring process through complaints to American authorities,[134] but the U.S. Department of Labor decided that the Toronto-based NHLPA did not fall under its jurisdiction, and when charges were referred to the National Labor Relations

---

[128]    On the collapse of a planned CDN $1 million donation to the NAC, see, "National Arts Centre reveals payoff deal" *The Globe and Mail* (Toronto: January 22, 1999) at A1, A3.

[129]    See Chapter 9, "National Hockey League", section C.

[130]    See, "Players took away their leader's baton", "Players appeased after lengthy meeting" *The Globe and Mail* (Toronto: July 22, 2005) at R7, R11, R12.

[131]    See, "Goodenow passes the torch" *The Globe and Mail* (Toronto: July 29, 2005) at R6, R10. Goodenow apparently received a payment of USD $8 million.

[132]    See, "Saskin gets majority vote of confidence from NHLPA" *The Globe and Mail* (Toronto: September 3, 2005) at S3.

[133]    See, "Players vote in favour of Saskin" *The Globe and Mail* (Toronto: December 21, 2005) at R11.

[134]    See: "NHLPA accused of 'illegal' activities in filing" *The Globe and Mail* (Toronto: September 29, 2005) at R9; "Dissident NHLers make their case" *The Globe and Mail* (Toronto: November 21, 2005) (Canadian Press, online).

Board they were substantially rejected.[135] A lawsuit in the name of Chris Chelios was similarly dismissed when the federal court in Illinois held that relevant events had not occurred within its jurisdiction.[136] The player representatives then agreed to refer Saskin's appointment to an investigation to be conducted by Toronto lawyer Sheila Block.[137]

While Block was conducting her inquiries, there were allegations that some NHLPA staff had intercepted players' and agents' emails through the association's Intranet system in an attempt to monitor dissenting factions.[138] The NHLPA placed Saskin and a senior director on paid leave in March 2007, while a second Toronto lawyer, Chris Paliare, was hired to investigate whether there was cause for dismissal in relation to the possible reading of emails.[139] After Paliare submitted a report in May 2007 indicating that surveillance had occurred, the NHLPA dismissed Ted Saskin as executive director.[140] The Block report dealing with the original hiring and other matters arrived a few months later.[141] The NHLPA conducted an extensive search and review of candidates prior to hiring its fourth executive director. In October 2007, the position was given to the Boston trial lawyer Paul Kelly, whose previous experience in hockey included the prosecution of Alan Eagleson.[142] Kelly's contract was for five years at an annual base salary of around USD $1.75 million.

At the time of Kelly's appointment, the NHLPA adopted a new constitution[143] establishing the 30 team representatives as members of an executive board and allowing the appointment of an ombudsman. The positions of executive director and general counsel are now held by different individuals, both of whom are non-voting members of the executive board. A further significant change involved the appointment of an advisory board whose members include persons with experience in corporate affairs, finance and marketing. The new structure gained prominence at the end of August, 2009 when the executive board in a

---

[135] See: "U.S. Department of Labor dismisses NHLPA complaint" *The Globe and Mail* (Toronto: January 23, 2006) (Associated Press, online); "Linden set to step down as president" *The Globe and Mail* (Toronto: July 12, 2006) at R9.

[136] See, *Chelios v. National Hockey League Players' Assn.*, 2007 U.S. Dist. LEXIS 4260 (N.D. Ill., January 18, 2007).

[137] See, "Block to head Saskin probe" *The Globe and Mail* (Toronto: January 27, 2007) at S3.

[138] See: "NHLPA facing renewed scrutiny" *The Globe and Mail* (Toronto: March 6, 2007) at R6, R10; "Who knew what, when?" *The Globe and Mail* (Toronto: March 9, 2007) at R6, R11.

[139] See: "Concern over lack of leader" *The Globe and Mail* (Toronto: March 13, 2007) at R10; "Players set to lower the boom on Saskin" *The Globe and Mail* (Toronto: May 10, 2007) at R8.

[140] See: "Players take 90 minutes to axe Saskin" *The Globe and Mail* (Toronto: May 11, 2007) at R6, R10; "Saskin agrees to $400,000 settlement" *The Globe and Mail* (Toronto: March 21, 2008) at R5.

[141] See, "Players get some late summer reading: the Saskin report" *The Globe and Mail* (Toronto: August 29, 2007) at R7.

[142] See: Chapter 3, "Organizations and Regulations", section A, 4; Chapter 9, "National Hockey League", section B, 1. See also, R. Conway, *Game Misconduct: Alan Eagleson and the Corruption of Hockey* (Toronto: Macfarlane, Walter & Ross, 1995, revised edition 1997); Conway notes Eagleson's associations with the Hon. Roy McMurtry at 101, 201-202, 260, 267.

[143] See, "NHLPA Members Approve New Constitution" (October 30, 2007), available at <http://www.nhlpa.com>, "Media Releases".

late-night session of their annual meeting decided to dismiss Paul Kelly following a majority vote by secret ballot.[144] The reasons for the firing were unexplained, although they appeared to be related to Kelly's reading the transcript of a confidential meeting in which the executive board renewed the contract of general counsel Ian Penny and discussed issues of trust and effectiveness in the operations of the association. Following Kelly's dismissal, Ian Penny briefly assumed the role of executive director on an interim basis but then joined other officials in resigning from the association. The NHLPA solicited a legal opinion from the Hon. Roy McMurtry that indicated that they had just cause to fire Kelly but then took a second opinion and resolved to negotiate a settlement. They also formed a committee to review their operations and constitutional structure.

An important function of the executive director is to take care of the finances of the association. The NHLPA is engaged in extensive commercial activities and recognizes various sponsors and promotional partners, including PepsiCo, Energizer, McDonald's, Scotiabank and Visa.[145] The designation of "official supplier" usually occurs in association with the league. By licensing cards and "player products" (*e.g.*, apparel, collectibles, video games), the NHLPA realises substantial revenue to fund its services and operations. The members also look to benefit from collective bargaining.

## C.    COLLECTIVE BARGAINING AGREEMENT (2005)

## 1.    Bargaining

With the CBA scheduled to end in September 2004, the league provided the NHLPA with financial information on four teams in 1999 in anticipation of an early start to negotiations. By June 2002, Commissioner Gary Bettman strongly maintained that there was a growing need to consider a new "economic system".[146] Bettman had received a mandate from the league's board of governors to seek "cost certainty", which seemed to translate to a desired annual payroll cap of USD $32 million, a figure that would require rollbacks by 20 of the NHL teams.[147] From the perspective of league management, player salaries now consumed an undue percentage of league revenue and were a contributing

---

[144] See: "Paul Kelly fired a palace coup" *The Globe and Mail* (Toronto: September 1, 2009) at S1, S3. See also, "Kelly fired with cause: Lawyer" *The Toronto Star* (September 30, 2009) (online) (legal opinion from the Hon. Roy McMurtry); "Executive board wants to settle with Kelly" *The Globe and Mail* (Toronto: October 6, 2009) at R6.

[145] See online: <http://www.nhlpa.com>, "Player Products" and "Corporate Sponsors".

[146] See, "Lack of labour talks bothers Bettman" *The Globe and Mail* (Toronto: June 7, 2002) at S3. On the hockey economy at this time, see: B. Dowbiggin, *Money Players: How Hockey's Greatest Stars Beat the NHL at its Own Game* (Toronto: McClelland & Stewart, 2003); M. Edge, *Red Line, Blue Line, Bottom Line: How Push Came to Shove between the National Hockey League and its Players* (Vancouver: New Star Books, 2004).

[147] See, "Union cools owners' zeal for salary cap" *The Globe and Mail* (Toronto: November 26, 2002) at S4 (interview with *The New York Post*).

factor in the bankruptcy of some franchises; the labour costs also disadvantaged the Canadian teams in small markets where revenues were in devalued Canadian dollars.[148] Bettman recognized that the CBA for 1993-2004 severely restricted free agency, but claimed that teams were under competitive pressures to spend in ways that did not make sense.[149] A new system might, therefore, save team owners from their own folly and from the distorting effects of extravagant decisions. On behalf of the NHLPA, Robert Goodenow declared that he was interested in receiving concrete proposals from the league but announced philosophical opposition to any form of salary cap. There was an imbalance in payrolls, but it was the position of the players that a "hard" cap was not the remedy. In October 2003, the payrolls of the Canadian teams ranged from USD $31 million for the Edmonton Oilers to USD $60 million for the Toronto Maple Leafs, and teams such as the New York Rangers, Dallas Stars and St. Louis Blues paid over USD $70 million. During the 2003-04 season, the range extended from USD $22 million for the Pittsburgh Penguins to USD $83 million for the Detroit Red Wings.

After a series of secret talks with the players in early 2003,[150] the league began to base its public position on more detailed financial data. The NHL claimed total losses of USD $300 million as payrolls had risen by 275 per cent while revenues increased by 163 per cent: the average salary in 2002-03 was USD $1.7 million, and 76 per cent of the league's revenue of USD $1.9 billion was spent on players.[151] Formal negotiation sessions began in October 2003 when it was revealed that the players were offering to take a 5 per cent cut in salaries and proposed a revenue-sharing system based on "taxing" payrolls above an agreed level; they were also agreeable to reductions in salaries at the entry level and to limits on bonuses.[152] The league then sought to bolster its claim of financial hardship through a study conducted by Arthur Levitt, a former chairman of the American Stock Exchange and the Securities and Exchange Commission. Levitt's report in February 2004 assessed NHL teams as poor investments and stated that 19 of them had a combined operating loss of USD $342 million, while 11 teams realised a total profit of USD $69 million.[153] The NHLPA dismissed the hiring of Levitt as a public relations exercise and maintained that the league's Uniform Report of Operations failed to include significant types of revenue

---

[148]   See further, Chapter 7, "The Business of Hockey", section B.

[149]   See, "Bettman chastises union" *The Globe and Mail* (Toronto: September 10, 2003) at S3 (address to Canada Sports Forum).

[150]   On the "Blue Fin Project", see, "Rejection of NHLPA proposals 'puzzling'" *The Globe and Mail* (Toronto: November 25, 2004) at R7, R11.

[151]   See, "The anatomy of an NHL showdown", "NHL claims teams lost $300M last year" *The Ottawa Citizen* (September 20, 2003) at F1, F6.

[152]   See, "NHL cool to offer by players" *The Globe and Mail* (Toronto: October 11, 2003) at S3. The NHLPA originally proposed a threshold of USD $40 million with an escalating "tax" of 10-30 per cent. This was modified in September 2004 to 20 per cent on payrolls above USD $50 million.

[153]   See, "NHL review says league in 'catastrophic' condition" *The Globe and Mail* (Toronto: February 13, 2004) at S1. In November 2004, *Forbes* magazine placed the league's losses at USD $96 million.

related to the ownership of franchises: the NHLPA's earlier review of data from four teams revealed a failure to include USD $52 million. The union placed itself in the ideological camp of the free market and declared its faith in the wisdom of hockey's entrepreneurs:

> We continue to believe that a market system, not a team of hired-gun accountants, provides the best measure of the value of the hockey business. In a market system, the owner decides how much to pay the players. The owner knows the value of the business better than any paid consultant or league employee and the owner uses this knowledge when he sets player salaries. In our view, there is no better indicator of the true value of the players and the business.[154]

In a set of "concepts" proposed in July 2004, the league preferred a new system of centrally negotiated contracts involving a grid of player categories and compensation based on performance.

The NHL refused to begin the 2004-05 season without an agreement in place and locked the players out on September 15, 2004, prompting the early exodus of about 200 of the league's 750 players to teams in Europe. At this time, the NHLPA renewed its proposal to reduce salaries and implement revenue-sharing through a "tax" on payrolls.[155] Public opinion largely favoured the team owners, and Gary Bettman offered the prospect of "affordable" ticket prices and more stable franchises if there was "cost certainty" through the reduction of players' salaries. (This theory would, however, be contrary to traditional analysis which maintains that ticket prices are determined by demand in the consumer market rather than costs in the labour market. The problem of weak franchises could also be explained by unwise expansion into locations that were not reliable sources of ongoing revenue.) In a tactical manoeuvre on December 9, 2004, the players offered a package that included a 24 per cent rollback on existing salaries, caps on entry-level salaries, reduced qualifying offers and adjustments to the salary arbitration system.[156] The proposed "luxury tax" system would begin with a rate of 20 per cent on payrolls over USD $45 million, rising to 50 cents on the dollar for payrolls over USD $50 million and 60 cents on the dollar for payrolls over USD $60 million. These rates were probably insufficient to deter the big spenders, although the rollback in salaries would result in cutting the total payroll in the league by USD $270 million. The league was pleased to accept some of the cost-cutting measures but rejected the players' concessions as the

---

[154] NHLPA Media Release, "Goodenow Comments on League Commissioned Report" (February 12, 2004), online: <http://www.nhlpa.com>. Levitt's fee as a "paid consultant" was USD $250,000.

[155] Besides the positions of the owners and the players, various hockey "brains trusts" offered solutions. A "TSN proposal" in October 2004 called for a USD $6-million cap on individual salaries, revenue redistribution through a 100 per cent "tax" on payrolls over USD $40 million, unrestricted free agency at 30 or after 10 years' service, qualifying offers at 75 per cent of the previous salary and an entry level cap at USD $1.7 million (salary and bonuses).

[156] See, "NHLPA's 24-per-cent olive branch" *The Globe and Mail* (Toronto: December 10, 2004) at R6, R10.

basis for settlement[157] Under the NHL's counter proposals, salary arbitration would be eliminated and the players would take an average of 54 per cent of hockey-related revenues, which would translate to an initial payroll cap of USD $34 million.

The next detailed proposal was made on February 2, 2005 when the league offered a six-year CBA incorporating the 24 per cent rollback on current contracts and including new rules in relation to salary arbitration, free agency and entry-level contracts. The proposed "economic system" would limit player costs to 55 per cent of revenues so that pay and benefits would fall within an adjustable range from USD $32 million to USD $42 million; 15 per cent of the payroll would be paid into an escrow account to ensure that salaries did not exceed the 55 per cent limit.[158] Since the offer included a cap tied to league revenue, it was promptly rejected by the NHLPA. Half of the association's members were now employed in European leagues,[159] and it was anticipated that the 2004-05 season would soon be cancelled. In an attempt to salvage the season, the league proposed that play should begin in accordance with the NHLPA's package from December 9, but the league's system of February 2 would be "triggered" by defined conditions related to continuing types of "excess" in payrolls.[160] As the end loomed, the players finally conceded a salary cap at USD $52 million (subject to exceptions) combined with "taxes" on payrolls, and the league was prepared to offer a cap at USD $40 million that was not linked to revenue.[161] The "final" positions soon evolved to USD $49 million on the side of the players, while the league proposed a "taxable" threshold ending with a "hard" cap of USD $42.5 million. In making this offer, Commissioner Bettman indicated that the "deal" for the players would only get worse as a result of further damage suffered by the business. Fearing that the payrolls of all teams would rise to USD $49 million,[162] Bettman found no basis for agreement and announced the cancellation of the season on the 154th day of the lockout, February 16, 2005.[163] An optimistic attempt to revive negotiations

---

[157] See: "Big-market owners backing Bettman in chess game" *The Globe and Mail* (Toronto: December 15, 2004) at R1; "Only a miracle will do now" *The Ottawa Citizen* (December 15, 2004) at B1, B6.

[158] See: "NHL poised to make sports history of the worst kind" *The Globe and Mail* (Toronto: February 2, 2005) at R12; "Last call for NHL hockey" *The Ottawa Citizen* (February 3, 2005) at C1, C8; "A closer look at the NHL's latest proposal" *The Globe and Mail* (Toronto: February 3, 2005) (online, Canadian Press).

[159] See, A.E. Reitz, "The NHL Lockout: The Trickle-Down Effect on European Hockey" (2006) 13 Sports Law. J. 179 (388 NHL players in Europe).

[160] See, "NHL: Zero hour looms" *The Globe and Mail* (Toronto: February 10, 2005) at A1, A15.

[161] See, "NHL: Hopes flicker", "Either way, the end is nigh" *The Globe and Mail* (Toronto: February 16, 2005) at A1, A3, R6, R7.

[162] See, "Economists question Bettman's calculations" *The Globe and Mail* (Toronto: February 17, 2005) at R7. Following the cut in salaries by 24 per cent, only seven payrolls exceeded USD $42.5 million, with six in excess of USD $49 million.

[163] See: "The End" *The Globe and Mail* (Toronto: February 17, 2005) at R6, R10; "League cancels hockey season in labor battle", "'This is a sad regrettable day'" *The New York Times* (February 17, 2005) at A1, D1-D3.

then proved futile.[164] As discussed in Chapter 1, "Lord Stanley and the Wednesday Nighters", the Stanley Cup was not contested in 2005, and the NHL suffered the rare distinction of losing an entire season to a labour dispute.

The suspension of business operations raised concerns about the financial condition of some teams, although the NHL as a whole was the subject of a USD $4 billion offer when Bain Capital Partners and GamePlan LLC proposed to buy the league and run it as a single entity.[165] Attention also focussed on the legal consequences of the failure to achieve a settlement, where Robert Goodenow fixed blame on the league and asserted that there had been nothing but "threats, ultimatums, take it or leave it tactics and refusals to negotiate".[166] Under American labour law, the NHL had the option of declaring an *impasse*, implementing its last offer and opening training camps, but it would be open to the NHLPA to charge that *impasse* had not been reached and that good faith bargaining had not occurred. The league was originally prepared to use replacement players, subject to limitations in provincial labour law,[167] although it subsequently declared that a new season would not begin until it reached agreement with the NHLPA.[168] The absence of a CBA presented further difficulties under antitrust law[169] in relation to the conduct of the 2005 entry draft. The league's plan was being watched with some interest by a junior player from Nova Scotia named Sidney Crosby, and again the decision was made to defer the draft until an agreement was in place.

Negotiations resumed in March 2005 when Gary Bettman was true to his word and offered less generous proposals involving either a cap at USD $37.5 million or a 54 per cent share of "hockey-related" revenue.[170] Subsequent meetings focussed on accounting practices and a proposal by the NHLPA linking payrolls to the revenues of individual teams and requiring a "floor" of USD $30 million.[171] By June 2005, both sides agreed that there would be a salary cap tied to revenue and a "floor" at some level, although the league was seeking a narrow range in the gap between teams.[172] The general contents of the economic

---

[164] See, "How the bottom line beat Gretzky and Mario" *The Globe and Mail* (Toronto: February 21, 2005) at A1, A8.

[165] See: "Skeptics take aim at trial balloon" *The Globe and Mail* (Toronto: March 4, 2005) at R6, R10; "Bid for NHL divides teams by market value" *The Globe and Mail* (Toronto: May 25, 2005) at B12.

[166] NHLPA Media Release, "NHL Cancels Season" (February 16, 2005), online: <http://www.nhlpa.com>.

[167] See Chapter 8, "Competition Law and Labour Law", section D.

[168] See, "NHL won't use replacement players" *The Globe and Mail* (Toronto: April 21, 2005) at R6, R11. The league had previously filed charges of unfair labour practices based on reports that the NHLPA would require replacement players to repay lockout stipends and would decertify any agent who represented a replacement player.

[169] See, Chapter 8, "Competition Law and Labour Law", sections A-C.

[170] See, "NHL's latest offer includes lower team cap" *The Globe and Mail* (Toronto: March 18, 2005) at R8.

[171] See, "Hint of optimism sneaks into NHL talks" *The Globe and Mail* (Toronto: May 21, 2005) at S3.

[172] See, "Signs of optimism in NHL meetings" *The Globe and Mail* (Toronto: June 3, 2005) at R6, R10.

settlement were soon in place, and negotiations moved on to other details of the CBA.[173] The lockout ended after 301 days when the parties signed the agreement on July 13, 2005.[174] The initial impression was that there had been a surrender by the players and that the CBA was a victory for the team owners.

After three years of labour economics and one lost season, thought was given to the hockey "product". Recognizing that a more exciting spectacle would be needed to entice the public back, the NHL introduced the shootout to eliminate ties during the regular season and enacted new rules to open the game up, reduce obstruction and stimulate offence. The league had imposed the lockout partly in the name of competitive balance, so that fans would have a new faith in the potential of their team to succeed. Those who would be funding the payroll ranges also deserved a game of speed and skill. A further pleasure that would eventually be on offer was the chance to study the 400 pages of the text of the new CBA.

## 2.  Agreement

### a.  *General*

The CBA[175] of 2005 supersedes all prior agreements and is entered into by the NHL and the NHLPA as "parties" (see, Preamble). By article 27 of the CBA, both sides agree to waive all legal claims arising from the lockout. The agreement is for a term of six years and then remains in force from year to year unless either party delivers a written notice of termination 120 days prior to September 15, 2011 (see, article 3.1(a)). The NHLPA may extend the agreement to 2012 and was given the right to terminate after four seasons (see, article 3.1(b)). The association resolved in January 2009 not to reopen the pact so that it will remain in operation at least through the 2010-2011 season.

The CBA includes general provisions relating to the labour relations process. The NHL recognizes the NHLPA as the exclusive bargaining representative of present and future players (see, article 2.1), and the NHLPA is authorized to hold meetings with players (see, article 2.2). The parties also agree that players acting individually or through certified agents[176] may negotiate contract terms consistent with the CBA (see, article 2.1). Teams must remit to the NHLPA the dues deducted from the salaries of those players who have authorized the deduction (see, article 4.2). The CBA forbids strikes, slowdowns or lockouts during its term (see, article 7.1) and forbids illegal discrimination, including

---

[173] See, "NHL sides agree on salary cap" *The Globe and Mail* (Toronto: June 9, 2005) at A1, A8.

[174] See: "NHL and players reach agreement" *The New York Times* (July 14, 2005) at D1, D7; "301 days $2-billion", "Puck peace - At last" *The Globe and Mail* (Toronto: July 14, 2005) at A1-A2, R5, R7, R9.

[175] See online: <http://www.nhlpa.com>, "Collective Bargaining Agreement". For discussion, see, M. Fournier and D. Roux, "Les relations de travail dans la Ligue nationale de hockey: un modèle de negociation collective transnationale?" (2008) 49 C. de D. 481.

[176] See Chapter 9, "National Hockey League", section G.

discrimination based on support for any labour organization (see, article 7.2). In the event of conflict between the CBA and "league rules", the CBA prevails (see, article 30.1). The teams and the league retain "management rights", including the right to determine how and where their hockey business will be operated (see, article 5).

## b.   *Payroll Range*

The central issue of overall compensation for players is addressed in article 50 of the CBA dealing with the "Team Payroll Range System". By article 50.4(b), the players are entitled to receive an "applicable percentage" of "Hockey Related Revenues" ("HRR"), as defined in article 50.1.[177] The league and the teams are obliged to make disclosure through the "HRR reporting package" developed by "independent accountants" who supervise and verify the books (see, article 50.12). The parties may also engage their own "independent auditors" to review records (see, article 50.12(g)).[178] Disputes regarding the calculation of HRR are normally resolved by the "independent accountants", although disputes over the interpretation of the CBA must be referred to arbitration (see, articles 48, 50.13). The "system arbitrator" might, for example, be called upon to determine whether a particular source of revenue constitutes HRR. The payroll range is further enforced through article 26 which requires the accurate reporting of team revenue and full disclosure of players' remuneration.[179] The arbitrator may, for example, impose a fine of up to USD $5 million in the case of a circumvention by a team or by a person acting on behalf of a team (see, article 26.13). Possible circumventions include the sale of media rights at less than market value and unauthorized or unearned payments to players, including arrangements made through team sponsors (see, article 26.15). Article 26 creates affirmative obligations to disclose circumventions and requires agents and general managers to make annual declarations that they have not been involved in any violation (see, articles 26.7, 26. 8; exhibits 31, 32).

The players' aggregate compensation is determined by revenues for the "league year", and by article 50.5 the payroll range must consist of a "lower limit" and an "upper limit". Under article 50.4(b), the "players' share" increases as follows according to the level of revenue and the "applicable percentage":

---

[177] On the revenues included and not included in HRR, see Chapter 7, "The Business of Hockey", section B, 2.

[178] See also, "Forensic accountant to examine teams' finances" *The Globe and Mail* (Toronto: February 5, 2008) at R6 (NHLPA hires Bob Lindquist).

[179] *Cf. Oliver v. Federal Commissioner of Taxation* (2001), 46 A.T.R. 1126 (A.A.T.A.) (Carlton Football Club used its "raffle account" to make payments to a company directed by the player's agent). In 2002, the Australian Football League imposed fines and loss of draft picks on Carlton for "rorting" the salary cap, and the National Rugby League stripped all points from the Canterbury Bulldogs so that they went from top of the competition to bottom.

HRR below USD $2.2 billion - 54%
HRR from USD $2.2 to USD $2.4 billion - 55/56%
HRR from USD $2.4 to USD $ 2.7 billion - 56/57%
HRR above USD $2.7 billion - 57%

The midpoint in the payroll range is calculated by considering "preliminary HRR" from the previous year, multiplying it by the "applicable percentage" and dividing it by the number of teams in the league. The figure is then adjusted upward by 5 per cent until actual HRR reaches USD $2.1 billion, at which point a further agreed "growth factor" applies. The "upper limit" of the payroll range is USD $8 million above the adjusted midpoint and the "lower limit" is USD $8 million below (see, article 50.5(b)).

Revenue for 2005-06 was projected at USD $1.8 billion but came in at USD $2.1 billion. Revenue then increased to USD $2.4 billion (2006-07) and USD $2.57 billion (2007-08). Reflecting the exact USD $16 million difference between lower and upper limits from 2006-07, the team payroll ranges during the first five seasons of the CBA were as follows:

2005-06: lower USD $21.5 million, upper USD $39 million
2006-07: lower USD $28 million, upper USD $44 million
2007-08: lower USD $34.3 million, upper USD $50.3 million
2008-09: lower USD $40.7 million, upper USD $56.7 million
2009-10: lower USD $40.8 million, upper USD $56.8 million

By 2008-09, the payroll minimum therefore exceeded the maximum from 2005-06. Total payroll costs reached USD $1.5 billion (compared to USD $1.3 billion before the lockout) as the strong value of the Canadian dollar until late 2008 contributed to growth in revenues requiring increases in salaries.

To ensure that the "players' share" does not exceed the "applicable percentage", teams withhold amounts from the compensation payable and place it in an escrow account (see, articles 50.4(d), 50.11). The deduction is calculated at the start of the season and then adjusted quarterly according to the aggregated midpoint of the "team payroll range". The amounts are withheld from the salary and bonuses of players being paid under standard player's contracts ("SPC"), except that there is special provision for deferred payments. Based on the aggregate compensation paid by the teams, there may be either a "shortfall" or an "overage" with respect to the required "players' share". In the event of a "shortfall", the funds in the escrow account and any necessary supplemental payments are released to the teams for payment to the players. An "overage" is released to the league for distribution to the teams, and if the funds in the escrow account are insufficient to make the reimbursement then a credit is deducted from the "players' share" for the following "league year". During the 2005-06 season, the players paid 7 per cent into the escrow account but recovered this at the end of the season, together with a "shortfall" payment. The deduction subsequently ranged between 10 per cent and 13.5 per cent, although the

NHLPA decided in the third quarter of the 2008-09 season to raise it to 22.5 per cent in anticipation of reduced league revenue.

To assist teams in meeting the lower limit of the payroll range, article 49 of the CBA establishes the "Player Compensation Cost Redistribution System" ("PCCR") which creates the categories of "contributing club" and "recipient club". The NHLPA's acceptance of the payroll range was conditional on the PCCR system, which is designed to enhance the ability of all teams "to spend sufficient amounts on Player Compensation Costs" (see, article 49, Preamble). Under PCCR, teams are ineligible recipients if they are in the top half of the ranking according to gross annual revenue of individual teams (see, article 49.3(b)). They are also ineligible if they are located in a designated market area of 2.5 million households or have available compensation "that exceeds the Targeted Team Player Compensation" for the year. From 2008-09, to qualify for a "full share" of PCCR a "recipient club" must meet "revenue performance standards" by having a growth rate in revenue above the league average and average paid attendance above either 14,000 or the league average (see, article 49.3(d)). First time and repeat "non-performers" suffer scaled reductions in the amounts that are redistributed. Articles 49.4 and 49.5 of the CBA incorporate detailed rules in relation to the calculation of PCCR and the sources and "phases" of funding. Particular responsibility to contribute falls on teams ranked in the top 10 according to individual team revenue.

### c.   *Managing the Cap*

Permissible spending is based on "averaged club salary" (see, article 50.5(d) and "illustrations"), which is the aggregated amount committed in the "league year" by each team to players' NHL salaries and bonuses, including buyout amounts (see, article 50.9(i))[180] and amounts offered in "qualifying offers" and "offer sheets" to "restricted" free agents.[181] In the case of multi-year contracts, the salary and bonuses are averaged over the length of the SPC. Deferred salary and bonuses are counted at their present value for the year in which the player performs the services (see, article 50.2(a)(b)). The permitted forms of compensation are referred to in article 50.2, which excludes from the payroll range and "players' share" certain "traditional hockey practices" such as modest gifts or benefits provided to family members.

Two important exceptions permit teams to have "averaged club salary" that exceeds the "upper limit".[182] By article 50.5(h), there is an allowable "cushion" of 7.5 per cent based on the earning of defined performance bonuses. Similarly, by article 50.10(a)(d), a team may replace a player who is suffering from a *bona fide* injury or illness that renders him unfit to play for 24 days or 10 regular season games. Ordinarily, the salaries and bonuses of

---

[180]   On the buyout of contracts, see also, SPC of NHL (2005), paragraph 13(d).

[181]   See further, Chapter 9, "National Hockey League", section C, 2, d.

[182]   By article 50.5(c)(ii)(B) of the CBA, "additional flexibility" up to 10 per cent is allowed during the off-season.

injured players count against the "upper limit", and the league may challenge the determination of the team's physician that the player's condition qualifies for the "long-term" exception. The salaries and bonuses of the replacement player or players may not exceed the amount being paid to the unfit player.

The "Team Payroll Range System" and the "upper limit" now require skilled "capology" as managers must calculate the "payroll room" available at particular times, familiarize themselves with the detailed accounting rules that deal with the averaging of payments and comply with other limits on compensation. (In a hockey variation of *capax imperii nisi imperasset*, there is the risk that managers will seem worthy of the job until they actually do it.) By article 50.5(e)(i),

> no Club may enter into or assume an SPC, enter into an Offer Sheet, extend a Qualifying Offer, or engage in any other Player transaction that commits the Club to Player Salary and Bonuses for which the Club does not have Payroll Room... A Club may not enter into a single year or multi-year SPC with a Player unless the Club has Payroll Room at the time the SPC is entered into equal to or in excess of the Averaged Amount of the Player Salary and Bonuses.

A team has available "payroll room" (see, article 50.5(e)) when "averaged club salary" is less than the "upper limit". Where a team wishes to create "payroll room", it may do so by trading or assigning players or through the waivers systems.[183] It may also buy out the contract, although the amounts paid under the buyout agreement are included in team salary.

Cap management involves determining the appropriate allocation of salaries and other payments within the range so as to differentiate players according to star status, experience, performance and other factors. It also requires adjusting the roster according to the team's current standing, immediate needs or long-term plan. Strategic cap calculations particularly arise when extending offers to free agents or determining to match offers received from other teams. The team with serious ambitions for the current season will wish to dispose of players who are a burden to payroll and performance in order to free up space for more productive talent. Although trading in "payroll room" itself is prohibited, the team may enjoy the cooperation of another team that is under the "upper limit". Since a team cannot retain an obligation to pay part of a traded player's salary (see, article 50.9(e)), the price of the accommodation is likely to be a first round draft pick. The expected future direction of the payroll range plays a particularly important role in the signing or disposal of contracts. By 2009, anticipating a reduction in the league revenues and the "upper limit", the prudent course was not to sign players to long-term contracts and not to accept the trade of players holding expensive SPCs.

---

[183] See further, Chapter 9, "National Hockey League", section C, 2, d. See also, SPC of NHL (2005), paras. 13, 14.

### d. *Systems, Rules, Contracts and Benefits*

Further provisions of the CBA deal with player allocation systems and free agency, contracts, benefits and other aspects of the conditions of work. These may be noted as follows:

1. entry draft and entry level;
2. waivers and loans to the minor leagues;
3. free agency;
4. contracts;
5. compensation and financial benefits;
6. pension plans;
7. insurance, medical plan and injury protection;
8. scheduling and rosters;
9. international games; and
10. dispute resolution.

1. *Entry draft and entry level*: The entry draft consists of seven rounds, with each round having the same number of selections as there are teams in the league (see, article 8.2). The selections and associated rights are a tradeable commodity that may be assigned to other teams (see, article 8.8). The choice of players in each round normally follows the reverse order of standing from the previous year, which in the case teams that did not make the playoffs is based on the totals of points from the regular season. To avoid the deliberate throwing of games to guarantee the selection of the year's *Wunderkind*, "non Playoff Clubs" participate in a lottery or draw to determine the first pick in round one. The draw is weighted to favour the lowest teams, and since no team may move up more than four places only the bottom five have the chance to take the first overall pick (see, exhibit 4). Players age 18 or older may be taken in the draft, except that free agents, players on reserve lists and players claimed in two prior drafts are ineligible (see, article 8.4). The drafting team holds exclusive rights of negotiation with an "Unsigned Draft Choice" until June 1 of the next calendar year, but may extend this to the second June 1 by making a "Bona Fide Offer" (see, article 8.6(a), (d)); additional rights relate to college players and drafted Major Junior players who have ceased to play in the juniors.[184] A team that loses rights to certain first round picks may be entitled to a compensatory selection (see, article 8.3).

The salaries of rookies and "Group 1" players are subject to the "Entry Level Compensation Limits". The SPC of an entry level ("Group 1") player is deemed to be a "two way" contract providing for minor league salary up to maximum amounts (see, article 9.4). The entry level extends for three years in the case of players signing their first SPC between the ages of 18 and 21, two years for players signing at 22-23 and one year for players signing at 24 (see, article 9.1). One year of service at the entry level is satisfied by playing 10 NHL games. The

---

[184] See Chapter 3, "Organizations and Regulations", section B, 3.

annual limits are USD $900,000 for 2009 and 2010 and USD $925,000 for 2011. These maxima relate to aggregate amounts for each year of the player's first SPC with respect to basic or "Paragraph 1" NHL salary, signing bonuses and "games played bonuses"(see, article 9.3). Players at the entry level may, however, earn specified performance bonuses, payable either by the team or the league, up to maximum amounts (see, article 9.5; exhibit 5).

2. *Waivers and loans to the minor leagues*: The waivers processes apply to the termination of SPCs (see, article 13.21) and the loaning of players to affiliated teams in the minor professional leagues, including loans for the purpose of conditioning (see, articles 13.8, 13.9). The loans primarily involve the American Hockey League (see, article 13.10), although there is special provision for the East Coast Hockey League (see, articles 9.7, 13.11). The recall of loaned players is subject to restrictions after the trade deadline, which occurs 40 days before the end of the regular season (see, article 13.12(j)-(m)).

Teams may not dispose of the services of their players without going through waivers, which involves notifying the NHL's Central Registry and declaring the availability of the player over a period of 24 hours on weekdays or 48 hours on weekends (see, articles 13.17, 13.18). Waivers are usually not required for younger players who have not yet played a specified number of NHL games according to a scale based on years since first signing (see, article 13.4). Another NHL team may acquire a player who is subject to waivers by paying the waiver price (see, article 13.16) and taking an assignment of his SPC (see, article 13.20(a)). Where two or more teams make claims, the transfer is to the team with the lowest standing in the league either for the current season or from the previous season (see, article 13.19). The involuntary relocation of players through loan or claim on waivers may be affected by the presence of a specially negotiated "no move" clause (see, article 11.8), and the claiming team can refuse the assignment of the contract if the Commissioner determines that the player is not physically fit (see, article 13.20(a)).

3. *Free agency*: Article 10 of the CBA modifies the five classes of free agency established in previous agreements[185] and switches them from Roman to arabic numerals. Groups 3, 5 and 6 are "unrestricted" free agents, while Groups 2 and 4 are "restricted". The free agency normally operates once the player's SPC has expired.

After 2008, Group 3 consists of players who have seven "accrued seasons" or who are 27 years of age with four "accrued seasons" (see, article 10.1(a)). A season is credited as "accrued" when a player is on the active roster for 40 regular season games (30 for goaltenders) during any "league year" (see, article 1). Group 5 consists of players who have completed 10 "professional seasons" (including minor leagues) and who in the final year of their SPC were not earning the average league salary (see, article 10.1(b)). Group 6 consists of players who are age 25, who have completed three "professional seasons" and who have played in less than 80 NHL games for skaters or less than 28 NHL games for goaltenders (see, article 10.1(c)). In the case of these "unrestricted" Groups, the free agency grants complete freedom to negotiate and sign with any

---

[185] See Chapter 9, "National Hockey League", section B, 3.

NHL team without a right of first refusal or any obligation to pay a penalty, compensation or equalization (see, article 10.1). Except for Group 5, a player may become an "unrestricted free agent" any number of times.

Players are eligible for Group 2 "restricted" free agency if they have three years of "professional experience" having signed their first SPC at 18-21, or two years having signed at 22-23, or one year having signed at 24 or older (see, article 10.2(a)(i)). At the expiry of the player's SPC, the previous team has the right at its option to receive a right of first refusal or draft choice compensation provided it "tenders" to the player the necessary "qualifying offer" by the required date in late June. This offer must be for one year, subject to salary arbitration where available, and in the case of players with a specified level of playing experience must be a one-way contract (see, article 10.2(a)(ii)(iii)). The "qualifying offer" must be at least on the following terms, depending on the previous year's basic or "Paragraph 1" NHL salary:

> Previous NHL salary less than USD $660,000 - offer at 110%.
> Previous NHL salary USD $660,000 to USD $1 million - offer at 105% but no more than USD $1 million.
> Previous NHL salary USD $1 million or more - offer at 100%.

Group 4 "restricted" free agents are "defected players" who have contracted with teams in unaffiliated leagues and subsequently become free of any obligation,[186] as determined by the Commissioner (see, article 10.2(b)(i)(ii)). A NHL team holds rights to a "defected player" by obtaining negotiation rights or because the player previously signed a SPC that was not completely fulfilled. The team obtains a right of first refusal by making a timely "qualifying offer" at the minimum salary level and within the range for entry level players where applicable (see, article 10.2(b)(vi)).

When a "restricted" free agent receives an offer from a new team that he wishes to accept, the previous team must be notified of its "principal terms" through an "offer sheet"[187] and then has seven days in which to exercise the right of first refusal (see, article 10.3(a); exhibits 3, 6). Failing such exercise, the new team and the free agent formalize a SPC containing all the terms of the offer sheet. The previous team is then entitled to compensation based on the average annual value of the principal terms. Compensation is in the form of draft picks that are actually available to the new team. The scale is as follows (see, article 10.4), although the dollar values are adjusted from 2007 according to percentage increases in the average league salary:

---

[186] On international transfers, see Chapter 3, "Organizations and Regulations", section C, 2, a.

[187] The "impartial arbitrator" determines disputes over the validity of the offer sheet; see, CBA of NHL (2005), articles 10.3(i); 11.6. On the Commissioner's authority prior to the CBA signed in 1995, see: *National Hockey League Players' Assn. v. Bettman*, 93 Civ. 5769 (S.D. N.Y., 1994) (disallowance of offer sheets devised by San Jose Sharks); A.N. Wise & B.S. Meyer, *International Sports Law and Business*, vol. 1 (The Hague: Kluwer Law International, 1997) at 183-93.

| **Offer** | **Draft Choice(s) and Round** |
|---|---|
| USD $660,000 or less | No compensation |
| USD $660,000 to USD $1 million | One third |
| USD $1 million to USD $2 million | One second |
| USD $2 million to USD $3 million | One first, one third |
| USD $3 million to USD $4 million | One first, one second, one third |
| USD $4 million to USD $5 million | Two first, one second, one third |
| Over USD $5 million | Four first |

In summary, the CBA of 2005 liberalizes the age qualifications for Group 3, but continues to limit free agency through the right of first refusal and the scale of compensation for "restricted" free agents.

4. *Contracts*: The CBA incorporates the standard form SPC as the required employment contract (see, article 11.1; exhibit 1) and deals with the filing and approval of contracts through Central Registry (see, articles 11.3, 11.5). Certain contract practices are approved, while others are prohibited. The SPC of a player who is or who will become a Group 3 "unrestricted" free agent may contain a no-trade or no-move clause (see, article 11.8). The sale or assignment of SPCs cannot be conducted through cash transactions (see, articles 11.16, 50.8(b)(ii)), and no SPC may contain an option clause, a voidable year or provision for the revision or reimbursement of salary (see, articles 11.13, 50.8). Compensation must be in the form of salary, deferred salary or authorized bonuses (see, article 50.2). Salary and bonuses must be "fixed", as opposed to indexed (see, article 50.6(b)), and a SPC may not provide for bonuses based on a team bonus plan or the performance of the team (see, article 11.7).

5. *Compensation and financial benefits*: From 2009, the minimum "Paragraph 1" NHL salary is USD $500,000 (USD $525,000 from 2011) (see, article 11.12(a)). SPCs must provide for compensation in American currency, except that compensation in the minor leagues may be paid in the "native currency" of the NHL team (see, article 11.17); the minimum in the minors is the greater of $35,000 in native currency or the minor league's minimum (see, article 11.12(b)). By article 50.6 of the CBA, no player may receive aggregate payments that are more than 20 per cent of the "upper limit" of the "team payroll range". In 2008-09, based on the limit of USD $56.7 million, the maximum salary was USD $11.34 million. Under the "100 per cent rule" relating to variations in payments in the later years of a SPC, the difference between the salary and bonuses in the first two years cannot exceed the lower amount paid, and the variation in subsequent years cannot exceed that amount (see, article 50.7 and "illustrations").

Besides salary, the CBA provides for further payments and benefits.[188] By 2005-06, the daily allowance for meals while "away" was USD $85, to be adjusted in subsequent years according to the American consumer price index (see, article 19). A 10-year professional who has played 600 NHL games is entitled to elect to have a single room on road trips (see, article 16.9). There is also provision for rental and moving expenses when assigned or traded (see, article 14), for travel and living expenses associated with training camp (see, article 15) and for the costs of travel and accommodation related to moves to or from the minors (see, article 13.12). Participation in the playoffs is rewarded from the very modest "player fund" of USD $6.5 million distributed by the NHLPA and derived from a lump sum payment from the league (see, article 28). Under the breakdown of playoff bonuses, players on the team winning the Stanley Cup receive about USD $75,000 each.

The CBA recognizes the sponsorship and licensing programs of the league and the NHLPA (see, article 25) and continues the joint licensing of cards showing current players in team uniform (see, article 25.5(d)). Players may not endorse tobacco products or alcoholic beverages, except that the endorsement or sponsorship of beer is permitted (see, article 25.1). When a player enters into an endorsement arrangement for himself, he may mention his team for identification purposes (see, article 25.2).

6. *Pension plans*: The CBA recognizes the established pension plans and requires at least half of the trustees to be appointed by the NHLPA; the association also has authority to designate administrators of the plans (see, articles 21.1, 21.6). The "senior player benefits" plan is eliminated (see, article 21.4).[189] Teams must make full contributions to the plans for players who are available for 82 games in any playing season and must make proportionate contributions for players who play less (see, article 21.3(a)). Where sufficient proceeds are realised from international hockey, one fourth of the credit allocations to the basic plan comes from the NHLPA's share of such proceeds (see, article 21.3(b)). A player who suffers permanent disability forcing premature retirement is entitled to pension benefits that are at least equivalent to contributions for five playing seasons (see, article 21.5).

7. *Insurance, medical plan and injury protection*: As noted in Chapter 6, "Play Safe: On the Ice", the annual exit physical must document injuries requiring treatment, and the player must be provided with a complete copy of his medical records (see, article 23.10).[190] Under the CBA, the teams and the NHLPA agree to maintain life insurance and disability policies (see, articles 23.1-23.3), and the teams agree to pay for a trust fund providing benefits under a medical and dental plan administered under the direction of the NHLPA (see, article 23.5). A player who is disabled through an injury sustained in the course of his employment is entitled to salary for the remaining stated term of his SPC (see, article 23.4); special provision relates to players injured in training camp (see, article 15.6). Where a player receives payments and claims "career ending

---

[188] See also, CBA of NHL (2005), article 50.3 ("benefits" for the purpose of "league-wide player compensation").

[189] See Chapter 9, "National Hockey League", sections B, 1, 2.

[190] On risks and injuries to players, see Chapter 6, "Play Safe: On the Ice", section A.

disability insurance", he must execute releases of liability relating to the claim and the injury (see, article 23.4; exhibits 10-12).

8. *Scheduling and rosters*: The "hours of work" include no more than nine exhibition games (see, article 15(2)(c)), and 82 regular season games scheduled over at least 184 days (see, articles 16.1, 16.3). Players can also be "asked to participate" in the All-Star Game and its related activities (see, article 16.14(a)). The playoffs consist of four rounds with a maximum of seven games, although the CBA provides for discussions regarding a further qualification round (see, article 16.2). Scheduling and travel are subject to "restricted days" and limits on flying (see, articles 16.5, 16.8), and practice sessions must be at reasonable times (see, article 16.6). With regard to "staffing requirements", the minimum playing roster is 18 skaters and two goaltenders, and the maximum active roster until the trade deadline is 23 players (see, article 16.4). The limit on active rosters is subject to exemptions relating to the replacement of players placed on the seven-day "Injured Reserve List" (see, article 16.11), the use of non-roster players (see, article 16.12) and the recall of goaltenders (see, article 16.13).

9. *International games*: The international committee of the NHL and NHLPA may organize international games, and the NHLPA is entitled to 50 per cent of the net proceeds (see, article 24.1). Players participating in these games receive a daily allowance and have the same rights and obligations as if they were playing in a league game (see, article 24.4). The CBA regulates selection to national teams for the IIHF world championships (see, article 24.6) and declares that players have the same injury protections during that event as if they were participating in a NHL game (see, article 24.7). The CBA also incorporates the commitment to participate in the Winter Olympics of 2006 and 2010 (see, article 24.8).

10. *Dispute resolution*: The CBA establishes arbitration procedures in relation to "grievances" (see, article 17) and "system grievances" (see, article 48) and provides for transfer to "system arbitration" if that is the proper process (see, article 17.18).

A "grievance" is any dispute involving the interpretation or application of the CBA or a SPC (see, article 17.1). Either the NHL or the NHLPA may initiate the grievance within 60 days of the event or within 60 days of the facts being known (see, article 17.2). Failing resolution by the grievance committee (see, article 17.4), cases are referred to the "impartial arbitrator" (see, articles 17.5, 17.6) who must issue a written decision within 30 days of the close of the record (see, article 17.13).

A "system grievance" is one that relates to "Player Compensation Cost Redistribution" under article 49 or the "Team Payroll Range System" under article 50 and includes issues bearing on entry level compensation, free agency or circumvention in so far as they may affect articles 49 and 50 (see, article 48.1). The "system arbitrator" is required to be experienced in financial matters (see, article 48.5(b)) and has particular jurisdiction over the reporting of "Hockey Related Revenue" (see, article 48.8).

Further important articles of the CBA deal with disciplinary powers,[191] doping control and the use of drugs,[192] the standard player's contract ("SPC"),[193] contract negotiation and salary arbitration,[194] and the certification of agents.[195] These topics are considered in the sections that follow.

## D.  DISCIPLINE

## 1.  General

The disciplinary process relates to the imposition of sanctions because of misbehaviour or wrongdoing. Since the persons or organizations accused of misconduct risk loss of status or financial harm, they are entitled to proper determinations according to established rules and fair procedures.[196] Disciplinary action in the context of employment also usually requires a scale of penalties allowing a proportionate response to the particular misbehaviour. Most disciplinary cases involve the employee players, although teams and their personnel are also bound by league regulations.

In the NHL, the traditional authority to impose discipline at the league level belongs to the Commissioner or his designee. This power has largely gone unchallenged,[197] but is subject to the general requirements of natural justice, including the accused's right to a proper hearing. In the case of professional leagues, various legal standards may be used to test the exercise of disciplinary authority. There are contractual aspects in that the SPC or league rules must allow for the regulation of the behaviour and the imposition of the sanction.[198] Competition law and restraint of trade principles are applicable because a league-wide suspension amounts to an exclusion or a denial of the right to work.[199] And the labour relations process is important because the CBA defines the recognized disciplinary powers and prescribes hearing and grievance procedures. Discipline and penalties affect terms and conditions of employment and are mandatory subjects of bargaining. It is a particular requirement that drug

---

[191]  See Chapter 9, "National Hockey League", section D.

[192]  See Chapter 9, "National Hockey League", section D, 3. See also, Chapter 3, "Organizations and Regulations", section D.

[193]  See Chapter 9, "National Hockey League", section E.

[194]  See Chapter 9, "National Hockey League", section F.

[195]  See Chapter 9, "National Hockey League", section G.

[196]  See further, Chapter 3, "Organizations and Regulations", section C.

[197]  See, T.J. Arkell, "National Hockey League Jurisprudence: Past, Present and Future" (1998) 8 Seton Hall J. Sport L. 135 at 152-57.

[198]  See, *Vancouver Hockey Club Ltd. v. 8 Hockey Ventures Inc.*, [1987] B.C.J. No. 2074, 47 D.L.R. (4th) 51 (B.C.S.C.) (maximum allowable fine against team under by-law 17.3).

[199]  See, Chapter 8, "Competition Law and Labour Law", sections A-C. See, for example, *Blalock v. Ladies Professional Golf Assn.*, 359 F.Supp. 1260 (N.D. Ga., 1973) (suspension imposed by committee of golfers who would be competing against Blalock; unfettered discretion and no hearing; illegal exclusion from market).

testing and doping control should be established in conjunction with the players' association.

The NHL and the individual teams base their disciplinary authority on the players' contractual agreement to behave as proper sportsmen, abide by rules and accept decisions. The authority relates to both "on-ice" and "off-ice" activity. By paragraph 2(e) of the SPC, the player agrees,

> to conduct himself on and off the rink according to the highest standards of honesty, morality, fair play and sportsmanship, and to refrain from conduct detrimental to the best interest of the Club, the League or professional hockey generally.[200]

Both the team and the player agree to be bound by league rules and by the CBA (see, SPC paragraph 18), and the player agrees that the team may put into effect any ruling by the league for his expulsion or for suspension with loss of pay (see, SPC paragraphs 15, 16). Teams may establish reasonable rules with respect to conduct and conditioning and may enforce them through fines or suspensions (see, SPC paragraphs 3, 4). Where the disregard of the rule constitutes a material breach of contract, the team may terminate the SPC[201] after the player has cleared waivers (see, SPC paragraph 14).

The SPC operates as a link to the disciplinary powers referred to in various league documents, including the playing rules and the system of "supplementary discipline" with respect to conduct on the ice.[202] This link is reinforced by the CBA which declares that both teams and players are bound by league rules (see, articles 30.1, 30.2) and enables teams to require players to abide by "Club Rules" (see, article 30.7; exhibit 14).[203] Standard disciplinary matters related to play are subject to articles 18.3 and 18.5 of the CBA which prescribe the right to fine and suspend players for conduct on the ice. Under article 6.3(j) of the NHL Constitution, the Commissioner may discipline any person connected with the league or a member team who has violated a league rule or been guilty of "conduct detrimental to the League or the game of hockey". The available

---

[200] See also, *Cimpean v. Payton*, [2008] O.J. No. 2665 (Ont. S.C.J.), leave to appeal granted, [2008] O.J. No. 4713 (Ont. S.C.J.) (clause 5 of Uniform Player Contract of NBA; alleged liability of Milwaukee Bucks and NBA for assaults committed by players at adult entertainment lounge).

[201] In the National Basketball Association, the power to combine termination of the contract with suspension by the league was considered in the case of Latrell Sprewell after he had attempted to choke coach P.J. Carlesimo during a practice session. An arbitrator found lack of "just cause", reinstated Sprewell and reduced the suspension by the league to a loss 68 games and USD $6.4 million. See: *NBA Players Assn. on behalf of Player Latrell Sprewell and Warriors Basketball Club and NBA* (March 4, 1998, J. Feerick, arb.) ("there is no history of both the League and a team imposing discipline for the same violent conduct"); *Sprewell v. Golden State Warriors*, 266 F.3d 979 (9th Cir., 2001) (arbitrator did not exceed his authority; no discrimination on the basis of race).

[202] See, Chapter 6, "Play Safe: On the Ice", section B, 5. See also, CBA exhibit 8.

[203] By article 30.8 of the CBA, a player may be fined for reporting to training camp overweight but may not be fined for "indifferent" play. Besides holding other rights under the SPC, by article 15.3(f) teams may make a specified pay deduction where a player does not report to training camp.

sanctions include expulsion, suspension, cancellation of contracts, fines or deprivation of draft choices. The Commissioner's determination is declared to be "final", subject to some right of appeal to the Board of Governors. Similarly, section 17 of the NHL By-Laws grants the Commissioner authority to discipline any person involved in intentionally losing a game (see, By-Law 17.2) or engaging in conduct or making statements that are "prejudicial" to the league or the game (see, By-Laws 17.3, 17.4). In association with the powers of teams, there is also authority to suspend players acting in breach of contract or agreement (see, By-Laws 17.5-17.7). Article 18.4 of the CBA is applicable where the league seeks to impose sanctions on a player for off-ice conduct or where it proposes to rely on evidence in addition to the videotapes of an on-ice incident. The league may investigate incidents and interview players, but may not impose discipline without holding a hearing at which affected parties, including the NHLPA, have the right to participate (see, article 18.4(d)). Where disciplinary action by the league results in a fine or the forfeiture of a player's salary, the proceeds are deposited in the NHL Players' Emergency Assistance Fund (see, article 18.7).

The NHL's power to sanction teams and management personnel has been considered in a number of notorious cases. In 1987, the league sought to impose a fine of USD $310,000 on the Vancouver Canucks after they had signed Pat Quinn as coach while he was still under contract with the L.A. Kings. In *Vancouver Hockey Club v. 8 Hockey Ventures Ltd.*,[204] the court examined the applicable league By-Law and determined that the maximum allowable fine was USD $10,000. The following year, the New Jersey Devils obtained a restraining order to prevent the suspension without a hearing of coach Jim Schoenfeld who had confronted the referee after a playoff game and delivered lines such as "fat pig" and "have another doughnut". NHL officials refused to serve at the next game which was officiated by amateurs wearing players' warm-up gear and yellow jerseys.[205] In 1993, Gary Bettman, newly appointed as Commissioner, imposed an authorized fine of USD $100,000 on the Ottawa Senators after their former owner made comments suggesting that they were tanking games late in the season in order to secure first pick in the entry draft; the Senators had failed to report the comments and the allegations that some players had not played to their potential.[206]

Cases related to players' off-ice conduct have traditionally involved gambling and the use of drugs.[207] The developing concern over crimes by athletes and other moral transgressions has now led the NHL to take a more general interest

---

[204] [1987] B.C.J. No. 2074, 47 D.L.R. (4th) 51 (B.C.S.C.).

[205] See: "Coach feels wrath of NHL" *The Globe and Mail* (Toronto: May 9, 1988) at A13; "Temporary peace reached in hockey war" *The Globe and Mail* (Toronto: May 10, 1988) at A15.

[206] See, "The verdict is delivered" *The Ottawa Citizen* (September 3, 1993) at F1. The players and coaches were found to have made every effort to win.

[207] See Chapter 9, "National Hockey League", sections D, 2, 3.

in personal misconduct.[208] In 2007, the league suspended Mark Bell for 15 games after he pleaded no contest in California to charges of drunk driving and leaving the scene of an accident.[209] In 2008, Sean Avery was suspended for six games after he invited media attention and then made crude sexual comments about players dating his former girlfriend.[210] Where a league seeks to condemn misconduct, it must show that it is acting to protect legitimate interests, including public relations. A league will be anxious to maintain a moral image and the continued favour of paying customers and usually declares that its players are role models whose private lives must stand up to public scrutiny. Although a long rap sheet rarely results in reduced revenue, the reputation of the league is clearly damaged by instances of violence, sexual assault, drunk driving or other serious crimes. There is, however, the risk that disciplinary action will be based on imprecise discretionary criteria or "romantic, even 'mid-Victorian' judgments of moral quasi-aesthetic value".[211] It would be inappropriate to sanction players who infringe conventional morality, lead unusual lifestyles or hold unpopular political opinions. Given the range of conduct prohibited by criminal law, the commission of an offence may not be a legitimate interest of the league, and sanctions cannot be applied in a manner that is arbitrary or discriminatory.[212] By article 7.2 of the CBA, the prohibited grounds of discrimination include membership or support of a labour organization.

Discipline based on off-ice behaviour calls for a careful balancing of the freedom of the player with the league's interest in the integrity of its game, and the system must show a consistent and principled approach to serious misconduct, not merely the "selective (and sometimes prejudiced) feelings of the powers that be".[213] If moral probity is to be demanded of the players, it is essential that similar standards are applied to team owners.[214] The character of the game is also relevant in showing "the highest standards of...morality...and sportsmanship". A league that tolerates and rewards fisticuffs and a violent style of play is hardly in a position to declare its unqualified disapproval of assault, including domestic violence. The charge of hypocrisy is also applicable where

---

[208] On sexual assault and other crimes, see, Chapter 5, "Be Safe: Off the Ice", sections C; D. See also, P.C. Weiler, *Leveling the Playing Field: How the Law Can Make Sports Better for Fans* (Cambridge: Harvard University Press, 2000) at 87-100.

[209] See, "Maple Leafs' forward suspended for 15 games", "Union rushes to Bell's defence" *The Globe and Mail* (Toronto: September 13, 2007) at R6, R10.

[210] See: "NHL right to act swiftly as Avery steps over the line" *The Globe and Mail* (Toronto: December 3, 2008) at R6; "Avery suspended six games" *The Globe and Mail* (Toronto: December 6, 2008) at S8.

[211] *Ali v. State Athletic Commission*, 308 F.Supp. 11 at 16 (S.D. N.Y., 1969), *per* Frankel D.J. See also, *Calzadilla v. Dooley*, 286 N.Y.S.2d 510 at 516 (1968) (refusal of wrestling licence to woman).

[212] See, *Ali v. State Athletic Commission*, 316 F.Supp. 1246 (S.D. N.Y., 1970) (boxer convicted for refusing induction into the army; abuse of discretion in denying licence; other applicants convicted of offences had received licences).

[213] P.C. Weiler, *Leveling the Playing Field: How the Law Can Make Sports Better for Fans* (Cambridge: Harvard University Press, 2000) at 91.

[214] On the history of team ownership in Canada, see Chapter 7, "The Business of Hockey", section B, 1.

the game is the foundation of betting systems,[215] centred on a culture of beer and a vehicle for advertising by breweries.

## 2.   Betting

Betting interests have played an important historical role in formalizing games and events since dedicated punters have a special stake in contests and wish to see them clearly defined, well regulated and honestly conducted. The financial commitment of gamblers and bookmakers can, however, lead to corruption as attempts are made to fix outcomes or influence the final score.[216] The corrupt insider risks criminal conviction because of involvement in illegal betting operations,[217] and professional leagues have sought to preserve competitive integrity through disciplinary action against players,[218] managers or officials who associate with gambling elements or bet on games. Under article 3.9 of the Constitution of the NHL, a franchise may be terminated for "countenancing" wagering or manipulating scores, and betting activities are subject to the general disciplinary authority of the Commissioner under article 6 and By-Law 17. By-Law 18 seeks to exclude "undesirable" employees, and article 31.1(a) of the CBA prohibits players from loaning money to officials.

In the NHL, betting is viewed as an egregious example of conduct "detrimental" or "prejudicial" to the league or the game, and paragraph 9 of the SPC makes special provision for payments based on the result of games,

> It is mutually agreed that the Club will not pay, and the Player will not accept from any person, any bonus or anything of value for winning or otherwise attempting to affect the outcome of any particular game or series of games except as authorized by the League By-laws.

Early instances of disciplinary action against players include the suspensions given to Walter "Babe" Pratt, Billy Taylor and Don Gallinger in the 1940s.[219] In 1946, president Mervyn Dutton initially expelled Pratt from the league for

---

[215]   See Chapter 7, "The Business of Hockey", section A, 5.

[216]   See: S. Gardiner *et al.*, *Sports Law*, 3d ed. (London: Cavendish Publishing, 2006) at 325-49; *Grobbelaar v. News Group Newspapers Ltd.*, [2002] 4 All E.R. 732 (H.L.) (libel action; series of articles claimed that goalkeeper had agreed to fix soccer games).

[217]   On the conviction of NBA referee Tim Donaghy, see: "Donaghy pleads guilty" *The Globe and Mail* (Toronto: August 16, 2007) at R11; "Donaghy sentenced to 15 months" *The Globe and Mail* (Toronto: July 30, 2008) at R9; *United States v. Donaghy*, 570 F.Supp. 2d 411 (E.D. N.Y., 2008) (NBA awarded USD $217,267 in victim restitution).

[218]   In relation to major league baseball, see: E. Asinof, *Eight Men Out: The Black Sox and the 1919 World Series* (New York: Henry Holt and Co., 1963); *Rose v. Giamatti*, 721 F. Supp. 906 (S.D. Ohio, 1989) (investigation into gambling by Pete Rose while he was manager of the Cincinnati Reds). In relation to the NBA, see: *Molinas v. Podoloff*, 133 N.Y.S.2d 743 (S.C., 1954) (injunction to lift suspension refused; lack of "clean hands" through admitted association with gamblers); *Molinas v. National Basketball Assn.*, 190 F.Supp. 241 (S.D. N.Y., 1961) (antitrust action denied; rule and suspension were reasonable and necessary).

[219]   See, "Hockey's first gambling face-off" *The Globe and Mail* (Toronto: February 11, 2006) at F7.

betting on hockey games, but this was reduced to loss of four weeks' pay following an appeal to the active gamblers who formed the NHL's Board of Governors.[220] (Pratt played for the Leafs, which at the time were owned by the horse racing enthusiast Conn Smythe.) To deter further involvement in unacceptable betting, the Board declared that in future there would be no appeal from the league president's decision.[221] In the cases of Taylor and Gallinger in 1948, president Clarence Campbell imposed permanent expulsions for associating with a known Detroit gambler and betting on hockey games.[222] Gallinger later admitted betting $1000 against his own team in a game in which he was instrumental in their victory.[223] The "life" suspensions were removed in 1970.[224]

The more recent example relates to former NHL player Rick Tocchet. In February 2006, Tocchet took a leave of absence from his position as an assistant coach with the Phoenix Coyotes after he was charged with playing a role in an illegal sports betting ring. "Operation Slapshot", conducted by police in New Jersey, detected a gambling enterprise that focussed on football and did not appear to handle hockey games; the business was relatively modest, taking in total bets of USD $1.7 million over one period of 40 days. Some media reports named Janet Jones, wife of Wayne Gretzky, as a client of the ring, and the investigations formed a major distraction as Team Canada prepared to play at the 2006 Winter Olympics in Turin.[225] Tocchet subsequently pleaded guilty to charges relating to the promotion of gambling and was sentenced to two years probation.[226] In November 2007, Commissioner Bettman announced that Tocchet would be permitted to resume coaching duties in February 2008 on condition that he not gamble and that he submit himself for evaluation under the Substance Abuse and Behavioural Health ("SABH") Program.[227]

## 3.  Drug Use and Doping Control

Discipline based on the use of prohibited substances traditionally focussed on illegal, recreational drugs rather than chemical means of enhancing athletic performance. The use of illegal drugs was subject to the discretionary authority

---

[220]  See: "Hockey expels 'Babe' Pratt for gambling on games" *The Globe and Mail* (Toronto: January 30, 1946) at 1; "'Babe' Pratt reinstated will play on Saturday" *The Globe and Mail* (Toronto: February 14, 1946) at 1.

[221]  See, "Pratt reinstated" *The Globe and Mail* (Toronto: February 14, 1946) at 15.

[222]  See: "NHL expels Taylor for life; Don Gallinger is suspended" *The Globe and Mail* (Toronto: March 10, 1948) at 1; "Hockey loop bars Bruins' Gallinger" *The New York Times* (September 29, 1948) at 38.

[223]  See, Dick Beddoes, *The Globe and Mail* (Toronto: August 29, 1970) at 29.

[224]  See, "Campbell says NHL still feels same about gambling" *The Globe and Mail* (Toronto: August 29, 1970) at 29.

[225]  See, "Gretzky: 'I didn't do it'" *The Globe and Mail* (Toronto: February 10, 2006) at A1, A6.

[226]  See, "No jail time for Tocchet" *The Globe and Mail* (Toronto: August 18, 2007) at S3.

[227]  See, "NHL commissioner extends Tocchet's ban until February" *The Globe and Mail* (Toronto: November 2, 2007) at R6.

of the Commissioner, including the powers under NHL By-Law 17.[228] In 1978, Don Murdoch was suspended for one season (later reduced to 40 games) after he pleaded guilty to possession of a small quantity of cocaine.[229] Ric Nattress received a 30-game suspension in 1983 after being convicted of possession of marijuana, Borje Salming received an eight-game suspension in 1986 after he admitted using cocaine five years earlier, and Bob Probert was subject to an indeterminate ban in 1989 following his conviction for importing cocaine. In 1990, Grant Fuhr admitted long-term use of cocaine and was suspended for one season, with the chance of reinstatement after 60 games.[230]

Various sanctions could, therefore, be applied where a player admitted using an illegal drug or was convicted by a criminal court. This unstructured, punitive system came to be regarded as inadequate as professional leagues dealt with repeated examples of drunk driving and the abuse of alcohol and drugs.[231] Reports of drug use in 1986[232] led Alan Eagleson and NHL president John Ziegler to recommend mandatory testing, but the scheme was rightly resisted by the players.[233] Unlike other major leagues,[234] the collective bargaining agreements negotiated in the NHL in 1990s did not incorporate drug testing, although the league and the NHLPA began negotiations on a system that would incorporate educational elements and programs for rehabilitation. The league also came under pressure to test for performance-enhancing substances as there were initiatives to strengthen national and international systems of doping control.[235]

In 1996, the NHL and the NHLPA established the Substance Abuse and Behavioural Health ("SABH") Program to assist players facing problems with drugs or alcohol and to provide counselling on issues such as domestic violence. Stage one of the program allows players to volunteer for a course of treatment and care while continuing to receive full salary and benefits; depending on their progress and compliance, the supervising medical personnel may make a recommendation for reinstatement. Where players suffer a relapse or do not

---

[228] NHL By-Law 17A has provided for a "Drug Audit" and disciplinary action against team employees in relation to the unauthorized use of prescription drugs or the failure to report the misuse of drugs.

[229] See: "NHL player reps say 'no sympathy' for Murdoch" *The Globe and Mail* (Toronto: July 26, 1978) at 27; E. McRae, "Coke on ice" *The Canadian* (October 14, 1978) at 5; "Ziegler lifts Murdoch's suspension at 40 games" *The Globe and Mail* (Toronto: January 4, 1979) at 41.

[230] See: "Oilers' Fuhr faces NHL drug hearing" *The Globe and Mail* (Toronto: September 1, 1990) at A16; A. Eagleson & S. Young, *Power Play: The Memoirs of Hockey Czar Alan Eagleson* (Toronto: McClelland & Stewart, 1991) at 284-94.

[231] On the death of John Kordic, see, "Kordic's death a microcosm of his career" *The Globe and Mail* (Toronto: August 10, 1992) at A13.

[232] See, for example, A. Keteyian & D. Ramsay, "The Joyless End of a Joyride" *Sports Illustrated* (May 12, 1986) 32 (rumours relating to the Edmonton Oilers).

[233] See: "NHL head, Eagleson urge tests" *The Globe and Mail* (Toronto: May 22, 1986) at A13; "Eagle's drug stance stirs up NHL players" *The Globe and Mail* (Toronto: May 30, 1986) at A12.

[234] See, for example, CBA of NBA (1999), article 33.

[235] See Chapter 3, "Organizations and Regulations", section D.

comply with prescribed conditions, they may be placed in the second or third stages of the program and suspended without pay.

The use of performance enhancing substances is now addressed in article 47 of the CBA which declares that the object is to combine educational elements with testing and disciplinary penalties. The costs of the Performance Enhancing Substances Program are the responsibility of the league, although salaries forfeited as a result of suspensions go towards this program and the SABH program. By article 47.2, the Program Committee reviews the list of banned substances maintained by the World Anti Doping Agency ("WADA") and makes recommendations as to which substances are relevant to hockey and so should be treated as "Prohibited Substances". Players who have participated in an orientation session may be subject to two no-notice tests during the period from training camp to the end of the regular season (see, articles 47.4, 47.6). Where a player tests positive, the following scale of penalties applies (see, article 47.7):

> First positive test: suspension for 20 NHL games without pay and mandatory referral to the SABH program.
>
> Second positive test: suspension for 60 NHL games without pay and mandatory referral to the SABH program.
>
> Third positive test: "permanent" suspension without pay, although the player may apply to the Committee after two years for discretionary reinstatement.

Appeals against positive tests are taken to the "impartial arbitrator" who may remove the period of suspension (see, article 47.8).

The in-house administration of the program and the schedule that excludes off-season testing did not impress Richard Pound, the chairman of WADA. In November 2005, the anti-doping czar declared his suspicion that one third of NHL players were using some form of performance-enhancing substance.[236] Pound was, however, unable to offer any evidence or statistical data on the point. The league's testing began in January 2006 and resulted in no positive results from the 1400 samples, although the program did not include testing for WADA's list of substances such as stimulants that are prohibited in-competition. Testing under the program in subsequent years brought just one failed test in 2007. As other sports have faced revelations relating to drug use and doping, the NHL has consistently maintained that steroids and other performance-enhancing drugs are not part of the culture of the game. A more intrusive regime of surveillance would probably yield more positives, but the particular merit of the league's program is that it is the result of collective bargaining with the players and so reflects their genuine consent. By incorporating the athletes' evaluation of the need for testing and sanctions, the program is superior to the "War on Drugs" coercion of the wider anti-doping movement.

---

[236] See: "NHL swift to deny Pound's charge" *The Globe and Mail* (Toronto: November 25, 2005) at R6; "Drug debate a hot topic in locker room" *The Globe and Mail* (Toronto: November 26, 2005) at S2.

# E. STANDARD PLAYER'S CONTRACT

## 1. General

The collective bargaining agreement ("CBA") recognizes that the system of employment allows for the individual negotiation of terms (see, article 2.1) but declares that the sole form of contract to be used in signing players is the standard player's contract ("SPC").[237] The 2005 form of the SPC is incorporated in the CBA as exhibit 1 and succeeds previous versions, except that contracts using the 1995 form remain valid until they expire (see, article 11.1). The SPC was originally developed by management to impose detailed obligations on players while granting sweeping powers to teams. Where uniform, "take-it-or-leave-it" contracts have been devised by trade associations, any ambiguity is interpreted against the drafting party,[238] although it may no longer be appropriate to apply this rule in the era of collective bargaining and professional agents.

The SPC of the NHL consists of 22 standard "paragraphs" that bind the player to play for and train with the team, maintain good physical condition and abide by league rules. The most important obligation of the employer is to pay the specified salary, the SPC being the sole basis for payments (see, article 11.9(b)). The terms of the contract are usually settled by the written record signed by the parties,[239] and the parol evidence rule limits the use of extrinsic material to modify the final text. Paragraphs 19 and 22 declare that the SPC contains the entire agreement and that there have been no undisclosed inducements or promises. The contract is, however, subject to league rules and the CBA, and it must be consistent with the CBA (see, paragraph 18).

The enforcement of contracts is subject to general principles of employment law, although interpretation and analysis may call for understanding of hockey terminology and recognition of practices or dealings peculiar to the industry.[240] Many disputes relating to players' contracts in professional leagues have resulted in litigation before the ordinary courts, and paragraph 6 of the SPC recognizes

---

[237] On the role of the players' association in negotiating the terms of the SPC, see, *Yashin v. National Hockey League*, [2000] O.J. No. 3306, 192 D.L.R. (4th) 747 (Ont. S.C.J.); see further, Chapter 9, "National Hockey League", section B, 3.

[238] See: *Johnson v. Green Bay Packers, Inc.*, 74 N.W.2d 784 (S.C. Wis., 1956) (ambiguity as to matters subject to arbitration); *Lemat Corp. v. Barry*, 275 Cal. App. 2d 671, 80 Cal. Rptr. 240 (C.A., 1972) (contract of adhesion to be construed strictly against team; renewal limited to one year).

[239] See: *Pinder v. Vancouver Hockey Club Ltd.*, [1972] B.C.J. No. 451, 28 D.L.R. (3d) 374 (B.C.S.C.) (oral guarantee not enforceable); *Sheehy v. Edmonton World Hockey Enterprises Ltd.*, [1979] A.J. No. 867, 105 D.L.R. (3d) 644 (Alta. Q.B.) (reason for inserting clause could not be used to explain contract term). But see: *Mandich v. North Star Partnership*, 450 N.W.2d 173 (Min. C.A., 1990); *Mandich v. Watters*, 970 F.2d 462 (8th Cir., 1992) (player bound by agent's oral side deal to take disability benefit and not claim salary).

[240] See, *In the Matter of...Philadelphia Flyers and Quebec Nordiques and New York Rangers* (June 30, 1992, L. Bertuzzi, arb.), relating to the trade of the draft rights to Eric Lindros, the arbitrator stated (at 3) that the dispute involved "a determination of whether two Clubs made a 'deal' in the way Clubs in the NHL have been making 'deals' for seventy-five years".

the team's right to apply directly for an injunction to deal with breach of the SPC, including "jumping" the contract and playing for another team.[241] The more common forum for contract issues is now the arbitration systems recognized in the CBA and the SPC (see, paragraphs 12, 18). Arbitration offers a private and specialized process aiming to bring final resolution to the case.[242] The decisions of labour arbitrators are subject to "a very high degree of deference", although the standard of review in relation to the jurisdiction of the arbitrator is correctness.[243] The named arbitrator may be the league commissioner or president or an impartial board.[244] Where parties prescribe arbitration for particular types of dispute, courts recognize the preferred process and will require that the case be dealt with in the chosen forum.[245] But if the dispute does not arise from an issue[246] or agreement[247] subject to arbitration, the matter may proceed as a court action.

---

[241] See further, Chapter 9, "National Hockey League", section E, 5. On the "sordid fight for football players" and the famous advice to Sam Etcheverry, see, *Detroit Football Co. v. Robinson*, 186 F.Supp. 933 (E.D. La., 1960).

[242] See: *Boston Celtics Limited Partnership v. Shaw*, 908 F.2d 1041 (1st Cir., 1990) (enforcement of arbitrator's decision); *National Football League Players' Assn. v. Pro-Football, Inc.*, 857 F.Supp. 71 (D. D.C., 1994).

[243] See, *Yashin v. National Hockey League*, [2000] O.J. No. 3306, 192 D.L.R. (4th) 747 (Ont. S.C.J.) (application for judicial review dismissed).

[244] See: *Dryer v. Los Angeles Rams Football*, 709 P.2d 826, 220 Cal. Rptr. 807 (S.C., 1991) (commissioner's power to remove issues did not invalidate arbitration process); *Morris v. New York Football Giants, Inc.*, 575 N.Y.S.2d 1013 (S.C. 1991) (neutral arbitrator appointed); *National Hockey League Players' Assn. v. Bettman*, 93 Civ. 5769 (S.D. N.Y., 1994) (authority to determine validity of offer sheets; no evidence of bias). See also, *Watson v. Prager*, [1991] 3 All E.R. 487, [1991] 1 W.L.R. 726 (Ch. Div.).

[245] See: *Cincinnati Bengals, Inc. v. Thompson*, 553 F.Supp. 1011 (S.D. Ohio, 1983) (player in bargaining unit bound by arbitration provision of expired collective agreement; player's right to pay during strike; arbitration promotes clarity and uniformity); *Brewer v. Maple Leaf Gardens Ltd.* (1985), 31 A.C.W.S. (2d) 73 and 74 (Ont. H.C.J.) (arbitration before president initiated; action stayed); *Krutov v. Vancouver Hockey Club Ltd.*, [1991] B.C.J. No. 3464 (B.C.S.C. (In Chambers)) (salary dispute to proceed to arbitration); *Smith v. Houston Oilers, Inc.*, 87 F.3d 717 (5th Cir., 1996) (claim alleging that rehabilitation program was "abusive" was governed by CBA); *Childs v. Meadowlands Basketball Associates*, 954 F.Supp. 994 (D. N.J., 1997) (alleged pre-contract misrepresentations subject to arbitration); *East Coast Hockey League, Inc. v. Professional Hockey Players Assn.*, 322 F.3d 311 (4th Cir., 2003) (disputes relating to salary cap and discipline subject to arbitration).

[246] See: *Johnson v. Green Bay Packers, Inc.*, 74 N.W.2d 784 (S.C. Wis., 1956) (arbitration limited to disputes relating to obligation to observe team and league rules); *Belanger v. Pittsburgh Penguins Inc.*, [1998] O.J. No. 427, 17 C.P.C. (4th) 245 (Ont. Gen. Div.) (injury grievance subject to arbitration, but claim for negligence and breach of duty allowed).

[247] See: *Hillman v. Sports Centrepoint Enterprises Ltd.*, [1977] 2 A.C.W.S. 104 (Man. C.A.) (dispute depending on supplementary agreement between teams not subject to arbitration); *Davis v. Pro Basketball, Inc.*, 381 F.Supp. 1 (S.D. N.Y., 1974) (modification of agreement subject to arbitration); *Spain v. Houston Oilers, Inc.*, 593 S.W.2d 746 (Tex. Civ. App., 1979) (team's arbitration rights waived by delay; state court action for injury grievance allowed).

## 2.    Formation and Avoidance

Disputes may occur over the basic issue of contract formation. A binding contract arises when final agreement is achieved through the acceptance of a subsisting offer. Whether a player's act of signing a contract amounts to a revocable offer or an acceptance of terms depends on the intent of the parties. Before holding that a contract is enforceable, a court will require proof that the parties reached agreement on matters such as the terms and duration of the service. If a signed document does not represent the understanding reached between player and team, or if an offer is withdrawn before there has been a final, operative acceptance, no binding agreement is reached.

In *Los Angeles Rams Football Club v. Cannon*[248] and *Detroit Football Co. v. Robinson*,[249] college players were able to repudiate signed "contracts" and accept competing offers because the SPC declared that the agreement became binding only when it was approved by the commissioner; that approval was, therefore, a condition precedent to the existence of a contract.

In the NHL, league By-Laws declare that agreement is reached when a player signs an authorized form, accepts a team's offer in writing or by telegraph[250] or gives a receipt for money advanced.[251] The CBA does, however, include detailed rules relating to the registration of SPCs and offer sheets and arbitration processes where a contract is rejected or challenged by the league (see, articles 11.5, 11.6). Article 11.3 declares that, "no SPC shall be valid or enforceable in any manner whatsoever unless and until it has been filed with Central Registry and approved by the League or the Arbitrator". The signing of documents is, therefore, not the last word, and the required additional review may result in the "reform" of a SPC or a player reverting to his previous contractual status, including free agency.

Even though parties have reached agreement, various circumstances may avoid the apparent obligations. The operation of the contract may be nullified where its terms are illegal (for example, for restraint of trade[252]) or where a party lacks the capacity[253] or age[254] to contract. A party may also claim that a contract was entered into under misrepresentation or fundamental mistake. In *Gabriel v.*

---

[248]    185 F.Supp. 717 (S.D. Cal., 1960).

[249]    186 F.Supp. 933 (E.D. La., 1960), affd 283 F.2d 657 (5th Cir., 1960).

[250]    See, "Wings' fax number key to suit" *The Globe and Mail* (Toronto: August 10, 1995) at C10 (offer by Detroit Red Wings to Mike Vernon accepted by fax).

[251]    See, NHL By-Law 2.1. See also, *Claude Lemieux v. New Jersey Devils* (September 29, 1995, G. Nicolau, arb.).

[252]    See Chapter 8, "Competition Law and Labour Law", section B.

[253]    See, *Spencer v. Milton*, 287 N.Y.S. 944 (S.C., 1936) (baseball player claimed that he was intoxicated when he signed).

[254]    See, *Toronto Marlboro Major Junior "A" Hockey Club v. Tonelli*, [1977] O.J. No. 2464, 18 O.R. (2d) 21 (Ont. H.C.J.), affd [1979] O.J. No. 4054, 23 O.R. (2d) 193 (Ont. C.A.); see further, Chapter 3, "Organizations and Regulations", section B, 3. See also, *Kitchener Dutchmen Inc. v. Russian Ice Hockey Federation*, [1998] O.J. No. 970 (Ont. Gen. Div.) (contracts with Torpedo Yaroslavl).

*Hamilton Tiger-Cat Football Club Ltd.*,[255] Tony Gabriel had signed a contract with the Ticats at a time when he was not aware that the playing schedule had increased from 14 to 16 games; the team's manager knew of the increase but he did not inform the player. The court held that in the circumstances there was no duty of disclosure and there was no misrepresentation or mistake that would avoid the contract.

## 3. Procuring Breach of Contract[256]

In 1853, an impresario persuaded the opera singer, Johanna Wagner, not to perform her contract at the plaintiff's theatre. In *Lumley v. Gye*,[257] the court recognized that the plaintiff could sustain an action against the person who "maliciously" induced the breach of a contract for professional services. The remedy was not limited to a claim in contract against the artiste. An action in tort could be brought against the person who had interfered with a subsisting contract. Two factors justified the need for a separate action: the other party to the contract might not be worth suing, and the damages in tort might be higher than those in contract. Where a representative of a rival league or team induces a player to "jump" a contract, the current team may therefore take action against both its player and the organization that procured the breach.

This legal remedy supplements internal disciplinary mechanisms applying to league members.[258] Within the NHL, negotiation and signing are regulated through the system of contract registration and the prohibitions on "tampering". By article 7.3 of the CBA a player may not negotiate with another team during the term of his SPC, and paragraph 10 of the SPC prohibits players from discussing present or future services that might be provided by players whose rights are held by other teams.

The tort of interference with contract[259] requires proof that a valid, enforceable contract existed; that the defendant deliberately procured its breach; that this breach was achieved by wrongful interference without justification; and that the plaintiff suffered actual damage as a result. The tort requires an intentional action to induce the breach of contract and injure the plaintiff. Such action may be direct persuasion (as in *Lumley v. Gye* where the defendant

---

[255] [1975] O.J. No. 2284, 8 O.R. (2d) 285 (Ont. H.C.J.).

[256] See: L.L. Stevens, "Interference with Economic Relations - Some Aspects of the Turmoil in Intentional Torts" (1974) 12 Osgoode Hall L.J. 595; L.N. Klar, *Tort Law*, 3d ed. (Toronto: Thomson Carswell, 2003) at 610-25; P.T. Burns & J. Blom, *Economic Interests in Canadian Tort Law* (Markham, ON: LexisNexis Canada, 2009) at 77-120.

[257] (1853), 2 E. & B. 216, 118 E.R. 749.

[258] On powers under NHL By-Laws 15 and 17, see, *Vancouver Hockey Club Ltd. v. 8 Hockey Ventures Inc.*, [1987] B.C.J. No. 2074, 47 D.L.R. (4th) 51 (B.C.S.C.) (Canucks signed Pat Quinn to become general manager after serving as coach of LA Kings).

[259] See, for example: *Versa Services Ltd. v. Toronto Blue Jays Baseball Club*, [1994] O.J. No. 139, 45 A.C.W.S. (3d) 228 (Ont. Gen. Div.) (inducing breach of contract to supply concession services at stadium); *Sports Corp. v. Svoboda*, [2004] A.J. No. 728, 49 C.P.C. (5th) 143 (Alta. Q.B.) (agent's representation agreement).

offered the singer more money) or some other intervention that disables the contracting party from performing.

In sports, the typical procurement action arises when a player, who is alleged to be bound by an existing contract, signs with a team in a rival league.[260] The remedy first sought is often the interim injunction. Usually the defendant is the team from the competing league that is trying to gain the player's services. Action may also be attempted against the league as a whole or against the individual agent who conducts the negotiations.[261] The league will probably prefer that the player discharge existing obligations and is unlikely to be involved in dealings leading to the signing of a player with a particular team;[262] in such circumstances, no remedy for procurement will be available against the league. However, when a league president or other representative conducts a general "recruiting drive" to encourage players to repudiate their contracts, the evidence will be sufficient to grant the plaintiff a remedy against that party.[263] In *Greig v. Insole*,[264] the wrongful interference took the form of resolutions by the established cricket governing body to disqualify players who served under contract with a rival commercial cricket league. The court found that the governing body "intended to apply pressure or persuasion to all players who had entered into contracts with World Series Cricket...whether or not they had lawful rights to withdraw".[265] In the circumstances, this amounted to a knowing and direct interference with the players' contractual relations.

There can be no action for procurement if a contract has not been formed[266] or if the contract is invalid and unenforceable, for example, for restraint of trade.[267] In *Toronto Marlboro Major Junior "A" Hockey Club v. Tonelli*,[268] the player signed a junior hockey contract while under the age of majority. On coming of age, he repudiated this contract in order to join the Houston Aeros of the World Hockey Association at a lucrative professional salary. The court found that the

---

[260] On international transfers, see Chapter 3, "Organizations and Regulations", section C, 2, a.

[261] See, *Toronto Marlboro Major Junior "A" Hockey Club v. Tonelli*, [1977] O.J. No. 2464, 18 O.R. (2d) 21 (Ont. H.C.J.), affd [1979] O.J. No. 4054, 23 O.R. (2d) 193 (Ont. C.A.).

[262] *Toronto Marlboro Major Junior "A" Hockey Club v. Tonelli*, [1977] O.J. No. 2464, 18 O.R. (2d) 21 at 37-38 (Ont. H.C.J.).

[263] See: *American League Baseball Club of New York, Inc. v. Pasquel*, 63 N.Y.S.2d 537 (S.C., 1946). See also, *World Football League v. Dallas Cowboys Football Club, Inc.*, 513 S.W.2d 102 (Civ. App. Tex., 1974); *News Ltd. v. Australian Rugby Football League Ltd.* (1996), 139 A.L.R. 93, 64 F.C.R. 410 (Fed. C. of Aust., Full Ct.).

[264] [1978] 1 W.L.R. 302, [1978] 3 All E.R. 449 (Ch. Div.).

[265] *Greig v. Insole*, [1978] 1 W.L.R. 302 at 344, [1978] 3 All E.R. 449 at 494-95 (Ch. Div.), *per* Slade J.

[266] But see, *Minnesota Muskies Inc. v. Hudson*, 294 F.Supp. 979 (M.D. N.C., 1969) (equitable aspects of signing player when current team intended to exercise option).

[267] See: *Boston Professional Hockey Assn., Inc. v. Gerry Cheevers Boston Professional Hockey Assn., Inc.*, 348 F.Supp. 261 (D. Mass., 1972); *Nassau Sports v. Hampson*, 355 F.Supp. 733 (D. Minn., 1972).

[268] [1977] O.J. No. 2464, 18 O.R. (2d) 21 (Ont. H.C.J.), affd [1979] O.J. No. 4054, 23 O.R. (2d) 193 (Ont. C.A.).

original junior contract was voidable as an unbeneficial infant's contract. No action could therefore succeed against Houston or against the player's agent:

> Since I have found that this was a voidable contract and that therefore Tonelli was able to carry out his intention to repudiate if his terms were not met, it cannot be said on the balance of probabilities that Houston induced him to breach an enforceable contract. The plaintiffs have also failed to satisfy the onus of proving that Houston conspired with Tonelli and others, including the other defendants, to bring about the repudiation. The most that can be said is that Houston was available if Tonelli made his election to repudiate.[269]

Where a valid and enforceable contract does exist, the plaintiff team must show that the defendant knew of the existence of such contract or had sufficient information to be put on inquiry and notice.[270]

A team is free to compete for the future services of a current player, provided it is not inducing breach of an existing contract. The present team cannot claim that the possibility of future departure will harm the player's or the team's current performance.[271] Merely signing for later service is not a breach of the duty of loyalty to the present team, although engaging in other promotional and publicity activities for the new team may be a breach.[272]

There was an unusual variation on procurement litigation in *Potechin v. Yashin*,[273] where an attempt was made to assert the interests of fans in contractual disputes.[274] In this case, a season ticket holder brought a class action against the player and his agent alleging that Alexei Yashin's holdout with the Ottawa Senators unlawfully interfered with season ticket holders' contractual relations with the team. The plaintiff claimed that it was an implied term of subscription that the Senators would include their elite players and so offer the best quality of entertainment; the holdout therefore prevented the team from fulfilling the bargain. By way of defence, Yashin denied any intent to inflict economic harm on fans although frankly admitting that his concern was personal gain. On a motion to strike out the statement of claim, Charbonneau J. held that the tort of unlawful interference required the plaintiff to show that he had an enforceable contractual right to have Yashin on the Senators' active roster. He found no promissory intent in the Senators' marketing campaign and dismissed the action

---

[269] [1977] O.J. No. 2464, 18 O.R. (2d) 21 at 39-40 (Ont. H.C.J.), *per* Lerner J.

[270] See, *Winnipeg Rugby Football Club, Ltd. v. Freeman*, 140 F.Supp. 365 (N.D. Ohio, 1955). See also, *Central Sports Army Club v. Arena Associates, Inc.*, 952 F.Supp. 181 (S.D. N.Y., 1997) (no knowledge that Sergei Samsonov was under any obligation to CSKA).

[271] See, *Cincinnati Bengals, Inc. v. Bergey*, 453 F.Supp. 129 (S.D. Ohio, 1974).

[272] See, *World Football League v. Dallas Cowboys Football Club, Inc.*, 513 S.W.2d 102 (Civ. App. Tex., 1974). On future services, see also, *Vancouver Hockey Club Ltd. v. 8 Hockey Ventures Inc.*, [1987] B.C.J. No. 2074, 47 D.L.R. (4th) 51 (B.C.S.C.).

[273] [2000] O.J. No. 1660, 186 D.L.R. (4th) 757 (Ont. S.C.J.).

[274] See, J.M. Popowich, "He Shoots, He Scores? The Potential for Future Success of Fan-Based Lawsuits following *Potechin v. Yashin*" (2001) 20 J.L. & Commerce 285.

with costs fixed at CDN $32,000. Not for the first time, the fan lost out and had to pay a steep price.

## 4. Contents: Rights and Obligations

The substantive provisions of the standard player's contract create rights or powers in both the player and the team. The following aspects are dealt with in this section:

1. the team's right to terminate the contract;
2. the team's right to assign the contract;
3. the player's right to compensation;
4. the player's entitlement in the event of injury; and
5. the option clause.

1. *The team's right to terminate the contract*: The SPC in most professional leagues grants the team the power to "cut"[275] the player with no further obligation to pay salary if, in the opinion of the head coach, the player does not display sufficient ability or quality of performance. Decisions about the composition of the roster are, therefore, largely at the discretion of the coach or manager.[276] The SPC of the NHL does not include a similar power to terminate for being useless on the ice, although paragraph 1 does declare that the player is employed as a "skilled" athlete. In the NHL, where the player's skills need improving, the remedy is to despatch him to the affiliated minor league team. By paragraph 14 of the SPC, the team has the right to terminate only where the player has been guilty of a material breach of the contract. This power may be exercised where the player fails to obey team rules relating to training or conduct or where he refuses to provide services under the contract. Termination for other reasons is subject to paragraph 13 of the SPC and results in the player becoming an unrestricted free agent. Under paragraph 13, the player is offered on waivers and is then entitled to the "buy-out" of the contract through payments over twice the remaining term of the SPC. The "buy out" price is one third of the value of the contract for players under age 26, and two thirds for players 26 or over. In the NHL, contracts and salaries are "guaranteed" to this extent.

2. *The team's right to assign the contract*: Teams frequently adjust their complement of personnel by exchanging players or trading them to other teams

---

[275] The power will not necessarily be implied; see, *Hawes v. Sherwood-Parkdale Metro Junior Hockey Club Inc.*, [1991] P.E.I.J. No. 145, 88 D.L.R. (4th) 439 (P.E.I.C.A.), affg [1990] P.E.I.J. No. 109, 86 Nfld. & P.E.I.R. 342 (P.E.I.T.D.) (player's claim for season's salary failed because contract was ambiguous). See also, *Di Ruocco c. Association de hockey mineur Les Étoiles de l'Est inc.*, [2007] J.Q. no 5725, 2007 QCCQ 5921 (C.Q.) (team undertook to retain Midget AAA player for the season; "l'assurance qu'il ne serait pas retrancher ou rétrograder"; damages of CDN $7500).

[276] See, J. Barnes, *Sports and the Law in Canada*, 3d ed. (Toronto: Butterworths, 1996) at 224-26 (termination), 233 (decision to use player).

in the league.[277] The power to trade derives from paragraph 11 of the SPC by which the team is given the right to assign the contract and the player agrees to accept the assignment and faithfully perform with the new team. The effect of a trade is to transfer the rights and duties specified in the SPC to the new team, which becomes entitled to the player's services and assumes the obligation to pay salary. The new team is also responsible for any addendum or special clause inserted in the SPC. In *Sheehy v. Edmonton World Hockey Enterprises Ltd.*,[278] the plaintiff originally entered into a contract with the New England Whalers that included a provision that he would be paid $10,000 if traded; on being first traded to the Edmonton Oilers, he received that sum. After two years in Edmonton, the Oilers traded the plaintiff to the Birmingham Bulls. Relying on the special clause in the original contract, the plaintiff claimed $10,000 from the Oilers in respect of this trade. In allowing the action, the court held that the effect of the assignment was to create a new contract containing all the terms of the original, including the obligation to make payment in the event of a trade:

> The position was as if the Oilers had been substituted for the Whalers in the contract and the Oilers in fact recognized this when they took advantage of the provisions of the contract and sent him to Birmingham and he complied.[279]

The CBA of the NHL prohibits assignments by way of cash transactions and prohibits teams from retaining an obligation to pay salary or bonuses (see, article 11.16). Normally, relocations will proceed without objection because of the express grant of the power of assignment and the common practice of making trades. A trade may even be permissible when the remuneration in the original contract includes a portion of the assigning team's gate receipts.[280] An assignment will cause particular hardship if it is made to a team that cannot afford the payments or that folds entirely; the player may then seek to hold the assigning team to its original obligations.[281] In some circumstances, assignment may be precluded by negotiating a "no-trade" clause, or a "no-move" clause which prevents involuntary relocation by trade, loan or claim on waivers (see, article 11.8(a)). By article 11.8(a), such clauses may be included in the contracts of players who qualify as Group 3 unrestricted free agents (*e.g.*, players over age 27). If the player is assigned before the clause takes effect, the acquiring team is

---

[277] On the transfer of players, see NHL By-Law 9. See also, *In the Matter of...Philadelphia Flyers and Quebec Nordiques and New York Rangers* (June 30, 1992, L. Bertuzzi, arb.) (trade of draft rights to Eric Lindros).

[278] [1979] A.J. No. 867, 105 D.L.R. (3d) 644 (Alta. Q.B.).

[279] *Sheehy v. Edmonton World Hockey Enterprises Ltd.*, [1979] A.J. No. 867, 105 D.L.R. (3d) 644 at 646 (Alta. Q.B.), *per* Steer J. See also, *Community Sports, Inc. v. Denver Ringsby Rockets, Inc.*, 240 A.2d 832 (S.C. Pa., 1968) (successor team bound by special agreement giving player right to join team in another league to "better" himself).

[280] See, *Washington Capitols Basketball Club, Inc. v. Barry*, 304 F.Supp. 1193 (N.D. Cal., 1969), affd 419 F.2d 472 (9th Cir., 1969).

[281] *Cf. Hillman v. Sports Centrepoint Enterprises Ltd.*, [1977] 2 A.C.W.S. 104 (Man. C.A.) (purported return to defunct team in Cleveland).

not automatically bound by the "no trade" or "no move" provision but may expressly agree to it (see, article 11.8(a)).

3. *The player's right to compensation*: The team's main obligation under the SPC is to pay the agreed salary: the player has the right to payment so long as the contract has not been properly terminated.[282] Payment is the responsibility of the employing team and there is no obligation on other league members or the league as a whole (see, article 11.14).[283]

Failure by the team to pay salary or failure to perform any other major obligation will enable the player to terminate the contract.[284] On termination, the player is entitled to compensation due until that date, and the player normally becomes a free agent.[285] In the NHL, an alleged default in paying compensation is subject to article 11.15 of the CBA, which is incorporated into the SPC as paragraph 12. The team or the league may dispute the claim through expedited arbitration, and the SPC remains in effect while the grievance is pending (see, paragraph 12(f)). Where the team fails to make payment, the player must give the team and league notice in writing of the default, and the team then has 14 days in which to remedy it (see, paragraph 12(a)). The player does, however, give the league the option of curing the default by guaranteeing payment for 21 days. This option may be assigned to another team, and if the original team does not cure the default the contract may be assigned to the team that makes the payment. The assignee assumes all rights and obligations under the SPC other than obligations not mentioned in the notice of default (see, paragraph 12 (b)-(e)).

The skate is on the other foot when the claim is brought by the team to recover payments from the player. Dispute may arise in relation to signing bonuses which are defined in article 1 of the CBA as "any compensation paid for signing an SPC".[286] On coming to contract terms and receiving the bonus, the player gives consideration in the form of an undertaking to go with the particular team.[287] The money is, therefore, "earned". Benefit accrues to the team because it gains the assurance of the player's availability and is able to promote its

---

[282] See, *Pinder v. Vancouver Hockey Club Ltd.*, [1972] B.C.J. No. 451, 28 D.L.R. (3d) 374 (B.C.S.C.) (no repudiation by player).

[283] See also, *United States Football League Players Assn. v. United States Football League*, 650 F.Supp. 12 (D. Ore., 1986).

[284] See, *Dewalt v. B.C. Lions Football Club* (1988), 9 A.C.W.S. (3d) 252 (B.C.S.C.), affd (1988), 13 A.C.W.S. (3d) 61 (B.C.C.A.) (reduction of salary was fundamental breach; player entitled to declaration of termination).

[285] See, *Oakland Athletics v. James A. Hunter* (December 13, 1974, Seitz, arb.); *American and National Leagues of Professional Baseball Clubs v. Major League Baseball Players Assn.*, 130 Cal. Rptr. 626, 59 Cal. App. 3d 493 (C.A., 1976) (failure to pay salary to Catfish Hunter in manner agreed; deferred compensation scheme).

[286] See, *Khabibulin v. Canada*, [1999] T.C.J. No. 686, 2000 D.T.C. 1426 (T.C.C.) (payment was for playing hockey, not signing bonus).

[287] Where a signing bonus is awarded to ensure that the player plays one professional sport rather than another, the team may seek an injunction to prevent the player from switching leagues during the term of the contract; see, *Toronto Blue Jays Baseball Club v. Boston Celtics Corp.*, 81 Civ. 5263 (S.D. N.Y., 1981) (signing bonus of USD $300,000 in return for not playing professional basketball).

operation by announcing the signing.[288] When there has been default by the team, it has been held that a player may rescind the contract and retain the signing bonus.[289] When the player refuses to provide services or is otherwise in breach of obligations and unable to perform, the recourse of management is to negotiate terms providing that payment is conditional on the fulfilment of the contract or requiring proportionate repayment of bonus money.[290]

4. *The player's entitlement in the event of injury*: Article 17.7 of the CBA, incorporated into the SPC as paragraph 5, includes important provisions relating to injury or unfitness and establishes procedures to determine the nature and cause of the condition.[291] Where injury occurs from the performance of duties with the team, salary and other benefits are payable, including career ending disability insurance (see, article 23).[292]

The SPC obliges the player to keep himself in good physical condition (see, paragraph 2(b)) and avoid any "athletic sport" (including hockey) that might impair his playing ability (see, paragraph 7). If it is the opinion of the team's physician that the player is unfit to play skilled hockey, the player may be suspended without pay for the period of the disability or unfitness (see, paragraph 5(b)). Where injury occurs in the course of employment, the player is entitled to receive hospitalization and medical expenses, together with salary and bonuses for the remaining term of the SPC so long as the disability is continuing (see, paragraphs 5(c)(d)). Besides the risks incurred on the ice,[293] the course of employment includes travel with the team and "business requested" by the team. Disputes as to whether the injury is related to hockey are referred to the "impartial arbitrator" (see, paragraph 5(m)).

Where the team physician determines that the player is fit or unfit to play, the player may give timely notice that he is seeking a second opinion. In the event of disagreement in the medical opinions, the issue may then be referred to an "independent physician" for a final and binding determination (see, paragraphs, 5(e)-(i)). If the player is declared unfit because of injury sustained in the course of employment, he is entitled to the benefits recognized in the CBA. If he is

---

[288]  See, *Alabama Football, Inc. v. Greenwood*, 452 F.Supp. 1191 (W.D. Pa., 1978) (contract repudiated prior to playing; failure of team and league imminent; player entitled to keep bonus).

[289]  See, *Alabama Football, Inc. v. Stabler*, 319 So. 2d 678 (S.C. Ala., 1975).

[290]  See: CBA of NFL (2006), article 14, section 9. See also, *Miami Dolphins and National Football League Management Council v. Ricky Williams and the National Football League Player Assn.* (October 5, 2004, R. Bloch, arb.); *White v. National Football League*, 533 F.Supp. 2d 929 (D. Minn., 2008) (Atlanta Falcons could not recover Michael Vick's earned roster bonus); D.C. Weiss, "How Terrell Owens, Collective Bargaining, and Forfeiture Restrictions Created a Moral Hazard that Caused the NFL Crime Wave and What It Meant for Michael Vick" (2008) 15 Sports Law. J. 279.

[291]  On injury grievances in football and other sports, see, J. Barnes, *Sports and the Law in Canada*, 3d ed. (Toronto: Butterworths, 1996) at 228-31.

[292]  See further, Chapter 6, "Play Safe: On the Ice", section A, 4. On liability, see, Chapter 6, "Play Safe: On the Ice", sections C, 5, 6.

[293]  See, *Belanger v. Pittsburgh Penguins Inc.*, [1998] O.J. No. 427, 17 C.P.C. (4th) 245 (Ont. Gen. Div.) (injury in pre-season game; claim for career-ending disability payments subject to arbitration procedures under CBA).

declared fit but refuses to play, he is liable to be suspended without pay (see, paragraph 5(j)). If the player is declared unfit because of an injury occurring outside the course of employment, he is not entitled to the benefits of the CBA until declared fit (see, paragraph 5(n)).

5. *The option clause*: The option clause is particularly associated with professional football where it permits the team to extend the period of service specified in the SPC for one year. In isolation, this power is not in restraint of trade,[294] although its restrictive effects may be enhanced by requirements to pay compensation or equalization after a player plays out the option and signs with another team.[295] The SPC in the NHL formerly included various option powers,[296] but article 11.13 of the CBA now specifies that SPCs shall not include any option clause. In relation to 18-or 19-year-old players who do not play 10 NHL games in a season, there is the power to extend the SPC by one or two years and so prolong the period at the entry level (see, article 9.1(d)).

## 5.   Remedies and Enforcement[297]

In an action by a team to enforce a player's service contract, the remedy most commonly sought is the injunction ordering the player not to commit a breach. By paragraph 6 of the SPC of the NHL, the team retains other rights and remedies but is also granted the right to go to court to enjoin the player by "appropriate injunctive proceedings" from playing hockey for another team. Such disputes, usually involving claims to player's services by teams from rival leagues, are not resolved by arbitration.[298] The breach may take the form of actions to be performed in the same country or on foreign territory. A Canadian team may therefore enjoin a player's service in the United States,[299] or an American team may take action to prevent a player performing in Canada.[300]

---

[294]   See, *Detroit Football Co. v. Dublinski*, [1955] O.J. No. 619, [1957] O.R. 58, 7 D.L.R. (2d) 9 (Ont. C.A.), revg [1956] O.J. No. 561, 4 D.L.R. (2d) 688 (Ont. H.C.J.).

[295]   See Chapter 8, "Competition Law and Labour Law", sections A, 2, 3; B; C, 2, 3.

[296]   See Chapter 9, "National Hockey League", section B, 3.

[297]   See: W.J. Lindal, "Negative Covenants in Sports Contracts" (1951) 23 Man. Bar News 91, 24 Man. Bar News 1; G.D. Finlayson, "Personal Service Contracts" in Special Lectures of the Law Society of Upper Canada, 1975, *Current Problems in the Law of Contracts* (Toronto: Richard De Boo, 1975) at 355; J. Weistart & C.H. Lowell, *The Law of Sports* (Indianapolis: The Bobbs-Merrill Co., 1979, Supplement 1985) at 334-96; C.I. Kyer, "A Case Study in Party Stipulation of Remedy: The N.H.L. Standard Player's Contract" (1981) 39 U.T. Fac. L. Rev. 1; J.P. McCutcheon, "Negative Enforcement of Employment Contracts in the Sports Industries" (1997) 17 L.S. 65.

[298]   But see, *Boston Celtics Limited Partnership v. Shaw*, 908 F.2d 1041 (1st Cir., 1990) (enforcement of arbitrator's order that player cancel contract with Italian team and play with domestic team).

[299]   See: *Winnipeg Rugby Football Club. Ltd. v. Freeman*, 140 F.Supp. 365 (N.D. Ohio, 1955); *Toronto Blue Jays Baseball Club v. Boston Celtics Corp.*, 81 Civ. 5263 (S.D. N.Y., 1991).

[300]   See, *Detroit Football Co. v. Dublinski*, [1955] 4 D.L.R. 176 (Ont. H.C.J.); W. Angus, "Negative Covenant in Service Contract" (1956) 14 U.T. Fac. L. Rev. 54.

The injunction is an extraordinary remedy that may be sought to prevent the infringement of legal rights; it will be granted only in cases where the order can work usefully, practically and effectively. The contractual right being protected must itself be lawful and enforceable. The use of the injunction is limited to cases where damages would not be an effective remedy,[301] for example, where the action to be restrained would cause irreparable injury. The remedy is equitable in nature and is granted at the discretion of the court.[302] If the applicant is guilty of delay, improper or oppressive conduct or otherwise does not come with "clean hands", the injunction will be denied.

An injunction may not operate in a way that amounts to ordering specific performance of a service contract.[303] It is a principle of equity that an employee will not be ordered to serve for a particular employer and that an employer will not be forced to take a particular employee.[304] This principle is based on a number of policy reasons: that enforced servitude infringes personal liberty,[305] that services performed under compulsion are obviously unsatisfactory and that a court would have difficulty assessing the quality of the services provided. In sport, it is obviously undesirable to have a reluctant performer on a team, and a court may not be well qualified to evaluate a player's effort or contribution if the team alleged that the order of specific performance had been breached.[306]

An injunction may, however, be granted to enforce express negative covenants in a service contract; such a covenant is a promise to give services exclusively to the employer during the term of the contract and not engage in similar work elsewhere. A player may not be ordered by a court to play for his team, but may be prevented by injunction from playing for another.[307] To ensure

---

[301] In appropriate circumstances, the injunction may be combined with damages; see, *Courts of Justice Act*, R.S.O. 1990, c. C.43, s. 99.

[302] At the height of the amateur ethic, Nottingham Forest were refused an injunction against Blackburn Rovers because they had engaged professionals merely "to satisfy their pride in winning their matches"; see, *Radford v. Campbell* (1890), 6 T.L.R. 488 (C.A.) (footballer had "jumped" contract paying £4 10s. a week).

[303] In *Kapp v. B.C. Lions Football Club*, [1967] B.C.J. No. 153, 61 W.W.R. 31 (B.C.S.C. (In Chambers)), the court refused a mandatory injunction that the team remove a player's suspension. Such an order would have the effect of restoring the player's employment and indirectly enforcing the contract; it would also be impossible for the court to supervise the performance of the player's duties.

[304] On reinstatement ordered by an arbitrator, see: *National Ballet of Canada v. Canadian Actors' Equity Assn. (Glasco Grievance)*, [2000] O.L.A.A. No. 209, 87 L.A.C. (4th) 1 (Ont. Lab. Arb.) (C. Albertyn, arb., March 16, 2000); *National Ballet of Canada v. Glasco*, [2000] O.J. No. 1071, 49 O.R. (3d) 223, 185 D.L.R. (4th) 372 (Ont. Div. Ct.); *National Ballet of Canada v. Glasco*, [2000] O.J. No. 2083, 49 O.R. (3d) 230, 186 D.L.R. (4th) 347 (Ont. S.C.J.).

[305] In *Yashin v. National Hockey League*, [2000] O.J. No. 3306, 192 D.L.R. (4th) 747 (Ont. S.C.J.), the court found that there was no compulsion when Alexei Yashin was required to perform the final year of his contract in order to become a free agent.

[306] For the view that the traditional rationales against specific performance are not persuasive, see, G.C. Rapp, "Affirmative Injunctions in Athletic Employment Contracts: Rethinking the Place of the *Lumley* Rule in American Sports Law" (2006) 16 Marq. Sports L.J. 261.

[307] See: *Lumley v. Wagner* (1852), 1 De G.M. & G. 604, 42 E.R. 687 (Ch.); *Philadelphia Ball Club, Ltd. v. Lajoie*, 51 A. 973 (S.C. Pa., 1902).

entitlement to injunctive relief, by paragraph 2(c) of the SPC the player agrees that he will "play hockey only for the Club" (see also, paragraph 6). An injunction will not be granted if it will prevent the defendant from working in *any* capacity or earning *any* livelihood. The injunction may prevent the person in breach of covenant from engaging in attractive employment, while allowing other types of work. In *Warner Bros. Pictures Inc. v. Nelson*,[308] the film actress Bette Davis agreed to act for the plaintiffs for a period of time during which she undertook not to act for anyone else without the plaintiff's written consent. When she entered into a contract to make films for a rival company, an injunction was granted to prevent her from breaking her original undertaking. She was not forced to act for the plaintiffs and was permitted to make a living by doing work other than acting. It is, therefore, no defence for a highly paid athlete to say that the injunction will prevent his earning a living: work other than professional sport is usually available.[309] The effect of this rule may be to put economic pressure on the athlete tantamount to specifically enforcing the original service contract.[310] If, however, there is uncontradicted evidence that professional sport is the athlete's only means of livelihood, the injunction will be denied.[311]

A negative covenant may, therefore, be enforced to restrain the defendant during the term of the contract from working for a competing organization; such a negative covenant protects legitimate interests of the original employer. Where the new employer is not a direct business competitor, the injunction may be denied. (In *Warner Bros. Pictures Inc. v. Nelson*, the relevant market was held to be the world film industry.) In *Detroit Football Co. v. Dublinski*,[312] a National Football League ("NFL") team was refused an injunction to restrain its player from playing in the Canadian Football League ("CFL") because the two organizations were not seen to be in competition: "The plaintiff obviously had an interest to be protected...but playing football and in fact a different kind of football, in another country where there is no competition with the plaintiff, in no way affects it".[313] However, the widespread broadcasting of NFL and CFL games

---

[308] [1937] 1 K.B. 209.

[309] See: *Buckenara v. Hawthorn Football Club*, [1988] V.R. 39 (S.C.) (player enjoined from playing for other teams in the same league; other work and other competitions available); *Hawthorn Football Club v. Harding*, [1988] V.R. 49 (S.C.).

[310] But see: *Page One Records Ltd. v. Britton*, [1968] 1 W.L.R. 157 (Ch. D.); *Warren v. Mendy*, [1989] 1 W.L.R. 853 (C.A.) (injunction refused where it might compel performance; considerations of special skill, mutual trust and length of service).

[311] In *Detroit Football Co. v. Dublinski*, [1955] 4 D.L.R. 176 (Ont. H.C.J.), unusual evidence to this effect was left uncontradicted.

[312] [1956] O.J. No. 561, [1956] O.R. 744 (Ont. H.C.J.), revd [1955] O.J. No. 619, [1957] O.R. 58, 7 D.L.R. (2d) 9 (Ont. C.A.).

[313] *Detroit Football Co. v. Dublinski*, [1956] O.J. No. 561, [1956] O.R. 744 at 753 (Ont. H.C.J.), *per* McRuer C.J.H.C. But see: *New England Patriots Football Club, Inc. v. University of Colorado*, 592 F.2d 1196 (1st Cir., 1979) (college football held to be in competition with professional football); *Toronto Blue Jays Baseball Club v. Boston Celtics Corp.*, 81 Civ. 5263 (S.D. N.Y., 1981) (basketball team enjoined from negotiating with player under contract with baseball team); *Boston Celtics Limited Partnership v. Shaw*, 908 F.2d 1041 (1st Cir., 1990) (contract with Italian team).

throughout North America may now suggest that both leagues are competitors in the same market. In hockey, the relevant market clearly includes both the United States and Canada and may now extend to European leagues.

An injunction will not be granted where damages are an appropriate remedy. Damages will be adequate relief if the team can, at a cost, find a replacement player equivalent to the defecting player. If, however, the player possesses such unique and superior skill that he cannot be replaced, then an injunction will be the appropriate remedy. Teams seek to ensure that the injunction will be available through the player's representation in paragraph 6 of the SPC that "he has exceptional and unique knowledge, skill and ability as a hockey Player, the loss of which cannot be estimated with certainty and cannot be fairly or adequately compensated by damages". The presence of such a clause may not be conclusive that, on the facts, the player did possess such unique ability.[314] Modern American decisions do, however, suggest that the mere fact of being signed to play professionally is substantial evidence of outstanding skill.[315]

The remedy of damages is always available where an employer or employee is in breach of a valid contract of service. The damage caused, for example, to a team through breach by a player is determined on ordinary principles, and the court estimates any losses on the basis of evidence actually presented. In *Detroit Football Co. v. Dublinski*,[316] the defendant had, in breach of contract, "jumped" from the Detroit Lions to play quarterback for the Toronto Argonauts. To acquire a new quarterback, the plaintiffs paid USD $10,000 and a player; the traded player's salary was USD $6,500. The new quarterback's salary called for USD $11,200, whereas Dublinski would have received USD $7,750. The expenses caused by the defendant's breach of contract were, therefore, USD $10,000 plus USD $11, 200. But the plaintiffs had made savings on two salaries of USD $6,500 and USD $7,750. The damages awarded were, therefore, USD $21,200 minus USD $14,250, *i.e.*, USD $6,950. Additional damages covering time and expense spent in training the defendant would have been recovered, but no evidence on this point was presented to the court. Neither was any evidence presented as to any loss of gate receipts, although the Ontario Court of Appeal noted that there might be difficulty in showing causal connection between such loss and the defendant's departure. The court commented generally on the seriousness of the plaintiff's loss and seemed reluctant that it could award only the sum that it did.

---

[314] See: *Warner Bros. Pictures Inc. v. Nelson*, [1937] 1 K.B. 209 at 220; *Detroit Football Co. v. Dublinski*, [1956] O.J. No. 561, [1956] O.R. 744 at 769 (Ont. H.C.J.); *Dallas Cowboys Football Club, Inc. v. Harris*, 348 S.W.2d 37 (Tex. C.A., 1961).

[315] See, for example, *Washington Capitols Basketball Club, Inc. v. Barry*, 304 F.Supp. 1193 (N.D. Cal., 1969), affd 419 F.2d 472 (9th Cir., 1969). But see, *Spencer v. Milton*, 287 N.Y.S. 944 (S.C., 1936) (minor league player; team must establish unique qualifications).

[316] [1955] O.J. No. 619, [1957] O.R. 58, 7 D.L.R. (2d) 9 (Ont. C.A.). An injunction to restrain Dublinski from playing for Toronto during the 1955 season had ceased to be relevant since the action did not reach trial until the following year.

## F.   REMUNERATION AND NEGOTIATION

## 1.   General

The matters for individual negotiation in a standard player's contract ("SPC") are the form and level of the compensation, length of service and special protections or guarantees. For tax purposes, players may also request that payments be made to a savings plan (see, article 50.8(e)). Negotiations are now constrained by the limits of the "Team Payroll Range System",[317] and the agreed compensation must comply with the collective bargaining agreement ("CBA") with respect to entry level compensation (see, article 9), minimum and maximum salary (see, articles 11.12, 50.6), escalation from year to year (see, article 50.7) and other rules and standards.[318]

By article 50.2(a)-(b), compensation may consist of salary or bonuses. "Paragraph 1" salary is the fixed amount payable on account of a particular year and may take the form of deferred salary paid after the SPC has expired.[319] Bonuses may also be deferred and may consist of signing, roster, reporting or performance bonuses: the payments are to be made within the period provided in the SPC or as soon as practicable (see, article 11.9(d)). An entry level ("Group 1") player may contract for a signing, "games played" or performance bonus, but the signing bonus may not exceed 10 per cent of the compensation for the year (see, article 9.3(b)).

Negotiated performance bonuses are payable where the player achieves an agreed benchmark related to individual or team performance during a particular year. Such bonuses are available to entry level players and may be included in one-year contracts signed by certain players who are over 35 or who have played over 400 games for pension purposes (see, article 50.2(b)(C)). Performance bonuses for entry level players are subject to article 9 and exhibit 5 of the CBA which prescribe maximum amounts for "Individual 'A' Bonuses" paid by teams and "Individual 'B' Bonuses" based on league-wide performances. For entry level forwards or defensemen, "A" bonuses may be based on ice time, goals, assists, points, points per game and plus-minus rating; defensemen may also be rewarded for blocked shots. Goaltenders' bonuses may be based on minutes played, goals against average, saves percentage, wins and shut-outs. All "entry-level" players may also receive performance bonuses based on selection for the All-Rookie team or selection for the All-Star game or as its MVP. The maximum amount payable for an individual "A" bonus is USD \$212,500, and the maximum aggregate is USD \$850,000. The category of "B" bonuses relates to winning or placing in league awards or trophies (*e.g.*, the Calder Memorial Trophy) and finishing among the top 10 forwards or defensemen or among the

---

[317]  See Chapter 9, "National Hockey League", sections C, 2, b, c.

[318]  See Chapter 9, "National Hockey League", section C, 2, d.

[319]  On "salary deferral arrangements" and the exception for professional athletes, see, *Income Tax Act*, R.S.C. 1985 (5th Supp.), c. 1, ss. 6(1)(a)(v), 6(11), 248(1).

top five goaltenders in the league. "B" bonuses may be paid according to a schedule of bonus amounts up to an aggregate maximum of USD $2 million.

Special protection in the form of the "no-trade" or "no-move" clause is permitted for Group 3 unrestricted free agents (see, article 11.8). The "no-cut" clause or "guaranteed" contract[320] is superseded by the buyout provisions in paragraph 13 of the SPC that require payment of either one third or two thirds of the value of the SPC when it is terminated. The main guarantee sought by NHL players is the "one-way" contract that precludes a lower level of compensation if the player's services are loaned to an affiliated minor league team.

Once terms have been agreed, the revision or reimbursement of salary and the renegotiation of the SPC are not permitted (see, articles 11.10, 50.8(a)(b)), and the value of payments and the duration of the contract may not be altered through "voidable years" (see, article 50.8(a)(ii)). However, during the final year of a SPC it is possible to negotiate an extension of the contract, except for any SPC at the entry level (see, article 50.5(f)).

As the upper limit of teams' payroll range reached USD $56.7 million in 2008-09,[321] total player costs in the NHL exceeded USD $1.5 billion, and since 2006 general managers have devoted the early days of July to spending sprees on free agents totalling an annual average of USD $345 million.[322] Individual playing skill is now rewarded with serious money as teams look to hire and retain the available elite talent. In 2008-09 Alexander Ovechkin received compensation of USD $9 million from his 13-year USD $124 million contract with the Washington Capitals, and Sidney Crosby also received USD $9 million from his six-year USD $43.5 million contract with the Pittsburgh Penguins. At the end of the 2008-09 season and the start of the 2009-10 season, the following players from the Canadian teams had annual compensation of USD $3 million or more:[323]

### Toronto Maple Leafs

| May 2009 | | October 2009 | |
|---|---|---|---|
| Pavel Kubina | USD $5.0m. | Jason Blake | USD $4.5m. |
| Jason Blake | USD $4.5m. | Phil Kessel | USD $4.5m. |
| Tomas Kaberle | USD $4.25m. | Michael Komisarek | USD $4.5m. |
| Vesa Toskala | USD $4.0m. | Tomas Kaberle | USD $4.25m. |
| Martin Gerber | USD $3.7m. | François Beauchemin | USD $4.2m. |
| Jeff Finger | USD $3.5m. | Vesa Toskala | USD $4.0m. |

---

320  See, *Barton v. Toronto Argonaut Football Club Ltd.*, [1978] O.J. No. 2721, 19 O.R. (2d) 634 (Ont. H.C.J.), affd [1979] O.J. No. 4003, 27 O.R. (2d) 734n (Ont. C.A.), affd (*sub nom. Barton v. Agincourt Football Enterprises Ltd.*), [1982] S.C.J. No. 33, [1982] 1 S.C.R. 666 (S.C.C.) (guarantee did not apply when the player signed with another team).

321  See Chapter 9, "National Hockey League", section C, 2, b.

322  For 2008, see, "Crazy busy, crazy money" *The Globe and Mail* (Toronto: July 2, 2008) at R6- R7.

323  See online: <http://www.nhlpa.com>, "The Players" (May 20, September 19, 2009).

| Mike Van Ryn | USD $3.35m. | Jeff Finger | USD $3.5m. |
|---|---|---|---|
| | | Lee Stempniak | USD $3.5m. |
| | | Mike Van Ryn | USD $3.35m. |
| | | Niklas Hagman | USD $3.0m. |

## Montreal Canadiens

| May 2009 | | October 2009 | |
|---|---|---|---|
| Andrei Markov | USD $5.75m. | Scott Gomez | USD $8.0m. |
| Mathieu Schneider | USD $5.75m. | Andrei Markov | USD $5.75m. |
| Roman Hamrlik | USD $5.5m. | Roman Hamrlik | USD $5.5m. |
| Alex Tanguay | USD $5.37m. | Michael Cammalleri | USD $5.0m. |
| Saku Koivu | USD $4.75m. | Brian Gionta | USD $5.0m. |
| Alex Kovalev | USD $4.5m. | Jaroslav Spacek | USD $3.83m. |
| Robert Lang | USD $4.0m. | Andrei Kastsitsyn | USD $3.25m. |
| Andrei Kastsitsyn | USD $3.25m. | | |

## Vancouver Canucks

| May 2009 | | October 2009 | |
|---|---|---|---|
| Roberto Luongo | USD $7.0m. | Roberto Luongo | USD $7.5m. |
| Mats Sundin | USD $5.62m. | Daniel Sedin | USD $6.1m. |
| Kevin Bieksa | USD $4.25m. | Henrik Sedin | USD $6.1m. |
| Pavol Demitra | USD $4.0m. | Pavol Demitra | USD $4.0m. |
| Sami Salo | USD $3.75m. | Sami Salo | USD $3.75m. |
| Daniel Sedin | USD $3.57m. | Kevin Bieksa | USD $3.5m. |
| Henrik Sedin | USD $3.57m. | William Mitchell | USD $3.5m. |
| William Mitchell | USD $3.5m. | Alexander Edler | USD $3.25m. |
| Mattias Ohlund | USD $3.5m. | Christian Ehrhoff | USD $3.15m. |

## Ottawa Senators

| May 2009 | | October 2009 | |
|---|---|---|---|
| Dany Heatley | USD $10.0m. | Jason Spezza | USD $8.0m. |
| Jason Spezza | USD $8.0m. | Daniel Alfredson | USD $7.0m. |
| Mike Fisher | USD $6.0m. | Alex Kovalev | USD $5.0m. |
| Daniel Alfredsson | USD $5.46m. | Mike Fisher | USD $4.0m. |
| Mike Comrie | USD $4.0m. | Pascal LeClaire | USD $3.6m. |

| Chris Phillips | USD $3.5m. | Jonathan Cheechoo | USD $3.5m. |
| Filip Kuba | USD $3.0m. | Filip Kuba | USD $3.5m. |
| Pascal LeClaire | USD $3.0m. | Milan Michalek | USD $3.5m. |
| | | Chris Phillips | USD $3.5m. |
| | | Anton Volchenkov | USD $3.2m. |

## Calgary Flames

| May 2009 | | October 2009 | |
|---|---|---|---|
| Miikka Kiprusoff | USD $8.5m. | Jay Bouwmeester | USD $7.0m. |
| Jarome Iginla | USD $7.0m. | Jarome Iginla | USD $7.0m. |
| Dion Phaneuf | USD $7.0m. | Miikka Kiprusoff | USD $7.0m. |
| Olli Jokinen | USD $5.25m. | Dion Phaneuf | USD $6.5m. |
| Daymond Langkow | USD $5.0m. | Olli Jokinen | USD $5.5m. |
| Robyn Regehr | USD $4.6m. | Daymond Langkow | USD $4.25m. |
| Adrian Aucoin | USD $4.0m. | Cory Sarich | USD $3.7m. |
| Michael Cammalleri | USD $3.6m. | Robyn Regehr | USD $3.5m. |
| Cory Sarich | USD $3.4m. | | |

## Edmonton Oilers

| May 2009 | | October 2009 | |
|---|---|---|---|
| Lubomir Visnovsky | USD $7.0m. | Shawn Horcoff | USD $7.0m. |
| Sheldon Souray | USD $6.25m. | Lubomir Visnovsky | USD $7.0m. |
| Dustin Penner | USD $4.25m. | Sheldon Souray | USD $5.5m. |
| Patrick O'Sullivan | USD $4.0m. | Ales Hemsky | USD $4.4m. |
| Ales Hemsky | USD $3.6m. | Dustin Penner | USD $4.25m. |
| Shawn Horcoff | USD $3.6m. | Nikolai Khabibulin | USD $3.75m. |
| Tom Gilbert | USD $3.5m. | Tom Gilbert | USD $3.5m. |
| Dwayne Roloson | USD $3.0m. | Denis Gresbeshkov | USD $3.15m. |

Where remuneration is on this scale, negotiations on the players' behalf should be conducted by competent representatives,[324] and professional assistance is also required by the many suffering stiffs forced to struggle on the minimum salary of USD $500,000. Preparations for negotiation sessions demand research into the player's expectations and preferences and an assessment of the importance of the

---

[324] See Chapter 9, "National Hockey League", section G.

signing to the team. The negotiator needs sound knowledge of the revenue and financial stability[325] of teams, available "payroll room" and the salary levels of comparable players. The NHLPA first revealed[326] contract figures in 1989-90, and the disclosure contributed to an increase in salaries. Now that compensation is constrained by the "upper limit" of the payroll range, effective individual representation is particularly required as players look to take the best slice of the limited total sum. This figure is further pinched when teams allocate a major percentage of salaries to the elite group, so that lesser and older players must be flexible about what is an acceptable team, an acceptable league or a living wage.

## 2.   Salary Arbitration

In the NHL and Major League Baseball ("MLB"), certain categories of veteran player are eligible to have compensation settled by interest arbitration, where a third party is called on to value the player's services for an upcoming year. This process serves as both an aid to negotiation and an alternative to negotiation:

> At the arbitration stage, it is impossible in practice to reproduce the leverage that the parties may have in negotiation. An arbitrator must rationalize his decision and...give greater weight to objective criteria...the arbitration process is helping the parties in their negotiation by laying out the ground rules which they can expect will be applied if they cannot agree. This forces both parties to be reasonable.[327]

In MLB, the arbitrator's power is limited to choosing either the proposal by the team or the proposal by the player: such "final offer selection" encourages both sides to devise the more acceptable package and leads to a particularly high rate of settlement. In the NHL,[328] where the arbitrator is free to structure the award, the parties may have exchanged reasonable positions during negotiations but will be tempted to go to extremes at the hearing.

Team owners have identified arbitration as a significant contributor to the inflation of salaries and have set the goal in collective bargaining of restricting eligibility, limiting allowable increases or eliminating the system entirely. The players have favoured retention, provided the process offers a transparent and impartial means of determining compensation. Salary arbitration began in the

---

[325]   Major leagues frequently limit the percentage of salary that can be deferred; see, for example, CBA of NFL (2006), article 28, section 11 (50 per cent of first USD $1 million, 75 per cent over USD $1 million), section 15 (funding of deferred salaries).

[326]   See, *Five Smiths, Inc. v. National Football League Players Assn.*, 788 F.Supp. 1042 (D. Minn., 1992) (no antitrust violation in exchange of salary information).

[327]   *National Hockey League Member Clubs (Boston Bruins) v. National Hockey League Players' Assn. (Bill Ranford)*, 1996 CanLII 330 (August 13, 1996, C.H. Foisy, salary arb.) at 10.

[328]   See: S.M. Yoost, "The National Hockey League and Salary Arbitration: Time for a Line Change" (2006) 21 Ohio St. J. Disp. Resol. 485; J. Lambrinos & T.D. Ashman, "Salary Determination in the National Hockey League: Is Arbitration Efficient?" (2007) 8 J. of Sports Econ. 192.

NHL in the 1970s,[329] although the NHLPA lost confidence in the established panel and process in 1991 following an adverse decision in the case of Doug Gilmour.[330] The strike in 1992 introduced important reforms, and eligibility and procedures were modified further in the CBA for 1993-2004 when teams gained the right to "walk away" from some awards.[331] Salary arbitration was the subject of discussion during the lockout of 2004-05, especially because of the practice of comparing salaries with those granted by free-spending teams in large markets. In the end, the settlement sought to control costs through the "upper limit" for teams rather than through substantial modification of the arbitration system.

The CBA of 2005 deals with salary arbitration in article 12 and declares that the process is limited to "restricted free agents" who have not signed an offer sheet (see, article 12.1(b)).[332] Players become eligible as follows:

| Age at Signing First SPC | Required Level of Professional Experience |
|---|---|
| 18-20 | 4 years |
| 21 | 3 years |
| 22-23 | 2 years |
| 24 and older | 1 year |

Players aged 18 or 19 earn the "professional experience" by playing 10 or more NHL games in a season; players over 20 are credited by playing 10 or more professional games under a SPC (see, article 12.1(a)). The eligible player must make the request for salary arbitration by July 5 (see, article 12.2). Once in the player's career, the player may also be subject to "club-elected" salary arbitration (see, articles 12.3-12.4). The party against whom the arbitration was filed elects whether the award is for one or two years, although there is provision for the shorter term where a player is within one year of becoming a Group 3 or Group 5 free agent (see, article 12.9(c)).

The panel of salary arbitrators is appointed by the league and the NHLPA and consists of eight members of the National Academy of Arbitrators, whose appointments are liable to be terminated (see, articles 12.6-12.8). The parties to the proceedings are the player and the NHLPA on one side and the team and the NHL on the other; the player is represented by the NHLPA, although the association may delegate its authority to the player's representative (see, article 12.9(a)(e)). Only the league and the NHLPA may communicate with the arbitrator, and written communications in connection with a proceeding must be

---

[329] See, *Philadelphia World Hockey Club, Inc. v. Philadelphia Hockey Club, Inc.*, 351 F. Supp. 462 at 482-85 (E.D. Pa., 1972). See also, CBA of NHL, 1975–1980 (May 4, 1976), article 10.

[330] See: "Jury still out on effectiveness of NHL arbitration process" *The Globe and Mail* (Toronto: December 17, 1991) at A13; J.M. Weiler, "Legal Analysis of the NHL Contract" (1992) 3 Marq. Sports L.J. 59 at 70-74.

[331] See: CBA of NHL (1993–2004), article 12; M. Lavoie, *Avantage numérique: L'argent et la Ligue nationale de hockey* (Hull: Éditions Vents d'ouest, 1997) at 168-72.

[332] On free agency, see Chapter 9, "National Hockey League", section C, 2, d.

sent to the other side (see, article 12.9(p)). The procedure consists of written submissions and oral presentations in which particular reliance is placed on official statistics and records of compensation held by the league and the NHLPA (see, article 12.9(g)(v),(h)). Evidence may be offered as to the player's overall performance and contribution, length of service, injuries or illnesses suffered and special qualities of leadership or public appeal (see, article 12.9(g)(ii)). The arbitrator may also consider the performance and compensation of other players, provided a party contends that the player is comparable. Some categories of evidence are inadmissible, including certain types of SPC and qualifying offers, offers made in previous negotiations, press reports and information as to the financial condition of the team or league (see, article 12.9(g)(iii)).

The arbitrator must issue the decision within 48 hours of the close of the hearing and provide brief reasons, including reference to the comparable compensation relied on (see, article 12.9(n)). The arbitrator must fix the term of the SPC, "Paragraph 1" NHL salary and any provision for minor league salary. The decision is normally "final and binding on the parties" and must be promptly incorporated into a SPC (see, article 12.5 (a)). With respect to arbitrations elected by players, teams have a limited number of "walk-away" rights where the player has been awarded salary of at least USD $1,042,173, adjusted after 2007-08 according to increases in the average league salary (see, article 12.10). Where the team renounces an award relating to a one-year SPC, the player immediately becomes an unrestricted free agent. Where the team renounces the second year of a two-year award, the player becomes an unrestricted free agent at the conclusion of the one-year SPC incorporating the compensation required by the award.

Where a player files for arbitration, the negotiation process continues and the majority of cases are settled before the hearing. Prior to the lockout the dispositions were as follows:

| Year | Cases Filed | Settled | Hearings |
|------|-------------|---------|----------|
| 1999 | 35 | 21 (60%) | 14 |
| 2000 | 32 | 18 (56%) | 14 |
| 2001 | 44 | 27 (61%) | 17 |
| 2002 | 40 | 29 (73%) | 11 |
| 2003 | 31 | 25 (81%) | 6 |
| 2004 | 66 | 47 (71%) | 19 |

By 2008, only 15 cases were filed of which 11 (73 per cent) were settled. Salary arbitration tends to be avoided because of the adversarial nature of the hearings and the use of invidious comparisons. A particular hearing may consist of the player pleading useful service and ingratitude, while management answers with allegations of inadequate performance and weakness of character. Since these postures do not make for harmonious employment, the parties usually prefer to structure their own deal and retain control of the compensation for the purpose of the "upper limit". After 2008, it was also questionable whether there was much comparative value in long-term contracts signed in more favourable economic conditions.

## G.   AGENTS

## 1.   General

Article 6 of the collective bargaining agreement ("CBA") recognizes the agent certification program maintained by the NHLPA. As the exclusive bargaining agent for players, the association is able to certify and regulate player representatives working in the negotiation of standard player's contracts ("SPC"). Teams may not negotiate with any person other than a "certified agent" (see, article 6.1), and they are further prohibited from making any payment to the representative (see, article 26.6).[333] Similarly, teams may not enter into a SPC and the league is prohibited from approving a SPC unless the player was represented by a "certified agent" or acted on his own behalf (see, article 6.2). By article 31.1(b) of the CBA, one player may not represent another player or be involved in any entity that represents players. In 2009, the NHLPA maintained a list of 153 approved agents, consisting of 152 men and one woman.[334]

The NHLPA began a voluntary registry of agents in 1991 and negotiated recognition of the certification program in 1995.[335] These measures were a response to a history of problems experienced in various professional leagues[336] as general legal and ethical standards failed to eliminate bad apples or guarantee proper representation. The client-agent relationship is open to abuse because the agent is the more experienced in the field and enjoys opportunities for self-serving behaviour.[337] Given this mismatch in knowledge, clients risk receiving poor service and may be the victims of transactions that benefit the agent's interests more than their own. The client can take legal action based on the agent's contractual and fiduciary duties, but the preferred course is to prevent abuses through special regulation. To improve standards of representation, two general types of control are available: monitoring mechanisms that supervise the qualifications and conduct of agents, and contracts that make the agent's

---

[333]   See also, NHL By-Law 2.9. On tax consequences, see, *Bure v. Canada*, [1999] T.C.J. No. 769, 2000 D.T.C. 1507 (T.C.C.) (Vancouver Canucks paid agent's fees to Ronald Salcer; fee of CDN $339,375 was a taxable benefit for Pavel Bure).

[334]   See online: <http://www.nhlpa.com>, "Certified Agents".

[335]   See, CBA of NHL (1993–2004), article 6.

[336]   In relation to North American leagues, see: E. Garvey, *The Agent Game: Selling Players Short* (Washington, D.C.: Federation of Professional Athletes, AFL-CIO, 1984); K.L. Shropshire & T. Davis, *The Business of Sports Agents*, 2d ed. (Philadelphia: University of Pennsylvania Press, 2008). For an international survey, see, R.C.R. Siekmann *et al.*, eds., *Players' Agents Worldwide: Legal Aspects* (The Hague: TMC Asser Press, 2007).

[337]   See: D.S. Mason & T. Slack, "Evaluating Monitoring Mechanisms as a Solution to Opportunism by Professional Hockey Agents" (2001) 15 J. of Sport Management 107; D.S. Mason & T. Slack, "Understanding Principal-Agent Relationships: Evidence from Professional Hockey" (2003) 17 J. of Sport Management 37.

compensation contingent on performance. Adequate performance is particularly required since the client pays professional fees in the expectation that these will be recouped from the increased salary and bonuses realized by the agent. Although various regulatory standards are now in place in Canada and the United States, disputes continue to arise between players and their agents. The extreme example of a troubled relationship may be the story of Mike Danton of the St. Louis Blues who was imprisoned in 2004 for initiating a bizarre conspiracy to murder in which the target may have been his agent David Frost.[338] The criminal justice system is ultimately available to sanction both players and agents, but other measures now offer the hope that things will not go that far.

## 2. Duties and Litigation: Eagleson Revisited

Agency is a recognized common law[339] relationship by which one person (the "principal") grants representative power to another (the "agent").[340] The client-principal authorizes the agent to act on his behalf, and the agent may then be in a position to bind the principal or change legal relations within the scope of the authority. Where the agent has been given express authority under seal, the agent holds "power of attorney". Agents are not employees because they do not work under the direct authority of the principal, but neither are they independent contractors because their authority is subject to the instructions received from the principal. The relationship is one of contract in that there are agreed services that must be competently performed. It is also one of trust, so that the agent is subject to fiduciary duties to act loyally in the client's best interests and not take unfair advantage of the position. The agent's contractual duties are to perform personally, to follow instructions and to exercise reasonable care and skill; the player agent[341] should, for example, show professional diligence in realizing market value in contract negotiations. The agent's fiduciary duties are to act in good faith, not to take secret profits and to make full disclosure. The main

---

[338] See, "Danton jailed for 7½ years in murder plot" *The Globe and Mail* (Toronto: November 9, 2004) at R6, R11. David Frost resigned as a "certified agent" in December 2005. On Frost's career as a coach, see Chapter 5, "Be Safe: Off the Ice", section F.

[339] The *Civil Code of Québec*, R.S.Q., c. C-91, recognizes a "Contract of Enterprise or for Services" (see, articles 2098-2109) and a contract of "Mandate" (see, articles 2130-2185); by article 2130, "the mandator, empowers another person, the mandatary, to represent him in the performance of a juridical act with a third person". See further, J. Brisebois, "L'univers de la relation contractuelle entre un athlète professionnel et son agent: Une analyse du droit québécois" (1999) 33 R.J.T. 589.

[340] See, G.H.L. Fridman, *Canadian Agency Law* (Markham, ON: LexisNexis Canada, 2009). On the creation of the agency relationship, see, *Bure v. Canada*, [1999] T.C.J. No. 769, 2000 D.T.C. 1507 (T.C.C.): "He gave instructions to Mr. Salcer who had previously represented him in 1991. He knew personal agents were paid. I find as a fact that the Appellant knew that Mr. Salcer was his agent and was being paid by the Canucks because he wanted the US $25 million for himself without any deduction to pay Mr. Salcer" (at para. 10, *per* McArthur T.C.J.).

[341] On the role of a "manager" in boxing, see, *Lalonde v. Coleman*, [1990] M.J. No. 355, 67 Man.R. (2d) 187 (Man. Q.B.).

responsibility of the principal is to pay the remuneration properly earned by the agent. The principal may revoke the agency at any time, although reasonable notice is required where the relationship is close to one of employment and has continued for a period of years.[342] In player agency, the practice is to specify a period of service and to allow either party to terminate the agreement on giving written notice.

Breach of legal responsibilities by an agent may give rise to both criminal and civil liability. The *Criminal Code*[343] includes general crimes of theft and fraud[344] and makes special provision in section 426 for agents who "corruptly" receive secret commissions. This crime is committed where the agent fails to make full and timely disclosure of the fact that services are being provided under the influence of material benefits received from a third party.[345] In the United States, criminal convictions have been recorded for "grand larceny"[346] and fraud,[347] although prosecutions have been less successful in relation to charges of tampering with contests[348] and racketeering.[349] In the American civil litigation, plaintiffs have alleged conflicts of interest,[350] breach of amateur regulations,[351] negligent representation[352] and misguided or irregular investment advice.[353]

---

[342] See, for example, *Marbry Distributors Ltd. v. Avrecan International Inc.*, [1999] B.C.J. No. 635, 171 D.L.R. (4th) 436 (B.C.C.A.) (reasonable notice required to terminate 10-year exclusive dealership for Reebok products accounting for high percentage of distributor's income).

[343] R.S.C. 1985, c. C-46, ss. 322 (theft), 325 (agent pledging goods), 331 (theft by person holding power of attorney), 332 (misappropriation of money held under direction), 336 (criminal breach of trust), 362 (false pretence or false statement), 366 (forgery), 374 (drawing document without authority), 380 (fraud), 386 (fraudulent registration of title).

[344] See, *Law Society of Upper Canada v. Eagleson*, [1998] L.S.D.D. No. 35 (Ont. Law Society Discipline Committee) (Alan Eagleson disbarred following convictions on three counts of fraud in relation to benefits obtained from the sale of rink-board advertising); see, further, Chapter 3, "Organizations and Regulations", section A, 4; Chapter 9, "National Hockey League", sections B, G.

[345] See, *R. v. Kelly*, [1992] S.C.J. No. 53, [1992] 2 S.C.R. 170 (S.C.C.) (investment advisor was receiving commissions from property developer).

[346] See: "$600,000 missing, athletes' agent charged" *The Globe and Mail* (Toronto: June 30, 1977) at 37; "What shook the sports establishment were crooked agent's gambling mates" *The Globe and Mail* (Toronto: October 19, 1977) at 44 (charges against Richard Sorkin). See also, *People of the State of New York v. Sorkin*, 407 N.Y.S.2d 772 (App. Div., 1978) (jail term affirmed).

[347] See: *Hilliard v. Black*, 125 F.Supp. 2d 1071 (N.D. Fla., 2000); *United States of America v. Piggie*, 303 F.3d 923 (8th Cir., 2002).

[348] See, *Abernethy v. State*, 545 So. 2d 185 (Ala. Cr. App., 1988) (contract with student-athlete).

[349] See, *United States v. Walters*, 711 F.Supp. 1435 (N.D. Ill., 1989); revd 913 F.2d 388 (7th Cir., 1990); 775 F.Supp. 1173 (N.D. Ill., 1991); revd 997 F.2d 1219 (7th Cir., 1993).

[350] See, *Detroit Lions, Inc. v. Argovitz*, 580 F.Supp. 542 (E.D. Mich., 1984) (agent signed Billy Sims to team in which he was part-owner; inadequate disclosure; Sims' contract with Houston Gamblers rescinded).

[351] See: *Walters v. Fullwood*, 675 F.Supp. 155 (S.D. N.Y., 1987) (action for fees by original agent; representation agreement in breach of NCAA rules not enforceable); *Total Economic Athletic Management of America, Inc. v. Pickens*, 898 S.W.2d 98 (Mo. C.A., 1995) (payments in breach of NCAA and NFLPA rules).

[352] See: *Zinn v. Parrish*, 461 F.Supp. 11 (N.D. Ill., 1977), revd 644 F.2d 360 (7th Cir., 1981) (agent's action for fees; adequate good faith efforts by agent); *Brown v. Woolf*, 554 F.Supp. 1206 (S.D. Ind., 1983) (contract negotiated with financially unstable team; full fee taken); *Bias*

Canadian cases on standards in player representation have centred on the affairs of R. Alan Eagleson who made his initial foray into hockey by providing legal services to professional players.[354] Eagleson achieved fame in 1966 when he represented Bobby Orr in negotiations with the Boston Bruins. After originally offering Orr around USD $10,250 for two years, the Bruins were eventually persuaded to come up with the unprecedented figures of a USD $25,000 signing bonus, USD $25,000 for the first year and USD $30,000 for the second.[355] Eagleson then assisted in the incorporation of "Bobby Orr Enterprises" and participated in investment decisions as a director of the company. During the 1970s, Eagleson's agency firms represented about 150 players or half the total in the NHL. While also serving as executive director of the NHLPA, Eagleson provided negotiation and management services through Sports Management Limited and Rae-Con Consultants Limited:

> The usual arrangements Eagleson made with his athlete-clients...were, the athlete would contract with Rae-Con. Rae-Con would bill the athlete, but Eagleson would provide the service of negotiating the athlete's contract with the team and bill Rae-Con for that service through his law firm. The offices of Eagleson's law firm, Rae-Con and the NHLPA were in the same building.[356]

Eagleson's control of the clientele was undermined in 1980 when his colleagues William Watters and Rick Curran left Sport Management Ltd. to operate their own company.[357] That year also saw the end of the business relationship with Bobby Orr who was in dispute with Eagleson over contract negotiations, investments and Orr's liability to pay income.[358]

---

v. *Advantage International, Inc.*, 905 F.2d 1558 (D.C. Cir., 1990) (death of Len Bias; no liability for failure to finalize insurance policy or endorsement contract). See also, *Day v. Rosenthal*, 217 Cal. Rptr. 89, 170 Cal. App. 3d 1125 (C.A., 1985) (malpractice by Doris Day's attorney); *Mandich v. Watters*, 970 F.2d 462 (8th Cir., 1992) (agent made undisclosed side-agreement that player would not claim salary if injured).

[353] See: *Washington v. Baenziger*, 673 F.Supp. 1478 (N.D. Cal., 1987); *Williams v. CWI, Inc.*, 777 F.Supp. 1006 (D. D.C., 1991) (investment through company owned by agent; breach of contract); *Jones v. Childers*, 18 F.3d 899 (11th Cir., 1994) (agent received secret commissions on players' high-risk, "tax shelter" investments); *Hendricks v. Thornton*, 973 S.W.2d 348 (Tex. C.A., 1998) (losses on trades in government securities; issues for trial).

[354] On Eagleson's roles in "Hockey Canada" and the NHLPA, see Chapter 3, "Organizations and Regulations", section A, 4; Chapter 9, "National Hockey League", sections B, 1-3.

[355] See: D. Clayton, *Eagle: The Life and Times of R. Alan Eagleson* (Toronto: Lester & Orpen Dennys, 1982) at 56-59; D. Cruise & A. Griffiths, *Net Worth: Exploding the Myths of Pro Hockey* (Toronto: Viking Penguin, 1991) at 194-95.

[356] *Gillis v. Eagleson*, [1996] O.J. No. 4214, 71 C.P.R. (3d) 292 at 296-97 (Ont. Gen. Div.), *per* O'Brien J. The NHLPA precluded Eagleson from acting as a player agent in 1990: D. Clayton, *Eagle: The Life and Times of R. Alan Eagleson* (Toronto: Lester & Orpen Dennys, 1982) at 324.

[357] See, D. Cruise & A. Griffiths, *Net Worth: Exploding the Myths of Pro Hockey* (Toronto: Viking Penguin, 1991) at 238-40.

[358] See: D. Clayton, *Eagle: The Life and Times of R. Alan Eagleson* (Toronto: Lester & Orpen Dennys, 1982) at 211-12, 218; R.A. Eagleson & S. Young, *Power Play: The Memoirs of Hockey Czar Alan Eagleson* (Toronto: McClelland & Stewart, 1991) at 186-96; W. Houston &

The services provided by Eagleson's firms were the subject of civil actions by Vaclav Nedomansky[359] and by player-turned-lawyer Michael Gillis. In *Nedomansky v. Eagleson,*[360] Nedomansky alleged that Sports Management Ltd. was in breach of duty for failing to obtain the prompt formalization of a contract worked out with the Detroit Red Wings in June 1979. The terms of this package were confirmed in a telex drafted by Eagleson, although negotiations had been conducted by William Watters. Nedomansky played the 1979-80 season without a signed contract when a dispute developed over undiscussed buy-out provisions. In September 1980, prior to an arbitration before the NHL president to determine the player's status, Eagleson arranged a new contract on terms less advantageous than the original package. The 1979 deal would have "fully guaranteed" major league play for five years and then provided for 10 years of service as a team scout. Instead, Nedomansky signed a four-year contract at more than USD $250,000 a-year with a buy-out at 60 per cent, which the Red Wings exercised after the 1981-82 season. Nedomansky terminated Eagleson's services in 1981 and brought action alleging negligence, breach of contract and breach of fiduciary duty; Eagleson counterclaimed for service fees owing. In 1984, Nedomansky's action was dismissed when Catzman J. held that the wording of the telex had not been defective and had not caused the failure to agree on the buy-out. Although the court agreed that there had been unreasonable delay, this did not cause the loss of the 1979 package because it was not clear that Detroit would have agreed to remove the normal buy-out rate of 33 per cent. Eagleson succeeded in the counterclaim for fees,[361] but was not awarded costs on Nedomansky's action because the court found a lack of professional "diligence and expedition" in finalizing his client's contract. In *Gillis v. Eagleson,*[362] Gillis was successful in an action against Eagleson and Rae-Con Consultants Limited and also prevailed in a counterclaim by Rae-Con alleging a fee-sharing arrangement with Gillis' agency firm. The court found breaches of contract and of "a long prior relationship of trust" when Eagleson improperly charged a fee of USD $41,250 for services relating to the recovery of compensation after Gillis' playing career was ended by injury. This disability claim was made under Lloyd's insurance policies held by the NHL, the NHLPA and Gillis. O'Brien J. recognized that Eagleson had done a lot of work on the claim "but never gave Gillis any details of what he was doing nor did he explain to him in what capacity he was working".[363] Knowing

---

D. Shoalts, *Eagleson: The Fall of a Hockey Czar* (Toronto: McGraw-Hill Ryerson, 1993) at 53-72.

[359] See, R.A. Eagleson & S. Young, *Power Play: The Memoirs of Hockey Czar Alan Eagleson* (Toronto: McClelland & Stewart, 1991) at 273-80.

[360] [1984] O.J. No. 473, 27 A.C.W.S. (2d) 327 (Ont. H.C.J.).

[361] In resisting the claim for fees, Nedomansky maintained that there had been "investment of the plaintiff's funds, without disclosure, in mortgages and projects in which Eagleson or members of his law firm or friends and associates had an interest": *Nedomansky v. Eagleson*, [1984] O.J. No. 473, 27 A.C.W.S. (2d) 327 at 84 (Ont. H.C.J.). No money was lost on the investments.

[362] [1996] O.J. No. 4214, 71 C.P.R. (3d) 292 (Ont. Gen. Div.). See also, *Gillis v. Eagleson*, [1995] O.J. No. 1160, 23 O.R. (3d) 164 (Ont. Gen. Div.) (stay of action pending criminal proceedings and law society hearings).

[363] *Gillis v. Eagleson*, [1996] O.J. No. 4214, 71 C.P.R. (3d) 292 at 320 (Ont. Gen. Div.).

that the claim would be settled and realizing that he had no fee agreement with his client, Eagleson misled Gillis "in a devious plan"[364] by advising him that lawyers had been retained to sue for the full amount. Gillis was entitled to recover the fee and was awarded CDN $30,000 in punitive damages because of Eagleson's serious breach of professional responsibilities when acting as Gillis' lawyer. At a later hearing, Gillis was also held entitled to complete indemnification of legal costs.[365]

## 3. Regulation

Given the history of "opportunistic" behaviour by agents and the uneven standards of representation and advice, various private and public systems of regulation have been attempted. In Canada, "The Agent in Amateur Sport" was the subject of a conference and series of consultations in 1985 and led to the publication of a guide book[366] dealing with the selection of agents and eligibility rules and commercial opportunities in high performance sport. The guide provided information about the desired qualifications of representatives and their legal responsibilities and included a suggested standard representation agreement. The conference did not recommend specific federal or provincial legislation[367] to deal with sports agency, so that the applicable responsibilities continue to be the general fiduciary duties of agents and the standards associated with recognized occupations and professions.[368]

Among the NHLPA's "certified agents", many are qualified lawyers who are subject to the rules of the relevant provincial law society. In Ontario, the *Law Society Act*[369] prohibits unlicensed practice (see, ss. 26.1-26.3)[370] and prescribes disciplinary sanctions for "conduct unbecoming a barrister or solicitor" (see, s. 33(1)).[371] The Rules of Professional Conduct (2000)[372] deal with matters such as the quality of service, confidentiality, conflicts of interest, preserving the client's

---

[364] *Gillis v. Eagleson*, [1996] O.J. No. 4214, 71 C.P.R. (3d) 292 at 319 (Ont. Gen. Div.), *per* O'Brien J. On Eagleson's credibility as a witness, see, *ibid.*, at 316-17.

[365] *Gillis v. Eagleson*, [1997] O.J. No. 2070 (Ont. Gen. Div.) (award of solicitor-client costs). See also, *Gillis v. Eagleson*, [1998] O.J. No. 147 (Ont. C.A.) (orders relating to payment of funds, security and examination of the appellant).

[366] J. Barnes, *The Amateur Athlete's Guide Book/Guide de l'athlète amateur* (Ottawa: Canadian Interuniversity Athletic Union, 1986).

[367] On the regulation of boxing, including managers' contracts, see, for example, *Athletics Control Act*, R.S.O. 1990, c. A.34; *General Regulation*, R.R.O. 1990, Reg. 52.

[368] See, for example: *Insurance Act*, R.S.O. 1990, c. I.8; *Public Accounting Act, 2004*, S.O. 2004, c. 8; *Real Estate and Business Brokers Act, 2002*, S.O. 2002, c. 30, Sched. C; *Securities Act*, R.S.O. 1990, c. S.5. Consumer protection legislation is largely inapplicable because the player has "business purposes"; see, *Consumer Protection Act, 2002*, S.O. 2002, c. 30, Sched. A.

[369] R.S.O. 1990, c. L.8.

[370] The *Law Society Act*, R.S.O. 1990, c. L.8, s. 1(5)-(8) defines the "provision of legal services".

[371] See, for example, *Re Cwinn and Law Society of Upper Canada*, [1980] O.J. No. 3548, 28 O.R. (2d) 61 (Ont. Div. Ct.) (sexual relations with teenage girls employed to ride and assist at horse shows; lawyer disbarred).

[372] See online: <http://www.lsuc.on.ca>, "Lawyer Regulation", "Rules of Professional Conduct".

property, fees, advertising, public responsibilities and sexual harassment. A fee must be "fair and reasonable and...disclosed in a timely fashion" (see, Rule 2.08(1)) and may be contingent on the successful disposition or completion of the matter for which the lawyer is retained (see, Rule 2.08(3)). Lawyers may advertise fees and may offer or market their services provided the means is not false or misleading and does not take advantage of the vulnerable (see, Rules 3.01, 3.02); when certified by the Law Society, they may also advertise that they are specialists in a specified field (see, Rule 3.03). Lawyers working as player agents are subject to supervision and discipline by provincial law societies and must comply with the associated professional standards.[373] Lawyers cannot maintain that their agency work (including the activities of partners and associates) is performed in a different capacity because the main reason that a player would choose a lawyer-agent is the further guarantee of competence and ethical probity associated with the professional accreditation.

In the United States,[374] a short-lived Association of Representatives of Professional Athletes ("ARPA") was founded in 1978 to create a voluntary system of registration and promulgate a code of ethics. More importantly, the eligibility rules of the National Collegiate Athletic Association ("NCAA") prohibit athletes from agreeing to use agents for the purpose of marketing and prohibit the acceptance of benefits from agents. These association rules began to be supplemented by legislation in 1981 when California adopted its *Athlete Agents Act*.[375] A fragmented pattern of legislation in different states then followed, creating jurisdictional complication through the various registration requirements. Although aimed at unscrupulous agents, these statutes largely deal with premature recruiting and seek to protect schools' investment in the continuing eligibility of their student athletes. A *Uniform Athlete Agent Act* ("UAAA") has been adopted in many states, and this has been supplemented at the national level by the federal *Sports Agent Responsibility and Trust Act* ("SPARTA").[376]

Agents based in Canada must address the issue of compliance with the American legislation and compliance with the different types of regulation operating in other jurisdictions,[377] including the countries that subscribe to the European Community Treaty.[378] Hockey agency in Germany, for example, is

---

[373] See, *Gillis v. Eagleson*, [1996] O.J. No. 4214, 71 C.P.R. (3d) 291 (Ont. Gen. Div.).

[374] See: J.T. Wolohan, "The Regulation of Sports Agents in the United States" (2004) 3-4 Int. Sports L.J. 49; J.T. Wolohan, "United States" in R. Siekmann *et al.*, eds., *Players' Agents Worldwide: Legal Aspects* (The Hague: TMC Asser Press, 2007) at 637.

[375] Cal. Labor Code, §§1500-1547.

[376] Public Law No. 108-304 (H.R. 361) (2004), 15 U.S.C. ss. 7801-7807.

[377] See, R. Siekmann *et al.*, eds., *Players' Agents Worldwide: Legal Aspects* (The Hague: TMC Asser Press, 2007), noting the regulation of agents in 40 countries, including Belarus, the Czech Republic, Finland, France, Germany, Italy, Russia, Slovakia, Sweden, Switzerland, the United Kingdom and the Ukraine.

[378] See, R.B. Martins, "The *Laurent Piau* Case of the ECJ on the Status of Players' Agents" in R. Siekmann *et al.*, eds., *Players' Agents Worldwide: Legal Aspects* (The Hague: TMC Asser Press, 2007) at 37. On the EC Treaty, see further, Chapter 8, "Competition Law and Labour Law", section E.

subject to the *Sozialgesetzbuch* (Code of Social Law), the *Rechtsberatungsgesetz* (law on giving legal advice), the *Bürgerliches Gesetzbuch* (Civil Code), the *Gewerbeordnung* (trade regulations) and the *Gesetz gegen den unlauteren Wettbewerb* (law against unfair competition).[379] Controls operating at national and international levels assume particular importance as the market for elite players takes on a global character.

In the North American major leagues, the principal form of supervision is the standards exercised by the various players' associations. This type of control began in 1983 when the National Football League Players' Association initiated its program and was followed by the Major League Baseball Players' Association in 1985[380] and the National Basketball Players' Association in 1986. The Canadian Football League Players' Association introduced "Regulations Governing Contract Advisors" in 1985 and added supervision of "Player Financial Advisors" in 2004. The NHLPA's program began operation in 1996. Courts have recognized the regulatory authority because of the associations' status as the exclusive bargaining agent for the players in matters relating to terms and conditions of employment.[381] In this system, the collective agent validates the personal agent for the purpose of individual representation: the "certified agent", as chosen by the player, is essentially the delegate of the players' association.

The NHLPA's "Regulations Governing Agent Certification" (June 25, 2002) deal with agents' conduct in negotiating contracts and in providing other advice and representation, including financial management (see, s. 1(B)). Only individuals are eligible for certification, although agents may work together through a corporation or other business entity (see, s. 2(A)). To obtain certification, the wannabe must represent either a current NHL player or an unsigned draftee, must submit an application and must pay an application fee and an annual fee. Applicants acknowledge that they will be required to report to the NHLPA all fees charged to players and agree to "save and hold harmless" the NHLPA from any liability resulting from their work as an agent. The "Application for Certification as an NHLPA Player Agent" consists of an extensive questionnaire that must be answered candidly, accurately and completely. Applicants are required to provide details of their education, business affiliations and employment history, their work on behalf of leagues or team officers and their experience in representing professional players or other celebrities. Further information relates to the services provided by the

---

[379] See, M. Schimke, "Germany" in R. Siekmann *et al.*, eds., *Players' Agents Worldwide: Legal Aspects* (The Hague: TMC Asser Press, 2007) at 227.

[380] See, *Rona v. Major League Baseball Players' Assn.* (October 22, 1993, Collins, arb.) (MLBPA attempted to refuse certification to former general counsel to management during the "collusion period" in MLB).

[381] See: *Collins v. National Basketball Players Assn.*, 850 F.Supp. 1468 (D. Colo., 1991), affd 976 F.2d 740 (10th Cir., 1992) (labour exemption applied); *Black v. National Football League Players Assn.*, 87 F.Supp. 2d 1 (D. D.C., 2000) (challenge to disciplinary proceedings); *White v. National Football League*, 92 F.Supp. 2d 918 (D. Minn., 2000) (allegation that agents were involved in negotiating undisclosed compensation in breach of the CBA). On the "labour exemption", see Chapter 8, "Competition Law and Labour Law", sections A, 3; C, 3.

applicant's firm, including financial management and bonding, referral arrangements with other businesses and systems for the payment of fees and expenses. Lawyers must indicate in which jurisdictions they are licensed and must provide details of any inquiries that called into question their fitness to practice; similar information must be provided by holders of other professional qualifications. The questionnaire calls for details of the applicant's involvement in legal or disciplinary proceedings and requires information about any proprietary or business connections with professional sport, including affiliations with the NHL, its teams or its management staff. The NHLPA may deny certification if the application includes any false statement or if the applicant has engaged in conduct adversely affecting "his credibility, integrity or competence to serve in a fiduciary capacity on behalf of players" (see, Regulations, s. 2(E)(5)). Particular grounds of refusal include the misappropriation of funds, unwillingness to comply with regulations, or suspension as an agent by a governmental entity or other players' association.

The "Regulations Governing Agent Certification" include a "Standard of Conduct for Agents" designed to maintain "the highest degree of professional competence and integrity" (see, s. 3). Agents must stay informed in relation to league structures, negotiation techniques and sports law and must report any violations of players' rights. They must keep comprehensive files recording the services they have performed and must provide the NHLPA with a copy of compensation agreements negotiated on behalf of players. The regulations list prohibited conduct that may result in disciplinary sanctions following a complaint and hearing process that also applies to denials of certification (see, s. 6). Agents are prohibited from providing valuable inducements to players to encourage them to use the agent's services and must avoid actual or potential conflicts of interest. Agents may not provide services to professional leagues or team officers and may not solicit or accept commissions from NHL teams. Other specific prohibitions include failing to disclose material facts, misusing confidential information and engaging in unlawful conduct.

The agent's services must be provided under a "Standard Player-Agent Contract" (see, Regulations, s. 4) that may be supplemented by mandatory clauses required by state legislation. The SPAC must be signed and submitted before the agent begins negotiations on behalf of the player. Automatic renewal provisions are not permitted, so that a new representation agreement is required for each contract negotiation or renegotiation. The SPAC continues for the period of the contract negotiated with the team, except that it may be terminated by written notice[382] or by the decertification of the agent. The specified services consist of negotiating compensation and enforcing the player's rights with the NHL team. Unlike the regulations operating in other leagues, the SPAC places no limits on fees, which may be charged as a percentage of income or at an hourly rate. Agents are not entitled to payment until the player has received the compensation on which the fee is based, although the player may choose to pay

---

[382] See, *Calabrese v. Weekes*, [2003] O.J. No. 4176 (Ont. S.C.J.) (arbitrator accepted that Kevin Weekes could provide verbal notice of termination; no fees were owing to original agent).

fees in advance, including fees related to deferred compensation. Expenses are normally the agent's responsibility, except that the player-agent contract may make specific provision for the reimbursement of documented expenses approved by the player. The SPAC is governed by the law of Ontario, and disputes relating to meaning, application or enforcement must be referred to arbitration under a special dispute resolution process. The NHLPA characterises such disputes as internal matters, and the Regulations prohibit the filing of a lawsuit where the matter is subject to the arbitration provisions (see, s. 3(B)(20)). The grievances referred to arbitration commonly involve claims by agents to be paid for services performed[383] and deal with issues such as the appropriate commission and the agent's entitlement when the player concludes the negotiations with the team.[384] In addressing the right to be paid, arbitrators consider the standard of service and whether the agent has met all required obligations.

Although it is not a comprehensive system, regulation by players' associations provides useful monitoring of services within particular major leagues and helps elite players in their selection of agents. The supervision is exercised by a labour organization and offers some guarantee that agents are qualified, competent and of good moral character. The main difficulty with the system is that the associations' power to exclude or discipline agents and restrict their commercial activities may be anti-competitive. Particular conflict arises when the individual player is at odds with the collective body and wishes to use an agent who is entirely unconstrained in pursuing the player's interests: if the association is hostile to a particular candidate it may be because that person is a very effective personal representative. While the various regulatory measures offer a patchwork of controls, further discipline is provided by the market for agents' services. The best test of an agent may well be business reputation and the ability to survive.

## 4.    The Agency Business

The hockey agency business that emerged in the 1970s had a buccaneering or *laissez-faire* character, although there was very little in it that was free-for-all. The period is particularly well known for a kickback scheme by which junior teams in Western Canada took payments for assigning players to particular agents.[385] The business quickly emerged as cut-throat and top-heavy. By 1979, 74 men were calling themselves hockey agents, and the competitiveness inevitably increased with the demise of the World Hockey Association.[386] Alan Eagleson's companies had charged fees of ten per cent of earnings, but this was challenged

---

[383] See, "DiPietro, Orr settle dispute" *The Globe and Mail* (Toronto: April 25, 2009) at S4 (SPAC not signed, but Rick DiPietro agreed to pay fee of USD $300,000).

[384] See, J. Brisebois, "L'univers de la relation contractuelle entre un athlète professionnel et son agent: Une analyse du droit québécois" (1999) 33 R.J.T. 589 at 628-29.

[385] See, D. Cruise & A. Griffiths, *Net Worth: Exploding the Myths of Pro Hockey* (Toronto: Viking Penguin, 1991) at 231-34.

[386] See Chapter 9, "National Hockey League", sections A, 2; B, 1, 3.

by agents who offered seven per cent or less.[387] The working environment often included disparagement of rivals, exaggerated claims about achievements and numbers of clients, client poaching, and the aggressive recruitment of increasingly younger players. New hopefuls entered the field during the 1980s and there were changes in the concentration of representation, but the business largely fell to a small number of firms. By 1991, "fewer than a dozen agents represent[ed] 75 percent of the 539 players ...in the NHL".[388]

The struggle for talent has led to frequent disputes arising from the migration of players from one agency to another. The original agent sometimes seeks fees from the ex-client[389] or alleges that the rival organization improperly induced breach of a representation agreement.[390] The inter-state and international nature of the business commonly present issues of jurisdiction.[391] In *Newport Sports Management Inc. v. Reichel*,[392] the well-known company made an oral agreement with Robert Reichel that Newport would be Reichel's agent in negotiations with NHL teams and would be entitled to three per cent of the seasonal salary and bonus income negotiated by Newport on the player's behalf. Newport negotiated a three-year contract with the Calgary Flames that provided for the possibility of an additional option year at CDN $160,000. Reichel paid the agreed fee for three years and then used another agent and salary arbitration to arrange a contract with the team for one year at CDN $700,000, plus a one-year option. When Newport claimed three per cent of the option year salary in the original contract, the court held that they were not entitled to further payment. Reichel's contract with Newport had terminated, and Reichel's new arrangement with the Flames amounted to a new contract that had not been negotiated by his original agent.

---

[387] See, D. Cruise & A. Griffiths, *Net Worth: Exploding the Myths of Pro Hockey* (Toronto: Viking Penguin, 1991) at 235. Eagleson's 10 per cent fee usually included financial management; see, *Gillis v. Eagleson*, [1996] O.J. No. 4214, 71 C.P.R. (3d) 292 at 297 (Ont. Gen. Div.).

[388] D. Cruise & A. Griffiths, *Net Worth: Exploding the Myths of Pro Hockey* (Toronto: Viking Penguin, 1991) at 226.

[389] See: *Walters v. Fullwood*, 675 F.Supp. 155 (S.D. N.Y., 1987) (agent's action dismissed); *Total Economic Athletic Management of America, Inc. v. Pickens*, 898 S.W.2d 98 (Mo. C.A., 1995) (jury awarded damages of only USD $20,000); *Calabrese v. Weekes*, [2003] O.J. No. 4176 (Ont. S.C.J.) (original agency properly terminated).

[390] See: *Speakers of Sport, Inc. v. Proserv, Inc.*, 178 F.3d 862 (7th Cir., 1999) (competition is not a tort); *Bauer v. The Interpublic Group of Companies, Inc.*, 255 F.Supp. 2d 1086 (N.D. Cal., 2003) (action dismissed); *Smith v. IMG Worldwide, Inc.*, 360 F.Supp. 2d 681 (E.D. Penn., 2005); *Steinberg, Moorad & Dunn v. David Dunn*, 2005 WL 712487 (9th Cir., 2005) (original award of USD $44.6 million; decisions affirmed and reversed in part and issues remanded).

[391] See: *Roundball Enterprises, Inc. v. Richardson*, 616 F.Supp. 1537 (S.D. N.Y., 1985) (jurisdiction of court in New York); *Landmark Sport Group Atlantic Ltd. v. Karpov*, [1995] N.S.J. No. 304, 142 N.S.R. (2d) 280 (N.S.S.C.) (jurisdiction of court in Nova Scotia); *Gandler v. Nazarov*, 1995 WL 363814 (S.D. N.Y., 1995) (jurisdiction of court in New York); *Sports Corp. v. Svoboda*, [2004] A.J. No. 728, 32 Alta. L.R. (4th) 272 (Alta. Q.B.) (jurisdiction of court in Alberta); *Sportrust Associates International, Inc. v. Sports Corp.*, 304 F.Supp. 2d 789 (E.D. Va., 2004) (court in Virginia lacked jurisdiction).

[392] [2000] O.J. No. 177 (Ont. S.C.J.).

The sports agency business consists of individual operators representing a small number of clients and major management companies that were sometimes formed through the consolidation of agencies.[393] The big players include the International Management Group ("IMG") and SFX, although IMG has withdrawn from representing players in team sports and now focuses on individual celebrities and the organization and broadcasting of events. In hockey, the leading agencies are the Newport Sports Management Inc. led by Donald Meehan and Patrick Morris, the Octagon hockey group led by Michael Liut and Larry Kelly, and the Orr Hockey Group; the IMG hockey group was formerly led by Pat Brisson and J.P. Barry who joined Creative Artists Agency in 2006. In 2004, the main representatives accounted for client payrolls of USD $166.5 million (Newport), USD $142.2 million (IMG), USD $78.5 million (Octagon) and USD $50.8 million (Orr).[394] The integrated organizations offer a range of legal, financial, investment[395] and tax services and assist prominent players in marketing and public relations. When arranging corporate sponsorships and endorsements,[396] the fee is usually around 20 per cent of the commercial earnings received.

Regulation and market forces have now brought some measure of stability to the business, so that the serious abuses and malpractices of the past are less likely. There is, however, continuing concern over conflicts of interest, especially when one agency holds a large stable of clients or represents different players on the same team who are each competing for the best slice of salary within the limited "upper range". Players associations are also limited in their capacity to "police" the market and investigate activities such as the payment of inducements or "advances on income" to potential clients. The obvious further problem is fees. A standard rate of compensation for negotiating contracts of employment is three per cent of the player's earnings,[397] which based on NHL payroll costs of USD $1.5 billion in 2008-09 would result in total annual payments to agents of USD $45 million. If this figure is thought to be excessive, the alternative is for players to pay flat fees or to base the account on hourly

---

[393] See, K.L. Shropshire & T. Davis, *The Business of Sports Agents*, 2d ed. (Philadelphia: University of Pennsylvania Press, 2008) at 37-52. On the break-up of a firm and the allocation of clients, see, *Weinberg v. Silber*, 140 F.Supp. 2d 712 (N.D. Tex., 2001).

[394] See, T. Davis, "United States" in R. Siekmann *et al.*, eds., *Players' Agents Worldwide: Legal Aspects* (The Hague: TMC Asser Press, 2007) 655 at 668, referring to the *SportsBusiness Journal*. The Winnipeg firm of Thompson, Dorfman, Sweatman comes in a close fifth with a client payroll of USD $49.8 million.

[395] On an action against fellow investors in a golf course, see, *Vanbiesbrouck v. Missere*, [2006] O.J. No. 3282 (Ont. S.C.J.) (John Vanbiesbrouck invested CDN $1.2 million in a venture that "has not been profitable").

[396] On the exploitation of "personality rights", see Chapter 7, "The Business of Hockey", section A, 4.

[397] The agent's fee is not deductible from the player's employment income, although the cost of negotiating personal endorsements and public appearances may be claimed against business income. See, IT-168R3, "Athletes and Players Employed by Football, Hockey and Similar Clubs" (May 13, 1991). See also, *Income Tax Act*, R.S.C. 1985 (5th Supp.), c. 1, s. 8(1)(b) (deduction limited to legal expenses incurred in collecting salary owed). *Cf. Spriggs and Riddell v. Commissioner of Taxation*, [2009] HCA 22 (H.C. of Aust.).

billings. With the possible concern about "money leaving the game", players' associations may move to a system of "union-hired agents"[398] or may cut out the middlemen entirely by making their own distribution of salaries according to experience, performance, position or other factors.[399] After checking that it is receiving the "players' share" of league revenue, it is open to the NHLPA to slice the spoils directly for the benefit of its members. However, for the foreseeable future professional players are likely to preserve individual representation and negotiations, and agents will continue to perform important functions in finding employment for upcoming or marginal players and in selling the services of free agents. It is unlikely that Canada's streets will soon be lined with decayed and dispossessed hockey agents soliciting a lucky loonie.

---

[398] See, R.T. Karcher, "United States" in R. Siekmann *et al.*, eds., *Players' Agents Worldwide: Legal Aspects* (The Hague: TMC Asser Press, 2007) 693 at 722-26.

[399] In 1982, the NFLPA proposed taking 55 per cent of gross team revenues which would then be distributed according to a wage scale based on years of service and playing time; see, R.C. Berry, W.B. Gould & P.D. Staudohar, *Labor Relations in Professional Sports* (Dover: Auburn House, 1986) at 130-34.

# Chapter 10

# CONCLUSION

And how do the players feel about it
this combination of ballet and murder?
For years a Canadian specific.[1]

This study has been an exercise in "sports law" in so far as the issues are peculiar to hockey. It has also been a case of "sports and the law" as legal doctrines are applied to different problems arising from the playing and organization of the national winter diversion. In rough order of appearance, the following are some of the legal subject areas that have intruded onto the ice: property rights and trusts, constitutional law, dispute resolution, human rights, administrative law, tort liability, criminal liability, commercial law, media law, competition law, labour law and contracts. The focus has been the common law of Canada, but the American legal system and international standards also exert their influence. The law of hockey may serve as a highway to further legal study, although the driver should be warned that many of the non-sporting side roads are not quite so exciting.

Al Purdy caught most of the issues in his famous poem:

What they worry about most is injuries...
Boys playing a man's game in a permanent childhood
with a screaming coach who insists on winning
sports-writer-critics and the crowd gone mad....
thinking of money in owners' pockets that might be yours.[2]

The power struggles of the game have always been there, and a wide array of legal problems will continue to be a staple of the sporting news. The law of hockey is not going away. Supported by government policies and legal services, disadvantaged groups can now claim equal opportunities to participate, equitable programs and a safe playing environment. Association members will seek recognition of their rights and fair procedures. Injured players and victims of

---

[1]   A. Purdy, "Hockey Players" in R. Brown, ed., *The Collected Poems of Al Purdy* (Toronto: McClelland & Stewart, 1986) at 54-56, modified from the original version published in *The Caribou Horses* (1965) at 60-62.

[2]   A. Purdy, "Hockey Players" in R. Brown, ed., *The Collected Poems of Al Purdy* (Toronto: McClelland & Stewart Ltd., 1986) at 54-56, modified from the original version published in *The Caribou Horses* (1965) at 60-62. In 1965, Purdy wrote, "Sports writers friendly but sometimes treacherous."

violence will seek redress through a variety of legal processes. And the high end of the business of hockey will see continued conflict over the validity of the figures and the division of the spoils. The future is likely to bring more of the same but with some novel twists brought on by technological innovations and the global reach of the game.

In the end, it is useful to go back to the beginning. The best known account of the original modern game in Montreal in 1875 comes from the *Gazette* newspaper, which recorded "an interesting and well-contested affair, the efforts of the players exciting much merriment as they wheeled and dodged each other".[3] However, *The British Whig*, of Kingston, had a different story to tell:

> A disgraceful sight took place at Montreal in the Victoria Skating Rink over a game of hockey. Shins and heads were battered, benches smashed, and the lady spectators fled in confusion.[4]

From day one, we see problematic masculinity and the tendency for the game to get a bad press. According to *The British Whig*, the brawl was "over" a game of hockey, and the most likely explanation is that the figure skaters wanted their rink back. Perhaps they tried to nip the game in the bud, but the tide of history was against them, not to mention the balance of brawn and muscle. Assuming that this foundation fracas actually happened, here was a splendid new game but it was one that had the potential for trouble. The lawyers have been doing well ever since.

---

[3]  "Hockey" *The Gazette* (Montreal: March 4, 1875) at 3.
[4]  "Canadian" *The British Whig* (Kingston: March 5, 1875) at 2.

# Appendix I

# Two Cases of Hockey Homicide[1]

## *R. v. Loney* (1905)[2]

This remarkable case arose from a local exhibition game played at Maxville in eastern Ontario on February 24, 1905.[3] The game was played against the Crescents club from nearby Alexandria which arrived with their own man as referee. Play began in slushy conditions, giving rise to a rough contest in which the visiting official called most of the fouls against the home club. After about 25 minutes, Alcide Laurin, of Alexandria, made a sweep up the ice and was checked hard by Maxville's Allan Loney. Laurin's stick was broken in the exchange and a mix-up took place between him and Loney; Laurin was then seen to fall after receiving a blow on the head from Loney's stick. Laurin died instantly from a fractured skull. Laurin, aged 24, was a star all-around amateur athlete from a well-known local francophone family. Loney was 19 years old and the son of a store owner who was prominent in the Orange movement. The case prompted intense local feelings that were often exacerbated by varying accounts in the outside English and French press.

Laurin's body was returned to Alexandria where a heavily attended inquest[4] took place at the local town hall. While these hearings were in progress, Loney was arrested in Maxville and taken to the county jail in Cornwall; an information alleging murder had been sworn by Leo Laurin, brother of the deceased. Witnesses at the inquest gave three different versions of the clash: that Loney raised his stick and struck Laurin deliberately, without justification; that he hit in self-defence; and, that it happened accidentally as he fell over. Maxville residents offered the latter accounts. The inquest jury eventually returned a verdict that, "Alcide Laurin came to his death by his being hit by a hockey stick in the hands of Allan Loney, of Maxville...the blow was given deliberately and

---

[1]   For a detailed study using judicial and archive records and newspaper accounts, see, J. Barnes, *Two Cases of Hockey Homicide: The Crisis of a Moral Ideal* (Paper presented to the North American Society for Sport History (NASSH), 1990). This Appendix is a modified version of the summary in J. Barnes, *Sports and the Law in Canada*, 2d ed. (Toronto: Butterworths, 1988) at 305-08; see also, *1990 NASSH Proceedings*, at 75-76.

[2]   See, J. Barnes, *Two Cases of Hockey Homicide: The Crisis of a Moral Ideal* (Paper presented to the North American Society for Sport History (NASSH), 1990) at 20-50.

[3]   On January 25, 1905, the Province had elected the Conservative government of James P. Whitney, putting an end to 33 years of Liberal rule. On the federal scene, Parliament was debating the separate schools provisions of the Autonomy Acts creating Alberta and Saskatchewan.

[4]   The coroner was Senator Donald McMillan, M.D. (1835-1914). During the later inquest sessions, questions were put by James Dingwall (1840-1923), who served as crown attorney from 1873 to 1916; in 1864, Dingwall had begun his articles in the law firm of the long-serving Liberal premier, Sir Oliver Mowat. Loney was represented by the local Conservative M.P., Robert A. Pringle (1855-1922), who acted for the defence throughout the subsequent proceedings.

not in self-defence". When the preliminary inquiry[5] was held in Cornwall on March 7, 1905, many people from both villages travelled to watch the proceedings. This time the evidence gave a picture of Laurin responding to the check and broken stick by raising his fists in the stance of a boxer; Loney then made his swing. It also emerged that this was the referee's first attempt at officiating. Loney was committed to trial on the murder charge and remanded to jail; he remained in custody for another three weeks until the Cornwall spring assizes opened on March 27, 1905.

Just before the trial, the prosecutor[6] decided to reduce the charge to manslaughter. Crown witnesses described how Loney had checked Laurin hard, broken Laurin's stick and then swung his own stick over his shoulder to strike Laurin down. Some conceded that Loney might have been responding to threats or punches from Laurin. Defence witnesses maintained that Loney had hit Laurin while stumbling forward trying to recover from blows struck by Laurin. The last man on the stand for the defence was the accused himself. Allan Loney gave this version:

> When I saw him coming down I went out to check him on the side of the rink. I got the puck, backed away and lifted the puck across the ice. As I was doing this, Laurin followed me and called me a 'son of a bitch' and then he hit me in the face...It dazed me. It was the blow which broke my nose and cut me. The blow caused me to stagger...I was in a dazed condition.

An emotional final address by Loney's lawyer brought loud applause from the packed courthouse crowd, but the summing-up by Teetzel J.[7] was very hostile to the accused's case. The judge asked the jury to consider whether it was necessary for Loney to kill Laurin in order to protect himself. He sought to discredit those witnesses who maintained that the death was accidental, and finally exhorted the jury to put aside all sympathy and do their duty. The jurors took four hours to consider their verdict. Late in the evening of March 29, 1905, the jury returned to a crowded, tense courtroom to announce a verdict of not guilty. Cornwall then witnessed a night of demonstration and celebration by Loney's supporters.

### *R. v. Masson* (1907)[8]

The 1907 season saw many brutal games[9] in the senior leagues, whose champions were recognized to challenge for the Stanley Cup.[10] Tragedy occurred

---

[5]   Before John A. McDougald, J.P.

[6]   F.J. French, K.C. (1847-1924), a Conservative from Prescott, led the prosecution at trial.

[7]   James V. Teetzel (1853-1926), a Liberal from Hamilton, was on the High Court bench from 1903 to 1914.

[8]   See, J. Barnes, *Two Cases of Hockey Homicide: The Crisis of a Moral Ideal* (Paper presented to the North American Society for Sport History (NASSH, 1990) at 51-72.

[9]   The game between the Ottawa Silver Seven and the Montreal Wanderers in the Eastern Canada Amateur Hockey Association on January 12, 1907 resulted in assault convictions for the Ottawa

at this level in an important game in the Federal Amateur Hockey League ("FAHL") played on March 6, 1907 between the Ottawa Victorias and Cornwall. In this case, Cornwall, Ontario, was the scene of both the death and the trial.

Early in the second period of a rough game, Owen "Bud" McCourt of the Cornwall team clashed with the Ottawa Victorias' player, Chamberlain, and then pursued him up the rink. Chamberlain's teammate, Charles E. Masson, was then seen to skate some distance up the ice, raise his stick and strike McCourt on the head. McCourt fell and a general mix-up followed. Teammates took McCourt to the dressing room for treatment but, rather than wait for the doctor to arrive, he resumed play. A few minutes later, McCourt collapsed and was carried off unconscious. He died in hospital the following day from a blood clot on the brain. McCourt, aged 22, was a distinguished and versatile athlete who features in official Stanley Cup records as the FAHL scoring champion for 1907.[11] Masson, also 22, had played his hockey with clubs in Ottawa and in the Maritimes and was the son of a former Ottawa alderman.

The day after the game, Charles Masson was taken into custody in Cornwall jail and charged with murder. When the inquest[12] was held in the courthouse on the evening of March 13, 1907, several hundred people attended. Witnesses described how McCourt took off after Chamberlain, apparently seeking reprisal for a blow received. They then described how Masson struck McCourt from behind with the blade of his stick. The medical evidence disclosed that McCourt had a thin skull; beneath a wound in the top of his head, the doctor found two blood clots. The verdict of the inquest jury was that McCourt "came to his death by a blow from a hockey stick in the hands of Charles Masson...there was no justification by personal provocation for the blow". The preliminary inquiry[13] held two days later heard similar evidence. Eventually, Masson was committed to trial on a charge of manslaughter, although the crown attorney vigorously opposed the reduction of the charge. On March 18, 1907, Masson was released on bail and returned to Ottawa. Much sympathy was felt for him in Cornwall.

When Masson's trial[14] took place at the Cornwall courthouse on April 10 and 11, 1907, the case aroused comparatively little interest.[15] The defence[16] made

---

players, Charlie Spittal and Alf Smith, who were each fined CDN $20, with CDN $38 costs, and required to keep the peace for one year. See: J. Barnes, *Two Cases of Hockey Homicide: The Crisis of a Moral Ideal* (Paper presented to the North American Society for Sport History (NASSH), 1990) at 15-16; S.L. Lorenz and G.B. Osborne, "'Talk About Strenuous Hockey': Violence, Manhood, and the 1907 Ottawa Silver Seven-Montreal Wanderer Rivalry" (2006) 40 J. Can. Studies 125.

[10] See Chapter 1, "Lord Stanley and the Wednesday Nighters", section B.

[11] See, C.L. Coleman, *The Trail of the Stanley Cup, Vol. 1, 1893-1926* (National Hockey League, 1966) at 141.

[12] Before Dr. C.J. Hamilton.

[13] Before Daniel Danis. The crown attorney was James Dingwall (see, note 4, above). At trial, the prosecution was led by D.H. Preston of Napanee.

[14] The trial judge was Justice James Magee (1846-1938) who served on the Ontario High Court from 1904 to 1933.

[15] In the newspapers, the trial lost out to coverage of the first Harry Thaw murder trial in New York, featuring jealousy for the affections of the showgirl Evelyn Nesbit. Thaw had shot the famous architect Stanford White at the roof theatre of the Madison Square Garden.

much of the fact that McCourt had been hit solidly by Chamberlain before Masson intervened and pointed out that many hard blows had been struck during this particularly strenuous game. Counsel also suggested that the accused might have been trying to protect his teammate from attack by McCourt. The jury took only half an hour to acquit Masson and was probably persuaded that it was unclear who had struck the blow to McCourt's skull.

## Contemporary Comments[17]

The Laurin-Loney and McCourt-Masson cases prompted a vigorous discussion of the state of the game and the causes of the violence. Most commentators welcomed Loney's acquittal, believing that he had suffered enough and should not atone for all of hockey's ills. When Masson was found not guilty in 1907, the feeling was that things had gone too far and stern punishment was now needed. The two deaths gave rise to official Grand Jury reports on the general problem of brutality in games, and public debate addressed the apparently degraded state of hockey. Observers expressed serious concern as they witnessed the transformation from a robust gentlemanly pursuit to a rougher commercial spectacle.[18]

Newspaper commentators and clergymen praised the sporting ideal, but warned against the dangers of fanaticism, greed and brutality. Subject to one exotic and aristocratic exception, hockey was extolled as the finest of all sports so that its moral value had to be preserved:

> Certainly hockey is a sport worth saving. There is nothing akin to it among the great games, unless it be polo...Among the games, hockey is unchallenged king: and it would be a crime against the enjoyments of our people if brutality were permitted to banish it from decent society.[19]

The game was conceived as a fine expression of "manliness" and a credit to the "British race", but it had to be cleansed of uncivilized elements, especially when ladies were present. Commentators spread the blame for the crisis in various directions. Many called for education to inculcate respectability and more enlightened standards among the spectators, who commonly approved of violence and lowered the social tone of events. The press were at fault for firing the imagination of "less level-headed spectators"[20] and indulging in home-town partisanship.[21] Professionalism and gambling were thought to drive teams to win-at-all-costs tactics, and leagues, associations and referees were condemned for

---

[16] Masson was defended by Robert A. Pringle (see, note 4, above) and by John A. Chisholm.

[17] See, J. Barnes, *Two Cases of Hockey Homicide: The Crisis of a Moral Ideal* (Paper presented to the North American Society for Sport History (NASSH), 1990) at 73-99.

[18] See Chapter 1, "Lord Stanley and the Wednesday Nighters", section B.

[19] "Hockey In Danger" *The Montreal Daily Star* (March 13, 1905) at 4.

[20] "The Assizes" *The Cornwall Standard* (March 31, 1905) at 4 (report of the Grand Jury).

[21] See, S.L. Lorenz and G.B. Osborne, "'Talk About Strenuous Hockey': Violence, Manhood, and the 1907 Ottawa Silver Seven-Montreal Wanderer Rivalry" (2006) 40 J. Can. Studies 125.

failing to take effective control by enforcing rules and imposing adequate penalties. Critics reserved harsh words for unprincipled entrepreneurs who promoted a violent style of play:

> ...it is the sordid management of clubs who encourage roughness in sport because it makes for a good "gate". While the better class of people who enjoy clean sport have been drawing away from the game it has increasingly attracted the element which would flock to a prize fight were such allowable under the law. As the management of clubs control the associations they take good care that proper rules are not made and carried into force which will stop "scrapping". These are the men who are morally responsible for the fatality.[22]

> "Why has hockey lost its prestige?"...It is because men have made these sports bloody, and brutal for money. We cannot develop our muscles to the glory of God, but men come in and say it must be for money. Scoundrels have got behind the whole business to rob men and women, and put the money into their own pockets.[23]

Besides the need for rule changes and moral renewal, commentators suggested practical precautions. One letter writer in 1907 thought there was a drug problem in the form of players taking strong alcoholic stimulants at half-time.[24] Another proposed protective head gear in the form of inflatable rubber tubing.[25]

Some commentators in 1905 and 1907 called for public regulation of hockey by special legislation[26] if the associations failed to make internal reforms. Criminal prosecutions were also viewed as an appropriate means of putting an end to violence. Charges were duly laid in the cases of Loney, Masson and others, but the actual outcomes are remarkably familiar. Faced with accused who were solid members of the middle class, the juries showed leniency, and the game continued on its rugged way. In the first decade of the twentieth century, society accepted rough action as a means of toughening the male population for the struggles ahead. Attitude and opinion therefore fell short of convicting and condemning individual warriors. One hundred years on, we repeat the postures of disapproval and still hold back from any serious interference with a violent spectacle that requires "proper levels of pugnacity, testosterone, truculence and

---

[22] "The Hockey Fatality" *The Evening Citizen* (Ottawa: March 8, 1907) at 6.

[23] "Scoundrelism Is Rampant" *The Evening Citizen* (Ottawa: January 14, 1907) at 11 ("Stirring Sermon by Rev. A.E. Mitchell").

[24] "The Hockey Brutalities" *The Montreal Daily Star* (March 29, 1907) at 13 (letter from, "One Who Knows the Dressing Rooms", who declared, "I am not a temperance crank").

[25] "Protection Against Rough Hockey" *Ottawa Free Press* (March 13, 1907) at 11 (letter from "J.M." suggesting "Pneumatic Appliance").

[26] The McCourt inquest jury recommended "that legislation be enacted whereby players and spectators engaging in or encouraging rough or foul play be sorely punished"; see: "Cornwall Jury Find That M'Court Was Killed By An Unprovoked Blow At The Hands Of Charles Masson" *The Montreal Daily Star* (March 14, 1907) at 1; "The Killing Of A Hockey Player" *The Globe* (Toronto: March 14, 1907) at 1.

belligerence".[27] The editorialist calls for the public to oppose "savagery", but the lingering fear is that men might go soft:

> Our race is a combative one, man is a fighting animal...It would be almost a national calamity if Canadian youth should discard their hockey and lacrosse sticks and puncture their footballs and grow deeply interested in croquet and "button, button, who's got the button".[28]

---

[27] "Burke officially joins Maple Leafs" (online) *The Globe and Mail* (Toronto: November 29, 2008).

[28] *Saturday Night* (Toronto: April 1, 1905) at 1.

# INDEX